STUDIES ON VOLTAIRE AND
THE EIGHTEENTH CENTURY

236

General editor

PROFESSOR H. T. MASON

Department of French
University of Bristol
Bristol BS8 1TE

ROBERT L. DAWSON

Additions to the bibliographies of French prose fiction 1618-1806

THE VOLTAIRE FOUNDATION

AT THE TAYLOR INSTITUTION, OXFORD

1985

ISSN 0435-2866

ISBN 0 7294 0327 0

Printed in England at The Alden Press, Oxford

Contents

Acknowledgements

I WOULD like to thank the following for the help they have given concerning different aspects of this bibliography: ferreting out information beyond my geographical reach, proffering advice, assisting with details of format and providing support of various kinds: Mildred Boyer, Andrew Brown, Lewis A. Dawson, Andrée Lhéritier, Georges May, Bruce Miller, David Paisey, John Thomas, William Todd, Jeanne Veyrin-Forrer, Uri S. Winterstein. Needless to say, all errors remain my own.

I am grateful to the University Research Institute of the University of Texas at Austin for providing some released time from university duties as well as funds for computer manipulation. My warm thanks also go to the National Endowment for the Humanities for help without which this book could not have been completed.

Introduction

THANKS to the efforts of first Silas Paul Jones,[1] then Professors Angus Martin, Vivienne G. Mylne and Richard Frautschi,[2] the entire eighteenth century has generally been covered for French prose fiction.[3] The seventeenth century also has an up-to-date bibliography devoted to its prose fiction by Maurice Lever.[4] While engaged in a careful examination of eighteenth-century French prose fiction in my own collections for a study of the Martin, Mylne, Frautschi bibliography,[5] I discovered that they contain many unique or very rare editions and issues. There are currently nearly two hundred and fifty of these, involving well over double that number of volumes (and many more titles), some extant elsewhere, but many here unique. I herewith make these known to the public, stressing that, had it not been for the remarkable efforts of Jones, then Lever and Martin, Mylne and Frautschi, it is quite likely that the following information would not now be coming to light. In my appraisal of the Martin-Mylne-Frautschi bibliography, I pointed out that it would surely give an impetus to further research in that field. The following presentation is, in a way, a direct result of the publication of the *Bibliographie du genre romanesque français*.

The limits of this bibliography are as follows: no attempt is made to contribute to a list of errata, for either Jones, Lever or MMF, although I have not hesitated to include prose-fiction works and editions which have escaped the attention of previous bibliographers of the genre. The main entries also include clarifications concerning entries that already figure in extant bibliographies of seventeenth- and eighteenth-century French prose fiction, for example Passerat's *Le Bel Anglais* (1695), Gueullette's *Mémoires de mademoiselle de Bontems* (the 1781 edition),

---

1. Silas Paul Jones, *A list of French prose fiction from 1700 to 1750* (New York 1939).

2. Angus Martin, Vivienne G. Mylne, Richard Frautschi, *Bibliographie du genre romanesque français: 1751-1800* (London, Paris 1977); abbreviated MMF.

3. For first editions, that is. Bibliographies of seventeenth-century prose fiction do not generally list later editions. Jones lists first editions, and then the re-editions by date alone which has led to the creation of many an error. Happily, MMF have listed editions of works which first appeared before 1751, but with few details (again by date alone and only if there was a re-edition of that work during the period covered by their bibliography). Thus there is no bibliography covering prose fiction works republished or reissued between 1700 and 1750, unless an edition occurs within the next fifty years. What is badly needed for the eighteenth century, in any case, is a bibliography which includes all works and editions of prose fiction, 1700-1800, with at least a minimal bibliographical record.

4. Maurice Lever, *La Fiction narrative en prose au XVIIème siècle: répertoire bibliographique du genre romanesque en France, 1600-1700* (Paris 1976). Lever makes no particular attempt to record all re-editions of the prose fiction works he lists, even for the seventeenth century. The Lever of course supersedes the previous bibliographies by Baldner and Williams and contains some excellent features, such as incipits and comprehensive indexes, including one of proper names in the titles. (Here are some details for the Baldner and Williams: Ralph Coplestone Williams, *Bibliography of the seventeenth-century novel in France*, New York 1931, and Ralph Willis Baldner, *Bibliography of seventeenth-century French prose fiction*, New York 1967.)

5. 'The Martin, Mylne, Frautschi *Bibliographie du genre romanesque français*' in *Eighteenth-century studies* 4 (1978), pp.497-508.

and the first eight volumes of the 1796 (and on) Leipzig edition of Florian's *Œuvres*.

Included in the text of the commentaries are addenda having to do directly with the main entries, largely culled from rare bibliographies, some of them never before used by modern French bibliographers of eighteenth-century French literature. For detailed explanations concerning some of those little-used bibliographies, see the commentaries on the Heinsius, Kayser, Messkatalog and related works in the list of abbreviations. (Poking about in various libraries, especially in the BL, has also turned up several items of interest.) It goes without saying that the existence of any edition described after a secondary source is open to a certain amount of suspicion until a copy of it is found. However, I have every confidence that most of the additional editions listed, culled from secondary sources, will eventually prove to have existed. I emphasise that the primary thrust of this bibliography is concerned with the main entries. Other addenda comprise information encountered as research progressed.

The items forming the main entries in the present bibliography derive from my own collections, with the exception of Baculard d'Arnaud's *Epreuves du sentiment* (1789), Contant Dorville's *Le Mariage du siècle* (1767), Mme de Graffigny's *Lettres d'une Péruvienne* (1774), and a 1771 edition of Le Tourneur's translation/adaptation of the *Méditations d'Hervey*. The first three are only extant – as far as I know – in the collections of the University of Texas at Austin (the Humanities Research Centre, the Benson Latin American Collection, etc.).

The books described below can be divided into three broad categories. There are new titles not to be found in previous bibliographies dealing with French prose fiction of the periods, usually because no other copy of the work is known (for example, *La Chatonciade*; *Dom Carlos, grand d'Espagne*; *Fantaisie nouvelle*; *Le Favori disgracié*; Chauveau's *Les Saisons*, and Meissner's *Mélanges de littérature allemande*). Then there are editions which have never been recorded (for example, *Les Mille et une nuits* 1790, *Le Passe-temps agréable*, and Musset and Bourgoing's *Correspondance d'un jeune militaire* 1798). Finally, I have listed editions which, although given a passing mention in, for example, the bibliographies of Gay, Quérard or Monglond (see the list of abbreviations below), are not generally to be found elsewhere. This of course does not mean that they do not exist in other collections, but that, with the sources at my disposal (especially the catalogues of printed books of the British Library and the Bibliothèque nationale, together with the NUC), they are not generally known to exist elsewhere. Even if listed by, for example, Tchemerzine, as is Diderot's *La Religieuse*, Seventh Year of the Republic (with an apocryphal 'suite', today unknown), it seems to me that more complete bibliographical data will be welcomed by not only all scholars interested in the novels of the period, but also by scholars interested in the specific authors involved. (See too, for example, Nougaret's *Lettre d'un mendiant au public* and Chevrier's *Histoire de la vie de H. Maubert*.) Occasionally a rare edition extant elsewhere (probably!) is listed in order to clarify confusion in Lever, Jones and/or MMF (for example, La Roche-Guilhen's *Histoire des favorites* 1708 and Prévost's *Doyen de Killerine* 1783-1784). When in doubt whether to include or not, I have chosen to include.

The following bibliography contains the description of quite a few unusual items illustrating various aspects of the history of the book. There are English piracies of French books (Mme de Genlis, *Les Veillées du château*, 1785), Parisian piracies of Swiss works (Haller, *Poésies*) and at least one case of a book trying to pass itself off as a work having been printed in Paris with a 'permission tacite' (Dorat, *Lettres, Œuvres*). It has been known that the 'Francfort' *Emile* (Rousseau) was printed in England. We now know who the printer was, and for whom it was printed, although I was unable to do much more than define the problems relating to the unusual imprint. This bibliography also contains a couple of examples of books printed during the last decade of the eighteenth century deliberately bearing false dates (Du Laurens, *Le Compère Mathieu* and Sterne, *Tristram Shandy*). By dint of going through documentary and manuscript sources for the booktrade or by comparing type, decorations and compositorial practices, I was able to identify the actual printer and/or publisher of various works: Didot for *Ismène et Isménias* (vide Eustathius) and for Voltaire's *Romans et contes*; the Société typographique (Neuchâtel) for Dorat's *Lettres, Œuvres*; Ballard the younger in Paris – in spite of the mention 'Bruxelles, veuve Tonnins' on the titlepage – for Marsy's *Semaines amusantes*, and so on. (For example, reasons are given for even the cancel titlepages of Gueullette's *Mille et une soirées* having been printed by Prault, in spite of the imprint.) There are examples of a hand-corrected edition (Gilbert, *Œuvres*), and of books still containing the slashed cancellantia with the leaves supposed to replace them (d'Auvigny with Desfontaines, *Mémoires de Barneveldt* and Lichtwehr, *Fables*). A couple of books, unique in their own right, have manuscript 'keys', which are transcribed and briefly discussed (d'Auvigny with Desfontaines, *Mémoires de madame de Barneveldt* and Fénelon, *Télémaque*, 1751). There are also several novels, or pseudo-novels with printed keys, three of which are centred on the life, times and loves of Louis XV: *Les Amours de Zéokinizul*, La Beaumelle's *L'Asiatique tolérant* and Toussaint's *Mémoires secrets pour servir à l'histoire de Perse*. Of the many piracies represented, there is at least one where the pirate nonchalantly transmitted the author's own complaints about the many illegitimate editions which were flooding the market (Bernardin de Saint-Pierre, *Etudes*, 1788-89). On the subject of piracies: there are several examples of legitimated, contraband books bearing the official guild-hall stamp and signature of the local police inspector (d'Arnaud, *Œuvres* 1777; Boiardo, *Roland l'amoureux*; Fénelon, *Télémaque* 1778; Lesage, *Gil Blas* 1771). Indeed, in the case of *Télémaque*, the book has undergone some of those mutilations which were not infrequent during the revolutionary period.

Listed are all works in my collections (pertinent to the stated scope of this bibliography) which might prove of significance to students of the French 'genre romanesque' of the seventeenth and eighteenth centuries. Thus I have also included a description of Pigault-Lebrun's four-volume periodical venture (which extends the list a bit beyond the chronological scope of MMF) together with a couple of other very rare periodicals containing prose fiction (for example, the *Nouveaux amusements sérieux et comiques* and Marsy's *Semaines amusantes*); a note on the first edition of the last volume of Lesage's *Gil Blas*; a note on a rare, early edition of Voltaire's *Candide*; explanations concerning the 1762 'Francfort' edition of Rousseau's *Emile*; one manuscript (the anonymous *Les Quêteuses*); a note on the 1746 'Paris' edition of Hamilton's *Mémoires du comte de Grammont*; and several books not in French: the anonymous *Secret memoirs of the late count Saxe* and various works by Baculard d'Arnaud translated into the Italian (which again carries the present bibliography slightly into the nineteenth century).

And what is meant by 'prose fiction'? The term as applied here is taken in the loosest possible sense: narration in prose, whether a tale of a paragraph or two, which would admit prose fables (see for example Lichtwehr) or novels in several volumes. Included are effusions in poetical prose when they contain fiction (either a plotline or fictitious characters). See for example Chauveau's *Les Quatre saisons*, Gessner's *La Mort d'Abel* and the entries devoted to Parny. What ought one do with fiction in dialogue form? I have excluded pastorals, but included Montesquieu's *Dialogue de Sylla et d'Eucrate*, which was printed with a very rare edition of the *Considérations sur les causes de la grandeur des Romains*, 1750. Thus, too, I have listed what appear to be unique copies of two editions of La Bruyère's *Caractères* (1724 and 1741) since he gives descriptions of fictitious characters, even if they were supposedly based on real-life people. (In any case, La Bruyère categorically denied the veracity of the various 'keys' with which he had to contend.) On the general subject of prose-fiction, see also, for example, the commentary on Voltaire's *Nouveaux mélanges*.

An interesting category of prose fiction which has often been neglected by bibliographers dealing with the genre is that of school editions and other works with a pedagogical bent. Well known is, for example, the large number of editions of Mme de Graffigny's *Lettres d'une Péruvienne*, published with the Italian translation and Deodati's pedagogical material. (See the Graffigny-Deodati entries below.) Less well known is the fact that Fénelon's *Aventures de Télémaque* went through many an edition with notes ('remarks') in German, 'à l'usage des écoles'. See the commentaries on the various editions of Fénelon's *Télémaque* in this bibliography. See too the anonymous *L'Art d'enseigner la langue française*; the commentaries on the many *Bélisaire*s listed below (Marmontel); the two works by David Etienne Choffin, and Berquin's *Ami des enfants*.[6]

In the few cases where a set contains one or more volumes reported in Lever,

---

6. A good example of an educator who composed all sorts of works and whose books are not listed in bibliographies of prose fiction is Jean Baptiste Perrin who was a French teacher in London (no dates known; active in the couple of decades preceding the Revolution). Ought not a bibliographer dealing with the 'genre romanesque' include *La Bonne mère* (1786)? As the title itself indicates, it contains 'de petites pièces dramatiques, chacune précédée de la définition, & suivie de la morale, entre la Bonne Mère & ses deux filles, avec des traits historiques & des anecdotes convenables' (Londres: B. Law, J. Robson, T. Cadell, P. Elmsly, 1786; BL). Perrin also composed some *Fables amusantes [en prose]: avec une table générale & particulière des mots, et de leur signification en anglois, selon l'ordre des fables, pour en rendre la traduction plus facile à l'écolier* (Londres: B. Law, T. Cadell, P. Elmsly, 1771: BL; 140 fables in prose, from a paragraph to a couple of pages each), *Contes moraux, amusans & instructifs, à l'usage de la jeunesse, tirés des tragédies de Shakespeare* (Londres: Law, Robson, Cadell, Elmsly, 1773), and other works with a pedagogical slant. Neither the plays nor the pieces of prose fiction are listed in Brenner or MMF. (An important precursor of the Lambs, the plays he abstracted – in the 1773 edition anyway – are *Hamlet, Coriolanus, King Lear, Romeo and Juliet, Othello, Macbeth, Julius Cesar, Anthony and Cleopatra, King John, Richard II, Henry IV, Henry V, Richard III, Cymbeline* and *Timon of Athens*.) For an incomplete list of his works, see Quérard vii.66-67. To complement Quérard, see especially the NUC and BLC. Although I could find precious little about the man, not even his dates, he seems to have enjoyed a considerable reputation in London and to have done quite well for himself. The verso of the table to *La Bonne mère* bears the following: 'N.B. L'auteur enseigne le François à raison de deux Guinées d'entrée, & de deux Guinées pour huit leçons', quite hefty prices for the time.

MMF or Jones, and one or more volumes largely only to be found in my collections, it has seemed wisest to describe all volumes, for example Bernardin de Saint-Pierre's *Etudes de la nature* 1788-1789 and Florian's *Œuvres* 1786-1801. Indeed, the problems involved with sorting out the individual and collected works of Florian have led me to adopt MMF's judicious system, that is, to list each work separately whether or not it was meant specifically for a collection (exception made of the 1796 *Œuvres* which constitute an obvious whole).

Descriptions of bindings have largely been omitted, except when of significance for dating a volume, indicating country of provenance (vs. country of physical origin or printing), or except when a collection has been uniformly bound. Such explanations are invariably perfunctory since they have little to do with the actual description of the printed book itself.

The presentation of each book, or set of books, differs from that of Lever, Jones and MMF. Since the quantity is strictly limited, the list is in alphabetical order, anonyms first, then by author, instead of in chronological sequence. For the convenience of the reader and so as not to clash with the order established by Jones and MMF, there is appended a chronological summary. Because we are dealing with a set of rare and in most cases unique books in a private collection, it was thought best to include considerably more information than given by either Lever, Jones or MMF.

I have chosen a modified, simplified method of transcription. Capitals are used only when logic so dictates: at the beginning of a sentence, after a period and for proper names. The italicisation or capitalisation of entire words is ignored, but every differentiated capitalisation is recorded. Thus, if a word begins with a letter bigger than the rest, that word is transcribed with an initial capital letter. Personal titles are not capitalised, including 'monsieur' and 'madame'. (However, in transcriptions of titlepages and halftitles, the abbreviation for 'monsieur' invariably remains 'M.'.) Lineation is recorded as well, since that can provide valuable clues to help identify similar, but non-identical editions.

All titlepage decorations are reported. The original spelling is strictly adhered to, including accentuation. If an accent has been dropped because the entire word is capitalised, or for whatever reason, it has not been restored. The same applies to the half titlepages, but catchmaterial is recorded only when deemed significant. All volume halftitles are transcribed. Particularly during the 1790s, it was the custom to include the names and addresses of publisher(s) and/or bookdealer(s) on the versos of volume half titleleaves. These too are recorded. Titlepages may be assumed to be printed in black; red is reported by the insertion of '*red* and black' at the beginning of the title, and the words so printed are italicised.

Brackets are used when a number or letter is inferred. This applies to signatures as well as to pagination. Thus, if pagination is reported within parentheses, the page number was so printed. If numbers and/or letters are positioned within brackets, this factor is explained. A gap in the pagination generally indicates the existence of a nonpaginated half titlepage. (Any discrepancies are explained.) For example, Tencin, *Mémoires du comte de Comminges* has '... [1]-74 + [77]-(137) ...' pp., meaning that pp.[75-76] represent a nonpaginated half titlepage. Sections contiguously paginated are linked by commas; otherwise a '+' is used.

Halftitles and titlepages excluded from the pagination are recorded as preliminary leaves, abbreviated 'pl'. If the pagination includes a leaf (or leaves), the indication of 'f.' (or 'ff.') for folio(s) is used, and the nature of these leaves is explained in parentheses. Any anomalies are noted. Unpaginated initial folios are generally part of preliminary gatherings. Again, discrepancies are noted. The number of pages of these items is recorded within parentheses. (Blank pages are disregarded.) Thus, for example, '8 ff. (13 + 2 pp.)' would mean that the eight folios consist of two items, the first 13 pp., the second 2 pp. (Since eight leaves contain 16 pages, that would ordinarily mean that page 14 or page 16 is blank).

I have paid careful attention to the illustrations. These can provide helpful clues concerning edition variants and different editions. Unfortunately, bibliographers in the past have not only left aside this aspect of a book, but have also generally been unaware of the enormous usefulness of bibliographies dealing with book illustrations, such as Reynaud's additions to and amplifications of Cohen. (See the list of abbreviations below.) For example, I firmly believed that my edition of Beauchamps's *Hipparchia* was the same as that in the rare-books room of the Bibliothèque nationale, since, for all practical purposes, the titlepages are identical. But the somewhat different states of the engravings suggested that I examine the copies minutely. And indeed, both proved to be copies of different editions. It is to be hoped that someone will take it upon himself to compose a proper bibliography dealing with the illustrated book of the eighteenth century.

An explanation concerning the term 'catchtome': there is no word currently in use to designate the volume indicator which sometimes appears after the text on the bottom of a page (usually to the left, on the rectos and at the beginning of signature sequences). Since 'catchword' is the term for the characters printed on the right, leading to the next page, the term 'catchtome' for the volume indicator seems a commodious and efficient way of referring to what is, after all, frequently a very important part of a bibliographical description. I have noted catchtomes where they are of significance in identifying the place of a work in a given collection. Particularly toward the end of the eighteenth century, books were issued as part of collected works and/or individually. (See for example Fanny Burney's *Evelina*, both editions, and Florian's *Œuvres*, 1792.) Halftitles were suppressed, titles cancelled and all too frequently the bibliographical muddle that ensued is difficult indeed to sort out. Catchtomes, while they usually do not resolve a problem, certainly help to clarify it.

A word about revolutionary dates: where it has been necessary to infer a Gregorian date from a revolutionary year, I have followed the practice of equating 'an Ier' (the first year of the French republic) with 1792, and so on, unless the revolutionary month and day are given as well. Since dates are also faithfully transcribed as they appear on the titlepages, this system should pose little problem for anyone consulting the present bibliography. The major source I have used for the revolutionary calendar in general is: Sébastien Louis Rosaz, *Concordance de l'annuaire de la république française avec le calendrier grégorien, formant 178 tableaux, qui commencent le 22 septembre 1793 (I.ᵉʳ vendémiaire an II), et se terminent au 31 décembre 1837* [...], *trente-deux ans après la suppression du calendrier républicain; avec la fixation des fêtes mobiles et la dénomination des jours et des saints de l'ère grégorienne, pour cette durée, précédée des lois, décrets* (Paris: Brunot-Labbe, Louis Fantin, Lenormant, 1810). This book not only gives tables with both calendars (up to 31 December 1837/10 nivôse an XLVI, particularly to help find later dates referred to or implied on legal documents), but also contains a thorough treatise on the revolutionary calendar and its development. Thus I have included a description of my copy of Nogaret's *Podalire et Dirphé* which is dated 'nivôse, [an] IX'. (That particular month ends the eighteenth century and ushers in the new).

Originally more bibliographical information was included with each item. At the request of the Voltaire Foundation editors and in the interest of conciseness, the entries were shortened. I would be pleased to answer readers' questions concerning all items in my own collections.

Indexes have been appended to the whole in order to render this presentation as useful as possible. Included is an index to the incipits. Where it is not really possible to assert that a novel commences with the beginning of the main text proper, or with one of the preliminary pieces, incipits for each are included. The incipits are for the beginning of the volume or volumes recorded; this does not always mean we are dealing with the beginning of the work, however. In the case of multiple works or *Œuvres*, incipits have been included for what have been deemed the more significant items of prose fiction. Lineation of incipits is recorded when it is felt that this might prove of further help in identifying different editions. Original spelling of incipits is strictly followed. The spelling in the index of incipits has, however, largely been modernised in order to facilitate consultation.

In their introduction, Professors Martin, Mylne and Frautschi state that 'nous serions surpris d'apprendre que nous avons recensé moins de 80 pourcent des rééditions, et nous aimerions penser que notre bilan est encore plus complet' (p.xxix). The following list contains works largely falling within the scope of the MMF, but does not particularly alter the conclusions which its authors have so elegantly described in their tables.

My own conclusions are these: the books described here derive from a modest library of mostly eighteenth-century French books, which includes all kinds of works. I was myself somewhat surprised to find that so many of the volumes would prove of interest to scholars concerned with the 'genre romanesque'. Since my collections are limited, it was possible to do the thorough kind of examination of them that would have proved too time-consuming for any major library's holdings. And I find, more and more, that current cataloguing practices are woefully inadequate for the purposes of even general seventeenth- and eighteenth-century bibliography, and that all copies must be examined *in manu*, as far as physically or financially possible. So many re-editions, including piracies, were copied from previous editions, often on a page-to-page basis, even line by line, that any bibliography of extended scope is bound to have omissions, some because works were not available, others because, with existing descriptions, it was improbable that copies presumed to be of the same edition represented two editions, never mind edition variants. Yet so often two copies presumed to be of the same edition are not. A bibliographical 'fingerprint' would go a long way to help resolve this problem. But, as has been pointed out, 'it cannot, of course, differentiate between two books of which one is a line-by-line reprint of the other; nor does regular cataloguing, however conscientious'.[7] That is the case with more than one item listed in this bibliography. See for example the various 1767, Merlin *Bélisaire*s (by Marmontel) and the editions of individual works by Florian with the same pagination.

One comes across a large number of editions mentioned particularly in nineteenth-century bibliographies and catalogues. Since they do not exist in any library (that one can presently ascertain), there is a natural tendency to think it a question of 'phantom' editions. More and more I am coming to believe that the bibliographers of a hundred years or so ago, while not enjoying the knowledge or notions of exactitude that we have today, were far more often correct than not. Bookshops in the nineteenth century (especially the first half) were filled with unwanted editions from the preceding centuries. Bibliographers were often bookdealers, as well as bibliophiles and purveyors of second-hand works. For the scholar who bothered, the living world outside the stolid halls of musty librairies held many a bibliographical treasure that could be had nearly for the asking. Libraries usually did not bother acquiring works of so little monetary value. And if, after passing from the hands of a dealer into those of a collector, they showed up again in the salesrooms, such rare works, but again of little value, would often be lumped together in large, poorly described lots, once more to disappear. As time wore on, more and more of these books disappeared forever (for all practical purposes). One need but think of the fate of the vast and priceless Soleinne collection of dramatic works.[8]

Then, too, many a nineteenth-century bibliographer relied on earlier sources, some of them more accurate and complete than the bibliographies that were supposed to supersede them! Let us take, for example, Quérard. His primary source of inspiration was the work of his German colleagues. As he writes in the 'Discours préliminaire' to *La France littéraire*: 'Nous trouvant en Allemagne, de

7. In *Computers and early books: report of the LOC project investigating means of compiling a machine-readable union catalogue of pre-1801 books in Oxford, Cambridge and the British museum*, with a preface by Robert Shackleton (London 1974), p.8. The interested reader should also consult John Jolliffe, 'Fingerprints and search codes: experiments in the union cataloguing of older books in project LOC', *Catalogue and index*, no. 15 (July 1969), pp.4-6; the various articles in *Les Fonds anciens des bibliothèques françaises* (Journées d'étude Villeurbanne, 13-15 novembre 1975, Association de l'Ecole normale supérieure de bibliothécaires, Villeurbanne 1976), and the latest issue of *Nouvelles des empreintes / Fingerprint newsletter*. The clue to the identification of hand-press books copied on a line-for-line basis lies, it seems to me, in the positioning of the signatures. See, for example, Coyer, *Lettre à une jeune dame nouvellement mariée* below. However, in many cases it would be difficult, even occasionally impossible, accurately to describe that position in relationship to letters/spaces supra. It is to be hoped that an inexpensive micro-photographic process be developed so that a card, or even eventually an entry, might reproduce the titlepage and 'key' interior pages.

I would like to take this opportunity to acknowledge two works dealing with aspects of descriptive bibliography which I have found of exceptional value (beyond such standard classics as those by McKerrow and Gaskell, together with the pioneering works by William Todd), viz: Giles Barber, 'Catchwords and press figures at home and abroad', *The Book collector* 9 (1960), pp.301-307, and R. A. Sayce, *Compositorial practices and the localization of printed books, 1530-1800*, a reprint from *The Library*, V, xxi, March 1966, with addenda and corrigenda (Oxford 1979).

8. The sales catalogue was compiled by the 'bibliophile Jacob', i.e. Paul Lacroix: *Bibliothèque dramatique de monsieur de Soleinne*, 1843-1844, indexes by Goizet (1845) and Brunet (1914), 7 vols in all.

1819 à 1824, nous eûmes l'occasion d'observer l'utilité que les savants et laborieux littérateurs d'au-delà du Rhin savent retirer de leurs livres de Bibliographie nationale; et combien ces ouvrages sont appréciés dans le commerce de la librairie de ces contrées: c'est alors que nous conçûmes la pensée de faire pour notre pays, ce que Heinsius, Ersch, Ebert et quelques autres ont fait pour l'Allemagne', and so on (p.ix; 1827). Quérard then goes on to explain that the major part of his labours has been directed towards the eighteenth and nineteenth centuries. One of the sources he relied on was Heinsius. And Heinsius in turn relied to a certain extent on the Messkataloge. Errors were created as Heinsius drew upon the Messkataloge, and these were sometimes further compounded as both Quérard and Kayser drew upon Heinsius.

Rather than return to some of the original bibliographies, the tendency in our time has often been to reject those secondary and tertiary sources: 'the older, the worse'. Few twentieth-century French bibliographers have even made good use of Heinsius and Kayser. (A notable exception is Monglond, who utilised Kayser, but tended to ignore Heinsius.) The present bibliography attests to the actual existence of several works listed in some of those older sources, even though they cannot be found in any other library (as far as I could ascertain). See, for example, Bernardin de Saint-Pierre's *Etudes de la nature* (Hambourg 1797); Choffin, *Amusements philologiques*; his *Récréations philologiques*, and Marmontel's *Contes moraux* (1775).[9] While far from claiming that every entry in the Messkatalog, for example, should be taken as proof-positive that a given edition (or work even) once existed, I do believe that most of those entries will eventually be shown to refer to books that were actually printed (taking into consideration certain reservations revolving around bibliographical principles utilised by the compilers. See the commentaries on the sources involved in the partially annotated list of abbreviations below).

9. Although the titlepages to Mme de Villeneuve's *Jardinière de Vincennes* bear 'se vend à Francfort en foire', those editions are not listed in the Messkatalog. But that is doubtless because pirates republished the novel many times, following the tradition of the first 'en foire' edition, so that these were not available at the fairs. Officially, anyway! (See the pertinent entries below.)

Annotated list of sources

Barbier: Antoine Alexandre Barbier, *Dictionnaire des ouvrages anonymes* (Paris 1882), 4 vols with a fifth volume supplement by Brunet (1889).

Barquissau: Raphaël Barquissau, *Les Poètes créoles du XVIIIe siècle: Parny, Bertin, Léonard* (Paris 1949).

BL: The British Library and the BL catalogue (BLC) of printed books, together with the various supplements.

BN: The Bibliothèque nationale and the BN catalogue (BNC) of printed books, with the various supplements.

Brenner: Clarence D. Brenner, *A bibliographical list of plays in the French language: 1700-1789* (Berkeley 1947).

Brunet: Jacques-Charles Brunet, *Manuel du libraire et de l'amateur de livres, contenant 1°. un nouveau dictionnaire bibliographique [...]; 2°. une table en forme de catalogue raisonné* (Paris 1860-1865), 6 vols.

Catalogue collectif: *Catalogue collectif des périodiques du début du XVIIe siècle à 1939, conservés dans les bibliothèques de Paris et dans les bibliothèques universitaires des départements* (Paris: Bibliothèque nationale, 1967-1981); the fifth and last volume comprises additions and corrections, and an index of collectivities.

Chapman: Robert William Chapman, *Cancels [...] with eleven facsimiles in collotype* (London, New York 1930); a volume of 'Bibliographia: studies in book history and book structure, 1750-1900', Michael Sadleir ed.

Charrier: Charlotte Charrier, *Héloïse dans l'histoire et dans la légende* (Paris 1933).

Chérel: Albert Chérel, *Fénelon au 18e siècle en France, Supplément: tableaux bibliographiques* (Fribourg 1917).

Cior. (or Cioranescu): Alexandre Cioranescu, *Bibliographie de la littérature française du XVIIIe siècle* (Paris 1969), 3 vols.

Cior. (Cioranescu), 17e siècle: Alexandre Cioranescu, *Bibliographie de la littérature française du dix-septième siècle* (Paris 1965-66), 3 vols.

Cohen: Henri Cohen, *Guide de l'amateur des livres à gravures du XVIIIe siècle, 6e édition, rev., corr. et aug. par Seymour de Ricci* (Paris 1912), 2 vols, consecutive columniation.

Conlon: Pierre M. Conlon, *Prélude au siècle des lumières en France: répertoire chronologique de 1680 à 1715* (Geneva 1970-1975), 6 vols.

Cordier: Henri Cordier, *Essai bibliographique sur les œuvres d'Alain René Lesage* (Paris 1910).

Corroënne: A. Corroënne, *Manuel du cazinophile: le petit format à figures, collection parisienne in-18* (Paris 1878).

Dawson: Robert L. Dawson, *Baculard d'Arnaud: life and prose fiction*, Studies on Voltaire 141-142 (1976), especially 'An annotated bibliography of [...] Baculard d'Arnaud', ii.609-712. (A few of the d'Arnaud items listed in this bibliography are also listed in Dawson. Since only a minimal bibliographical description was included in the latter, it was deemed best not to omit them here. In any case, those items are not in MMF.)

Drujon: Fernand Drujon, *Les livres à clef: étude de bibliographie critique et analytique pour servir à l'histoire littéraire* (Paris 1888), 2 vols, consecutive columniation.

Dufour: Théophile Dufour, *Recherches bibliographiques sur les œuvres imprimées de J.-J. Rousseau, suivies de l'inventaire des papiers de Rousseau conservés à la Bibliothèque de Neuchâtel* (Paris 1925), 2 vols.

Ersch: Johann Samuel (Jean Samuel) Ersch, *La France littéraire, contenant les auteurs français de 1771 à 1796 / Das Gelehrte Frankreich, oder Lexicon der franzoesischen Schriftsteller* (Hamburg 1797-1806). 5 vols, including various supplements. (There is a Slatkine reprint, 1971).

Escoffier: Maurice Escoffier, the cover titlepage reads *Vente du 12 au 15 novembre 1934 et du 27 novembre au 1er décembre 1934, Me Edouard Giard, commissaire-priseur. Catalogue d'une bibliothèque représentant le mouvement romantique, 1788-1850; essai de bibliographie synchronique et méthodique provenant d'une réunion formée par M. M. E. précédé d'une lettre à l'académie française sur l'édition originale et suivi de notes et documents sur le même sujet* (Paris 1934). The internal titlepage starts with *Le Mouvement romantique, 1788-1850: essai de bibliographie*, with no mention of the sale. The imprint varies, cover titlepage: Paris, L. Giraud-Badin; internal titlepage, Paris, maison du bibliophile.

ESTC: the Eighteenth-century short-title catalogue, in course of compilation (data-base).

Gay: Jules Gay, *Bibliographie des ouvrages relatifs à l'amour, aux femmes*, 4e édition, edited by J. Lemonnyer (Paris, Lille 1894-1900), 4 vols.

Gesamtk.: *Gesamtkatalog der preussischen Bibliotheken mit Nachweis des identischen Besitzes der bayerischen Staatsbibliothek in Muenchen und der Nazionalbibliothek in Wien* (herausgegeben von der preussischen Staatsbibliothek; Berlin 1931-1939), 14 vols. From vol. ix on, titled *Deutscher Gesamtkatalog.* ('A' to 'Beethordnung').

Gesamtverzeichniss: *Gesamtverzeichniss des deutschsprachigen Schrifttums (GV), 1700-1910*, bearbeitet unter der Leitung von Peter Geils und Willi Gorzny. Bibliographische und redaktionelle Beratung: Hans Popst und Rainer Schoeller, later with Hilmar Schmuck, et al. (Munich, New York, London, Paris 1979 and on, in course of publication). This important work is for a large part a photo-montage culled from many sources, including Heinsius, Kayser and the *Gesamtkatalog der Preussischen Bibliotheken*. Although a remarkable work, and one that will be used to advantage by future French bibliographers of the period, it far from supersedes the German sources for the eighteenth century utilised in the current bibliography. Because it is a recent work, and in course of publication, I have only been able to make very limited use of it. Reference is given to the volume and page number. The left-hand columns are indicated by an 'a' following the page number; a 'b' indicates those to the right. Reported is information pertinent to the entries in this bibliography that I could not find in other sources listed here (especially Heinsius and Kayser).

Girardin: Fernand, marquis (or comte) de Girardin, *Iconographie des œuvres de Jean-Jacques Rousseau pour faire suite à l'iconographie de Jean-Jacques Rousseau, suivie d'un addendum à cette iconographie* (Paris [1910]).

Giraud: Yves Giraud, *Bibliographie du roman épistolaire en France des origines à 1842* (SEGES no. 23, Suisse 1977).

Graesse: Jean Georges Théodore Graesse, *Trésor de livres rares et précieux, ou nouveau dictionnaire bibliographique* (Berlin 1922). 7 vols. (There is a 1971 reprint by Slatkine.)

Harrisse, 1877: Henry Harrisse, *Bibliographie de 'Manon Lescaut' et notes pour servir à l'histoire du livre*, seconde édition, rev. et augm. (Paris 1877).

Harrisse, 1896: Henry Harrisse, *L'Abbé Prévost: histoire de sa vie et de ses œuvres d'après des documents nouveaux* (Paris 1896).

Hatin: Eugène Hatin, *Bibliographie historique et critique de la presse périodique française, ou catalogue systématique et raisonné de tous les écrits périodiques* (Paris 1866).

Heinsius: Wilhelm Heinsius, *Allgemeines Buecher-Lexikon, oder vollstaendiges alphabetisches Verzeichnis der von 1700 bis zu Ende 1810 erschienenen Buecher, welche in Deutschland und in den durch Sprache und Literatur damit verwandten Laendern gedruckt worden sind. Nebst Angabe der Druckorte, der Verleger und der Preise* (Leipzig 1812-1813; rprt. Graz, Austria 1962), 4 vols with a separately paginated volume of addenda at the end of iv containing two major sections for *Romane* and *Schauspiele*.

The Heinsius, Kayser and Messkatalog (for which see below) are particularly useful for Germanic imprints of eighteenth-century French works and editions which do not exist in major libraries west of the Rhine. (The same holds true for works in English, Italian and other languages.) The Heinsius, while not that easy to use (no index for example; works are whimsically listed under spurious authors, 'main word' in title, related authors or works, etc.), is well worth the trouble of consulting. This series was continued, but the sequel is not relevant to the present bibliography. For further information, see the commentary on the Kayser below which largely applies to the Heinsius. (See too the Messkatalog.) Eventually the Heinsius, Kayser, Gesamtk. and other works will be replaced (in principle!) by the *Gesamtverzeichniss des deutschsprachigen Schrifttums*; see Gesamtverzeichniss above.

Heinsius, *Handbuch*: Wilhelm Heinsius, *Handbuch für Litteratoren, oder allgemeine alphabetische Uebersicht der gesamten gangbaren in- und ausländischen Litteratur nebst Anzeige des Druckorts, der Verleger und der Ladenpreise der Bücher* (Magdeburg 1794). This work has an interesting foreword by the publisher, Johann Christian Giesecke.

Heinsius, 1793 and Heinsius, 1798: *Allgemeines Buecher-Lexicon, oder alphabetisches Verzeichniss der in Deutschland und den angrenzenden Laendern gedruckten Buecher, nebst beygesetzten Verlegern und Preisen* (Leipzig: Buchhandlung des Verfassers, 1793), 4 vols, 'Livres françois' in iv.[473]-562. Together with a supplement (same format): *Erstes Supplement, erster Band; enthaltend die erschienenen Buecher vom Jahr 1793 bis Ende des Jahres 1797* (Leipzig 1798). This is indicated as Heinsius, 1798. Items are priced. This work contains several items listed in the current bibliography that are nowhere else to be found, as far as I am able to ascertain. The 1812-1813 Heinsius is largely considered the best source for the period covered, but, what seems to be the case, is that Heinisus eliminated from future listings books that were then no longer available. Thus, unfortunately, Heinsius (1812-1813) does not supersede Heinsius 1793 and 1798.

Jones: Silas Paul Jones, *A list of French prose fiction from 1700 to 1750* (New York 1939).

Kayser: Christian Gottlob Kayser, *Index locupletissimus librorum qui inde ab anno*

MDCCL usque ad annum MDCCCXXXII in Germania et in terris confinibus prodierunt /
Vollstaendiges Buecher-Lexicon enthaltend Alle von 1750 bis zu Ende des Jahres 1832 in
Deutschland und in den angrenzenden Laendern gedruckte Buecher. In alphabetischer
Folge, mit einer vollstaendigen Uebersicht aller Autoren, der Anonymen
sowohl als der Pseudonymen, und einer genauen Angabe der Kupfer und
Karten, der Auflagen und Ausgaben, der Formate, der Druckorte, der
Jahrzahlen, der Verleger und der Preise (Leipzig 1834-1838), 9 vols.

Although this important work is usually cited as being in seven volumes, it
is actually in nine, for, after the sixth volume, paralleling the Heinsius, are to
be found two more: one for 'Schauspiele' and another for 'Romane', neither of
which bears a volume indicator. The last volume is a 'Sachregister', which
also does not bear any volume indication on the titlepage. Vols i-vi are so
indicated in the following bibliography, with the addition of 'a' or 'b' to the
page number to indicate left- and right-hand columns. The volume dealing
with novels is given as 'Romane'. Thus 'Romane, p.38a' means the volume
dealing with novels, p.38, left-hand column.

Since it is not the easiest of works to use, I have reported what information
of interest I could find in the Kayser, dealing with the works/authors described
in the following bibliography. For example, to find Mme de Souza's *Adèle de*
Senange, those in the know would first try 'Senange', then 'Adèle', then 'Souza'
and finally the alternative possibilities for the author's name. Then this
process would have to be repeated for the volume dealing with novels. The
'Sachregister' is of virtually no help at all. Yet Kayser's and Heinsius' bibliographies, together with the Messkatalog, are invaluable for French literature
of the period, and not that hard to use (once you get used to them!).

There is a fairly high error margin, of the typographical variety at least, in
the Heinsius and Kayser. *Cave*, too, early nineteenth-century bookdealers
confused with eighteenth-century publishers. Nevertheless, these sources are
essential for Germanic imprints of French works of the period not to be found
in many major western European or American libraries. Like the Heinsius,
the Kayser was continued, but the continuation is of no particular relevance
to the present bibliography. A good deal of the information concerning French
works in the Heinsius is duplicated in the Kayser, but the two works complement each other. (Although it is not a review of the Heinsius and Kayser, the
interested reader might consult Bernhard Fabian, 'Heinsius, Kayser und die
Bibliographie des achtzehnten Jahrhunderts', *Zeitschrift für Bibliothekswesen und*
Bibliographie, 1980, 4, xxvii.[298]-302.) For further information, see Messkatalog below. See too the end of the commentary on Heinsius.

Krauss-Fontius: Werner Krauss and Martin Fontius, *Französische Drucke des*
18. Jahrhunderts in den Bibliotheken der Deutschen Demokratischen Republik, vol. i:
Bibliographie (in thematic order); vol. ii: *Register*. Both comprise vol. i of *Deutsche*
Akademie der Wissenschaften zu Berlin: Schriften des Instituts für Sprachen und Kultur
(Berlin: Akademie Verlag, 1970).

Le Petit: Jules Le Petit, *Bibliographie des principales éditions originales d'écrivains*
français du XVᵉ au XVIIIᵉ siècle (Paris 1888).

Lever: Maurice Lever, *La Fiction narrative en prose au XVIIème siècle: répertoire*
bibliographique du genre romanesque en France, 1600-1700 (Paris 1976).

Messkatalog: *Allgemeines Verzeichniss der Bücher, welche in der Frankfurter und Leipziger Ostermesse (Michael[is]messe) des* [date] *Jahres entweder ganz neu gedruckt, oder sonst verbessert, wieder aufgeleget worden sind, auch inskünftige noch herauskommen sollen.* Information derived from the 1790 volume. This was the title under which this series appeared for most of the second half of the eighteenth century. It began as the *Catalogus universalis* in the early seventeenth century, although there were other catalogues before. (For the other titles and for further publication details, see the sources listed below).

This is a highly important and rare series that began publication in the sixteenth century (in various forms) and continued well beyond the eighteenth. Each year of the Messkatalog is divided into two sections, for the Ostermess and the Michaelismess, respectively. I give the sections abbreviated as OM and MM, followed by the date and page(s), or folio(s) if that volume or year is not paginated. This is a source which Kayser and Heinsius relied upon, to a certain extent, and French bibliographers of the nineteenth century seem not infrequently to have made some use of it as well as borrowing from Heinsius and Kayser. Because there is no copy in the BN (or in Paris that I know of), aside from a few odd volumes, this highly important series has largely been ignored by twentieth-century bibliographers of French literature.

Those interested in further information concerning the Messkataloge should consult Berhard Fabian's most interesting 'Die Messkataloge des achtzehnten Jahrhunderts' in *Wolfenbütteler Schriften zur Geschichte des Buchswesens* 4 (Hamburg 1981), pp.[321]-342. This article provides, among much else, a discussion of the bibliographical 'modus operandi' of the Messkatalog and contains, too, valuable notes for those interested in pursuing the matter.

In addition to the sources cited in Fabian, I might suggest that the reader also consult: Michael S. Batts, *The Bibliography of German literature: an historical and critical survey* (Bern, Las Vegas 1978; no. 19 of Kanadische Studien zur deutschen Sprache und Literatur / Etudes canadiennes de langue et littérature allemandes), especially pp.42ff., *et passim*; and Albert Ward, *Book production: fiction and the German reading public, 1740-1800* (Oxford 1974).

I read through as many pertinent years of the Messkatalog as I had access to. Here is a list of those Messkataloge I was able to consult (in the British Library):

1704-1728 (excluding MM 1706; MM 1717; OM 1719; MM 1723; OM 1724; MM 1725; OM 1726; all of 1727; MM 1728)

1742-1801

I might here state that there is a section for books printed in languages other than German and Latin for each 'Messe'. It is particularly towards the latter part of the second quarter of the eighteenth century that the Kataloge begin to take on a definite importance, listing quite a few works in French. (Although French predominates in the 'foreign' section, the Messkatalog is also of paramount interest for especially English, Italian, Spanish and Polish language publications.) Many of the works listed in the Messkatalog are not to be found in western libraries. Since a large number indeed of works in French was published across the Rhine, the Messkatalog is vital for especially the second half of the century.

But the Messkatalog is important for the entire eighteenth century. For example, there is an entry for some 'Histoires plaisantes & recreatives Francois & allemand, par Matth. Mouchand, 12mo. Hannov. chez Nic. Förster', MM 1714 (f.G4r), not listed in prose-fiction bibliographies (or printed library catalogues). A couple of years later, we have a 'Recueil de quelques contes divertissants, de quelques Entretiens, de plusieurs lettres & de quelques maximes de morale tirees de plusieurs Autheurs françois par M. Gotschling [surely Caspar Gottschling]. 8vo. chez *Renger à Halle*' (MM 1716, f. F3v). I could not find this in the usual sources. Or one finds an entry for 'Le Modele des Meres ou Memoires de Madame la marquise de Bezire. 8. [octavo] Paris et Dresde, chez Walther' (OM 1770, p.82; also in Heinsius, *Handbuch*, p.811, with no mention of Paris). This work is not listed in any modern bibliography I have consulted. Surely it is a novel? Yet again, in the OM for 1798, one finds: 'Colons, les, de toutes couleurs; histoire d'un établissement nouveau à la côte de Guinée, par Mr. de Texier. 3 Vol. avec fig. 12. [duodecimo] à Berlin, l'auteur. (à Leipsig, Rabenhorst en comm[ission].)' (p.225). Although not listed in modern bibliographies dealing with French prose fiction, this is a novel. (The BLC even kindly informs us that it is one. The imprint indicates: Berlin, 1798. Imprimé chez George Decker.) Or MMF list 'Walzik ou lettres d'un philosophe à madame la comtesse de Claveinden', Altona, Hammerich, 1799, in-8°, as a possible translation (99.38). Their source is Monglond, 'qui cite Kayser'. The Messkatalog was quite possibly Kayser's source in turn: 'Walzik ou lettres d'un philosophe à la Comtesse de Claweinden. gr.-in-8. à Altona, Hammerich' (OM 1799, p.218). Or, again: MMF cite some 'Contes nouveaux en prose, tirés des meilleurs auteurs et publiés à l'usage de la jeunesse. Brunswick, Thomas, 1797, in-12', by F.-Th. Kuehne, after Monglond and Quérard (97.39). The Messkatalog entry gives a more complete title, also indicating that this was the first volume of a collection: 'Contes nouveaux en prose, tirés des meilleurs auteurs et publ. à l'usage de la jeunesse et de tous ceux qui aiment une lecture facile et amusante, p[ar] F. T. Kühne. Tom. 1r. 8. Bronsvic, Thomas', OM 1797, p.225. And so it goes.

The Messkataloge are also very important for the scholar who might want to study the diffusion and availability of a given work, as Fabian has emphasised: 'So sind die Messkataloge Quellen für den Bibliographen wie für den Literarhistoriker, für den Verlagshistoriker wie für den allgemeinen Kulturhistoriker' (p.337). Indeed, Ward has carefully examined the Messkataloge in establishing a good portion of his data concerning the interrelationship of the novel, booktrade and reading public in Germany (chapter 2 *et passim*).

My original intention had been to abstract all editions and items of interest to students of French prose fiction from the Messkatalog for at least the revolutionary period. But there was simply too much material and the scope of the present bibliography would have altered considerably. So I have limited myself to listing editions (sometimes works, too) directly relevent to the entries in this bibliography.

Since the Messkatalog is currently so rare, and in order to transmit something of the flavour of the series, original spelling has been retained (as far as my notes have permitted).

A few words of caution concerning works in French listed in the Messkatalog are in order. (What follows is based on having read well over a half century of the fair catalogues and having checked all novel entries – ascertainable as such – for 1790-1800.) Although the entries are fairly accurate (barring spelling errors of varying degrees of importance), occasionally a bookdealer is confused with the publisher. The date of entry does not always exactly correspond to what appears on the titlepage(s). It was often the custom to postdate a book (to increase the period of its 'marketability'), so that a book appearing in lateish 1765 (for example) might carry the date of 1766, but would be listed in the Messkatalog for 1765 (in all likelihood). For example, there is an entry in the Messkatalog for Prévost's *Mémoires et aventures d'un homme de qualité*, a 'Nouvelle éd. aug. 8 vol. 12. à Amsterdam et à Leipsic, chez Arkstée & Merkus. Avec Privilege' MM 1758, p.920. Harrisse lists a 'n. éd. rev. & cons. aug.', 8 vols in-12°, Amsterdam; Leipzig: Arkstée et Merkus, 1759. Avec Priv. de S. M. le Roi de Pologne, Elect. de Saxe (Harrisse 1896, p.399). This is probably the same edition as that listed in the Messkatalog.

Entries, while recording place (city usually) of origin, often follow with the Germanic cities and dealers where the work was available. Thus 'à Paris et à Leipsic chez Fleischer' might refer to a Paris publication (omitting the name[s] of the Parisian publishers), available at Fleischer's. There is for example: 'Religieuse, la, Ouvrage posthume de Diderot. 12mo. à Paris. A Leipsig, Rabenhorst' (OM 1797, p.237), the next entry being 'le même livre. 12mo. à Bâle, Decker (Leipsig, *Leo* en comm[ission])'. This possibly (dare I write 'probably'?) constitutes an edition (or issue) printed in Paris or bearing 'Paris' on the titlepage. However, it should be noted that MMF list no duodecimo edition for 1797. But see the commentary on Diderot's *La Religieuse* below. 'En commission' (often abbreviated 'en comm.') seems generally to refer to a joint publication *venture*, though not necessarily a joint publication proper. Sometimes too a work is listed rather perfunctorily in one 'Messe', and then an expanded entry is included for the next fair. Of course many a work was published in Germanic countries with 'Paris' indicated on the titlepage, together with other places, so it is possible that discounting entries listing 'Paris', for example (if a 'Paris' edition is known for that date), might mean omitting mention of a different edition. I have all taken these factors into consideration when reporting additional editions in this bibliography.

Professor Fabian, who was kind enough to provide me with an offprint of his article, is preparing a microform edition of the Messkataloge which will make this important reference source available to a wide public. (Part of this has been completed and is available. See Fabian's article, note 6, p.338).

MMF: Angus Martin, Vivienne G. Mylne, Richard Frautschi, *Bibliographie du genre romanesque français: 1751-1800* (London, Paris 1977).

Monglond: André Monglond, *La France révolutionnaire et impériale: annales de bibliographie méthodique et descriptive des livres illustrés* (Grenoble, Paris 1930-1963), 9 vols with an index to i and ii in a separate volume and a succinct index to the entire series by Mme Th. Monglond, comprising vol. x of a Slatkine reprint (Geneva 1978).

Nicoletti: Gianni Nicoletti, ed. of Mme de Graffigny's *Lettres d'une Péruvienne*

(Bari 1967), especially the bibliography (pp.[49]-67).

NUC: *National union catalog, pre-1956 imprints*, of the Library of Congress. The supplement is abbreviated 'NUC:S'.

OCLC: an acronym for what used to be known as the Ohio College Library Centre, now the On-line Computer Library Centre. This is one of the major cataloguing tools in the US and Canada. It consists of a computer data bank, containing well over eight million entries (as of autumn 1983). As the over two thousand libraries which use it acquire new materials (or indulge in retrospective cataloguing), these entries are keyed into the OCLC. Needless to say, the OCLC will play an ever increasing rôle in all kinds of bibliography. There is another major data base in the U.S. and abroad to which, unfortunately, I have not had access: RLIN (acronym for Research Libraries Information Network). This is part of the Research Libraries Group, Inc., a partnership organisation of some of the most important libraries in the U.S. (The ESTC has tied in with the group.) The RLIN data base is just as important as OCLC's and has many excellent search capabilities, far exceeding those of OCLC.

pl: preliminary leaf or leaves. These are invariably halftitles and titlepages excluded from the initial gathering of text or excluded from the pagination. Discrepancies are noted. See the introduction for further information.

Plomer: Henry R. Plomer, G. H. Bushnell, E. R. McC.Dix, *A dictionary of the printers and booksellers who were at work in England, Scotland and Ireland from 1726 to 1775* (Oxford 1932; there are other volumes in this series, but they are not pertinent to the present bibliography).

Primo cat(alogo): *Primo catalogo collettivo delle biblioteche italiane* (Rome 1962-1975), 8 vols. (A to Balmus, to date).

Quérard: J.-M. Quérard, *La France littéraire, ou dictionnaire bibliographique* (Paris 1859-1864), 12 vols.

Quérard SD: J.-M. Quérard, *Les Supercheries littéraires dévoilées* (seconde édition, Paris 1869-1870), 3 vols.

Reynaud: Henri J. Reynaud, *Notes supplémentaires sur les livres à gravures du 18ᵉ siècle* (Genève, Lyon 1955).

Rochedieu: Charles Alfred Emmanuel Rochedieu, *Bibliography of French translations of English works, 1700-1800*, with an introduction by Donald F. Bond (Chicago 1948).

Sabin: Joseph Sabin, *Bibliotheca americana: a dictionary of books relating to America, from its discovery to the present time* (New York 1868; reprt. Amsterdam 1961), 29 vols. A *New Sabin* is in course of publication, compiled by Lawrence Sidney Thompson (Troy, N.Y. 1974-), but it is not yet relevant to the present bibliography.

Sénelier: Jean Sénelier, *Bibliographie générale des œuvres de J.-J. Rousseau* (Paris 1950).

Tchemerzine: Avenir Tchemerzine, *Bibliographie d'éditions originales et rares d'auteurs français des XVᵉ, XVIᵉ, XVIIᵉ et XVIIIᵉ siècles* (Paris 1927-33), 10 vols. There is also a reprint, 'reproduction de l'édition originale publiée par Marcel Plée, 1927-1933, avec annotations de Lucien Scheler' (Hermann 1977).

Toinet: Paul Toinet, *'Paul et Virginie': répertoire bibliographique et iconographique* (Paris 1963).

Vian: Louis Vian (under the pseudonym of Louis Dangeau), *Montesquieu: bibliographie de ses œuvres* (Paris 1874).

Weller: Emil(e) Weller, *Die Falschen und fingierten Druckorte / Dictionnaire des ouvrages français portant de fausses indications des lieux d'impression et des imprimeurs* (Leipzig 1864).

Zambon: Maria Rosa Zambon, *Bibliographie du roman français en Italie au XVIIIe siècle: traductions* (Florence, Paris 1962).

Additional information concerning many of the more generalised sources listed above can be found in Dawson, ii.609-21.

The reader is also somewhat hesitatingly referred to Constance Mabel Winchell, *Guide to reference books* (8th edition, Chicago 1967; three supplements by Eugene P. Sheehy carry the work to 1970) and to Eugene Sheehy, with Rita G. Keckeissen and Eileen McIlvaine, *Guide to reference books* (9th edition of the Winchell, Chicago 1976; suppl. 1980). The latter work does not entirely supersede the first. (Although it is a useful guide and reference tool, there are inaccuracies, false directions and not a few omissions.) The primary source for finding bibliographies remains, of course, Theodore Besterman's *World bibliography of bibliographies*, with the supplements.

Additions to the bibliographies of French prose fiction 1618-1806

I

Anonymous?: *Les Amours de Zéokinizul, roi des Kofirans*, 1779

Anonymous, but see the commentary: Les / amours / de / Zeokinizul, / roi des Kofirans; / Traduits de l'Arabe du Voyageur / Krinelbol. / [composite ornament, largely a square laid on its side with various flowers] / A Constantinople, / De l'Imprimerie de Sa Hautesse. / [double rule: thick, thin] / M. DCC. LXXIX.

12°: 2 ff. (halftitle and titlepages) + [v]-vij + [1]-107, (108)-(109) pp.

Commentary: The pagination reflects a preface, the novel, and two pages of a 'Clef des noms'. The volume halftitle reads 'Les / amours / de / Zeokinizul, / roi des Kofirans.'

Tchemerzine lists this work as by Crébillon, fils (iv.193). Cioranescu also gives Mme de Vieuxmaisons (no.21748; under Crébillon's name), but has no rubric for 'Vieuxmaisons'. Quérard puts it under Crébillon (ii.333-34), mentioning that *L'Asiatique tolérant* is by La Beaumelle, in spite of having been attributed to Crébillon. (See La Beaumelle below.) Jones lists it under Crébillon, fils (1746), stating that he could not find the 1740 and 1745 editions listed by Gay. (Tchemerzine also gives 1746 and reproduces the titlepage of that edition; iv.192.) Drujon implies the work is by La Beaumelle (i.36), in spite of being attributed to Crébillon. Erroneously he states that the work went through about ten editions, the last dated 1770. He also reproduces a key to the novel (i, cols.36-39).

The only trace of the edition described here I could find is mentions in Gay and Tchemerzine. Jones lists after those sources. And MMF (57.R1) list after Jones. (It is more than likely that Tchemerzine lists after Gay).

This book was possibly produced in Holland or in Switzerland (perhaps in Germany), and seems to have been printed by the same firm that did La Beaumelle's *Asiatique tolérant*, 1779. (See that entry below.) Both works are 'romans à clef', dealing with the private life and reign of Louis XV.

Incipit: 'Quelques soins que se soient / donnés nos meilleurs Acadé- / miciens'.

2

Anonymous: *Apparition du cardinal Bellarmin*, ca.1760

(head title) [double rule] / L'apparition / Du Cardinal Bellarmin au Révérend Pere / Ricci Général des Jésuites, la nuit du / 5 Janvier 1760. / [rule] / Ouvrage traduit de l'Italien.

12°: 1-10 pp. + 1 f. (blank)

Commentary: There is no titlepage for the present copy and there probably never was one for the work. It consists of a single gathering, A1-A12; f.[A12] is a blank. I went through Carlos Sommervogel's (*et al.*) monumental and poorly indexed *Bibliothèque de la compagnie de Jésus* (12 vols, 1890-1930), but could find no trace of the *Apparition* in it. Not listed in the BLC, the NUC does record two copies of presumably this edition (University of Minnesota, Princeton

University), and there is one copy (again I assume of this edition) in the BN (Ld39.331). The verso of the marbled, second end paper of the volume containing the above copy carries what appears to be a scribbled, eighteenth-century library annotation. A contemporary manuscript table of contents lists the *Apparition* with the date of 1760. I see no reason to doubt the unknown owner's accuracy. This piece was doubtlessly composed in French, and there would thus be no Italian original.

Incipit: 'Eh! Vive Dieu, mon cher Confrere, tout est perdu parmi nous'.

3

Anonymous?: *L'Art d'enseigner la langue française / L'Arte d'insegnare la lingua francese*, 1684

Anonymous? (See the commentary). Double titlepages, beginning with the left, verso, i: L'arte d'insegnare / la lingua / franzese, / per mezzo dell'italiana, / o vero / la lingua italiana / per mezzo / della franzese, / Che contiene con un nuovo Metodo la / Teorica, e la Pratica generale delle / due medesime Lingue. / All'illvstrissimo signore / marchese Pier Antonio / Gerini, / Gentilhuomo Tratte-nuto del / Granduca di Toscana. / [small, symmetrical woodcut ornament, same for both titlepages] / In Lione, / E si vende / in Firenze, / Per Jacopo Carlieri, Libraio, all'Insegna / di San Luigi. / [rule] / M. DC. LXXXIV. / Con Licenza de' Superiori.

ii: L'art d'enseigner / la langue / françoise, / par le moyen de l'italienne, / ov / la langue italienne / par la françoise; / Comprenant par une nouvelle Methode / la Theorie & la Pratique generale / de ces deux Langues. / A monsievr / le marquis Pierre Antoine / Geriny, / Gentilhomme Entretenu du / Grand Duc de Toscane. / [woodcut ornament] / A Lyon, / Et se vend / a Florence, / Chez Jacques Charlier, Libraire / à l'Enseigne de S. Loüis. / [rule] / M. DC. LXXXIV. / Avec Permission des Superieurs.

12°: 2 pl (two titlepages facing each other) + 12 ff. (4 + 2 + 9 + 8 + 1 pp.) + 1-264, 265-270, 271-356 pp.

Commentary: The pagination reflects:
  1. a dedicatory letter to Gerini, signed Jacq. Charlier / Jacopo Carlieri;
  2. 'L'imprimeur au lecteur';
  3. 'L'autheur au lecteur';
  4. a 'table';
  5. 1 p. of legal material;
  6. all the sundry pieces of grammar, dialogues, etc. (pp.1-264);
  7. 'Au lecteur' (pp.265-70);
  8. Contes (pp.271-356).

The legal documents comprise a permission for Pierre Guillimin to print the work (Lyon, 16 January 1684, signed 'Deseve') and a 'consentement' ('Je consens pour le Roy à l'impression requise. A Lyon le 8. Janvier 1684. Vaginay'). The 'Autheur au lecteur' indicates that there was a larger format, anterior edition, printed in Florence, but out-of-print, and that the current book is the same, barring a few additions concerning verbs. (The additions are also mentioned in the 'consentement').

I list this work because it contains, at the end, pieces of prose fiction, and also serves as an excellent exemplum of the many pedagogical works printed in France and abroad containing items of interest to students of the 'genre romanesque'. I could find no trace of this edition anywhere.

As for the author: the BN has a similar edition as far as the contents are concerned (Venise: Joseph Prodocine, 1701; X.11528), which is listed in the BNC under the name of Michele Berti, a work 'corrigée, et augmentée dans cette derniere impression par L.D.L. [Louis (de) Lépine]' ([12] + 1-368 pp. in-12°). There is also a Bologne: Longhi, n.d. [end seventeenth century?] in the BN (X.11539; [17] + [1]-396 pp. in-12°, possibly also in the NUC with locations for Allegheny College in Pennsylvania and the Union Library Catalogue of Pennsylvania; conceivably the union catalogue refers to the Allegheny copy). However, from the dedicatory letter to Gerini in the 1684 edition, it would seem that this book is by Charlier, or that the latter at least had a hand in its composition: 'Ce petit Ouvrage revient au jour pour la seconde fois sous vos favorables auspices; Son Auteur ne pouvoit luy choisir un plus illustre protecteur, qu'en le consacrant aux merites incōparables d'un Gentil-homme autāt estimé que vous l'étes', etc.

All the introductory material is bilingual (columns in French and Italian on each page). The same holds true for much of the book, including the dialogues and tales.

Concerning the tales: in the 'L'Autheur au lecteur', the author explains that he wrote them first in French, then translated them into Italian. The introduction to the tales proper further elucidates: 'J'ay tiré le Recueil de ces Contes de plusieurs livres Latins, Italiens, & Anglois, & les ay mis en langue Françoise'. The author then goes into some detail concerning his style and the pedagogical value of stories in a foreign language. These short tales (a paragraph or so each) are:

1. 'Le chien fidelle à son maître';
2. 'Le borgne, & le bossu, qui se mocquent l'un de l'autre';
3. 'Autre réponce à propos';
4. 'Le chien, qui se trompe';
5. 'Une femme se mocque adroitement de son mary';
6. 'Le renard flatteur';
7. 'La vengeance malheureuse';
8. 'Le malade guery par hazard';
9. 'Le savetier medecin';
10. 'L'orage de la mer';
11. 'Le plus habile d'entre tous les bouchers';
12. 'Le fou sage';
13. 'Adresse d'un predicateur';
14. 'Hardiesse d'un filou';
15. 'Un vieillard qui souhaite de mourir appelle la mort, mais il se repent aprés de l'avoir appellée';

16. 'Un homme qui a de l'esprit, demande à boire de l'eau & ne boit que du vin, & pourquoy';
17. 'Réponce [*sic*] d'un maréchal, qui pensoit [*sic*] le cheval d'un medecin';
18. 'Une femme fait semblant d'aimer son mary, qui luy joüe une piece';
19. 'Le voleur redoutable par son adresse';
20. 'Il ne faut pas oublier de rendre ce que l'on emprunte';
21. 'Le trompeur trompé';
22. pp.321-22 have been removed from the book; no title available;
23. 'Le songe heureux';
24. 'Un homme conte une piece, qu'il avoit joüée à des païsans';
25. 'Un homme jeune joüe une piece a deux aveugles gourmans, & débauchez';
26. 'Un païsan fait le recit d'une avanture, qui luy étoit arrivée';
27. 'Un autre fait le recit d'une tromperie faite à un cabaretier';
28. 'Le cheval aveugle';
29. 'Le juge avaricieux';
30. 'Le Suisse malade'.

Incipit: ('Le chien fidelle à son maître') 'Un voleur tâchoit d'êtrer pēdant la nuit dans une maison, pour emporter quelque chose.'

4

Anonymous: *L'Asile des Grâces*, 1796

This piece of prose fiction is contained in the following volumes by the comte [Jean Bapiste] Charles [Henri] Hector d'Estaing (1729-1793); Julien Offray de La Mettrie (1709-1751); and the abbé Favre of the Société littéraire of Metz; edited and published by Claude François Xavier Mercier, called Mercier de Compiègne (1763-1800):

i: Le plaisir, / poëme / en VI chants, / Par feu le Comte d'Estaing. / Nouvelle édition. / [rule] / L'égalité finit où sont les passions. / Chant IV, page 82. / [rule] / A Paris, / Chez C. Mercier de Compiègne, / rue Coq-Honoré, n°. 120. / [short rule] / M. DCC. XCVI.

ii: L'école / de la volupté, / les quatre heures / de la toilette / des dames, / et / l'asile des Graces; / poëmes / pour servir de suite a celui / du plaisir. / Nouvelle édition. / [rule] / Æneadum genitrix et rerum diva voluptas! / [rule] / A Paris, / Chez l'éditeur, Imprimeur-Libraire, / Rue du Coq-Honoré, n°. 120. / [short rule] / M. DCC. XCVI.

32°, i: 2 pl (halftitle page, and titlepage with 'Avis de l'éditeur' verso) + [1]-(127), [128] pp.

ii: 1 pl (titlepage with 'Avis' verso) + [j]-iv, [5-6], [7]-(136) pp.

Commentary: The first volume contains the halftitle: 'Le plaisir, / poëme.'; titlepage (with the 'Avis...' verso); an 'Épitre dédicatoire au désœuvrement' (pp.[1]-(3)). A 'sommaire' continues p.(3); then follows the poem with, at the end (p.[128]), an interesting catalogue of 'Ouvrages qui se trouvent chez le même' (i.e., Mercier de Compiègne).

The second volume contains the titlepage, with the 'Avis' verso; a 'Préface' (pp.[j]-iv); 'A ma chere amie' (pp.[5-6]); *L'Ecole de la volupté* (pp.[7]-(64)); *Les Quatre heures de la toilette des dames* (pp.(65)-(118)); *L'Asile des Grâces, conte érotique* (p.119) [*sic*]-(136)).

There is a pretty, allegorical frontispiece to vol. i, captioned and not signed. (Not in Cohen or Reynaud).

The one unequivocal piece of prose fiction in these two volumes is *L'Asile des Grâces*. MMF (85.4) list this tale as 'L'asile des Grâces, étrennes aux jolies femmes de Paris, conte érotique publié par un Parisien' for 'Cythère & Paris, Royez, 1785, pet. in-12' after Gay. They further remark that 'selon Gay, ce conte serait en prose'. They also mention another edition for '1786, pet. in-12', once again according to Gay. This information is so given in Gay (i, col.292), who also notes that those editions contain an engraving.

Gay further remarks that this tale 'a été réimprimé à la suite de l'*Ecole de la Volupté*, en 1796'. The entry for *L'Ecole de la volupté* is as follows: '*Ecole (l') de la volupté* (en prose) et l'*Isle de Calypso*. Cologne (Paris), P. Marteau, 1742, 1746, 1747, in-12 [ill.] [...] Suivi de la *Nouvelle Messaline*, 1758 [...] Genève, 1783 [...] Paphos, 1764 [...] Suivi des *Quatre heures de la toilette des Dames* et de l'*Asile des grâces* (par La Mettrie). Paris, Mercier, 1796, in-16 de iv et 136p. – Les notes mythologiques et l'épître dédicatoire à Madame de Lamballe sont retranchées. L'*Asile des grâces*, conte érotique, est en prose; 17 pages' (ii, cols.55-56). A cross reference then leads to the *Tableau du plaisir et de la volupté* (Paris: Mercier, an VII), which is given as 2 vols. in-18, with the same contents as the collection listed here (iv, col.1170). Gay somewhat enigmatically remarks: 'Nouvelle édition, augmentée du recueil intitulé: l'*Ecole de la volupté*'. Since the contents appear to be the same, I do not know why he indicates that the 'an VII' edition is augmented. Under *Le Plaisir, rêve*, the same source gives 1785, then 'Paris, 1794, 1796, in-18, avec titre gravé (de Saint-Denis et Mallet ...)'. Gay adds: 'la dernière édition seule, qui est publiée par Mercier de Compiègne, n'est pas anonyme. – Réimprimé dans le *Tableau du plaisir et de la volupté*'.

Gay's entry for *Les Quatre heures de la toilette des dames* gives editions for 1779, 1780, 1783, 1793 and 1882, the latter having only 500 copies printed. (That is probably a mistake, his having meant 1880, 600 copies printed; BNC, OCLC, etc.)

Although Gay indicates that *L'Asile des Grâces* is by La Mettrie, he is wrong (La Mettrie died in 1751), probably having confused the facts somewhat. *L'Ecole de la volupté* is generally attributed to La Mettrie (first edition, Cologne: Pierre Marteau, 1746; Barbier ii, col.15d), and not *L'Asile des Grâces*.

Gay's errors, and others' as well, seem to stem from the fact that they derived their information from secondary sources (largely sales catalogues). I could find no other copy of the volumes listed here, or indeed of the 'an VII' edition.

Mercier's 'Avis de l'éditeur' to *Le Plaisir* is of considerable interest, for, from it, we learn that he was directly acquainted with d'Estaing: 'Ce fut dans les cachots de la conciergerie, au mois de Pluviôse, que je vis l'auteur de cet ouvrage, avant que la hache décemvirale le punît d'avoir joui d'un grand nom. Ce fut là que je le forcai [*sic*] de m'avouer qu'il était l'auteur de ce poëme, et que je lui promis de lui donner, comme poëte, un rang qu'il avait rougi d'avouer quand la sottise lui donnait celui de la noblesse. Je publierai par la suite une édition de ses romans et autres ouvrages. La première édition de ce poëme, parut en 1755 *n*-12 [*sic*] et *in*-8°. A Otiopolis, chez Daniel Songecreux, à l'Apocalypse' (i, verso of the titlepage).

An 'Avis' on the verso of the titleleaf to vol. ii explains the relationship between the two volumes: 'Le poëme du Comte d'Estaing [...] que nous venons de publier, pouvant ne pas remplir entierement le but que se proposeraient nos lecteurs [...] nous nous empressons de les en dédommager, en leur offrant ce recueil de poëmes choisis sur la volupté [...]. Ces deux volumes sont donc inséparables: et le relieur doit intituler le tome 1ʳ. *Le Plaisir*. Et celui-ci, *La Volupté*, tome. 2ᵉ'.

The preface to volume ii is actually Favre's to the *Quatre heures de la toilette des dames* (compared to the first edition, 1779). As for Favre's paeon to the ladies' toilette table: Mercier explains that the work was published in 1780, in-16, '*chez J. F. Bastien*. Nous avons supprimé les notes mythologiques et l'épître dédicatoire à madame de Lamballe' (ii.(65), note). That work actually first appeared in 1779, magnificently illustrated and is, today, of considerable rarity.

Incipit: (*L'Asile des Grâces*) 'L'amour est un Dieu malin: qui ignore sa / malice, ne l'a jamais connu.'

5

Anonymous: *La Chatonciade*, 1757

La / chatonciade, / poëme / heroï-comique. / [double rule] / Honni soit qui mal y pense. / [double rule] / [small woodcut decoration: two curious little busts haloed by rays] / A Provins, / De l'Imprimerie de la Veuve Louis / Michelin, Imprimeur-Libraire. / [double rule] / M DCC LVII. / Avec permission.

12°: 1 f. (titlepage) + [3]-45 pp.

Commentary: I could find no trace of this work, never mind edition, anywhere. It is a burlesque prose-poem of sorts in four canti, and somewhat confusing. It opens with an invocation. Then comes a description of the rivalries and jealousies of the gods on Olympus. (The author mixes mythologies, which doesn't much help the reader keep the plot straight.) When Juno tries to enlist the aid of her august spouse in her squabbles with 'Cythérée' (and others), Jupiter impatiently answers: 'Venés vous allumer de nouveau le flambeau de la discorde? Tant de guerres, de meurtres, de tempêtes, ou de villes saccagées n'ont pû vous satisfaire? Un léger affront que vous croyez avoir reçu vous enflamme d'une colere implacable? Vengés vous donc, mais sans éclat' (p.15).

The human counterparts to the gods are Damon and Licidas. They are well received at the court of Venus, particularly since they arrive while the goddess is happily ensconced with a novel: 'Cette lecture venoit sans doute de rendre quelque chose de vif & d'enjoué à son caractere; son abord fut doux & gracieux, & les mortels heureux furent honorés d'un demi souris [*sic*]' (p.22). To make a rather long story short: there is a huge battle centred on a couple of regal felines. The cats' fortress is stormed, with the aid of 'la cour de Cupidon' (p.34). Enters one Eglé, 'la plus aimable des Nymphes du canton' (p.38). Damon and Licidas fall into disgrace with their divine friends, and the story ends with a sort of moral exhortation to the rest of mortaldom. The reader is left with the impression that he has just visited Pope in Bedlam.

Incipit: 'Je chante l'illustre journée où les Chats acquirent une gloire immortelle'.

6

Anonymous: *Complaisances amoureuses*, 1758

Complaisances / amoureuses / faites, / à madame / la / comtesse de G*** / par / Mr le comte de S*** / [rule] / Aux dépens du Beau-Sexe. / MDCCLVIII.

12°: 1 f. (titlepage) + [III]-IV, [V]-XI, [XII]-XIV + [1]-58 pp.

Commentary: The first item is an 'Avant-propos du libraire'; the second, a 'Préface'; the third, a 'Lettre de madame la comtesse de G** [*sic*] á [*sic*] l'editeur' (dated at the end, 'à Paris ce 28 Septembre 1757'), and finally the *Complaisances* themselves. On the verso of the titlepage is an epigraph: 'Curribus Automedon [...] Ovid. de arte amandi, lib. I.' Signatures are consecutive throughout (A12-C12), in spite of the pagination. Catchwords on every page.

The only other copy I could find is in the BL (012331.de.24).

This work is marginal to the 'genre romanesque', the main text consisting of prose aphorisms dealing with love, followed by briefer poetical statements dealing with the same particular topic. However, the preliminary material directly parallels the prose-fiction subterfuges of the time, and is interesting to the 'genre romanesque' precisely because those subterfuges are applied to what is basically a non-fiction work. The 'Avant-propos' opens with the usual lie: 'On va croire, que la préface & l'ouvrage sont de la même main: mais je dois avertir en conscience, qu'on se trompe: le livre est de l'Officier, à qui on l'attribuë', etc. From what follows, it is obvious that the 'libraire' and 'auteur' are one and the same. (Absurd claims made that the 'préface' was composed by 'un homme du Seiziéme Siécle: je m'y connois, croïez, qu'il ne cache ainsi sa Vieillesse, qu'avec l'Elixir de Paracelse, ou le breuvage d'Eson' [p.IV], etc.) Then the preface was supposedly written by the editor, and not the author. The original manuscript was found on the body of of a Gascon officer killed in the Battle of Hastenbeck (which took place 26 June 1757: d'Estrées beat Cumberland), and so it goes, making of the preliminary material itself a definite piece of prose fiction!

Incipit: 'Je ne sai, si les Chagrins de l'Amour ne sont pas à préferer aux Ennuis de ces Cœurs'.

7

Anonymous: *Délibération extraordinaire des charbonniers de la communauté de Quaix*, 1764

(head title) [double rule] / Délibération extraordinaire / des Charbonniers de la Communauté de / Quaix en Dauphiné, au sujet du retour / du Parlement. / Du Vendredi 2 Mars 1764.

12°: 1-27 pp.

Commentary: At the end of the text, there is a legal statement: 'Permis d'imprimer. A Grenoble ce 3 mars / 1764. Vallet, Lieut. Gén. de Pol.' There is also a colophon: 'A Grenoble, / Chez Andre' Arnaud, Imprimeur-Libraire, / rue Brocherie.' This is a satirical piece which might be considered marginal to the 'genre romanesque'. It sets on stage some thirty coalmen who dialogue principally with one 'R....'. The overtones are political, and the style humourous.

I could find only one other copy of this work (a different edition), in the BN. Although there is no card for it in the 'fichier des anonymes', it is listed in the *Catalogue de l'histoire de France* (Paris 1855, rprt. 1968), ii.422 and in the *Table générale alphabétique des ouvrages anonymes: table des noms de lieux* (1931), xii.194. The BN edition is [1]-24 pp. in-12° (8vo.Lb38.950). It too carries Vallet's permission and Arnaud's colophon.

Incipit: 'Comme Consul je vous ai fait assembler. Les Seigneurs de Parlement rentreront au Palais le 20 de ce mois'.

8

Anonymous: *Dom Carlos, grand d'Espagne*, 1711

(titlepage in *red* and black) Dom / *Carlos* / grand / *d'Espagne*. / Nouvelle / *galante*. / [woodcut ornament: two cupids shaking hands over the winged head of another] / *A La Haye*, / Chez Jean Swart, Matchand [*sic*] Li- / braire dans le Korte Poote, à l'En- / seigne d'Ovide. / [rule] / *M. DCC. XI.*

12°: 1 f. (titlepage) + 3-158 pp.

Commentary: This novel is not listed in any bibliography I have consulted, except Weller (see below). The only other copy of this edition I have been able find is in the BN (Y2.27988). The probable reason it escaped the attention of Lever and Jones is that they thought it an edition of Saint-Réal's well known historical novel, *Dom Carlos, nouvelle historique* which first appeared in 1672 (Lever, pp.142-43). The *Dom Carlos, grand d'Espagne, nouvelle galante* described above has nothing to do with Saint-Réal's work. It is set in a much later time, and takes place mostly in France. The earliest edition of this novel I could find is in the rare-books room of the University of Florida, Gainesville: A Cologne, Chez Pierre Marteau. [no address, rule] M. DC. LXXXVIII. (listed in the NUC under 'Saint-Réal'). Indeed, it seems quite probable that my copy is a reissue with Swart's cancel titlepage. And quite possibly Swart also published the 1688, 'Cologne', 'Marteau' edition. Although I was unable to juxtapose the copies, mine seems to match the Florida copy. In fact, it is possible to see the folded-over edge of the titlepage leaf in my copy. (My thanks go to the University of Florida library staff for their cooperation.)

For what it's worth, Weller lists a *Dom Carlos, grand d'Espagne, nouvelle galante* under Saint-Réal's name, with editions for 1686, 'Cologne, P. Marteau (La Haye)' and 'ib. 1712' (p.40).

Incipit: 'Un homme de la premier [*sic*] Qualité de toute l'Espagne, étant devenu Maitre de grans biens à l'âge de dix-huit ans par le decés de ses pere & mere, fit resolution d'aller en France, pour voir non-seulement le Païs, mais encore pour apprendre ses Exercices.'

9

Anonymous: *Essais de mon ami*, 1788

Essais / de mon ami, / publiés / par moi. / [rule] / Omne tulit punctum, qui miscuit utile dulci. / Hor. / [rule] / [decoration comprising three stars] / A Londres, / Et se trouve à Paris, / Chez les marchands de Nouveautés; / Et à Caen, / Chez Poisson, Imprimeur-Libraire, rue / Froide-rue. / [rule] / 1788.

8°: 1 pl (titlepage) + 3 ff. (1 + 3 pp.) + [1]-104 pp.

Commentary: This work is not listed in the usual bibliographies or in any printed library catalogue I have consulted. The only modern mention of it is to be found in Monglond, under the heading of 'Poésie', 1789, incorrectly as 'Essais à mon Ami, publiés par ...' (i, col.525), after the *Mercure de France*, April 1789. The information given by the *Mercure* is as follows: '*Essais à mon Ami*, publiés par ..., Brochure in-8°, de 104 pages. Prix, 24s. A Londres; & se trouve à Paris, chez les Marchands de Nouveautés; & à Caen, chez Poisson, Imp-Lib. rue Froide-Rue: on en trouve des exemplaires chez Cailleau, Lib Imp. rue Galande; & Lacroix, à l'orme St-Gervais. Ce petit Volume est composé de Poésies fugitives, & de petits Contes en prose fort courts. Les vers en sont souvent foibles; mais il y a dans la poésie & dans la prose en général de la facilité & un but moral' (p.94). In spite of the divergent listing, I do not doubt that we are dealing with the same work and the same edition. It is also listed in the *Journal de la librairie, ou catalogue hebdomadaire* as 'Essais de mon ami, publiés par moi', and it is stated that it was available at Cailleau's – 'published by' is implied – in Paris (1788, xxvi, no.41, art.5).

The three preliminary leaves consist of a one-paragraph 'Avis de l'éditeur', and 2 ff., 3 pp. of a 'Table'. The book is signed in 4s. The contents are in prose and verse, short prose pieces and poems. Many of the prose pieces are meditations, some with a tenuous plot of sorts, à la Gessner. The 'Avis', a short paragraph, claims the work is by a friend which the 'editor' has put in order 'au hazard'. Here are the prose pieces, according to the head titles:

1. Le bon conseil, conte oriental, p.[1].
2. Ma solitude, pp.2-5.
3. Le difficile, conte oriental, pp.10-11.
4. A l'année commençante, pp.12-13.

5. La curieuse, conte arabe, pp.15-20.
6. Les envieux. Conte oriental, p.26.
7. Le pere malheureux, anecdote, pp.30-34.
8. Le retour de Sémur, conte oriental, p.38.
9. La fille séduite, anecdote, pp.40-54.
10. La consolation des mechans, conte oriental, p.57.
11. L'indulgence, conte oriental, p.59.
12. Le riche, anecdote, pp.61-66.
13. Les épitaphes, conte oriental, p.68.
14. Le suicide, anecdote, pp.69-75.
15. Reponse d'Amenides, p.76.
16. La prudence, conte oriental, p.77.
17. L'exemple dangereux, anecdote, pp.79-84.
18. Le duel, conte oriental, pp.85-86.
19. Le départ de Sémur, conte oriental, p.91.
20. Il est minuit, pp.93-94.
21. La consolation, conte oriental, p.95.
22. Harangue d'Abbas, conte oriental, p.97.
23. La modération, conte oriental, pp.100-101.

Incipit: ('Le bon conseil') 'Le jeune Sélim avait composé un ouvrage qu'il soumit à la critique du sage Abbas.'

10

Anonymous: *Evénements historiques choisis*, 1691

Evenemens / historiques / choisis. / Divisés en deux Parties. / [woodcut of a rose] / Suivant la copie de Paris. / A Bruxelles, / Chez Jean Leonard, Libraire / & Imprimeur ruë de la Cour. / [rule] / M. DC. XCI.

12°: 1 pl (titlepage) + 3 ff. (4 + 2 pp.) + 1-182 + halftitle + 185-394 pp. + 3 ff. (5 + 1 pp.)

Commentary: There are two 'parties' (consecutive pagination and signatures), separated by a half titlepage reading simply 'Seconde / partie.' This work first appeared in 1690, as far as I know (copies in the BN, G.23394, and New York Public Library [NUC]; listed in Conlon i.574, no.4654). I know of no other copy of this edition. It is marginal to the 'genre romanesque', consisting of short extracts from all kinds of historical works, but since the authenticity of many of the works cited is open to question – or, at the very least, the incidents reported – I have chosen to include the *Evénements historiques choisis*. The editor and/or author cites his sources at the end of each 'history', such as the *Histoire métalique de la république de Hollande*, *Relation de Groenland*, *Mémoires du baron de Sirot*, etc.

The first item is a dedication, 'A sa majesté britanique', signed 'J. Leonard' (presumably the bookdealer); the second is an interesting 'Avertissement'. Then follow the 'histoires', a 'Table' and finally an 'Extrait du privilege' (to Daniel Hortemels, 1 September 1689; registered 27 September 1690, signed 'J. Cramoisy'; 'achevé d'imprimer' for the first time, 20 October 1690). The dedication to the king of England is signed 'J. Leonard' (as mentioned), but it seems doubtful that Léonard was the editor, since it is clearly indicated that he was simply republishing a work (presumably by someone else).

The 'Avertissement' is of interest to historians of the 'genre romanesque' and its relationship to history: 'Quelque instruction & quelque plaisir que puisse donner le Roman, l'Histoire ne laisse pas d'avoir sur luy le même avantage que le veritable a sur le chimerique. Si nous cherchons des exemples dans les livres pour regler nôtre conduite, ceux que nous sçavons être faux, pouront ils jamais avoir de l'Empire sur nôtre esprit, les actions Heroïques que nous lirons dans la Cleopatre [by La Calprenède], par exemple, auront elles l'autorité de nous en faire entreprendre de semblables, & prendrons nous pour modele des personnes imaginaires. Il n'en est pas de même de l'Histoire, & sa lecture produit des effets plus certains', etc. The editor then proceded to chose the most 'romanesque' possible tidbits from the 'histories' at his disposal, paying careful attention to shipwrecks, capture into slavery, to the exotic in Turkish stories, Italian, Danish, Egyptian, etc.! Each tale is headed by a titillating title: 'Passion violente', 'Innocence opprimée', 'Fortune tragique', 'Le Tombeau des amants', and so on.

Incipit: ('L'Amour foudroyant') 'Magdelaine de Senneterre veûve de Guy de Saint Exupery Seigneur de Miraumont, êtoit de la Religion, & faisoit sa retraite à Miraumont, Château dans le Limouzin.'

II

Anonymous: *Fantaisie nouvelle*, ca.1750

(head title) [line of ornamentation] / Fantaisie / nouvelle / a / madame de M***. / [rule]

12°: (1)-(183) pp.

Commentary: This is a piece of epistolary fiction for which there is no titlepage (in the present copy at least). The head title is repeated at the beginning of each letter. The signatures are consecutive, albeit highly irregular. For some reason or other, the printers seem to have had considerable difficulty correctly signing the 4th, 5th and 6th folios of most of the gatherings.

The first four gatherings consist of one letter each; at the end of each is the following indication: A12v, p.(24) '*Prix six sols.*'; B12v, p.(48) '*Prix six sols.*'; C12v, p.(72) '*P rix six so. [sic]*'; D12r, p.(95) '*Prix six sols.*' Then there must have been a change of issuing policy, because letters 5 and 6, very disproportionate in length – 97)-(117) and (118)-(183) pp.; p.96 is blank – take up the remainder of the novel, as extant. Letter 5 does not even comprise an entire gathering and thus was never intended to be issued separately. Also there is no indication of price at the end of letters 5 and 6. The head title decorations are identical for letters 1-4; then there is a change for both 5 and 6.

In light of the above, it seems probable that we are dealing with two separate printings, in spite of the consecutive signatures, and that the first four letters were issued separately, as a kind of serialised novel. Perhaps the author and/or publisher were disappointed with the results, and tried to hasten the completion of their endeavour. In any case, this novel is incomplete. Possibly no more of it appeared.

The only trace of this novel that I have been able to find is the first gathering, letter 1, pp.(1)-(24) in the BN rare books room (Rés. Y2.2639), which also has no titlepage. As for the date, the best I can suggest is ca. 1750, or shortly thereafter, due to typography, spelling and printing. Indeed, in the novel, the author mentions Mme de Graffigny's *Lettres d'une Péruvienne* (1747), J. F. R. de Bastide's *Causes célèbres de Cythère* (1750) and his *Confessions d'un fat* (1749, without a doubt, in spite of what Quérard records; see Jones p.78). No authors or dates are mentioned. (It might be noted that the *Confessions d'un fat* and the *Tribunal de l'amour* are listed in the Messkatalog for Francfort, Franz. Varrentrapp, MM 1749, ff.E4r and F1r respectively. The latter is also in OM 1750, but with no place of publication or publisher mentioned; p.54. New editions of the *Tribunal*, or copies of the 'Cythère' [Paris], first edition?)

Since this work is in the vein of those by Bastide – indeed the *Tribunal de l'Amour, ou les causes célèbres de Cythère* (Jones p.100, same for 1749 and 1750) is incomplete – it seems possible to suggest Bastide's name as the author. (I am not familiar enough with his works to make a positive statement either way.) The author of the *Fantaisie nouvelle* refers to the above two novels by Bastide in the following terms: 'ma tante qui sçavoit que rien n'est plus propre à faire des impressions durables que les traits semés dans des livres dont le fonds est relatif à nos penchans, m'en prêta deux qui paroissoient nouvellement & de la méchanceté desquels elle pouvoit tout se promettre. (C'étoit les Causes célébres de Cythère & les Confessions d'un Fat.)' (pp.(32)-(33)). He continues: 'Ces livres, quoique écrits avec esprit sont, comme vous sçavez, de purs libelles contre les femmes.'

Indeed, the *Fantaisie nouvelle* is scarcely complimentary towards women. It deals with the coming-of-age of a young man, and more particularly his seduction by, and contact with various rather nasty, immoral and highly unscrupulous women. The end result, rather than being a school for scandal, is a school for corruption, hypocrisy and perfidy. The letters of the novel are addressed by Saint-Fer (as he is later named) to a beautiful woman, who enjoys all the appearances of virtue. From the start, the tone is set: 'on est le maître de sa réputation; les vertus & les vices ne sont rien par eux-mêmes, c'est le ton que l'on prend qui décide leur valeur & leur succès? L'art de cacher un caractère infâme est un moyen plus sûr de réussir dans le monde que les plus grandes vertus qu'on ne sçait pas faire valoir' (p.(5)).

To shorten: his ageing aunt finds him rather attractive, lures him to her country estate, and seduces him. In the meanwhile, she has said so many nasty things about women that Saint-Fer grows to hate the entire sex, except for his aunt of course! The aunt's decrepit neighbour also finds Saint-Fer attractive, but the two decide to share him, rather than become enemies and both lose him. Saint-Fer has to return to Paris (death of his father) and falls for the comtesse de Rainsable, who is a rather curious creature, both for her peculiar kind of beauty and for her disguised nastiness. After a long talk, she ends by treating him as the inexperienced adolescent that he is. Saint-Fer decides to leave in the middle of the night, and to write her 'une lettre bien impertinente, bien ridicule & très-conforme à l'extravagance de ma résolution' (p.(183)). And there the present copy of this curious novel ends. One can only speculate as to its continuation!

Incipit: 'Dois-je me fier à vos sermens? Songez-vous au poids immense de tout secret essentiel'.

12

Anonymous: *Le Favori disgracié*, 1678

Le / favory / disgracie', / nouvelle. / [large woodcut ornament: vase/basket of flowers] / A Cologne, / Chez Jean Stoupen. / M. DC. LXXVIII.

12°: 1 pl + 1-128p.

Commentary: I could find no trace of this work anywhere (NUC, BLC, NUC, Arsenal, Lever, Gay, Weller, etc.). The head- and runningtitles read 'Histoire nouvelle'.

Signature sequences are in 6s (4 + 2, arabic: title-leaf + A-A4, [A5-6], B-B4, [B5-6] ... L-L3, [L4]).

Because of the uniqueness of this volume, it seems appropriate to enter into a brief analysis of its contents. The tale takes place during the aftermath of William of Normandy's conquest of England. Montalant the elder, also of Normandy, is poorly recompensed for his warrior services. With his son, he lives in retirement. Montalant junior becomes good friends with prince Henry, son of the king of France, and has fallen for Floride, daughter of the marquis de Douvre whose twin brother had been kidnapped shortly after birth. (Long political and emotional explanations surround that episode.) Eventually the perfidious prince Henry meets Floride, succumbs to her beauty and graces, and attempts to carry her off. Montalant intervenes, but the two lovers are forced to flee. The father joins them in Flanders. Much goes on, but the three are eventually captured by Scottish privateers and locked up in Edinburgh Castle. (Floride and Montalant pass themselves off as brother and sister.) Montrose, the king of Scotland's favourite, falls for Floride. A new Andromaque, she decides to marry Montrose (thereby freeing Montalant and his father), and then to kill herself. Suspense mounts, centred on Montalant's agony, although he knows nothing about her final plan. Floride is more or less dragged to the nuptial altar, but a distinctive birthmark on Montrose's hand reveals that he is her long-lost twin brother. Floride and Montalant eventually marry, and all ends happily.

The tale is well told, incorporating letters, poems, and proverbs set off in the narrative, which is largely third-person. There are exciting battles, good character development, castles hidden away in dark forests, tempests, and an alternance of despair and happiness. Although the French is far from matching the best of the classical period, I would be surprised if further editions – perhaps in collections – of this historical novel do not turn up.

Finally I might point out that there are numerous typographical errors. Some of these follow certain patterns that might be indicative of regionalisms: 'croid' for 'croit' (p.22); 'vid' for 'vît' (p.24); 'void' for 'voit' (p.35), and so on. Sometimes the 'v' replaces a 'u', and the tilde is irregularly used to help justify the margins.

Incipit: 'Ce n'est pas d'aujourd'huy / que nous voyons le merite / & les grandes actions des / Capitaines sans recom- / pense, le temps present nous en four- / niroit des preuves assez convain- / quantes'.

13

Anonymous: *Histoire de la duchesse de Châtillon*, 1712

(*red* and black titlepage) *Histoire* / galante / *et veritable* / de la / *duchesse* / de / *Chatillon.* / [woodcut sphere] / *A Cologne.* / Chez Pierre Marteau. / [rule] / *M. DCC. XII.*

12°: 1 f. (titlepage) + 3-192 pp.

Commentary: Thanks to the proper-name index and to the valuable inclusion of incipits in Maurice Lever's bibliography of seventeenth-century French prose fiction, I was able to identify this rare work as the *Histoire véritable de la duchesse de Châtillon* (Cologne: P. Marteau, 1699, BN; Lever p.218; also Conlon, ii.456, no.9092). I was unable to juxtapose my copy with the two in the BN for 1699. Since the pagination is the same, one might surmise that my copy is a reissue and that the publisher simply later added a new titlepage, probably in an effort to sell left-over copies. (In support of this is the fact that the head title matches the title of the first edition. Also a tell-tale strip of paper is a visible indication that the titlepage was tipped in.) The novel is a distant cousin of the *Princesse de Clèves*, although the style is so convoluted in parts that the entire effect is rather comical. The only mention I have been able to find of this edition is in Weller, p.61. He lists: 'Histoire galante et véritable de la Duchesse de Chatillon. Cologne, P. Marteau (Hollande) [1699]; n. éd. ib. 1712'. He was obviously copying his information from the second(?) edition, but where he found a copy of that, I wouldn't know. Gay remarks that the duchesse de Châtillon was the maréchal de Luxembourg's sister and that she also made an appearance in Bussy-Rabutin's *Histoire amoureuse des Gaules* (ii, col.583. True: the *Histoire d'Angélie et de Ginolic* is that of Mme and M. de Châtillon).

Incipit: 'Je ne sçai pourquoi il y en a tant qui prennent plaisir à médire du beau Sexe'.

14

Anonymous: *Histoire des quatre fils d'Aymon*, ca.1785

(head title) [line of ornamentation] / Histoire / Des Nobles & vaillans Chevaliers, / les quatre Fils d'Aymon.

8°: 3-112 pp.

Commentary: This is a 'livre de colportage' (chapbook), probably forming part of the 'bibliothèque bleue de Troyes' or one of its analogues. There are numerous woodcut illustrations nearly a half-page in size, some repeated. From the paper, printing, typography, spelling and woodcut decorations to be found at chapter ends, etc., it is possible to hazard a date of ca. 1785, bearing in mind the general quality of the book. I have listed this work since it is not to be found, as far as I can gather, in Alfred Morin, *Catalogue descriptif de la Bibliothèque bleue de Troyes, almanachs exclus* (Geneva 1974). F.A1 is missing, which was doubtless the titlepage. The style matches the illustrations and general printing, i.e. rather primitive, but interesting (if one likes that sort of thing!). I do not bother with an outline. The *Histoire des quatre fils d'Aymon* was one of the most popular and most often republished of the neo-medieval epics that Cervantes so ably fought against, but was unable to render extinct, on the popular level anyway.

Incipit: 'Dans l'Histoire de Charlemagne, nous lisons qu'un / jour de Pentecôte, il tint une grande Cour à Paris, / après qu'il fut venu d'Italie où il vainquit les Sarrasins'.

15

Anonymous: *Histoire secrète du voyage de Jacques II*, 1696

(titlepage in *red* and black) *Histoire* / Secrette du Voyage de / *Jaques II.* / a Calais / Pour passer en / *Angleterre;* / Où l'on voit les Voyes cachée [*sic*] / que ce Prince a tenu pour ce dessein. / Et la maniere que le Conseil / Privé de / *Louis XIV.* / En avoit ordonné suivant le De- / cret des reverends Peres Jesuites, / Et son retour à Boulogne. / [small woodcut decoration] / *A Cologne,* / Chés Andre' Pitou, à l'I- / mage St. Vigort. / [rule] / *M. DC. XCVI.*

12°: 1 f. (titlepage) + [3-6], 7-(214) pp.

Commentary: The first item is an 'Avis aux lecteurs' ('[...] au lecteur' for the running title). Then follows the 'history'. There appears to be a copy of this edition in the BN which I have been unable to examine (I was told that it would not return from the binder's for quite some time), and copies at Berkeley and in the Folger, possibly, and another in the BL (610.a.39[1]). It is also listed in Krauss-Fontius, with a location for the Universtäts- und Landesbibliothek Sachsen-Anhalt, Halle (no. 6528). There are variants in the NUC listing which are probably the result of careless recording. 'Secrette' is spelled 'secrète'; 'Jaques', 'Jacques'; 'II.', 'II'; 'où', 'ou'; and 'XIV.', 'XIV'. (Krauss-Fontius modernise.) Conlon lists this work accurately, giving a location for the BL (ii.253, no.7457). Weller has the following entry for 1696: 'Histoire secrete du voyage de Jacques II à Calais pour passer en Angleterre, etc. et son retour à Boulogne. Cologne, André Pilon (Hollande)' (p.58). I have chosen to include this work since it is not listed in Lever.

The 'Avis' claims that the story is true, further adding that the author is a Protestant converted to Catholicism (without believing in it). Moreover the unknown author was an actual witness to the events. The 'Avis' ends with: 'j'ai hasardé pour mon plaisir premierement & pour celui des autres; les risque [*sic*] qu'il y a d'écrire en France des choses de cette nature; mais étant trés sûr que personne ne le sçait que moi, je défie le plus penetrant qui soit de m'en accuser, à moins que le Diable qui fourre son né par tout ne s'en mêle'. Fact or fiction? Aside from the 'history' itself, with its dialogues, biting sarcasm, etc., the opening of the preliminary piece is a dead giveaway: 'Messieurs mes Amis, je vous envoye une petite Histoire que vous ne serés pas fachés de voir, à cause de l'entreprise secrette du Roi Jaques, ci-devant Roi d'Angleterre, que l'on a tenuë cachée dans un antre qui est bati sous l'Eglise des Jesuites, de la maison professe de Paris, que l'on appelle la Chambre Noire'.

There was apparently an eighteenth-century edition (or issue) of this piece of prose fiction: 'Histoire secrette de Jaques II pour passer en Angleterre; où l'on voit les voyes cachée [!] que ce prince a tenu pour ce dessein. Cologne, André Pitou, 1737.' 214 pp. (NUC, NH0397533: Brown University). This edition is incorrectly cited in Graesse, who, after mentioning that the first edition dates to 1696 ('Cologne, André Pilon [*sic*]'), according to the Mac-Carthy and La Bédoyère sales catalogues, remarks: 'Reproduit à *Cologne* 1737. in-12 (1 fl. 12 kr. Scheible)' (iii.297).

Incipit: 'Il y a eu de tout tems dans les Etats, & dans les Royaumes les plus florissans & les plus malheureux d'honnêtes gens qui ont eu de l'horreur pour les conspirations'.

16

Anonymous (Galland transl.): *Les Mille et une nuits*, 1790

Antoine Galland (1646-1715) translator: Les / mille et une nuits, / contes arabes; / Traduits en François par M. Galland. / Nouvelle édition, / Corrigée & augmentée. / [double rule] / Tome premier [second, troisième, quatrième, cinquième]. / [double rule] / [woodcut decorations, symmetrical for i, v; radiant sun? on ii, iv; small crown, etc. on iii] / A Genève [À Genève for i, v], / Chez Barde, Manget & Compagnie, / Imprimeurs-Libraires. / Et [& for iii] se trouve à Paris, / Chez Cuchet, Libraire, rue & hôtel Serpente. / [double rule] / M. DCC. XC.

12°, i: 2 ff. (halftitle and titlepage) + [5]-8, [9]-482, [483]-490 pp.
  ii: 2 ff. (halftitle and titlepage) + [5]-478, [479]-487 pp.
  iii: 2 ff. (halftitle and titlepage) + [5]-525, [526]-528 pp.
  iv: 2 ff. (halftitle and titlepage) + [5]-582 [for 584], [585] pp.
  v: 2 ff. (halftitle and titlepage) + [5]-505, [506] pp.

Commentary: Vol. i.[5]-8 contains an 'Avertissement'. The last sets of pages indicated above are the 'Tables'. At the end of the text of each volume is found: 'Fin du septième [huitième, neuvième, dixième, onzième] volume'. There are half titlepages bearing 'Les / mille et une nuits. / [rule] / Tome premier [second, troisième, quatrième, cinquième]. / [rule]'.

We have here what might seem to be a reissue, with new title- and half titlepages, of the *Arabian nights*, from that popular compendium, *Le Cabinet des fées, ou collection choisie des contes des fées...* (MMF 85.R4), forming vols vii-xi of the duodecimo edition. However, a comparison of the pertinent volumes of the Indiana University copy of the *Cabinet des fées* (Lilly Library) and the books described here reveals quite marked differences, although many pages are duplicated word-for-word. My thanks go to Professor Diana Guiragossian-Carr who was kind enough to examine the Indiana *Cabinet des fées* in detail and supply me with photocopies of pertinent pages.

I have not been able to find another copy of the 1790 edition anywhere, or indeed any mention of it. However, there seems a good possibility that the edition (or issue) described here is a reissue of a five-volume, duodecimo edition of the *Mille et une nuits*, a 'nouv. éd., corrigée, augmentée et enrichie de très belles figures gravées par M. de Launay d'après les dessins de M. Marillier', same places of publication indicated as above, same publishers, 1787 (Monglond, ii, col.1125). Monglond further remarks: 'Médiocre reproduction des fig. que Marillier avait dessinées pour les tomes vii à xi du *Cabinet des fées*' (for which see below).

Included in this issue are the fine engravings after Marillier for the 1785 edition (see Cohen and Reynaud). Although this issue was unknown to them, I dispense with a description of the illustrations, since they are the same as those for 1785, albeit in a somewhat poorer state. In my collection, these volumes are uniformly bound with Cazotte (*et al.*), *Continuation des Mille et une nuits, contes arabes* (1788-1789, 4 vols in-12, MMF 88.40), also with illustrations after Marillier. The *Mille et une nuits* first appeared from 1704-1717 (MMF 68.R4). There are some half dozen errors in signature signing for the five volumes and certain irregularities with the catchwords. Catchtomes are for vols vii-xi. In iv, pp.[553-84] are printed as 552-582, etc.

There are several 'Cabinets des fées' and editions of them listed in modern bibliographies: one which appeared in 1717 (possibly; see Jones pp.28 and 44), another in 1731-35 (Jones p.44; possibly another edition or collection in or about 1735: see Jones p.44), a reissue of the first volume of the 1731-35 edition in 1754 (Jones p.44; MMF 54.R2), a *Cabinet de fées et des génies*, 14 vols, Bruxelles: Le Francq, 1785 (MMF 85.R3) and the well known 41 vol. *Cabinet des fées* edited by Charles Joseph Mayer (i-xxxvii) and Cazotte (xxxviii-xli), 1785-89 (MMF 85.R4), of which there were two issues, in-8 and in-12 (Amsterdam and Paris, and Geneva).

To all these, to the editions elsewhere mentioned in the current bibliography and to editions mentioned in MMF, I would add the following five editions and/or issues listed in Heinsius (Romane, col.38), following his order:

1. *Cabinet des fées*, 1792. 'XLI Vol. avec 150 pl. gr. form. Berne, Typogr. Soc. [1]792'. Kayser specifies two issues: 'gr[and] [in-]8' and 'gr[and] [in-]12' (under 'Kabinet', Romane p.71b); see no. 2 just below.

2. *Cabinet des fées*, 1792. '–le même. gr. [in-]12. ibid. [1]792'.

3. *Cabinet des fées*, 1785. 'av[ec] fig. XXXI Vol. gr. [in-]12. Génève, Haller. [1]785'. (Also in Heinsius, *Handbuch*, p.777).

4. *Cabinet des fées*, 1762. 'av[ec] fig. IX Tom. Nürnb. Raspe. [1]762'. The first three volumes of this edition are listed in the Messkatalog, with more complete information: 'Le Cabinet des Fées contenant les contes des Fées par Mad. *d'Aunoy* en neuf Volumes. T. I. II. av[ec] fig. 8. Nuremb. chez G. N. Raspe', OM 1762, p.264; the same, 'T. III av. fig. 8. Nuremb. chez G. N. Raspe', MM 1762, p.305. (This collection is not mentioned in MMF; for 'd'Aunoy', read 'd'Aulnoy'.)

5. *Cabinet des fées*, 1792. 'av[ec] fig. Tom. I. [in-]8. Vien. Keyserer [for Kaiserer?]. [1]792'. (Also in Heinsius, *Handbuch*, p.777.)

I have listed these without attempting to identify which particular collection of the *Cabinet des fées* each belongs to, since the entries in Heinsius do not record details that would enable one to do so.

There were of course other collections containing fairy tales in the eighteenth century, with different titles. Heinsius has the following entry for a rare collection of fairy tales (not listed in MMF, or for that matter in BLC, NUC and Barbier):

'Contes de fées, destinés à servir d'amusement et d'instruction aux Enfans et aux jeunes gens, ornés de 3 Figures. [in-]8. Vien. Kaiserer. (Kohler à Lpz.) [1]796' (Romane, col.44). Kayser has the following entry in his list of 'contes': '[Contes] des fées destinées [*sic*] à servir d'amusement et d'instruction aux enfans et aux jeunes gens. Ornées [*sic*] des [*sic*] 3 fig. [in-]8. Lpz. [Leipzig] [1]796. Köhler' (i.480b).

Finally I might add that there are a couple of other editions of the *Mille et une nuits* listed in the Messkatalog which have escaped the attention of modern bibliographers:

1. *Les Mille et une nuits*, 1776. 'Les Mille & une Nuit. Contes Arabes, par *Galland*. 8 Vol. 12. Avignon & à Dresde, chez Ge. Conr. Walther', OM 1776, p.96.

2. *Recueil des plus jolis contes*, 1778. 'Recueil des plus jolis Contes tirés des mille & une Nuit à l'usage des écoles, par Jean Theoph. *Schoummel*. 2 Tomes. 8vo. à Magdebourg & à Leipsic, chez l'Editeur & chez S. L. Crusius', Messkatalog, MM 1778, p.581. Heinsius, *Handbuch* has: '[Recueil] des plus jolis Contes tirés des mille & une nuits par Schoummel, II Tomes, 8vo. Lips. [*sic*] Crusius, [1]780' (p.819).

For additions concerned with 'contes', see the commentary on Marmontel's *Contes moraux*, 1775.

Incipit: 'Les chroniques des Sassaniens, anciens rois de Perse, qui avoient étendu leur empire dans les Indes'.

17

Anonymous: *Nouveaux amusements sérieux et comiques*, 1735

Nouveaux / amusemens / serieux / et comiques. / Tome I [II]. / [woodcut ornament: i, trophy of the arts on a plinth; ii, symmetrical bouquet of stylised flowers] / A Paris, / Chez Charles Guillaume, à l'en- / trée du Quay des Augustins, du côté / du Pont S. Michel, à S. Charles. / [rule] / M. DCC. XXXV. / Avec Approbation & Privilege du Roy.

12°, i: 1 f. (titlepage) + 3-4, [5]-288 pp.
    ii: 1 f. (titlepage) + 3-144 pp. + 6 ff. (12 pp.) + 145-286 pp. + 1 f. (2 pp.)

Commentary: The pagination of the first volume reflects an 'Avertissement' and then the first part of the work. The second volume contains the first part of the book; six folios tipped in of twelve unnumbered pages; then the continuation, with a two-page set of 'tables' to both volumes at the end.

This is actually a periodical venture which I list because of its rarity and because of the large number of prose-fiction items it contains. Also, since it was issued as a whole, one might well consider this work a compendium of miscellaneous pieces containing short stories.

Although not listed in Hatin's annotated bibliography of periodicals, there is an entry for the *Nouveaux amusements* in the recent *Catalogue collectif des périodiques*, with only one location given (Bibliothèque de l'Opéra, a department of the Bibliothèque nationale: Opé. *pi*719). However, the *Catalogue collectif* gives the date of 1735, whereas the volumes in the Opéra bear Paris, no name, 1737 for vol. i, and then Paris, Guillaume, 1735 for vol. ii (as described here).

It appears there was only one edition (printing) of the *Nouveaux amusements sérieux et comiques*, but that there were at least three issues. The first is that described here. (I was unable to find another complete copy of it.) The second, for La Haye, chez Gosse et Neaulme, MDCC. XXXVI., cancel titlepages in red and black (with an engraved, emblematic device: two cows pulling an agricultural machine, prodded by a boy; a gleaner is in front). The vignette carries the following motto: 'serere ne dubites'. Two full-page engravings were added, the first a sort of emblematic titlepage including the portrait of Democritus, repeating the title of the collection. The second is meant to illustrate vol. ii, p.284, and bears 'scotin sculp.' at the bottom right. (Not in Cohen or Reynaud.) This information is derived from the Arsenal copy (8vo B.L.31200[1-2]). The only other copy I could find of this issue (assuming it be the same) is listed in the NUC with a location for the University of Illinois at Urbana. The entry notes that this work is attributed to Charles, sieur de la Rivière Du Fresny. Such an attribution is quite wrong, for the *Nouveaux amusements sérieux et comiques* have nothing to do with Dufresny's *Amusements sérieux et comiques* (first edition: 1699; many subsequent editions). The work listed here is also not to be confused with the *Nouveaux amusemens sérieux et comiques, ou l'art de suppléer à l'esprit par la mémoire* (1776; for further information see, for example, the latest edition of the BLC, vii.331, col.2).

The third issue is represented by the first volume of the Opéra copy. Since no publisher is indicated, one can only surmise that Guillaume made an attempt to get rid of left-over copies in 1737. But why Néaulme would have participated in such a venture in 1736 remains a mystery. (The cancel titlepages added in 1736 do seem genuinely his.)

Note that the original titlepages bear 'avec approbation et privilège du roi'. The approbation is printed with the work, 7 September 1735, signed 'Maunoir' (i.4). Perhaps officials had originally promised a privilege, but I could only find an indication that a 'permission simple' was accorded this work, to the sieur Guillaume, 8 October 1735 (permission simple no. 3609). Here is the essential of that information, as it has come down to us in one of the registers of the 'Communauté des libraires et des imprimeurs de Paris' (B.N., ms F.F.21956, p.177): 'Louis par la grace de Dieu ... salut notre bien amé Charles Guillaume Libraire a Paris nous ayant fait supplier de luy accorder nos lettres de Permission pour l'Impression des Nouveaux amusemens serieux et Comiques. Offrant pour cet effet de le faire imprimer en bon papier ... Nous luy avons permis et permettons par ces presentes de faire imprimer les dit livres cy dessus specifié en un ou plusieurs vol. conjointement ou separement et autant de fois que bon luy semblera et de les vendre faire vendre et debiter par tout notre Royaume pendant le temps de trois années consecutives a compter du jour de la datte des presentes faisons defenses ... Donné a Versailles le vingt sixeme [*sic*] jour du mois de septembre [... 1735] Par le Roy en son Cons. [conseil] signé Bonneau'. Unfortunately no mention is made of an author. Very hesitently indeed one might propose Guillaume as a major editor. (A comment: it is curious that Sainson is the signer of all other documents in that register for October 1735; Bonneau was only concerned with the *Nouveaux amusements*).

Each volume contains twelve issues ('numéros') of the work, each comprising a duodecimo gathering of twelve folios (twenty-four pages), except for no. 18 which has six leaves tipped in at the end (as mentioned above). What is not without interest is that nearly all the issues end with various indications: Nos. 1-3, 5, 21 bear 'fin' at the end. Nos. 4, 8-10, 14-15, 22-23 bear nothing. Nos. 6-7, 11, 13, 17, 20 indicate a 'suite' for the next number. Nos. 12 (end of vol. i), 18-20 and the end of the table (ii.[288]) have a colophon for Guillaume, with his address. No. 16 bears at the end a short advertisement for the *Almanach des Dames Sçavantes Françoises*, 'pour l'année 1736 ... chez C. Guillaume'. At the end of vol. ii, before the tables (p.286), one reads: 'Fin Du second Volume'. This would lead one to assume that each number was issued separately, the first of each volume with the titlepage, presumably in order to encourage members of the public to acquire the entire thing. Each volume bears catchtomes for tomes I and II, respectively. No. 9 is mislabled '8', and a marginal note makes the reader aware of this. (That leaf, H1 is asterisked, indicating a cancel: *H[1].)

This work contains bits and pieces of all kinds: in praise of ants, bees, flies and Normands; a critical view of Paris and its inhabitants; some poetry; curious etymologies, and so on. Here, according to the headtitles, is a list of prose-fiction items (where ascertainable as probably being fiction), with incipits in order to facilitate future identification:

    1. 'Le double mariage', i.40-48; 'Une aimable héritiere d'une des meilleures familles de Rouen, avoit pris de la tendresse pour un jeune Chevalier'.

    2. 'Le retour imprevu. Histoire', i.59-71; 'Chacun se dit malheureux, & tout le monde semble avoir raison, tant il y a de la fatalité'.

    3. 'L'heureux intendant, ou la Constance récompensée par l'Amour', i.97-114; 'Mademoiselle de B..... née avec tous les avantages dont la nature peut favoriser une jeune personne'.

    4. 'Le mal sans remede. Avanture aussi naturelle que plaisante', i.115-18; 'L'experience que l'on fait de certaines choses est sans doute au-dessus de tous les raisonnemens des meilleurs Philosophes.' (This is perhaps not fiction.)

    5. 'La trahison punie, ou l'Heureux Traître. Histoire', i.158-68, 199-202; 'S'il est certain qu'on n'aime pas quand on veut, il ne l'est pas moins qu'on ne cesse point d'aimer quand la raison le conseille'.

    6. 'Le Jaloux généreux, ou la surprise agréable. Histoire', i.210-20; 'Une jeune personne, belle, & brillante, & qui avoit de quoi toucher le cœur le plus insensible'.

    7. 'Les apparences trompeuses', i.241-48; 'L'Amour a été de tous les siécles'.

    8. 'L'amant ventousé', i.248-53; 'Un jeune Gentilhomme renfermé jusqu'à

l'âge de vingt ans dans le fonds de sa Province'.

9. 'Trait d'avarice', i.253-55; 'Si les uns meurent sans avoir le tems de songer qu'ils vont mourir, il y en a d'autres'.

10. 'La belle Normande', i.255-64, 265-67; 'On a beau prendre des précautions contre l'adresse des Belles'.

11. 'Le faux religionaire', ii.30-35; 'Un Cavalier se promenant seul aux Thuilleries, y vit une jeune Demoiselle'.

12. 'La loterie de l'himen, Ou l'union des Rivaux', ii.40-48; 'Dans les conjonctures embarassantes, le secours d'un ami prudent'.

13. 'L'Amant généreux préféré', ii.60-69' 'L'Interêt est la pierre de touche de l'amour'.

14. 'Le blond postiche', ii.90-93; 'Il y a une espece de fureur dans la passion du jeu'.

15. 'Le trompeur obligeant, Avanture galante', ii.97-107; 'Une Veuve assez jolie, vivoit sans inquiétude, & ne songeoit qu'à se divertir'.

16. 'Avanture Sur les Placets des Amans contre les Filoux', ii.211-114 [i.e. 214]; 'Les Amans ayant fait faire un Placet galant contre les Filoux'.

17. 'Le prince Kouchimen, histoire tartare', ii.265-86; 'La Tartarie est un des plus grands Empires du monde qui s'étend'.

'La princesse Sophie, Ou les troubles de Russie arrivés sous la minorité du Czar Pierre I. surnommé le Grand, dernier régnant' seems to be real, in spite of being written in a lively, 'romanesque' style (i.131-44, 145-58; incipit: 'Le Czar Theodore, fils du Czar Alexis-Samelinik, étant tombé dans de grandes maladies').

In the 'Avertissement' the editor (and/or author) complains that too often authors allow members of the public to languish after having whetted their appetite with the beginning of some work or other. Interestingly he places himself in the tradition of serialised fiction by choosing to praise the assiduity of Mme Gomez: 'L'on pourroit nommer ici quelques Ouvrages modernes qui ont eu grand cours par leur bonté, & par l'attention des Auteurs à remplir leur engagement avec le Public. Madame de Gomez nous en donne un bel exemple dans son exactitude à donner sans interruption les suites de ses cent Nouvelles', etc. It is then stated that the *Nouveaux amusements* will appear every Monday and Friday, without interruption, and that the editor/author's sole goal is to entertain.

18

Anonymous: *Le Passe-temps agréable*, ca.1740

Anonymous, but variously attributed to J. de Rochefort or Cartier de Saint-Philip (see the commentary): (titlepages in *red* and black) Le / *passe-tems* / agre'able, / ou / *nouveaux choix* / de / *bons mots*, / de pense'es ingenieuses, / *de Rencontres Plaisantes,* / Dont une partie n'avoit point encore été mise au jour, / *enrichi* / D'une Elite des plus Vives Gasconnades, / *Qui ne sont point dans le Gasconniana,* / Et de quelques Nouvelles Histoires Galantes, / *Le tout avec des Réflexions* [*Réfléxions* for ii]. / Nouvelle

Edition augmentée de plus du double. / *Tome premier* [*second*.; a printing accident
has cut half of the second 'r' in 'premier', together with the probable period] /
[small woodcut decorations: what look like two hands pointing at each other,
same for both volumes] / *A Rotterdam*, / Chez *Jean Hofhout*. / [rule] / Imprimé cette
Année presente.

12°, i: 1 pl (titlepage) + 4 ff. (2 + 2 + 1 + 2 + 1 pp.) + 1-228 pp.
    ii: 1 pl + 1-216 pp.

Commentary: This work contains: 1. a kind of dedication titled: 'A messieurs***';
2. a preface; 3. a one-page 'Avertissement Touchant la seconde & troisiéme
Edition'; 4. a 'Liste particuliere' which contains the names of the people to
whom are attributed the 'bons mots' (2 pp.); 5. a list (one page) of some of the
authors who figure in the work; 6. then the two volumes of the work proper.
(The preliminary pieces are misbound towards the end of volume i.) At the end
of vol. ii are three tales: *L'Insensible touché. Histoire* (pp.178-91), *La Belle cure.
Histoire véritable & Galante* (pp.191-201) and *Dorimène. Nouvelle galante* (pp.202-
16). These first appeared in a 1715 edition, according to Jones (p.17). The
'Avertissement' gives some explanations about the augmentations, stating that
the present work is something like twice as large as the original. This work first
appeared in 1709 (Jones p.16; Conlon iv.132, no. 14903), and was very successful. It consists largely of bits and pieces culled from various histories and
other compendia, varying from a couple of lines to a page or two in length,
including excerpts or sayings from or by Rabelais, Cicero, Louis XIV, Boileau,
Bassompierre and many others.

   The *Passe-temps agréable* has variously been attributed to a J. de Rochefort or to
a Cartier de Saint-Philip. I have listed it as anonymous because no bibliographer
seems sure of either attribution. Barbier explains: 'en tête d'une édition d'*Amsterdam*, 1753, on assure que c'est un sieur de Rochefort, petit-fils de l'auteur de
"l'Histoire des îles Antilles", et ce qu'il y a de remarquable, c'est que cette
indication ne se trouve plus dans les éditions postérieures à 1753. [...] Formey,
en rendant compte de l'édition de *La Haye*, 1742, 2 vol. in-8, dit: "Il paroit, par
certains endroits de ce 'Passetemps', qu'il est de l'auteur du 'Je ne sçai quoi',
c'est-à-dire de Cartier de Saint-Philip"' (iii, cols.801-802; see also Gay, iii,
cols.659-60).

   The only possible trace of the edition described here I have been able to find
is an edition with no date listed in Jones (pp.16-17; location: Harvard college
library). Jones gives no details; MMF list after Jones. That edition is not listed
in the NUC or NUC:S (although two dated editions are listed with locations
for Harvard). I have tentatively dated my book to ca.1740, based on type
style, woodcut decorations, spelling, accentuation and frequency of catchwords.
Although it seems certain that we are dealing with another edition, the Messkatalog has the following entry: 'Passe-tems agreable ou nouveau Choix de bons-
mots, cinquieme Edit. 8. [octavo] chez les memes [Ar[k]stée et Merkus, Leipzig]'
(OM 1742, f.G2*v*).

   There is also a 'Passe tems agreable ou nouveaux contes à rire. 8. Amsterdam
& se trouve à Leipsic, chez la veuve H. Merkus' listed in the Messkatalog for
the MM 1779, p.785.

It might also be pointed out that there were various versions of this collection, for example a 'Passetems agreable et instructif en diverses langues, en Prose & en Vers. 8. Hambourg, chez Hen. Chret. Grund', OM 1774, p.724. (The next entry is for an English-oriented version or edition of the same, though it is of course possible that we are dealing with double titlepages: 'Passetime agreable & instructive in divers Languages both in Prose and Verse. 8. Hamburg, by [a mistake for 'bei'?] Hen. Chr. Grund', *loc. cit.*).

Incipits: (*Le Passe-temps agréable*) 'Se taire & parler à propos, est un / secret très-peu pratiqué'.

(*L'Insensible touché*) 'On trouve dans le monde des personnes / d'un caractére bien différent à l'égard / de l'Amour.'

(*La Belle cure*) 'On ne sçauroit nier que l'Amour n'ait une / puissance absolue sur le cœur'.

(*Dorimène*) 'Ce n'est pas toujours la constance, la fi- / délité, les services, le mérite'.

19

Anonymous: *Le Passe-temps agréable*, ca.1740

anonymous, but variously attributed to J. de Rochefort or Cartier de Saint-Philip (see the commentary on the previous entry): (titlepages in *red* and black) Le / *passe-tems* / agre'able, / ou / *nouveaux choix* / de / *bons mots*, / de pense'es ingenieuses, / *de Rencontres Plaisantes*, / Dont une partie n'avoit point encore été mise au jour, / *enrichi* / D'une Elite des plus Vives Gasconnades, / *Qui ne sont point dans le Gasconniana*, / Et de quelques Nouvelles Histoires Galantes, / *Le tout avec des Réflexions.* / Nouvelle Edition augmentée de plus du double. / *Tome premier.* [*second.*] / [small woodcut decorations: what look like two hands pointing at each other, same for both volumes] / *A Rotterdam*, / Chez *Jean Hofhout.* / [rule] / cette Année presente.

12°, i: 1 pl (titlepage) + 4 ff. (2 + 2 + 1 + 2 + 1 pp.) + 1-228 pp.
ii: 1 pl + 1-216 pp.

Commentary: The contents of this volume are the same as for the preceding entry, including preliminaries and the three tales at the end of vol. ii (same pagination). For further information, see the *Passe-temps agréable* listed just above.

These two volumes seem to have been printed by the same firm that did the ones described in the preceding entry. (Decorations are repeated, for example, the one on the titlepages. Also the headpiece for i.1 – repeated on ii.1, for the volumes described in this entry – is the same for both editions; it is signed 'PLSF'.) I am unable to ascertain which *Passe-temps* was printed first.

Here are a couple of obvious differences that should permit bibliographers and cataloguers to differentiate between the two editions: note that the date indication does not here bear 'Imprimé'. Vol. i, pp.1-2 here are f.B3; the corresponding pages for the preceding item are f.A[1], with a catchtome for 'Tome I.' Note too the different spellings in the incipits.

Incipits: (*Le Passe-temps agréable*) 'Se taire & parler à propos, est un / secret très-peu pratiqué'.

(*L'Insensible touché*) 'On trouve dans le monde des personnes / d'un caractere bien different à l'égard / de l'amour.'

(*La Belle cure*) 'On ne sçauroit nier que l'amour n'ait une / puissance absoluë sur le cœur'.

(*Dorimène*) 'Ce n'est pas toûjours la constance, la fi- / délité, les services, le mérite'.

20

Anonymous: *Les Quêteuses*, ca.1740

(head title) Les Quêteuses / Avanture

8°: 1-102 pp. (or 51 ff.)

Commentary: This is a manuscript of 54 ff., the last three blank, with two preliminary leaves and two at the end (added by the binder). There are catchwords every sixteen pages (8 ff.). I include this manuscript novella, hoping that the description will enable someone to identify it. There are numerous corrections in a different hand, with certain words and passages struck out. (Many deletions are barbs against the church: references to the archbishop of Paris, and so on.) The spelling and penmanship would indicate a date of ca.1730-1740.

The tale deals with a M. and Mme de G*** and their daughter. The ex-army officer and his wife fall upon hard times, so the mother and daughter decide to disguise themselves as nuns in order to beg money in churches for their 'convent'. Various incidents occur, and the upshot is that the two women desist, having been warned about possible trouble by two kindly intended knights. A wealthy uncle dies, leaving all his goods to an unknown woman, 'de basse condition'. So the family decides to sue. In order to make some money, M. de G*** now dons a cowl and goes a-begging. (More adventures, including one with a couple of ladies of the night and their musketeers.) Finally the two knights turn out to be suitably connected, vis-à-vis the trial; money is won, and one of the love-stricken knights marries Mlle de G***. The tale ends with a long apology of 'la quête', and explanations absolving the G***s from any culpability. (There is also a description of the bliss of the new couple.) Perhaps someone will be able to identify *Les Quêteuses*.

As this book was in the press, I was able to identify this novel as the *Histoire nouvelle et galante de deux aimables questeuses, et d'un frere questeur, de même famille*, Paris: veuve N. Oudot, 1727 (Arsenal; Jones, p.39). I was not able to ascertain exactly how alike the printed version and the manuscript are.

Incipit: 'Les personnes de mérite et de naissance seroient souvent exposées aux malheurs, que la misére cause, si elles n'étoient retenues par des sentimens [d'honneur: struck] qui n'abandonnent jamais les [grandes: added] [belles: struck] ames: Cependant la necessité en diminue beaucoup la noblesse; elle nous entraîne quelquefois dans une bassesse [populaire: struck], dont nous ne pouvons nous défendre, lorsque nous avons l'esprit abattu par des traverses, sur tout par celles qui nous privent de ce qui est le plus nécessaire à la vie.'

21

Anonymous: *Secret memoirs of the late count Saxe*, 1752

Secret / memoirs / Of the Late / Count Saxe, / Marshal of France, / and / General of the French Army, / during the late Wars in / Flanders: / with / A particular Account of his / Amours and Gallantry in his younger / Years. / Translated from a French MSS. / [rule] / Trahit sua quemque Voluptas. / [double rule] / London: / Printed for J. Wren, at the Bible and / Crown, near Great Turn-stile, Holborn. / [rule] / MDCCLII.

12°: 2 pl (halftitle and titlepage) + [25]-[48] + [1]-[208] pp. (all page numbers are enclosed in brackets) + 2 ff. (4 pp.)

Commentary: I have not been able to find any trace of this work in any bibliography, including those connected with French history of the period and more particularly with Maurice, maréchal-comte de Saxe (1696-1750). Neither is it mentioned or referred to by any historian I have consulted who has written about this illegitimate son of Aurora von Königsmark and Frederick Augustus I, elector of Saxony, later Augustus II, king of Poland. That is strange because Maurice was one of the most famous men of his time and was much discussed then and afterwards. The only other copy of this book I have been able to locate is in the BL (12603.a.29). It was, for a very long time and until just recently, erroneously classified; it is now properly listed under Maurice of Saxony. (Accession date: 10 November 1900.) One might surmise that, because of its contents – dealing with the highest French nobility, and royalty even, in a scandalous setting at a time when France and England were having their difficulties – the *Secret memoirs* was pulled from the market before much of any distribution took place.

Because of its rarity and hitherto inaccessibility, it seems appropriate to enter into a discussion of the contents. The titlepage tantalisingly claims that the book was 'translated from a French mss', but unfortunately there is no preface or preliminary material which might have offered some explanations. The first set of pages reported above consists of a duplication of gathering C (C[1]-[C12]), an exact duplication which includes the press figure '2' on p.48 (C12v). The text of the novel begins with pp.[1]-[2], f.B[1]. However the first gathering of text for eighteenth-century English books is often signed 'B', so that is no clue as to the possibility of there having been an initial gathering of preliminary material. (The BL copy is the same, barring the duplication of gathering C.)

There is a half titlepage present as follows: '[rule made of a row of small 'flowers'] / Secret / memoirs / Of the late / Count Saxe, / Marshal of France, &c. / [rule similar to the first]'.

As for the contents: the events described are in keeping with Saxe's life-style and the way he behaved. But I was unable to verify the authenticity of the private events recounted, even by dint of going through quite a few memoirs of the period, with especial emphasis on those by people set on stage in the *Secret memoirs*. What seems to be the case is that we have here one of those memoir novels, semi-authentic in nature, which often appeared after a famous person's demise, especially if he (or she!) was known for his/her gallant exploits.

The authenticity of the novel – I will call it that until reasons emerge for *not* terming it so – is further corroborated by the use of initials, or beginning/end letters for the character/people's names. And there can be little doubt that the real people placed in the novel are made to behave as they probably did, in general. Thus the princess *C—i* is doubtless the princesse de Conti. The princess *C—n* would be a harder nut to crack, but the author obligingly spells her name with an 'an' at the end a couple of times, permitting the reader to identify the very wealthy and equally well connected princesse de Carignan. When the novelist writes that everyone knows 'that the Princess *C—n* is so complaisant as to tickle Cardinal *F—y's* Toes' (p.74), the reader needs little discernment to substitute 'Fleury' for '*F—y*'. The duke of *R—u* would be, of course, that wily rake, the duc de Richelieu. The archbishop of *R—n* is presumably either Louis de La Vergne de Tressan (archbishop of Rouen from 1723 to 1733) or possibly his successor, Charles Nicolas de Saulx-Tavanes (source: the *Almanach royal*) who, 'having a little of the *Italian* Gusto, takes a particular Pleasure in seeing half a dozen naked boys tumbling over one another in a large Bathing Tub, which is a more agreeable Sight to this good Prelate, than so many *Venus*'s without draperies' (p.75).

Is this a work translated from the French? I doubt it. The style contains numerous examples of French-turned syntax, and even word use (such as cognates not quite exactly used), but so did many of the English novels and plays of the period. And when French terms are used in the text, they are translated usually in the text itself, which seems a deliberately artificial way of trying to make the reader believe the original was composed in French, for example, the comte de Saxe 'is deservedly stiled, *Le brave Conte a quatorze*; i.e. *The brave Count of Fourteen*' (p.77, for sleeping on a regular basis with fourteen different women each day; note the atrocious French spelling). And there is a very heavy-handed compliment paid to Marlborough at the very beginning of the work, which would never have found its way into a 'French mss' of the period authored by a patriotic Frenchman. (See the incipit below.)

In spite of the information given by the titlepage, the tale is told not by the comte de Saxe himself, but by one Monbrun, who is finally named on p.32. To lend further credence to the fact that the author was most certainly not French, or at least not Parisian (which Monbrun is, or at least that is where he lives and has lived for a long time in the novel) are the couple of instances when the author has either done his research poorly or forgotten that he is supposed to be translating from a French original. When Monbrun and Saxe are to duel, they are first to meet in the Tuileries, then to walk through the Champs-Elysées in order to carry out the purpose of the assignation in the bois de Boulogne! The fact that the actual duel never takes place is immaterial. If it had, however, it is doubtful whether the duelists would have had the energy to carry out their fight.

Sometimes, too, the author sounds very much like a foreigner in his native

SECRET
MEMOIRS

Of the Late

COUNT *SAXE*,

MARSHAL of *France*,

AND

GENERAL of the *French* Army,
during the late WARS in
Flanders:

WITH

A particular ACCOUNT of his
Amours and Gallantry in his younger
Years.

Tranſlated from a *French* MSS.

Trahit ſua quemque Voluptas.

LONDON:

Printed for J. WREN, at the *Bible* and
Crown, near *Great Turn-ſtile*, *Holborn.*

MDCCLII.

1752

No 21: *Secret memoirs of the late count Saxe,* 1752

Paris: 'At the usual Hour of Dinner, I went to his House [Saxe's], where I found the Count *de F—e*, the Marquis *d'O—l*, and the Chevalier *de M—r*, all Musquetaires [*sic*], who had come to dine with the Count without Invitation, a Thing common in *Paris* among Friends' (p.62). A French text would never have contained an explanation of such a common custom.

Towards the beginning of the book, the author states his purpose: 'it is not not my Design in this little Piece, to follow our General through his political Labyrinths, in which he was often bewildered, nor to the Field of *Mars*, where his military Exploits have been so pompously cried about in our Streets, and confirmed by *Te Deums* in our Churches: I shall make it my principal Business to trace him through the softer Scenes of Life, to all which I was privy, and can with Confidence affirm, that I religiously adhere to Truth; but tho' his Amours and Gallantries are what I principally aim at, yet there was such a Connection betwixt his Political, Military and amorous Characters, I must sometimes attend him in the Closet, the Council-Table, and the Field, as well as in the Circles and at the Toilets' (pp.4-5).

The novel gives Saxe's background, and we are then rapidly advanced to his teenage years: 'Scarce was our Hero initiated into Love's Mysteries, when *Billets Doux* came crowding upon him from all Quarters, and he extremely willing, as well as capable to oblige, had no Notion of breaking any Girl's Love-sick Heart by denying her the proper Remedy; and I can safely say that before he entered his Seventeenth Year, he was in great Reputation, and had performed wonderful Cures on Females troubled with languishing Distempers' (etc; p.9-10). The author informs us how Saxe became the lover of the princesses C—i and C—n, who united to help his advance, in spite of their rivalry; even the cardinal de F—y did his bit, cajoled by his mistresses, who were Saxe's too!

And so it goes, from one love affair to another, with special emphasis being placed on the carnal side of love. The comte de Saxe at one point is forced into hiding under a bed and is nearly squashed to death when a couple makes very boisterous love over him. Love is viewed as a battle between the sexes, with the undoing of the fair half causing the victory of both. Thus a love-duel is arranged between Saxe and one of his lady friends; each has, of course, to bring seconds. As Miss P—re writes at one point (a large number of letters exchanges hands, and of course Monbrun obtains them all, originals or copies): '"As I look upon your Affair and mine to be a sort of a Duel not so bloody, nor so dangerous, indeed, as where nothing but Death can satisfy the Combatants; yet as you are a terrible Man, and have a terrible unbending Weapon, and as the Fortune of War is dubious, I shall bring a Couple of Female Friends along with me, on whose Courage I can depend as well as my own; and I desire that you may bring the same Number of Males"' (p.131). Thus an orgy is arranged. (But Saxe is betrayed. The two princesses are invited to the brothel, and things become quite complicated indeed!)

Our anonymous author does not neglect the novel's political background. He describes in some detail the cardinal de Fleury's plans to drive a wedge between the king and queen of France by having the queen refuse to bed with Louis. The cardinal then debauches the latter. The last part of the novel is taken up with these affairs, and their relationship to Saxe himself, his life and loves. There is here a certain amount of narration founded on fact, enough to insure that the book would have caused an international scandal of sorts. Its rarity today probably reflects its rarity in the eighteenth century.

The book ends with preparations for war; the narrator explains that since his interest is the private life of the comte de Saxe, he will stop there. The last few lines of this curious work are: 'as I only proposed in these Memoirs to recount his Exploits in the Field of *Venus*, I shall leave the martial Part of his Life to some abler Pen; and only add, that if Justice be done him, it must be allowed even by his Enemies, That *France* has not produced a greater General since *Turenne*'s Days. / FINIS.'

The last four pages of the book – these are bound in after the titlepage in the BL copy – comprise a list of 'Books Printed for and sold by J. Wren, at the Bible and Crown, near Great Turn-Stile, Holborn', 44 items, including a 'Life of Cardinal de Fleury' for 1 shilling, 'stitch'd'. Plomer lists J. Wren as a 'bookseller and publisher in London over against the New Exchange Building in the Strand, 1764-5' (p.272), and mentions four works put out by Wren. The date on the titlepage is 1752, and I see no particular reason to question it. Indeed, there is every reason to believe it. Saxe died in 1750, and it is doubtful that anyone would have bothered to compose (or to publish) such a work some fifteen years later, when the Seven Years' War had totally eclipsed the events of the '30s and '40s. And the author himself indicates that Saxe's body was not quite stone-cold in the grave. (The binding covering my copy is contemporary: English speckled calf.) Vide the incipit, which is deliberately longer than usual. Thus a correction to Plomer is called for.

Incipit: 'Our brightest Pens are now, no doubt, at work to celebrate, with all the pompous Strokes of Rhetorick, and with the most refined Encomiums which delicate Flattery can suggest, the Fame and Glory of our late General; but would they take my Advice, I would have them, before they attempt to eternize the Memory of their Hero, look into the Annals of the late Reign, at that Period, where our *grand Monarch* [Louis XIV] had the Misfortune of having his Armies beat, his Towns taken, and his whole vast and extensive Kingdom at the Mercy of a conquering Enemy; by a comparative View they then must see, that our General, even in his most renown'd Actions, could not, without fulsome Flattery, be represented, but as a faint Copy of an *English* Original:*' (a note refers to Marlborough).

22

Anonymous: *Testament de Gille Blasius Sterne*, 1788

Testament / de / Gille Blasius / Sterne. / [rule] / Traduit du hollandois. / [rule] / [composite woodcut decoration] / A Lausanne, / Chez [open brace] Jean Mourer, Libraire. / A Paris, / Guillaume de Bure l'ainé, / Libraire, Hôtel Ferrand, rue / Serpente, N°. 6. [end of material set off by brace] / [rule] / 1788.

12°: 2 pl (halftitle and titlepage; see the commentary) + (3)-VIII, (IX)-XIII + [1]-185 pp.

Commentary: The preliminary pages listed above are a 'Préface du traducteur au *Testament de G.B.S.*' and the 'Préface de l'auteur'. There is a half titlepage for 'Testament / de / Gille Blasius / Sterne.' which seems to be actually f. H10. (The last gathering bound in the book is H-H5, [H6-9] and external evidence points to the half titlepage having been kept for some time contiguous to f.H9. The preliminary material is signed a, aij, aiij, [a4-6], indicating, in spite of the pagination, a preliminary leaf or leaves. The binding is contemporary and no further evidence is obtainable from the book in its present state).

This work is not listed in nearly all reference works I have consulted, including Drujon and Quérard:SD. But there is an entry for it in the *Journal de la librairie ou catalogue hebdomadaire, contenant* [...], vol. xxvi, 1788 in no. 32 (Saturday, 9 August 1788), under the rubric of 'Livres nationaux, avec privilége', art. no. 21. Only Paris and 'Debure' are mentioned. There is every reason to doubt that the above volume was printed in Paris; it seems possibly to have been printed in Lausanne. Perhaps there was another edition or issue? However, Weller has the following entry, in which only Lausanne is mentioned: 'Testament de G. B. Sterne, trad. du holland. Lausanne (Paris)', for 1788 (p.238).

The only other copy I could find of this book is tucked away in the BN, listed in the BNC under the name of Gille Blasius *Sterne* (Y2.9592). The name on the titlepage is obviously a pseudonym. 'Gille Blasius' is a version of 'Gil Blas', and the 'Sterne' is wilfully, in the text and preliminary material, associated with Lawrence Sterne: 'plusieurs lecteurs taxeront peut-être l'auteur d'être trop présompteux, de se dire un descendant de Sterne; mais si une certaine origina-lité dans les idées, jointe au ton de sensibilité qui regnent dans l'ouvrage, ne suffisent pas aux Yoricks pour le reconnoître de leur famille; je crois cependant que les personnes impartiales y trouveront des traits de ressemblance, qui leur feront au moins suspendre leur jugement' (p.VI). In the text, the author declares himself the brother of Richard Jonathan Sterne (p.66) and the grand-nephew of 'Yorick' Sterne himself (pp.80 and 96-97), with suitable references to the *Sentimental journey*. The author owes a considerable, but not overwhelming debt to Sterne, both for form and style (chapter headings, the mixture of adventure and reflection, humour, use of direct dialogue, etc.).

The 'translator' claims that the 'but de l'auteur étoit, de faire une espece de critique des divers abus qui regnent en Hollande, relativement à la jurisprudence civile & criminelle' (p.IV). And indeed, many of the pages castigate, among other abuses, that of the arbitrary incarceration of suspects, that of the lack of speedy – never mind fair! – trials, etc.

I have been unable to find a Dutch original. But perhaps there never was one. The translator claims: 'Le petit ouvrage dont j'offre la traduction au Public, parut en Hollande en 1784, c'est-à-dire, peu après la courte guerre que ce pays eût à soutenir contre l'Angleterre, & durant laquelle se formerent les divisions intestines qui ont amené la révolution de 1787, en faveur de la maison d'Orange' (pp.(3)-IV).

Incipit: 'Mon ame est-elle toujours active durant le sommeil? Rêve je sans discontinuer, quoique à mon insçu?'

23

Anonymous: *Vie du roi Isaac Chapelier*, 1790

Vie privée / et politique / du roi / Isaac Chapelier, / Premier du nom, & Chef des Rois de France / de la quatrième Race, en 1789, / Louis XVI étant roi des Français. / Précédée d'une Introduction, & ornée du / Portrait de Sa Majesté. / [rule] / Se trouve a Rennes, / Chez l'Auteur, Historiographe de Sa Majesté. / Et chez tous les Libraires de Province. / [rule] / 1790.

8°: 1 f. (titlepage with an 'Avant-propos' verso) + [iij]-viij, [9]-81 pp. + 1 f. (1 p.)

Commentary: The first two pieces are an 'Avant-propos' (verso of the titlepage) and an 'Introduction'. The last page is a 'key' to the work. This satirical work is listed in Monglond, i, col.782 (for 113 pp. in octavo, no mention of an illustration), in Lawrence S. Thompson, *A bibliography of French political pamphlets on microfiche* (Troy, N.Y. 1974) for 112 pp. (p.648), in Krauss-Fontius (xvi, 96 pp., 'unvollst.', that is, incomplete; no. 6370; location: Universitäts- und Landesbibliothek Sachsen-Anhalt, Halle), and in Weller, for 'Vie privée et politique du roi Isaac Chapelier, I du nom, et chef des rois de France de la 4ᵉ race. Rennes, chez l'auteur, historiographe de S. M. (Paris)', for 1790 (p.249). The BN copy of this work (Lb39.3100) has 112 pp., in-8 (no illustration, no key). The BL copy (same pagination) has a leaf, 1 p., of 'Clefs des personnages' tipped in, between p.80 and 81 (shelf mark: F.445[2]). The copy described here contains no illustration; perhaps there never was one? The *Vie privée et politique*, in spite of having a printed key appended to it, is not listed in Drujon.

This is a rather venomous satire directed against the 'député' Chapelier. The author enters into considerable detail concerning the 'hero's' illegitimate background, describes with relish many scandalous peccadilli, and, in general, condemns the events of 1789 and 1790: 'si *Mirabeau* étoit le Rousseau du crime, *Isaac* étoit le *Fréron* de la vertu' (p.36). In the 'Avant-propos', the author claims: 'Nous pouvons certifier qu'il n'est pas, dans cette histoire, un fait, une anecdote qui ne soit vraie. Nous avons embelli, peut-être, mais nous nous sommes défendu l'invention. Qu'on écrive en Bretagne, & l'on verra jusqu'à quel point nous avons poussé le respect envers la vérité.' The techniques employed by the author are interesting: the work contains long quotations from particularly poetical works (Voltaire, Gresset, Boileau, etc.) incorporated directly into the narrative, and cleverly so.

The head title is of interest for its connection with Rousseau: '[treble rule] / Vie privée / et politique / du roi / Isaac Chapelier, / premier du nom. / [rule] / Je veux montrer, à mes semblables, un homme dans / toute la véracité de la nature; & cet homme, ce / sera lui.... Je n'ai rien tu de mauvais, rien ajouté / de bon;... Je l'ai montré tel qu'il fut; vil, quand / il l'a été... Etre éternel! rassemble autour de lui / l'innombrable foule de ses semblables: qu'ils écou- / tent, gémissent & rougissent; & qu'un seul te dise, / s'il ose, je fus meilleur que cet homme-là. / Confess. de J. J. Rousseau, liv. I, pag. 1 & 2. / [rule]'.

Incipit: 'Le jeune Isaac avoit reçu *une éducation conforme à sa naissance*, à l'abbaye de St.-Melaine'.

24

Arnaud: *Amélie*, 1787

François Thomas Marie [de] Baculard d'Arnaud (1718-1805): Amélie, / histoire / angloise. / Par M. d'Arnaud. / [symmetrical woodcut ornament: lyre in centre] / A Paris, / Chez Le Jay, Libraire, rue Saint- / Jacques, au grand Corneille. / [double rule, thick thin] / M. DCC. LXXXVII.

18°: 2 ff. (halftitle and titlepages) + [5]-(103) pp. + 1 f. (blank)

Commentary: This edition is not separately listed in Dawson, or in MMF (80.9 and 70.21).

The novella first appeared in 1780, and was intended for inclusion in d'Arnaud's collection, *Les Epreuves du sentiment*. (For further details concerning the *Epreuves*, see Dawson. Also listed in that source is a collection of 'épreuves' which might include the ones currently listed; cf. pp.691-92.) The similarity of type and format leaves little doubt that the publisher meant this work, and others like it listed in the present bibliography, to be available separately, and as a collection. See *Julie*, 1788; *Liebman*, 1788, *Lucie et Mélanie*, 1788; *Makin*, 1789; and *Sélicourt*, 1788.

It is highly unlikely that these books were printed by Le Jay, one of d'Arnaud's major publishers of the mid-late '60s and early '70s. (Indeed, I doubt they were produced in Paris.)

The volume halftitle reads 'Amelie, / histoire / angloise.' Like the other similarly printed tales by d'Arnaud listed in this bibliography, the halftitle is framed in a sort of oval made of small decorations.

Incipit: 'Nos moralistes s'élevent avec vi- / gueur contre les passions'.

25

Arnaud (transl. unknown): *Biblioteca sentimentale*, 1806

François Thomas Marie [de] Baculard d'Arnaud (1718-1805), translator unknown: (engraved titlepages) Biblioteca / sentimentale / ossia / produzioni / del sig. d'Arnaud / Scritte per sollievo del Cuore. / Tomo I [same for all volumes] / Venezia, MDCCCVI / nella stamperia Graziosi. / [double rule] / Con Approvazione.

8°, i: [1]-181 pp.
   iii: 1-148 + [1]-102 pp.
   iv: 1 f. (titlepage; see the commentary) + 5-102 + 1-93 pp. + 1 f. (1 p.)

Commentary: These three volumes contain various novelle from d'Arnaud's two best known collections, the *Epreuves du sentiment* and the *Nouvelles historiques*. I have found no trace of this edition or issue anywhere. As mentioned, the engraved titlepages (excluded from the pagination recorded) all bear 'Tomo I', with inked in modifications to indicate the presumably correct volume (information echoed on the spines). The 'CVI' of the date is sharper, and could have been added to the plate later, possibly to replace an eighteenth-century date: 'MDCC?'.

Vol. i contains *Il Principe di Bretagna, ossia i tristi effetti delle passioni dominanti* (*Le Prince de Bretagne*, a 'nouvelle historique' which first appeared in 1777). Vol. iii contains *Salisbury, ossia la vedova non sedotta* (the first 'nouvelle historique' which first appeared in 1774) and *Ermanzia, ossia lo specchio delle mogli* (*Ermance*, an 'épreuve du sentiment', first French edition 1775; pp.1-148 and [1]-102 respectively). Vol. iv opens with *Liebman* (an 'épreuve du sentiment', 1775), with its own titlepage: 'Liebman / ossia / gl'effetti funesti / della / gelosia / del signor / d'Arnaud. / [symmetrical woodcut decoration] / In Venezia / M, DCCC, XIII. / [rule] / Nella Stamperia Graziosi a S. Silvestro / al Ponte dei Meloni N. 1374.' The text of this piece begins with f.A3. However, it is possible to ascertain, in the present copy, that a blank leaf extant before the engraved titlepage is conjugate with f.[A8]. Thus all leaves are present and accounted for. The second piece in volume iv is another 'épreuve', *D'Almanzi, ossia la vittima degli errori di una cieca e malvagia gioventù* (*D'Almanzi*, 1776).

The last folio of the last volume described here – it's part of the last gathering, f.[F8] – contains a page of legal material: a permission for Antonio Graziosi to print and distribute the third volume of the *Biblioteca sentimentale*, but mention is made only of *Salisbury*. (This is dated 10 May 1792.) These volumes seem to have been printed sometime at the very end of the eighteenth century or early in the nineteenth century, possibly at different dates. See the commentaries on d'Arnaud, *Prove del sentimento*, and the *Ricreazioni dell'uomo sensibile*.

Zambon lists a *Biblioteca sentimentale* for Venezia, 1791-1793, 5 vols (no publisher given), in the Biblioteca comunale di Verona (p.5, no. 13). A couple of the tales described above might be the same translation, but I doubt they would be of the same edition.

Incipits: (*Il Principe di Bretagna*) 'Giovanni V. (1) duca di Bretagna era morto, lasciando della sua moglie, sorella di Carlo VII (1)'. (Notes give historical information.)

(*Salisbury*) 'L'Inghilterra riprendeva il suo ascendente sopra la Scozia.'

(*Ermanzia*) 'Ci viene ogni giorno presentato come uno de' più grandiosi oggetti del gran quadro dell'antichità'.

(*Liebman*) 'Chiamato in Germania da motivi, di cui poco importa al Pubblico essere informato'.

(*D'Almanzi*) '–No, amico mio, no, non sono felice!'

26

Arnaud: *Les Epoux malheureux*, 1758

François Thomas Marie [de] Baculard d'Arnaud (1718-1805) for the prose fiction, Charles Huchet de La Bédoyère *et al.* for the legal material, i, ii: Les epoux / malheureux, / ou / histoire / de / monsieur et madame / de la Bedoyere, / Ecrite par un Ami. / Tome premier [second]. / [symmetrical woodcut decoration, different for each volume] / A la Haye, / [double rule] / M. DCC. LVIII.

iii, iv: Recueil / de / toutes les pieces / du / procez / D'entre Mr. & Madame de la Be- / doyere; Mr. de la Bedoyere, leur / Fils; Agathe Sticcotti [Sticotti for iv], &c. / Avec / L'Extrait du Plaidoyé de Mr. l'Avocat / Général du Parlement de Paris, & / le précis de l'Arrêt qui est intervenu. / Tome troisieme [quatrieme]. / [symmetrical woodcut decoration; the decorations are identical for vols i, iii and ii, iv] / A la Haye, / [double rule] / M. DCC. LVIII.

12°, i: 1 pl + (1)-(2), [3]-(76), [77]-(154) pp.

ii: 1 pl + (1)-8, [9]-(72), [73]-(135) pp.

iii: 1 pl + (3) [for (1)]-175 pp.

iv: 1 pl + (1)-(142) pp.

Commentary: The first two volumes (the novel) actually have four 'parties'. The first two pages in vol. i are an 'Avis de l'éditeur'. The novel first appeared in 1745, and the legal documents, in this compact form, in 1749. (For further information, see Dawson, ii.682-88.) Suffice it to say that this was one of the most popular novels of the day; in the preface to the second version (1783), d'Arnaud claimed that there had been over sixty editions of the first version alone! The novel did not have official government approval in France, dealing with important, titled people in a then scandalous setting, and the legal documents, together with the novel, were probably not regarded with much official approval either, within that context. (For an account of the events surrounding the trial and novel, see Dawson, i.73-120.)

I have not been able to locate another complete copy of this edition. The only other possible copy I could find is listed in the Gesamtk. (Very few details are given; location: Universitätsbibliothek, Göttingen.) Curiously there exists in the BN a very similar – and probably identical – edition of the novel alone (16°: Y2.17992) which has four titlepages – for the novel (2) and the legal material (2) – distributed before each 'partie' of the novel. I can only surmise that the legal material was supressed in the BN copy because, juxtaposed with the novel, it would have offended a powerful noble family. In support of this is the following. The end of the novel bears 'Fin de la quatriéme & derniere Partie', which would enable those volumes to stand alone. At the end of vol. iv is found 'Fin du dernier Tome', which permitted the addition of vols iii and iv. The woodcut vignettes at the head of the text in i-ii are single block designs (some repeated) of the kind popular in the '20s and '30s (going into the '40s and beyond, especially outside of Paris). The corresponding woodcut vignettes in iii-iv are composite (same for each volume). The signatures in i-ii are numbered in arabic; those in iii-iv, in roman. Thus there is a good chance that these volumes were printed by different firms.

It might be pointed out that Jones lists a 1758 edition after Barbier (Jones p.91). MMF list after Jones (58.R6). Barbier has 'Nouvelle édition, 1758, 1780, 2 vol. in-12' (ii, col.166f). Barbier gives a reference to Quérard, who makes no mention of a 1758 edition (i, col.302c).

Incipit: 'Quoi, Monsieur, il est encore un cœur ouvert aux cris des malheureux?'

27

Arnaud: *Les Epoux malheureux*, 1792

François Thomas Marie [de] Baculard d'Arnaud (1718-1805): Les époux / malheureux, / ou / histoire / de monsieur et madame de ***. / Nouvelle Édition, / Corrigée, augmentée de deux nouvelles / Parties, qui sont la conclusion de / l'Histoire, avec figures. / Par M. d'Arnaud. / [rule] / Premiere [seconde, troisieme, quatrieme] partie. / [rule] / [small woodcut decoration, same for all volumes] / A Avignon, / Chez Joly, Imprimeur-Libraire. / [rule] / M. DCC. XCII.

18°, i: 1 pl + [1]-(232) pp.
   ii: 1 pl + [1]-(156) pp.
   iii: 1 pl + [1]-(163) pp.
   iv: 1 pl + [1]-(180) pp.

Commentary: This is the entirely refurbished version of d'Arnaud's highly successful, fictionalised reportage, the original version of which first appeared in 1745. The augmented version first appeared in 1783. MMF list an edition for 1792, with no explanation. Monglond lists a 1792 edition for Avignon (no publisher mentioned), 4 vols in-8 (ii, col.670) after Quérard and the *Mercure de France*, 11 January 1794. The edition listed in the *Mercure français*, 11 January 1794/22 nivôse l'an deuxième, is for an edition which appeared in Paris, 4 parts, small duodecimo, 'chez Lepetit, commissionnaire en librairie, quai des Augustins, no. 32' in 1792 (p.52; the review extends to p.59). This is an edition to be found hither and thither. Both the *Mercure* and Quérard are probably in error, concerning format at least. However, there were obviously two editions for 1792 (Paris and Avignon). The edition described here is not to be found in the NUC, BLC, or BNC.

Each volume has a frontispiece, and these are imitations of four of the fine engravings after Eisen which appeared with an octavo, 1783 edition. No. 1 is after the second engraving, 2 after the fourth, 3 after the seventh, 4 after the ninth. This edition lacks the preface which d'Arnaud composed for the 1783 version. (There are two signature errors in vol. i.)

For further information, see Dawson, ii.682-88, and d'Arnaud's *Œuvres*, 1795-1815 below.

Incipit: 'Quoi, monsieur! il est encore un cœur ouvert aux cris des malheureux!'

28

Arnaud: *Les Epreuves du sentiment*, 1789

François Thomas Marie [de] Baculard d'Arnaud (1718-1805): Épreuves / du / sentiment, / Par M. d'Arnaud. / [double rule] / Tome premier [second, troisieme, quatrieme, cinquieme, sixieme, septieme, huitieme, neuvieme, onzieme]. / [double rule] / [woodcut decoration, different for each volume] / A Paris, / Chex [Chez for v, vii and xi] Le Jai, Libraire, rue St. Jacques [Saint-Jacques for v; S. Jacques for vi; Saint Jacques for vii and xi; St. Jacques with no comma after it for viii], /

au-dessus [au dessus for ii and vii] de celle des Mathurins, / Au Grand Corneille. / [double rule] / M DCC. LXXXIX. [M. DCC. LXXXIX. for v, vii and xi] / Avec Approbation & Privilege du Roi.

12°, i: 2 ff. (halftitle and titlepage) + [v]-xvj + [1-2: half titleleaf for 'Fanny, / histoire angloise.'], [3]-102, [103-104: half titleleaf for 'Lucie et Mélanie, / nouvelle.'], [105]-175, [176] pp.

  ii: 1 f. (titlepage) + [3]-84, [85]-184 pp.

  iii: 1 f. (titlepage) + [3]-100, [101]-192 pp.

  iv: 1 f. (titlepage) + 3-106, 107-213, [214] pp.

  v: 1 f. (titlepage) + [3]-105, [p.[106] is blank], [107]-254, [255] pp.

  vi: 1 f. (titlepage) + [3]-166, 167-189, [p.[190] is blank], 191-283, 284 pp.

  vii: 1 f. (titlepage) + [3]-126, [127]-278 pp. + 1 f. (1 p.)

  viii: 1 f. (titlepage) + [3]-107, [p.[108] is blank], 109-225, [226] pp.

  ix: 1 pl + [1]-111, [p.[112] is blank; p.[113-114] comprise a half title for 'D'Almanzi, / anecdote françoise.'], [115]-216 pp.

  x: [1]-108, [p.[109-110] comprise a half titleleaf for 'Makin, / anecdote angloise.'], [111]-238 pp.

  xi: 1 pl + [1]-112, [p.[113-114] comprise a half title for 'Daminville, / anecdote.'], [115]-296 pp.

  xii: [1]-197 pp.

Commentary: There are no titlepages in the present copy for vols x and xii. The last, unnumbered pages represent tables of contents, for those volumes which have them. (However the 'table' to vol. vi is on a numbered page.) The preliminary pages in vol. i comprise the preface which d'Arnaud composed for the first, duodecimo Le Jay edition. It seems impossible to tell which firm published the edition described here, probably not Le Jay in any case, but the books were perhaps produced in Paris.

There is a half titlepage at the beginning of vol. i bearing: 'OEuvres / de / M. d'Arnaud. / [double rule] / Épreuves du sentiment. / [double rule] / Tome premier.' What seems to be the case is that this particular edition was to have formed part of a larger collection of the *Œuvres*, and these *Epreuves* could well have been available separately. They match in size and format the Moutard edition of the *Epreuves du sentiment* and various editions of the *Délassements de l'homme sensible*. There are catchtomes throughout which match the appropriate volumes.

These books are in the collections of the University of Texas at Austin (the Humanities Research Centre). I could find no trace of them elsewhere. There are numerous typographical errors throughout. No legal documents are present.

There is a very mediocre frontispiece engraving designed by P. Peyron and engraved by F. Guibert le jeune, dated 1785. The present twelve tomes (bound into six) do not contain the entire collection of the *Epreuves du sentiment*. (*Valmiers*, 1779 and *Amélie*, 1780 are missing.) At the end of volume xii, which instead of containing two 'épreuves' only contains one, is to be found: 'Fin du douzieme volume.' Perhaps this edition was continued? For the contents and first dates of publication of the individual pieces, see the incipits below. And for further information concerning the individual pieces and the collection, see Dawson.

To the editions of individual 'épreuves' found in modern bibliographies, I would add (in alphabetical order):

1. *Clary*, 1771. 'Clary, ou le retour à la vertu; histoire angl. [in-]8. Frankf. [1]771. Gebhardt et K[ayserer?]' (Kayser, i.106b). This is probably a reedition of the 'Francfort, Compagnie, 1768' edition listed in MMF (67.15).

2. *Julie*, 1771. 'Julie ou l'heureux répentir, anecdote historique. 8vo. Frkf. [Francfort] a[m] M[ain]. [1]771. Gebhard u[nd] K[ayserer?]' (Gesamtverzeichniss, v.556a).

3. *Lucie et Mélanie*, 1771. 'Lucie et Melanie, ou les deux sœurs généreuses, anecdote histor. [in-]8. Frankf. a. M. [1]771. Gebhard et K[ayserer?]' (Kayser *loc. cit.*). This is probably a reedition of the 'Francfort, Compagnie, 1768' edition listed in MMF (67.17).

4. *Sidnei et Silli*, 1766. '[...] Ou la bienfaisance et la reconnaisance. Histoire anglaise, suivie d'odes anacréontiques. Par l'auteur de Fanni [...]. Frankfort: Eslinger 1766. 112 [pp.]' (Gesamtverzeichniss, v.556b).

5. *Sidnei et Silli*, 1767. '[...] Francfort: Eslinger 1767. 112 [pp.]' (Gesamtverzeichniss, v.556b).

See too the end of the commentary on d'Arnaud's *Œuvres complètes* (1777) and La Fontaine's *Les Amours de Psyché et de Cupidon* (1793).

It might be worth mentioning that MMF list several 'épreuves' in and about 1792, for Hamburg and/or Paris. My copy of *Sargines*, Hambourg: Fauche; Paris: Lepetit, 1793 (MMF 72.11, after the only other copy known in the BN which I was not able to examine) carries an advertisement on the verso of the titlepage: 'Ouvrages du même Auteur qui se trouvent chez le même Libraire'. It seems logical to assume that the three additional volumes (and there might well have been more) all carried 'A Hambourg, chez Fauche. A Paris, chez Lepetit [...]' on the titlepages. MMF were unable to locate copies of some of these and cite them with varying imprints after several periodicals of the time. In the commentary appended to the entry concerned with the collection (70.11), MMF remark: 'Des articles dans FC [la *Feuille de correspondance du libraire*] 92 XVII 3703, 3704, XIX 3889, semblent indiquer une collection comprenant au moins *Adelson*, *Lucie*, *Nancy* et *Anne Bell*, publiée à Hambourg, in-18, en 1792'. As is obvious, this collection extends at least to 1793. (See too the end of the commentary on d'Arnaud's *Loisirs utiles* and on La Fontaine's *Psyché et Cupidon*).

The 'épreuves' mentioned in the advertisement are as follows:

1. *Adelson et Salvini*. 'Adelson et Salvini, histoire anglaise, in-18, 2 fig.'.

2. *Lucie et Mélanie*; *Clary*. 'Lucie et Mélanie, suivie de Clary, histoire anglaise, in-18, 4 fig.'.

3. *Nancy*; *Anne Bell*. 'Nancy et Anne Bell, histoires anglaises, in-18, 4 fig.'.

Each listing comprises one volume. (The price is included for each item.) My copy of *Sargines* has two illustrations, unsigned. (The second is an adaptation of the original Eisen design.) Moreover, the *Feuille de correspondance du libraire* makes no mention of Fauche, puts 'Paris' between parentheses, so it seems likely that these small volumes were Paris-printed.

Incipits, i: 1. (*Fanny*, [1762], 1764) 'Le Lord Thaley entroit dans l'âge des passions; il étoit né avec une ame droite'.

i: 2. (*Lucie et Mélanie*, [1761], 1767) 'La mort de Louis XII avoit, en quelque sort, changé l'esprit de la nation.'

ii: 1. (*Clary*, [1765], 1767) 'Aprés la vertu, objet immuable de nos hommages, ce qui doit produire le plus cette considération personnelle'.

ii: 2. (*Julie*, 1767) 'Le systême avoit entraîné la ruine de beaucoup de familles'.

iii: 1. (*Nancy*, [1760], 1767) 'Des maladies cruelles qui affligent l'esprit humain, l'imprudence & la jalousie'.

iii: 2. (*Batilde*, 1767) 'La puissance des maires étoit deveune [*sic*] presque égale à celle des rois.'

iv: 1. (*Anne Bell*, 1769) 'La vertu & l'honnêteté, en exigeant des jeunes personnes'.

iv: 2. (*Sélicourt*, 1769) 'Le chevalier de Sélicourt sortoit d'une famille distinguée dans la province'.

v: 1. (*Sidney et Volsan*, [1765], 1766; 1770) 'J'étois avant hier, selon mon usage, au caffé de Guillaume.'

v: 2. (*Adelson et Salvini*, 1772) 'Rome paroît, en quelque sorte, avoir conservé ses droits sur l'admiration & sur les hommages des autres peuples'.

vi: 1. (*Sargines*, 1772) 'Philippe-Auguste imprimoit le sceau de sa grandeur sur l'empire François'.

vi: 2. (*Zénothémis*, 1773; includes the 'Extrait de l'histoire de Marseille, jusqu'à sa prise par Jules César', pp.167-89) 'Marseille, en fléchissant sous la fortune de César, n'avoit perdu que les apparences du plein pouvoir'.

vii: 1. (*Bazile*, 1774) 'La sensibilité, est sans contredit, la qualité la plus précieuse de l'homme'.

vii: 2. (*Lorezzo*, 1775) 'Trapani, anciennement Drépanum, est une des plus jolies villes de la Sicile'.

viii: 1. (*Liebman*, 1775) 'Appellé en Allemagne par des motifs dont il importe peu au public d'être instruit'.

viii: 2. (*Rosalie*, 1775) 'Rosalie devoit le jour à des commerçants estimables.'

ix: 1. (*Ermance*, 1775) 'On nous présente tous les jours, comme un des objets les plus imposants du grand tableau de l'antiquité'.

ix: 2. (*D'Almanzi*, 1776) '–Non, mon ami, non, je ne suis point heureux.'

x: 1. (*Pauline et Suzette*, 1777) 'Une femme de la campagne, veuve, & n'ayant qu'un seul enfant, avoit nourri la fille de gens de condition'.

x: 2. (*Makin*, 1777) 'On ne peut nier que l'ambition & l'avarice n'aient porté nos Européens sur les mers inconnues des Indes Orientales'.

xi: 1. (*Germeuil*, 1777) 'La province a été de tout temps l'objet du dédain & des froides plaisanteries'.

xi: 2. (*Daminvil[l]e*, 1778) 'Monsorin étoit du nombre de ces parvenus que la richesse corrompt & dénature'.

xii: (*Henriette et Charlot*, 1779) 'La même femme, qui devoit être la complice, ou plutôt l'auteur d'une catastrophe'.

29

Arnaud: *Julie*, 1788

François Thomas Marie [de] Baculard d'Arnaud (1718-1805): Julie, / nouvelle. / Par M. d'Arnaud. / [woodcut ornament: largely grapes and vines] / A Paris, / Chez Le Jay, Libraire, rue Saint-Jacques, / au-dessus de celle des Mathurins, / Au Grand Corneille. / [double rule, thick thin] / M. DCC. LXXXVIII. / Avec Approbation & Privilege du Roi.

18°: 2 pl + [1]-(108) pp.

Commentary: The halftitle ('encadré') reads 'Julie, / nouvelle.'

This edition is not separately listed in Dawson or in MMF (67.16). For further information, see d'Arnaud's *Amélie*, 1787 above.

Incipit: 'Le systême avoit entraîné la ruine / de beaucoup de familles'.

30

Arnaud: *Liebman*, 1788

François Thomas Marie [de] Baculard d'Arnaud (1718-1805): Liebman, / histoire / allemande. / Par M. d'Arnaud. / [composite woodcut ornament: four general parts, each with a fleur-de-lys] / A Paris, / Chez Lejay, Libraire, rue S. Jacques, / au grand Corneille. / [ornamental rule] / M. DCC. LXXXVIII.

18°: 2 pl + [1]-(91) pp. + 1 f. (blank)

Commentary: The halftitle ('encadré') reads 'Liebman, / histoire / allemande.'

This edition is not separately listed in Dawson or in MMF (75.14). For further information, see d'Arnaud's *Amélie*, 1787 above.

Incipit: 'Appelé en Allemagne par des motifs / dont il importe peu au public d'être ins- / truit'.

31

Arnaud: *Les Loisirs utiles*, 1794-1796

François Thomas Marie [de] Baculard d'Arnaud (1718-1805), i: Les / loisirs utiles. / [rule] / Linville / ou / les plaisirs / de la vertu / par d'Arnaud. / Avec figures. / Tome premier. / [woodcut monogramme 'LP' intertwined in a wreath] / A Paris, / Chez Lepetit, Libraire, quai des / Augustins, N°. 32. / [rule] / L'an deuxième de la République Française.

ii: Les / loisirs utiles. / [rule] / Eugénie, / ou / les suites funestes / d'une première faute. / Par d'Arnaud. / Avec figures. / Tome second. / [same decoration] / A Paris, [... same as for i].

iii: Les loisirs utiles. / [rule] / Belleval, / ou / l'amour egoïste. / Par d'Arnaud. / Avec figures. / Tome troisième. / [same decoration] / A Paris, chez Lepetit, Libraire, / Quai des Augustins, N°. 32. / A Niort, chez Dugrit, Libraire, / Rue de la Révolution. / A Tours, chez Plasmame, Libraire. / [rule] / L'an troisième de la République Française.

iv: Les loisirs utiles. / [rule] / Selvile, / ou / le véritable amour. / Par d'Arnaud. / Avec figures. / Tome quatrième. / [same decoration] / A Paris, chez Lepetit, Libraire, / Quai des Augustins, N°. 32. / A Niort, chez Dugris [*sic*], Libraire, / Rue de la Révolution. / A Tours, chez Plasmame, Libraire. / [rule] / L'an quatrième de la République Française.

18°, i: 2 pl (but see the commentary) + [j]-vij + [1]-139, [140] pp.

ii: 2 ff. (halftitle and titlepage) + [5]-148 [for 138] pp.

iii: 2 ff. (halftitle and titlepage) + [5]-156 pp.

iv: 2 ff. (halftitle and titlepage) + [5]-97 + [99]-141, [142] + [1]-(2) pp.

Commentary: MMF list the first two volumes largely as per the above description, 94.3. The only location they cite for vols iii and iv is for the Château d'Oron, and those two volumes differ from the above if the information reported is exact (MMF 95.8).

My four volumes contain five illustrations of nice, if not exciting quality. Each volume has a half titlepage for 'Les / loisirs utiles.' In spite of the pagination, the first two pages in vol. i (pp.[j]-ij) comprise f.A3 and the half title- and titlepages are the first two leaves of the first gathering. (F.[A3] of vol. iv is signed 'G2'.) Vol. iv contains, at the end, a shorter novella, *Valmont et Julie, ou la faute réparée* (pp.[99]-141). Vol. iv.[142] also contains the following 'Avis': 'Les Personnes qui desireront se procurer les deux premières Anecdotes du même auteur, qui forment les deux premiers volumes de cet Ouvrage, les trouveront chez le même Libraire.' The last, added leaf, 2 pp. of vol. iv is an interesting catalogue of 18° novels available at Lepetit's. iv.141 carries at the end: 'De l'Imprim. de Conort et Galland, Rue de la Harpe, n.ᵒˢ 6 et 152.'

The reverse of the half titlepage to vol. i has the following announcement: 'On trouve chez le même Libraire, les dix volumes suivant [*sic*] du même Auteur'. The list contains *Lucie [et Mélanie]*, *Adelson [et Salvini]*, *Nancy*, *Sargines*, *Comminges* (probably Mme de Tencin's novel with d'Arnaud's play; see Tencin, *Mémoires*, below), *Fanny* and *Les Epoux malheureux* (each entry comprising one volume in-18, except for the latter: 4 vols in-18). At the end of the list is information available on the titlepages of iii and iv: 'A Niort, chez Dugrit, Libraire, / rue de la Révolution. / Et à Tour [*sic*], chez Plasmame, Libraire.' For further information, see Dawson, ii.699-700.

Incipits: (*Linville*) 'J'arrivois à cette époque de la vie où les sens paraissent être dans un continuel délire.'

(*Eugénie*) 'C'est de mon lit funèbre où j'acheve le peu de jours que j'ai à vivre'.

(*Belleval*) '–Comment, Belleval? auriez-vous des prétentions sur la fille de Monsieur *Dorsoi*?'

(*Selvile*) 'Nous venons d'exposer un tableau dont les teintes sombres auront affecté, peut-être, trop vivement la sensibilité'.

(*Valmont et Julie*) 'Valmont et Julie(1) avoient été réunis selon l'usage reçu'. (A note introduces the tale and its theme: the evils of divorce).

32

Arnaud: *Lucie et Mélanie*, 1788

François Thomas Marie [de] Baculard d'Arnaud (1718-1805): Lucie / et / Mélanie, / nouvelle. / Par M. d'Arnaud. / [woodcut ornament: spray of flowers with large one in centre] / A Paris, / Chez Le Jay, Libraire, rue Saint-Jacques, / au-dessus de celle des Mathurins, / Au Grand Corneille. / [double rule: thick, thin] / M. DCC. LXXXVIII. / Avec Approbation & Privilege du Roi.

18°: 2 pl + [1]-(76) pp.

Commentary: The halftitle ('encadré') reads 'Lucie / et / Melanie, / nouvelle.'

   This edition is not separately listed in Dawson or in MMF (67.17). For further information, see d'Arnaud's *Amélie*, 1787 above.

   Incipit: 'La mort de Louis XII avoit, en / quelque sorte, changé l'esprit de la / nation.'

33

Arnaud: *Makin*, 1789

François Thomas Marie [de] Baculard d'Arnaud (1718-1805): Makin, / histoire / anglaise. / Par M. d'Arnaud. / [symmetrical woodcut ornament: generally circular, with revolving cog, asterisk in centre] / A Paris, / Chez Le Jay, Libraire, rue Saint- / Jacques, au grand Corneille. / [double rule, thick thin] / M. DCC. LXXXIX.

18°: 2 ff. (halftitle and titlepages) + [5]-(107) pp.

Commentary: The halftitle ('encadré') reads 'Makin, / histoire / anglaise.'

   This edition is not separately listed in Dawson or in MMF (77.10). For further information, see d'Arnaud's *Amélie*, 1787 above.

   Incipit: 'On ne peut nier que l'ambition & / l'avarice n'aient porté nos Européens sur / les mers inconnues des Indes orientales'.

34

Arnaud: *Œuvres complètes*, 1777

François Thomas Marie [de] Baculard d'Arnaud (1718-1805) (*et al.*; see the commentary): (titlepages in red and black) Œuvres / completes / de M. d'Arnaud. / Nouvelle édition, / Contenant tous ses Ouvrages, & plus / ample que celles qui ont paru jusqu'à / présent. / [rule] / *Tome premier* [*second, troisieme, quatrieme, cinquieme, sixieme*]. / [rule] / [woodcut ornament, same general design, but different for all volumes] / *A Amsterdam,* / Chez Marc-Michel Rey. / [double rule] / *M. DCC. LXXVII.*

12°, i: no. 1, Julie, / anecdote historique. / [rule] / Huitieme Edition. / [rule] 1 f. (half titlepage) + [3]-56 pp.

no. 2, Fanni, / ou / l'heureux repentir, / histoire angloise. / [woodcut decoration] / A Londres, / [double rule] / M. DCC. LXXVIII. 1 f. (titlepage) +·[iij]-jv ('Avis des editeurs'), [5]-54 pp.

no. 3, Nancy, / nouvelle angloise. / [rule] / Huitieme Édition. / [rule] (half titlepage) + [3]-56 pp.

no. 4, Lucie et Mélanie, / nouvelle. / [rule] / Huitieme édition. / [rule] (half titlepage) + [3]-40 pp.

no. 5, Clary, / histoire angloise. / [rule] / Huitieme édition. / [rule] (half titlepage) + [3]-46 pp.

no. 6, Batilde, / ou / l'héroisme de l'amour, / anecdote historique. (half titlepage) + [3]-(48) pp.

no. 7, Adelson et Salvini, / anecdote angloise. (half titlepage) + [3]-80 pp.

ii: no. 1, Sargines, / nouvelle. (half tiltepage) + [3]-91 pp.

no. 2, Sidney et Volsan, / histoire angloise. (half titlepage) + [3]-55 pp.

no. 3, Les / amans malheureux, / ou / le comte / de Cominges, / drame. / Par M. d'Arnaud, / Conseiller d'Ambassade de la Cour de Saxe, / de l'Académie royale des Sciences & Bel- / les-Lettres de Prusse, &c. / [rule] / .... Et qui pungit cor / Profert sensum. Ecclesiastic. cap. xxij. v. 24. / [rule] / Sixieme édition. / [woodcut decoration] / A la Haye, / Chez Pierre Gosse junior, & Daniel Pinet. / [double rule] / M. DCC. LXXVIII. (titlepage) + [3]-50 ('Discours préliminaires'), 51-58 ('Idée de La Trappe') + [59]-130 (play including halftitle) + [131]-(190) (Tencin, *Mémoires du comte de Comminges*) pp. + (next item)

no. 4, Lettre / du comte / de Cominges / a sa mere, / suivie / d'une lettre de Philomele / a Progné. / [woodcut decoration] / A La Haye, / Chez Pierre Gosse junior, & Daniel Pinet. / [rule] / M. DCC. LXXVIII. (titlepage; but nos. 3 and 4 are part of the same printed book, with consecutive signatures and pagination; these are two heroids by Dorat) + [193]-199 ('Extrait des Memoires du comte de Cominges') + [203]-216 + [219]-228 pp.

no. 5, Anne Bell, / histoire angloise. / [rule] / Par M. d'Arnaud. / [rule] / [woodcut decoration] / Yverdon. / [double rule] / M. DCC. LXXVIII. (titlepage) + [3]-44 pp.

iii: no. 1, Fayel, / tragédie. (half titlepage) + Fayel, / tragédie, / Par M. d'Arnaud. / [rule] / ..... Furis [*sic*], æstuat, ardet. / [rule] / [woodcut decoration] / A Paris, / Chez Lejai, Libraire, rue S. Jacques, au-dessus / de celle des Mathurins, au Grand Corneille. / [double rule] / M. DCC. LXXVIII. / Avec Approbation & Privilege du Roi. 2 pl (halftitle and titlepage) + 1-26, + [28], [29]-108 + [111]-120 pp.

no. 2, Euphémie, / ou / le triomphe / de la religion. / [double rule] / Drame. (half titlepage) + Euphémie, / ou / le triomphe / de la religion, / drame. / Par M. d'Arnaud. / Sonitus terroris semper in auribus. / Job. ch. / [woodcut decoration] / A Paris, / Chez Le Jay, Libraire, Quai de / Gêvres, au grand Corneille. / [rule] / M. DCC. LXXVIII. / Avec Approbation & Permission. 2 ff. (halftitle and titlepage) + 5-12 + [14], [15]-80 + [83]-138, 138-145, 146-148 + [151]-236 pp.

no. 3, Selicourt, / nouvelle. (half titlepage) + [3]-54 pp.

iv: no. 1, Mérinval. / [double rule] / Drame. (half titlepage) + Mérinval. / Drame. / Par M. d'Arnaud. / [woodcut decoration] / A Paris, / Chez Le Jay, Libraire, rue S. Jacques, au dessus / de celle des Mathurins, au grand Corneille. /

[rule] / M. DCC. LXXVIII. / Avec Approbation & Privilege du Roi. 2 ff. (halftitle and titlepage) + 5-18 + [20], [21]-88 + [91]-122 pp.

no. 2, Nouvelles / historiques. (half titlepage) + Nouvelles / historiques. / Par M. d'Arnaud. / [woodcut decoration] / A Paris, / Chez Delalain, Libraire, rue de la Comédie / Française. / [double rule] / M. DCC. LXXVIII. / Avec Approbation & Privilege du Roi. 2 ff. (halftitle and titlepage) + [5]-24 + [27]-111 pp. (preface and *Salisbury*).

no. 3, Zenothemis, / anecdote marseilloise. (half titlepage) + Zenothemis, / anecdote marseilloise. / Par M. d'Arnaud. / [woodcut decoration] / A Paris, / Chez Le Jai, Libraire, rue S. Jacques, au-dessus / de celle des Mathurins, au Grand Corneille. / [double rule] / M. DCC. LXXVIII. / Avec Approbation & Privilege du Roi. (titlepage); 2 pl (halftitle and titlepage) + [1]-20, [21]-72 pp.

no. 4, Lorezzo. / Anecdote sicilienne. / [double rule] (half titlepage) + [3]-93 pp.

v: no. 1, Bazile, / anecdote française. / [double rule] (halftitle) + [3]-70 pp. (All items described from here to end have only half titlepages which are pp.[1-2], comprising the first folios of the initial gatherings).

no. 2, Ermance. / Anecdote française. / [double rule] + [3]-59 pp.

no. 3, Rosalie, / anecdote. / [double rule] + [3]-64 pp.

no. 4, Liebman. / Anecdote allemande. / [double rule] + [3]-59 pp.

no. 5, D'Almanzi, / anecdote française. / [double rule] + [3]-55 pp.

no. 6, Varbeck. / [double rule] + [3]-134 pp.

vi: no. 1, Le / sire de Crequi. / [double rule] + [3]-90 + 93-118 pp.

no. 2, Le prince / de / Bretagne. / [double rule] + [3]-102 pp.

no. 3, Pauline et Suzette, / anecdote française. / [double rule] + [3]-60 pp.

no. 4, Makin, / anecdote angloise. / [double rule] + [3]-68 pp.

no. 5, Germeuil, / anecdote. / [double rule] + [3]-60 pp.

Commentary: Each volume has a preliminary leaf, 1 p., of a 'Table' at the beginning. Those, together with the volume titlepages, are not part of the printing of any of the works in the volumes. Generally speaking, the individual titlepages and half titlepages are part of the initial gathering of each piece contained in the six volumes. Those pieces with their own titlepages are dated 1778 whereas the volume titlepages carry 1777. Many of the sheets are watermarked with the date 1777.

On the first endpaper to vol. i is glued a contemporary label: 'Se vend chez Fontaine, Libraire à Libourne.' There is a curious stamp: 'Rouen [sunburst] 1777', with the signature of the provincial inspector for the book trade, Havas on the first page of the first piece (*Julie*, p.[3]). This is the same as that to be found in the edition of Lesage's translation of Boiardo's *Roland l'amoureux* (1776) and in the *Gil Blas* (1771) described below, being the marks affixed to contraband works or editions which were thereby legalised by royal decree. See too Fénelon, *Les Aventures de Télémaque*, 1778. (For further information, see Anne Boës and Robert L. Dawson, 'The legitimation of contrefaçons and the police stamp of 1777', *Studies on Voltaire* 230, 1985, pp.461-84). I also have another copy of vols iii and iv. These match in all respects the volumes described here except for some missing blank leaves and several of those discrepancies ordinarily involved with handpress books.

As for the contents: these *Œuvres* are by no means complete, in spite of the claim made on the titlepages. They contain four of d'Arnaud's major plays (*Coligny* is missing) and tales from his two major collections, the *Epreuves du sentiment* and the *Nouvelles historiques*. Included is the preface to the latter; missing is the preface to the former since Rey copied the octavo editions. Rey was one of the more rapacious pirates of his time, and very effective too, much to the regret of d'Arnaud and his Parisian publishers. For further details and information concerning the first editions of all the pieces listed above, see Dawson, ii.609-712.

The above volumes reflect an aspect of d'Arnaud's *Œuvres* which occurred with increasing frequency as the century progressed: Rey individually printed each piece, copying faithfully, for the most part, the contents and titlepages of the works he was pirating. These were then presented as a collection for those who wished to buy the whole, and doubtlessly were sold separately as well. Hence, for example, the reason that the preface of the *Epreuves du sentiment* is missing. Rey copied the octavo, individual (and collected) editions, and not the first, legitimate, Le Jay duodecimo edition which contains the preface. Rey kept the indication of legal rights on the titlepages, perhaps to help increase the possibility of circulation in France. The titlepages lie of course, as none of the material was printed in Paris. The above description of these *Œuvres* will help in identifying individual pieces as they turn up.

MMF list an *Œuvres*..., Amsterdam, Marc-Michel Rey, 1777, 6 vols in octavo (70.21) for the Bibliothèque royale de Belgique. (I have never seen a Rey, octavo edition of d'Arnaud's *Œuvres*.) And in the Primo cat. we find '*Œuvres complètes* [...] vol. iv. Amsterdam, M. M. Rey, 1777, 16°, pp.[407: pag. varia]', with the remark 'Théâtre' (location for the Biblioteca nazionale, Milan). There is, too, a good possibility that the edition described here was continued by Rey & co. I have also seen various copies of what appear to be part of these *Œuvres* containing only the plays.

This collection contains works not by d'Arnaud. Related to the 'genre romanesque' are:

1. C.-A. Guérin de Tencin: *Mémoires du comte de Comminges* in ii, no.3, pp.[133]-(190). See Tencin, *Mémoires* below.

2. Antoine François Prévost, called Prévost d'Exiles: *Effets de la vengeance, relation d'un religieux* in iv, no. 1, pp.[91]-122, from his *Monde moral*... (1760), as inserted by Mlle Uncy into her four-volume collection, *Contes moraux*... (1763); for further information, see Dawson, ii.670-71.

3. *Extrait du 'Spectateur anglais'*, iii, no. 2, pp.138-145.

4. *Extrait des 'Variétés curieuses* ['sérieuses', actually] *et amusantes'*, iii, no. 2, pp.146-148 (C. Sablier, author and compiler; see Dawson, ii.663).

By d'Arnaud, and related to the 'genre romanesque' are:

1. *Extrait de l'histoire du châtelain de Fayel* in iii, no. 1, pp.[111]-120.

2. *Mémoires d'Euphémie* in iii, no. 2, pp.[83]-138.

The volumes described here also contain two heroids by Claude-Joseph Dorat, ii, no. 4. For further information, see Tencin, *Mémoires du comte de Comminges* below.

In passing, I might mention that MMF list an *Œuvres complètes de M. d'Arnaud*, Amsterdam: Marc-Michel Rey, 1775 (i-iv)-1776 (v), 70.21. The Gesamtk. lists this edition (apparently), with an additional volume for 1777 (vol. vi; location: Staats- und Universitätsbibliothek, Breslau).

MMF list an edition of the *Nouvelles historiques* for Maestricht: Dufour et Roux, 1785, vol. i only located (University of Michigan; 74.8). The Messkatalog has the following: 'Nouvelles historiques par Mr. *d'Arnaud*. Tome 4 [4 vols]. 12 [in-12°]. Mastricht & Francfort, chez J. J. Kessler', MM 1784, p.748.

And here are some more editions of works by d'Arnaud not listed in MMF, in chronological order:

1. *Julie*, 1768. 'Julie, ou l'heureux Repentir; Anecdote historique par Mr. *d'Arnaud*. av. fig. 8. Francfort, chez Garbe', OM 1768, p.983. The 'Francfort, Compagnie, 1768' editions of *Batilde*, *Clary*, *Lucie et Mélanie* and *Nancy* listed in MMF (67.14, 15, 17, 18) are all listed in the Messkatalog (OM 1768) for Francfort, chez Garbe.

2. *Œuvres philosophiques et morales*, 1768. 'Œuvres philosophiques & morales par Mr. *d'Arnaud*, où se trouvent les sept Romans publiées [*sic*] par l'Auteur. 8. à Paris & à Zullichau en commiss. de la mais[on] des Orphelins & Frommann', MM 1768, p.1040. Krauss-Fontius list the following, with the indication of 'Teils.', or *Œuvres choisies*: 'Œuvres philosophiques et morales. - (Paris: L'Escla-part, Duchesne, 1768)' with separate pagination for the items; location: the Universitäts- und Landesbibliothek Sachsen-Anhalt, Halle (no. 4513). That volume contains: *Fanni, ou l'heureux repentir* (no. 4491); *Clary, ou le retour à la vertu récompensé* (no. 4506); *Julie, ou l'heureux repentir* (no. 4507). According then to the Messkatalog, the collection (evidently a 'recueil factice') actually included four more tales.

3. *Romans moraux*, 1769 (2 editions probably). 'Romans moraux pour servir de supplement à la Bibliotheque de Campagne, 1 & 2 Partie. 8. Francfort sur le M. chez Franc. Varrentrapp', OM 1769, p.1128. The next entry is for 'Le même livre. gr. 12. Amsterd. & à Leipsic, chez Arkstée & Merkus'. MMF list a five-volume collection for 1771 (71.R12), of which vols iii and iv comprise *Sidnei et Silli* and *Anne Bell*. See *Lucile* right below.

4. *Lucile*, 1769. 'Lucile ou les Progres de la vertu. Anecdote historique attribuée à Mr. *d'Arnaud*, ou Tome sec. des Romans moraux. 8. Francfort, chez J. G. Garbe.' The next entry is for 'Le même Livre, à Liège chez C. Plomteux & à Leipsic chez Heinsius', OM 1769, p.1125. This is actually by Restif de La Bretonne. There is no *Lucile* in the 1771 collection of *Romans moraux* listed in MMF (71.R12). This edition could comprise one of the three Francfort editions of the novel listed in MMF (68.50), especially the one indicating 'aux dépens de la compagnie'.

5. *Mémoires d'Euphémie*, 1769. 'Mémoires d'Euphemie par M. *d'Arnaud*. 8. Berne, chez la Société typographique', OM 1769, p.1126. (Not in MMF 68.12).

6. *Mémoires d'Euphémie*, 1769. Amsterdam: Changuion, 1769. 204 pp. Krauss-Fontius (no. 3909), with a location for the Universitäts- und Landesbibliothek Sachsen-Anhalt, Halle. (Not in MMF, 68.12).

7. *Dona Elmira*, 1777. 'Dona Elmira, ou la fidelité à l'épreuve par Mr. *d'Arnaud*. gr. 8. à Bale, chez C. A. Serini', OM 1777, p.285. This is not by d'Arnaud and the edition here is possibly a reissue of the 1774 edition. See Dawson, 'A note on *Dona Elmira*', *The Yale University library gazette* (1978), liii.18-25.

8. *Epreuves du sentiment*, 1787. 'Epreuves du sentiment par M. *d'Arnaud*. 15 Vol. 12. à Lyon, chez Piestre et de la Molliere', OM 1787, p.637. (Not in MMF, 70.21).

9. *Epreuves du sentiment*, 1788. 'Epreuves du sentiment, par *d'Arnaud*. 3 Vol. 8. à Vienne, en commiss. chez R. Graeffer et Comp.', OM 1788, p.144. Could this be part of a seven-volume edition listed in Heinsius (varia) and Kayser: 'Epreuves du Sentiment, p. M. d'Arnaud. 7 T[omes]. gr. [in-]8. Wien, Schrämbl. (Sammer.) [1]787-88' (Heinsius, 1798 [p.486]; Heinsius, Romane [col.59]; information repeated in Kayser, Romane [p.11a]).

See too the end of the commentary on the *Epreuves du sentiment* listed above and on the *Ricreazioni dell'uomo sensibile* below, and the *Répertoire de bibliographie française mentionnant tous les ouvrages … 1501-1930* (Paris 1941, fasc. x; discussed in Dawson ii.609-10).

Incipits followed by the first date(s) of publication:

(*Julie*), 'Le systême avoit entraîné la ruine de beaucoup de familles', 1767.

(*Fanny*) 'Le Lord *Thatley* entroit dans cet âge que l'on peut nommer', 1762, 1764.

(*Nancy*) 'Des maladies cruelles qui affligent l'esprit humain', 1767.

(*Lucie et Mélanie*) 'La mort de Louis XII avoit en quelque sorte', 1761, 1767.

(*Clary*) 'Après la vertu, objet immuable de nos hommages', 1765, 1767.

(*Batilde*) 'La puissance des Maires étoit devenue presque égale', 1767.

(*Adelson et Salvini*) 'Rome paroît, en quelque sorte, avoir conservé ses droits', 1772.

(*Sargines*) 'Philippe-Auguste imprimoit le sceau de sa grandeur', 1772.

(*Sidney et Volsan*) 'J'étois avant-hier, selon mon usage', 1765, 1766, 1770.

(*Mémoires du comte de Comminges*, Mme de Tencin) 'Je n'ai d'autre dessein, en écrivant les Mémoires de ma vie', 1735.

(*Anne Bell*) 'La vertu & l'honnêteté, en exigeant des jeunes personnes', 1769.

(*Mémoires d'Euphémie*) 'Oui, ma chere fille, car ma tendre amitié me permet de vous donner ce nom', 1768.

(*Sélicourt*) 'Le Chevalier de Sélicourt sortoit d'une famille distinguée', 1769.

(*Effets de la vengeance*, abbé Prévost) 'Ma naissance est noble, & mon nom'; for dating, see Dawson ii.670-71.

For the rest of the incipits, see d'Arnaud, *Œuvres*, 1795-1815 below.

35

Arnaud: *Œuvres*, 1795-1815

François Thomas Marie [de] Baculard d'Arnaud (1718-1805): Oeuvres / de / d'Arnaud. / Contenant / [vol. i] Zénothemis, Bazile, Lorezzo. [ii: Liebman, Rosalie, Germeuil.; iii: Maxin, Dalmanzi, Valmiers.; iv: Pauline et Suzette,

Amélie, Daminville; v: Ermance, Henriette et Charlot.; vi: Salisbury, Varbeck.; vii: Le S. de Créqui, Le P. de Bretagne.; viii: La D. de Chatillon, le C. de / Strafort.; ix: Eudoxie, le C. de Glechein.; x: […] / Contenant Fayel.; xi: les époux malheureux.; xii: les époux malheureux.] / Tome premier [second-douzième]. / [rule] / Avec figures. / A Paris, [Paris. for vols iv-vi, ix-xii] / Chez Laporte, Libraire, rue Christine. / [double rule for i-ii, vii-viii; swell rule for iii-vi, ix-xii] / M. DCC. CXV. [for vols i, v-vii, xi-xii; M. DCC. XCV. for the rest]

8°, i: 2 ff. (two preliminary leaves: a. 'Catalogue…', see the commentary; b. Œuvres / de / M. d'Arnaud. / [double rule] / Nouvelles historiques. / [double rule] (half titlepage) + 1 f. (volume titlepage described above)

no. 1, Nouvelles / historiques. / Par M. d'Arnaud. / [double rule] / Tome premier. / [double rule] / [woodcut ornament: heart with two arrows through it surmounting what might be a stylised quiver, bow and arrow; symmetrical plant-like flourishes swooping to either side below it, with a finial at the bottom] / A Paris, / Chez Delalain, Libraire, rue de la Comédie / Française. / [double rule] / M. DCC. LXXIV. / Avec Approbation & Privilège du Roi. 1 pl (titlepage) + j-xxij pp. ('Préface') + 1 f. (2 pp.: the privilege, registration and an erratum for *Salisbury*).

no. 2, Zénothémis, / anecdote marseilloise. (half titlepage) + 3-26, [27]-104 pp. (for the *Extrait de l'histoire de Marseille jusqu'à sa prise par Jules-César* and the novella proper).

no. 3, Bazile. / Anecdote française. / [double rule] (half titlepage) + [107]-208 pp.

no. 4, Lorezzo. / Anecdote sicilienne. / [double rule] (half titlepage) + [211]-340 pp.

ii: no. 1, Liebman. / Anecdote allemande. / [double rule] (half titlepage) + [343]-428 pp.

no. 2, Rosalie. / Anecdote. / [double rule] (half titlepage) + [431]-522 pp. + 1 f. (1 p.: 'Table du tome troisième').

no. 3, Germeuil, / anecdote. / [double rule] (half titlepage) + [365]-456 pp. + 1 f. (1 p.: 'Table du tome quatrième') + j-viij pp. (The last 8 pp. are the music, by Desaugiers, Simon and Rochefort, of the 'Romances siciliennes' meant to accompany *Lorezzo*, i, no. 4 above.)

iii: no. 1, Makin, / anecdote anglaise. / [double rule] (half titlepage) + [261]-362 pp.

no. 2, D'Almanzi. / Anecdote française. / [double rule] (half titlepage), + [91]-168 pp.

no. 3, Valmiers, / anecdote. / [double rule] (half titlepage) + [315]-448 pp.

iv: no. 1, Pauline et Suzette, / anecdote française. / [double rule] (half titlepage) + [171]-258 pp.

no. 2, Amélie, / anecdote anglaise. / [double rule] (half titlepage) + [451]-542 pp. + 1 f. (1 p.: 'Table du Tome cinquième').

no. 3, Daminvile, / anecdote. / [double rule] (half titlepage) + [3]-152 pp.

v: no. 1, Ermance, / anecdote française. / [double rule] (half titlepage) + [3]-88 pp.

no. 2, Henriette et Charlot, / anecdote. / [double rule] (half titlepage) + [155]-312 pp.

vi: no. 1, Salisbury. / [double rule] (half titlepage) + [3]-128 pp.

no. 2, Varbeck. / [double rule] (half titlepage) + [131]-324 pp.

vii: no. 1, Le / sire de Créqui. / [double rule] (half titlepage) + [327]-452 + (Romance, / contenant l'histoire / du sire de Créqui, / Composée vers 1300.; half titlepage) + 455-456 (untitled preface), [457]-486 pp. + 2 ff. (3 pp. of music by Le Boucher Ducrosco and Moncriff, 'Complaintes du sire de Créqui') + 1 f. (1 p.: 'Table du tome premier').

no. 2, Le / prince de Bretagne. / [double rule] (half titlepage) + [3]-160 pp.

viii: no. 1, La duchesse / de Châtillon. / [double rule] (half titlepage) + [163]-254 + (half titlepage: Anecdote, / Contenant les détails du passage de Charles II / en France, après la bataille de Worcestre, / tirée des Mémoires de Clarendon.) + [256] ('Avertissement' verso the half-title), [257]-280 pp.

no. 2, Le comte / de Strafford. / [double rule] (half titlepage) + [283]-404 pp. + 1 f. (1 p.: 'Table du Tome second').

ix: no. 1, Eudoxie. / [double rule] (half titlepage) + [3]-112 pp.

no. 2, Le comte / de / Gleichen. / [double rule] (half titlepage) + [115]-224 pp.

x: Fayel, / tragédie. (half titlepage) + Fayel, / tragédie, / Par M. d'Arnaud. / Nouvelle édition. / [rule] / .....Furit, æstuat, ardet. / [rule] / [woodcut decoration: spray of flowers] / A Paris, / Chez Delalain, Libraire, rue de la Comédie / Françoise. / [rule] / M. DCC. LXXVII. / Avec Approbation & Privilége du Roi. 2 ff. (halftitle and titlepage) + [v]-xl pp. + 1 f. (pp.[1-2], half titlepage: Fayel, / tragédie., with 'Personnages' verso) + [3]-110 + (half titlepage: Extrait / de l'histoire / du châtelain de Fayel. / [double rule]) + 113-126 pp.

xi (A confusing array of half title- and titlepages, as follows):

1. Œuvres / de M. d'Arnaud. / [double rule] / Les / époux malheureux. / [double rule] (half titlepage).

2. (Vol. titlepage as described above.)

3. Les / époux malheureux, / ou / histoire / de monsieur et madame de ***; / nouvelle édition, / Corrigée, augmentée de deux nouvelles Parties, qui sont la / conclusion de l'Histoire, enrichie de belles Estampes, &c. / Par M. d'Arnaud. / [double rule] / Tome premier. / [double rule] / [small woodcut decoration: sprig of flowers] / A Paris, / Chez la Veuve Ballard & Fils, Imprimeurs du Roi, / rue des Mathurins. / Et chez Laporte, Libraire, rue des Noyers. / [rule] / M. DCC. LXXXIII. / Avec Approbation & Privilége du Roi. (titlepage).

4. Œuvres / de M. d'Arnaud. / [double rule] / Les / époux malheureux. / [double rule] (half titlepage, considerably different from the first half titlepage).

5. Les / époux malheureux, / ou / histoire / de M^r et Mme de ***; / nouvelle édition, / Corrigée, augmentée de deux nouvelles Parties, qui / sont la conclusion de l'Histoire, enrichie de belles / Estampes, &c. / Par M. d'Arnaud. / [double rule] / Tome premier. / [double rule] / [small woodcut decoration: quiver and torch?, crossed, tied with two flowers] / A Paris, / Chez Laporte, Libraire, rue des Noyers. / [rule] / M. DCC. LXXXIII. (titlepage); (various pl as described) + [j]-xij ('Avertissement des éditeurs').

6. Les / époux malheureux, / ou / histoire / de monsieur et madame de ***. / Premiere partie. / [rule] / Tome premier. / [rule] (half titlepage) + [3]-86 + (half

titlepage for '[...] Seconde partie. [...]') + [89]-174 + (half titlepage for '[...] Troisieme partie. [...]') + [177]-288 pp. + 1 f. (1 p. 'Errata Pour le premier Volume').

xii (Similar confusion prevails):

1. Œuvres / de M. d'Arnaud. / [double rule] / Les / époux malheureux. / [double rule] (half titlepage corresponding to xi, 1).

2. (Volume titlepage as described above.)

3. Les / époux malheureux, / ou / histoire / de monsieur et madame de ***; / nouvelle édition, / Corrigée, augmentée de deux nouvelles Parties, qui sont la / conclusion de l'Histoire, enrichie de belles Estampes, &c. / Par M. d'Arnaud. / [double rule] / Tome second. / [double rule] / [small woodcut decoration, same as for vol. xi, no. 5 above] / A Paris, / Chez la Veuve Ballard & Fils, Imprimeurs du Roi, / rue des Mathurins. / Et chez Laporte, Libraire, rue des Noyers. / [rule] / M. DCC. LXXXIII. / Avec Approbation & Privilége du Roi. (titlepage corresponding to xi, no. 3).

4. Les / époux malheureux, / ou / histoire / de monsieur et madame de ***. / Quatrieme partie. / [rule] / Tome second. / [rule] (half titlepage) + [3]-82 + (half titlepage, '[...] Cinquieme partie. [...]') + [85]-180 + (half titlepage, '[...] Sixieme et derniere partie. [...]') + [183]-238 [for 256] pp. + 1 f. (1 p., approbation: 18 December 1782, signed 'Cardonne'; 'Le Privilége se trouve à la fin des Œuvres de M. d'Arnaud.') + 1 f. (1 p.: 'Errata Pour le second Volume') + 1 f. (2 pp.: 'Avis aux relieurs, Pour placer les Estampes').

Commentary: These twelve volumes are most whimsically bound into six tomes. The contents provide the items promised for on the titlepages, but the actual contents comprise a wide range of the individual editions of d'Arnaud's prose fiction, including one of his major plays (*Fayel*) in the second, legitimate, refurbished edition. The items through volume ix contain novelle from d'Arnaud's two, major collections, the *Epreuves du sentiment* (from *Zénothémis* to *Henriette et Charlot*) and all the *Nouvelles historiques* (from *Salisbury* to *Le Comte de Gleichen*).

The editor made no attempt to group the tales in the order they were originally issued; the firm of Laporte probably assembled a collection of the *Œuvres* in order to use up stock which either the firm had left over, or which it acquired from other publishers for that purpose. The sheets added by Laporte (the preliminary leaves to vol. i and all volume titlepages) are of cheap paper. The actual contents are printed on fine paper, of different kinds. Signatures follow the individual pieces, presumably as originally issued, and are as diverse as the pagination. In any case, there were other editions by Laporte of d'Arnaud's *Œuvres* for the end of the eighteenth century, beginning of the nineteenth, some of which were specifically republished and reprinted for that purpose. (See Dawson, especially ii.630-34.) Note that the woodcut decorations for the title-pages of xi, no. 5 and xii, no. 3 are the same, which leads one to believe that the same firm printed both titlepages, for copies meant to be sold by different publishers. Curiously xi, no. 5 bears no mention of legal affairs. (Its counterpart for the second volume of the novel is not here present.)

The first folio of volume one is a leaf added by Laporte containing a 'Catalogue De diverses Anecdotes et autres Pièces de d'Arnaud que l'on a réunis [*sic*] en

12 vol. in-8°, ornés d'environ 90 Gravures, prix en feuilles pour la totalité, 180 l. Les personnes qui voudront se les procurer séparement les payeront; SAVOIR:'; follows a list of the contents with the price for each piece.

Why did Laporte not mention the exact number of engravings to be found with this collection? In all likelihood for the reason that he had available several different editions of some of the pieces, not all of which carried the 'correct' number of engravings. Thus there would be, without a doubt, a considerable number of edition variants. Reynaud, under the rubric of 'Œuvres d'Arnaud, chez Laporte', states: '1ere édition 1795. [...] Collection recherchée pour les jolies illustrations par Eisen, Marillier, Le Barbier et autres, qu'elle contient au nombre de 34 fig. hors-texte et 38 vignettes, en-têtes et culs-de-lampe. [...] Certaines vignettes sont changées, des culs-de-lampe n'ont pas été imprimés, enfin certaines figures ont été refaites en contrepartie et mal gravées, non signées' (col.32). This means that, in spite of the artists' signatures on the plates, some of the illustrations differ from those issued with the original editions of the individual works. Reynaud then mentions that there exist two additional editions for 1795, one with 33 full-page engravings, 22 headpieces and 14 tailpieces, and the other with a frontispiece, and 46 illustrations, 32 vignettes and 14 culs-de-lampe. Moreover the latter edition has ten pages of engraved music. Reynaud also mentions a twelve-volume, octavo, 1815 edition, with 33 illustrations: 21 vignettes and 11 culs-de-lampe. This is an edition 'constituée des éditions Delalais [*sic*, for Delalain], 1773 à 1783, auxquelles le libraire a ajouté un titre de relais. Epreuve en premier tirage dont il avait la lettre de ces figures qui sont de la plus grande beauté. Grand papier' (col.33). Reynaud makes no mention of a 1795-1815 *Œuvres*, and none is listed in the BNC, BLC or NUC.

Reynaud might have mentioned that the 1795 editions are also constituted from previous printings, with cancel titlepages added by the publisher, as is the case here. (I have never seen an edition of either the 1795 or 1815 *Œuvres* with all the engravings in the first state; the 1815 edition described by Reynaud is obviously from a specific copy, which was possibly, if not probably unique.)

The engravings in the above edition, with names of artists, engravers, titles and dates (when included with the plate), are as follows: 1. Frontispiece for the 'Nouvelles historiques' (Eisen-De Longueil, 1774). 2. Frontispiece for 'Zénothémis' (Eisen-de Launay). 3. Headpiece (Eisen-Ponce, 1773). 4. Tailpiece (Eisen-Ponce, 1773). 5. Frontispiece for 'Bazile' (Eisen-De Longueil, 1773). 6. Headpiece (Eisen-Née). 7. Tailpiece (Eisen-De Launay). 8. Frontispiece for 'Lorezzo'; unsigned, a poor imitation. 9. Headpiece (Marillier-Mesquelier, 1774). 10. Frontispiece for 'Liebman'; unsigned, a poor imitation. 11. Headpiece (Marillier-De Ghendt). 12. Frontispiece for 'Rosalie'; unsigned, a poor imitation. 13. Headpiece (Marillier-Le Roy, 1774? [nearly illegible]). 14. Frontispiece 'Germeuil' (Marillier-Halbou, 1776). 15. Headpiece (Marillier-Le Grand). 16. Tailpiece (Marillier-Le Grand). 17. Frontispiece for 'Makin' (Marillier-Halbou, 1776). 18. Headpiece (Marillier-Maillet, 1776). 19. Tailpiece (Marillier-De Ghendt). 20. Frontispiece for 'D'Almanzi'; unsigned, a poor imitation. 21. Headpiece (Marillier-De Longueil). 22. Frontispiece for 'Valmiers' (Marillier-Fessard, 1779). 23. Headpiece (Marillier-Texier). 24. Tailpiece, unsigned. 25. Frontispiece for 'Pauline et Suzette' (Marillier-De Launay, 1776). 26. Headpiece

(Marillier-De Launay, 1776). 27. Tailpiece (Marillier-De Launay, 1775; the engraver got a bit confused; De Launay's name is to the left, Marillier's to the right, and the date is a mirror image of what it should be.) 28. Frontispiece for 'Amélie' (Le Barbier-Godefroy). 29. Headpiece (Le Barbier-Ponce). 30. Tailpiece (Le Barbier-mme Ponce). 31. Frontispiece for 'Daminvile' (Marillier-Halbou, 1777). 32. Headpiece (Marillier-Halbou, 1777). 33. Tailpiece (Marillier-Halbou, 1776). 34. Frontispiece for 'Ermance'; unsigned, poor imitation. 35. Headpiece (Marillier-Ponce, 1772). 36. Frontispiece for 'Henriette et Charlot' (Marillier-Halbou, 1777). 37. Headpiece (Marillier-De Ghendt). 38. Tailpiece (Marillier-De Ghendt). 39. Frontispiece for 'Salisbury' (Eisen-Née). 40. Headpiece (Eisen-Helman, 1773). 41. Tailpiece (Eisen-Helman, 1773). 42. Frontispiece for 'Varbeck' (Eisen-Née, 1774). 43. Headpiece (Eisen-Née, date illegible). 44. Tailpiece (unsigned). 45. Frontispiece for 'Le Sire de Créqui' (Eisen-De Launay, 1775). 46. Headpiece (Eisen-Née, 1774). 47. Tailpiece (Eisen-Née). 48. Frontispiece for 'Le prince de Bretagne' (Marillier-Lingée, 1776). 49. Headpiece (Marillier-Lingée, traces of a date). 50. Tailpiece (Marillier-Lingée, 1776). 51. Frontispiece for 'La duchesse de Chatillon' (Le Barbier-Ponce, 1780). 52. Headpiece (Marillier-Fessard). 53. Tailpiece (Marillier-[Halbou?], date illegible). 54. Frontispiece for 'Le comte de Strafford' (Le Barbier-Halbou). 55. Headpiece (unsigned). 56. Tailpiece (unsigned). 57. Frontispiece for 'Eudoxie' (Le Barbier-Triere, 1782). 58. Headpiece (Le Barbier-Triere, 1782). 59. Tailpiece (Le Barbier-Triere, 1782). 60. Frontispiece for 'Le comte de Gleichen' (Le Barbier-Halbou, 1783). 61. Headpiece (Le Barbier-Halbou). 62. Tailpiece (Le Barbier-Halbou). 63. Frontispiece for [*Fayel*]; this is the mediocre engraving issued with the first edition of the play (1770). 64. Full-page engraving facing xi.13, bears '2^e'; unsigned. 65. Full-page engraving facing xi.39, bears '3^e'; unsigned. 66. Full-page engraving facing xi.67, bears '4^e'; unsigned. 67. Full-page engraving facing xi.115, bears '5'; unsigned. 68. Full-page engraving facing xi.219, bears '6'; unsigned. 69. Full-page engraving facing xi.232 (Eisen-Guttenberg); bears '8'. 70. Full-page engraving facing xii.21, bears '11.^{e}'; unsigned. 71. Full-page engraving facing xii.47, bears '12.^{e}'; unsigned. 72. Full-page engraving facing xii.193 (Eisen-Macret); bears '18.e'. 73. Full-page engraving facing xii.251 (Eisen-Guttenberg); bears '19.e'.

Containing a collection of 73 engravings, it is possible that we have here what Reynaud describes as the first, 1795, Laporte edition. The Delalain 'épreuves' and 'nouvelles historiques' (and Le Jay's before that) each carried a full-page frontispiece plate, a vignette and a cul-de-lampe, in the first, octavo editions. I suspect that the titlepages were printed in 1795, with some of them accidentally having the 'XC' juxtaposed. Printing a date for 1815 as M. DCC. CXV. would be unusual. And the type is reminiscent of the fonts used in the later '90s (but which continued in use well into the nineteenth century).

Concerning the last ten engravings listed above: these are the fine illustrations for the first edition of the second version of *Les Epoux malheureux*, and seem to be in the first state. There were at least two octavo issues or editions in 1783 (date of the first edition of the second, greatly revised version of the novel), by Laporte and Ballard (or Laporte and Ballard/Laporte). Both of these included the illustrations. Although only three of the engravings are signed, the 'Avertissement des éditeurs' at the head of the novel (doubtlessly authored by d'Arnaud) explains: 'l'Édition *in-8°* est enrichie de Dessins du célebre Eysen, & ce sont ses dernieres productions en ce genre' (p.xij). Eisen died in 1778, so, although more engravings were originally planned (which is easy to deduce from their numbering), the artist did not have time to finish his work. The 'Avis aux relieurs' bound in at the very end explains: 'On prévient les Relieurs que les planches, qui sont au nombre de dix, n'étant pas numérotées exactement, on doit se conformer à l'ordre qui suit'. Then follows a brief description of each plate, with the explanation of where it should go. At the end is a 'nota': 'Les Relieurs observeront que cette page volante est pour leur instruction, & qu'ils la déchireront lorsqu'ils auront placé les Estampes'. (The one-folio errata sheet for the first volume of the novel, and the last three folios in vol. ii are made of paper different from the preceding gatherings, and have been tipped in.)

And, indeed, the binders seem to have carefully followed this advice, for I know of no other copy of the *Epoux malheureux* containing this sheet. However, M. Pereire did find a copy with the instructions to the binder (conceivably the same copy described here), and made it the subject of a short article, in which he transcribed the two pages in their entirety (*Bulletin du bibliophile et du bibliothécaire*, 15 May-15 June 1921 [nos 5-6], pp.[118]-124). The numbers appearing on the plates have led many a bibliographer to suppose that the *Epoux malheureux*, in the fine, 1783 octavo edition, was supposed to have had nineteen or twenty pictures. I might add that the illustration engraved by Macret after Eisen is of exceptionally fine quality.

Incipits, followed by the first date of publication:

(*Zénothémis*) 'Marseille, en fléchissant sous la fortune de César' (1773).

(*Bazile*) 'Nos livres sont remplis de déclamations contre cette opiniâtreté presque invincible de la nature' (1774).

(*Lorezzo*) 'Trapani, anciennement Drépanum, est une des plus jolies villes de la Sicile' (1775).

(*Liebman*) 'Appellé en Allemagne par des motifs dont il importe peu au public d'être instruit' (1775).

(*Rosalie*) 'Rosalie devoit le jour à des commercants estimables' (1775).

(*Germeuil*) 'La province a été, de tout temps, l'objet du dédain & des froides plaisanteries' (1777).

(*Makin*) 'On ne peut nier, que l'ambition & l'avarice n'ayent porté nos Européens' (1777).

(*D'Almanzi*) '–Non, mon ami, non, je ne suis point heureux!' (1776).

(*Valmiers*) 'La justice & la bonté, ces deux vertus si nécessaires aux hommes' (1779).

(*Pauline et Suzette*) 'Une femme de la campagne, veuve, & n'ayant qu'un seul enfant' (1777).

(*Amélie*) 'Nos moralistes s'élèvent avec vigueur contre les passions' (1780).

(*Daminvile*) 'Monsorin étoit du nombre de ces parvenus que la richesse corrompt & dénature' (1778).

(*Ermance*) 'On nous présente tous les jours comme un des objets les plus imposants' (1775).

(*Henriette et Charlot*) 'La même femme, qui devoit être la complice ou plutôt l'auteur d'une catastrophe' (1779).

(*Salisbury*) 'L'Angleterre reprenoit son ascendant sur l'Ecosse.' (1774).

(*Varbeck*) 'Le dénouement presque honteux, d'une intrigue conduite avec toutes les précautions' (1774).

(*Le Sire de Créqui*) 'Il est de ces fortes secousses qu'un siècle reçoit' (1776).

(*Le Prince de Bretagne*) 'Jean V, duc de Bretagne, étoit descendu au tombeau' (1777).

(*La Duchesse de Châtillon*) 'La malheureuse journée de Worcestre sembloit avoir mis le sceau' (1780).

(*Le Comte de Strafford*) 'Les devoirs du sujet envers le souverain, ce qu'à son tour le souverain doit au sujet' (1781).

(*Eudoxie*) 'Athenes sembloit se survivre à elle-même, & sa mémoire' (1783).

(*Le Comte de Gleichen*) 'Mélédin, malgré tous ses efforts' (1784).

(*Les Epoux malheureux*) 'Quoi, monsieur! il est encore un cœur ouvert aux cris des malheureux!' (1783).

36

Arnaud (transl. unknown): *Prove del sentimento*, 1780

François Thomas Marie [de] Baculard d'Arnaud (1718-1805), translator unknown: (engraved titlepages) Prove / del / sentimento / del sig^r d'Arnaud / tomo I [same for all volumes; however the engraved 'I' seems to have been added later, and vestiges of other marks remain in front of it] / Venezia, MDCCLXXX / nella stamperia Graziosi. / [double rule] / Con Approvazione.

8°, i: 1. (head title) Zenotemi novella del signor d'Arnaud; (engraved titlepage) + [3]-64 pp.

2. (head title) Basilio annedoto Francese, 1-80 pp.

3. (head title) Makin, aneddoto inglese, 1-78 pp.

ii: (head title) 1. Fanni del signor d'Arnaud. Novella; (engraved titlepage) + 3-64 pp.

2. (head title) Daminvile, ossia l'uomo virtuoso nelle avversità, 1-116 pp.

iii: (head title) 1. Adelson e Salvini novella del signor d'Arnaud; (engraved titlepage) + [3]-100 pp.

2. (head title) Sydney e Volsan novella del signor d'Arnaud, 1-64 pp.

3. (head title) Batilde del signor d'Arnaud novella, 1-62 pp.

iv: (head title) 1. Anna Bell novella del signor d'Arnaud; (engraved titlepage) + 3-69 pp. + 1 f. (blank).

2. (head title) Giulia del signor d'Arnaud novella, 1-67 pp.

3. (head title) Selicourt del signor d'Arnaud novella, 1-68 pp.

4. (titlepage) Lucia / ossia / il modello della più rara e della / più sublime generosità / novella / del sig. d'Arnaud. / [rule] / Traduzione dal Francese. / [rule] / [small woodcut decoration: stylised flower] / Venezia / MDCCCXII. / Nella Stamperia Graziosi. / S. Silvestro Ponte dei Meloni N. 1374. / [rule] / Prezzo

Centesimi sessantacinque.; (head title: Lucia del signor d'Arnaud novella): 1 f. (the titlepage) + 3-48 pp.

v: (head title) Aneddoti diversi, 1-221, 222 pp.

Commentary: Each of the above items has its own signatures and was separately printed. The volume titlepages are again makeshift titlepages, with the volume number inked in, information which is echoed on the spines. However, each titlepage bears an engraved 'I', as mentioned; see d'Arnaud, *Biblioteca sentimentale* and *Ricreazioni dell'uomo sensibile*. (These titlepages are excluded from the pagination recorded.) There is a blank sheet preceding the tipped in titlepages in volumes i-iv. In the present copy, it is possible to see that they are all conjugate to the respective f.[A8]. The first folios of text for the first items in vols i-iv begin with p.3, f.A2r. The preliminary blanks are thus f.[A1]. Note that this pattern is repeated for *Lucia* (iv, no. 4) except that A1 is the item titlepage. The rest of the pieces, beginning with p.1, begin with f.A[1].

The French titles and first dates of publication (in French) for the items in the first four volumes are as follows:

1. *Zénothémis, anecdote marseillaise*, an 'épreuve du sentiment', 1773.
2. *Bazile*, an 'épreuve', 1774.
3. *Makin*, an 'épreuve', 1777.
4. *Fanni, ou l'heureux répentir, histoire anglaise*, an 'épreuve', 1762, 1764.
5. *Daminvile*, an 'épreuve', 1778.
6. *Adelson et Salvini, anecdote anglaise*, an 'épreuve', 1772.
7. *Sidney et Volsan, histoire anglaise*, an 'épreuve', 1765, 1766, 1770.
8. *Batilde, ou l'héroïsme de l'amour, anecdote historique*, an 'épreuve', 1767.
9. *Anne Bell, histoire anglaise*, an 'épreuve', 1769.
10. *Julie, ou l'heureux repentir, histoire anglaise*, an 'épreuve', 1767.
11. *Sélicourt, nouvelle*, an 'épreuve', 1769.
12. *Lucie et Mélanie, ou les deux sœurs généreuses, anecdote historique*, an 'épreuve', 1767.

As for the fifth volume: it contains tales from the *Délassements de l'homme sensible*, mostly from vols iii and iv. For the French titles, see MMF 83.14. The Italian titles are as follows: 'La Vera nobiltà, ovvero la nobiltà dell'animo'; 'Sibilla e Lusignano, ovvero il nuovo esempio dell'amor conjugale'; 'Il Vile senza saperlo'; 'I Vantaggi dell'economia'; 'La Nuova Lucrezia'; 'Il Principe degno di esserlo, ossia l'uomo veramente grande'; 'Heredia, ovvero il gran maestro di Rodi'; 'L'Insalata di Sisto Quinto'; 'Il Genio della liberalità'; 'La Voce della giustizia'; 'I Lamenti paterni'; 'L'Artigiano benefico, e la dama riconoscente'; 'Alla memoria di Bertinazzi, detto Carlino, ovvero il debito della sensibilità'; 'Le Due età'; 'Teodelinda, ovvero l'amore vittima del dovere'; 'La Morte di Zomeny, ovvero il fine dell'uomo dabbene'. This volume has nothing to do with the *Ricreazioni* listed in Zambon (pp.10-11, no. 41).

The last page of this fifth volume is a table ('Indice'). At the end of the text is the price of the volume ('Il suo prezzo è Lire 3').

It is not possible to tell when these volumes were actually printed, but they were probably issued in the late eighteenth century, possibly early in the nineteenth. Note that *Lucia* (vol. iv, no. 4) has its own titlepage for 1812. The titlepages were probably hastily added, from a previous edition (or editions). Zambon lists two editions for the *Prove del sentimento*: Venice, Graziosi, 1780-1781 (5 vols in-8), but she could only find vols i and iv in the Biblioteca comunale di Verona, an edition which has nothing to do with the one described here. (Although the pagination for *Basilio* and *Anna Bell* coincide, the edition described in Zambon consists of volumes with consecutive pagination, and the titles vary; p.8, no. 38.) The other edition listed for the *Prove del sentimento* is in thirty-three volumes, Florence, Stecchi, 1797; this again seems to have nothing at all to do with the edition described here (p.9, no. 39).

I would make the following correction to Zambon: vol. xxiii of the 1797 *Prove del sentimento* contains the *Memorie del conte di Comingio*, 'relativo del dramma intitolato: *Gli Amanti infelici*', which is, of course, a translation of Mme de Tencin's popular novel, the *Mémoires du comte de Comminges*. See d'Arnaud, *Œuvres*, 1775, and Tencin, *Mémoires* infra.

There are several other editions of the *Prove del sentimento* listed in the Primo cat. (at least four, some forming part of the *Opere*), not listed in Zambon. Zambon's bibliography and the long article devoted to d'Arnaud in her *Les Romans français dans les journaux littéraires italiens du XVIIIᵉ siècle* (Florence, Paris 1971), together with the additional entries listed in the Primo cat., the NUC (etc.) amply demonstrate that d'Arnaud was one of the most widely read French novelists in Italy in the eighteenth century; I do not doubt but that further research will underscore this phenomenon.

Incipits: (*Zenotemi*) 'Marsiglia, cedendo alla fortuna di Cesare'.

(*Basilio*) 'I Nostri Libri sono ripieni di declamazioni'.

(*Makin*) 'Non può negarsi, che l'ambizione e l'avarizia'.

(*Fanni*) 'Il Lord Thaley entrava nell'età delle passioni'.

(*Daminvile*) 'Monsorin era uno di quegli uomini di ventura'.

(*Adelson e Salvini*) 'Roma sembra in certo modo aver conservato'.

(*Sydney e Volsan*) 'Io era [*sic*] l'altro jeri, secondo l'usanza mia'.

(*Batilde*) 'La (*) potenza de' prefetti del Palazzo era divenuta'. (A note gives further historical information.)

(*Anna Bell*) 'La virtù e l'onestà esigendo dalle fanciulle'.

(*Giulia*) 'Il Sistema tratto avea seco la rovina di molte famiglie'.

(*Selicourt*) 'Il Cavaliete [*sic*] di *Selicourt* usciva di una distinta, e ragguardevole famiglia nella Provenza'.

(*Lucia*) 'La morte di Luigi XII. aveva in certo modo cangiato lo spirito della nazione.'

(vol. v, 'La Vera nobiltà') 'Ci prendiamo di nuovo la libertà di presentar sulla scena'.

37

Arnaud (transl. unknown): *Ricreazioni dell'uomo sensibile*, 1803

François Thomas Marie [de] Baculard d'Arnaud (1718-1805), translator unknown: (engraved titlepage) Ricreazioni / dell'uomo / sensibile / del sig.ʳ d'Ar-

naud / Traduzione / dal Francese. / Tomo I / Venezia MDCCCIII / nella stamperia Graziosi / [double rule] / Con Approvazione

8°, i: engraved titlepage + 1, (p.2 is blank), 3-220, 221, 222 pp.

Commentary: This is a translation of part I of the first volume of d'Arnaud's
Délassements de l'homme sensible which first appeared in 1783, in the French. (The
last tale is the first of vol. i, part II.) The titlepage is a make-shift, albeit pretty
engraved sheet which was in all likelihood added in 1803 to a book printed and
published in 1800. The first page is a brief 'Prefazione dell'autore' (p.2 is a
blank). Then follow the *Ricreazioni*, with a head title for 'Aneddoti diversi', from
'Alfredo il grande' to 'Il Trionfo della virtù' and a one-page 'Indice' with, on
the verso, some legal material and additional information. The approbation is
dated 26 June 1800 for the volume described here, 'Gradenigo Segr.' At the
bottom of the page is found: 'Il suo prezzo è Lire 3. Si stampa presentemente il
Tomo Secondo.'

The only translation of the *Délassements de l'homme sensible* listed in Zambon is
for Genoa, Caffarelli, 1789, in eight volumes, by an unknown translator. (And
the only copy Zambon could find is missing vols i and vii. In any case, all the
'délassements' are not included.) The NUC has two entries for the *Ricreazioni*,
both for the New York Public Library: Ricreazioni dell'uomo sensibile; ovvero
Aneddoti diversi del Sig. d'Arnaud. Tradotti da*........ Tomo 1-2 (Genova: nella
stamperia Caffarelli, 1786, in-12) and, same title, twelve vols, for 1786-1793.
The only 'ricreazioni' listed in the Primo cat. are for volumes v-x of the *Opere*,
10 vols in-24, Napoli: V. Orsino, 1791-1801. The following dates are given: v-
vi, 1801; vii, 1799; viii-ix, 1800; x, 1801. These volumes most likely consist of
an amalgam of various editions, not having anything to do with the '1803' book
here listed.

From the publisher's notice at the end of the volume described here, it seems
clear that this is the first of a series which was supposed to be longer. However,
perhaps no more of it appeared?

The tales contained in this volume are: 'Alfredo il grande'; 'L'Uomo unico';
'Il Potere della pietà; 'L'Origine del priorato detto dei Due Amanti'; 'La Nuova
Clementina'; 'Montagu e Randall'; 'L'Ingenuità dell'innocenza'; 'Il Ricco degno
di esserlo'; 'Marlborough'; 'L'Amante inglese'; 'L'Impero della natura'; 'La
Morte di Carlo I, re d'Ingilterra [*sic*]'; 'Felicia'; 'L'Uomo giusto e sensibile'; 'Il
Bisogno di esser amato'; 'La Marchesa di Spadara, ovvero l'esemplare
dell'amore materno'; 'Il Grand'uomo'; 'Il Trionfo della virtù'. For more 'délassements' rendered into the Italian, see d'Arnaud, *Prove del sentimento* above. See,
too, d'Arnaud, *Biblioteca sentimentale*. (For the French titles of the 'délassements'
described here, see MMF 83.14.) For further information concerning the *Délassements* as a collection, see Dawson.

To the various editions of the *Délassements* listed in modern bibliographies, I
would add: 'Délassemens de l'homme sensible, ou anecdotes diverses, p. d'Arnaud. 9. Tom. en 17 parties. gr. [in-]8. Vien. Schrämbl. (Sammer [for Sommer?])
[1]787-88' (Heinsius, Romane col.48). The publisher, dates and format match
an edition of the *Epreuves du sentiment* mentioned above (end of the commentary

on the *Œuvres complètes*, 1777). Perhaps these two collections formed part of an *Œuvres*?

Kayser mentions a 'Délassement [*sic*] de l'homme sensible etc. XII. Part. en VI Vols. [in-]12. Frankf., Varrentrapp' (i.106b). This edition probably dates to the eighteenth century. I have not been able to find any 'délassements' published by Varrentrapp, or any mention of such an edition. I mention this because Varrentrapp was a major publisher of French works and could well have done an edition of the *Délassements*.

There is also a *Délassements* listed in the Messkatalog, an edition which has escaped the attention of modern bibliographers: 'Dilassemens [*sic*] de l'homme sensible ou Anecdotes diverses par Mr. *d'Arnaud*. 6 Parties. 12. à Leipsic, chez la même [veuve H. Merkus]', OM 1784, p.900. However, since the next entry for the *Délassements* is for 'Tom. IV. parties 7 & 8. à Paris & à Leipsic, chez [la veuve H. Merkus]', MM 1784, p.1003, there is a good chance that we are dealing with a Paris edition available in Leipzig.

There is also a 'Delassemens de l'homme sensible, ou anecdotes diverses, par *d'Arnaud*. 6 Tom. XII. Part. 8. à Vienne, chez R. Graeffer et Comp.', OM 1788, p.143 not listed in the usual bibliographies. It is however mentioned in Heinsius, 1798, but as '9 Tom. en 17 parties, gr. 8vo. Wien, Schrämbl (Sammer) [1]787. 88' (p.484). This might have been published as part of, or with some *Epreuves*. See the commentary on the *Œuvres complètes*, 1777.

Incipit: ('Alfredo il grande') 'Fra tutti i generi di letteratura la Storia è forse quel solo, nel quale siasi meno adoperato di Filosofia'.

38

Arnaud: *Sélicourt*, 1788

François Thomas Marie [de] Baculard d'Arnaud (1718-1805): Selicourt, / nouvelle. / Par M. d'Arnaud. / [woodcut ornament: largely grapes and vines] / A Paris, / Chez Le Jay, Libraire, rue S. Jacques, / au-dessus de celle des Mathurins, / Au Grand Corneille. / [double rule, thick thin] / M. DCC. LXXXVIII. / Avec Approbation & Privilege du Roi.

18°: 2 pl + [1]-(114) pp.

Commentary: The halftitle ('encadré') reads 'Selicourt, / nouvelle.'

This edition is not separately listed in Dawson. MMF list a small, in-octavo edition, same place and publisher, 114 pp. (Monglond's library at the Université de Clermont, Clermont-Ferrand; 69.13). Although Monglond's book possibly represents the same edition as mine, I include this description in order to complete a series of 'épreuves' as extant in my collection. Without a doubt more tales than those described in the current bibliography were printed for this 'collection', since the *Epreuves du sentiment* comprise twenty-five novelle in all. For further information, see d'Arnaud's *Amélie*, 1787 above.

Incipit: 'Le chevalier de Sélicourt sortoit / d'une famille distinguée dans la pro- / vince'.

39

Aulnoy: *Histoire d'Hypolite, comte de Duglas*, ca.1775

Marie Catherine Jumelle de Berneville [de La Mothe], comtesse d'Aulnoy (?-1705): Histoire / d'Hypolite / comte / de Duglas. / Par madame d'Aulnoy. / Nouvelle Édition. / Tome premier [second]. / [curious elaborate, composite ornament, same for both volumes] / A Amsterdam, / Chez Abraham Wolfgan. / [rule] / Avec Approbation.

12°, i: 1 f. (titlepage) + 2 ff. (3 + 1 pp.). + [9]-132 pp.
  ii: 2 ff. (halftitle and titlepages) + [5]-164 pp.

Commentary: The preliminary pages are an 'épître': 'A son altesse serenissime madame la princesse de Conty', and a one-page approbation (Paris, 5 March 1708, signed Danchet).

Although a leaf seems to be missing from volume i, it is not. It is possible to ascertain in the present copy that what would at first glance appear to be an end paper is actually f.[A1]. Indeed, the only signature for the first gathering of that volume is A5 for p.[9]-10. Vol. ii ends with gathering G: G-Gij, [Giij-iv], Gv, [Gvj-Gx], according to the text. In the present copy, it is possible to ascertain that [Gxj] is actually the final guard leaf, and that [Gxij] has been glued down onto the back board of the binding. The signature pattern follows that of the last gathering, i.e. ff. 1, 2 and 5 are signed. Curiously the signatures in vol. i are in arabic, and for vol. ii in lower-case roman.

Vol. ii has the following halftitle page: Histoire / d'Hypolite / comte / de Duglas. / Par madame d'Aulnoy. / Tome second.

It is unlikely that this book was produced in Holland. The general appearance is quite primitive (including the contemporary calf binding). The few woodcut ornaments are even reminiscent of those to be found in books produced for the so-called 'bibliothèque bleue'. (Without excluding a nordic country, Denmark or Sweden perhaps, I would suspect a small Germanic town, from a press with a limited production).

MMF (56.R11) list a dateless edition for [1764], after Raymond Foulché-Delbosc's edition of d'Aulnoy's *Relation du voyage d'Espagne* (Paris 1926). That edition has nothing to do with the one listed here (Limoges, n.d. [1764], 2 vols in-12; Foulché-Delbosc p.111). I have dated this volume to ca. 1775 based on the fact that it is a contrefaçon, and on the binding, type, decorations and general compositorial practices. The last end-paper (actually f.[Gxij]) contains the following manuscript remark: 'Ce livre apartien a françois joseph Verdelet a bourg le 8 septembre 1788'. I see no reason to doubt Verdelet's scribbled date. Thus this book certainly would not postdate 1788.

Hypolite first appeared in 1690 (Lever, MMF, etc.).

To editions of works by Mme d'Aulnoy listed in MMF, I would add: 'Les Contes des fées. Cont[ient] tous leurs ouvrages en 9 vol. par Mme d'Aunoy. Nouvelle éd. avec fig. T. [1.]2. Nuremberg: Raspe 1762' (Gesamtverzeichniss, vi.401b).

Incipit: 'Sous le regne d'Henry VII. Roi / d'Angleterre, George de Neüilly, / Comte de Burgen'.

40

Auvigny, with Desfontaines: *Mémoires de madame de Barneveldt*, 1732

Jean du Castre d'Auvigny (1712-1743), with the abbé Pierre-François Guyot Desfontaines (1685-1745), but see the commentary: Memoires / de madame / de / Barneveldt. / Tome premier [second]. / [woodcut ornament: symmetrical, different for each volume] / A Paris, / Chez [open composite, curved brace] Michel Gandouin, Quay / de Conty, aux trois Vertus. / Et / Pierre-François Giffart, / ruë s. Jacques, à Ste Therese. [end of material set off by brace] / [rule] / MDCCXXXII. / Avec Approbation & Privilege.

12°, i: 2 pl (halftitle and titlepage, ff.[aj], [aij]) + 10 ff. (8 + 12 pp.) + [1]-288 pp.

    ii: 2 pl (halftitle and titlepage) + [i]-lxvi + 1-250 pp. + 3 ff. (6 pp.)

Commentary: This novel is listed by Jones (p.48), and is extant in the Arsenal Library and the BN (no copies listed in the NUC or BLC). Gay, Quérard, Drujon and Jones report that Desfontaines revised the novel, originally by d'Auvigny.

Jones only lists one edition (as above) of this novel. But the Gesamtk. lists another for the same year: 2 vols, Amsterdam: Aux dépens de la Compagnie, 1732 (location: the Prussian State Library, Berlin). It is also listed in Krauss-Fontius (no. 3657), with a location for the Universitäts- und Landesbibliothek Sachsen-Anhalt, Halle. I have managed to track down a copy in the U.S. (in the Rice University libraries): *Memoires* / de madame / de / *Barneveldt*. / Tome premier [second]. / [i: engraved vignette, 'vis unita major'; ii: woodcut version of the same] / *A Amsterdam*, / Aux depens de la Compagnie. / *M. DCC. XXXII.* in-12°, i: 2pl + 6ff. (8 + 4 pp.) + [1]-199 pp. ii: 2pl + 4ff. (8pp.) + [1]-227, [228] pp. There are halftitles for 'Memoires / de madame / de / Barneveldt. / Tome premier [second].' (The last page contains Jolly's approbation, copied from the first edition). The 'Rice' edition follows the refurbished version (for which see below).

I list my copy of this hard-to-come-by novel because my copy contains an extra leaf and because it is interfoliated with a 'clef'. The first eight pages in i are an 'Avertissement'; the next ten, a 'Sommaire' of both volumes. The first two sets of pages in vol. ii are the second part of the novel. The last six pages contain 1 p. of some 'Fautes à corriger', a one-page 'Avis du libraire', and the last four pages are legal material. First a flattering approbation dated 10 July 1731, signed 'Joly'. Then a privilege to Michel Gandouin for the novel by 'le sieur Dauvigni', 8 August 1731, signed 'Sainson'. Follows a document in which half the rights were ceded by Gandouin to Giffart (10 August 1731). Registered 10 August 1731 by the 'syndic' P. A. Le Mercier.

The 'Avis du libraire' explains: 'Comme on avoit obmis les trois premieres feüilles du second volume, on a été obligé de les imprimer après avoir imprimé les feüilles suivantes; c'est ce qui fait qu'après le chiffre lxvj. on trouve les chiffres 1. 2. 3. &c.' That is, however, not true. In the above copy, not only are there added leaves with manuscript annotations, but between ii.lxiv and ii.lxv there is an additional printed leaf, bearing the signature A[1] for 'Tome II.', the verso paginated '2'. This offers an entirely different direction to the beginning of the second half of the novel.

The first volume ends with Mme de Barneveldt having just embarked in Monte Carlo on a boat to Livorno, the final words being: 'je jouissois d'un état tranquille, & jene [*sic*] croyois pas qu'il pût jamais être troublé.' As the discerning reader very well knew (and knows!), that is but a foreshadowing of trouble to come. Indeed, the orginal version of vol. ii begins: 'Mon bonheur étoit trop parfait pour qu'il pût durer'. The characters re-embark in Livorno. 'Des songes affreux' trouble Mme de Barneveldt's husband. Lo, and behold! On the third day, their boat is pursued by a Tunisian ship. And there p.2 ends. This sheet has been slashed through the middle, meaning it was supposed to have been cancelled. (For another example of sheets slashed, but not cancelled, vide the entry devoted to Lichtwehr).

In light of the above, I propose that Desfontaines, possibly, decided to alter the novel radically, adding to its piquancy by changing things around so as to be able to incorporate references to his contemporaries. He even included some compliments for himself! This theory is supported by the gap between the date of publication, even if early in 1732, and that of the legal material. The beginning of the second version of volume ii has the characters remain in Italy (in and about Florence), enabling them to visit especially seigneur Martini's salon. And it is in the salon that Desfontaines introduces us to his contemporaries, under assumed names of course.

Drujon (cols 598-99) lists the novel (no mention of F. Giffart) and remarks: 'Ces mémoires, rédigés par Jean du Castre d'Auvigny, ont été revus et corrigés par l'abbé Desfontaines'. He mentions that Née de La Rochelle had left some information in his '"Récréations bibliographiques" laissées en manuscrit'. He refers to the *Œuvres posthumes* of Quérard. Brunet, in the 'Avant-propos' to Quérard's *Œuvres posthumes*, i: *Les Livres à clef*, gives a sort of history of research on 'les livres à clef' in which he notes: 'Née de La Rochelle, bibliographe zélé, né en 1751, mort en 1838, avait laissé, parmi de nombreux manuscrits, des *Récréations bibliographiques*, où se trouvaient des recherches sur divers ouvrages', including the one that interests us here. No further information is given.

The *Mémoires de Mme de Barneveldt* were announced in the *Nouvelliste du Parnasse*, letter XLIX, 15 January 1732: 'Les *Memoires de Madame de Barneveldt* paroissent; ils contiennent des choses très-singulieres, qui méritent que je vous en entretienne plus au long' (p.24), but the periodical stopped before that wish could be fulfilled. The *Journal littéraire* devoted several pages to a rather lackadaisical review of the novel (1732, tome xix, seconde partie, p.440-44). The *Mercure de France* praised the *Mémoires* with respect to style, contents and morality (January 1732, p.106). The most interesting review, from our point of view, is the not very flattering one which appeared in the *Mémoires pour l'histoire des sciences et des beaux-arts* (the *Mémoires* or *Journal de Trévoux*). It deserves citing (August 1732, pp.1487-89):

'L'Auteur, qui réfléchit d'une part que ce tître de *Mémoires* promet des faits particuliers, des intrigues de Cour, des secrets de Cabinet, des anecdotes intéressantes & curieuses, & que le nom de *Barneveld* fait encore plus attendre quelquechose de tout cela; et d'autre part, que son Ouvrage ne contient rien de pareil, a cru qu'il étoit de la probité de ne pas tromper son Lecteur par le tître, sans l'en avertir, & c'est par où il commence. A son exemple, le Libraire donne aussi un avis au sujet d'une lacune qui sépare les deux tomes. Pour remplir le nombre stipulé de pages, l'Auteur a fourni après coup quelques portraits satyriques, où il s'est peint lui-même comme un homme à qui le Public en veut, quoiqu'il n'en veüille qu'aux particuliers, ne s'attachant même qu'aux personnes de mérite. Quant à ceux qui pourroient trouver à redire, qu'un homme de son état & de sa profession ait encore fait un Roman, il peut leur prouver par toutes les régles d'un Roman, que celui-ci n'en est pas un. L'invention, peut-il dire, n'a rien de neuf ou de curieux; on ne voit dans l'exécution ni ordre, ni conduite; les événemens sont peu vraisemblables; les épisodes presque toûjours hors du sujet. [...] L'Auteur ne se nomme pas dans le Livre; mais il y a répandu tant d'expressions extraordinaires, qu'on peut se douter que c'est quelqu'un, qui a intérêt de grossir le Dictionnaire néologique.'

Indeed, the fact that the *Mémoires de Mme de Barneveldt* had had a 'key' inserted in them seems to have been common knowledge. Looking no further than Voltaire's correspondence, we find that Jean Baptiste Nicolas Formont wrote to Pierre Robert Le Cornier de Cideville: 'Il paroit depuis 2 jours des mémoires de M^de de Barneveld, Roman de l'abé des Fontaines, ou il y a Beaucoup de portraits Des Beaux ou prétendus beaux esprits de Paris. Je ne L'ay pas encor Lu' ([16 January 1732], Best.D458). Note that Formont attributes the work to Desfontaines, with no mention of d'Auvigny.

The object of what follows is simply to transcribe the manuscript notes found on the leaves bound in with the text of the novel. Space precludes a discussion of those notes. They date to the eighteenth century (as does the binding), but it seems impossible to affirm that these are strictly contemporary with the printing of the novel. The book (both volumes are bound in one) has a later note glued onto the second endpaper, remarking 'exemplaire ayant annotations curieuses'. There is also a library shelf mark, '124g'.

Facing i.14: 'la liberté des hommes'.

Facing i.90 (meant for pp.90-91): 'Les Ministres, et gens d'affaires'.

Facing ii.ii: 'Mr Crozat le Riche; ou bien le Marquis de Nel, chés lequel s'assemblent, mangent tres souvent un certain nombre de Beaux esprits'.

Facing ii.vi: 'M^r. Boindin'.

Meant for ii.vii-viii: 'L'abbé souchet de l'academie des Belles-Lettres; il est l'auteur de L'ausonne. Cet abbé est l'amant de la veuve Pissot Marchande-libraire sur le Quay de Conty.'

Facing ii.viii: 'Camuzat cydevant Bibliotecaire de M^r le marechal d'Estrées qui publie partout que Camuzat est un fripon. Camuzat est auteur du Ciaconnius Biblioteque des auteurs Ecclesiastiques. Il est aussi auteur de quelques Journaux des sçavans.'

Meant for ii.ix: 'Rousseau, un des plus fameux Poette qu'ait eu la France.'

Facing ii.x: 'Arroüet de Voltaire.'; 'oudart de la motte'.

Meant for ii.xi: 'Crebillon reçû a l'academie françoise en 1731.'

Meant for ii.xi: 'Nericault des Touches auteur de plusieurs Pieces de Théatre qui ont êtés fort goûtées.'

Facing ii.xi: 'Joly approbateur de ces memoires'.

Facing ii.xii: 'L'abbé des fontaines auteur de ces Memoires.'

Meant for ii.xiii: 'Remond de Saint Marc, fils de Remond fermier général surnommé Remond le Diable, son fils est surnommé le Petit Metaphysicien.'

Meant for ii.xv: 'Terrasson auteur du Roman de Sethos'.

Meant for ii.xxi: [same as for ii.xiii]

Facing ii.xxii: 'Dumont porte manteau du Roi l'histoire du Regiment de la Cotte l'a fait tres fort connoistre.'

Meant for ii.lv: 'L'abbé Alary, il est de l'Academie des Belles-lettres; et fils d'un apoticaire de la Montagne de Sainte-Geneviève à paris'.

Facing ii.30: 'La Constitution Unigenitus'.

Bound in after the first volume is a folding sheet, in a different hand, largely repeating the information contained on the interfoliated sheets. (Or perhaps the interfoliated sheets repeat the information to be found on the folding sheet?) Of interest are the first lines: 'L'abbe desfontaines auteur des memoires / Dauvignÿ qui passe pour l'auteur des memoires est le ganimede de l'abbe des fontaines'. It is further claimed that the Martini in the novel is 'Me Croisat', with no mention of the 'marquis de Nel'. If we were to believe the manuscript information, that means that Desfontaines alone composed the novel, and used his lover, d'Auvigny, as a figurehead. It seems to me that the question remains open, with particular emphasis on the rôle – if any – played by d'Auvigny in the composition of the novel. I have listed the *Mémoires de madame de Barneveldt* under 'Auvigny', with the participation of Desfontaines, because that is the way it is usually entered; perhaps the names of d'Auvigny and Desfontaines ought to be inverted.

All copies I have examined carry half titlepages for the novel ('Memoires / de madame / de / Barneveldt. / Tome premier [second].') Some bear, at the end of vol. ii, the following colophon: 'De l'Imprimerie de Claude Simon' (e.g. BN Y2.52530 and Y2.52528; the present copy has no colophon). Rather than a different edition, this seems to indicate an edition variant. No other copies examined carry any annotations pertaining to a key, and none has the 'real' first leaf of the second volume.

Here is a list of names mentioned in the key, in modern French. Not listed are obvious names (Destouches, Voltaire, etc.) or the ones I could not identify (Dumont and Nel [Nesle?]).

Alary, abbé Pierre-Joseph

Ausone, Decimus Magnus (or Decius)

Boindin, Nicolas

Camusat, Denis-François

Ciacconius, the Latin for Alonso Chacon

Crozat, Joseph-Antoine (in all likelihood; possibly his father, Antoine Crozat, marquis Du Châtel)

Rémond de Saint-Mard, Toussaint

Souchay, Jean-Baptiste

Terrasson, abbé Jean

Incipits: (vol. i) 'Je suis née au milieu de la forêt des Ardennes, & je dois mon éducation à un Solitaire'.

(vol. ii, original version) 'Mon bonheur étoit trop parfait pour qu'il pût durer.'

(vol. ii, second version) 'Mon beau-pere & ma belle-mere avoient pour moi beaucoup de complaisance & d'amitié'.

4 1

Barthélemy: *Voyage du jeune Anacharsis en Grèce*, 1790

abbé Jean Jacques Barthélemy (1716-1795): Voyage / du jeune Anacharsis / en Grèce [Grece for vol. vi, Gréce for vol. vii], / dans le milieu du quatrième [quatrieme for ii] siècle / avant l'ère vulgaire. / [rule] / Troisième édition. / [rule] / Tome premier [second, troisième, quatrième, cinquième, sixième, septième]. / [thin swell rule] / A Paris, / Chez De Bure l'aîné, Libraire de Monsieur, Frère / du Roi, de la Bibliothèque du Roi, et de l'Académie royale / des Inscriptions; hôtel Ferrand [Ferran for ii], rue Serpente, n°. 6. / 1790.

8°, i: 2 pl (halftitle and titlepages) + [v]-xvj + [1]-248 pp.
  ii: 2 pl + 1 f. (two-page 'table' with 'errata' at end] + [1]-350 pp.
  iii: 2 pl + 1 f. (two-page 'table') + [1]-332 pp.
  iv: 2 pl + 1 f. (two-page 'table') + [1]-339 pp.
  v: 2 pl + 1 f. (two-page 'table') + [1]-336 pp.
  vi: 2 pl + 1 f. (one-page 'table') + [1]-313 pp.
  vii: 2 pl + 1 f. (two-page 'table') + [1]-78, [79-80] + [j]-lxiv + [i]-cxxxix, [cxl] pp.

Commentary: Each volume has a halftitle for 'Voyage / du jeune Anacharsis / en Grèce. / Tome premier [second, etc.].' Vol. i contains an 'Avertissement' (pp.[v]-vj); 'Ordre chronologique du voyage d'Anacharsis' (pp.[vij]-viij); 'Division de l'ouvrage' (pp.[ix]-xvj); then the 'Introduction' with notes at the end. Vols. ii-vii, through p.78 of vii, contain the didactic novel (with notes at the end of each volume and notes in vii.[66]-78). Then follows a whole series of tables concerned with antiquity, preceded by an 'Avertissement...' (vii.[79]) and a 'table' of the tables (p.[80]). The second series of pages in lower-case roman numbers is a general index. At the very end (vii.[cxl]) is a brief 'Extrait des registres de l'Académie royale des inscriptions et belles-lettres. Du Vendredi 18 août 1786' in which the academy cedes its privilege for the *Voyage* to Barthélemy (Paris, in the Louvre, 18 August 1786, 'Dacier, Secrétaire perpétuel de l'Académie').

This long-winded, yet highly popular work first appeared in 1788. MMF (88.27) list two editions for 1790: a 'troisième édition' for Paris, 7 vols in-8°, after BN, Quérard and Maurice Badolle, *L'abbé Jean-Jacques Barthélemy ... et l'hellénisme en France dans la seconde moitié du 18ᵉ siècle* (Paris 1927). The other edition listed is for Paris, Debure, in-12, after BN and Badolle. (An octavo, seven-volume, 1790 edition is listed in OCLC for the University of Cincinnati, Athens, and there is also one in the BL [584.e.4-10]).

The edition listed here differs markedly from the seven-volume, octavo edition in the BN. For one thing, the pagination is entirely different. Perhaps my copy represents a piracy of that in the BN (or vice-versa)? The *Voyage du jeune Anacharsis* was often printed with a separate volume of maps, which does not appear to be the case here. (The BN edition also has no maps present.)

I could find no trace of my books elsewhere, assuming the University of Cincinnati and BL books are not the same.

Here are a few more editions not listed in MMF:

1. *Voyage du jeune Anacharsis*, 17??. Heinsius lists an edition without a date, but that could very well antedate the nineteenth century; MMF list no edition with that imprint: '[...] 9 Vol. 12mo. Lpz. [Leipzig] Hinrichs' (i, col.180).

2. *Voyage du jeune Anacharsis*, 1790. Aspin lists an edition in 7 vols, large in-12, Liège: Bassompierre, 1790 (J. Geoffrey Aspin, cat. no. 71 [1983?], p.5, no.42).

3 and 4. *Voyage du jeune Anacharsis*, 1790 (two editions). Gesamtverzeichniss (viii.320b) lists an edition for 'Gotha [1]790. 7 Vol. 12mo'. The same source also has an entry for 'X Vols. Avec Atlas. 12mo. Strasb. [1]790. Levrault', which would indicate another edition.

5. *Voyage du jeune Anacharsis*, 1791. Heinsius lists '[...] 7 Vol. 12. Hamb[ourg,] Fauche. [1]791' (i, col.180). Gesamtverzeichniss has the same, and 'T.1-9. Hambourg [usw. (etc.)]: Fauche 1791. 8vo' (viii.320b).

6. *Voyage du jeune Anacharsis*, 1793. '[...]9 Vol. av[ec] Atlas 12mo. Lpz [Leipzig] Sommer. [1]793' (Heinsius, i, col.180).

7. *Voyage du jeune Anacharsis*, 1796. Heinsius lists '[...] 9 Vol. av[ec] Cart. gr. 12mo. Bern. Typ. Soc. [Société typographique] [1]796' (i, col.180).

8. *Voyage du jeune Anacharsis*, 1799. Gesamtverzeichniss has 'Ed. IV [quatrième édition]. publ. par St. Croix. Paris [1]799. 7 Vol. 8vo. (12mo) et un atlas in[-]4' (viii.320b).

Incipit: 'Anacharsis, Scythe de nation, fils de Toxaris, / est l'auteur de cet ouvrage qu'il adresse à ses amis.'

42

Barthélemy: *Voyage du jeune Anacharsis en Grèce*, ca.1800

abbé Jean Jacques Barthélemy (1716-1795): Voyage / du / jeune Anacharsis / en Grèce, / dans le milieu du quatrième siècle / avant l'ère vulgaire. / [rule] / Tome premier [deuxième, troisième, quatrième, cinquième, sixième, septième, huitième, neuvième]. / [rule] / A Paris, / Chez Richard, Caille et Ravier, / Libraires, rue Haute-feuille, N°. 11.

12°, i: 2 pl + [1]-(381) pp.
ii: 2 pl + [1]-(390) pp.
iii: 2 pl + [1]-(394) pp.
iv: 2 pl + [1]-(364) pp.
v: 2 pl + [1]-(398) pp.
vi: 2 pl + [1]-(383) pp.
vii: 2 pl + [1]-(392) pp.
viii: 2 pl + [1]-(400) pp.
ix: 2 pl + [1]-(337) pp.

Commentary: The volume halftitles read 'Voyage / du / jeune Anacharsis / en Grèce.'

Type, binding (full contemporary calf), presentation, etc., all indicate a late eighteenth-century edition of about 1800. Also Caille, Richard and Ravier were in association at about that time.

This edition is not listed in MMF and neither could I find it listed in the usual library catalogues. For further information concerning this work, see the preceding entry.

Incipit: 'Anacharsis, Scythe de nation, fils / de Toxaris, est l'auteur de cet ouvrage / qu'il adresse à ses amis.'

43

Baudot de Juilly: *Histoire de Catherine de France, reine d'Angleterre*, 1706

Nicolas Baudot de Juilly (1678-1759): Histoire / de / Caterine / de France, / reine / d'Angleterre. / [woodcut ornament: spray of flowers] / A Paris, au palais, / Chez Damien Beugnie', dans / la Grand'Salle, au Pilier des Consul- / tations, au Lyon d'or. / [rule] / M. DCCVI. / Avec Privilege du Roy.

12°: 1 pl + 1 f. (2 pp.) + 1-349 pp.

Commentary: The two-page leaf at the beginning contains the legal material: an 'Extrait du privilege du Roy' to Guillaume de Luyne to print 'ou faire imprimer par qui il lui plaira' the work for ten years, given in Paris 9 April 1696, the original signed Le Fevre; registered 20 April 1696, 'Auboüyn, Syndic'; 'Achevé d'imprimer pour la seconde fois le 4. Decembre 1700'. The legal depository was supposedly accomplished: 'Les Exemplaires ont été fournis.'

This work first appeared in 1696 (Lever p.191-92). The edition described here is not listed in Lever, NUC, NUC:S, BLC (and supplements), and does not exist in the BN. (Gay only lists editions for 1696 and 1697.) I could find no trace of it in the usual sources.

MMF (61.R2) list an edition which appeared in the *Bibliothèque de campagne* (1761) and go into explanations concerned with other editions of that collection and its analogues. The NUC lists *Caterine de France* for the 'nouvelle édition' of the *Bibliothèque de campagne*, 1749 (in ii.[321]-489; Library of Congress and also on microfilm). The NUC supplement has the same work, same title ('par monsieur Baudot de Juilli') as apparently extant in a Bruxelles, 1785 edition/version of the *Bibliothèque de campagne* (in ii.[1]-132). This is described after a microform edition, the general collection title of which reads *Eighteenth-century French fiction* (reel 13, item 7[a], General microfilm company, Cambridge, Massachussetts). However, there is no cross-reference to the *Bibliothèque de campagne* or to the microform collection, and the information given is ambiguous.

Incipit: 'La Province de Galles / en Angleterre, a dé- / fendu sa liberté con- / tre les Anglois avec un cou- / rage invincible'.

44

Beauchamps: *Hipparchia, histoire galante*, ca.1748

Pierre-François Godard (or Godart) de Beauchamps (1689-1761): Hipparchia, / histoire / galante, / traduite du grec, / divisée en trois parties, / Avec une Préface très-interessante, & / ornée de Figures en taille-douce. / [double rule] / Premiére partie. / [double rule] / [symmetrical woodcut ornament] / A Lampsaque. / [rule] / L'an de ce monde.

12°: 1 pl (titlepage) + 1 f. (1 p.) + j-xvj + 1-63 + 1 f. (half titlepage) + 65-115 + 1 f. (half titlepage) + 117-152 pp.

Commentary: The first folio reported after the titleleaf contains a one-page key: 'Clef Pour l'intelligence de la Préface & de l'Ouvrage'. The second item reported is a 'Préface très-interessante', and then follow the three 'parties' of the novel, with leaves tipped in preceding parts ii and iii, consisting of half titlepages: 'Hipparchia, / ou / la courtisanne / grecque. / [rule] / Seconde [Troisiéme] partie. / [rule]'. These half titlepages are not part of the gatherings or pagination. Also each part ends with a complete section of a gathering, resulting in an unusual sequence of what would ordinarily be a consecutive set of gatherings, if the book were printed as a whole, even assuming *8 and A4 to be the first gathering (2 pl + *8, A4, B8, C4, D8, E4, F4 + 1 f. + G8, H8, I4, K6 + 1 f. + L8, M4, N6). The running title is for 'Hipparchia, [versos] / Histoire Philosophique. [rectos]'. There are four libertine engravings, of fairly mediocre quality (a frontispiece and then a picture for each part). These are copies, or a different state of the illustrations accompanying the BN edition (for which see below). The first edition of this piece of prose fiction dates to 1748, with the title of *Aihcrappih, histoire grecque* (Jones, p.96).

Jones lists what appears to be the edition described here, as per the BN copy. (There is also a copy of this work, xvi + 152 pp., listed in Krauss-Fontius, under 'Richard'; no.4604.) However, the BN copy (Réserve, Enfer 231), while very similar indeed to my copy, does not represent the same edition, although the above description matches it perfectly. Here are a couple of the more obvious differences which should enable future bibliographers and cataloguers to distinguish between the two editions. The one-folio key in my copy has a catchword, 'PRE-' leading to the preface; no catchword for the BN copy. The composite head title woodcut vignette, p.1, in my copy has three repeated sets of decorations, with a sun in the middle, in an ornamental border; the BN copy has a vignette formed of 3 sets of decorative lozenges, with one in the centre (decorative border). Mine: asterisk signature, p.j, is under the second 'c' of 'caractére'; BN: star under the 'ra' (closer to the 'a'). Etc. The differences in type are slight, and would be most difficult to describe. This work has also been attributed to the abbé Jerôme Richard. (See Gay; see below also.)

Drujon devotes a fairly long article to this novel (i, cols.428-29; mention is also made of the attribution to Richard). Drujon reports that the small, duodecimo book which he describes (XII + 160 pp., four illustrations) appeared in Paris, which is not here likely. This is information he might have gleaned from Weller, who also attributes the work to Richard ('Comp. par J. Richard'; p.121).

Krauss-Fontius indicate '[Paris 1748]' (no. 4604). Drujon also briefly discusses the contents, with respect to the 'people-characters'. And if Drujon is accurate in reporting the pagination of the copy he describes (which he probably isn't), that means there were three editions of *Hipparchia* for 'Lampsaque, l'an de ce monde'.

This satirical novel relates events concerning the court of Versailles, and puts on stage such noteworthies as the duchesse de Villeroy, that wily rake, the duc de Richelieu, the cardinal de Bissy, the duc de Brancas and others. Curiously, Drujon reports that 'suivant Barbier, le duc de Brancas serait un des personnages mis en scène' when the duke's name appears explicitly in the key. And curiously too, Barbier mentions a manuscript key that he found inserted in a copy of the novel, and makes no mention of the printed 'clef' (i, col.86a-b).

The key runs as follows. For 'C. de P.' read 'cour de Versailles'. For 'C. de R.' read 'duchesse de Villeroi'; for 'D. de S.', the 'marquise d'Alincourt'; for 'M. de B.', the 'duc de Richelieu'; for 'D. de B.', the 'duc de Brancas'; for 'C. de V.', the 'cardinal de Bissi.'

Barbier also attributes this work to Richard, according to a manuscript note by the abbé [de] Papillon in the latter's personal copy of the *Bibliothèque de Bourgogne*. (Quérard, i.235, largely repeats information given by Barbier.) However, even a cursory examination of the works of Beauchamps and Richard leads one to believe that the former is the most probable author. (And he was also the maréchal de Villeroy's secretary.) The preface states: 'le caractére d'Hipparchia, quoique naturel, révoltera bien des gens. On veut de la bienséance aux dépens même de la vérité; mais se fâche qui voudra, je traduis les faits tels qu'ils sont dans l'Original; ils doivent paroître d'autant moins extraordinaires, que notre siécle nous a fourni des exemples, sinon semblables, du moins équivalens' (pp.j-iij). The preface then describes, in graphic detail, 'M. de B.', Richelieu's rape, aided by the 'C. de R.' (duchesse de Villeroy) of 'D. de S.' (the marquise d'Alincourt). I might point out that the 'clef' only refers to the 'préface très intéressante'. The main body of the text sets different characters on stage, or at least characters with different names.

Incipit: 'Ma façon de penser,* la Secte dont je suis, & la vie que j'ai menée jusqu'ici'. (A note refers to various editions of Bayle's dictionary.)

45

Bérenger: *La Morale en action*, 1789

Laurent Pierre Bérenger (1749-1822): La morale / en action, / ou / élite de faits mémorables / et d'anecdotes instructives, / Propres à faire aimer la Vertu & à former les / Jeunes Gens dans l'Art de la Narration. / Ouvrage utile à Messieurs les Éleves des Écoles / Militaires et des Colleges. / [woodcut ornament: flying cupid bearing a basket] / A Lyon, / Chez les Freres Perisse, Imprimeurs-Librai-res, / Grande rue Merciere. / A Paris, / Chez Louis Perisse, Libraire, Pont-Saint-/ Michel, au Soleil d'or. / [rule] / 1789. / Avec approbation et Privilege.

12°: 1 f. (titlepage) + [iii]-xxiv + [1]-444, [445]-455, [456] pp.

Titre.

HIPPARCHIA,
HISTOIRE
GALANTE,
TRADUITE DU GREC,
DIVISÉE EN TROIS PARTIES,
Avec une Préface très-interessante, &
ornée de Figures en taille-douce.

PREMIÉRE PARTIE.

A LAMPSAQUE.

L'AN DE CE MONDE.

No 44: Beauchamps, *Hipparchia, histoire galante*, ca.1748

Commentary: The first item is the preface; the second, the work; the third, a 'table'; the fourth, which continues from p.455, an approbation (20 July 1782, signed 'Guidi') and a 'Privilege général N°. 2628' to the brothers Perisse of Lyon, dated 24 July 1782 (signed 'Le Begue'). Registered 13 August 1782, 'Le Clerc'. The head title of the work reads: 'La morale en action, ou Choix d'Anecdotes, de Traits intéressans, de Contes Moraux, de Narrations historiques & d'Apologues'. The opening of the preface explains the scope and utility of the work: 'La premiere édition de ce Recueil a obtenu un si grand succès dans les maisons d'éducation, il a été si agréable à la Jeunesse, en réunissant pour elle l'amusement à l'instruction, que nous avons été encouragés à l'accroître considérablement, à le refondre en entier, & à le mettre dans un ordre plus amusant & plus varié.' (Most of the remainder of the preface is taken from Rollin, with acknowledgment.)

This work first appeared in 1783 (MMF, 83.17). MMF cite what might be this edition, with no details (other than the date '1789'), after Quérard and Robert Reboul, *Un littérateur oublié* [L.-P. Bérenger] (Paris 1881). Reboul lists 'La Morale en action, ou élite de faits mémorables et d'anecdotes instructives propres à faire aimer la vertu. Lyon, Périsse, 1783, 1787, 1789, 2 vol. in-12' and makes no mention of Quérard (p. 45).

Quérard lists: 'Morale (la) en action, ou Elite de faits mémorables et d'anecdotes instructives. Lyon, Périsse frères, 1783, 1787, 1789, 2 vol. in-12' and remarks: 'Le premier vol. est de Bérenger, et le deuxième, intitulé *Manuel de la jeunesse française*, est du père Guibaud' (i.28). The *Almanach littéraire, ou étrennes d'Apollon* (1787, by Aquin de Château-Lyon) lists *La Morale en action* 'chez Perisse le jeune, en face du Marché-Neuf, près S. Germain-le-Vieux, in-12' (p.270). No second volume is indicated, nor is a city of publication although Paris is implied.

The volume described here carried 'Fin.' at the end (p.455) and, at the end of the table, 'Fin de la Table.' which seems to indicate that a second volume was not planned. Having found no trace of this particular edition in the NUC, BLC or BNC, I have chosen to include it.

It might be pointed out that there were many more than three editions of this work and that the contents vary somewhat.

Incipit: (no. 1, 'Le Paysan du Danube') 'Pendant que j'étois Consul, dit Marc-Aurele, un pauvre Paysan du Danube vint à Rome'.

46

Bernard: *La Gazette de Cythère*, 1775

François Bernard (fl.1770-1789): La / gazette / de / Cythere, / ou / avantures / galantes et recentes, / Arrivées dans les principales Villes / de l'Europe. / Traduite de l'anglais. / à la fin de laquelle on a joint le Précis / historique de la Vie de Mad. la / Comtesse du Barry, / avec son Portrait. / [rule] / Aeneadum genetrix, hominum, divûmque voluptas, / Alma Venus &c. &c. &c. / Lucrece. / [rule] / Londres, / M DCC LXXV.

and

Precis [possibly Précis] / historique / de la vie / De mad. la comtesse / du Barry, / avec son portrait. / [woodcut ornament: two cupids on either side of what looks like a mirror, one crowning it with a wreath] / à Paris, / [rule] / MDCCLXXV.

8°, i: 1 f. (titlepage) + [III]-(VIII) + [1]-262 pp. + 1f. (2 pp.)
    ii: 1 f. (titlepage) + [3]-88 pp.

Commentary: These two pieces first appeared in 1774 (MMF 74.12). Martin, Mylne and Frautschi remark, concerning the first edition, that the second item 'qui a une pagination séparée, semble être une simple biographie, défavorable mais non pas romancée'. Under 'autres éditions', they list: 'Londres, 1775, in-8, viii + 262 pp.' with locations/references for BL, Barbier, Delcro, Gay, Quérard, stating that 'malgré la mention du *Précis* à la page de titre, cette édition ne contient que la *Gazette*'. As can be seen by the above, that is not true, through no fault of the bibliographers of course. Although I was unable to juxtapose my *Gazette* with the BL copy (012331.gg.8), they both appear to be the same. I might mention, too, that the *Précis* described here differs entirely from the 1775 edition which appeared as *Gazette de Cythère, ou histoire secrète de madame la comtesse du Barry*, Londres: P. G. Wauckner, 1775, titleleaf + [3-4], [5]-(104) pp. in-8°. (The titlepage is 'encadrée'; printed in Brussels?) Although I was unable to juxtapose my copy with a copy of the first edition of the *Précis historique*, it was easy to ascertain that my copy differs radically from the octavo, BL, 1774 edition (12237.cc.10); thus my copy of the *Précis* is a new edition, versus a reissue.

Weller lists the first edition, with no explanation concerning the *Précis*, further adding 'Londres (Paris); n. éd. ib. 1775', again with no explanation (p.195). Gay notes that 'dans l'édition de 1775, le 2ᵉ titre est: ou *Histoire de la comtesse du Barry*' (ii, col.395). The volumes described here were certainly not printed in Paris. The 1774 *Gazette* reads 'Londres, / MDCCLXXIV.' on the titlepage. The *Précis* which follows it reads 'Paris 1774.' Neither of these, nor my copies described here, was printed in London or Paris: everything suggests that they were printed in a Germanic state.

In support of this is the fact that I could find only one correct entry for the *Précis* (with a variant for the imprint), and that in the Messkatalog: 'Precis historique de la Vie de Mad. la Comtesse du Barry, avec son portrait. 8vo. à Londres' OM 1775, p.888. There is also an entry for *La Gazette de Cythère* (p.884).

Heinsius, *Handbuch* lists yet another edition of the *Précis* for 1775: '[*Précis*] historique de la Vie de Madame la Comtesse du Barry, 8vo. Francf. Varren-trapp, [1]775' (p.817).

A breakdown of the contents in the works described here is as follows: 'Epitre dedicatoire a Venus. Grande reine!' (head title). Then the *Gazette* (with a head title for the first piece). The last folio contains the 'Table', 2 pp., at the end of which is a 'nota bene'. Then there is the next major item, with its own pagination and signatures. There is a frontispiece to each part: i, an allegorical picture captioned 'Tableau du monde' and ii, a portrait of our countess. (These interesting, but somewhat primitive illustrations are copies or adaptations of those issued with the first edition; not in Cohen or Reynaud.)

MMF mention that there is an 'annonce' after the 'épître dédicatoire'. This is the note, here printed after the table, which runs as follows: 'Au moment que

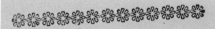

CLEF

Pour l'intelligence de la Préface & de l'Ouvrage.

C. de P. *veut dire* Cour de Versailles.
C. de R. - - - - Duchesse de Villeroi.
D. de S. - - - - Marquise d'Alincourt.
M. de B. - - - - Duc de Richelieu.
D. de B. - - - - Duc de Brancas.
C. de V. - - - - Cardinal de Bissi.

PRE-

PRÉFACE

TRÈS-INTERESSANTE.

LE Public si fa-vorable à tous les Traducteurs, n'au-ra, peut-être, pas pour moi autant d'indul-gence qu'il en a eu pour ceux qui m'ont précé-dé dans ce genre d'é-crire ; le caractère

I. Partie.

No 44: Beauchamps, *Hipparchia, histoire galante*, ca.1748

nous finissons ce Volume, un de nos Correspondans nous a envoyé *le Précis historique de la Vie de Madame la Comtesse du Barry*. Cette pièce nous a paru si relative au Plan que nous nous étions formé, que nous avons cru devoir en augmenter le nombre de celles qui composent ce Volume, nous l'eussions mise à la tête, si la chose eut été, possible, l'Héroïne devoit sans doute avoir le pas sur celles qui la précèdent dans ce Tome: mais nous espérons qu'entre Camarades elles s'accommoderont sur la préséance, d'autant mieux que Mad du Barry doit voir actuellement, d'un oeil assez indifférent les honneurs de ce monde périssable. Note du Traducteur.' Before the 'nota bene' and at the end of the 'Table' is to be found the following statement: 'Suit le Prêcis de la Vie de Md. la Comtesse du Barry.'

Barbier attributes the *Gazette de Cythère* to Jean-Frédéric Bernard. Octave Uzanne, in his edition of the *Gazette* – he excluded the life of Mme Du Barry – (Paris 1881), attributes it to François Bernard (p.VI), without, however, seeming too sure about his attribution. Uzanne sees in the *Gazette* a possible 'livre à clef': 'il faudrait peut-être voir là un Livre à clef; mais dans quel labyrinthe d'impossibilités ne devrions-nous pas nous engager et nous perdre pour chercher cette clef qui n'aurait assurément pas à ouvrir une bien grande porte sur l'histoire!' (p.VII). This work is not mentioned in Drujon.

Here is a breakdown of the above, 1775 edition of the *Gazette*, as per the head titles: 1. Les amans ingénus. Swansey.... 1773, pp.[1]-23; 2. Frere Modeste de Capo-Corso, capucin, &c. &c. &c. Rome...... 1773, pp.24-59; 3. Avanture galante de lord M***. Londres... 1773, pp.60-66; 4. La revenge de lord B–. sur le lord G–. Londres Janvier... 1774, pp.66-80; 5. Le juif petit-maitre et Co.... U... Londres Octobre.. 1773, pp.80-84; 6. Marie C***. ou l'orgueil puni. Londres..... 1773, pp.84-103; 7. Abrege historique des memoires de la celebre mademoiselle D. V. Trouvé dans son Portefeuille après sa mort prématurée Paris Decembre... 1773, pp.103-12; 8. Le negociant pris sur le fait. Amsterdam..... 1773, pp.113-23; 9. Le matelot et la Liegeoise Catherine. Amsterdam...... 1774, pp.124-28; 10. L'Italienne trompeuse et trompee. Amsterdam..... 1773, pp.128-60; 11. Le peintre et son modele. La Haye.... 1774, pp.160-74; 12. Les plaisirs de l'amour bien superieurs a ceux de Bacchus. Extrait d'une Lettre de Melle G– à M^{r}. B– son Amant. Angleterre.... 1774, pp.175-89; 13. La coquette dupee par un religieux B*** et par un marquis. Toulouse..... 1773, pp.190-229; 14. La jeune veuve de C–, ou l'amour vertueux et malheureux. Londres ce..... 1774; Extrait d'une Lettre de Mr. P. à l'Auteur, pp.230-62.

A couple of remarks: the physical page size of the second item (or volume) is smaller than that of the first. The last four and a half pages of the *Précis historique* have smaller characters than the rest.

Incipits: ('Epître dédicatoire') 'Il n'est presque pas d'Etat sur la terre qui n'ait pas son Gazettier propre & particulier'.

('Les Amans ingénus') 'Jaques Lloyd fils d'un honnête Négociant de Swansey'.

('Précis historique') 'Quoiqu'on ne donne au Public la Vie de ceux qu'on juge dignes d'avoir place dans les fastes de l'histoire, qu'après leur mort'.

47

Bernardin de Saint-Pierre: *Etudes de la nature*, 1788-1789

Jacques Henri Bernardin de Saint-Pierre (1737-1814): (titlepages for i-iv), Etudes [Études ii, iii, iv] / de / la nature, / par Jacques-Henri-Bernardin / de Saint-Pierre. / Troisieme Édition, revue, corrigée / & augmentée. / [rule] / ... Miseris succurrere disco. Æneid. Lib. 1. / [rule] / 4 vol. in-12 fig. / Tome premier [second, troisieme, quatrieme]. / [woodcut decorations, i: bagpipe; ii: hive; iii: flowers; iv: vase with flowers] / A Bruxelles, / Chez B. Le Francq, Imprimeur-Libraire, / rue de la Magdelaine. / [rule] / M. DCC. LXXXVIII.

v: Études / de / la nature, / par Jacques-Bernardin-Henri / de Saint-Pierre. / [rule] / ...Miseris succurrere disco. Æneid. lib. 1. / [rule] / Tome cinquieme. / [woodcut of flying cherub with torch and wreath] / A Bruxelles, / Chez B. Le Francq, Imprimeur-Libraire, / rue de la Magdelaine. / [rule] / M. DCC. LXXXIX.

12°, i: 2 pl + [1]-24 + [j]-xlviij + [1]-36 + 73-357 pp.
 ii: 2 pl + [1]-361 pp.
 iii: 2 pl + [1]-398 pp.
 iv: 2 pl + [1]-361 pp. + 2ff. (2 + 1 pp.)
 v: 2 pl + [j]-liv + 1f. (2 pp.) + [1]-148 + [150], [151]-227 + [229]-236, [237]-328, [329]-344 pp.

Commentary: There are numerous mistakes and irregularities in the pagination and signatures. However, there is no material missing from vol. i, as the errata on p.xlvij explain. (v.[228] is blank.) The first item in i is an 'Avis sur cette seconde édition et sur cet ouvrage'. The second is the 'Explication des figures', including, at the end, an 'Avis au relieur' and 'errata' (p.xlvij), and 'Tables' (for i and ii, p.xlviij). Then follow four volumes of the *Etudes*. The items at the end of iv are a 'Table', 'Explication des figures' (2 pp.) and legal material (1 p.). Vol. v contains: 1. 'Avis sur cet ouvrage et sur ce nouveau volume'; 2. 'Paul et Virginie. Avant-propos'; 3. 'Etudes de la nature. Paul et Virginie'; 4. a half titlepage for 'L'Arcadie.', with an untitled notice on the verso; 5. a 'Fragment servant de préambule à l'Arcadie', pp.[151]-236; 6. some notes (pp.[229]-236); 7. the *Arcadie* proper; 8. notes to the *Arcadie*.

The first four volumes of the *Etudes de la nature* seem to be the same as those in the BN (16°: R.9205[i-iv]). The end of the table to vol. iv bears 'Fin de la Table du Tome IV & dernier volume'. However, the fifth volume described here, containing *Paul et Virginie* and the *Arcadie*, has a quite different titlepage from the copy in the BN (16°: R.9205[v]). The type characters differ slightly, as does the ornamental rule setting off the date, and, what is more obvious, the woodcut decoration is entirely different. The pagination for vol. v, BN (MMF 88.101) matches my copy, but I doubt we are dealing with a reissue. (I was unable to juxtapose the copies.)

In the interesting 'Avis' which opens the fifth volume, Bernardin de Saint-Pierre explains why he chose the duodecimo format and also complains about the piracies of his work. Why, the second edition 'a été contrefaite, avec ses augmentations, approbations, privilége, & jusqu'aux titres où on lit l'adresse

LA GAZETTE DE CYTHERE,

OU AVANTURES

GALANTES ET RÉCENTES,

Arrivées dans les principales Villes de l'Europe.

TRADUITE DE L'ANGLAIS.

à la fin de laquelle on a joint le *Précis historique* de la Vie de Mad, la Comtesse DU BARRY, avec son Portrait.

Aëreadum genitrix, hominum, divûmque voluptas, Alma Venus &c. &c. &c.   LUCRECE.

LONDRES,
M DCC LXXV.

TABLEAU DU MONDE.

No 46: Bernard, *La Gazette de Cythère*, 1775

No 46: *Précis historique de la vie de Mad. la comtesse du Barry,* 1775

de mes libraires' (p.iij)! On the next page, he mentions a new, unauthorised edition published in Brussels, in 4 volumes. As is obvious, the fifth volume was not added until later, so at the time he wrote the 'Avis', Bernardin could not have been aware of it. Le Francq was at least honest enough to include Bernardin de Saint-Pierre's complaints about his piracy in his piracy! Indeed, for the fourth (legitimate!) edition of the *Etudes*, Bernardin had special paper for the titlepages manufactured with his name incorporated into the watermark. (See Tchemerzine, v.648.)

Since there were at least two editions (we seem to have here a new edition and not a reissue) of the fifth volume, what might have happened is that the first edition of the fifth volume of this pirated edition, with its popular novels, was soon out of print. Le Francq then, perhaps in order to help sell off the first four volumes of the *Etudes*, republished the two novels. Still assuming that the first four volumes in my collection are the same as those in the BN, it also appears certain that the fifth volume was available separately.

There are illustrations in the first four volumes, some of them folding, which I do not bother to describe. The fifth volume contains no illustrations, and is printed on the same flimsy paper as the first four. The two novels in vol. v first appeared in 1788 (MMF 88.101). Legal documents are included with this piracy, but there is no question that they carried no legal effect. Approbations: 11 March 1784 (Sage); 6 April 1784 (Lourdet). For the additions, 18 March 1786 (Sage). (Printed at the end of vol. iv.) Each volume has a half titlepage for 'Etudes [Études for ii-v] / de / la nature, [nature. for v] / tome premier [second, troisieme, quatrieme, cinquieme].'

Further, there are several editions of the *Etudes* and of *Paul et Virginie* which warrant clarification:

1. *Etudes*, 1791. MMF list an edition of the *Etudes de la nature* for 'Munster, Coppenrath, 1791, 7t.' (88.101). The commentary for Toinet's entry (MMF's source) is as follows: 'Edition signalée uniquement par M[onglond]. Il faut lire probablement 7 vol. in-16, car le texte ne suffirait pas à remplir 7 vol. in-12. Ne se trouverait-on pas en présence de la même édition que la précédente chez un autre éditeur, le dernier volume ayant disparu?' (p.15, no.9). The preceding entry is for a 6 + 2 vol. edition in-16, Paris [etc.] 1791-1793 (for which see no.2 directly below). Heinsius lists '8 Vol. av[ec] Fig. [in-]12. Münster, Coppenrath. [1]791' (i, col.259; also Kayser v.11a). Since the source for Monglond's information was Kayser, more than one error can be attributed to Monglond's mistake. Toinet's supposition is, however, probably at least partially correct, although his information is wrong (and idea concerning format erroneous): that the Coppenrath edition derives from an eight-volume, Paris edition. Conceivably, the last two volumes of the Coppenrath edition bear the date of 1792 or 1793. The last two volumes of eight-volume editions of the *Etudes* usually comprise the *Vœux d'un solitaire*. (For the first edition of the *Vœux d'un solitaire*, see MMF 92.38). Finally, Gesamtverzeichniss has an entry which would indicate that this edition was also available in-octavo: 'le même ouvrage. 5 Vol. 8vo. ibid. [Münster, Coppenrath, [1]791]' (xiii.316b).

2. *Etudes*, 1791-1793. Etudes de la nature, par Jacques-Henri-Bernardin de Saint-Pierre. 2[ᵉ] éd., rev., corr. & augm. Paris: chez P. F. Didot, 1791-93. 8

vols., ill. 15 cm (OCLC: State University of New York, Stony Brook). The title
varies: 'Etudes de la nature' for vols i-vi; vii: 'Vœux d'un solitaire, première
partie'; viii: 'Suite des vœux d'un solitaire, deuxième partie'. This is possibly
Toinet no. 8 (p.15; he possessed the only copy he could find), who lists: 'Etudes
de la nature, seconde [*sic*] édition revue, corrigée et augmentée; Paris, de
l'imprimerie de Monsieur, P. F. Didot le jeune et Méquignon l'aîné. 6 vol. in-
16, suivis normalement de 2 vol. contenant les Vœux d'un Solitaire, pour faire
suite aux Etudes de la nature, MDCCXLIII [surely an error for MDCCXCIII],
sans illust. Au tome VI, pp.1-167, *Paul et Virginie*'. MMF list a '... seconde
édition [*sic*], Paris, imprimerie de Monsieur, 1791, 6t. in-16', citing a location
for the Universiteitsbibliotheek, Amsterdam. (No mention is made of a sequel,
or of a corresponding edition of the *Vœux d'un solitaire* for 1793.) For further
information, see the entry for *Paul et Virginie*, 1789.

  3. *Etudes*, 1793. MMF list an *Etudes* for 'Paris, 1793, 10t. in-16' (88.101).
Toinet lists the same, a 'troisième édition revue, corrigée et augmentée' (more
details are included), with a location for the Musée de la France d'Outre-mer
(p.17, no. 18). Heinsius lists what appears to be the same edition, but in-18
(indicating after Paris: '(Sommer in Leipz.)'; *loc. cit.*).

  4. *Etudes*, 1796. London: Spilsbury, 1796, 2 vols (NUC and OCLC: Cleveland
Public Library). Toinet, no. 27, lists: '*Etudes de la nature*, nouvelle édition revue,
corrigée et considérablement augmentée; Londres, imp. de W. et C. Spilsburg,
chez Ch. Dilly, Poultry, 1796. 2 vol. in-8 [...]' (p.18; 'Spilsburg' is obviously an
error for 'Spilsbury', and 'Poultry' is part of the address, and not a publisher.
Maxted lists several Spilsburys and no Spilsburg: Ian Maxted, *The London book
trade, 1775-1800: a preliminary checklist of members*, London 1977.) MMF list
'Londres, Dilly, 1796, 2t. in-8' (after Toinet; Toinet's location is his own
collection). All these comprise without a doubt: 'Etudes / de / la nature. / Par /
Jacques-Henri-Bernardin / de Saint Pierre. / [double rule] / Nouvelle édition, /
revue, corrigée et augmentée. / [double rule] / ....Miseris succurrere disco. Æneid.
lib. 1. / [double rule] / Tome premier [second]. / [double rule] / A Londres: / de
l'imprimerie de W. & C. Spilsbury. / Chez Charles Dilly, Poultry. / [double
rule] / 1796.' In-8°, i: 1 pl (titlepage) + 2 + [i]-xvi + [1]-500 pp. ii: 1 pl
(titlepage) + 2 + [1]-504 pp. *Paul et Virginie* is ii.(299)-300, (301)-390; *L'Arcadie*,
ii.(393)-436, (437)-504, pp. [391-92] comprising a halftitle, with an 'avis' verso
(BL: 1509/2003).

  5. *Etudes*, 1799. Londres: Imprimerie de Baylis, 1799, 1 vol. (NUC: Library
of Congress). The pagination given is xii + 288 pp., 'format' 17 1/2 cm. This
is surely BL 1507/767: 'Études / de / la nature: / abrégé / des œuvres / de / Jacques-
Henri-Bernardin / de Saint-Pierre. / [double rule] / Miseris succurrere disco. –
Æneid. lib. 1. / [double rule] / A Londres: / de l'imprimerie de Baylis, / Se trouve
chez Vernor & Hood, No. 31, Poultry, & / Boosey, Broad-Street, près de la
Bourse-Royale. / [rule] / 1799.' In-12°: titleleaf + [iii]-(xii) + [1]-(288) pp., with
a frontispiece engraving. This book does contain excerpts from Bernardin's
novels, for example, 'La Négresse marronne', pp.(155)-(168). (The short preface
is in English, pp.[iii]-vi. The editor intended that his elegant extracts be read
by the young to help them with their French studies and to inculcate in them

the principles of morality and virtue.) This edition is not listed in Toinet or MMF.

Toinet lists a *Paul et Virginie*; Londres, imp. de Beylis [presumably for Baylis], se trouve chez Vernor et Hood, n° 31, Poultry; et Boosey, Broad St.; près de la Bourse Royale, 1797' (no. 33, p.19; various locations). His commentary includes a list of three ulterior 'réimpressions' – 1799, 1803, 1811 – which he hastens to call new editions vs. reprints. Toinet lists the (or *a*) 1797 edition for iii and 171 pp., differing markedly from the edition extant in the Library of Congress (NUC). Thus the latter would constitute yet *another* edition. (MMF list 'Londres, Bayliss, 1797, in-12, iii + 171p.'.)

For those interested, full information concerning the 1799 Baylis edition of *Paul et Virginie* is as follows: Paul / et / Virginie. / [rule] / Par / Jacques-Bernardin-Henri de Saint-Pierre. / [double rule] / ....Miseris succurrere disco. Æneid, lib. i. / [double rule] / [woodcut ornament of nest with two eggs in branches] / À Londres: / de l'imprimerie de Baylis, / Et se trouve chez Vernor & Hood, N°. 31, Poultry; / & Boosey, Broad-Street, près de la Bourse-Royale. / [rule] / 1799. 1 pl + [i]-(iv) + [1]-172 pp. in-8, 'papier vélin', 5 plates (the first four by Liagec, the last by Lefevre), published by Vernor and Hood, 1796 (various days and months). This information is derived from the Texas copy (Humanities research centre, University of Texas at Austin); a BL copy has no introductory material (1490.l.19).

6. *Paul et Virginie*, 1789. Here is another edition not listed in Toinet or MMF: Paul et Virginie, par Jacques-Bernardin-Henri de Saint-Pierre. Paris: Didot, 1789. xxxv + 243 + [1] pp., ill., 13 cm (OCLC: Ohio University, Athens).

MMF list an edition for 'Paris, Imprimerie de Monsieur, 1789, in-16, 180 p.' (88.101; what they probably mean is 'in-18'). Krauss-Fontius list a *Paul et Virginie* simply for 'Paris 1789. 181 p.', with locations for the Universitätsbibliothek at Leipzig and the Stadtbibliothek of Ballenstedt (no.4366).

7. *Paul et Virginie*, 1793. MMF (88.101) and Toinet (no. 19, p.17) list an edition for Paris: Libraires associés, 1793, xiii + 212 pp. in-16. Toinet states that the only location he knows is for the Musée de la France d'Outre-Mer. (MMF list after Toinet.) The OCLC has the following: Paul et Virginie. Par Jacques-Bernardin-Henri de Saint-Pierre. Nouvelle éd. Paris: Libraires Associés, 1793. vii + 235 pp., 14 cm (University of Notre Dame). If both Toinet and OCLC are correct, then there were two similar but different editions for Paris 1793.

8. *Paul et Virginie*, 1795. The following escaped the attention of MMF: Paolo e Virginia / Paul et Virginie. Firenze / Florence: Nella Stamperia Molini, 1795. 2 vols in-16 (14 cm): viii + 259 and 259 pp. Titlepages in French and in Italian; bilingual edition with text in each language on facing pages. The information for this has been reconstructed from Toinet, no. 308 and OCLC: University of Alabama. NUC lists what appears to be a parallel, Italian-only edition: Paolo e Virginia, del signor J. B. H. de Saint-Pierre. Firenze, Nella stamperia Molini, 1795. 3 pl + [3]-260 [for 250] pp. (various locations including University of Virginia, Yale, Harvard; this edition is not in Toinet).

9. *Paul et Virginie*, 1796. 'Paul et Virginie. Nouv. Ed. [in-]12. Lausanne [1]796. (Fr. Fleischer in Leipz.)' (Kayser v.11b). Toinet (no.26) and MMF (after

Toinet) list a Lausanne, Giegler, 1796 edition (250 pp.), but in-16. Toinet remarks that Monglond 'signale [iii, col.743] à cette date sans autres précisions une édition: Lausanne (Leipzig, ER. [*sic*; surely for 'Fr.'] Fleischer). Je crois à une erreur d'impression'. It is of course a question of Monglond citing Kayser, together with the publisher/book-dealer where the novel was available.

Incipits, i: 'Je formai, il y a quelques années, le projet d'écrire une histoire générale de la nature'.

v: (*Paul et Virginie*) 'Sur le côté oriental de la montagne qui s'élève derrière le Port Louis de l'île de France'.

(*L'Arcadie*) 'Un peu avant l'équinoxe d'automne, Tirtée, berger d'Arcadie'.

48

Bernardin de Saint-Pierre: *Etudes de la nature*, etc., 1791

Jacques Henri Bernardin de Saint-Pierre (1737-1814): i-iv: Études / de / la nature, [nature. for iii, iv, and the type varies considerably for this line from i-ii to iii-iv] / par [Par for iii, iv due to full stop after 'nature'] Jacques-Henri-Bernardin [Jacques-Bernardin-Henri for iv] / de Saint-Pierre. / Quatrieme édition, / Revue, corrigée & augmentée. / [rule] / ....Miseris seccurrere [*sic*] disco. Æneid. lib. 1. / [rule] / Tome premier [second, troisieme, quatrieme]. / [woodcut ornament: sprays of foliage, rays, ball with three fleurs-de-lys surmounted by a crown; a device associated with Didot and the comte d'Artois, or an imitation of it] / A Paris, / de l'imprimerie de monsieur. / [thick swell rule] / Chez [open brace] / P. F. Didot le jeune, Libraire, quai des Augustins. / Mequignon l'aîné, Libraire, rue des Cordeliers. [end of material set off by brace] / [rule] / M. DCC. XCI. / Avec approbation et privilege du roi.

v: Vœux / d'un / solitaire, / pour servir de suite / aux études de la nature; / par Jacques-Bernardin-Henri / de Saint-Pierre. / [rule] / ...Miseris succurrere disco. Æneid. lib. 1. / [rule] / Tome cinquieme. / [same woodcut decoration] / A Paris, / de l'imprimerie de monsieur. / Chez [open brace] P. F. Didot le Jeune, Libraire. [possibly Libraire,] quai / des Augustins. / Méquignon l'aîné, Libraire, rue des / Cordeliers. [end of material set off by brace] / [rule] / M. DCC. XCI.

vi: La / chaumiere / indienne. / Par Jacques-Bernardin-Henri / de Saint-Pierre. / [rule] / ...Miseris succurrere disco. Æneid. lib. 1. / [rule] / Tome cinquieme. / [same woodcut decoration] / A Paris, / de l'imprimerie de monsieur. / Chez [open brace] P. F. Didot le Jeune, Libraire. quai / des Augustins. / Méquignon l'aîné, Libraire, rue des / Cordeliers. [end of material set off by brace] / [rule] / M. DCC. XCI.

6 vols in-12, i: 2 pl (halftitle and titlepage) + [j]-xxiv + [1]-499, [500] pp.

ii: 2 ff. (halftitle and titlepage) + [5]-508, 509-510 pp.

iii: 2 ff. (halftitle and titlepage) + [5]-490, 491-492 pp. + 2 ff. (1 + 3 pp.)

iv: 2 ff. (halftitle and titlepage) + [v]-lxxxviij + [1]-426 pp. + 3 ff. (1 + 4 pp.)

v: 2 pl (halftitle and titlepage) + [j]-xl + [1]-218 pp. + 1 f. (one-page table)

vi: 1 f. (titlepage) + [3]-32 + [1]-63 pp.

Commentary: These volumes contain:

i: An 'Avis sur cette quatrieme edition et sur cet ouvrage'; *Etudes*; a one-page table.

ii: More *Etudes* and a two-page table.

iii: The end of the *Etudes*; 'Explication des figures', pp.435-90; a two-page table (pp.491-92); 2 ff., 4 pp. containing:

a. 'Avis au Relieur';

b. 'Approbations Des Censeurs Royaux' (first for the *Etudes*, 11 March 1784, signed 'Sage'; second for the same, 6 April 1784, 'Lourdet, Professeur Royal'; third for 'les Additions faites à la seconde édition des *Etudes...*', 18 March 1786, 'Sage');

c. 'Privilege du roi', to Bernardin de Saint-Pierre for the *Etudes*, 'pour lui & ses hoirs à perpétuité' (with explanations concerned with legal alternatives, based on the laws of 30 August 1777), 7 May 1784, 'Le Begue';

d. Registration: 28 May 1784, signed 'Valleyre jeune, Adjoint'.

iv: a. 'Avis sur cet ouvrage et sur ce quatrieme volume', pp.[v]-lxxxij;

b. a halftitle for 'Paul / et / Virginie.';

c. 'Avant-propos', pp.lxxxv-lxxxviij;

d. 'Études de la nature. [swell rule] Paul et Virginie', pp.[1]-189;

e. halftitle for 'L'Arcadie.', with an untitled notice on the verso;

f. 'Fragment servant de préambule a l'Arcadie', pp.[193]-271;

g. 'Notes', pp.272-82;

h. 'L'Arcadie', pp.[283]-400;

i. 'Notes', pp.401-26;

j. 3 ff., 5 pp. of legal material. First, the three approbations as per volume iii. Second, an approbation for the third edition and fourth volume of the *Etudes*, 8 March 1788, 'Sage'. Third, the same privilege as above. Fourth, the same registration.

v: 'Préambule', pp.[i]-xl; 'Vœux d'un solitaire', pp.[1]-218; one-page table.

vi: 'Avant-propos', pp.[3]-23; 'Notes', pp.24-32; 'La chaumiere indienne', pp.[1]-63.

These volumes contain the usual illustrations (some folding), including a poor-quality imitation of Moreau's frontispiece titled 'Philocles dans l'Ile de Samos' at the head of volume i. (This is a mirror image of the original engraving.)

I could find no trace of this particular edition anywhere. Toinet lists a fourth edition of the *Etudes* for Paris: imprimerie de monsieur, 1790 (five vols in-12°) after two copies in the BN and Monglond. He remarks: 'Cette édition date de 1790 et a été réimprimé en 1791 et 1792. Les deux réimpressions portent comme mention d'éditeurs: P. Didot le jeune, quai des Augustins, n° 82; Née de La Rochelle, rue de Hurepoix, n° 13. Desenne, au Palais-Royal, arcades 1 et 2'. Furthermore he adds that the BN 'possède deux exemplaires: un hétérogène, t. I, II et III, 1791 (R.11680-1-2), t. IV, 1790 (R.11683), t. V, 1792 (R.11684); un homogène, 1792 (8 R.25895)' (no. 7, p.13). The BNC lists: 'Études de la nature, par Jaques[*sic*]-Bernardin-Henri de Saint-Pierre. 4e édition... Paris, P.-F. Didot le jeune, 1791. In-12. T.II-III [seuls]' (R.11681-82). I was able to examine vols i-iii, v of this collection in the B.N., and they have nothing to do with the volumes described here.

The NUC has an *Etudes*, 4th edition, 'rev., cor. et aug.' for Didot frères, 1791, 3 vols, ill., 22 cm. (location: University of North Carolina, Chapel Hill). The size would indicate an octavo or 'grand in-12'. The page size of the books described here (bound) is 16 cm. In any case, those books would have nothing to do with the edition recorded here if the NUC entry be exact. And there is another edition listed in the same source, a 4th edition, 'rev., cor. et augm.' for 'Paris, P. F. Didot [etc.; perhaps the 'etc.' stands for Née de La Rochelle and Desenne?], 1791-1792', 5 vols, ill. (location: University of Washington, Seattle). There seems little likelihood that any listing in the NUC refers to volumes forming part of the edition described here. At best, a volume or two might be the same. BLC has a '–Quatrième édition. 5 vol. Paris, 1791, 92. 12°.' (733.bb.2), which I have not been able to see. Finally, Tchemerzine states: 'Quérard signale encore: Suite des Vœux d'un solitaire, avec la Chaumière indienne pour servir de complément au Ve volume des Études de la nature. Paris, Née de la Rochelle, 1791, in-12. Nous n'avons pas rencontré ce volume' (x.148). This information is in Quérard, viii.367a. Before, the latter source reports: 'Chaumière (la) indienne. Paris, Née de la Rochelle, 1790 in-8 [probably a mistake for the date at least], et 1791, in-12. Impr. aussi à la fin de la Suite des Vœux d'un Solitaire.... l'édition de 1791 n'est qu'un tirage à part du volume en question' (viii.363a).

As is obvious, my books comprise an entirely different edition. I do not know whether the imprint reflects the true printer and publishers. (There is a good chance that the edition described here is a piracy.)

There is a possibility that volume vi is listed in the OCLC: 'La chaumi'ere indienne[.] Jacques-Bernardin-Henri de Saint-Pierre. Paris: P. F. Didot, 1791. 63 p.; 16 cm. Bound with the author's Vœux d'un solitaire' (location: Miami University, Ohio). The entry for the *Vœux d'un solitaire* is for 218 pp. – no mention of preliminaries – Paris: P. F. Didot, 1790, which, if accurate, is certainly not part of the edition described here. (A cross-reference leads to the *Chaumière indienne* just mentioned.) Note that there is no mention of a volume v, which appears on the titlepage in the edition listed here, or of the 'imprimerie de monsieur' and Méquignon. In any case, MMF list nothing similar (either to the copy described here or that listed in the OCLC; 91.43).

There is a distinct change in titlepage layout for vols v and vi from the preceding ones. Vol. vi seems to have been tacked on to vol. v as an addendum. The last two volumes are bound together (contemporary calf), and, although vol. vi has its own pagination and sequences of signatures (in two series: for the prelims and the main text), each gathering sequence bears a catchtome for 'Tome V.', echoing the catchtomes of vol. v. Vol. vi, bearing the indication of vol. v on the titlepage, and with catchtomes to match, was obviously intended as a sequel or addendum to vol. v.

Paul et Virginie first appeared in 1788, as did *L'Arcadie*; the *Chaumière indienne*, in 1791. (See Toinet and MMF).

To editions of *La Chaumière indienne* listed in MMF, I would add:

1.*1791*. 'Chaumiere, la, indienne, par C. de la Pierre [*sic*], gr[and] 12mo. ibid. [i.e., Strasb[ourg], König.] [17]91' (Heinsius, *Handbuch*, p.778).

2. *1791*. MMF list a *Chaumière indienne* for 'Paris, de l'imprimerie de Monsieur, Didot jeune, 1791, xlvii + 127p.' (location: Harvard). The BNC ten-year

supplement (1960-69) lists what is surely the same, but for xlviii-127 pp., specifying the format: in-12° (Rés. p.Y2.2565). *Cave*: the BNC lists under 'Saint-Pierre', the supplement under 'Bernardin'. As this work was in the press, I was able to examine that book. It is in-18: 1 f. (titlepage) + [v]-xlvij, [xlviij] + [1]-127 pp. One leaf is missing, presumably a halftitle. In any case, the titleleaf is a cancel.

3. *1791*. After a description of the first edition of *La Chaumière indienne* (mentioning that 'il a été tiré des ex. sur papier vélin d'Essone'), Tchemerzine records the following edition which has escaped the attention of MMF: 'Il en a été fait la même année une contrefaçon portant la même adresse, du même format, en xlj-94 pp.' (x.151)

And a final clarification concerning an undated edition of *Paul et Virginie*: MMF list: 'Paris, Lepetit et Guillemard, 1792, in-16, 284p. Gumuchian cite une édition: Paris, Lepetit et Guillemard, s.d. [vers 1791], pet. in-12; c'est vraisemblablement cette édition de 1792' (88.101). Gumuchian does give this information, commenting that this edition is a 'copie de l'édition originale, ornée d'un charmant titre-frontispice gravé et de 5 figures non signées, dont 4 de bonnes copies des figures de *Moreau le Jeune* pour la 1re édition (1789). La préface est celle de 1789. A la fin se trouve la comédie "Paul et Virginie" [par Fr. de Favières]' (*Les Livres de l'enfance du XVe au XXe siècle*, préface de Paul Gavault. [Paris], en vente à la librairie Gumuchian et Cie [catalogue XIII], [1931], no. 5049). Note in any case the different format. Gumuchian is without a doubt correct. The BNC ten-year supplement has a *Paul et Virginie* together with another work, which might possibly be the undated edition Gumuchian refers to: 'Paul et Virginie, par Jacq. Bernardin-Henri de Saint-Pierre. [*suivi de*: Paul et Virginie, comédie en 3 actes, en prose, mêlée d'ariettes, par Edmond Guillaume François de Favières. [Paris, Comédiens italiens, 15 janvier 1791.] –Paris, Lepetit et Guillemard ainé, s.d. In-18, 346p. titre et [5] pl. gr. sur cuivre. ... Contrefaçon de l'éd. Cazin, 1793, d'après Tchemerzine. 4 pl. ont été copiées sur celles de Moreau-le-Jeune et de Joseph Vernet' (Rés. p.Y2.2449).

However, according to what Toinet reports in his commentary, it seems fairly certain that there were two undated Paris, Lepetit et Guillemard editions (which probably appeared not too far distant in time from one another). Toinet remarks, after listing a *Paul et Virginie*, ill., same publishers, 1792: 1 vol. in-16, conforme en tous points, format, caractères, composition et illust., aux éditions n° 10 et 15 [both probably Cazins according to Toinet], sauf titre et date. [...] Le titre se présente suivant les exemplaires sous deux formes: soit titre imprimé conforme à l'indication ci-dessus, soit titre gravé portant au lieu de "avec fig." la mention "Prix: 4 livres" encadrée dans une guirlande de fleurs et *sans date* [Toinet's emphasis]' (no. 11, pp.15-16). Among other details given is that this edition is paginated like his entry no. 10, which includes the play, pp.271-346. This undated issue would seem to match the BNC supplement copy mentioned above. In any case, there was more than one, undated, Paris edition (or issue) for around 1792. (Toinet mentions a format in-16, the BNC:S in-18. Although it is sometimes difficult to differentiate between the in-18 and in-24 formats, that in-16 presents few problems of identification.)

As this work was in the press, I was able to examine B.N., Rés. p.Y2.2449, which is in-18. It has an engraved titlepage for 'Paul / et / Virginie, / Par Jacq. Bernardin-Henri / de Saint Pierre / ... Miseris succurrere disco. AEneid. lib. 1 / [rule] / Prix 4. liv. / [rule] / A Paris. / Chez le Petit. et / Guillemard, aîné / Commissionnaires en librairie, / Rue de Savoye, n°. 10.'; 1 f. (engraved titlepage) + [1]-33, [34: blank], [35]-284, [285-86: play halftitle with 'personnages' verso], [273 *sic*], 274-346 pp. Differences in pagination recorded from this edition doubtless stem from the pagination error in the book itself.

Moreover, Tchemerzine lists the illustrated, Paris, Didot, 1789 edition as the first, reproducing the titlepage of the edition variant bearing 'Avec figures': 'In-18 de xxxv-243 pp. et (1) p. [approbation], plus 4 figures de *Moreau le Jeune* et *Joseph Vernet*, gravées par *Girardet, Halbou* et *De Longueil*' (x.149). He further remarks that the 'édition de 1789 a été contrefaite la même année, sous la même adresse, en un vol. in-18, de 181 pp., avec 3 figures copiées sur celles de *Moreau*. Le texte du roman est suivi de l'adaptation de *Paul et Virginie* par E. de Favière, en trois actes en prose mêlés d'ariettes, occupant 69 pp. paginées séparément, mais dont les signatures font suite à celles du roman. Autres éditions: *Londres*, [*Paris, Cazin*] 1793, in-18 de 284 pp. plus 76 pp. chiff. [271]-346, titre gravé avec vignette et 5 fig. non signées dont 4 copies sur Moreau [Le texte est suivi de la comédie; contrefaçon de l'éd. de 1789]. –*Paris, Le Petit et Guillemard aîné, s.d.* [1793], in-18 [Même éd. que la précédente; seul le titre gravé est différent]. –*Avignon, Jean-Albert Joli*, 1793, 2 vol. in-18 de 143 et 136 pp. –*Londres, de l'impr. de Biggs et Cottle; Vernor et Hood*, 1803, in-12 de (1) f. titre, iv-172 pp., (1) f. [annonces], titre gravé, frontisp. et 4 fig.' (x.150).

Paul et Virginie first appeared in 1788, as did *L'Arcadie*; the *Chaumière indienne*, in 1791. (See Toinet and MMF).

For further information concerning works by Bernardin de Saint-Pierre, see the other entries in this bibliography under his name.

Incipits, i: 'Je formai, il y a quelques années, le / projet d'écrire une histoire générale de la / nature'.

iv: (*Paul et Virginie*) 'Sur le côté oriental de la montagne / qui s'éleve derriere le Port-Louis de l'île / de France'.

(*Arcadie*) 'Un peu avant l'équinoxe d'automne, / Tirtée, berger d'Arcadie'.

vi: (*La Chaumière indienne*) 'Il y a environ trente ans qu'il se forma / à Londres, une compagnie de savants / Anglois'.

49

Bernardin de Saint-Pierre: *Etudes de la nature*, etc., 1797

Jacques Henri Bernardin de Saint-Pierre (1737-1814): i-v: Etudes / de / la nature, / par Jacques-Henri-Bernardin / de Saint-Pierre. / Nouvelle édition. [possibly 'edition.' with no accent for i] / [rule] / ... [.. for v] Miseris succurrere disco. Enéid. [Enéid for v] liv. 1. [1 for v] / [rule] / Tome premier [second, troisième, quatrième, cinquième]. / [short swell rule; short straight rule for v] / [ornamental swell rule; an ordinary, larger swell rule for ii, iii] / à [A for ii, iii; the 'A' for v is a small capital] Hambourg, / chez P. F. Fauche, Imprimeur-libraire. / 1797.

[/ chez P. F. Fauche, et Comp. Impri- / meurs-libraires. / 1797. for iv; / chez P. F. Fauche, et Comp. / Imprimeurs-libraires. / 1797. for v]

vi: L'Arcadie. / Par Jacques-Henri-Bernardin / de Saint-Pierre. / Suivie de la chaumière indienne. / Nouvelle edition. / [rule] / ...Miseris succurrere disco. Enéid. liv. 1. / [rule] / Tome sixième. / [short swell rule] / [ornamental swell rule] / à Hambourg, / chez P. F. Fauche, et Comp. / Imprimeurs-libraires. / 1797.

vii: Vœux / d'un / solitaire. / Par / Jacques-Henri-Bernardin / de Saint-Pierre. / Suivis de l'explication des figures pour / les études de la nature. / Nouvelle édition. / [rule] / ..Miseris succurrere disco. Enéid. liv. 1. / [rule] / Tome septième. / [short swell rule] / A Hambourg, / chez P. F. Fauche, et Comp. / Imprimeur-libraire [*sic*]. / 1797.

7 vols in-18, i: 1 pl (titlepage) + [1]-(4) + [1]-337, [338] pp. (The last page is a table.)
    ii: 1 pl (titlepage) + [1]-336 pp. + 1 f. (one-page table)
    iii: 1 pl (titlepage) + [1]-378 pp. + 1 f. (two-page table)
    iv: 1 pl (titlepage) + [1]-342 pp. + 1 f. (two-page table)
    v: 1 pl (titlepage) + [1]-418 pp. + 1 f. (one-page table)
    vi: 1 pl (titlepage) + 1 f. (halftitle for 'L'Arcadie.') + [3-4], [5]-244 pp. and 1 f. (halftitle for 'La chaumière [there seems to be a period after 'chaumière'] / indienne.') + [iij]-lvj + [1]-61 pp. + 1 f. (one-page table)
    vii: 1 pl (titlepage) + 1 f. (halftitle for 'Vœux / d'un / solitaire.') + [3]-418 pp. + 2 ff. (2 + 1 pp.)

Commentary: The first four pages in volume i are a 'Table générale des matières, contenues dans la collection des œuvres de Jacques-Henri-Bernardin de Saint-Pierre'. Then follows a breakdown for the seven volumes. The catchtomes throughout the volumes are for 'Tome I [II, etc.].', with no mention of 'œuvres'. And no volume halftitles are present. Yet this edition comprises more than just the original *Etudes* and is also termed an *Œuvres* in the Messkatalog (for which see below).

Volumes i-iv contain 'études' 1 through 13.

Volume v contains: a. 'étude' 14, pp.[1]-104; b. 'Avis sur la quatrième édition', pp.[105]-142; c. 'Avis sur les études de la nature', pp.[143]-218; d. 'Paul / et / Virginie.', halftitle; e. 'Avant-propos', pp.[221]-224; f. the novel, pp.[225]-404; g. 'Le café / de Surate.', halftitle; h. the tale, pp.407-18; i. a table, p.[419].

Vol. vi contains: a. 'L'Arcadie.', halftitle; b. untitled notice, pp.[3-4]; c. 'Fragment servant de préambule a l'Arcadie', pp.[5]-84; d. 'Notes', pp.85-98; e. 'L'Arcadie', pp.[99]-214; f. 'Notes', pp.215-44; g. 'La chaumière[.] / indienne.', halftitle; h. 'Avant-propos', pp.[iij]-xx; i. 'Notes', pp.[xxj]-xxxj; j. 'Préambule de la chaumière indienne', pp.[xxxij]-lvj; k. 'La chaumière indienne', pp.[1]-61; l. table, p.[63].

Vol. vii contains: a. 'Vœux / d'un / solitaire.', halftitle; b. 'Préambule des vœux d'un solitaire', pp.[3]-22; c. 'Vœux d'un solitaire', pp.[23]-222; d. 'Suite / des vœux / d'un / solitaire.', halftitle; e. 'Suite[...]', pp.[225]-340; f. 'Explication / des / figures, / pour / les études de la nature.', halftitle; g. 'Explication [...]', pp.343-418; h. 'Avis au relieur' and 'Avis pour placer les figures', p.[419]; i.

'Nachricht an den Buchbinder' and 'Nachricht wegen der Kupfer', p.[420]; j. table, p.[421].

This edition is not listed in Toinet or MMF. I could find no other copy of it, and only two mentions of it, the first in the Messkatalog, as follows: 'Œuvres complettes de J. Bern. Henry de St. Pierre. Nouv. edit. 7 Vol. [in-]18. Hambourg, Fauche' (OM 1797, p.235). It is also in the 1798 edition of Heinsius as '[Œuvres] de J. H. B. de St.-Pierre. 7 Vols. avec fig. 12. Hbg. Fauche. [1]797' (p.495). There are no engravings present in the books described here, and none seems ever to have been present with the copy in hand (contemporary full calf). The Messkatalog makes no mention of any, so possibly none was issued with this edition in spite of the bilingual notice to the binder (in English and in German; vol. vii, items h and i above).

In vol. vi, *La Chaumière indienne* has its own pagination, but the signatures are consecutive for the entire volume, with catchtomes for 'Tome VI.'. There is every possibility that this edition was copied from the 1791 edition described here (or one of its analogues), which would explain this discrepancy.

There was an 'official' edition in 1797, one printed in Basel ('Tourneizen', 5 vols in-8°, with a permission to sell it in Paris on the verso of the titlepage; Toinet, no. 29, p.19). NUC lists: 'Etudes de la nature, par ... ... Nouv. ed... Bale, Chez Tourneizen, 1795-1797. 5v.' (University of Michigan, Ann Arbor); perhaps this is some sort of a composite edition? MMF list an *Etudes* as a '... nouvelle édition, Bâle, Tourneizen, 1795' after the Michigan copy (personally examined by the authors), remarking: 'Le premier tome porte la date de 1797' (88.101) which implies that the other volumes bear 1795. (No mention is made of the number of volumes or the format). I have seen vols iv and v of these *Etudes de la nature* (including the *Vœux d'un solitaire*, the *Chaumière indienne*, etc.) in a bookshop, both bearing the date of 1797.

Escoffier lists a 'traité passé entre B. de Saint-Pierre et l'éditeur Poignée pour la vente d'une édition des Etudes de la Nature en 5 vol., parue à Bâle en 1797; la pièce semble de la main de B. de Saint-Pierre et porte sa signature' (no. 14, p.5). Thus the Basel edition is the 'official' one in the sense it was printed (or at least distributed) with the knowledge and consent of the author.

There was also supposed to have existed an edition of the *Œuvres* for Leipzig, Fleischer, same year (1797). Toinet lists an *Œuvres complètes*, Leipzig: E. Fleischer, 1797, after the 'bibliographie de l'édition Crès (no. 214), sans cotes' and Monglond. He notes that the former source lists 18 vols, the latter, 7 vols in-18, and further remarks that he has never seen such an edition (no. 30, p.19). MMF list 'Leipzig, E. Fleischer, 1797, 7t. in-18' after Toinet (88.101). Monglond (iv, col.166) lists that information, after Kayser. In the latter we find: '*de Saint-Pierre*, Bernardin J. B. H., œuvres complett. VII Vols [in-]18. Leipz. [1]797. Er. Fleischer' (v.11a). Since these entries revert ultimately to Kayser, since the 'Fleischer' edition is not listed in Heinsius (or Heinsius, *Handbuch*) or in the Messkatalog, there does seem a good possibility that Kayser has made an error, perhaps (if not probably) listing after the Hambourg edition described here (since the Bâle edition comprises 5 vols in-8°), his having neglected to record the imprint after which he would have inserted 'Leipzig, Fleischer' within parentheses to indicate the bookseller. In any case, the first edition of the *Œuvres complètes* listed in the NUC, BLC and BNC dates to 1818.

Paul et Virginie first appeared in 1788 as did *L'Arcadie*; the *Chaumière indienne*, in 1791 and the *Café de Surate* in 1792 (probably; see Toinet and MMF).

For further information concerning works by Bernardin de Saint-Pierre, see the other entries in this bibliography under his name.

Incipits, i: 'Je formai, il y a quelques années, le pro- / jet d'écrire une histoire générale de la na- / ture'.

v: (*Paul et Virginie*) 'Sur le côté oriental de la montagne qui / s'élève derrière le Port-Louis de l'île de / France'.

(*Le Café de Surate*) 'Il y avoit à Surate un café où beaucoup / d'étrangers s'assembloient l'après-midi.'

vi: (*L'Arcadie*) 'Un peu avant l'équinoxe d'au- / tomne, Tirtée, berger d'Arcadie'.

(*La Chaumière indienne*) 'Il y a environ trente ans qu'il se / forma, à Londres, une compagnie de sa- / vans anglais'.

50

Bernardin de Saint-Pierre: *Paul et Virginie*, 1789

Jacques Henri Bernardin de Saint-Pierre (1737-1814): Paul / et / Virginie, / Par Jacques-Bernardin-Henri / de Saint-Pierre. / ...Miseris succurrere dico [*sic*]. Æneid. lib. I. / [rule] / Prix, broché, 1 liv. 10 sols. / [rule] / [simple, symmetrical woodcut ornament in the form of two Ls intertwined] / A Paris, / de l'imprimerie de monsieur. / M. DCC. LXXXIX. / Avec approbation et privilége du roi.

18°: 2 ff. (halftitle and titlepage) + [v]-viij, [ix]-xxxj + [1]-238 pp.

Commentary: The pagination reflects an 'Avant-propos', an 'Avis sur cette édition' and the novel proper. There is a halftitle for 'Paul / et / Virginie.', f.[A1]. In spite of the pagination, the book is continously signed (A12, B6 to P-P5, [P6-9]). The titlepage is a cancel of different paper (no chainlines). In the present copy it is possible to see the matching strip of paper comprising the extension of this leaf. The binding is contemporary.

The pagination does not match any edition for 1789 of the novel I have examined or which is recorded in the usual bibliographies. And I could find no trace of this edition anywhere (BN, BL, NUC, Toinet, etc.). It does seem to represent a Paris printing, and the type is quite similar to the fonts used by Didot at the time. Quérard, perhaps somewhat rashly, states that 'Le succès de cette production [*Paul et Virginie*], ainsi que de celle des deux premiers livres de l'*Arcadie*, fut encore plus éclatant que celui des *Etudes*. Dans l'espace d'un an, on publia plus de cinquante contrefaçons de *Paul et Virginie*' (viii.365). I do not know whether the above edition is a 'contrefaçon' or not: its rarity would certainly make one think so however.

I might take this opportunity to clarify a question concerning one of the first (doubtless *the* first) illustrated edition of *Paul et Virginie*. MMF list an edition for 'Paris, imprimerie de Monsieur, 1789, in-16, xxv + 243 pp.' (They further remark: 'Cohen ajoute le nom du libraire, P. Fr. Didot, et donne "in-18" au lieu de "in-16"'. By 'xxv' they surely mean 'xxxv' pp.; I have never seen a Paris, Didot, 1789 edition with even similar pagination in-16.) There were two issues of this edition (in-18° however), one on fine paper, with pictures after Moreau le jeune, bearing on the titlepage the mention 'avec figures'. This corresponds to, for example, BL C.44.a.6 and BN Rés.p.Y2.1715. Tchemerzine further explains that this edition 'existe sur divers papiers: en papier vélin avec figures avant la lettre; en papier vélin d'*Essone*, coûtant 6 livres; en papier écu fin, à 4 livres' (v.649). Tchemerzine reproduces the titlepage of the 'avec figures' issue. Toinet reproduces the other (p.10, no.3). Toinet also erroneously records xxv preliminary pages and was unaware of the different issues. For further information, see Cohen cols.931-32. See too Reynaud col.485.

For more editions of *Paul et Virginie*, see the commentary on the first Bernardin de Saint-Pierre entry *et passim*.

Incipit: 'Sur le côté oriental de la montagne qui s'élève derrière le Port-Louis de l'île de France'.

51

Berquin: L'Ami des enfants, 1798

Arnaud Berquin (1747-1791), edited by Nic[h]olas Salmon: L'ami / des / enfans, / par / M. Berquin. / [small ornamental rule in swell form] / Nouvelle édition, / revue et corrigée avec soin, / Par Nicolas Salmon. / [double rule] / Tome premier [second, troisième, quatrième]. / [double rule] / [woodcut ornament: musical trophy with lyre and trumpet in centre] / [small ornamental rule in swell form] / À Londres: / Chez J. Johnson; C. Dilly; J. Sewell; F. & C. Rivington; / J. Stockdale; Vernor & Hood; C. Law; / & W. Creech, Edinburgh. / [short rule] / 1798.

12°, i: 1 f. (titlepage) + [iii]-iv, (v)-xiii, [xiv: blank], [xv]-xvi + [1]-207 pp.
  ii: 1 pl (titlepage) + 1 f. (2 pp.) + [1]-206 pp.
  iii: 1 pl + 1 f. (2 pp.) + [1]-235 pp.
  iv: 1 pl + 1 f. (2 pp.) + [1]-212 pp.

Commentary: The pagination reflects a 'Prospectus' for the *Ami des enfants* (i.[iii]-iv); an 'Avis au public' (p.(v)-xiii); a 'table' for vol. i (p.[xv]-xvi) with a list of 'Fautes d'impression' at the end; then the work proper. Each of the remaining volumes is preceded by a one-folio, two-page 'table', with a list of errata at the end.

The prospectus seems to have been authored by Berquin himself. A note explains that 'il a paru, sous le même titre un Ouvrage de M. Weisse, l'un des plus célébres Poëtes de l'Allemagne. On en tirera des morceaux choisis, ainsi que des Ouvrages de MM. Campe & Salzmann'. Exactly how much of this work is taken from those authors I do not know.

The 'Avis au public' is authored by Salmon himself, and is very interesting from more than one point of view. From it we learn that the edition bearing 1797 on the titlepages (presumably Londres, Robinson [etc. without a doubt] as listed in MMF, 82.14) actually appeared in 1798. (If this is true, that would constitute a rare example of a legitimate edition appearing after the indicated date.) Salmon complains about the many errors, both typographical and of language, that besmirch all previous editions. So what Salmon proposed to do was correct the original French (many examples are given), and standardise the spelling following the dictionary of the Académie française. The editor also enters into considerable detail concerning mistakes made by English compositors setting a French book: what these are and why they are unavoidable when one takes into account the processes undergone by hand-press book production.

But why go to all this trouble, not only concerning the material presentation of his edition, but also concerning the purity of the language? 'Je regarde [...] L'Ami des Enfans comme un ouvrage très-propre à mettre entre les mains des jeunes personnes qui étudient la langue Françoise. C'est pour le rendre encore plus propre à produire l'effet que l'on peut en attendre, que je me suis permis de corriger les fautes que j'ai aperçues contre la Syntaxe ou le génie de la langue Françoise' (p.(ix)). Salmon was a lexicographer, gramarian and educator; his preface is proudly signed 'N. Salmon Auteur d'un Dictionnaire Etymologique Latin, intitulé *Stemmata Latinitatis*, d'un ouvrage intitulé *The first Principles of English Grammar*, &c.' ('St. John's Square, N° 23, Clerkenwell, 1798').

My copy is printed on 'papier vélin' (no chainlines), of a quality quite inferior to that generally used by French printers at that time, however. These books were obviously printed in Great Britain: press figures throughout; first gathering of text in each volume signed with 'B' (B-B6, [B7-12]); catchwords on each page, etc. There are forty-three most charming engravings by Cook: 'Cook sc.' (A couple of these are in a curious state.) This is probably Thomas Cook (1744-1818) who worked on, among other things, Bell's edition of the British poets. (See Emmanuel Bénézit, *Dictionnaire critique et documentaire des peintres, sculpteurs [...], nouv. éd.*, iii.149 [Paris 1976]).

MMF (82.14) list a *Pièces choisies de l'Ami des enfans* for 'Londres, 1798 (PPL, PPULC)'. This information is so given in the NUC, with the same locations (Library Company of Philadelphia and Union Library Catalogue, Pennsylvania; NB.0371201). That edition or version would seem to have little to do with the edition described here. OCLC has the following entry: 'L'ami de enfants et des adolescents par Berquin. Nouv. éd., revue et corr. avec soin par Nicolas Salmon. Londres: J. Johnson, C. Dillu [*sic*], J. Sewell, F. & C. Rivington, J. Stockdale, Vernor & Hood, C. Law, 1798. 4 v. ill. 18 cm.' (Michigan State University, East Lansing). This might coincide with my books. But no mention is made in the latter of *L'Ami des adolescents* (either on the titlepages or in the preliminary material), and it would be surprising were a cataloguer to transcribe the names of eight London bookdealers, and then leave out the last, with the mention of a different city (Edinburgh). That entry was keyed into OCLC 1 January 1978. (The edition described here is not listed in the BLC and supplements, the new edition of the BLC or in the BNC and all supplements. It is also not mentioned in Cohen or Reynaud.)

As for the contents: these four volumes seem to contain all of the original *Ami des enfants* and some, or all, of the *Ami de l'adolescence*. Although I do not have access to many editions of works by Berquin at this writing, according to Brenner some of the plays contained in the present collection first appeared in the *Ami de l'adolescence*, for example, *Le Retour de croisière* (iii.(37)-61; Brenner 3668), *L'Ecole des marâtres* (iv.[54]-70; Brenner 3649), and so on. To Brenner's list of plays by Berquin, I would add *Le Père de famille* with more of the same play under the title of *La Séparation*, both translated 'du Père de Famille Allemand par L'Edit.' (iv.46-49, [51]-53). Some of the plays in the *Ami des enfants* are adaptations or translations from German originals by G. Stéphanie, J. J. Engel and Friedel. (See Brenner for more details.) These are acknowledged in the text; perhaps more of the plays are adaptations from foreign sources?

What seems to be the case is that Berquin's two periodical ventures, *L'Ami des enfants* and *L'Ami de l'adolescence* were often grouped together under the collective title of *L'Ami des enfants*, and editors simply did not deem it necessary, or noteworthy even, to enter into explanations concerning that. Also the tales, plays, dialogues, occasional poems and so forth that comprise the collections were often published in a different order, and often abstracted to form collections of various sizes. It might also be noted that certain characters recur, such as the rather saccharine little Caroline. At one point the latter's handwriting is imitated typographically, which carries children's letters, as composed by Jean Jacques Rousseau for example, to their ultimate development! (This occurs in the epistolary tale titled *La Tendre mère*, iv.174.)

To editions of works by Berquin listed in MMF, I would offer the following additions and comments (in chronological order):

1. *L'Ami des enfants*, 1782-83. 'Londres, Chez M. Elmsley, 1782-83, 24 nos. in 12 v. Published each month from January 1782 to December 1783' (OCLC: University of South Florida, Tampa). MMF (82.14) give 'Londres 1782-83, 4t. in-32 (Gumuchian)' and 'Londres, M. Elmsley, 1783, 12 t. in-16' (BL; for Gumuchian see the commentary on Bernardin de Saint-Pierre, *Etudes de la nature*, 1791). So it would appear that Elmsley did indeed publish a complete run of the periodical.

2. *L'Ami des enfants*, 1782-1783. '24 Vol. [in]-12. Leipz. Dyk. [1]782-[1]783' in Gesamtverzeichniss (GV), xiv.2. Not in MMF.

3. *L'Ami des enfants*, 1788. 'Ami, l', des Enfans, par Rochow, II tomes, 8vo. Leips. Schneider, [1]788' (Heinsius, *Handbuch*, p.774). Heinsius has '[Ami] l', des Enfans à l'usage des Ecoles, traduit de l'Allemand de Rochow. II. Tom. 8vo. Berl[in] et Strasb[ourg]. (Linke Leips.) [1]788' (Heinsius, i, col.64). Kayser, under the title, has: '[...] enfans à l'usage des écoles, (trad. de l'Allemand de Rochow par S. H. Cat.). II Tom. 8vo. Berl. et Strassb. [1]788. (Linke in Leipz.)' (i.52a). This is not Berquin's work, but a translation of Friedrich Eberhard von Rochow (1734-1805), *Kinderfreund* (1776-77). I have not been able to examine that work, and list it for two reasons: to avoid future confusion concerning the French and German 'Ami des enfants', and because it could well contain items of prose fiction. (This edition is not listed in the NUC and NUC:S, BNC and all supplements, BLC and all supplements.) The BLC (and all supplements) do not list a French *Kinderfreund*. The first French version in the NUC is for 1826, translated by François Bock. The BNC has an entry for *L'Ami des enfans, ouvrage destiné à exercer les enfants à la lecture et à les rendre attentifs à ce qu'ils lisent* (Brandenbourg: Leich, 1796), translated by Hauchecorne and Catel. That is the first French edition listed in the BNC. There were many subsequent

editions. (The Hauchecorne and Catel version is not listed in the NUC or the BLC, including all supplements.)

4. *L'Ami des enfants*, 1789. A 'nouvelle éd. en douze volumes, ornés de cent trente-deux gravures. A Paris: Au Bureau de l'Ami des Enfans, 1789. 12 v. ill. 14 cm. "Cette édition [...] comprend les 24 vol. de l'Ami des enfans, & les 12 vol. de l'Ami de l'adolescence". Avis de l'éditeur, p.xv'. The illustrations are 'after designs by M. Borel, by MM. Delaunay, de Longueil, Ponce, Guttenburg [*sic*, for Guttenberg probably], Delignon, *et al.*, cf. pp.xv-xvi' (OCLC: Indiana University, Bloomington). This edition is not listed in MMF or, surprisingly, in Cohen and Reynaud. (The latter mention the Paris, an XI (1803) *Œuvres complètes*, with over two hundred illustrations, some of which are perhaps reissues from the 1789 edition.)

5. *L'Ami des enfants*, 1790. '[...] par Berquin, avec fig. années 1782-83. XII Part. en VI Vol. 8vo. Berne, Haller, [1]790.' (Heinsius, *Handbuch*, p.774). Not in MMF.

6. *L'Ami des enfants*, 1794. MMF list a 1794 edition for Lausanne, Hignou (Indiana University, Harvard, University of Michigan; 82.14). This is so described in the NUC. Kayser has what is doubtless the same edition, with further information: Lausanne, [no name], 1794, 8 vols in-12, adding '(Haller in Bern)' (i.228b).

7. *Suite des Amis des enfants*, 1796. OCLC has such a main-title entry, for 'Geneve: [s.n.] 1796', 207 p. ill.; 14 cm. Bibliotheque des enfans, t. x' (U.S. Naval Academy, Annapolis). There is no such title or collection mentioned in MMF.

8. *L'Ami des enfants et des adolescents*, 1798. '[...] Nuremberg 1798. H[erausge-ber]: Meynier, Joh. Heinr. (Ky [Kayser, 1834-]) (MGT [Hamberger and Meusel, *Das Gelehrte Teutschland, oder ...*, 1799-1831])', Gesamtverzeichnis (GV), xiv.2. The next entry in the same source doubtless refers to the same edition: '[...] Adolescens, ouvrage aussi intéressant qu'agréable, enrichi de l'explication des Mots et des Phrases les plus difficiles en faveur de la jeunesse allemande. II. Vol. 8vo. Nürnb. Grattenauer. [1]798.' Kayser gives much the same information, adding the name of the editor/adaptor and that of the bookdealer: '[...] en faveur de la jeunesse allem. (par J. H. Meynier). II Vols. 8vo. Nürnb. [1]798. (Eichhorn)' (i.228b; also i.52a). Heinsius also lists this edition, but does not give the name of the editor (i, col.64). There were several other editions of this version during the first half of the nineteenth century.

Incipit: ('Le petit frère') 'FANCHETTE s'étoit un jour levée de grand matin, / pour aller cueillir des fleurs'.

52

Bitaubé: *Joseph*, 1768

Paul Jérémie Bitaubé (1732-1808): Joseph, / en neuf chants, / Par M. Bitaubé, / De l'Académie Royale des Sciences / & Belles-Lettres de Prusse. / [extensive woodcut ornament: musico-war trophy on ruined wall; large sunburst] / A

Paris, / Chez [open brace] / Prault, Imprimeur, Quai de Gêvres. / Le Clerc, Libraire, au Palais. [end of material set off by brace] / [rule] / M. DCC. LXVIII. / Avec Approbation & Privilege du Roi.

12°: 2 pl + [j]-xxiv + [1]-295, [296] pp.

Commentary: This volume contains a dedication 'A son altesse royale monseigneur Fréderic-Guillaume, prince de Prusse, &c. &c. &c.' (pp.[j]-iv; signed 'S.P', for Samuel Pitra); a 'Discours préliminaire' (pp.[v]-xxiv); *Joseph*, with a one-page approbation at the end (p.[296]). The latter is for a submitted printed book (and not a manuscript): '*Joseph, Poëme en prose, en neuf Chants*, par M. Bitaubé, deux volumes *in*-8vo. imprimé à Berlin, chez Samuel Pitra, Libraire, 1767', Paris, 27 July 1767, signed Albaret. (As is obvious, the first edition is the octavo Berlin one.) The volume halftitle bears 'Joseph, / en neuf chants.'

This book is a contrefaçon of the Paris, Prault and Leclerc edition, and is possibly Switzerland-printed (or possibly produced in Germany).

The only edition MMF list of this work for 1768 is Paris, Prault, in-12, after the printed catalogue of the Bibliothèque municipale of Rennes (2nd part, 1823-28, by D. Maillet; 67.12). I was unable to consult the Rennes book. It is conceivable that the edition described here is the same. In any case, I could find no other copy of my book.

In passing, I might mention that OCLC lists yet another edition for 1768: a self-proclaimed second edition, chez Prault and Leclerc, 350 pp., 15cm (location: California State University, Chico). Krauss-Fontius also list an edition that has escaped the attention of bibliographers of the 'genre romanesque': a '3ᵉ éd.', Neufchâtel: Sinnet, 1772, 318 pp. (no. 3460; location: Universitäts- und Landesbibliothek Sachsen-Anhalt, Halle).

And an entry in Gesamtverzeichniss indicates that there was a 1785, Paris edition: 'Joseph II, poeme en IX Chants. II Vols. 8vo. Berl[in]. [1]767. N. Ed. 12mo. Neufchatel [1]772. Ed. V [cinquième édition]. 12mo. Paris [1]785' (xvi.291a).

Incipit: 'Long-temps j'osai répéter les ac- / cords belliqueux du Poëte'.

53

Boiardo (Lesage transl.): *Nouvelle traduction de Roland l'amoureux*, 1776

Matteo Maria Boiardo, or Bojardo (ca.1440-1494), Alain René Lesage, trans. (1668-1747): Nouvelle traduction / de / Roland / l'amoureux, / de / Matheo Maria Boyardo, / Comte di Scandiano. / Par Monsieur Le Sage. / Tome premier [second]. / Nouvelle édition. / [woodcut ornament: basket of flowers in decoration for i; symmetrical, with baldaquin for ii] / A Paris, / Chez Caillau, Libraire, rue du Foin, / à Saint-André. / [double rule] / M. DCC. LXXVI. / Avec Approbation & Privilege du Roi.

12°, i: 2 ff. (halftitle and titlepage) + v-xij + [1]-295, 296-299 pp.
    ii: 2 pl + [1]-296, 297-302 pp. + 2 ff. (3 pp.).

Commentary: The preliminary material in vol. i is the 'Préface du traducteur'. The paginated items at the end of each volume are the 'Tables'. There are half titlepages reading 'Nouvelle traduction / de / Roland / l'amoureux. / Tome premier [second].' The last three pages in vol. ii are the legal documents: approbation for 22 August 1768 ('Crébillon'); privilege to François Babuty, 8 November 1768 ('Le Begue'); Babuty shares the rights with 'Barois, Guillin, Caillau, Bailly, veuve David' the 5th December 1768; registered 6 December 1768 ('Briasson, Syndic'). From these, it would appear certain that we are dealing with a counterfeit edition, copied from that described in Cordier for Paris: David, 1769 (Cordier no. 909, p.329). Underscoring this probability are the legal stamp for Rouen, 1777 and Havas' signature to be found on i.[1], f.A[1]*r*. (For further information, see for example the commentaries on Lesage, *Gil Blas* 1771 and on d'Arnaud, *Œuvres* 1777.)

I have found no trace of this edition elsewhere, except possibly in MMF who list an edition for 1776, extant in Neuchâtel (no details given, 69.R17; I can only surmise it might be the same edition). This is a translation, which first appeared in 1717, of Boiardo's *Orlando innamorato*, 1476-1494 (MMF 69.R17).

Incipit: 'Le Roi Gradasse étoit le plus vaillant Prince de son siecle.'

54

Boufflers: *Œuvres*, 1782

Chevalier Stanislas de Boufflers (1738-1815): Œuvres / du / chevalier / de / Boufflers. / [symmetrical woodcut decoration] / A la Haye, / Chez Detune, Libraire. / [double rule] / M. DCC. LXXXII.

24°: 2 ff. (halftitle and titlepage) + [5]-150 pp.

Commentary: Contains 'La reine / de Golconde, / conte.' (half titlepage), with the preliminary poem ([5]-8, 9-56 pp.). MMF (61.6) note that Gay cites 'La Haye ou Genève'. Gay further remarks that the work in question is a Cazin, with an engraving by [after] Marillier, in-18, 178 pp. (iii.542). The edition described here differs markedly from the Cazin edition and, in the present copy, does not seem ever to have had an engraving. There is obviously a mistake on Gay's part since he does not record two different editions. (The contents of this volume include Boufflers' 'Voyage / en / Suisse.' [half titlepage], various poems, and even verse by Voltaire.) *La Reine de Golconde* first appeared in 1761 (MMF 61.6).

The final leaves of this book are signed G, G2, G3. Since the book is signed in 12s (A12-F12, G3), there is every likelihood of there having been more of it printed, or at least planned for, perhaps to contain works by the marquis de Villette.

To the editions of Boufflers' *Œuvres* listed in MMF, I would add four octavo editions for 1780, an edition for 1782 and another for 1786:

1. *Œuvres*, 1780. 'Francf. Academ. Buchhandl. [1]780' (Heinsius, i, col.392; also Kayser i.325a). Heinius, 1793 lists '8. Francf. Kunze. [1]780' (iv.537). See also no.4 below.

2. *Œuvres*, 1780. 'Œuvres du Chevalier de *Boufflers*; jolie Edition. 8. [La] Haye,

& se trouve à Leipsic, chez la Veuve H. Merkus', Messkatalog, OM 1780, p.920.

3. *Œuvres*, 1780. 'Œuvres de [*sic*] Chevalier de *Bouffleurs* [*sic*], Edition revue & corrigée. 8. Francfort sur l'Oder, chez Strauss', Messkatalog, MM 1780, p.1014.

4. *Œuvres*, 1780. '[Œuvres] de Chevalier de Bouffleurs, 8vo. Frcf. [Francfort] Kunze [1]780' (Heinsius, *Handbuch*, p.814).

5. *Œuvres*, 1782. 'Genève 1782. 168 pp.' (Krauss-Fontius, no. 935, with a location for the Universtäts- und Landesbibliothek Sachsen-Anhalt, Halle).

6. *Œuvres diverses*, 1786. 'Œuvres diverses en prose et en vers de Mr. le Cheval. de *Bouffler*. 8. à Lausanne, chez J. H. Pott et Comp.', Messkatalog, OM 1786, p.387.

Nos 1, 3 and 4 could conceivably refer to the same edition.

Incipit: (*La Reine de Golconde*) 'Je m'abandonne à vous, ma plume: jusqu'ici mon esprit vous a conduite'.

55

Brantôme: *Mémoires…*: *Vies des dames galantes*, 1689-1690

Pierre de Bourdeille, seigneur de Brantôme (1540?-1614): Memoires / de / Messire Pierre de Bourdeille, / Seigneur de / Brantome, / contenans / Les Vies [Vices for ii] de [des for ii] Dames Galantes de son / temps. / Tome I [II]. / [woodcut ornament of a sphere] / A Amsterdam, / [rule] / Chez Jean de la Tourterelle. [Tourterelle, for ii] / M. DC. LXXXIX [M. DC. LXXXX. for II].

12°, i: 1 pl (titlepage) + 2 ff. (3 + 1 pp.) + [1]-358 pp.
    ii: 1f. (titlepage) + 3-408 pp.

Commentary: The first piece is a dedicatory letter to the duke of Alençon and Brabant, count of Flanders, signed 'de Bourdeille'; the second, a notice 'Au lecteur'; then the *Vies* – or *Vices*, depending on which volume's title one follows! – through the sixth 'discours'. At the end of vol. i, one reads: 'Fin du Premier Tome'; at the end of ii, 'Fin', which seems to indicate that these two volumes were published as a complete entity, and not as part of a larger whole. Vol. i.358 and vol. ii.313 to the end (for both volumes) have smaller type and more lines per page (gatherings O-R in vol. ii), an obvious attempt by the publisher to squash all his material into two, similarly sized volumes.

I have found no trace of this edition anywhere. This work first appeared in 1665 (Tchemerzine, iii.111) and might be considered somewhat marginal to the 'genre romanesque', depending on how much of it one chooses to believe! It is actually a vivacious and libertine blend of fact and fiction.

Incipit: ('Discours premier sur les Dames qui font l'amour') 'D'Autant que ce sont les Dames, qui ont fait la fondation du Cocuäge, & que ce sont elles qui font les hommes Cocus'.

MEMOIRES

DE

Meſſire Pierre de Bourdeille,

Seigneur de

BRANTOME,

CONTENANS

*Les Vices des Dames Galantes de ſon
temps.*

TOME II.

A AMSTERDAM,

Chez Jean de la TOURTERELLE,
M. DC. LXXXX.

No 55: Brantôme, *Mémoires*, 1689-1690

56

Bret and Damours or Crébillon fils: *Mémoires sur la vie de mademoiselle de Lenclos*; *Lettres de Ninon de Lenclos au marquis de Sévigné*, 1761

Antoine Bret (1717-1792) for vol. i, Louis Damours (1720?-1788) or Claude Prosper Jolyot de Crébillon fils (1707-1777) for ii and iii:

i: Mémoires / sur / la vie / de mademoiselle / de Lenclos. / Par M. B*****. / [rule] / Premiére partie. / [rule] / [woodcut decoration] / A Amsterdam, / Chez François Joly. / [double rule] / M. DCC. LXI.

ii and iii: Lettres / de mademoiselle / de / Ninon de Lenclos, / au marquis / de Sévigné. / Felix qui potuit rerum cognoscere causas! / Virg. Georg. Liv. II. / [rule] / Seconde [Troisiéme] partie. / [rule] / [woodcut ornament, identical for ii and iii] / A Amsterdam, / Chez François Joly. / [double rule] / M. DCC. LXI.

12°, i: 1 pl + [j]-v + [1]-116 pp.

ii: 1 pl + [j]-vj + [1]-120 pp.

iii: 1 pl + [1]-128 pp.

Commentary: The first piece is universally attributed to Antoine Bret. It is largely factual, so at the least must be considered quite marginal to the 'genre romanesque'. The epistolary novel is attributed to Damours or Crébillon fils, depending on which bibliographer is consulted. The *Lettres de Ninon de Lenclos au marquis de Sévigné* first appeared in 1750; the *Mémoires sur la vie* in 1751, or possibly 1750. See Jones p.104. Neither Jones nor MMF (51.R13) mentions a 1761 edition and I have found no trace of one. The preliminary piece in vol. i is a dedicatory preface, 'A monsieur Lant..... de Damm....'. Vol. ii is preceded by an 'Envoi' to an unnamed lady, who was supposed to have kept the letters to herself. At the end of the 'Envoi' is an 'Explication d'embléme', decoding an engraving not here present.

To the editions of the Bret-Damours material listed in most modern bibliographies of eighteenth-century prose fiction, I would add the following:

1. *1754*. – Amsterdam: F. Joly, 1754. 3 vols, 19 cm [in-12?], NUC: University of Virginia. Krauss-Fontius list what is probably the same edition, with a location for the Universitäts- und Landesbibliothek Sachsen-Anhalt, Halle, no. 3788. (Not in Jones p.104, MMF 51.R13, or Giraud.)

2. *1754-1763*. – Amsterdam: F. Joly, 1754-63, 3 vols, NUC: Harvard University. (Not in Jones, MMF or Giraud. This is probably an amalgam of two editions, perhaps of no. 1 above and no. 5 below.)

3. *1758*. 'Lettres & Memoires de Madelle Ninon de Lenclos, 3 vols. 12. [Dresde & Leipzig implied], chez George Conrad Walther', Messkatalog, OM 1758, p.879. An Amsterdam: Joly, 1758 edition in three volumes is listed in Krauss-Fontius, with a location for the Universitäts- und Landesbibliothek Sachsen-Anhalt, Halle (no. 3789). MMF list a 1758 edition (ex libris Professor Morris Wachs), with no details.

4. *1759*. – Amsterdam: F. Joly, 1759, 3 vols, ill., 16 cm [in-12?], NUC: Cornell

University. (Not in Jones or MMF; Giraud lists simply 'A., Joly, 1759, in-12', 1750.3.f, p.39.)

5. *1763*. 'Mémoires sur la vie de Mademoiselle de Lenclos par M. B***. Amsterdam, François Joly, 1763, 2 ff. n.ch., viii, 120 pp., portrait. –[Damours (Louis).] Lettres de Mademoiselle de Ninon de Lenclos au marquis de Sévigné... Ibid., id., 1763, 1 f. n.ch., viii, 120 pp. [... vol. iii:] 1 f. n.ch., 128 pp.' Vols numbered 'première' to 'troisième partie'. (Paul Jammes, Librairie Paul Jammes, *Livres anciens et modernes*, cat. no.238, 1981, no.1058; the precision and value of Jammes catalogues require no clarification.) The only trace of this edition I could find – assuming it be the same edition – is in Krauss-Fontius, no. 3790 (with a location for the Universitäts- und Landesbibliothek Sachsen-Anhalt, Halle). But see no. 2 just above.

6. *1763*. 'Lettres de Ninon de Lenclos au Marquis de Sevigné, avec sa vie. Nouv. edit. revue exactement. 2 Voll. 8. à Paris & se trouve à Leipsic chez Gasp. Fritsch', Messkatalog, OM 1763, p.368. This could conceivably be the same as no. 5 above, assuming the latter is a Parisian edition with a false imprint and, what seems a bit farfetched, assuming the editors of the Messkatalog were aware of this. (I do not know whether the Messkatalog sometimes records place of publication based on provenance.)

7. *1781*. 'Lettres de Ninon de Lenclos au marquis de Sévigné avec sa vie par M. B.***. Nouvelle édition, revue, corrigée et augmentée. A Amsterdam, chez François Joly, 1781, 3 parties de viii, 111 pp.; xii, 112 pp.; 2 ff. n.ch., 122 pp.' (Jammes, cat. cit., no.1059). I could find no other copy or trace of this edition.

8. *1787*. 'Lettres de *Ninon de L'enclos* au Marquis de Sevigné. Nouv. Edit. 2 Vol. 8. à Leipzig, chez G. Fritsch', Messkatalog, OM 1787, p.640. Also in Heinsius, *Handbuch* as : '[Lettres] de Ninon de Lenclos au Marquis de Sévigné, avec sa vie, II Vol. 8vo. Leips. Fritsch [1]787' (p.803).

Incipits: (*Mémoires sur la vie*) 'La naissance de Ninon (a) ne fut point obscure'. (A note points to the date: 1615.)

(*Lettres de Ninon*) 'Moi, Marquis, me charger de votre éducation!'

57

Burney d'Arblay: *Evelina*, 1786

Frances (Fanny) Burney d'Arblay (1752-1840): Évelina, / roman / Nouvellement traduit & rédigé avec / beaucoup de soin d'après l'Anglois. / [rule] / Tome I [II]. / [rule] / [woodcut decoration, i: blindfolded cupid seated with bow and arrow; ii: putto playing drums] / A Londres, / Et se trouve à Paris chez les Libraires / qui vendent des nouveautés. / [rule] / M. DCC. LXXXVI.

12°, i: 2 ff. (halftitle and titlepage) + [v]-viij + [1]-264 pp.

ii: 2 pl (halftitle and titlepage) + [1]-216 pp.

Commentary: The half titlepages carry: 'Œuvres / de miss / Burney. / [rule] / Tome V [VI]. / [rule].' The end of vol. i reads: 'Fin du premier Volume'; that of ii, 'Fin du second & dernier Volume.' The catchtomes appearing to the far left of the first signature for each sequence bear 'Tome I.' and 'Tome II.' respectively.

Tom. 1. *Evelina.*

J'ai saisi son bras, et suis tombée
moi-même sans connaissance.

ÉVELINA;

ROMAN

Nouvellement traduit et rédigé avec
beaucoup de soin d'après l'Anglois
de Miss BURNEY.

TOME PREMIER.

A PARIS,

Chez LEPRIEUR, Libraire, rue
Savoie, Nᵒ 12.

L'an IV de la République franç.

No 58: Burney d'Arblay, *Evelina*, 1796, t.1

MMF list an *Œuvres de Miss Burney* for the same apparent place and publishers (79.7; 1785-86 actually), but in six octavo volumes, the pertinent volumes having 391 and 392 pp., a copy which the authors personally examined (Bibliothèque publique de Neuchâtel). The above is then a hitherto unrecorded edition. I do not believe that the two volumes were printed in Paris, certainly not in London.

The translation does not appear to be by the two translators of *Evelina* cited by MMF, Henri Renfner (MMF 79.7) or Antoine-Gilbert Griffet de La Baume (MMF 84.8). See the next entry. Although MMF list only two translations of *Evelina*, according to Gabrielle Buffet there was also an anonymous one which appeared in 1784 (*Fanny Burney: sa vie et ses romans*, Paris 1962, especially ii.[441]). The 'Avant-propos' in this edition of *Evelina* (i.[v]-viij) gives a short outline of what incited Fanny Burney to compose her novel.

This is a translation of *Evelina, or the history of a young lady's entrance into the world*, which first appeared in 1778 (Rochedieu, p.44; MMF 79.7).

To the editions of the French translations of *Evelina* listed in MMF (79.7, 84.8) and herein, I would also add: '[Evelina,] roman, nouvellement traduit et rédigé. II Vol. [in-]12. Berne, Haller. [1]786' (Heinsius, Romane, col.65; same information also in Heinsius, *Handbuch*, p.789 and in Heinsius, 1793: iv.503).

Incipits: (Lady Howard to M. Villars) 'Je viens, Monsieur, de recevoir / une lettre de Mme. Duval. Cette mere / dénaturée de feu lady Belmont vou- / droit, ce semble, réparer sourde- / ment les maux qu'elle a faits, & en / même tems passer aux yeux du public / pour en être innocente.'

ii: (Evelina to Miss Mirvan) 'Vous serez surprise, ma chere miss, / d'apprendre que je suis à Bristol; / mais j'ai été bien malade, & M. Vil- / lars qui croyoit entrevoir du danger'.

58

Burney d'Arblay: *Evelina*, 1796

Frances (Fanny) Burney d'Arblay (1752-1840): Évelina, / roman / Nouvellement traduit et rédigé avec / beaucoup de soin d'après l'Anglois / de Miss Burney. / [double rule] / Tome premier [second]. / [double rule, followed by a swell rule] / A Paris, / Chez Leprieur, Libraire, rue / Savoie, N° 12. / [double rule] / L'an IV de la République franç.

18°, i: 1 f. (titlepage; halftitles missing; see the commentary) + [v]-x, [11]-264 pp.

ii: 1 f. (titlepage) + [5]-312 pp.

Commentary: MMF list translations by Henri Renfner (79.7) and by Antoine-Gilbert Griffet de La Baume (84.8; see too Rochedieu, pp.44-45). The 'Avant-propos' is signed 'Rousseau, de Toulouse', presumably Pierre Rousseau, author of *Les Faux pas* (MMF 55.41), several plays (including *L'Année merveilleuse*; see Coyer and Le Prince de Beaumont below), a chief editor and author of the *Journal encyclopédique*, etc. (But Rousseau died in 1785.) In any case, this is not a re-edition of the first French translation of *Evelina*. The 'Avant-propos' is exactly the same as that for the previous entry, up to the end of the anecdote which gave rise to the composition of the novel. In this version/edition, there follow two additional paragraphs explaining that the translator has shortened the work and edulcorated Fanny Burney's language. The last paragraph reads: 'Cet ouvrage, entiérement corrigé d'après la traduction qui en a paru, et réduit aux deux tiers, ne peut manquer de plaire aux lecteurs délicats, puisqu'il a eu le bonheur de réussir avec tous ses défauts'. This is, however, the same translation as the previous item. The last letter is numbered LXXI. This is an error; no. LXI is numbered LI, and an 'X' has been dropped from all successive numbers. There are two pretty frontispiece engravings, one for each volume, with the following captions, i: 'J'ai saisi son bras, et suis tombée / moi-même sans connaissance.'; ii: 'J'ignore, Monsieur de quelles espérences / vous parlez;'. (Not in Cohen or Reynaud.)

There are no half titlepages in the present copy. However, f.A1 is missing in each volume. (The titlepages are ff.A2, unsigned.) The end of vol. i reads: 'Fin du Tome premier'; that of ii, 'Fin'. There are catchtomes for 'Tome I. [II.]'. But we are in all likelihood dealing with *Œuvres* available as a collection, the individual items also being sold separately, parallelling the 1786 *Evelina* listed above. For further information, see the preceding entry.

Incipit, i: (Lady Howard to M. Villars) 'Je viens, Monsieur, de recevoir une / lettre de Mme Duval. Cette mère dé- / naturée de feu lady Belmont vou- / droit, ce semble, réparer sourde- / ment les maux qu'elle a faits, et en / même temps passer, aux yeux du pu- / blic, pour en être innocente.'

ii: (letter XLVIII, Evelina to M. Villars) 'J'ai payé cher le bonheur passager / d'une courte matinée! Les Brangh- / ton proposèrent hier une partie pour / les jardins de Kensington'.

59

Bussy-Rabutin: *Lettres*, 1700-1702

Roger de Rabutin, comte de Bussy, also known as Bussy-Rabutin (1618-1693), *et al.*, edited by his son, Amé (sometimes Amable) Nicolas, marquis de Bussy-Rabutin: (titlepages in *red* and black) Les / *lettres* / de messire / *Roger de Rabutin* / comte de Bussy, / Lieutenant General des [Des for iii and iv] Arme'es / Du [du for iii and iv] Roi, et Mestre de Camp Ge- / neral [Gene- / ral for iii and iv] de la Cavalerie Françoi- / se et Etrangere. [Françoise et / Etrangere. for iii and iv] / Troisiéme édition [edition for ii] avec les Réponses, & des nouvel- / les [nouvelles / for iii and iv] Lettres [lettre for ii] qui n'étoient pas dans les precedentes. / *Tome premier* [*second, troisie'me, quatrie'me*]. / [woodcut decorations: symmetrical basket of flowers, same for all volumes] / *A Paris*. / Chez Florentin Pierre Delaulne [Florentin et Pierre Delaulne for ii, iii and iv]. / [rule] / *M. DCC*. [for i and ii; *M. DCCII*. for iii and iv]

12°, i: 1 pl (titlepage) + 2 ff. (2 + 2 pp.) + 1-424 pp.
 ii: 1 f. (titlepage) + 5-306 + 2 ff. (4) pp.
 iii: 1 f. (titlepage) + 5-336 + 6 ff. (12) pp.
 iv: 1 f. (titlepage) + 3-396 + 6 ff. (12) pp.

Tom. 2.　　　*Évelina*

J'ignore, Monsieur de quelles espérences vous parlez ;

ÉVELINA,

ROMAN

Nouvellement traduit et rédigé avec
beaucoup de soin d'après l'Anglois
de Miss Burney.

TOME SECOND.

A PARIS,

Chez Leprieur, Libraire, rue
Savoie, N° 12.

L'an IV de la République franç.

No 58: Burney d'Arblay, *Evelina*, 1796, t.2

Commentary: The first two pages are an 'Avertissement', the next two, a 'Table'. The last sets of pages in vols ii-iv are tables. The text of vols ii and iii begins with p.5, which is A2r. No leaves are missing, for the frontispiece illustrations at the head of vols i-iii are part of the pertinent gatherings. There are catchwords on every page. The signatures are numbered in arabic, further indicating a non-Parisian printing, and thus a piracy of some sort.

The short 'avertissement', presumably by the publisher (or possibly editor), runs as follows: 'On peut dire, sans dessein d'imposer à personne, que le stile simple, noble, délicat, & naturel qu'on trouve dans les Lettres de feu Monsieur le Comte de Bussy, les rendent des Originaux en ce genre d'écrire, où personne n'a encore atteint. Un autre agrément unique de ce recueil, c'est qu'il est diversifié par des réponses qui ont aussi leurs beautez, & qui en donnant l'intelligence des Lettres de Monsieur de Bussy, font voir un commerce d'esprit fort amusant, & qui pourroit bien faire regreter au Public comme au Libraire, qu'il n'ait pas duré davantage'. But it did, in a sense, and other, augmented editions were published as the century progressed.

The first volume contains a portrait frontispiece by A. de Blois after Le Febure (signed). A similar engraving, bearing the same signatures, faces the titlepage to vol. iii. At the head of vol. ii is a nice engraving, unsigned, depicting Mercury flying over a city harbour. In his left hand is a sheet bearing the title 'Lettres de Cour'. At the bottom there seems to be an erased caption. Evidently the engravings at the head of vols i, ii and iii are included in the pagination. (It was sometimes the custom to use the first leaf of a gathering for an engraving, especially in Germanic countries.)

I have located what appear to be two other copies of this edition, at the Johns Hopkins University (NUC) and in the BL (10910.aaa.24). I have included the above volumes because they are not listed in bibliographies dealing with prose fiction, in Charrier, or in César Rouben, *Bussy-Rabutin, épistolier* (Paris 1974). Cioranescu (17e siècle) makes no mention of a 'troisième édition' and cites a 'Paris, 1700. 12°. 4 vol.' edition (i.499, no. 17101).

These volumes contain several items of interest to the 'genre romanesque'. In volume i: *Les Remèdes contre l'amour: imitation d'Ovide*, which is a piece in alternating prose and verse (i.51-61). This was actually an adaptation which Bussy-Rabutin enclosed with a letter to Mme de Sévigné dated 7 September 1668, according to this edition. In the Pléiade edition of Mme de Sévigné's correspondence, the following: 'Cependant je vous envoye une imitation des Remedes d'amour d'Ovide, qui ne vous déplaira pas. Il faut bien s'amuser.' (above edition, i.50), has been replaced by 'Il n'est pas difficile de savoir mes sentiments sur le sujet de feue mon *Iris*; je ne cache guère ni mon amour ni ma haine. Mais il faudrait se parler pour tout dire; ce sera un jour la matière de quelques-unes de nos conversations, qui ne sera pas la moins agréable' (Roger Duchêne ed., *Correspondance*, Paris 1972, i.104). The Lalanne edition of Bussy-Rabutin's correspondence presents another variant of the letter as transcribed in the 1700-1702 edition (Ludovic Lalanne ed., *Correspondance de Roger de Rabutin, comte de Bussy avec sa famille et ses amis, 1666-1693*, n. éd. [...], Paris 1858-1859, 6 vols, i.131, no. 129).

Next is a *Fragment de Pétrone* containing the *Histoire de la matrone d'Ephèse* which accompanied a letter to his friend Corbinelli, actually sent care of Mme de Sévigné, dated 20 August 1677 (i.232-36). The text of the letter presents several variants from that given by Duchêne. And the end of Duchêne's text reads: '[...] car vous savez que naturellement il me fait du bien, et du mal par complaisance' (ii.531). The 1700-1702 edition gives: 'Car j'ai dans la tête, heureusement pour ma consolation, que naturellement il me feroit du bien & du mal sur les mauvais offices qu'on me rend auprés de lui. [paragraph] Je vous envoye une traduction de la Matrône d'Ephese. Le grand nombre des traductions qui en ont paru, ne m'ont point rebuté' (i.232). This is also to be found in Lalanne, iii.331, no. 1136. (Lalanne dates the letter to Corbinelli to the 21st August.) The *Matrone d'Ephèse* is, of course, a fragment from Caius Petronius Arbiter's *Satiricon*.

Then, in the next volume, the editor included Bussy-Rabutin's famous, whimsical 'translations' of some of the Abelard and Heloïse material, which had actually been sent to Mme de Sévigné with a letter dated 12 April 1687 (ii.45-69; also Lalanne, vi.61, no. 2336 and vi.62-63, no. 2338 for Bussy-Rabutin's reply to Mme de Sévigné). This material comprises a brief, historical introduction, Heloïse's first letter to Abelard, the latter's reply, and a reply from Heloïse to Abelard. None of this is to be found in Duchêne's edition, so Bussy-Rabutin's letter to Mme de Sévigné, and the latter's reply are worth transcribing, even if the possibility exists that they be apocryphal: 'A Chaseu, ce 12. Avril 1687. / Il n'est pas, ma chere Cousine, que vous n'ayez ouï parler d'Abelard & d'Heloïsse; mais je ne croi pas que vous ayez jamais vu de traduction de leurs lettres: pour moi je n'en connois point. Je me suis amusé à en traduire quelques-unes qui m'ont donné beaucoup de plaisir. Je n'ai jamais vu un plus beau Latin, sur tout celui de la Religieuse, ni plus d'amour & d'esprit qu'elle en a. Si vous ne lui en trouvez point, ma chere Cousine, ce sera ma faute. Je vous prie que notre Ami Corbinelli vous les lise en tiers avec la belle Comtesse [Mme de Grignan], & je reglerai l'estime de mon amusement sur les sentimens que vous en aurez tous trois' (ii.44). And here is his cousin's reply: 'A Paris, ce 18. Avril 1687. / Nous croyons, la belle Comtesse & moi, que vous avez tout au moins donné de l'esprit à Heloïsse, tant elle en a. Notre ami Corbinelli qui connoît l'Original, dit que non, mais que votre François a des délicatesses & des tours que le Latin n'a pas; & sur sa parole nous n'avons pas cru le devoir apprendre pour avoir plus de plaisir à cette lecture, car nous sommes persuadez, comme lui, que rien n'est au dessus de ce que vous écrivez' (ii.70; also Lalanne, vi.62-63, no. 2338).

Volume ii also contains a *Traduction d'un fragment de Théophile* (pp.195-98), which had also been enclosed with a letter to his famous cousin, Mme de Sévigné (2 December 1692). Bussy explains: 'Les petits contes ne vous déplaisent pas, ma chere Cousine. En voici un que Theophile a écrit en Latin, qui m'a paru assez bon pour être traduit, & pour vous réjoüir' (ii.194). *Larisse* is a much shortened adaptation of a Latin text by Théophile de Viau first published in 1621, in the *Œuvres*. (See Duchêne, iii.1616, commentary on no. 1272.) Duchêne also remarks that Bussy's letter to Mme de Sévigné, and her reply (10 December 1692) 'sont peut-être, comme beaucoup de textes analogues dans l'édition, de simples artifices de présentation ajoutés après coup par Amé-Nicolas [marquis de Bussy-Rabutin] pour introduire les œuvres de son père' (*loc. cit.*).

The three pieces are set off from the main text of the letters, with their own head titles. They were first published in 1697, date of the first edition of the *Lettres de messire Roger de Rabutin, comte de Bussy* (Charrier p.606, no. 50; Lever p.248; BN Z.14556-57-58-59).

It might here be mentioned that the Messkatalog records an edition of Bussy-Rabutin's letters which does not appear to exist in the BL or BN, and is not listed in the NUC: 'Les plus belles lettres de Mess. Roger de *Rabutin* Comte de *Bussy*. Nouv. Edit. augmentée de courtes notes par D. E. *Choffin*. 8. à Halle, à la maison des Orphelins', OM 1764, p.482.

Incipits: (*Les Remèdes contre l'amour*) 'L'Amour n'eut pas lû le titre de cet ouvrage, qu'aussi-tôt alarmé'.

(*Fragment de Pétrone*) 'Eumolpe qui venoit de mettre la paix parmi nous, voulut entretenir notre gayeté par des contes agréables.'

(*Histoire de la matrone d'Ephèse*) 'Il y avoit autrefois à Ephese une Matrône d'une si grande réputation'.

(Heloïse to Abelard) 'Il y a quelque temps que l'on m'apporta par hazard une lettre que vous écriviez à un de vos amis.'

(*Traduction d'un fragment de Théophile*) 'Larisse aimoit à conter & contoit bien. Un jour'.

60

Cailhava de l'Estendoux (or d'Estendoux): *Contes en vers et en prose*, 1798

Jean-François Cailhava de l'Estendoux (or d'Estendoux), 1730-1813: Les contes / en vers et en prose / de feu / l'abbé de Colibri, / ou / le soupé, / conte / composé [compose for ii] de mille et un contes. / Tout conteur est un sot / S'il n'embellit la chose en esquivant le mot. / Partie I [II]. / [rule] / Les Estampes sont de la main de l'Auteur. / [rule] / A Paris, / de l'imprimerie de Didot jeune. / L'an VI.

18°, i: 1 f. (halftitle) + 1 f. (1 p.) + 1 f. (titlepage) + [7]-10, [11]-16, [17]-22, [23]-30, [31]-155, [156]-157 pp.

ii: 1 f. (halftitle) + 1 f. (1 p.) + 1 f. (titlepage) + [7]-144, [145]-148, [149]-152 pp.

Commentary: The first two leaves in each volume are a half titlepage and a description of engravings. Together with the titlepages, these form the first three leaves of the first gatherings. The half titlepages bear: 'Les contes / en vers et en prose / de feu / l'abbé de Colibri, / ou / le soupé.' The versos of the half titlepages bear: 'A Paris, / Chez P. N. F. Didot, imprimeur-libraire, / quai des Augustins, n.° 22.' Following the order of the pagination recorded above, the contents consist of i: no. 1, 'Introduction'; 2, 'Epître dédicatoire à madame de ....'; 3, 'Envoi'; 4, 'Avant-propos'; 5, 'Le soupé, conte composé de mille et un contes'; 'Epilogue'. ii: no. 1, 'Le soupé [...]'; 2, 'Postface'; 3, 'Table' (for both volumes). MMF include this work with the reeditions of *Le soupé des petits-maîtres* (see the following entry) after the BN copy, Gay and Quérard, with no explanation

(70.32). Quérard lists '[...] ou le soupé. Paris, Didot le jeune, 1797, 2 vol. in-8' (ii.15b). Gay lists 2 vols in-18° (iii, col.1140).

I list this work to comment on the authorship and because there are two leaves missing from the BN copy. (There is also a copy listed in Krauss-Fontius, no. 4530, with a location for the Thüringische Landesbibliothek Weimar; no details are given.)

The only other complete copy of this edition I know of is in The Humanities Research Centre at the University of Texas, Austin. No copy examined contains any illustrations, but my copy and the HRC's have descriptions of the two engravings that were supposed to have accompanied this work, but which were probably never executed. The descriptions are as follows: 'Estampe du tome I. Le Dessin offre son crayon à l'Auteur. La Gravure lui présente son burin. Il les remercie par un signe de tête obligeant, et leur montre sa plume dont il écrit: "Anch'-io son pittore."' 'Estampe du tome II. Vénus s'est élancée des bras d'une Naïade sur un lit de gazon, qu'elle presse mollement. Les Grâces la couvrent des fleurs qui naissent autour d'elle; et la Volupté, en les effeuillant sur mille charmes divers, agace le Desir. Sur la droite, le timide Adonis, poussé par l'Amour vers un myrte fleuri, n'ose faire un pas pour s'en couronner. Il respire à peine; son ame et ses yeux jouissent délicieusement. A gauche, en opposition, un Satyre hideux, ivre de luxure, et les deux joues enflées, voudrait, d'un souffle impur, enlever jusqu'à la plus petite des feuilles qui s'opposent à l'avidité de ses regards. Dans le lointain, Diane, feignant d'être scandalisée, rougit, porte la main sur son front, écarte les doigts, lorgne Adonis, mesure de l'œil le Satyre, et entraîne Endymion dans un taillis toufu.' To my knowledge, Cailhava never applied himself to the art of engraving. (He is not listed or cited in Cohen, Bénézit, or in Reynaud that I could ascertain.)

Concerning the authorship of this work: it is a different version of *Le Soupé*, containing a large number of variants of varying degrees of importance, deletions and a considerable amount of additions, notably the verse which is generally not to be found in the original. Some of the poetry is quite amusing: 'Le cul prophète', 'Le cordelier escamoteur, ou la fille métamorphosée en moulin', 'Le pucelage nageur', etc. The latter anyway appeared separately in 1766 (BNC, Quérard, Cior., etc.), and it seems likely that the others too were published before 1798, probably in various compendia. There are no explanations to be found with the work.

In his preface to the *Contes de l'abbé de Colibri* (Paris 1881), Charles Monselet mentions the 'mystification' of the engravings, further reporting that 'l'édition dont nous nous sommes servis pour donner celle-ci est l'édition de Didot jeune (an VI), imprimée sur très beau papier fort, et qui prouve que le membre de l'Institut, successeur de Fontanes, bien que continuant à garder l'anonyme, ne reniait pas les péchés fripons et inoffensifs de sa jeunesse' (p.I). The thing is that Monselet gives the text of the *first* version of the *Soupé*, and not that of 'l'an VI'. Two possibilities exist: that there was indeed an 'an VI' edition of the *Soupé*, with a modified title and unchanged contents, or that Monselet deliberately constructed his own mystification.

Monselet is the likely source for inaccuracies on the part of later bibliographers and scholars who have claimed that the *Contes en vers et en prose* are the same as the *Soupé*. Gay remarks that *Le Soupé* was published in 1782, in Cazin's *Bibliothèque amusante*, comprising 'une petite édition remaniée et augmentée de quelques contes en vers' (iii, col.1140). Gay also mentions the an VI, Didot edition, 'augmentée de plusieurs chapitres et de plusieurs contes, et, en même temps, élaguée de quelques longueurs; elle est jolie et recherchée' (*loc. cit.*). And Monglond lists what *appears* to be the edition described here, yet in-octavo (in the section devoted to 'La littérature nouvelle: œuvres nouvelles'; no pagination given; transcription of the titlepage abbreviated, etc., iv, col.663).

Incipits: ('Introduction') 'Il est midi. Un Abbé assez semblable à une poupée de quatre pieds de haut'.

('Epître dédicatoire', in verse and prose) 'Toi qu'Hébé, que Cypris verraient avec envie'.

('Envoi') 'L'abbé va au Palais-Royal. Le chevalier de ***, jeune mousquetaire'.

('Avant-propos') 'Le Chevalier s'empressa de joindre l'Abbé.'

(chapter I, 'Le double qui-pro-quo') 'Nous étions à la fin du mois d'août'.

61

Cailhava de l'Estendoux (or d'Estendoux): *Le Souper des petits-maîtres*, ca.1771

Jean-François Cailhava de l'Estendoux (or d'Estendoux), 1730-1813: Le soupé / des / petits-maitres, / ouvrage / moral. / [rule] / Premiere [Seconde] partie. / [rule] / [i: woodcut decoration of roses on a mantel of sorts; ii: putti embracing over two glowing hearts pierced by an arrow, further decoration] / [double rule] / A Londres.

12°, i: 1 f. (titlepage) + [iij]-vj, [vij]-x, [xj]-xvj, [xvij]-xxiv, [25]-(141), [142]-(144) pp.

ii: 1 f. (titlepage) + [iij]-iv, [5]-(96), (97)-(100), (101)-(103) pp.

Commentary: Most bibliographers give the date of the first edition as ca. 1772 (but see MMF, 70.32, who list it for 1770 after Gay). For example, Quérard has 'Soupir [*sic*] (le), ouvrage moral. Londres et Paris, Bastien, 1772, 2 part. in-12' (ii.16a). The *Catalogue hebdomadaire*, 'Catalogue des livres nouveaux', for 8 July 1771, lists 'Souper (le); Ouvrage moral: 1 vol. in-8 br[oché]. A Londres, & à Paris, chez Le Jay, L. [libraire] rue Saint-Jacques' (1771, no. 23, art. 16). Thus 1771 seems to me the most probable first date of publication. It might be noted that the *Catalogue des livres nouveaux*, for 14 March 1772, lists 'Soupir [*sic*] (le); Ouvrage moral: 2 Part. in-12 Br. A Londres, & à Paris, chez Bastien, L. rue du Petit-Lion, Fauxbourg Saint-Germain', in no.11. It is impossible to tell the date of the edition described here. A pencilled note on the second end paper reads: 'Vers 1770'; another note in pencil to the right of the imprint on the titlepage of volume i indicates 1782. (Both appear to be modern.) There are no clues to be had from the binding. In any case, these two volumes were not printed in London.

The four preliminary pieces in vol. i are: 1. 'Introduction'; 2. 'Épitre dédicatoire a madame de....'; 3. 'Envoi'; 4. 'Avant-propos'. The second volume is preceded by an 'Avis au lecteur', and pp.(97)-(100) are a 'Post-face'. Both volumes have tables at the end.

Incipits: ('Introduction') 'Il est onze heures du matin. Un Abbé, assez semblable à une poupée de quatre pieds de haut'.

('Epître dédicatoire') 'Toi, qu'Hébé, que Cypris verraient avec envie'.

('Envoi') 'L'abbé va au Palais-Royal. Il est abordé par le Chevalier de ***, jeune Mousquetaire'.

('Avant-propos') 'Le Chevalier s'empressa de joindre l'Abbé.'

(chapter I: 'Joli soupé manqué') 'Nous étions à la fin du mois d'Août.'

62

Cailleau *et al.*: *Lettres et épîtres amoureuses d'Héloïse et d'Abeilard*, ca.1780

André Charles Cailleau, editor and author (1731-1798), with Roger de Bussy-Rabutin (1618-1693), Pierre François Godard (or Godart) de Beauchamps (1689-1761), Charles Pierre Colardeau (1732-1776), Claude Joseph Dorat (1734-1780), Aimé Ambroise Joseph Feutry (1720-1789), Louis Sébastien Mercier (1740-1814), Sébastien Marie Mathurin Gazon-Dourxigné (?-1784), Bernard Joseph Saurin (1706-1781), Jean Baptiste Guys, Alexander Pope (1688-1744) *et al.*, and Abelard (1079-1142) and Heloïse (1101-1164) [possibly!]: Les lettres / et / épîtres amoureuses / d'Héloïse / et d'Abeilard, / traduites librement en Vers et en Prose, / Par MM. de Bussy Rabutin, de Beauchamps, / Pope, Colardeau, Dorat, Feutry, / Mercier, G**. Dourxigné, Saurin, &c. / précédées / De la Vie, des Amours & Infortunes de ces célebres / & malheureux Epoux, par M. C**. / Nouvelle édition / Corrigée & augmentée de plusieurs Lettres & Epîtres, / & d'une Préface Historique; par le même. / Tome premier [second]. / [woodcut decoration: flying angel (or cupid) bearing swaddled bouquet, rays in background; same for both volumes; traces of a signature, Papillon's; see Montesquieu, *Considérations...*, 1750; both titlepage vignettes are miror images of each other] / [rule] / Au Paraclet.

12°, i: 1 f. (titlepage) + iij-xiv, [xv] + [1]-61, 62-197 pp.

ii: 2 pl (titlepage and halftitle for Cailleau's translation, in prose, of Pope's heroïd, with an 'avis' verso) + (another halftitle), 2 (an 'Avant-propos' on the verso of the halftitle), [3]-211, 212-214 pp. (The first two pages of text are, as indicated, a halftitle, with a paginated 'avant-propos' verso).

Commentary: The items contained in vol. i, following the pagination recorded above, are a 'Préface historique et apologétique' (including a letter by Voltaire, dated 13 April 1774, Best.D18888, to Cailleau); an unpaginated 'Table'; 'La vie, les amours et les infortunes d'Abeilard et d'Héloïse'; then the various pieces in prose and verse. The second volume contains further material relating to Abelard and Heloïse, with a 'Table' (pp.212-14) at the end. Vol. i.[j]-[xvj] consists of eight preliminary folios, [a6] + [b2] (including the titlepage). Then follow A6, B6 to R2, S1. Vol. ii has two preliminary leaves (including the titlepage), then A12-S4, T1. (There are numerous half titlepages scattered throughout.)

The above volumes are considerably different from BN Z13820-21, are not listed in the BNC, BLC or NUC and differ in all likelihood from the entries to be found in Charrier's bibliography (nos 88 and 90, especially from the latter). For further information regarding this interesting collection, see the 1796, 3 vol. edition described below. I do not know when the above volumes were printed, so, following the tradition of bibliographers referring to the 'Paraclet' editions of the last part of the eighteenth century, I hazard ca. 1780. The signatures are numbered in lower-case roman, which would indicate a Parisian printing, a probability supported by type, rules, catchword frequency and woodcut ornaments.

Incipits: ('Lettre d'Abeilard à son ami', p.63) 'Après le triste récit que vous m'avez fait des malheurs'.

('Lettre d'Héloïse à Abeilard', p.75) 'Il y a quelque tems que l'on m'apporta par hasard une lettre que vous écriviez à un de vos amis'.

63

Cailleau *et al.*: *Lettres et épîtres amoureuses d'Héloïse et d'Abeilard*, 1780

André Charles Cailleau, editor and author (1731-1798), with Roger de Bussy-Rabutin (1618-1693), Pierre François Godard (or Godart) de Beauchamps (1689-1761), Charles Pierre Colardeau (1732-1776), Claude Joseph Dorat (1734-1780), Aimé Ambroise Joseph Feutry (1720-1789), Louis Sébastien Mercier (1740-1814), Sébastien Marie Mathurin Gazon-Dourxigné (?-1784), Bernard Joseph Saurin (1706-1781), Jean Baptiste Guys, Alexander Pope (1688-1744) *et al.*, and Abelard (1079-1142) and Heloïse (1101-1164) [possibly!]: Lettres / et / épîtres amoureuses / d'Héloïse / et d'Abeilard. / [rule] / Nouvelle Édition. / [rule] / Tome premier [second]. / [woodcut ornament: bouquet of three flowers, same for both volumes] / A Londres. / [decorative rule] / M. DCC. LXXX.

18°, i: 2 ff. (halftitle and titlepages) + [v]-xxiv + [1]-201 pp.
ii: 2 ff. (halftitle and titlepages) + v-viij + [1]-240 pp.

Commentary: The preliminaries in vol. i are a 'Préface historique et apologétique' which ends with an extract from a letter by Voltaire (Ferney, 13 April 1774). See the preceding entry for further information.

This edition is not listed in Charrier (especially p.609, no.82 and no.85).

There are pretty portrait frontispieces, one for each volume, unsigned and captioned. Vol. i's is that of Abelard, and ii's that of Heloise. (Heloise's portrait is after a picture by Gardner.)

The volume halftitles read 'Lettres / et / épitres amoureuses / d'Héloïse / et d'Abeilard. / [rule] / Tome Ier [second]. / [rule]'. Some of the sheets are of blue-tinted paper.

This collection contains several pieces of prose fiction. Indeed, the 'original' correspondance between Abelard and Heloise is probably not original at all.

For further information, see the other Cailleau entries in this bibliography, especially the 1796 edition below.

Incipits: ('Lettre d'Abeilard à son ami [Filinte or Philinte]', i.[63]) 'Après le triste récit que vous m'avez fait / des malheurs'.

('Lettre d'Héloïse à Abeilard', i.[75]) 'Il y a quelque temps que l'on m'apporta / par hasard une lettre que vous écriviez à un / de vos amis.'

('Lettre amoureuse d'Héloïse a Abeilard', Pope's heroid rendered into prose, ii.[1]) 'Dans cette solitude paisible, séjour où / la contemplation tourne constamment'.

64

Cailleau *et al.*: *Lettres et épîtres amoureuses d'Héloïse et d'Abeilard*, 1796

André Charles Cailleau (ed. and author) 1731-1798, with Roger de Bussy-Rabutin (1618-1693), Pierre François Godard (or Godart) de Beauchamps (1689-1761), Charles Pierre Colardeau (1732-1776), Claude Joseph Dorat (1734-1780), Aimé Ambroise Joseph Feutry (1720-1789), Louis Sébastien Mercier (1740-1814), Sébastien Marie Mathurin Gazon-Dourxigné (?-1784), Bernard Joseph Saurin (1706-1781), Jean Baptiste Guys, Alexander Pope (1688-1744), and Abelard (1079-1142) and Heloïse (1101-1164) [possibly!]: Lettres / et / épitres [ii, iii: epitres] amoureuses / d'Héloïse [ii, iii: d'Heloïse] / et d'Abeilard, / Précédées de la Vie, des Amours et Infortunes de / ces célèbres et malheureux Époux. / Nouvelle édition augmentée; / par / A. C. Cailleau. / Tome I [II, III]. / [rule] / A Paris, / de l'imprimerie de Didot jeune. / M. DCC. XCVI.

18°, i: 2 ff. (halftitle and titlepage) + [5]-8, [9]-44, [45]-123, [124]-229, [230] pp.

    ii: 2 ff. (halftitle and titlepage) + [5]-216 pp.

    iii: 3 ff. (halftitle, titlepage and halftitle) + [7]-163, [164] pp.

Commentary: The pagination reflects various preliminary pieces and halftitles, some with material on the versos. The last pages, vols i and iii, are tables. This material is not listed in MMF. Since it contains quite a few pieces of prose fiction (indeed the authenticity of the original Abelard and Heloïse correspondence is itself more than subject to question), I have included this edition, which exists in no public library that I know of. The only approximation of a listing I have been able to find is in Cohen, col.642. His titlepage transcription extends only to 'nouvelle édition', with no mention of Cailleau. His imprint is Paris: Didot, 1796, 3 vols in-18, Cohen also notes that there are two portraits and four illustrations by Quéverdo, engraved by Villerey.

There are six engravings as follows in the volumes described here: i, frontispiece portrait of Abelard, by Villerey and a second illustration, facing p.73, by Villerey after Quéverdo; ii, two illustrations by Villerey, after Quéverdo for the first (p.78) and no artist mentioned for the second (p.147; this is actually a copy of the fine engraving designed by Eisen and engraved by Marillier that accompanied the first edition of Colardeau's imitation of Pope's heroid, 1766);

iii, frontispiece portrait of Heloïse by Villerey (no artist mentioned, but this is a portrait after Gardner; a similar engraving is reproduced in Charrier, pl. 28, facing p.482) and a second engraving by Villerey after Quéverdo (p.159). All of these have captions, some quite long, which I have not transcribed.

The volume half titlepages bear: 'Lettres et epitres / amoureuses / d'Héloïse / et / d'Abeilard. / Tome I [II, III].' The versos of these half titlepages indicate: 'A Paris, / chez Lepetit, quai des Augustins, N°. 32. / L'an IV.-1796.' The verso of the first half titlepage also has an announcement stating that there is an ever increasing number of piracies, so the publisher has signed copies 'sorties de nos presses'. This copy bears no signature. The 'Avis' on the verso of the first titlepage mentions that 'Les éditions in-12 et in-18 que nous publions, sont beaucoup plus amples et plus correctes que les précédentes' (i.[4]). There are numerous half titlepages throughout the three volumes which I have not bothered to transcribe.

Those interested in the first editions of the extensive material contained in these three volumes should consult Charlotte Charrier's very interesting work, especially pp.606-10. The first edition of the Cailleau collection appeared in 1774 (Charrier no. 82), and was republished several times. (Charrier makes no mention of this edition.)

Incipit: ('Extrait de la lettre d'Abeilard à Philinte son ami') 'Après le triste récit que vous m'avez fait des malheurs que vous avez éprouvés'.

65

Champion de Pontalier: *Variétés d'un philosophe provincial*, 1767

François Champion, called Champion de Pontalier (1731-1812): Variétés / d'un philosophe / provincial, / Par M. Ch..... le jeune. / [rule] / Premiere [Seconde] partie. / [rule] / [composite woodcut ornament, different for each volume] / A Bruxelles, / Chez la Veuve Vasse; / A Paris, / Chez H. C. De Hansy, Libraire, / rue Saint-Jacques. / [double rule] / M. DCC. LXVII.

12°, i: 2 pl + 2 ff. (2 + 1 pp.) + [1]-273 pp.
    ii: 1 pl + 1 f. (1 p.) + [1]-224 pp. + 2 ff. (4 pp.)

Commentary: Vol. i has a halftitle for 'Variétés / d'un philosophe / provincial.' (There is no halftitle for vol. ii.) The pagination reflects a two-page 'Avis au lecteur' at the head of vol. i; then follows a 'table'. Vol. ii is preceded by a table as well. At the very end is a list of 'Livres nouveaux qui se trouvent chez le même Libraire'. This is the first edition of this work. It is marginal to the 'genre romanesque', consisting of philosophical discussions, among other things. (It is not mentioned in MMF.) However, there are two sections, one per volume, dealing with portraits and character sketches (i.[51]-96 and ii.[35]-88). Most of these set fictitious characters on stage. A couple even have titles and might be considered short stories, for example *L'Avare et l'emplâtre, fable* (i.84-88), *Anecdote égyptienne* (ii.82-88).

My copy differs from the copies to be found in the BN and the Royal library of Belgium – no copies in the NUC or BLC – in that the the letter of the first signature of each gathering is preceded by an asterisk (* A[1], * B[1], etc.). I am grateful to Professor Hasquin for checking the Brussels copy for me (VB37379/a). I do not know why my copy has asterisks. If the reason were that copies meant for the Parisian (or Brussels) trade were to be so differentiated, surely the Brussels copy would differ from the BN copy? As this book was in the press, Professor Wallace Kirsop was kind enough to share with me the fact that asterisks were often used in this way to differentiate special-paper copies from those printed on ordinary paper. That is probably the case here. Furthermore, Chapman remarks that the 'appearance of a star or dagger does not necessarily imply a cancel. These signs were used also instead of "figures" (to identify the press used to print a sheet or a forme). They were used, too, to distinguish printings' (etc.; p.23, note).

Incipits: ('De l'éducation') 'On ne considere point assez les enfans chez la plûpart des nations.'

('Caracteres et portraits', vol. i, no. 1) 'Clitus sonne: aussitôt deux grands pages entrent dans son appartement'.

('L'Avare et l'emplâtre, fable') 'En comptant ses écus, un avare avait oublié parmi les avantages qu'ils pouvaient lui procurer'.

('Anecdote egyptienne') 'On trouva à quelque distance du Caire, parmi les débris d'une colonne'.

66

Chauveau: *Les Quatre saisons*, 1800

J. Chauveau: Les / quatre saisons, / poëme; / par J. Chauveau, / Membre du Lycée du Département / de la Vienne. / [rule] / Je viens de leur richesse avertir les humains. / St.-Lambert. / [rule] / Suivi / d'un petit mot aux dames, / et d'un dialogue sur le / célibat. / [rule] / Allez mes vers. / [rule] / A Chatelleraud, / Chez P. J. B. Guimbert, Imprimeur. / An VIII.

12°: 1 f. (titlepage) + [iij]-vij + [1]-197 pp.

Commentary: This volume contains:

1. a 'Discours préliminaire';
2. the *Quatre saisons* proper (pp.[1]-177);
3. a poem, 'Un petit mot aux dames, lu au lycée des sciences et des arts de Poitiers, à une séance publique' (pp.[179]-186);
4. another poem, 'Dialogue sur le célibat' (pp.[187]-197).

I could find no trace of this work anywhere, including such contemporary sources as the *Journal typographique et bibliographique*, *Journal général de la littérature de France*, etc. And I do not know who Chauveau was. By using a line from Saint-Lambert for his epigraph, the author deliberately associated his work with that of the author of the famous verse adaptation of Thomson's *Four seasons*. (For a hitherto unrecorded edition of a prose translation of Thomson's *Seasons*, see below.) Chauveau's *Quatre saisons* is a prose-poem of sorts, a series of meditations à la Gessner in style, interwoven with plot lines dealing with fictitious characters (Mélidor, Araminte, Lycas, Philis, etc.). The author also puts his own family on stage. Chauveau invokes Gessner, Florian and Fénelon (pp.149-50). All this is set to the background of the four seasons and change. 'Winter', the last of the seasons, ends with a melancholy reference to current troubled times. (Earlier there had been praise of Napoleon, pp.61-62.)

There are corrections in my copy (contemporary or early nineteenth-century binding), both in the prose and verse, which might be by Chauveau himself. (The only previous ownership record is a later, engraved bookplate for the 'Bibliothèque du Château des Ormes'.)

Incipit: 'Je laisse aux voix fortes à emboucher la trompette retentissante de la renommée'.

67

Chavigny: *La Religieuse cavalier*, 1717

François de Chavigny (sometimes Chauvigny) de La Bretonnière (?-1698): (*red and black titlepage*) La / *religieuse* / cavalier, / *epoux et chanoine*. / Histoire Galante & Tragique. / [woodcut decoration of a sphere] / *A Cologne,* / Chez Pierre le Jeune. / [rule] / *M. DCC. XVII.*

12°: 1 pl (titlepage) + 2 ff. (4 pp.) + 1-138 pp.

Commentary: The first four pages comprise a dedicatory letter to the prince of Naussau, Henri Casimir, signed 'de Chavigny'. This novel first appeared in 1682 (Lever, p.369), and went through several editions. Conlon lists the first edition for 1692, an edition not listed in Lever (ii.41, no.5669). However, the location given by Lever is for the Royal Library at The Hague and the 1682 book could easily have escaped Conlon's attention. The one described here is not to be found in the NUC, BLC or BNC.

Gay seems to list this edition under the title of 'La Religieuse cavalier, mémoires galants' (under the first edition) and then again, as a separate entry (implying a different work) under the title of 'La Religieuse, épouse et chanoine' (iii, col.995). He further indicates, for the latter entry, that 'Cologne' is a false imprint and that the book was actually printed in Paris. Weller has the following somewhat enigmatic entry under the date of 1717: 'Religieuse, La, cavalier; mémoires galants (par de Chavigny). Cologne' (p.83; Weller reports the place of publication as printed, but offers no alternative). Gay also mentions that the 1717 edition is illustrated. Quite possibly we are dealing with a different work, or at least two different editions for 1717. Yet the incipit recorded here matches that given by Lever. (Understandably, Jones has no entry for *La Religieuse cavalier*.)

Incipit: 'L'Europe étoit calme, Mars & Bellone las de semer le carnage & l'horreur, avoient rendu aux délices d'une vie rustique & tranquile, un de leurs plus braves Favoris.'

68

Chevrier: *Le Colporteur*, ca.1762

Antoine François Chevrier (1721-1762): Le / colporteur, / histoire morale / et critique, / par / M. de Chevrier. / Des jeunes gens d'un ton, d'une stupidité... / Des femmes d'un caprice & d'une fausseté... / Des Ouvrages vantés, qui n'ont ni pieds ni têtes, / Des Protégés si bas, des Protecteurs si bêtes, / Des réputations on ne sait pas pourquoi, / Tant de petits talens où je n'ai pas de foi.... / Gresset, Com. du Méch. / [woodcut decoration of flowers] / A Londres, / Chez Jean Nourse, / [double rule] / L'An de la Vérité.

12°: 1 f. (titlepage) + [3]-6, [7]-12, [13]-(216), [217]-(224), (225)-(228) pp.

Commentary: This very popular satirical work went through many editions. I have checked the above copy against the copies to be found in the British Library and the BN, and mine is different (BL: 12512.bb.22; BN: Li3.28D, Li3.28C, Li3.28B, Li3.28A, Li3.28, Z17213). It seems hardly credible that all these editions appeared during the same year as that of the first edition (1762, MMF 62.11), so it is impossible to date my copy accurately. What seems to be the case is that the various publishers simply copied the date of the preceding editions, 'L'An de la Vérité', since that is in keeping with the contents. Moreover, many of the scandals reported do seem true. The one major difference between the various editions is that Chevrier's name boldly appears on the titlepages of some; on others, a prudent discretion seemed to the publishers the wiser course to follow. In any case, Chevrier died in 1762, so it would not have made much difference to him.

For the dating of *Le Colporteur* and further bibliographical information concerning the editions, see the references given in MMF 62.11. Weller has the following entry: 'Colporteur, Le, histoire morale et critique par M. de Chevrier. Londres, J. Nourse (Bruxelles) [1752]; n. éd. ib. 1762' (p.131). See the end of this commentary. Quérard erroneously gives 1753 as the date of the first edition (ii.186). It is highly unlikely that all editions of the *Colporteur* were published in Brussels, if indeed the first one was. The volume described here was most certainly not printed in London and most likely not in Brussels, but I do not know where it appeared. The publisher obviously copied the imprint. What probably lent further credence to the false information given on the titlepage is the fact that John (or Jean) Nourse was a well known London bookdealer of that period (Plomer: 'bookseller and publisher in London, Lamb without Temple Bar, 1730(?)-1780 [...] Dealt in French literature, and made a feature of scientific works' p.183).

The contents are as follows: 1. 'Epître dédicatoire'; 2. 'Avertissement de l'auteur'; 3. 'Le Colporteur [...]'; 4. 'Postface servant de réponse à la lettre que le sieur Carraccioli [...]'; 5. 'Errata'.

To this edition and to those listed in MMF, I would add the following:

1. *Le Colporteur, histoire morale et ctitique* [*sic*], *par M. de Chevrier*. [...] A Londres, Chez Jean Nourse. L'An de la Vérité. 2 ff. (halftitle and titlepage) + 5-8, 9-12, (13)-(161), (162)-(169), (170)-(172) pp. in-12°. BL: 1607/2655. This edition could very well have been printed in Brussels and could thus conceivably be

the first, were one to place one's faith in Weller.

2. 'Le Colporteur. Histoire morale & critique par Mr. de *Chevrier*. 8. Francf. sur le Meyn, chez Knoch & Esslinger', Messkatalog, MM 1762, p.305. Heinsius, 1793 has 'Colporteur, le; histoire morale et critique, par Chevrier. 8. Francf. Esslinger. [1]762' (iv.484). Aside from the imprint indication, note the format. I have found no octavo *Colporteur* for that probable date.

Incipits: ('Epître dédicatoire') 'Monsieur *Parisot*, ci-devant Capucin de la Province de Lorraine'.

(*Le Colporteur*) 'Ah! c'est vous, Chevalier, dit la Marquise de *Sarmé*'.

69

Chevrier: *Histoire de la vie de H. Maubert*, 1761

François Antoine Chevrier (1721-1762): Histoire / de la vie / de / H. Maubert, / soi disant / chevalier de Gouvest, / gazettier a Bruxelles, / et auteur de plusieurs / libelles politiques. / [double rule] / Mise en lumiere pour l'utilité Publique. / [double rule] / A Londres, / Chez les Libraires associés. / [treble rule] / M. DCC. LXI.

8°: 1 f. (titleleaf) + 2 ff. (3pp.) + (7)-(54) pp.

Commentary: MMF list this work, which is a libellous 'life' of Maubert de Gouvest, with the date of 1763 (63.22). They state that Quérard and Gillet list an edition for 1761. Gillet, in his 'Notice historique et bibliographique sur Chevrier' (in *Mémoires de l'Académie de Stanislas*, 1863 [Nancy 1864]), mentions 'Londres (La Haye), 1761, 1 vol. in-12', in the author's collection (no. 51, p.285). To the sources listed by MMF, one must add Weller who lists it as follows: '[for 1761] Histoire de la vie de H. Maubert, soi-disant chevalier de Gouvest, Gazettier à Bruxelles [...] Londres [Bruxelles]; nouvelle éd. ib. 1763' (p.159).

The copy described here certainly settles the date of the first edition. (It must be borne in mind that Chevrier died in 1762, and there seems little likelihood that someone would have published such a work after his death.) Perhaps the 1761 edition was issued in duodecimo and in octavo, or perhaps there were two editions for that year. I see no reason to doubt Gillet's exactitude, especially in light of his general meticulousness. In support of there being two editions for 1761 is the fact that Weller and Gillet list two different, real places of publication. Although Weller is often inexact and does not list his sources, I am inclined to believe that the volume described here was printed in Brussels rather than in The Hague. (It was certainly not printed in London.)

The preface, the three preliminary pages titled an 'Avis de l'éditeur', opens with: 'Repandre des Libelles Satyriques, est presque toujours un Crime de Léze-Société, que la Misantropie, l'Envie ou la Vengeance fait commettre, & il n'est pas permis d'attaquer par un de ces motifs, qui que ce soit, fut-ce le moindre individu de l'Espece Humaine'. And that seems to be just what Chevrier, in his own inimitable fashion, proceded to do in the text, even if the 'éditeur' is careful to note: 'On louera l'exactitude avec laquelle on a ramassé les Anecdotes qui forment cette Histoire. On ne s'est pas permis la plus legere Addition. On n'a fait que debrouiller & mettre en ordre les differens Memoires qui ont été envoiés sur ce sujet'. Dubious tales and disclaimers have even been put in the notes! For a discussion of the contents, and their relationship to the real life of Maubert, see Enea Balmas, *Les 'Lettres iroquoises' de J.-H. Maubert de Gouvest* (Paris, Milan 1962), especially pp.8-18.

The *Histoire de la vie de H. Maubert* is not to be confused with *L'Espion, ou l'histoire du faux baron de Maubert*, by one Saint-Flour, first published in 1759 (Barbier ii, col.178c and MMF 59.23). There was another edition in or about 1762, unknown to modern bibliographers: 'L'Espion ou l'histoire du faux Baron Maubert. Nouv. edit. 8. Amst[erdam] et à Jena, chez J. Chr. Fischer' (Messkatalog, OM 1762, p.265; same information in Heinsius, 1793: iv.499).

Incipit: 'Henri Maubert est né à Rouen en Normandie'.

70

Chevrier: *Mémoires d'une honnête femme*, 1763

François Antoine Chevrier (1721-1762): Mémoires / d'une / honnéte femme, / écrits / par elle-méme, / et publiés / Par M. de Chévrier. / [rule] / Il en est jusqu'à trois que je pourrois citer. / DEsp. [Desp. for ii and iii] Sat. des F. / [rule] / Premiere [Seconde, Troisieme] partie. / [largely symmetrical woodcut decoration, same for all titlepages] / A Amsterdam, / Chez H. Constapel, Libraire. / M.DCC.LXIII, [M.DCC.LXIII. for iii]

12°, i: 1 f. (titlepage) + 1 f. (2 pp.) + [1]-58 pp.

ii: 1 f. (titlepage) + [61]-117 pp.

iii: 1 f. (titlepage) + [121]-191 pp.

Commentary: This book is continuously signed and paginated, and the text begins on f.A3. The first two folios of vol. i are f.[A1] and [A2], respectively. The titlepages preceding sections ii and iii are part of the pertinent gatherings and occupy the pertinent unnumbered pages. After the titlepage to the first tome follows f.A2, 2 pp., a letter 'A madame madame de P****.' A contemporary hand has supplied '[P]ompadour', which is surely not true.

I could find no other copy of this edition and no mention of it. MMF cite an edition for 1763, after BL (copy personally examined), BN and Gillet (53.10). Both the BL (12510.aaaa.4) and BN (Y2.7818) copies are the same, and differ radically from the one described here. The titlepages of that edition are in red and black for part i (in black alone for ii and iii), and the pagination runs as follows: 2 pl + 1f. (2 pp.) + [1]-62 + [67]-126 + [131]-206 pp. + 5 ff. (10 pp.). Each section has a halftitle as well as a titlepage. The last ten pages are an interesting catalogue of books available at Constapel's. This list includes 'Chevriade (la) ou l'Observateur des Enfers, par Mr. G***. 8vo. *Paris* 1762', a *Colporteur* for Londres, 1762 and, '*sous presse*', an 'Essai sur la maniere de juger les Hommes, par Mr. de Chevrier, 8vo'. (The reader is reminded that Chevrier died in 1762.) The *Chevriade*, which is not listed in the usual bibliographies (Gay, Quérard, BLC, Quérard: SD, etc.) does exist (Paris: N. B. Duchesne; Amsterdam: Adrien Hupkes, 1762; NUC: Boston Public Library). The BN, BL,

HISTOIRE

DE LA VIE

DE

H. MAUBERT,

SOI DISANT

CHEVALIER DE GOUVEST,

GAZETTIER A BRUXELLES,

ET AUTEUR DE PLUSIEURS LIBELLES POLITIQUES.

Mise en lumiere pour l'utilité Publique.

A LONDRES,

Chez les Libraires associés.

M. DCC. LXI.

No 69: Chevrier, *Histoire de la vie de H. Maubert*, 1761

Gillet edition of the *Mémoires d'une honnête femme* also seems to be listed in the NUC (Library of Congress).

Incipit: 'Qui! moi devenir Auteur? Y pensez-vous, Madame?'

71

Choffin: *Amusements philologiques*, 1764 and 1766

David Etienne Choffin (1703-1773), author and editor: (titlepages in *red* and black) *Amusemens* / philologiques; [philologiques: for ii] / ou / *Mélange agréable* / de diverses pièces [the accent is between the 'i' and 'e'], / Concernant / *l'histoire des personnes célèbres,* / les Evènemens mémorables, les Usages & les Mo- / numens [Monu- / mens for ii] des anciens, [Anciens, for ii] la Morale, la Mytho- / logie, & l'Histoire [Mythologie, & l'Hi- / stoire for ii] Naturelle. [Naturelle, avec quelques pièces de Poë- / sies & un Indice général. for ii] / *Troisième edition,* / Revue, corrigée & augmentée. [Revue & corrigée. for ii] / [rule formed of little decorations, different for each volume] / Tome I [II]. / [rule] / Avec Figures. / [engraved vignette, different for each volume, but the same emblem, both bearing 'illo splendente levabor'] / [interesting decorative rule for i; none for ii] / à Halle, / *a la maison des orphelins,* [*orphelins.* for ii] / MDCCLXIIII. [MDCCLXVI. for ii]

8°, i: 1 pl + 14 ff. (4 + 8 + 16 pp.) + [1]-480 pp.
    ii: 1 pl + 10 ff. (4 + 4 + 12 pp.) + [1]-448 pp. + 15 ff. (30 pp.)

Commentary: The titlepage of each volume is conjugate with the frontispiece. The pagination for volume i reflects:

1. A dedicatory letter to Frederick William, prince of Prussia, signed 'David Etienne Choffin' (4 p.);
2. A preface (8 pp.);
3. The table (16 pp.);
4. The work proper.

The second volume contains:

1. A dedicatory letter to prince Frederick Henry Charles of Prussia, again signed 'David Etienne Choffin', 4 pp.;
2. An 'avertissement', 4 pp.;
3. The table, 12 pp.;
4. The continuation of the work proper;
5. A 'Table générale et alphabétique des amusemens philologiques', 30 pp.

The verso of each titlepage carries an epigraph. I: 'Est-ce une raison décisive, / D'ôter un bon mets d'un repas? / Parce qu'il s'y trouve un Convive, / Qui, par malheur, ne l'aime pas. / Il faut que tout le monde vive; / Et que les mets pour plaire à tous / Soient différens comme les goûts.' II: '*Conseils de l'Amitié*, p.218. / Ce n'est pas précisément pour savoir qu'on / étudie; c'est pour devenir meilleur: on y / parvient lorsqu'on en a la volonté.' In spite of the reference, the latter citation is not to be found on p.218 of either volume described here.

This work first appeared in 1749-1750, or at least I could find no earlier edition. See, for example, NUC with locations for Library of Congress, University of

Oklahoma, Harvard; also Krauss-Fontius no. 664. (The latter list 2 vols 1749-50, with a third volume, 1761. Also the title recorded is slightly different.) Vol. i is listed in the Messkatalog, Halle, à la maison des Orphelins (OM 1749, f.H2*v*). However, vol. ii is also listed for 1749 (MM 1749, f.E4*r*), leaving the possibility that vol. ii was printed in 1749, yet dated 1750. There were various editions, probably with varying contents. For example, the NUC lists a 1755-1761 edition (doubtless a copy or copies consisting of two or more editions; Louisiana State University and University of Chicago). The Messkatalog lists: '*Choffin*, D. E. Introduction aux Amusemens philologiques. 8. [octavo] à Halle, aux depens de la maison des orphelins (MM 1761, p.191). The supplement ('Anhang') of this work is apparently a *Dictionnaire abrégé de la fable* [...] (Gesamtverzeichniss, xxiv.118a).

In addition to editions listed in the more accessible bibliographies, Heinsius, *Handbuch* has: 'Amusemens Philologiques, IV Part. par Choffin, 8vo Halle, [à la maison des] Orphel[ins,] 1784' (p.774). Heinsius, 1793 includes '4 Part. 8vo. Halle, Orphanotr. [1]784' (iv.476). And Gesamtverzeichniss has editions for 1762, 1767, 1784, 1785-89, 1787, 1789, 1795 (xxiv.118a).

I could find no mention of the edition described here in any modern bibliography, with the possible exception of vol. ii. (Krauss-Fontius list a '3. éd. I-III. Halle [etc.], 1766; location: the Universitäts- und Landesbibliothek Sachsen-Anhalt, Halle.) It is probably in three volumes, for the Messkatalog lists: 'Amusemens philologiques ou Melange agreable de diverses Pieces. T[ome]. I & III. Nouv. Ed. 8vo. à Halle, aux depens de la Mais. des Orphelins (OM 1764, p.478). Vol. ii is then listed the following year, with a different title: 'Amusemens philologiques en Prose & en Vers par Mr. *Choffin*. Tome II. Ed. nouv. 8. Halle, aux depens de la maison des Orphelins' (MM 1765, p.644).

This work consists of short 'histories' based on rumour, fact and imagination. There are also occasional poems, dialogues, scientific explanations of natural phenomena and so on. The first volume is divided into four 'centuries', each containing a hundred items. Vol. ii has three 'centuries'. In the preface to vol. i, Choffin insists upon the pedagogical value of his compilation, whose audience was supposed to consist primarily of children, women and soldiers. Further: 'Les principaux Auteurs d'où j'ai tiré ces matières sont des Ecrivains du prémier ordre & des plus connus. Messieurs de Fènelon, La Fontaine, Rollin, l'Abbé d'Olivet, l'Auteur du Spectacle de la Nature [l'abbé Pluche] & autres, seront mes garants' etc. Choffin then gives some detailed instructions on the use of his book.

Each volume has a frontispiece engraving depicting a palace and an allegorical garden. Vol. ii has three illustrations, one folding. Both titlepage vignettes are signed 'Gr:sc.'

Choffin was a professor of French at Halle and the editor/author of numerous works with a pedagogical bent, including 'Les plus belles Fables d'Esope, de Phedre & d'autres auteurs. 8 [octavo]. Halle, aux depens de la maison des Orphelins' (Messkatalog, MM 1754, p.542; an entry for 1755 further elucidates 'Recueil des Fables en prose & en vers, tirées des meilleurs Auteurs avec des notes allemandes. 8. [octavo] Halle, aux depens de la maison des Orphelins, OM 1755, p.592). He also composed a 'Dictionnaire abrégé de la Fable ou de

la Mythologie servant de Supplement aux Amusemens philologiques. 8vo.
Halle, a la maison des Orphelins' (Messkatalog, OM, 1750, p.51), some 'Amusemens littéraires, ou Magazin de la belle littérature tant en prose qu'en Vers
[...]. 8vo. à Brandenbourg, chez les freres Halle' (OM, 1772, p.395).

Since so many of his works were published to benefit the Halle orphanage, it
seems not too farfetched to assume that there was some sort of arrangement
between the professor (or perhaps the university) and that charitable institution.
See the next entry.

For those who might wonder about the word 'philologique' used in the title:
'philologie' had a more generalised meaning in the eighteenth century: 'C'est
une espèce de science composée de Grammaire, de Rhétorique, de Poëtique,
d'Antiquités, d'Histoire, & généralement de la critique & interprétation de tous
les Auteurs; en un mot, une littérature universelle qui s'étend sur toutes sortes
de sciences & d'Auteurs' (*Dictionnaire universel françois et latin*, the *Dictionnaire de
Trévoux*, Paris 1771, vi.736).

Incipit: ('Conduite du jeune Cyrus, à la cour d'Astyage, son grandpère')
'Cyrus, qui devint ensuite un si grand Monarque, étoit bien fait de corps, &
encore plus estimable par les qualités de l'esprit'.

72

Choffin: *Récréations philologiques*, 1767

David Etienne Choffin (1703-1773), author and editor: (titlepages in *red* and
black) *Re'cre'ations / philologiques, / ou / me'lange agre'able / de / diverses pièces, /* concernant / l'histoire des personnes célè- / bres, la morale, la poésie, les évé- / nemens
mémorables et l'hi- / stoire naturelle. / *Pour servir de suite / aux / amusemens philologiques.* / Tome prémier [second]. / [a rather lovely, extensive, rococo engraved
vignette bearing 'lux / post tene- / bras', presumably Mezlar's device; on the
bottom, the intitials 'JBM' intertwined on a 'rocaille'] / A' Stougard / *chez Jean
Benoit Mezler.* / MDCCLXVII.

8°, i: 1 f. (titlepage) + 1 f. (p.[3-4]) + [5]-366 pp.
    ii: 1 pl + [I]-XVI + [1]-302 pp.

Commentary: P.[3-4] of vol. i are an 'Avertissement'. P.[I]-XVI at the head of
vol. ii are a table for both volumes. There is a pretty frontispiece engraving by
Tyroll [?] after J. J. Preissler at the beginning of vol. i. The titlepage to vol. i
should comprise f.[A1], were one to believe the evidence of the signatures. (The
'Avertissement' leaf is signed A2.) However, pp.[3]-14 comprise six leaves of a
gathering and the titlepage is conjugate with the frontispiece. In vol. ii, the
titlepage should comprise f.[*1], according to the signatures, since the first leaf
of the table is signed *2. However, the first gathering would then have nine
leaves. The title leaf is conjugate with either the last or penultimate leaf of the
preliminary material, and the other leaf has been tipped in.

This work is not listed in Barbier, or in any other modern bibliography I
have consulted, for that matter. Although there is no editor/author name
indicated in this compilation, it seems certain that it is by (or edited by rather)

Choffin. The end of the 'avertissement' reads: 'Le but que j'ai dans cette nouvelle collection, est le même que celui que j'ai eu dans les précédentes, savoir d'instruire la Jeunesse par manière d'amusement, & lui faciliter en même temps la connoissance de la Langue françoise. C'est un but que j'ai fort à cœur, & je n'ai garde de m'en écarter'. Choffin was a professor of French at Halle, and wrote/compiled many other works of a pedagogical nature. (See, for example, the preceding entry.)

The only mentions of this work I could find are in the Messkatalog and in Heinsius, 1793 (the latter in iv.545; the information given here is transcribed from the former): 'Recreations philologiques ou melange agreable de diverses pieces concernant l'histoire des Personnes celebres, la Morale, la Poesie, les evenemens memorables & l'histoire naturelle. T[ome]. I. 8. [octavo] à Stuttgard, chez J. B. Mezler (MM 1766, p.769). The following year there is an additional entry, indicating that this work is a sequel to the *Amusements philologiques*: '[...] pieces pour servir de suite aux Amusemens philologiques. Tome II. 8. Stouccard [!], chez J. B. Mezler' (OM 1767, p.854). Either there were two editions of vol. i at least, or, more probably, vol. i appeared late in 1766, bearing a date for 1767.

The work might be considered marginal to the 'genre romanesque', containing bits and pieces from various histories (ersatz and real), dialogues, poems, and so forth, by Choffin and culled by him from a wide variety of sources. Without acknowledgment, he also included Coyer's *Lettre à une jeune dame angloise nouvellement mariée. Critique ou satyre des travers des dames de France* (according to the headtitle, i.306-19; see Coyer, *Lettre...* below).

Incipits: ('Les grands événemens ont souvent de petites causes') 'Robert & Henry, enfans de Guillaume le Conquérant, étant venus visiter le Roi Philippe I. à Constans sur l'Oise'.

(*Lettre à une jeune dame anglaise nouvellement mariée*) 'Si vous étiez née à Paris, l'éducation vous auroit sauvé bien des ridicules'.

73

Choisy, after d'Urfé: *La Nouvelle Astrée*, 1713

François Timoléon, abbé de Choisy (1644-1724), after Honoré d'Urfé (1567-1625): (titlepage in *red* and black) La / nouvelle / *Astrée,* / dediée / *a son* / altesse royale / *madame*. / [symmetrical woodcut decoration with crown on top] / A Amsterdam, / Chez *Pierre Humbert*. / [rule] / M DCC XIII.

12°: 2 ff. (halftitle and titlepage) + [5-12], 13-216 pp.

Commentary: This novel first appeared in 1712 (Jones, p.20 and Conlon, iv.284, no.16237). The first two pages of text (pp.[5-6]) are the dedication 'A son altesse royale madame'; then follow an 'Avertissement' (pp.[7-11]), the 'Approbation' (12 May 1712, signed 'Fontenelle', p.[12]), and the novel. The whole is preceded by a half titlepage for 'La / nouvelle / Astrée.' Jones lists an edition bearing the date of 1613, for 1713 (copies in the BN, Arsenal and BL). Although he mentions no edition bearing the date 1713, the one described here does exist in the BN.

Jones also remarks that Choisy mentions in the 'Avertissement' that he is attempting a reduced adaptation of d'Urfé's interminable original (which first appeared from 1607 on. There were two 'suites' by Gomberville and Balthazar [de] Baro; see Lever pp.78-81).

However, this work must be listed under both Choisy's name – assuming he is the adaptor; see below – and d'Urfé's, since the plot follows fairly closely the main lines of the principal action of the original *Astrée*. Occasionally too the original language is used, or a very close approximation. In the 'Avertissement' the adaptor explains that a lady friend had first given him/her the idea for a *New Astrée*: 'Elle avoit oüi dire, qu'une jeune persone, qui veut avoir de l'esprit, doit lire & relire le Roman d'Astrée, & cependant, malgré sa prévention & son courage, elle n'avoit jamais pu aller jusqu'à la fin du premier Volume. Les Episodes continuels, l'affectation d'une vaine science', etc., all this and more made of the original an unbearable book. But she did not dare entirely dismiss the opinion of the public at large. So, continues the adaptor, 'je lui proposé [*sic*] d'en ôter tous les défauts qu'elle avoit sentis par un bon goût naturel, d'en faire un petit Ouvrage de galanterie champêtre, d'en adoucir certains endroits un peu libres, que la pudeur scrupuleuse de nôtre siecle ne sauroit souffrir dans les Livres, de le purger de Theologie, de Politique, de Medecine, de Poësie; d'en éloigner tous les personages inutiles, de n'y jamais perdre de vûë Astrée & Celadon, & d'éviter par-là l'écueil de tous les longs Romans, où le Héros & l'Héroïne ne paroissent sur la Scene que rarement; ce qui empêche, qu'on ne s'affectionne à la suite de leurs avantures [...]. Il a fallu de plus changer le stile, quoiqu'il eut beaucoup de force dans l'Original. Cent ans dans une Langue vivante, mettent tout hors de mode. J'ai pourtant conservé certains traits qu'on remarquera assez aux mots antiques, & encore mieux à la beauté des sentimens.'

And indeed, in the text itself, the adaptor does not hesitate to mention d'Urfé, when upon occasion the latter's own words are used (e.g. pp.57, 191). And on one or two occasions, the reader is reminded that the adaptor is not too far away. For example, when Celadon, separated from his beloved Astrée, decides to write the object of his affections, the adaptor shows a sense of humour when he interpolates: '(Les Bergers avoient toujours dans leur panetiere une écritoire & du papier.)'.

Concerning the identity of the adaptor: Jones, doubtless after Gay and Barbier, lists this work solely under Choisy. However, the dedication reports that the *Nouvelle Astrée* is 'un petit Ouvrage composé par une persone du beau sexe, qui a trouvé le moyen de le purger de tout ce qui pouroit offenser la pudeur la plus scrupuleuse. MADAME y verra partout la bonne morale suivie, le merite récompensé, & la vertu couronnée.' Could the adaptor have been a woman? What seems more likely is that the abbé de Choisy perpetrated a small mystification.

Incipit: 'La nature avoit rendu le petit païs de Forêt, le plus délicieux des Gaules'.

74

Contant Dorville: *Le Mariage du siècle*, 1767

André Guillaume Contant Dorville (or d'Orville), 1730?-1800?: Le / mariage / du siécle, / ou / lettres / De Madame la Comtesse de Castelli, / à Madame la Baronne de Fréville. / Par M. Contant d'Orville. / Premiere [Seconde] Partie. / [woodcut decoration: shell motif, same for both volumes] / A Lille, / Par la Société. / [rule] / M. DCC. LXVII.

12°, i: 1 f. (titlepage) + [iij]-iv, [v]-viij, [ix]-xij + [1]-154 pp.
    ii: 1 pl + [1]-204 pp.

Commentary: Vol. i.[iij]-iv is an 'Epître à l'une des plus vertueuses & des plus respectables femmes de Paris'; the next item is the 'Avis de l'éditeur'; then follow a 'Lettre de madame la baronne de Fréville, à l'éditeur', and the first part of the novel. This novel first appeared in 1766 and went through another edition in French for 1767. I could find no other trace of the edition described here. The only copy of it I could find is in the Humanities Research Centre of the University of Texas, Austin.

In passing, I might mention that this novel was translated into the English, German and the Italian, and went through two editions (or possibly translations) for the latter language alone. This now identifies the novel listed under Contant Dorville's name in Josephine Grieder, *Translations of French sentimental prose fiction in late eighteenth-century England: the history of a literary vogue* (Durham 1975), p.91. Grieder lists 'French original unidentified'. The English title is: *Pauline, or the victim of the heart, from the French of Dorville*. 2 vols. London: printed for William Lane at the Minerva Press, 1794. (In 'The Translator to her countrywomen', the adaptor explains her deviations from the original. This is signed 'a woman'.) I am grateful to Professor Georges May for supplying me with information and xeroxes of the titlepages and introductory material (derived from the Yale copy).

The Messkatalog lists 'Mariage du Siecle. 2 Parties. 12. Paris & à Leips. ch. Arkstée & Merkus', OM 1767, p.852. This probably refers to one of the 'En France' editions listed in MMF.

Incipit: 'Qui pourra remplacer dans mon cœur ma chère Baronne?'

75

Courtilz de Sandras: *Mémoires de la marquise de Fresne*, 1706

Gatien de Courtilz, sieur de Sandras (1644-1712): Memoires / de / madame / la / marquise / de / Fresne. / Enrichi de Figures. / [woodcut sphere] / A Amsterdan [*sic*], / Chez Jean Malherbe, sur le / Vygendam. / [rule] / M. D. CCVI.

12°: 1 pl + 2 ff. (4 pp.) + 1-482 (for 402) pp.

Commentary: The first four pages listed are a preface. This novel first appeared in 1701 (Jones, p.3; Conlon iii.144, no. 10633). The NUC lists what appears to be the same edition for the William Andrews Clark Memorial Library at the University of California, Los Angeles. The differences (pagination errors, signatures, etc.) between that copy and mine seem to be a result of sloppy recording. I have listed this edition since it has escaped the attention of all bibliographers whose works I have consulted. This volume is illustrated with 29 engravings, of mediocre quality, although I find the artist's use (or misuse rather) of perspective rather amusing. There are numerous errors in pagination and a couple of mistakes in the signatures.

Incipit: 'L'Affaire que j'ai euë malheureusement avec mon mary, a fait assez de bruit dans le monde'.

76

Coyer: *Lettre à une jeune dame nouvellement mariée*, 1749

Abbé Gabriel François Coyer (1707-1782): (head title) [double rule] / Lettre / a une jeune dame / nouvellement mariée. [1749].

4°: 1-8 pp.

Commentary: This is a work which might be considered marginal to the 'genre romanesque'. But it is a piece of prose fiction (not in Jones), dealing with a young Englishwoman and her silliness – ironically intended – in not following the fashions of the day. In pointing out her 'ridicules', Coyer is sarcastically attacking women and their foibles: 'plût au Ciel vos ridicules fussent-ils bornés aux murs de votre Hôtel! Vous en portez dans les cercles. Vous y entrez avec les couleurs de la nature sur le visage. Ainsi se présente la femme du Suisse qui vous a ouvert la porte: repassez la mer si vous voulez paroître telle que vous êtes' (p.3). Or: 'il s'en faut deux pouces que vos girandoles ne descendent assez bas: si vous pouviez suspendre un lustre à chaque oreille, vous seriez au parfait. On vous a vuë à l'Opera coëffée en *Comète*, lorsque depuis deux jours on étoit en *Rhinoceros*' (p.6). Etc. the resulting portrait of the young bride is amusing, if somewhat conventional. Barbier attributes this *Lettre* to Coyer (ii, col.1124c). In conclusive support of this claim is Le Prince de Beaumont's *Réponse d'une jeune femme nouvellement mariée à Paris. A M. l'abbé C**** (8 pp. in-4° BN Z.Beuchot 1902(15)). A note p.2 refers sarcastically to the *Année merveilleuse* in terms which confirm Barbier's attribution. (See too Fréron's *Année littéraire*, i.338-40.)

On the last page of the *Lettre à une jeune femme nouvellement mariée* recorded here is the following date: '*A Paris le 7. Août* 1749'.

This is one of the pieces resulting from the rather tempestuous battle of the sexes surrounding Coyer's *Année merveilleuse*. For more information, see Le Prince de Beaumont's *Lettre en réponse à l''Année merveilleuse'* and *Arrêt solennel de la nature* below. The *Lettre à une jeune dame nouvellement mariée* was translated into the English, and appeared together with the French in a bilingual edition (NUC: Newberry Library).

There are three copies of the *Lettre* in the BN. However, although the BNC lists them all as being the same edition, they comprise two separate editions: Z.Beuchot 1902(15) and Li3.17 carry signature 'A' under the 'a' of 'réputation' (p.[1]), and p.8, up two lines from the bottom, one finds '[...] nous? allons-nous [...]'. In BN Z.Fontanieu 254 the signature 'A' is under the 'n' of 'réputation' and p.8 up two lines from the bottom reads '[...] nous? Allons-nous [...]'. I have two copies of the above described *Lettre*, both identical, and which match the two identical BN copies (probably; I was unable to juxtapose my copy with those in the BN). I know of no other copies. (Gay lists this work after Barbier, ii, col.799.)

For another edition of Coyer's *Lettre à une jeune dame nouvellement mariée*, see Choffin, *Récréations philologiques*, 1762 above.

Incipit: 'Madame, / Si vous étiez née à Paris, l'éducation vous auroit sauvé bien des / ridicules'.

77

Crébillon fils: *Le Sopha*, ca.1745

Claude Prosper Jolyot de Crébillon, fils (1707-1777): (titlepages in *red* and black) Le / *sopha*, / conte moral. / *Premier* [*Second*] *volume*. / [woodcuts, i: long-tailed birds facing centre of flowers on extensive decoration; ii: what looks vaguely like a large artichoke centred in a symmetrical, floral design] / *A Gaznah*, / De l'Imprimerie du Très-Pieux, Très- / Clément & Très-Auguste Sultan / des Indes [Indies for ii]. / [double rule] / L'an de l'Hegire *M. C. XX*. / Avec Privilege du Susdit.

12°, i: 1 f. (titlepage) + [iii-iv], [v]-(xii) + [1]-([1]36) pp.

ii: 1 pl + 1 f. (2 pp.) + [1]-(128) pp.

Commentary: There were several editions of this tale parallelling Fougeret de Monbron's *Le Canapé couleur de feu* (see under that author below) for 'Gaznah'. The above volumes are rare enough that I could find no other copy of this edition or mention of it. The novel is in two volumes, as indicated, bound in speckled, contemporary English calf. A pencilled note states that this is the first edition, 1745. The comment is wrong. The first edition appeared in 1742 (Jones), and this particular edition probably appeared between 1742 and 1745, if not later. It is a counterfeit edition, printed in England (probably London), as is more than obvious by not only the paper, type, signatures, woodcut decorations and frequency and kind of catchwords, but by the fact that press figures appear throughout. Also vol. ii is preceded by two preliminary, unsigned leaves (the titlepage and 'Table'), and the volume then begins with gathering B. (The preliminary pagination for vol. i represents a 'Table' and an 'Introduction', which, together with the titlepage, constitute ff. [A1], A2, A3, [A4-6] of the first signature sequence.) For further information concerning the dating of *Le Sopha*, see D. A. Day's interesting 'On the dating of three novels by Crébillon fils', *MLR* (1961), pp.391-92.

It might be noted that Gay reports a 1763 edition, with no details. This information is repeated in MMF (51.R12). Jones makes no mention of a 1763 edition. Kayser supplies additional details, remarking that this edition – if it be the same that Gay saw – is in-8°: Jena, Fischer ('Sopha, ou conte moral. [in-]8. Jena [1]763. Fischer', Romane p.29b). This information is also given in Heinsius ('Jena' spelled 'Jene'), who might have been the source for Kayser's corrected entry (Heinsius, Romane col.200). It is also in Heinsius, 1793 (iv.552). Weller,

LE
SOPHA,

CONTE MORAL.

PREMIER VOLUME.

A GAZNAH,

De l'Imprimerie du Très-Pieux, Très-Clément & Très-Auguste Sultan des Indes.

L'an de l'Hegire M. C. XX.

Avec Privilege du Susdit.

No 77: Crébillon fils, *Le Sopha*, ca. 1745

in the fairly extensive and confusing list of editions of *Le Sopha* gives '[...] *Pékin* (Paris). 1762; ib. (Jena). 1763; ib. 1770 [...]' (p.112). Perhaps then 'Pékin' appeared on the titlepage of the 'Jena' edition? I mention this because I could find no copy of that edition (BNC, NUC, BLC, etc.).

To editions of works by Crébillon listed in Jones and MMF, I would add the following:

1. *Le Sopha*, 1751. 'Crebillon, le Sopha, Conte Moral, 2 parties, [in-]12. Francf. chez Fr. Varrentrapp', Messkatalog, OM 1751, p.165. Jones gives an edition after the BN (repeated in MMF). The BNC lists two copies for Gennes, aux dépens du public, 2 tomes en 1 vol. (Y2.9221-22 and Y2.68990-91). I was unable to consult these. Furthermore, Krauss-Fontius list a two-volume, 'Francfort: Libraires, 1751' edition, with two locations (the Universitäts- und Landesbibliothek Sachsen-Anhalt, Halle and the Stadtbibliothek of Ballenstedt; no. 4242). MMF list after Krauss-Fontius (51.R12).

2. *La Nuit et le moment*, 1756. 'Nuit, la, et le moment, ou les matinées de Cythère, dialogue. [in-]12. Berl[in]. [1]756' (Heinsius iii, col.72). MMF (55.16) list a *Nuit et le moment* for 'Londres, 1756, in-12' after the Library of Congress copy and Gay. The NUC entry for the Library of Congress indicates that Paris was the real place of publication. So I do not doubt that we are dealing with two different editions (if the information given be exact).

3. *Le Sopha*, 1763. Jones, and MMF after Jones list an edition for 1763, after Gay. Gay lists by date alone (iii, col.1135). Gesamtverzeichniss has: 'Sopha, ou conte moral. 8vo. Jena [1]763. Fischer' (xxvi.169a).

4. *Œuvres complètes*, 1772. Gesamtverzeichniss has an entry for 'Collection compl. de ses Œuvres. 7 Vol. 8vo. Londres. (Varrentrapp, Francf.) [1]772' (xvi.169a). (I would strongly suspect that the 'Londres' is a false indication of the actual printing place of the volumes).

5. *Le Hasard au coin du feu* with *La Nuit et le moment*, 1779. Le hasard au coin du feu, dialogue moral. Par M. de Crébillon, fils. Maestricht: J.-E. Dufour & P. Roux, 1779. 311 p., 18 cm. A note remarks that *La Nuit et le moment, ou les matiné[e]s de Cythère* is to be found on pp.[151]-311 (OCLC: Johns Hopkins University).

Incipit: 'Sire, votre Majesté n'ignore pas que, quoique je sois son sujet, je ne suis pas la même Loi qu'elle'.

78

Desforges: *Anecdotes de M. Duliz*, 1752

(no first names known) Desforges: Anecdotes / des / avantures galantes / de M. Duliz, / Devenuës tragiques, après la catastrophe / de celle de Mademoiselle Pélissier, / Actrice de l'Opéra de Paris. / Avec le Triomphe de l'Intérêt, / Comédie. / [stylised, symmetrical woodcut ornament] / A Lisbonne, / De l'Imprimerie de la Juiverie. / M. DCC. LII.

12°: 1 pl (titlepage) + [1]-206 and 1 f. (halftitle) + [3]-66 pp.

Commentary: The novel first appeared in 1739 (Jones, p.69). The play, by Laus de Boissy, was first performed 8 November 1730 and first published in 1734 (Brenner, no. 3908). Jones reports that there were two editions for 1752, according to Gay. The head title of the present copy matches the title of the first edition and subsequent editions as reported by Jones and other bibliographers, viz. *Mémoires anecdotes des avantures galantes de M. Duliz, Devenuës tragiques, après la catastrophe de celle de Mademoiselle Pelissier, Actrice de l'Opéra de Paris* (as per the head title from the above copy). Gay indicates, under the title of *Mémoires anecdotes…*: 'Lisbonne, de l'imprimerie de la Juiverie, 1752'.

In the NUC is listed an edition, as per Gay's title, same general pagination as described above, and a note states that the comedy 'has special t.-p. [titlepage] with same imprint as the preceding *Mémoires*'. The volume described here has no special titlepage for the second item (Boissy's play), but a half titlepage reading 'Le / triomphe / de / l'intérêt, / comédie.' (f.[R8], p.[1-2] of the second item). The signatures for both pieces are consecutive (1f. + A8, B4-Z4), and none of the leaves is missing.

Incipit: 'Je ne donne point ces Mémoires au Public par un esprit de vengeance contre M. Duliz'.

79

Diderot: *Les Bijoux indiscrets*, 1797

Denis Diderot (1713-1784): Les / bijoux / indiscrets. / Par Diderot. / [rule] / Tome premier [second]. / [rule] / A Paris, / Chez tous les marchands de nouveautés. / [double rule] / 1797.

18°, i: 2 pl + [1]-177, [178] pp.
  ii: 2 pl + [1]-199, [200] pp.

Commentary: Unfortunately I only have vol. i of this edition. The information pertaining to vol. ii derives from a copy of this edition seen in a bookstore. There are pretty, engraved frontispieces by Blanchard to each volume, with captions. The only mention I have been able to find of this edition of Diderot's licentious flight of fancy is in Reynaud, col.130, who writes 'nouveauté' instead of the plural and mentions that it is '2 tomes in 1 vol. in-18', with two frontispieces by Blanchard. My copy of vol. i is in a contemporary trade binding, so Reynaud is obviously reporting from a specific copy. (The last page in each volume is a 'Table'.) There are half titlepages for 'Les / bijoux / indiscrets. / [rule] / Tome premier […]. / [rule]. This novel first appeared in 1748.

Drujon has some interesting information concerning it as a 'roman à clef' (i, cols.136-37). Gay gives an outline of some of the legal difficulties encountred by this work in the nineteenth century (i, cols.401-402).

Incipit: 'Hiaouf Zélès Tanzai régnoit depuis longtems dans la grande Chéchianée'.

80

Diderot (and anonymous): *La Religieuse* (and a 'Continuation'), 1799

Denis Diderot (1713-1784) for the novel, anonymous for the 'Continuation': La religieuse, / par Diderot; / nouvelle édition, / ornée de figures, / et ou l'on trouve une conclusion. / Tome premier [second]. / [rule] / A Paris, / Chez [open brace] Deroy, Libraire, rue Haute-Feuille, [Haute-Feuille. for II] n.° 34, au coin / de celle des Poitevins. / Moller, Imprimeur-Libraire, rue des Francs-Bourgeois, / n.° 129, place Michel. / Mongie, l'aîné, Libraire, Palais-Égalité [Egalité for ii], galerie de / bois, n.° 224. [end of material set off by a brace] Et à Belleville, chez Dupréel, Graveur, rue Franciade, / n.° 122. / [rule] / An VII de la république.

8°, i: 1 pl + [1]-4, [5]-72 + [1]-157 pp.

ii: 1 pl + [1]-158, 159-186 pp.

Commentary: MMF list this edition (97.22; the novel first appeared in 1796) after Tchemerzine, Gay, Quérard, Saint-Fargeau (*Revue des romans*, 1839) and three periodicals. Cohen also cites it (col.305) as does Reynaud (col.131). The former notes that the illustrations are the same as in the *Œuvres*, Paris: Desray et Deterville, 1798 (15 vols in octavo) and as in *La Religieuse* (Paris: Rousseau [etc.], an XIII.-1804). There are five engravings all told: a portrait frontispiece and four illustrations. The latter are reproduced in Georges C. May, *Diderot et 'la Religieuse': étude historique et littéraire* (New Haven, Paris 1954; the reproductions derive from the 1804 edition). Here are the illustrations:

1. Portrait frontispiece of 'Diderot' by Dupréel after Aubry.

2. Facing i.25(2), by Dupréel after Le Barbier: 'Messieurs, et vous sur-tout mon père et ma / mère, je vous prends tous à temoins....'.

3. Facing i.45, meant for ii.43, by Giraud jeune after Le Barbier: 'Elle joue et chante comme un ange.'

4. Facing ii.116, meant for i.146, by Dupréel after Le Barbier: 'Eh bien, madame? / Elle répondit: je l'ignorais.'

5. Facing ii.176, meant for i.61, by Dupréel after Le Barbier: 'Approchez toutes que je vous embrasse; ve- / nez recevoir ma bénédiction et mes adieux.........'.

Monglond also lists this edition, after Cohen and the *Mercure français* (iii, col.729). He remarks that this edition 'm'est demeurée introuvable'. I have found no other copy either.

At the end of vol.ii is the following colophon: 'De l'imprimerie de Suret, rue Hyacinthe.' The two volumes contain an 'Avis de l'éditeur', 'Extrait de la Correspondance littéraire de M.*** année 1770', the novel, and, in ii.159-86, the 'Continuation'.

Concerning the 'Continuation': this is apocryphal and was first published, as far as I know, with this edition of *La Religieuse*. I do not know who composed it, but there was a deliberate effort made to imitate Diderot's style, mood and even to follow his intentions. This 'Continuation' was also published with the 1804 edition or issue of the novel.

Curiously it has remained largely unknown to Diderot scholars, and no mention is made of it in nearly all modern editions of the works or the novel I have consulted (for example, the André Billy edition of the *Œuvres* [Paris, 'Pléiade', 1951], the recent chronological edition of the works, 'Le club français du livre', iv, 1970, etc., or even in Assézat-Tourneux). The one editor to have noticed the sequel is Jean Hervez in an otherwise not very interesting edition: *L'Œuvre de Diderot*, 2ᵉ partie, *Réproduction intégrale de l'édition de 1796 avec la 'Continuation' publiée dans l'édition de 1804* (Paris, Bibliothèque des curieux, 1920, series: 'Les maîtres de l'amour'). Hervez mentions that the 1804 edition of the 'works' is 'fort prisée', not only for the illustrations, but because 'elle publie (tome ii, pages 159-186), sous le titre *Continuation*, la suite et la fin du roman, sans l'attribuer à Diderot, certes, mais aussi sans indiquer aucune paternité à ces pages' (p.7). He continues: 'Mais c'est par pure curiosité que nous publions cette *Continuation*, qui ne nous paraît, en aucune façon, pourvoir être attribuée à l'auteur de *la Religieuse*. Nous nous contentons de faire observer qu'il est regrettable que Naigeon, alors âgé de 66 ans, si bien informé[!], n'ait pas jugé à propos de dire un mot de ces pages évidemment apocryphes, et que Léon Godard ou Maurice Tourneux n'aient pas eu la pensée de contrôler, à ce point de vue, les manuscrits de Pétersbourg', etc. While I agree that the sequel is apocryphal, it is obvious that the editor of the 1804 book did not have it composed for that edition, as Hervez proposes.

As this bibliography was in the press, I was able to compare some photocopies of the 1804 *Religieuse* (BN) with my volumes, and it would appear that the former is a reissue, with cancel titleleaves.

The *Journal général de la littérature de France*, lists '*La Religieuse par Diderot, où l'on trouve une Conclusion*; nouvelle édition, 2 voll. in-8, fig. [...] *Deroy*'. A laudatory comment ensues: 'La *Conclusion* qui manque à toutes les autres éditions, termine cet ouvrage d'une manière très satisfaisante, & doit lui assurer un succès complet' (messidor, an VII / June or July 1799, p.209).

There is also a brief, yet interesting article in the *Mercure* (décadi, 30 messidor an VII [18 July 1799]) devoted to 'La Religieuse, par Diderot, avec une conclusion. Jolie édition, 2 volumes in-8°. avec cinq figures, y compris le portrait de Diderot, d'après le dessin de Barbier l'aîné, destinés à faire suite aux Œuvres du même auteur. Prix 4 francs, et 5 francs, franc de port'. (Follows a list of the publishers/bookdealers, with no mention of Mongie however.)

The two-paragraph review runs as follows:

'Il est inutile de ramener l'attention sur le roman de *Diderot*; ceux qui l'ont lu, savent avec quelle simplicité forte il est écrit, avec quel talent les caractères sont dessinés, et quel intérêt touchant, il inspire d'un bout à l'autre. C'est ainsi qu'un observateur, un homme de génie fait un roman; il voit se qui se passe autour de lui, prend la plume, et en paraissant n'écrire qu'une fiction, c'est le tableau même du monde qu'il esquisse. Ce bel ouvrage cependant est imparfait; Diderot l'avait peut-être jugé indigne de lui. Une main qui ne se fait point connaitre, a osé ajouter quelques traits à ceux d'un maître, sa touche n'est point la même; elle n'est cependant pas à dédaigner; il y a de la chaleur, quelque vigueur même; et le lecteur qui, auparavant, s'arrêtait dans une situation touchante et s'en prenait à l'auteur de n'avoir point achevé le plaisir qu'il lui donnait, saura quelque gré au continuateur d'avoir conduit l'attention jusqu'à la fin de cette histoire qui déchire l'ame.

Au surplus, cette édition est la plus jolie qu'on ait encore donnée de *la Religieuse*; elle est ornée de cinq jolies figures, dessinées par le citoyen Barbier l'aîné, et gravées par le citoyen Dupréel, tous deux connus avantageusement chacun dans leur art. Les possesseurs de l'édition *in*-8°. des *Œuvres de Diderot*, doivent la rechercher, et ils le peuvent d'autant plus facilement que le prix en est très-modique.'

This article, and the others, are reproduced in J. Th. de Booy and Alan J. Freer, '*Jacques le fataliste*' et '*La Religieuse*' *devant la critique révolutionnaire (1796-1800)*, Studies on Voltaire 33 (1965).

I would add the following editions to those mentioned in MMF (97.22):

1. *La Religieuse*, 1797. 'Religieuse, la, ouvr. posth. de Diderot. [in-]12. Basle, (Tourneisen, a[uch] Levrault à Paris. [However, Levrault was a Strasbourg-based publisher and dealer.]) [1]797' (Heinsius, Romane, col.171).

2. *La Religieuse*, 1797. La / religieuse. / [swell rule] / Ouvrage posthume / de / Diderot. / [swell rule] / À Paris, / chez les marchands de nouveautés. / 1797. in-12°: 1 f. (titlepage) + [3]-246, 247-288 pp. The second set of pages represents the *Correspondance littéraire* matter. Page numbers have hyphens on either side. The first gathering is [titlepage], A, A2, [A3-7], B, B2, [B3-4]. BL: 1607/5221.

The Messkatalog has the following entries: 'Religieuse, la, Ouvrage posthume de Diderot. 12. à Paris. A Leipsig, Rabenhorst.' (OM 1797, p.237). The next entry is for 'le même livre. 12. à Bâle, Decker (Leipsig *Leo* en comm[ission].)' (ibid.) This should mean that a Paris edition was for sale at Rabenhorst's in Leipzig, and that an edition printed for Decker in Bâle was also printed for (and available from) Leo in Leipzig. (The Decker edition is not mentioned in MMF.) It could be a case of an error in the Messkatalog, and that a Paris edition was available in Bâle, at Decker's. But this does not appear particularly likely, especially since it is listed in Heinsius, 1798: '12mo. Decker et Rabenhorst. [1]797' (p.497). MMF list no 1797 edition in-duodecimo. However, this entry might refer to the book in the BL, recorded just above (no. 2).

In passing: Heinsius mentions another edition of the Diderot-Gessner *Contes moraux et nouvelles idylles* which is not listed in modern prose-fiction bibliographies: '[in-]12. Lausanne. Pott et Comp. [1]773' (i, col.680; also Kayser ii.44a).

And although 1797 is sometimes given as the first edition of *Jacques le fataliste* (e.g. MMF, 97.21), it first appeared in 1796, and Gesamtverzeichniss has: '*Diderot*, le fataliste Jacques et son maitre. II Vols. 8vo. Basel [1]796. Decker' (xxviii.408b). Although the date is possibly an error, MMF list no Basel edition.

Incipits: (*La Religieuse*) 'La réponse du marquis de Croismare, s'il m'en fait une, me fournira les premières lignes de ce récit.'

(*Continuation*) 'L'impatience double le tems et les maux. J'ai écrit à M. le marquis de Croismare.'

81

Dorat: *Lettres en vers et œuvres mêlées*; *Collection complète des œuvres*, 1775

Claude Joseph Dorat (1734-1780): (titlepage to vol.i) Lettres / en vers, / et / œuvres mélées / de M. Dorat, / Ci-devant Mousquetaire; / Recueillies par lui-même. / [large woodcut ornament: vase with handle, wreath thrown over it; grape vines and grapes cast hither and thither] / A Paris. / [segmented double rule with finials] / M. DCC. LXXV.

8°, i: 2 ff. (halftitle and titlepages) + 5-430 pp.

Commentary: This book has a halftitle for a 'Collection / complete / des / œuvres / de M. Dorat. / [rule] / Tome premier. / [rule]'. Here are the contents:

    1. 'Lettre de l'auteur', pp.5-8;

    2. *Lettre de Barnevelt*, pp.[9]-25;

    3. *Lettre du comte de Comminges*, pp.26-49 (with an 'Extrait des *Mémoires du comte de Comminges*' as a preface);

    4. *Lettre de Philomèle à Progné*, pp.[50]-61;

    5. 'Lettre a madame de C**', pp.62-72;

    6. *Lettre de Zéila*, with Valcour's reply (both in verse), and liminary material, pp.[73]-108;

    7. 'Apologie de l'héroïde', pp.109-18;

    8. *Lettre de Valcour à son père*, pp.[119]-128;

    9. various heroids and poems with liminary material, pp.129-76;

    10. 'Lettres / d'une chanoinesse / de Lisbonne, / a Melcour, / officier françois. / Tome I. M [catchmaterial]' (halftitle), pp.[177]-270 (includes halftitle leaf and liminaries);

    11. *Ma philosophie*, pp.[271]-295;

    12. *Idylles de Saint-Cyr, ou l'hommage du cœur*, pp.[296]-313 (a play; includes list of characters);

    13. *Lettre d'un philosophe*, pp.[314]-338;

    14. a series of shorter pieces, in prose and verse (including the *Epître à Catherine II* and *Les Tourterelles de Zelmis*), pp.[339]-428;

    15. 'Table Des Pieces contenues dans ce premier volume', pp.[429]-430.

I could find no trace of these *Œuvres*. In spite of the imprint, it is possible to affirm that this volume was produced in Neuchâtel by or for the 'société typographique'. I was able to compare this volume with those in the BN for the *Œuvres*, Neuchatel: De l'Imprimerie de la Société Typographique, M. DCC. LXXVI. (8vo Z17641[1-6]). The type is the same, and many of the handsome woodcut ornaments (figurative and composite) are repeated, albeit in a different order. The dispostion of the contents in the edition represented by the BN copy is different, as is the pagination (vol i: 1 pl [titlepage, with quote verso] + [1]-422 pp., in-8vo), but the signatures follow the same pattern (signed in 8s, lower-case roman, with terminal 'j's). For those who might wonder if the 1776 edition might not bear a false place-name of publication: the volume described here and the set in the BN were definitely produced in Switzerland. That is obvious from the type and ornaments alone. Since the mention of 'Paris' on a titlepage with no name of a publisher was a common practice of Parisian publishers when they printed (or had printed) works which had received a 'permission simple' or 'tacite' from the authorities, perhaps we have here an example of Swiss publishers deliberately trying to beat the French at their own game?

I have little doubt but that the 1775 edition includes more than the volume described here. In spite of the titlepage for the collection of largely verse in this volume alone, there are catchtomes for 'Tome I.'. The end of the text bears 'FIN du Tome premier.' (At the very end: 'FIN de la Table.')

I could find no trace of this edition anywhere.

Incipit: ('Extrait des *Mémoires du comte de Comminges*) 'Le comte est obligé, pour des / intérêts de famille, de se rendre à l'abbaye de / R***.'

82

Dorat: *Les Malheurs de l'inconstance*, 1793

Claude-Joseph Dorat (1734-1780): Les / malheurs / de l'inconstance, / ou / lettres / de / la marquise de Syrce [Syrcé for ii] / et du comte / de Mirbelle; / Par Dorat. / [rule] / Première [Seconde] partie. / [rule] / A Paris, / Chez Leprieur, Libraire, quai / Voltaire, N.° 12. / [rule] / 1793.

18°, i: 2 ff. (halftitle and titlepage) + [v]-xiv, [15]-251 pp.

ii: 1 f. (titlepage; a leaf is missing, see the commentary) + [5]-216 pp.

Commentary: The first item in vol. i is an 'Avant-propos'. This epistolary novel first appeared in 1772 (MMF 72.19). MMF list this edition after Quérard's quite inadequate entry and Aspin's catalogue no. 45. (This was the Aspin copy.) Giraud lists what appears to be this edition for 2 vols in-12 (1772.2.d). Since it does not exist anywhere else that I know of, I have included it.

There are two fine engravings (a frontispiece for each volume) which, curiously enough, are adapted from the excellent Marillier engravings issued with the first edition of another novel by Dorat, *Les Sacrifices de l'amour*, 1771 (MMF 71.25). The first frontispiece to the *Malheurs* corresponds to the second in *Les Sacrifices*, and the second to the *Malheurs* is the first in *Les Sacrifices*. Monglond lists a *Sacrifices de l'amour* for 1793, 2 vols in-12 (after Cohen), with two illustrations by Blanchard (ii, col.999). But the entry in Cohen is for 1792, 2 vols in-8, with two illustrations by Blanchard (col.322). Quérard lists a 'IIIe édition' for 2 vols in-12, 1793 (ii.578). And Drujon mentions a '2e édition: Paris, 1793, 2 vol. in-12' (i, col.1112). Perhaps the unsigned engravings in the edition described here have something to do with the Blanchard pictures meant for the 1793 edition of *Les Sacrifices de l'amour*? The reduced adaptations are mirror images.

The half titlepage to vol. i reads: 'Les / malheurs / de / l'inconstance. / [rule] / Première partie. / [rule]'. F.A1 of vol. ii is missing (presumably the half titlepage), so there is no half titlepage in the present copy for that volume. Monglond lists yet another edition of *Les Malheurs de l'inconstance* for 1793: a 'nouvelle édition', Paris, Delalain, 2 vols in-12, after Quérard (ii, col.999; Quérard ii.578). That edition is not listed in MMF.

To editions of *Les Malheurs de l'inconstance* listed in MMF (72.19), I would add:

No 82: Dorat, *Les Malheurs de l'inconstance*, 1793, frontispiece to vol. i

Dorat, *Les Sacrifices de l'amour*, 1771, frontispiece to vol. ii

'Les Malheurs de l'Inconstance, ou lettres de la Marquise de Circé & du Comte de Mirbelle. II Parties. 12. Bern & à Leipsic, chez Hertel en commiss.', Messkatalog, OM 1773, p.560. This is conceivably (but not probably) the same edition as listed in MMF (72.19) and in Krauss-Fontius (no. 3953), for Neuchâtel: Société typographique, 1773.

And to editions of *Les Sacrifices de l'amour* recorded by MMF (71.25), one might add:

1. 1771. 'Les Sacrifices de l'amour, ou lettres de la vicomtesse de Senanges et du chevalier de Versenay, suivies de Sylvie et Moléshoff. 2 vols. Amsterdam; Paris: Delalain, 1771', Krauss-Fontius (no. 3951), with a location for the Landesbibliothek Gotha. The first edition of the novel with *Sylvie et Moléshoff* listed in MMF is dated 1772.

2. 1772. *Les Sacrifices de l'amour, ou lettres de la vicomtesse de Senanges et du chevalier de Versenai, suivies de 'Sylvie et Moléshoff'*. Amsterdam; Paris: chez Delalain, 1772. 2 pl + [j]-vi (for iv), [v]-xvj + [1]-(235) pp. and 2 pl + [1]-(186), [187-188; halftitle with an announcement verso], [189]-(205) pp. in-8°, two poor fontispieces (imitations of the original illustrations), BL: 11475.df.25. (This is a piracy, probably German or Swiss.)

3. 1784. 'Sacrifices de l'amour, ou Lettres de la Comtesse de Senanges & du Chevalier de Versenay par Mr. Dorat. 2 Voll. 12. à Lausanne, chez Jul. Hen. Pott & comp.', Messkatalog, OM 1784, p.907.

Incipit: 'Vous me demandiez hier d'où venoit ma tristesse, et si j'avois à me plaindre de vous.'

83

Dubois (transl. and editor): *Histoire des amours et infortunes d'Abelard et d'Eloise*, 1703

François Nicolas Dubois, translator and editor; Pierre Abailard (1079-1142) and Heloise (1101-1164), possibly: (titlepage in *red* and black) *Histoire / des / amours / et infortunes / d'Abelard / et / d'Eloise, / avec / Les Lettres qu'ils s'écrivirent l'un à l'autre. / Quatriéme edition, / Revûë, corrigée & augmentée de deux lettres, / qui n'ont point encore paru. / [small woodcut ornament: basket of flowers] / A la Haye, / Chez Meydert Uytwerf, Marchand / Libraire, das le Hof-straet, / près de la Cour. / [rule] / M. DCCIII.*

12°: 1 pl + 6 ff. (12 pp.) + 1-334 pp.

Commentary: This book contains a preface, an *Histoire des amours et infortunes d'Abélard et d'Eloise* (pp.1-133); 'Lettres / d'Abélard / et / d'Eloïse.' (halftitle, pp.[135-36], and then the work, including an introduction, p.137-334). At the end of the text, p.334, there is a list of errata.

The preface gives some interesting information. After stating that the first edition appeared in 1693 at The Hague, it is claimed that 'L'Edition en a été renouvellée trois fois, & débitée avec une promptitude, qui a fait juger que l'Ouvrage étoit bon'. Then the editor states that the Dutch edition, with its preliminary history of Abelard and Heloise, leaves out most of the essentials.

As for the Paris edition, the long introduction is 'une espèce de Roman, où l'Auteur, en s'égayant lui-même, a plûtôt cherché à divertir le Lecteur. [...] Il s'est contenté de décrire deux ou trois des principaux événemens de leur Vie, ausquels il a joint quelques fictions'. Dubois (assuming it be he) then goes on to tout the accuracy of his own introduction. He also gives interesting information concerned with the previous publication of some of the material contained in the work.

Charrier lists the first edition of this collection for La Haye, chez Louis van Dole, 1695, in-12, remarking that that book was 'réimprimé en 1697, 1700, 1703, 1705, 1709, 1711, 1722', also in-12 (p.605, no.44). There is no way of telling whether Charrier came across the edition described here, or another one. Note that she seems to indicate that the later editions were for The Hague, van Dole as well. (Indeed, the self-styled fifth edition is for La Haye: chez L. & H. van Dale [*sic*; possibly a transcription error], M. DCC. XI.; NUC for the Library of Congress, ND 0392700). Since I could not find my book in any library (or library-union catalogues), I have chosen to include a description of it.

There is a pretty frontispiece engraving, depicting the castration of Abelard: 'CPL [intwined] Sluyter Schulp:'.

Little if any of the material in this book is probably by Abelard and Heloise. See the commentary on the 1796 Cailleau entry above for further clarification.

Incipit: (*Histoire des amours et infortunes...*) 'Pierre Abélard, natif de / Palais* en Bretagne, / vivoit dans le douziéme / Siécle.' (A note gives the location of Palais).

('Lettre d'Abélard a Filinte') 'La derniére fois que nous / fûmes ensemble, Fi- / linte'.

84

Du Laurens: *Le Compère Mathieu*, 1793

Henri Joseph Du Laurens (1719-1797): Le compère [compere for iii-iv] / Ma- thieu. [Mathieu, for iii-iv] / ou [Ou for i-ii because of the preceding period] / les bigarrures / de l'esprit humain. / Nouvelle édition. / Ornée de belles Figures. / [rule] / Tome premier [second, troisieme, quatrieme]. / [small symmetrical orna- ment in the form of a short rule] / A Hambourg, / Chez Fauche, [Fauche. for iii- iv] / Et à Paris, chez Lepetit, Libraire, / Quai [quai for iii-iv] des Augustins, N°. [n° for iii-iv] 32. / [short rule] / 1793.

18°, i:1 f. (titlepage, with quote from the work verso) + 1 f. (2 pp.) + [5]-238 pp.

ii: 1 f. (titlepage, no quote verso) + [3]-210 pp.

iii: 1 f. (titlepage, with quote verso) + [3]-228 pp.

iv: 1 f. (titlepage, with quote verso) + [3]-220 pp. + 1 f. (two-page table)

Commentary: The two preliminary pages are an 'Avis de l'éditeur'. There are four pretty frontispiece plates by Louvion. The citation verso of the titleleaves is taken from the work itself and varies somewhat.

MMF list a 1793-1797, Paris and Hamburg edition, 4 vols. in-16, after a M. Rossignol sales' catalogue (no.97). They remark that Princeton has an edition for Paris: Dufart, 1793, in 4 vols, 'qui pourrait être la même' (66.21). I have no idea whether the Rossignol copy represents the same edition described here. The BLC lists an edition for 1793-1795, in-16 (no further information given; 012550.de.72).

MMF further list an edition for Paris: Bouqueton, 1793, 4 vols in-18, after an ms catalogue by Edouard Tricotel in the BL. That edition exists in the Eleuthe-rian Mills Historical Library (Delaware), and is succinctly described in OCLC. It is also listed in Krauss-Fontius (no.3888), with a location for Universitäts-und Landesbibliothek Sachsen-Anhalt, Halle.

Furthermore, Krauss-Fontius list an edition which has escaped the attention of bibliographers of the 'genre romanesque': 'I-III. -Londres: Comp. 1782, [I (is) 1772.]' (no. 3886; location: Stadtbibliothek Ballenstedt [I.II.]).

Incipit: 'Lecteur, tu vas lire l'histoire de mon / *compere Mathieu*, la mienne et celle / de quelques autres personnages'.

85

Duvernet: *Les Dîners de M. Guillaume*, 1788

Abbé Théophile Imarigeon Duvernet (or Du Vernet; 1734-1796): Les diners / de / M. Guillaume, / avec / l'histoire / de / son enterrement. / Par l'auteur de la vie de Voltaire. / [small symmetrical woodcut ornament] / [double rule] / M. DCC. LXXXVIII.

12°: 1 f. (titlepage) + [3]-97, [98] pp.

Commentary. MMF (88.49) list this work after the BN copy, with a different title, 108 pp. in-12. Reynaud, in his faulty description, lists this work largely as described here. However, there are two editions in the BN, and mine matches Z. Bengesco 799. (The MMF entry obviously derives from BN Y2.27751, Z27459.) The confusion doubtless stems from the fact that the BNC lists the 108 pp. edition with the mention of '3 exemplaires' and the shelf marks for the three BN copies, actually comprising two editions (vol. xlvi, col.311). I describe my copy to help clarify the bibliographical confusion. The edition listed above contains a nice engraving which is similar to, but not the same as the engraving by Ransonnette issued with the edition listed in MMF.

The contents of the two editions are pretty much the same, with a couple of changes concerning the ordering of the items, except that the 'Dawson-Bengesco' edition contains an additional, interesting paragraph in the 'Note de l'éditeur', printed on the last, unnumbered page. The entire note reads: 'Parmi les manuscrits de M. *Guillaume* on trouva un petit *catéchisme* qu'il avait composé pour la conversion de feu M. l'abbé *Rabatier*, qui, comme tous les languedociens savans, avait eu le malheur de tomber dans l'athéisme. M. *Guillaume*, si M. l'abbé n'était pas mort, espérait lui faire croire en Dieu. Il était déjà parvenu à lui apprendre le commencement du Credo. [paragraph] On trouva aussi parmi les papiers de M. *Guillaume* plusieurs de ses après-dîners; nous les imprimerons si nous voyons le public content de ses dîners.' No 'après-dîners' were ever published, that I know of. MMF mention that the *Dîners* are a continuation ('suite') of Duvernet's *Monsieur Guillaume, ou le disputeur* (81.18). The *Dîners de M. Guillaume* sets real people on stage (Préville, Du Gazon, La Place, Vestris, Le Mière (or Le Mierre), Mercier, Benjamin Franklin and others), and is not very kind to most of them.

Incipit: 'Les conseils d'une femme aimable qui donne peu de conseils, ont toujours un bon effet'.

86

Eustathius Macrembolites (Beauchamps transl.): *Ismène et Isménias*, 1780

Eustathius (sometime Eumathius) Macrembolites (12th century), translated by Pierre François Godard (sometimes Godart) de Beauchamps (1689-1761): Ismene / et / Ismenias. / Roman grec. / [extensive allegorical woodcut ornament with head in centre, signed 'Beugnet inv.'] / A Paris. / [short rule] / M. DCC. LXXX.

18°: 2 pl (halftitle and titlepages) + [1]-115 pp.

Commentary: The halftitle reads 'Ismene / et / Ismenias.' The type seems to be Didot's. Chainlines are vertical. The book is signed in 6s, with no catchwords at all. It is elegantly produced, with wide margins (in the present copy; contemporary 'cartonnage' of superior quality). Aside from the titlepage vignette and a modest, yet elegant composite ornament at the beginning of p.[1], there are no decorations. This ornament is the same as that for Voltaire's *Romans et contes*, i.[174] (*Les Aveugles juges des couleurs*) and iv.[167] (*Bababec*). See the pertinent entry below for further information.

Jones (1729, p.42), and MMF after Jones (56.R24), list an edition of this work for 1780. That edition, represented by a copy in the BL for example, is different from the one recorded here. It is part of the famous collection printed by Didot for the comte d'Artois and bears Didot's name on the titlepage. I could find no trace of the edition (or issue) described here, aside from my copy.

I do not know whether Godard de Beauchamps translated from the original Greek, or from the Latin, but here are those titles (the Greek transliterated): 'To kath' Hysmenian kai Hysminen drama' and 'De Ismeniae et Ismenes amoribus'.

Incipit: 'La ville d'Eurycome est située dans un / pays charmant : la mer l'environne d'un / côté ; de l'autre, d'agréables prairies, ar- / rosées de rivieres'.

87

Fénelon: *Les Aventures de Télémaque, fils d'Ulysse*, 1710

François de Salignac de La Motte (or de La Mothe) Fénelon (1651-1715): (titlepage in *red* and black) Avantures / de / *Telemaque,* / fils d'Ulysse; / ou / suite du quatriéme livre / de l'Odyssée / *d'Homere*. / Par Monseigneur François de

Salignac, de la / Mothe Fenelon, Archevêque Duc de Cambrai, / Prince du St. Empire, Comte du Cambresis, ci- / devant Precepteur de Messeigneurs les Ducs de / Bourgogne, d'Anjou & de Berri, &c. / Servant d'Instruction à Monseigneur le / *duc de Bourgogne*. / Derniere Edition, plus ample & plus exacte que les precedentes. / [woodcut sphere] / *A la Haye*, / Chez Adrien Moetjens, Marchand Libraire, près / de la Cour, à la Librairie Françoise. / [rule] / *M. DCC. X*. / Avec privilege.

12°: 1 f. (titlepage) + iij-iv, v-xxix, xxx-xxxv, xxxvj-xlij, xliij-xliv + 1-430 + 433, 434-448 pp.

Commentary: The contents are as follows:

   1. a 'Privilegie' in Dutch to Adriaen Moetjens for fifteen years, starting in 1699, signed 'vt. H. Hensius. Ter Ordonnantie van de Staten Simon van Beaumon';

   2. a preface;

   3. various poems by different authors, concerning the *Aventures de Télémaque*, beginning with La Fontaine's 'Le serpent et la lime', 'addressée [*sic*] aux auteurs qui ont critiqué les Avantures de Telemaque';

   4. two poems of a dedicatory nature, in Latin (pp.xxxvj-xlij);

   5. 'Sommaire du premier livre' (pp.xliij-xliv);

   6. the novel proper;

   7. a halftitle for 'Les / avantures / d'Aristonoüs.' (pp.[431-32]), an 'Avertissement du libraire' (p.433) and *Aristonoüs* (pp.434-48).

I was unable to find a reference to this edition anywhere. Chérel mentions a La Haye: Moetjens, 1710 edition, in one volume in-12°, ill., which is an edition quite different from the one described here. The edition listed by Chérel can be found hither and thither. He states that the preface is by the abbé de Saint-Rémi (the abbé Jean Baptiste de La Landelle de Saint-Rémy), which must here be the case. (The preface first appeared in 1701 and was often reprinted particularly with editions put out by Moetjens.) The copy described here, bound in contemporary calf, contains no illustrations, and none seems ever to have been included.

The last piece first appeared in 1699, as did the *Aventures de Télémaque* (the initial version, that is; see Lever and Chérel). Chérel mentions that *Les Aventures d'Aristonoüs* first appeared under the title of *Sophronime* (or *Sophronyme*; p.29). *Sophronime* is not listed in Lever. The dialogues often included with *Télémaque* are absent from this edition. (Concerning this, and other bibliographical points, see the extensive article devoted to Fénelon and *Télémaque* in Quérard, iii.89-102.)

The edition described here conceivably represents a German piracy of a legitimate Dutch edition, possibly the Moetjens, 1708 edition (BL: 634.a.7) or one of its analogues. The contents of the 1708 edition are the same as the 1710 one described here, right down to the privilege (which is the same). The pagination varies somewhat. The 1708 edition carries Moetjen's device on the titlepage: woodcut decoration of a stork in a tree-top, over a book held open by an angel and a warrior, the whole enclosed by a wreath. Outside there is the slogan: 'Amat libraria curam'. (The arrangement of the lettering on the titlepages of both editions is similar, although not identical, and both are in red and black.)

There are several editions of *Télémaque* which do not seem to be listed in modern bibliographies dealing with prose fiction (or in Chérel), as follows:

1. *1709*. 'Avantures de Telemaque, Fils d'Vlysse, ou svite du quatrieme Livre de l'Odyssée d'Homere par Mr. François de Salignac, de la Mothe Fenelon, derniere Edition, plus ample & plus exacte que les precedentes. aux depens de Daniel Bartholomy [*sic*].' Messkatalog, OM 1709, f.G2*v*.

2. *1718*. 'Avantures de Telemaqve fils d'Ulysse. Composées par feu Messire François de Salignac, de la Mothe Fenelon, nouvelle edition Augmentie [*sic*] sur le manuscrit original de l'Auteur. 8. A Jene. Aux dépens de *Jean Felix Bielcke*.' Messkatalog, MM 1718, f.E4*v*.

3. *1719*. 'Les Avantures de Telemaque, Fils d'Ulysse composées par feu Messire François de Salignac, de la Motte Fenelon, Precepteur de Messeigneurs les Enfans de france. Et depuis Archevêque-Duc de Cambray, Prince du Sr. [*sic*] Empire. Derniere Edition. Augmentée & Corrigée sur le Manuscrit Original de l'Auteur. Imprimée suivant la Copie de Paris. 8. avec & sans figures. Aux depens de Daniel Barthelemy. 1719. Avec Privileges.' Messkatalog, MM 1719, f.F3*r*. This is conceivably the Rotterdam: D. Barthélemy, 1718 edition listed in Chérel. I write 'conceivably' because there is a listing in the 1718 Messkatalog (vernalibus 1718, f.D4*v*) for a edition (or issue) similar to that cited by Chérel.

4. *1732*. MMF list two editions for 1732, after Chérel and Quérard. Chérel's entry is for a 2 vols, in-12, 'Londres' edition. (Quérard lists a Londres, 1732 edition and gives further information about it; iii.90b.) Quérard also has a Hambourg, Abraham Van-den-Hoeck, 1731 edition, with a 1732 reprint (possibly a reissue, although the latter possibility is unlikely; iii.91a). Gesamtverzeichniss has two editions for 1732. The first is '[le même] av[ec] remarq. p. M. Plat. 8vo. Francf. Brönner. [1]732' (xxxvii.128b).

5. *1732*. The other edition listed in Gesamtverzeichniss (*loc. cit.*) is for '[...]. Nouvelle édition corrigée, & enrichie de belles remarques allemandes par Joseph Antoine d'Ehrenreich. [Ulm?] Aux dépens de Jean Conrad Wohler, 1732. 8vo. 5 BL [ff.] 344 & 296 S. [pp.] 23 BL. [ff.] und 24 hübsche Kupfer. [...]' (*loc. cit.*). A fairly extensive note explains that this is the first 'Ehrenreich' edition. (He was a professor at the Stuttgart 'Gymnasium'.) Importantly the note states that 'Die späteren Drucke dieser Ausgabe erschienen mit französ.-deutschem, oder nur deutschem Titel, in Ulm'. It is mentioned that the engravings are nice copies (reductions) of those appearing with the Paris, 1730 edition.

6. *1745*. 'Les Avantures de Telemaque Fils d'Ulysse, corrigée [!] & enrichie de belles Remarques allemandes, par Jo. Ant. d'Ehrenreich, avec Figures, 8. Ulm, chez *J. C. Wohler*.' Messkatalog, MM 1745, f.E3*v*. (An entry in Gesamtverzeichniss states that this is the second edition; xxxvii.128b.)

7. *1747*. 'Les Avantures de Telemaqué [!] avec remarques Allemandes & figures. 8. Ulm, chez *JC Wohler*. Mit allergn. Privilegio.' Messkatalog, OM 1747, f.H1*r*.

8. *1747*. 'Les avantures de Telemaque, fils d'Ulysse. Par Fen [!] Mre François de Salignac, de la Mothe-Fénelon... Nouv. éd. conforme an [!] manuscrit original, & enrichie de figures en taille-douce. Amsterdam, J. Westein [*sic*] &

G. Smith, & Z. Chatelain, 1747. [10] xl, 487 p. front. (port.), plates. 17cm.'
NUC supplement (New York Public Library).

9. *1749*. 'les Avantures de Telemaque, composées par Fr. de Sal. de la Motte
Fenelon, avec remarques allemandes & figures, 8. chez *Jean Conrad Wohler*, mit
allergn. Priv.' Messkatalog, OM 1749, f.H2*v*.

10. *1752*. 'Les Avantures de Telemaque fils d'Ulysse par Fenelon &c. enrichie
de belles remarques alemandes [!] par Ios. Ant. d'Ernreich avec fig. 8. à Ulme,
chez I. C. Wohler, mit allergn. Privileg.' Messkatalog, OM 1752, p.268. There
is a similar edition listed in the NUC (four locations) for 1751. Perhaps the one
listed in the Messkatalog is the same?

11. *1761*. 'les Avantures de Telemaque fils d'Ulisse. Nouv. Edit. av. Fig. 8. à
Ulm chez Dan. Barthelemy et fils.' Messkatalog, MM 1761, p.191. The edition
listed in the NUC (University of Utah) is 16cm. That would be a small
duodecimo, unless that copy has been drastically cropped. I record the Messkatalog entry since it could well represent a different issue.

12. *1762*. 'Les Avantures de Telemaque, fils d'Ulysse. Nouv. éd., rev., corr.
et enrichie de belles remarques allemandes, par Joseph Antoine d'Ehrenreich.
[Stuttgart] J. C. Wohler, 1762. 2 v. in 1. illus., map.' NUC supplement (Indiana
University). Concerning the attribution of the place of publication to Stuttgart:
Wohler was an Ulm based publisher, and there were many editions put out by
him bearing no mention of place of publication.

13. *1769*. 'Les Avantures de Telemaque fils d'Ulysse, avec des notes allemandes. Nouv. Ed. corrigée & augmentée. 8. à Ulm, chez J. Conr. Wohler.'
Messkatalog, OM 1769, p.1121. An entry in Gesamtverzeichniss has 'N. Aufl.,
mit verb. deutschen Noten u. e. Chrestomathie, (v. J. Köhler). 8vo. Ebd.
[Ulm] [1]769' (xxxvii.128b).

14. *1777*. MMF list two editions for that year, after Chérel. The latter source
indicates editions for Genève [Lyon] and Paris, Barrois. Gesamtverzeichniss
has an entry for 'le même. 12mo. Venice. (Tourneysen. Basel.) [1]777'
(xxxvii.128b), meaning that there were at least three editions for 1777.

15. *1778*. 'Les Avantures de Telemaque fils d'Ulysse, mit ganz neuen und
durchaus verbesserten deutschen Noten, auch neuen Kupfern. 8. Ulm, chez J.
Conr. Wohler.' Messkatalog, MM 1778, p.577. (An entry in Gesamtverzeichniss,
evidently gleaned from a modern sales catalogue, gives many more details
conerning this edition; xxxvii.128b.)

16. *1780*. 'Les Avantures de Telemaque, fils d'Ulysse par feu Mess. Franç. de
Salignac de la Motte de Fenelon. 2 Tomes. Nouv. Edit. gr. 12. à Porto & Leipsic,
chez Char. Fred. Schneider en commiss.' Messkatalog, OM 1780, p.912.

17. *1787*. Les aventures de Telemaque [...] soigneusement corrigee par J.
Perrin [Jean Baptiste Perrin]. Londres. Chez C. Nourse, J. F. & C. Rivington,
T. Longman, B. Law [etc.], 1787. xxviij + 372 p. + 1 f. (2 pp. of advertisements)
in-12° (BL 1607/2336).

18. *1799*. 'Avantures, les, de Télémaque, fils d'Ulysse, par Fr. de Salignac de
la Motte Fénélon. Nouv. édit. 8. à Leipsig, Rabenhorst.' Messkatalog, OM
1799, p.202.

19. *1799*. 'Avantures, les, de Telemaque, fils d'Ulysse, mit deutschen Anmerk.
von Jos[eph] Ant[on] v. Ehrenreich u. Joh. Ludw. Röhker. Neue verb. Aufl. 8.

Ulm, Wohlersche Buchhdl.' Messkatalog, OM 1799, p.202. There is an edition (Ehrenreich's notes, Ulm: Wohlersche Buchhandlung, 1798) listed in the NUC (Detroit Public Library, St. John's University [Minnesota]). Perhaps it is the same as that referred to in the Messkatalog?

It might further be remarked that MMF list a 1723 edition after the NUC (presumably), with a location for Harvard. The NUC listing is for 'Les aventures de Telemaque, fils d'Ulysse. Nouv. éd. cy-devant rev. & corr. Paris, Bartelemy, 1723, xxxiii, 505 pp. ill.' There is an entry in the Messkatalog which, if it refers to the same edition, indicates that this edition was not printed in Paris: 'Les Avantures de Telemaque, Fils d'Ulysse composées par feu Messire François de Salignac, de la Motte Fenelon, nouvelle edition, Cy-devant revue & corrigée sur le manuscrit original de l'auteur. A present augmentée d'une table genealogique de Telemaque, & des remarques morales, politiques, & historiques, regardants[!] la fable ou l'histoire ancienne, tisées[!] des Meilleurs Auteurs, Lexicographes, & glossaires. 8. Imprimé suivant la copie de Paris. Aux depens. De Daniel Bartelemy, MDCCXXIII. avec Privilege de S.M. Imperiale, de S.M. le Roy de Pologne & de S.A.S. l'Electeur de Saxe.', OM 1723, f.G2 (recto and verso). The NUC entry perhaps omits the highly important qualifier, 'suivant la copie'.

MMF mention an edition for 1772, after the copy in the Gemeente Bibliotheek, Rotterdam which I was unable to consult. (This is not listed in Chérel.) Heinsius lists an edition as follows: '[Aventures] de Telemaque, p[a]r de Sal. de la Motte Fenelon franc. & allemand, avec fig. gr. 8[vo]. ibid. [Ulm] Wagner, [1]772' (*Handbuch*, p.776).

For perhaps further editions of *Télémaque*, see Gesamtverzeichniss, xxxvii.128b et seq.; I was only able to do a cursory examination of the entries listed in that source.

Incipits: (*Les Aventures de Télémaque*) 'Calypso ne pouvoit se consoler du départ d'Ulysse: dans sa douleur elle se trouvoit malheureuse d'être immortelle.'

(*Les Aventures d'Aristonoüs*) 'Sophronime ayant perdu les biens de ses Ancêtres par des naufrages, & par d'autres malheurs, s'en consoloit par sa vertu dans l'Isle de Delos.'

88

Fénelon: *Les Aventures de Télémaque, fils d'Ulysse*, 1751

François de Salignac de La Motte (or de La Mothe) Fénelon (1651-1715): i: Les / avantures / de / Telemaque, / fils d'Ulysse. / Par feu Messire François de Salignac / de la Motte Fenelon, Précepteur / de Messeigneurs les Enfans de France, & / depuis Archevêque-Duc de Cambrai, / Prince du saint Empire, &c. / augmentéees, / Des Avantures / d'Aristonous. / Nouvelle edition / conforme au Manuscrit original. / Enrichi de Figures en Taille douce. / Tome premier. / Londres: / Chez J. Brotherton, G. Innys, R. Ware, J. Wal- / thoe, G. Meadows, T. Cox, J. & P. Knapton, / S. Birt, C. Hitch, T. Astley, E. Austen, J. Hodges, / J. Osborn, & J. Ward. MDCCLI.

ii: Les / avantures / de / Telemaque, / fils d'Ulysse. / Nouvelle edition / conforme au Manuscrit original. / Enrichi de Figures en Taille douce. / Tome second. / Augmentées, / des / avantures / d'Aristonous. / Londres: / Chez [...; same as vol. i]

18°, i: 2 ff. (halftitle and titlepages) + [v]-vii, [viii: blank], [ix]-xii + [1]-28, 29, [30: blank], [31]-250 pp.
 ii: 2 pl + [1]-215 + [219]-230, [231]-236 pp.

Commentary: These volumes contain:
  1. a dedication 'Au roy', signed 'Fenelon' (pp.[v]-vii);
  2. an 'Avertissement' of the editor(s) (pp.[ix]-xii);
  3. a 'Discours de la poesie epique, et de l'excellence du poeme de Telemaque' (pp.[1]-28);
  4. an approbation: 1 June 1716, signed 'de Sacy' (pp.28-[29]);
  5. the novel (i.[31]-250, plus a blank leaf);
  6. the rest of the novel (ii.[1]-215);
  7. a halftitle for 'Les / avantures / d'Aristonous.' (pp.[217-18]);
  8. *Aristonoüs* (pp.[219]-230);
  9. an 'Ode' (pp.[231]-236).
I could find no trace of this edition anywhere. The office of the ESTC in London was kind enough to check the records for the Short-title catalogue, and there is nothing in them corresponding to the edition described here (as of August 1982). This edition is clearly British printed, probably as indicated by the imprint.

Pages 6 and 12 in vol. i (both versos) bear an asterisk at the far left. I do not know what they signify.

The *Aventures de Télémaque* first appeared in 1699, as did *Aristonoüs*. For further information, see the preceding entry.

The 'Discours' is by Andrew Michael Ramsay. The brief 'avertissement' explains, concerning it and the poem appended to the end of vol. ii: 'L'on a cru ne devoir pas laisser plus longtems à la tête de cet Ouvrage une Préface qui a paru, & que l'Auteur de Telemaque n'a jamais approuvée. On a mis en sa place le Discours suivant, où l'on tâche de déveloper les beautés de ce Poëme, sa conformité aux regles de l'art, & la sublimité de sa morale. On a cru devoir ajouter à cette Edition, les Avantures d'Aristonoüs. [...] On a joint à la fin de cette Edition une Ode de l'Auteur composée dans sa jeunesse. Elle fera voir son talent naturel pour la versification' (pp.xi-xii).

The approbation contains some of the highest praise I have ever read concerning a piece of fiction. That is presumably why the 1751 publishers included it, leaving out the rest of any legal material.

There are halftitles for 'Les / avantures / de / Telemaque, / tome premier [second].' The two volumes contain twenty-five plates: a portrait-frontispiece by N. Parr after Vivien and twenty-four pictures, one for each book, by N. Parr, numbered and bearing the 'book' indication. The information printed on the plates is in English and Latin. At the head of the 'Discours' there is a folding map. (This edition is not listed in Cohen or Reynaud).

On the verso of the binder's leaf (contemporary calf) is a manuscript 'clef':

'Telemaque has been imagined to be a satire against the government and reign of Lewis XIV. with whom Fenelon was in disgrace on account of his defence of Quietism, or the doctrines of Madame Guion [Guyon] –

Calypso supposed to be Madame Montespan
Eucharis... Mademoiselle de Fontange
Telemachus[,] The Duke of Burgundy
Mentor[,] The Duke of Beauvilliers
Antiope[,] The Duchess of Burgundy
Protesilaus[,] Louvois
Dominius[?,] King James 2ᵈ
Sesostris[,] Lewis 14ᴿ'.

Fénelon never intended that his didactic novel revolve around a key. See Drujon, ii, col.925-26 and Albert Cahen's introduction to his edition of the work (Paris 1920, 'Grands écrivains de la France'), especially p.xcviii et seq.

Incipits: (*Les Aventures de Télémaque*) 'CALYPSO ne pouvoit se consoler du départ d'Ulysse.'

(*Les Aventures d'Aristonoüs*): 'SOPHRONIME ayant perdu les biens de ses Ancêtres par des naufrages, & par d'autres malheurs, s'en consoloit par sa vertu dans l'isle de Delos.'

89

Fénelon: *Les Aventures de Télémaque, fils d'Ulysse*, 1778

François de Salignac de La Motte (or de La Mothe) Fénelon (1651-1715): Les / aventures / de / Télémaque, / fils d'Ulisse. / Par feu Mre. François de Salygnac, / de la Motthe-Fénélon, Précepteur de / Messeigneurs les Enfans de France, / & depuis Archevêque, Duc de Cambrai, / Prince du Saint-Empire. / Nouvelle édition corrigée, / Conforme au Manuscrit original, & enrichie de / Figures en taille-douce. / [symmetrical woodcut ornament] / A Paris, / Par la Compagnie des libraires. / [segmented double rule, with finials] / M. DCC. LXXVIII. / Avec Approbation & Permission.

12°: 1 f. (titlepage) + [iij-iv], v-xl + [1]-464 pp.

Commentary: This book contains a dedication to the king, signed Fénélon; a 'Discours De la poésie Epique, & de l'excellence du Poëme de Télémaque' (translated from Ramsay's English); the novel, to p.445; 'Les / aventures / d'Aristonoüs.' (half titlepage, p.[447]); 'Avertissement du libraire' (p.[448]); *Aristonoüs* (p.[449] to the end).

MMF cite two editions of this work for 1778, after Chérel and presumably the NUC (locations in the USA). Chérel's entry is for Leyde, Wetstein, 2 vols in-12, ill. The NUC (with locations as given by MMF) lists Londres: J. Hourse [*sic*; an error for 'Nourse'?], 1778, xxxii, 386, [16] pp., ill. Obviously neither of those corresponds to my book. I could not find another copy.

On p.xxiv there is the stamp of the local guild office of Marseille, 1777, with inspector Durand's signature (struck), indicating that this is a legitimate copy of a pirated edition. (For further information concerning this matter, see Anne

Boës and Robert L. Dawson, 'The police stamp of 1777 and the legitimation of contrefaçons', *Studies on Voltaire* 230, 1985, pp.461-84.)

There are an allegorical frontispiece portrait by Faure and ten primitive, unsigned engravings (one for each book), together with a folding map. Titles of nobility and mentions of the king have been struck in the dedicatory letter, probably during the revolution when such mutilations were frequent. (That also probably accounts for Durand's name having been crossed out.)

This book was certainly not produced in Paris. All indications are of a Marseille printing (by Mossy?).

Incipits: (*Les Aventures de Télémaque*) 'Calypso ne pouvoit se consoler / du départ d'Ulysse: dans sa dou- / leur, elle se trouvoit malheureuse / d'être immortelle'.

(*Les Aventures d'Aristonoüs*) 'Sophronime ayant perdu les / biens de ses ancêtres par des nau- / frages, & par d'autres malheurs, / s'en consoloit par sa vertu dans / l'isle de Delos.'

90

Fiévée: *La Dot de Suzette*, 1798

Joseph Fiévée (1767-1839): La dot / de Suzette, / ou / histoire / de Mme de Senneterre, / racontée par elle-mème. / [rule] / A Paris, / Chez Maradan, Libraire, rue du Cimetière- / André-des-Arts, n°. 9. / [rule] / An sixième.

18°: 2 ff. (halftitle and titlepage) + [v]-xij + [1]-222 pp.

Commentary: The pagination reflects a preface and the novel. There is a halftitle bearing 'La dot / de / Suzette.' MMF list a xii, 222-page edition after copies in the BN and BL (claiming they are in-24, erroneously [98.41]; the novel first appeared in 1798).

I list my book to remark that there were two editions, same format, same pagination, same year. The other edition is represented, for example, by BL 012511.a.6, the titlepage reading 'La dot / de Suzette, / ou / histoire / de Mme de Senneterre, / racontée par elle-mème. / [rule] / A Paris, / Chez Maradan, Libraire, rue Pavée- / André-des-Arts. n°. 9. / [rule] / An sixième.' 1 f. (titlepage) + [v]-xij + [1]-222 pp. in-18. (The BL copy has no halftitle, but f.[a1] is missing.) Cohen mentions the in-18 edition (Paris, Maradan), remarking that there is a 'jolie figure non signée. Rare.' He also states that there is a 'contrefaçon sous la même date. Les caractères sont plus petits et la figure est en contre-partie, Mme de Senneterre étant à gauche et Suzette à droite' (col.397). This description would fit the BL copy, although it is by no means certain the latter is a piracy.

There is a frontispiece in my copy (chain lines horizontal) bearing 'la Dot.' at the top left, with a caption: 'Madame de Seneterre [*sic*]! Ô! Ciel Madame de / Senneterre!'. (Figure in white to the left, figure in black to the right). The caption in the BL frontispiece reads: 'Madame de Senneterre! Ô Ciel! Madame / de Senneterre.'

There is an edition listed in Krauss-Fontius which has escaped the attention of bibliographers of prose-fiction: 'La Dot de Suzette, ou mémoires de Mme de

Senneterre, par elle-même. Paris 1798. xii, 243 pp.' (no. 4054), with two locations.

Incipit: 'Je suis née à Saint-Domingue. A dix ans, mon père me fit passer en France'.

91

Florian: *Estelle*, 1788

Jean Pierre Claris de Florian (1755-1794): Œuvres / complettes / de Mr. de Florian. / Capitaine de Dragons, et Gentilhomme / de S. A. S. Monseigneur le Duc de / Penthièvre, des Académies de / Madrid, de Florence, de Lyon, de / Nisme, d'Angers, etc. etc. / Tome neuvième. / Contenant Estelle. / [symmetrical woodcut ornament] / A Paris; / Et se trouve à Bruxelles, / Chez Emmanuel Flon, Imprimeur / Libraire, rue des Fripiers. / [double rule] / M. DCC. LXXXVIII.

18°: 2 pl + [j]-xxxvj + [1]-197, [198]-227 pp.

Commentary: Pagination reflects the 'Essai sur la pastorale', the novel, and the notes. There is a halftitle reading: 'Œuvres / complettes / de Mr. de Florian.' The halftitle and titlepage are tipped in (chainlines horizontal) and probably replaced the original halftitle and titlepage.

This volume is part of a 'recueil factice' of the *Œuvres* put together by Flon, with books he may or may not have printed (or had printed), although they do seem to be products of Brussels press[es]. Flon apparently just added his own titlepages and halftitles. Flon might also have had a separate titlepage for *Estelle* done up, assuming he made an attempt at being consistent. If this held true for the works by Florian included in Flon's collection, the publisher could then have issued the several items as a whole or individually, a practice especially common for the works of Florian (as has been pointed out elsewhere in this bibliography).

For other volumes from this collection, see *Galatée*, 1786; the Flon *Mélanges de poésie et de littérature*, 1787; the Flon, 1789 *Six nouvelles*.

MMF list what might be the same edition of this volume ('Paris & Bruxelles, Flon, 1788, in-8'), with locations for the château d'Oron and Utrecht (88.53). Note that they report an octavo. If this be correct, and if we are dealing with the same edition, there were then at least two issues in different formats. I could find no other trace of this book.

Needless to say, this collection was more extensive than indicated by the four volumes recorded in the present bibliography. The NUC has an entry for the 'Œuvres complettes de M. de Florian ... Paris; et se trouve à Bruxelles, chez Emmanuel Flon, 1789. v, fronts. 14 cm t.3-5. Théatre italien' (NF.0201009; location: University of Virginia). The size recorded would match the format of my four books. MMF (86.34) list a *Numa Pompilius* for 'Paris & Bruxelles, Flon, 1789, 2t. in-24, 224, 245p.', with locations for the Royal library at Brussels, Amherst College and the Boston Public Library. (I have little doubt but that we are dealing with an in-18 in spite of MMF's data.)

I could find no other volumes of the Flon *Œuvres complètes* other than the theatre and *Numa Pompilius* mentioned just above, and the other volumes described in this bibliography. (See the commentaries on the pertinent entries in this bibliography.) There were obviously at least nine volumes issued and nine volumes are accounted for (assuming *Numa Pompilius* forms part of the collection). It seems very likely that this collection was continued, probably copying one of the Didot editions of the time. It would have extended into the 1790s. None of the Florian, Flon items in this bibliography bears catchtomes.

In spite of the mention of Paris in the imprints, there is no doubt but that the four volumes from the Flon collection described in this bibliography were printed in Brussels.

Krauss-Fontius have the following enigmatic entry: 'Œuvres complètes. I-IX[?]. Paris, Brüssel. Flon 1789', with a location for the Romanisches Seminar der Universität Jena (no. 989).

Incipit: 'J'ai célébré les bergers du Tage; j'ai / décrit leurs innocentes mœurs, leurs / fidèles amours'.

92

Florian: *Estelle*, 1792

Jean Pierre Claris de Florian (1755-1794): Estelle, / roman pastoral; / par M. de Florian, / De l'académie françoise, de celles de / Madrid, Florence, etc. / [rule] / Rura mihi, riguique placent in vallibus amnes: / Flumina amo, silvasque inglorius. / Georg. lib. 2. / [rule] / A Paris, / de l'imprimerie de Didot l'ainé. / 1792.

18°: 2 ff. (halftitle and titlepage) + [v]-xxxiv + if. (halftitle for 'Estelle. / Livre premier.') + [1]-184 + [187]-209 pp.

Commentary: The first item recorded by the pagination is the 'Essai sur la pastorale.' Then follow the novel and some 'Notes / historiques.' (halftitle, pp.[185-86]). In spite of the pagination, signatures are consecutive throughout. There are no catchtomes. The volume indication on the spine is for vol. ix.

There is a halftitle for the 'Œuvres / de / M. de Florian.' This edition forms part of a 1792 *Œuvres*, for which see below. There is a frontispiece bearing, at the top: 'Estelle et Némorin.' (Not in Cohen or Reynaud.) This is a somewhat primitive copy of the picture designed by Quéverdo and engraved by de Longueil issued with various editions of *Estelle*, and meant to illustrate book 1 of the novel.

This novel first appeared in 1788 (MMF 88.53). I have not been able to find another copy of this edition anywhere, or any trace of it for that matter. (There is, however, a possibility that this is the same edition listed somewhat enigmatically in the NUC for '1 p.l., (i)vi-xxxiv, 1 l., 209p., 1 pl. 8°. 24°.', New York Public Library. Note that neither format listed is in-18°.)

To editions listed in MMF, I would add:

1. *Estelle*, 1788. 'Estelle; roman pastoral, par M *de Florian*. 12. à Bâle, chez C. A. Serini, et chez J. J. Flick, et à Berne, en comm[ission] chez E. Haller', Messkatalog, OM 1788, p.145. Heinsius reports: 'Estelle, roman pastoral, p[ar] de Florian. [in-]12. Basel, Flick. [1]788' (Romane, col.63; same information also in Heinsius, *Handbuch*, p.789 and in Heinsius, 1793: iv.502).

2. *Estelle*, 1793. Estelle, roman pastoral, par M. Florian. Lille: chez C. F. J. Lehoucq, 1793. 213 pp., frontispiece, 14 cm [in-18°?], with pp.[5]-31 containing the *Essai sur la pastorale* (OCLC: University of California at Los Angeles, Tulane University). MMF list an edition for 'Lille, 1793, in-12 (Leyde, Nimègue)' which might be the same (88.53).

3. *Estelle*, 1798. Estelle, pastorale. Par M. de Florian. Londres: Impr. de Baylis, pour A. Dulau, 1798. 244 pp., 16 cm (in-18° or in-12°, probably the former), with 'Notes', pp.[222]-244. Source: OCLC, Wayne State University.

4. *Estelle*, 1800. 'Estelle, roman pastoral. [in-]8. Strasb[ourg]. Levrault. [1]800' (Heinsius, i, col.899).

Incipit: 'J'ai célébré les bergers du Tage; / j'ai décrit leurs innocentes mœurs, leurs fi- / dèles amours'.

93

Florian: *Estelle*, 1793

Jean Pierre Claris de Florian (1755-1794): Estelle, / pastorale. / Par M. de Florian, / De l'académie françoise, de celles de Madrid, / Florence, etc. / Troisieme édition. / Rura mihi riguique placent in vallibus amnes: / Flumina amo sylvasque inglorius. / Georg. lib. 2. / [woodcut decoration in the neoclassical style, oval centre with intertwined initials 'PD'] / A Paris, / de l'imprimerie de P. Didot l'aîné. / 1793.

18°: 2 ff. (halftitle and titlepage) + [5]-32 + [35]-236, [237]-260 pp.

Commentary: The first item in this book is the 'Essai sur la pastorale'. Then follow the poetic novel and some notes. MMF list a 'troisième édition', 260 pp. in-24°, with locations for the Library of Congress, Harvard, Brooklyn College and Rotterdam: Gemeente Bibliotheek. Cohen seems to list this edition, in-18°, as here extant (col.398). (MMF have possibly made a mistake concerning format, or the edition[s]/issue[s] described in the NUC are different from mine.) I list this edition since it is part of a collection of Florian's works, 1786-1801. See the corresponding *Œuvres* entry for more information.

There is a half titlepage for the 'Œuvres / de / M. de Florian.' The verso bears: '[rule] / A Paris, / Chez Girod et Tessier, rue de la / Harpe, au coin de celle des Deux- / Portes, n°. 162; / Où se trouvent toutes les œuvres de / l'auteur en collection et séparé- / ment, dans les deux formats in- / 8°. et in-18.' There are no catchtomes present.

There are six very pretty engravings after Quéverdo included with this book: 1. facing p.[35], by de Longueil; 2. facing p.[70], by Dembrun; 3. facing p.[101], by Delignon; 4. facing p.[133], by Hubert; 5. facing p.[167], by Delignon; 6. facing p.[202], by Dembrun.

All the pictures are signed, captioned and bear the book part. It might be noted that Moreau was apparently supposed to have designed some pictures for this work, but probably never did. See Reynaud, col.182.

Incipit: 'J'ai célébré les bergers du Tage; / j'ai décrit leurs innocentes mœurs, / leurs fidèles amours'.

94

Florian: *Galatée*, 1784

Jean Pierre Claris de Florian (1755-1794): Galatée, / roman pastoral, / imité / de Cervantes, / par M. de Florian, / Capitaine de Dragons, & Gentilhomme / de S. A. S. Mgr. le Duc de Pen- / thievre, des Académies de Madrid / & de Lyon. / [rule] / On peut donner du lustre à leurs inventions, / On le peut, je l'essaie; un plus savant le fasse. / La Fontaine, II. 1. / [rule] / A Bievre. / [double rule] / M. DCC. LXXXIV.

18°: 1 f. (titlepage) + [3]-4, 5-21, 22-36, [37]-192 pp.

Commentary: The first item is a verse dedication to the duchess of Chartres; the second, a 'Vie de Cervantes'; the third, an analytical 'Des ouvrages de Cervantes'. Then follows the novel. MMF (83.26; the novel first appeared in 1783) list this edition after the copy in Professor Morris Wachs's personal collection. I know of no other copy, and thus list mine with complete information. (And it is of course possible that the above book differs from Professor Wachs's; no format is mentioned in MMF.) There are no catchtomes present.

To editions of *Galatée* not recorded by MMF I would add the following:

1. *Galatée*, 1792. Galatée, roman pastoral; imité de Cervantès. 4th ed. Paris: Didot l'aîné, 1792. 192 pp., frontisp., 14 cm (OCLC: State University of New York, Stony Brook). MMF list a 'Paris, Didot l'aîné, 1792, in-12, 139p.' edition (BN), which I was unable to consult.

2. *Galatée*, 1800. '[in-]18 et [in-]8. Strasb[ourg]. Levrault. [1]800' (Heinsius i, col.900; Romane col.78).

See the next entries as well.

Incipit: 'Avant que le soleil ait éclairé nos / plaines'.

95

Florian: *Galatée*, 1784 [or 1799?]

Jean Pierre Claris de Florian (1755-1794): Galatée, / roman pastoral; / imité / de Cervantes / par M. de Florian, / Capitaine de dragons, et Gentilhomme de S. A. S. / Mgr le Duc de Penthièvre; des aca- / démies de Madrid et de Lyon. / Troisième édition. / [rule] / On peut donner du lustre à leurs inventions, / On le peut, je l'essaie, un plus savant le fasse. / La Fontaine, II. 1. / [woodcut ornament resembling a fireplace on a mantle, oval cartouche in centre with intwined initials; see the comentary] / A Paris, / de l'imprimerie de Didot l'aîné. / M. DCC. LXXXIV.

8°: 1 f. (titlepage) + 1 f. (2p.) + 1 f. (halftitle: 'Vie / de Cervantes.') + [3]-32p. + 1 f. (pp.[33-34], halftitle: 'Galatée. / Livre premier.') + [35]-171 pp.

Commentary: The first item after the titleleaf is a dedication (in verse) to the duchess of Chartres; the second, a life of Cervantes. Then comes the novel proper.

Although the pagination and general titlepage description matches the similar edition listed in MMF, I was able to compare my book with the BN copy, and it is quite different. For example, the signature numbers appear on different pages: '2' BN on p.9, '2' my copy on p.17; '3' BN on p.17, my copy has no no.3; '4' BN on p.25, '4' my copy on p.49, and so on. The titlepage transcribed here so reads. That in the BN reads: '[...] Mgr le Duc de Penthievre; des académies / de Madrid et de Lyon. [...]' and the word 'troisieme' has no accent (BN Y2.36191; copy on 'papier vélin', no halftitle for the *Œuvres*). The BL has a 171-page, octavo edition which I have not been able to see. (It lacks the titleleaf and contains ms notes by Florian; Cerv.552.)

My book is illustrated with a series of beautiful engravings, emanating from various editions of *Galatée*. This volume is not listed in Cohen, and there is no way of telling whether this edition was issued with the engravings or whether they were added by the binder at the owner's request. (The binding is late eighteenth, early nineteenth century, full mottled calf, usual gilt decorations; one of the titlepieces bears 'Œuvres / de / Florian', with no indication of volumniation.) Note that the first engraving is dated 'an 7' [1799]. I feel certain that the rest of the engravings were executed at about the same time, and suspect strongly that the book was, too. This sort of thing was not infrequent during the 1790s. For another example of this, see Sterne, *La Vie et les opinions de Tristram Shandy*, 1784 [or ca.1794]. Although Cohen does not list this edition, Reynaud has an entry for what *might* be this book, as follows: 'Galatée 1784. In-18. Dans Œuvres. On possède une édition in-8, Imprimerie de Didot l'aîné. 3e édition avec portrait, front. et 4 figures par Flouest, gravées par Guyard, in-18, tirées avec cadres' (col.183). Note that there are five pictures listed here by Guyard after Flouest. Moreover the size of the pictures certainly exceeds the 18mo format.

Here are the illustrations in the copy described here:

1. the first frontispiece, bound in before the titlepage: 'Front. de / Galatée.' on the top; 'lebarbier fec. / lan.7 / L. M. halbou sculp' on the bottom.

2. the second frontispiece, facing the first: 'Galatée. / Pastorale' in the picture; 'Dupréel Sculp' at the bottom.

3. facing p.[3]: elaborate portrait of Cervantes, 'Flouest del.', 'Guyard Sculp.'.

4. facing p.[35]: 'Lebarbier inv.', 'De Launay. sc.'.

5. facing p.40: 'Flouest inv.', Guyard Sculp.'.

6. facing p.[65]: 'Le Barbier inv', 'De Launay sc.'.

7. facing p.75: 'J. Flouest inv.', 'J. B. Guyard Sculp.'.

8. facing p.[104]: 'le barbier inv', 'Bacoy sc.'.

9. facing p.111: 'Flouest inv.', Guyard Sculp.'.

10. facing p.[136]: 'Le Barbier inv', [de Launay; barely legible]'.

11. facing p.[143]: 'Flouest inv.', 'Guyard Sculp.'.

A few remarks: all engravings are on heavy paper with horizontal chainlines. The pictures generally bear the mention of their place in the book with respect to the 'livres'. They all bear captions, sometimes with misspellings. There are finials to the bottom left and right of each picture, forming part of the elaborate engraved borders. They all bear the letters 'G' (to the left), and 'E' (to the right), except for the first illustration which bears two 'E's, presumably by mistake. The Le Barbier pictures are signed 'à la pointillé'; those after Flouest, in 'normal' script.

Incipit: 'Avant que le soleil ait éclairé nos plaines'.

96

Florian: *Galatée*, 1786

Jean Pierre Claris de Florian (1755-1794): Galatée, / roman pastoral; / imité / de Cervantes / Par M. de Florian, / Capitaine de Dragons, et Gentilhomme de / S. A. S. Mgr. le Duc de Penthievre. / [rule] / On peut donner du lustre à leurs inventions: / On le peut, je l'essaie; un plus savant le fasse. / La Fontaine, II. 1. / [symmetrical composite woodcut ornament swirling upwards with rose in centre top] / A Bruxelles, / Chez Em. Flon, Imprimeur-Libraire. / [double rule] / M DCC. LXXXVI.

18°: 3 pl (halftitle followed by two titlepages) + 1 f. (2 pp.) + 1 f. (halftitle for 'Vie / de Cervantes.') + [1]-24, [25]-135 pp.

Commentary: This volume belongs to a collected edition of Florian's *Œuvres* put together by Flon and has the following titlepage for the collection: 'Œuvres / complettes / de / M. de Florian, / Capitaine de dragons, et Gentilhomme / de S. A. S. Mgr. le duc de Pen- / thievre; de Académie de Ma- / drid, &c. / Tome premier, / Contenant Galatée, roman pastoral. / [symmetrical woodcut ornament: sun-burst] / A Paris; / Et se trouve à Bruxelles, / Chez Emmanuel Flon, Imprimeur- / Libraire, rue de la Putterie. / [double rule] / M. DCC. LXXXIX.' Preceding this titlepage is a halftitle for the collection: 'Œuvres / complettes / de / M. de Florian.' Both of these leaves have horizontal chainlines and were tipped in. (The paper is somewhat different from the rest of the book as well.) The next three leaves comprise the volume titlepage as transcribed above, a dedication to the duchesse de Chartres (2 pp., in verse) and a halftitle for the *Vie de Cervantes*. The introductory material is divided between the *Vie* (pp.[1]-13) and 'Des ouvrages de Cervantes' (pp.[14]-24).

At the head of the preliminary material there is a pretty frontispiece portrait of Cervantes by De la Rue, after Flouest (signed and captioned). This is a copy of that designed by Guyard. (See the 1788, Didot *Galatée* below.)

MMF list a 'Bruxelles, 1786, in-12, 135p. (BL)' edition (83.26) which might well be this edition. But note the different format. I list my copy because it is part of the Flon *Œuvres*. These *Œuvres* were issued by Flon over a period of years. What might have been the case is that Flon began by printing individual works (in the mid '80s) and, a few years later, began issuing the works (with left over copies and/or volumes especially printed). For other volumes from this collection, see *Estelle* 1788; the Flon *Mélanges de poésie et de littérature*, 1787; the Flon, 1789 *Six nouvelles*. Aside from the BL edition referred to by MMF which might be the same (I was unable to examine it), I was unable to find any trace of the book described here. In any case, should the BL copy prove to be the same edition, I doubt it would have the collection halftitle and titlepage, for surely the cataloguers would have remarked upon the additional titlepage at least (not to mention that a different format is indicated).

Incipit: 'Avant que le soleil ait éclairé nos plaines'.

97

Florian: *Galatée*, 1788

Jean Pierre Claris de Florian (1755-1794): Galatée, / pastorale; / imitée / de Cervantes, / par M. de Florian, / Lieutenant-Colonel de dragons, Gentilhomme / de S.A.S. Mgr le duc de Penthievre, / de l'Académie Françoise, etc. / Cinquième édition. / [rule] / On peut donner du lustre à leurs inventions: / On le peut, je l'essaie; un plus savant le fasse. / La Fontaine, II, 1. / [rule] / A Paris, / de l'imprimerie de monsieur. / M. DCC. LXXXVIII.

18°: 3 ff. (halftitle, titlepage and halftitle for 'Vie / de Cervantes.') + [7-8], [9]-36, [37]-59 + [63]-214 pp. + 1 f. (1 p.)

Commentary: The first item after the three first folios is a verse dedication to the duchesse d'Orléans. The second and third are a 'Vie de Cervantes' and an analytical 'Des ouvrages de Cervantes'. Then follow the novel and a one-page, priced list of Florian's works in-8° and in-18°.

There is a half titlepage for the 'Œuvres / de / M. de Florian.' On the verso is the following indication: '[rule] / A Paris, / Chez Guillaume, rue du Bacq, n°.940; / Fabre, rue du Hurepoix, n°. 11.' There are no catchtomes present.

MMF list what is probably this edition; the only location mentioned is for the BN (83.26). I was unable to see the BN copy. It might also be listed in the NUC (locations: Library of Congress, Harvard and Indiana University), and in OCLC for the University of Arizona, Tucson. The latter source records eight plates after Flouest. I list this edition because it forms part of a 1786-1801 collection. See the *Œuvres* for that date.

This volume contains five pretty engravings by Guyard after Flouest (portrait-frontispiece, then facing p.[63], [96], [140], [176]). All the pictures are signed, captioned and the last four bear the book indication.

Incipit: 'Avant que le soleil ait éclairé nos plaines'.

98

Florian: *Galatée*, 1792

Jean Pierre Claris de Florian (1755-1794): Galatée, / roman pastoral; / imité / de Cervantes, / par M. de Florian, / De l'académie françoise, de celles de / Madrid, Florence, etc. / Quatrieme édition. / [rule] / On peut donner du lustre à leurs inventions: / On le peut, je l'essaie; un plus savant le fasse. / La Fontaine, II. 1. / [rule] / A Paris, / de l'imprimerie de Didot l'ainé. / 1792.

18°: 3 ff. (halftitle, titlepage and halftitle for 'Vie / de Cervantes.') + [7-8], [9]-27, [28]-42 + [45]-192 pp.

Commentary: The first item after the first three folios is a dedication to the duchess of Chartres. The second, a 'Vie / de Cervantes.' (halftitle preceding the dedication, pp.[5-6]). The third is the analytical 'Des ouvrages de Cervantes'. Then comes the novel proper.

This book has a halftitle for the 'Œuvres / de / M. de Florian'. The half titlepage bears the catchtome '1.' and signature 'a'. Catchtomes throughout the volume are for no.1, which is echoed on the spine. The only trace I have been able to find of this edition, assuming it is the same, is in OCLC for SUNY at Stony Brook. The novel first appeared in 1783 (MMF 83.26). This edition is part of a complex and very rare collection of Florian's works; see the *Œuvres*, 1792 for further details.

There is a pleasant frontispiece reading, at the top, 'Galatée.' (Not mentioned in Cohen or Reynaud.) This is a copy of the picture designed by Flouest and engraved by Guyard issued with various editions of *Galatée*, meant to illustrate book 1.

Incipit: 'Avant que le soleil ait éclairé nos plaines'.

99

Florian: *Gonzalve de Cordoue*, 1792

Jean Pierre Claris de Florian (1755-1794): Gonzalve / de Cordoue, / ou / Grenade reconquise. / Par M. de Florian, / De l'académie françoise, de celles de / Madrid, Florence, etc. / Seconde Edition [Édition for ii]. / Tome premier [second, troisieme]. / [woodcut decoration in the neoclassical style, oval centre with initials 'PD' intertwined] / A Paris, / de l'imprimerie de Didot l'aîné. / 1792.

18°, i: 3 ff. (halftitle, titlepage and halftitle for 'Précis / historique / sur les Maures / d'Espagne.') + [7]-11 + [13]-231, [232]-282 pp.

ii: 2 pl + 1 f. (halftitle for 'Gonzalve / de Cordoue. / [rule] / Livre premier.', 'sommaire' verso) + [3]-254 pp.

iii: 2 pl + 1 f. (halftitle for 'Gonzalve / de Cordoue. / [rule] / Livre sixieme.', with 'sommaire' verso) + [3]-252 pp.

Commentary: The first item in vol. i is a 'Tableau chronologique des souverains arabes ou maures qui régnèrent en Espagne'. The second is a 'Précis historique sur les Maures d'Espagne', followed by some notes. The novel actually occupies vols ii and iii.

MMF list this edition, but in-24°, after the BL copy (91.21). However, the BL copy is in-18° and is the same as mine (634.a.27-29). This edition is also conceivably listed in the NUC (various locations). I list this edition since it forms part of a collection of Florian's works. See the *Œuvres*, 1786-1801 for further information.

There are half titlepages for the 'Œuvres / de / M. de Florian. [no period for ii and iii]'. On the versos, we find: '[rule] / A Paris, / Au magasin des ouvrages de l'auteur, / chez Girod et Tessier, rue de la / Harpe, au coin de celle des Deux- / Portes, n° 162, [162; for ii] / Et chez Debure, rue Serpente, hôtel / Ferrand.' There are no catchtomes on the halftitles; those in the volumes are for 1., 2. and 3., respectively.

Although not mentioned in Cohen (but probably listed in Reynaud, col.183), these volumes contain some very pretty illustrations by Hubert, Delignon, Gaucher, Dambrun (or Dembrun) and Ingouf after Quéverdo (fourteen in all). Each engraving is signed, captioned and bears an indication of its place in the work. The NUC entry mentions fourteen illustrations and a frontispiece by Patas after Monsiau. The latter was possibly if not probably issued at a later date. For other examples of this sort of thing, see the entries for the *Mélanges de poésie et de littérature*, Didot, 1787 and the *Six nouvelles*, 1786, below.

Incipit: (vol. ii, the novel proper) 'Chastes nymphes, vous qui bai- / gnez les tresses de vos longs cheveux / dans les eaux limpides du Guadal- / quivir'.

100

Florian: *Gonzalve de Cordoue*, 1792

Jean Pierre Claris de Florian (1755-1794): Gonzalve / de Cordoue, / ou / Grenade reconquise. / Par M. de Florian, / De l'académie françoise, de celles / de Madrid, Florence, etc. / Troisiéme Édition. / Tome premier [second]. / A Paris, et a Liège, / Chez Lemarié, Libraire et Imprimeur / de Son Altesse, sous la Tour. / [double rule] / 1792.

12°, i: 2 ff. (halftitle and titlepage; see the commentary) + 1 f. (halftitle for the first book of the novel; 'sommaire' verso) + [5]-248 pp.
    ii: 2 ff. (halftitle and titlepage; see the commentary) + 1 f. (halftitle for the sixth book of the novel; 'sommaire' verso) + [5]-250 pp.

Commentary: In spite of the pagination, the volume halftitles and titlepages comprise preliminary leaves. The halftitle for the first book is f.[A1]. Then follow ff.A2, A3, etc. (signed in 12s). This edition does not contain the preliminary volume forming the *Précis historique sur les Maures*. (The end of volume i bears 'Fin du livre cinquiéme'; that to ii, 'Fin.')

The volume halftitles bear: 'Gonzalve / de / Cordoue. / [rule] / Tome premier [second]. / [rule]'.

MMF list a '...*troisième édition*, Paris & Liège, Lemarié, 1792, 2t. in-32, 248, 250p. (Bruxelles)' (91.21). The different format recorded would suggest at least a different issue. Although possibly the same edition as that extant in Bruxelles, I have chosen to list it because of its rarity and because of the many items of Florian interest in the present bibliography.

Incipit: 'Chastes Nymphes! vous qui bai- / gnez les tresses de vos longs vheveux / dans les eaux limpides du Guadal- / quivir'.

101

Florian: *Gonzalve de Cordoue*, 1792

Jean Pierre Claris de Florian (1755-1794): Gonzalve / de Cordoue, / ou / Grenade reconquise. / Par M. de Florian, / De l'académie françoise, de celles de / Madrid, Florence, etc. / [rule] / Tome premier [second, troisieme]. / [rule] / A Paris, / de l'imprimerie de Didot l'ainé. / 1792.

18°, i: 3 ff. (halftitle, titlepage and halftitle for 'Précis / historique / sur les Maures /

d'Espagne.') + [vij]-xvj, [17]-222, [223]-156 [for 256, or so it seems: the ink is smeared] pp.

ii: 3 ff. (halftitle, titlepage and halftitle for 'Gonzalve / de Cordoue. / [rule] / Livre premier.', with 'sommaire' verso) + [7]-232 pp.

iii: 3 ff. (halftitle, titlepage and halftitle for 'Gonzalve / de Cordoue. / [rule] / Livre sixieme.' with 'sommaire' verso) + [7]-232 pp.

Commentary: I have found no mention of the above volumes anywhere. The half titlepages read 'Œuvres / de / M. de Florian.' This *Gonzalve* was meant to form part of an edition of Florian's works, the individual items of which were sold separately. The volume indication (catchtomes) on the half titlepages reads [10; barely legible], 11 and 12 for the respective volumes (presumably). However, in the volumes themselves, the catchtomes are for volumes 1., 2., 3. The half titles were probably meant to be cancelled for copies of the three volumes issued as a complete entity. I have two copies of this edition: one forms part of a uniformly bound *Œuvres* (see Florian's *Œuvres* for 1792, 12 vols), bearing the indication of vols 10-12 for the collection and 1-3 for the item on the spines. The other copy, complete with the halftitles, bears the indication for vols 1-3 on the spines (contemporary speckled calf), and none for any collection.

This historical novel first appeared in 1791 (MMF 91.21; Monglond ii, col.401) and was enormously successful. The first item in vol. i is a 'Tableau chronologique des souverains arabes ou Maures qui régnèrent en Espagne', the second a 'Précis historique sur les Maures d'Espagne', and, at the end, the notes. The first pages of ii and iii are 'sommaires', found on the versos of the half titlepages for the first and sixth books, respectively.

In the copy bound for the 1792, Didot edition of the *Œuvres*, there is a pleasant frontispiece to vol. i, 'Queverdo del'-'J J Hubert. Sc'. On the top is 'Precis Histor'-'Ire. Epoque.' The caption at the bottom reads: 'Dieu de Mahomet, tu le vois; &c.' (Not in Cohen or Reynaud.) This is a copy of the original engraving illustrating the first 'époque' of the introductory *Précis historique*.

I might mention that Heinsius lists a *Gonzalve de Cordoue* for Leipzig: G. Fleischer, 1800, 2 vols in-8. This is also to be found in MMF (91.21). Heinsius further gives '(Levrault in Strasb. a[uch] Tourneysen in Cassel)' (i, col.900 and Romane col.91). Perhaps there were copies with Levrault's (and maybe too Tourneisen's) own titlepages? However, it is probably just the case of Levrault and Tourneisen having copies of the Fleischer edition for sale, since the information that Heinsius and Kayser report in parentheses seems to refer to dealers rather than publishers. In any case, the Leipzig edition is part of an *Œuvres*; see MMF 83.26 and 91.21. See too the *Œuvres*, 1796, below.

Incipit: (vol. ii, the novel proper) 'Chastes nymphes, vous qui bai- / gnez les tresses de vos longs cheveux / dans les eaux limpides du Guadal- / quivir'.

102

Florian: *Guillaume Tell*, 1801

Jean Pierre Claris de Florian (1755-1794): Guillaume Tell, / ou / la Suisse libre, / par M. de Florian, / De l'académie française, de celles de Madrid, / Florence, etc. / Ouvrage posthume, / Précédé de son discours de réception à l'Académie / française, de la vie de l'Auteur, par Jauffret, et / orné de cinq jolies gravures, dessinées par Monnet / et Laplace, et gravées par Gaucher. / [woodcut ornament in the neoclassical style, centre having oval with intertwined initials] / De l'imprimerie de Guilleminet. / A Paris, / a la librairie économique, / rue de la Harpe, n° 117. / [rule] / an IX.

18°: 2 ff. (halftitle and titlepage) + [5]-231 pp.

Commentary: This book contains the following pieces:
1. Vie de Florian, pp.[5]-70;
2. Poésies diverses, pp.[71]-[76];
3. Discours prononcé par J. P. Florian, à sa réception à l'Académie Française, le 14 mai 1788, pp.[77]-93;
4. Guillaume Tell, ou la Suisse libre, pp.[95]-231.

There is a halftitle for the 'Œuvres / de Florian.' This volume, as extant in my collection, forms part of a 'recueil factice' of Florian's works, 1786-1801. There are no catchtomes present in this edition. It first appeared with the title of *Œuvres posthumes de Florian...* in 1800. MMF do not mention this edition (00.69). Cohen mentions an edition which could conceivably be the same (col.403). However, MMF mention an edition for 1801, 'Paris, imprimerie de Guilleminet, 1801 [for an IX?], 141p. (U. of Amsterdam, Indiana University)' which might correspond to Cohen's entry. It certainly doesn't to mine.

Guillaume Tell is a prose poem of sorts, a kind of 'Gessnerised' counterpart to *Gonzalve de Cordoue*.

Although the titlepage promises five engravings, there are actually six. The first is a frontispiece portrait by Clément after Laplace (quotation in the picture). The second, facing p.69, is a captioned picture by Quéverdo, titled 'Le tombeau de Florian, à Sceaux.' These are followed by four more engravings by Gaucher after Monnet, each illustrating a book of the 'epic' (facing pp.[95], [137], [166], [201]). The last four engravings bear the pagination, which does not match this edition at all (pages 125, 140, 182, 200 indicated, respectively). The last two pictures are dated 'An VII'. Cohen calls for six pictures and mentions that these are the same as for the 'vers 1800' edition. Possibly the portrait frontispiece was an afterthought or issued sometime after the other five. (For other possible examples of this, see the first *Gonzalve de Cordoue* listed above, the first *Mélanges* listed below, and the *Six nouvelles*.) There was also an 'an X' edition with eight illustrations. MMF list two issues, in-18 and in-8, after Quérard. Reynaud only lists the octavo one (col.185). MMF indicate (after Quérard I assume) that this edition appeared under the title of *Œuvres posthumes*. Reynaud gives the full title for *Guillaume Tell, ou la Suisse libre* (etc.).

Incipit: 'Amis de la liberté, cœurs magnani- / mes, ames tendres, vous qui savez / mourir pour votre indépendance'.

103

Florian: *Mélanges de poésie et de littérature*, 1787

Jean Pierre Claris de Florian (1755-1794): Mélanges / de / poésie et de littérature. / Par M. de Florian, / Capitaine de dragons, et Gentilhomme de S.A.S. / Mgr le duc de Penthièvre; des acad. de Madrid, / de Florence, de Lyon, de Nismes, d'Angers, etc. / [woodcut decoration in neoclassical style, oval centre bearing initials intertwined] / A Paris, / de l'imprimerie de Didot l'aîné. / M. DCC. LXXXVII.

18°: 3 ff. (halftitle, titlepage and halftitle for 'Ruth, / églogue / tirée de l'ecriture sainte, / Couronnée par l'académie françoise / en 1784.') + [7]-222, [223]-224 pp. + 2 ff. (3 + 1 pp.)

Commentary: The pagination reflects the various pieces in this volume as a whole, a table, three pages of legal material and one page of advertisement, listing works by Florian, in-8° and in-18°, fine paper, ordinary paper, with and without illustrations. In the section titled 'Imitations / et / traductions.' (halftitle), this volume contains *Léocadie, nouvelle espagnole imitée de Cervantès*, p.[145]-168.

That is a piece of prose fiction mentioned in MMF. The latter do not cite *Louis douze au lit de mort*, which, even if designated an 'éloge', is actually a romanticised life, or piece of historical prose fiction, although one might consider it somewhat marginal to the 'genre romanesque'. As Florian himself explains, after stating that the Académie française 'blâma la forme que j'avois adoptée': 'j'osai conduire son peuple [de Louis XII] jusques à son lit de mort, pour donner une image forte et touchante de l'amour si tendre et vrai que ce peuple portoit à son roi. Quant aux fautes de mon héros, je voulus, pour les affoiblir, en mettre l'aveu dans sa propre bouche; je voulus qu'il s'en accusât lui-même, afin qu'on les excusât davantage; et je pensai que le moyen de rendre ses erreurs pardonnables, étoit qu'il ne voulût pas se les pardonner' (pp.[37] and 39-40; the 'avant-propos' and 'éloge' occupy pp.[35-36], [[37]-40, [41]-92). The first two pages recorded comprise a halftitle: 'Éloge / de Louis douze, / roi de France, / surnommé pere du peuple. / [rule] / Nec magis sine illo nos esse felices quàm ille sine nobis potuit. / Plin. panég. de Trajan.'

The legal material comprises an approbation for Florian's *Œuvres* (13 December 1786, Suard), a privilege to Florian for his *Œuvres* (29 October 1783, Le Begue) and the registration (11 November 1783, Leclerc, syndic).

MMF (87.41) list a 227 pp. edition, in-16 with copies in the Arsenal and the BN (last copy examined in manu) for Paris: Didot, 1787, with *Léocadie* occupying the same pages as in the book listed here. It is perhaps a question of errors on their part. (I was unable to examine the BN or Arsenal copy.) Cohen's description matches my copy, '224 pp., 2 ff. n. ch., plus 1 frontispice gravé par Dupréel et 6 charmantes figures par Quéverdo, gravées par Dambrun, Delignon et de Longueil' (col.401).

I list my copy since it is part of an interesting collection of Florian's works. There is a halftitle bearing 'Œuvres / de / M. de Florian.' On the verso is: '[rule] / A Paris, / Chez Guillaume, rue du Bacq, n°.940; / Fabre, rue du Hurepoix, n°.

11.' There are no catchtomes present in this volume. For further information, see the *Œuvres*, 1786-1801 below.

My copy has six engravings. Cohen lists seven, including a frontispiece by Dupréel (col.401). The NUC lists what is conceivably this edition, with the portrait frontispiece (various locations). Reynaud remarks: 'Le frontisp., gravé par Dupréel, manque parfois dans certains exemplaires en reliure de l'époque' (col.184). This leads one to surmise that it was issued at a later date. For other examples of this sort of thing, see Florian's *Six nouvelles* below and the first *Gonzalve de Cordoue* above. (See too *Guillaume Tell*.) My book contains the following pictures after Quéverdo: 1. facing p.[7], by Dembrun; 2. facing p.[25], by de Longueil; 3. facing p.[41], by de Longueil; 4. facing p.[95], by Delignon; 5. facing p.[145], by de Longueil; 6. facing p.[171], by Delignon.

There is no frontispiece in my copy, as indicated, but the picture illustrating 'Ruth' is the one usually bound in at the head of the book. This poem first appeared separately in 1784. (See for example the other *Mélanges* listed in this bibliography.) All the engravings are signed, captioned and bear the title of the piece they illustrate at the top left. (The second, for 'Voltaire et le serf du mont Jura', which first appeared separately in 1782, is of special interest to Voltairean iconography. It depicts a smiling patriarch surrounded by grateful peasants in a mountainous landscape.)

To editions of the *Mélanges* listed in MMF and in this bibliography, I would add:

'Melanges de poésie et de litt., par *de Florian*. 8. à Lausanne et à Berne, chez F. Seiger [Seizer?] et Comp.', Messkatalog, OM 1788, p.147.

See too the 1796 *Œuvres complètes* described below.

Incipits: (*Louis douze*) 'Louis XII, après dix-sept ans de / regne, au moment où son hymen / avec Marie d'Angleterre lui donnoit / un allié puissant'.

(*Léocadie*) 'Une nuit d'été, par un beau clair / de lune, vers les onze heures à-peu- / près, un pauvre vieux gentilhomme'.

104

Florian: *Mélanges de poésie et de littérature*, 1787

Jean Pierre Claris de Florian (1755-1794): Mélanges / de / poésie et de littérature. / Par M. de Florian, / Capitaine de dragons, et gentilhomme de S.A.S. / Mgr le duc de Penthievre; des acad. de Madrid, / de Florence, de Lyon, de Nismes, d'Angers, etc. / [woodcut decoration in neoclassical style, oval centre bearing the initials 'FAD' intwined] / A Paris, / de l'imprimerie de Didot l'aîné. / M. DCC. LXXXVII.

18°: 3 ff. (halftitle, titlepage and halftitle for 'Ruth, / eglogue / tirée de l'écriture sainte, / Couronnée par l'académie françoise / en 1784.') + [7]-222, [223]-224 pp. + 2 ff. (3 + 1 pp.)

Commentary: The pagination reflects the various pieces in this volume as a whole (including a halftitle for the 'Œuvres / de / M. de Florian.'), a table (pp.[223]-224), three pages of legal material and one page of an advertisement, listing works by Florian, in-8° and in-18°, fine paper, ordinary paper, with and without illustrations. In the section titled 'Imitations / et / traductions.' (halftitle), this volume contains *Léocadie, anecdote espagnole imitée de Cervantes*, pp.[145]-168. The 'Eloge / de Louis douze, / roi de France, / surnommé pere du peuple. / [rule] / Nec magis sine illo nos esse felices quàm ille sine nobis potuit. / Plin. panég. de Trajan.' (halftitle) occupies pp.[35]-92 (including the halftitle leaf and preliminaries).

The legal material comprises an approbation for Florian's *Œuvres* (13 December 1786, Suard), a privilege to Florian for his *Œuvres* (29 October 1783, Le Begue) and the registration (11 November 1783, Leclerc, syndic).

This edition is illustrated with the same pictures as to be found in the preceding *Mélanges* except that they are the 'originals', and those to be found with the 1787 edition listed just above are very clever copies. A couple of the engravings contain easily describable differences. In the picture facing p.[41], the title 'Eloge de Louis XII.' appears to the upper right; in the preceding item, that appears to the left and the king's name is spelled 'Louis XIII'. Facing p.[169] (bound in before p.[171] in the preceding item), 'Jnès de Castro' is to the right here; in the preceding item, it is to the left, reading 'Ines de Castro'. Cohen lists a frontispiece (Dupréel) and six engravings by Dambrun, Deligni and de Longueil after Quéverdo (col.401; see the preceding item as well).

Instead of a very cleverly executed contrefaçon, could it be that we have here a case of one work published by and for Guillaume (the first item: the intials on the titlepage decoration seem to read 'MRG') and the other by and for Didot? (The halftitle page of this item bears no mention of Guillaume.) In any case, there are some printing errors in the first book, which are not found in the second. For example, the running title p.52 reads 'loge' instead of 'Éloge'; p.58, running title reads 'Eloge' instead of 'Éloge', etc. The two books are very close to being line-by-line reprints with rules of about the same thickness and length in the same positions (etc.). Which is a reprint of which cannot be said for sure, but the evidence of the engravings would lead me to give chronological precedence to the edition described in this entry.

Here is an easy way of differentiating between the two editions. The note beginning p.52, although textually identical, is not typographically so. I give beginning and end words of that note, on a page-by-page basis, starting with the preceding item:

'(1)Les commissaires pousserent ... XII ne se soumit / qu'avec beaucoup ... touchantes : les / voici mot à ... eût pu venir aucun / "procès entre monseigneur ... du divorce.)'.

'(1)Les commissaires pousserent ... XII ne se soumit qu'avec / beaucoup de ... touchantes : les voici mot à / mot: ... eût pu venir aucun / "procès entre monseigneur ... du divorce.)'.

Incipits: (*Louis douze*) 'Louis XII, après dix-sept ans de / regne, au moment où son hymen / avec Marie d'Angleterre lui donnoit / un allié puissant'.

(*Léocadie*) 'Une nuit d'été, par un beau clair / de lune, vers les onze heures à-peu- / près, un pauvre vieux gentilhomme'.

105

Florian: *Mélanges de poésie et de littérature*, 1787

Jean Pierre Claris de Florian (1755-1794): Mélanges / de / poésie et de littérature, / par M. de Florian, / Capitaine de dragons, et Gentilhomme de / S. A. S. Mgr. le duc de Penthievre; des / académies de Madrid, de Florence, de / Lyon, de Nismes, d'Angers, etc. / [woodcut decoration: vase of flowers] / A Geneve. / [rule] / M. DCC. LXXXVII.

24°: 3 ff. (halftitle, titlepage, halftitle for 'Ruth, / églogue / tirée de l'écriture sainte, / Couronnée par l'académie françoise / en 1784.') + [7]-201, [202]-203 pp.

Commentary: Among the various pieces contained in this edition are the *Eloge de Louis douze*, pp.[33]-84, including halftitle and 'avant-propos' – for an explanation concerning this piece, see the commentary on the first *Méanges* listed above – and *Léocadie, anecdote espagnole imitée de Cervantès* (pp.[129]-150). The halftitle for the former reads: 'Éloge / de Louis douze. / Roi de France, / surnommé pere du peuple. / [rule] / Nec magis sine illo nos esse feliccs [*sic*] quam ille sine / nobis potuit. / Plin. panég. de Trajan. / B5 [signature]'. MMF list what might be this edition (87.41) after A. Corroënne, *Petits joyaux bibliographiques...* 1e série: *Livres-bijoux précurseurs de Cazin* (Paris 1894). This edition is not listed by any other bibliographer I have examined, is not in Cohen or Reynaud, in spite of the pretty frontispiece, not in NUC, BLC, BNC, etc. Because of its extreme rarity and because Corroënne's description is inexact (still assuming we are dealing with the same edition), I have chosen to list it.

There is a half titlepage as follows: 'Œuvres / de / M. de Florian.' This is preceded by a fine engraving, unsigned, after Quéverdo, probably by Dembrun (no artists' signatures). This is a mirror image of the engraving by Dembrun after Quéverdo to be found with the Didot, 1787 edition. It bears at the top left: 'Ruth.' (The first piece in the collection is a poem, 'Ruth, églogue tirée de l'écriture sainte'; this first appeared separately in 1784.) At the bottom is the following caption: 'Dieu pour se faire aimer doit / prolonger tes ans.' 1787 is the date of the first edition of *Léocadie*, in the Didot edition of Florian's *Mélanges* (MMF 87.41). The second item listed in the pagination reported above is the 'Table'.

There are no catchtomes in this volume.

Incipits: (*Louis douze*) 'Louis XII, après dix-sept ans de / regne, au moment où son hymen / avec marie d'Angleterre lui donnoit / un allié puissant'.

(*Léocadie*) 'Une nuit d'été, par un beau clair / de lune, vers les onze heures à-peu- / près, un pauvre vieux gentilhomme'.

106

Florian: *Mélanges de poésie et de littérature*, 1787

Jean Pierre Claris de Florian (1755-1794): Mélanges / de / poésie et de littérature. / Par M. de Florian, / Capitaine de dragons, et Gentilhomme / de S. A. S. Mgr. le Duc de Pen- / thievre; des Académies de Ma- / drid, de Florence, de Lyon, de / Nismes, d'Angers, etc. / [symmetrical woodcut ornament] / A Paris; / Et se trouve à Bruxelles, / Chez Emmanuel Flon, Imprimeur- / Libraire, rue des Fripiers. / [double rule] / M. DCC. LXXXVII.

18°: 1 pl (halftitle) + 3 ff. (2 titlepages and a halftitle for *Voltaire et le serf du mont Jura*) + [vij]-xij, [13]-208 pp. + 1 f. (2 pp.; a table)

Commentary: The first pages comprise an 'Avant-propos nécessaire' for *Voltaire et le serf du mont Jura*. The collection halftitle bears: 'Œuvres / complettes / de / M. de Florian.' Then follows a titlepage, also for the collection: 'Œuvres / complettes / de / M. de Florian, / Capitaine de dragons et Gentilhomme / de S. A. S. Mgr. le duc de Pen- / thievre; de Académie de Ma- / drid, & c. / Tome huitième, / Contenant les Mélanges de lit- / térature. / [symmetrical woodcut ornament: sun-burst] / A Paris; / Et se trouve à Bruxelles, / Chez Emmanuel Flon, Imprimeur- / Libraire, rue de la Putterie. / [double rule] / M. DCC. LXXXIX.'

Both the collection halftitle and titlepage have been tipped in. (Chainlines horizontal.) The volume titlepage is f.[A2]. What probably happened is that Flon suppressed a halftitle (possibly a collection halftitle for the *Œuvres*) in or about 1789 of a book printed in 1787 (assuming the information on the volume titlepage be accurate). In any case, there really was a collection of Florian's *Œuvres* issued by Flon in the late 1780s, which in all likelihood continued into the 1790s. None of the Florian, Flon items in this bibliography bears a catchtome. For further clarification, see the commentary on the Flon, 1788 *Estelle* listed above.

The volume described here is not listed in modern bibliographies (either as an entity or as part of a collection), and I could find no other copy of it anywhere.

The item of prose fiction contained in this collection is *Léocadie, anecdote espagnole imitée de Cervantès*, pp.[131]-152 in a section with a halftitle for 'Imitations / et / traductions.' Also pertinent to the 'genre romanesque' is the 'Éloge / de Louis douze, / roi de France, / surnommé père du peuple. / [rule] / Nec magis sine illo nos esse felices / quàm ille sine nobis potuit. / Plin. panég. de Trajan. / B [signature]' (halftitle) + pp.[27]-30, [31]-77. For further information, see the first *Mélanges* listed above.

Incipits: (*Louis douze*) 'Louis XII, après dix-sept ans de / règne, au moment où son hymen avec / Marie d'Angleterre lui donnoit un allié / puissant'.

(*Léocadie*) 'Une nuit d'été, par un beau clair / de lune, vers les onze heures à-peu- / près, un pauvre vieux gentilhomme'.

107

Florian: *Mélanges de poésie et de littérature*, 1792

Jean Pierre Claris de Florian (1755-1794): Mélanges / de / poésie et de littérature, [possibly a period instead of a comma] / par M. de Florian, / Des Académies de Madrid, de Florence, de Lyon, / de Nismes, etc. / [rule] / A Paris, / de l'imprimerie de Didot l'aine [conceivably ainé]. / [double rule] / 1792.

18°: 3 ff. (halftitle, titlepage and halftitle for 'Ruth, / églogue / tirée de l'écriture sainte. / Couronnée par l'académie françoise / en 1784.') + [7]-202, [203]-204 pp.

Commentary: I could find no other copy of this edition or trace of it. This edition is present in my collection as vol. 8 of a very rare edition of some collected works. For the pieces included in this collection, see the *Œuvres*, 1792 below. The half titlepage ('Œuvres / de / M. de Florian.') bears the signature 'a' and the catchtome '7.' Curiously the catchtomes in the rest of the volume read '8.' F.[a3], p.[5-6] is a halftitle for the first piece, the poem *Ruth*, which first appeared separately in 1784.

This volume, in the section titled 'Imitations / et / traductions' (halftitle) contains *Léocadie. Anecdote espagnole imitée de Cervantès*, pp.[135]-158, a piece of prose fiction which first appeared in a 1787 *Mélanges* (MMF 87.41). It also contains the 'Éloge / de Louis douze, / roi de France, / surnommé pere du peuple. / [rule] / Nec magis sinè illo nos esse felices, quàm ille sinè / nobis potuit. / Plin. Panég. de Trajan.' (halftitle + pp.[35]-38, [39]-90). (For further information concerning *Louis XII*, see the commentary on the first entry for the *Mélanges* above.)

There is a not very exciting frontispiece bearing, at the top, 'Mélanges.' which has nothing to do with Quéverdo's design for the first edition (for which see the 1787, Geneva edition above). This edition is not listed in Cohen or Reynaud.

Incipits: (*Louis douze*) 'Louis XII, après dix-sept ans de / regne, au moment où son hymen / avec Marie d'Angleterre lui don- / noit un allié puissant'.

(*Léocadie*) 'Une nuit d'été, par un beau clair / de lune, vers les onze heures à-peu- / près, un pauvre vieux gentil- / homme'.

108

Florian: *Mélanges de poésie et de littérature*, 1794

Jean Pierre Claris de Florian (1755-1794): Mélanges / de poésie / et de littérature, / par J. P. Florian. / Nouvelle édition. / [circular woodcut ornament forming two circles: a wreath in the outside circle, 'LP' intertwined in the inner circle] / A Paris, / Chez Lepetit, Libraire, quai des Augustins, N°.32. / Berry, Libraire, rue Nicaise, N°. 12. / A Niort, chez Dugrit, Libraire. / [rule] / An II de la République françoise.

18°: 2 ff. (halftitle and titlepage) + [5]-178, [179]-180 pp.

Commentary: The last two pages comprise a 'table'. The only possible trace I have been able to find of this edition is a defective copy listed in the BNC (lii, col.978): 'An II. (Paris, J. J. Lepetit.) In-16, 180 p., front.' (8° Z.10399). The editors remark 'Œuvres de J. P. Florian. Le titre manque'. The mention of 'J. J. Lepetit' could well have been derived from the information to be found on the verso of the halftitle (for which see below). Since the BNC lists 'in-16', perhaps the BN copy represents a different issue (still assuming that it be the same edition)? I was unable to examine the BN copy.

Among the various pieces (largely in verse) contained in this volume are *Louis douze au lit de mort* (pp.[27]-72, including the 'avant-propos') and *Léocadie, anecdote espagnole imitée de Cervantès* (pp.[116]-135). As mentioned above, *Louis XII* might be considered marginal to the 'genre romanesque'. (See the first entry for the *Mélanges* above.)

There is a halftitle for 'Œuvres / de J. P. Florian.' On the verso is an interesting document, titled 'Avis aux citoyens': 'D'après le traité fait entre nous J. P. Florian, auteur de *Mélanges de poésie et de littérature*, et J. J. Lepetit, Libraire, nous déclarons que cet ouvrage est notre propriété commune, conformément aux clauses dont nous sommes convenus. Nous le plaçons sous la sauve-garde des loix et de la probité des citoyens, et nous poursuivrons devant les tribunaux tout contrefacteur et tout distributeur qui, au mépris de la propriété et des loix existantes, mettroit au jour des éditions contrefaites. / A Sceaux-l'Unité, ce 10 Floréal, l'an second de la République françoise, une et indivisible [29 April 1794]. / J. P. Florian. / J. J. Lepetit.'

From this it would seem that publishers (legitimate publishers, that is!) negotiated sometimes on a volume-to-volume basis for works by Florian, even when they were to form part of an *Œuvres*. However, in spite of the halftitle, it is by no means certain that Lepetit, in conjunction with Berry and Dugrit, went much further with the publication of a collection of Florian's *Œuvres*.

There is a mediocre frontispiece captioned: 'Il court vers elle, il hennit de plaisir.' This is a poor imitation of the pretty plate designed by Quéverdo and engraved by Delignon originally meant to illustrate the first verse tale in the *Mélanges*, 'Le Cheval d'Espagne' (in this edition, pp.[73]-85).

Incipits: (*Louis douze*) 'Louis XII, après dix-sept ans de regne, / au moment où son hymen avec Marie / d'Angleterre lui donnoit un allié puissant'.

(*Léocadie*) 'Une nuit d'été, par un beau clair de / lune, vers les onze heures à-peu-près, un / pauvre vieux gentilhomme'.

109

Florian: *Nouvelles nouvelles*, 1792

Jean Pierre Claris de Florian (1755-1794): Nouvelles / nouvelles. / Par M. de Florian, / De l'académie françoise, de celles de / Madrid, Florence, etc. / [rule] / Non potes in nugas dicere plura meas / pse [*sic*] ego quàm dixi. / (Mart. Epigramm. lib. XIII.) / [rule] / [woodcut decoration in the neoclassical style, oval centre with the initials 'PD' intertwined] / A Paris, / de l'imprimerie de Didot l'aîné. / 1792.

18°: 2 ff. (halftitle and titlepage) + [5]-304 pp.

Commentary: This book contains the following tales:

1. *Selmours, nouvelle angloise*, pp.[5]-70;
2. *Sélico, nouvelle africaine*, pp.[71]-100;
3. *Claudine, nouvelle savoyarde*, pp.[101]-158;
4. *Zulbar, nouvelle indienne*, pp.[159]-190;
5. *Camiré, nouvelle américaine*, pp.[191]-252;
6. *Valérie, nouvelle italienne*, pp.[253]-304.

MMF (92.13) list an edition or issue for Paris, Didot, 1792, but in-24 (304 pp.), with locations for Oron, Utrecht, Harvard, University of Massachusetts (Amherst) and the Detroit Institute of Arts. (The first three were examined by the authors; 92.13.) I was unable to see any of the above copies. Mine forms part of a curious collection of Florian's works. See the *Œuvres*, 1786-1801 for further information.

There is a half titlepage for the 'Œuvres / de / M. de Florian.' On the verso, we find: '[rule] / A Paris, / Au magasin des ouvrages de l'auteur, / chez Girod et Tessier, rue de la / Harpe, au coin de celle des Deux- / Portes, n° 162; / Et chez Debure, rue Serpente, hôtel / Ferrand.' (This matches the information given in the NUC.) There are no catchtomes present.

There are six very pretty illustrations after Quéverdo in the books described here, all signed, captioned and bearing the title of the piece illustrated. Most are dated: 1. facing p.[5], by Gaucher, dated 1792; 2. facing p.[71], by Dambrun, dated 1792; 3. facing p.[101], by Dambrun, dated 1792; 4. facing p.[159], by de Longueil (no date); 5. facing p.[191], by Dambrun, dated 1792; 6. facing p.[253], by de Longueil (no date).

These engravings do not all seem to be in the first state. Perhaps then the edition described here is not the first and differs from the edition described by MMF (allowing for the fact that the latter have probably made an error concerning format).

Incipits: (*Selmours*) 'C'est une belle et respectable / nation que la nation angloise.'

(*Sélico*) 'Si l'on pouvoit supposer, comme / les Parsis le disent, que cet univers / est soumis'.

(*Claudine*) 'Au mois de juillet 1788, me re- / trouvant dans ce Ferney qui, depuis / la mort de Voltaire'.

(*Zulbar*) 'Vous ne me tromperez plus, / perfides et lâches humains!'

(*Camiré*) 'Je reprochois un jour à un Espagnol / nouvellement arrivé de Buenos-Ay-/ res'.

(*Valérie*) 'On fait semblant dans le monde / de ne plus croire aux revenants'.

110

Florian: *Nouvelles nouvelles*, 1792

Jean Pierre Claris de Florian (1755-1794): Nouvelles / nouvelles. / Par M. de Florian, / De l'Académie françoise; de celles de / Madrid, Florence, etc. / [rule] / Non potes in nugas dicere plura meas / Ipse ego quàm dixi. / (Mart. Epigramm. lib. XIII.) / [rule] / A Paris, / de l'imprimerie de Didot l'ainé. / 1792.

18°: 2 ff. (halftitle and titlepage) + [5]-288 pp.

Commentary: There is a halftitle for the 'Œuvres / de / M. de Florian.' which bears the signature 'a' and a catchtome for vol. '13.' There are identical catchtomes throughout the book. The information on the spine indicates that it was supposed to be vol. 4 of a collection. For further information concerning this very rare Didot edition and collection, see the *Œuvres*, 1792 below. I could find no trace of this particular edition anywhere.

There is a very pretty frontispiece engraving to vol. i bearing, at the top, 'Selmours.' and the caption (at the bottom): 'When the sheepare [*sic*] in the fauld. &c.' No artists' signatures are present. This represents a very fine state of the engraving designed by Quéverdo and engraved by Gaucher issued with various editions of the *Nouvelles nouvelles*. This state is not mentioned by either Cohen or Reynaud, and neither is this specific edition.

This book contains the following tales:

1. *Selmours. Nouvelle angloise*, pp.[5]-66;
2. *Selico. Nouvelle africaine*, pp.[67]-94;
3. *Claudine. Nouvelle savoyarde*, pp.[95]-150;
4. *Zulbar, nouvelle indienne*, pp.[151]-180;
5. *Camiré. Nouvelle américaine*, pp.[181]-238;
6. *Valérie. Nouvelle italienne*, pp.[239]-288.

This collection of stories first appeared in 1792 (MMF 92.13).

Incipits: (*Selmours*) 'C'est une belle et respectable na- / tion que la nation angloise.'

(*Sélico*) 'Si l'on pouvoit supposer, comme / les Parsis le disent, que cet univers / est soumis'.

(*Claudine*) 'Au mois de juillet 1788, me re- / trouvant dans ce Ferney qui, depuis / la mort de Voltaire'.

(*Zulbar*) 'Vous ne me tromperez plus, / perfides et lâches humains!'

(*Camiré*) 'Je reprochois un jour à un Espagnol / nouvellement arrivé de Buenos-Ay- / res'.

(*Valérie*) 'On fait semblant dans le monde de / ne plus croire aux revenants'.

III

Florian: *Nouvelles nouvelles*, 1793

Jean Pierre Claris de Florian (1755-1794): Nouvelles / nouvelles, / par / M. de Florian, / De l'Académie Françoise, de celles / de Madrid, Florence, &c. / Ornées de 6 jolies Figures en taille-douce. / [rule] / Non potes in nugas dicere plura mea[s?] / Ipse ego quàm dixi. / (Mart. Epigramm. lib. XIII.) / [rule] / [symmetrical woodcut ornament] / A Liege, / Chez J. F. Desoer, Imprimeur- / Libraire, à la Croix d'or, / sur le Pont-d'Isle. / [rule] / 1793.

18°: 1 pl + 1 f. (table; 1 p. with catchword 'NOUVELLES' on verso) + [1]-281 pp. + 1 f. (see the commentary)

Commentary: MMF list what is possibly this edition, in spite of the different format recorded: 'Liège, J. F. Desoer, 1793, in-24, iii + 281p.', with locations for the Royal library at Brussels and the central public library of Liège (92.13). I know of no other copies and list mine because of its rarity.

The very last folio recorded consists of a curious kind of halftitle, comprising: '[heavy bar] / Nouvelles / nouvelles. / Par Florian. / [heavy bar]'. The print is very small, the bars very heavy and the entire effect is unusual. This halftitle seems more to have as its function a binder's or printer's instruction. But there is no volume indication for a collection, catchtomes or otherwise.

This volume contains:

1. *Selmours, nouvelle angloise,* pp.[1]-62;
2. *Sélico, nouvelle africaine,* pp.[63]-90;
3. *Claudine, nouvelle savoyard,* pp.[91]-144;
4. *Zulbar, nouvelle indienne,* pp.[145]-174;
5. *Camiré, nouvelle américaine,* pp.[175]-232;
6. *Valérie, nouvelle italienne,* pp.[233]-281.

Each tale is preceded by a full-page plate, captioned, bearing a short title and correct pagination. The last only is signed 'H. Godin Sculp.' (These are mirror-image adaptations of the original designs by Quéverdo for which see the first 1792, Didot edition above.)

Incipits: (*Selmours*) 'C'est une belle & respectable na- / tion que la nation angloise.'

(*Sélico*) 'Si l'on pouvoit supposer, comme les / Parsis le disent'.

(*Claudine*) 'Au mois de Juillet 1788, me re- / trouvant dans ce Ferney qui, depuis la / mort de Voltaire'.

(*Zulbar*) 'Vous ne me tromperez plus, perfides / & lâches humains!'

(*Camiré*) 'Je reprochois un jour à un Espagnol / nouvellement arrivé de Buenos-Ayres'.

(*Valérie*) 'On fait semblant dans le monde de / ne plus croire aux revenans'.

112

Florian: *Numa Pompilius,* 1786

Jean Pierre Claris de Florian (1755-1794): Numa Pompilius, / second / roi de Rome. / Par M. de Florian, / Capitaine de dragons, et Gentilhomme de S.A.S. / Mᵍʳ le Duc de Penthievre; de l'académie / de Madrid, etc. / Seconde Édition. / Tome premier [second]. / [woodcut decoration in the neoclassical style, oval centre with intertwined initials] / A Paris, / de l'imprimerie de Didot l'aîné. / M. DCC. LXXXVI.

18°, i: 2 ff. (halftitle and titlepage) + [5-6], [7-8, halftitle for 'Numa Pompilius. / Livre premier.', with 'sommaire' verso], [9]-240 pp.

ii: 3 ff. (halftitle, titlepage and halftitle for 'Numa Pompilius. / Livre septieme.', with 'sommaire' verso) + [7]-269, [270-72] pp. + 2 ff. (4 pp.)

Commentary: The first two pages recorded for vol. i are a verse dedication to Marie-Antoinette. Then follow a halftitle and the novel. The last three pages of vol. ii are the legal material. At the very end are four pages of 'Ouvrages imprimés chez Didot l'ainé ...'. There are halftitles for the 'Œuvres / de / M. de Florian.', with, on the versos, '[rule] / A Paris, / Chez Guillaume, rue du Bacq, n°.940; / Fabre, rue du Hurepoix, n°. 11.' The catchtomes are for vols 1. and 2. of the novel. None are present for the *Œuvres*.

MMF list a 'seconde édition', Didot, 1786, 240 and 269 pp., with a location for Harvard and after Cohen and Quérard (86.34; the NUC lists Harvard and Indiana University). I list my copy since it is part of a curious collection of Florian's collected works. See the *Œuvres*, 1786-1801 below for further information. (*Numa Pompilius* first appeared in 1786, in-octavo; see MMF.)

The above volumes are illustrated with twelve pretty engravings by Dambrun after Quéverdo: facing i.[9] (dated 1785); i.[49] (dated 1785); i.[85]; i.[121]; i.[157] (dated 1785); i.[199] (dated 1785); ii.[7]; ii.[47] (dated 1785); ii.[95]; ii.[141]; ii.[183]; ii.[229]. All engravings are signed, captioned and bear the book number. (Some of the dates might conceivably read '1783' instead of '1785').

To editions of *Numa Pompilius* listed in MMF and in this bibliography, I would add: *Numa Pompilius, second roi de Rome*, 3ᵉ éd. Paris: Didot l'aîné, 1787. 418 pp., 19 cm (in-12°?), ill. Part of an 'Œuvres de M. de Florian'. Source: OCLC, University of Alabama (University, Alabama).

Incipit: 'Non loin de la ville de Cures, dans / le pays des Sabins, au milieu d'une / antique forêt'.

113

Florian: *Numa Pompilius*, 1786

Jean Pierre Claris de Florian (1755-1794): Numa Pompilius / second / roi de Rome. / Par M. de Florian, / Capitaine de Dragons, et Gentilhomme / de S. A. S. Mgr. le Duc de / Penthievre; de l'Académie de / Madrid, etc. / [symmetrical woodcut ornament: stylised flower with foliage] / A Paris, / Et se trouve / A Mastricht, / Chez Dufour, Libraire. / [rule] / M. DCC. LXXXVI.

12°: 1 f. (titlepage) + [3]-4, [5]-374 pp.

Commentary: pp.[3]-4 comprise a verse dedication to Marie-Antoinette.

MMF list an edition for 'Paris & Mastricht, Dufour, 1786, in-18, 314p.', after the Bruxelles copy (86.34). The edition described here obviously differs radically. I could find no other copy of it.

For further information concerning this work, see the other entries devoted to it.

Incipit: 'Non loin de la ville de Cures, dans / le pays des Sabins, au milieu d'une / antique forêt'.

114

Florian: *Numa Pompilius*, 1792

Jean Pierre Claris de Florian (1755-1794): Numa Pompilius, / second / roi de Rome. / Par M. de Florian, / De l'académie [Académie for ii] françoise, [françoise; for ii] de celles de / Madrid, Florence, etc. / Troisieme édition. / [rule] / Tome premier [second]. / [rule] / A Paris, / de l'imprimerie de Didot l'ainé. / 1792.

18°, i: 2 ff. (halftitle and titlepage) + [5-6], [7-8], [9]-240 pp.

ii: 3 ff. (halftitle, titlepage and halftitle for 'Numa Pompilius. / Livre septieme.', with 'sommaire' verso) + [7]-252 pp.

Commentary: The first two pages recorded in vol. i are a verse dedication to

Marie-Antoinette. Then follow a halftitle ('Numa Pompilius. / Livre premier.'), with a 'sommaire' verso, and the novel. There is a frontispiece to vol. i. (Not in Cohen or Reynaud.) This is a somewhat primitive copy of the frontispiece designed by Quéverdo and engraved by Dambrun found at the head of various editions of *Numa Pompilius*. (The book held by Athena does not bear 'Telemaque' as the original does.)

Each volume has a halftitle for 'Œuvres / de / M. de Florian.' Each bears the signature 'a' and a catchtome for '3.' and '4.' respectively, catchtomes which are to be found throughout the books as well. The information on the spines is for vols ii and iii of the collection, and for i and ii of the novel. These books are part of a rare, 1792 Didot edition and were doubtless sold separately (with and without the halftitles), and with the set. The end of vol. i reads 'Fin du tome premier.'; the end of ii bears just 'Fin.' I was unable to find any trace of this edition anywhere. The novel first appeared in 1786 (MMF 86.34).

For further explanations, see the 1792, Didot *Œuvres* below.

Incipit: 'Non loin de la ville de Cures, dans / le pays des Sabins, au milieu d'une / antique forêt'.

115

Florian: *Œuvres*, 1786-1801

Jean Pierre Claris de Florian (1755-1794): (half titlepages) Œuvres / de / M. de Florian.

15 vols in-18°, Paris 1786-1801. See the commentary for details.

Commentary: This is a collection of various works by Florian, emanating from different editions (largely Didot's), uniformly and most elegantly covered with contemporary bindings. A few of these works appear to be hitherto unrecorded editions, and the rest are, in any case, very rare. So I have chosen to list them all. These volumes, all of which contain halftitles for the *Œuvres*, are an excellent example of the bibliographical muddle created by eigthteenth- and early nineteenth-century owners collecting Florian's works willy-nilly, and having them uniformly bound. (See the NUC for nine of these 'recueils factices'.) None of the bindings in the collection described here bears a volume indication for the collection. All read 'Œuvres / de / Florian', give a short title, and a volume indication for the piece, where applicable.

Here is a list of the items contained in this collection, in chronological order:
1. *Numa Pompilius*, 1786;
2. *Les Six nouvelles*, 1786;
3. *Mélanges de poésie et de littérature*, 1787;
4. *Galatée*, 1788;
5. *Théâtre*, 1791;
6. *Fables*, 1792;
7. *Gonzalve de Cordoue*, 1792;
8. *Nouvelles nouvelles*, 1792;
9. *Estelle*, 1793;

10. *Guillaume Tell*, 1801.

For the pieces of prose fiction, see the main entries in this bibliography. Here is a description of the volumes falling outside of the 'genre romanesque' and thus excluded from the list of main entries, although *Héro et Léandre* could be considered marginal. (See below.)

Théâtre:

Théâtre / de / M. de Florian, / De l'académie françoise, de celles de Madrid, / Florence, etc. / Quatrième Édition. / Tome premier [second, troisieme]. / [rule] / Tous les genres sont bons, hors le genre ennuyeux. / Voltaire. / [woodcut ornament in the neoclassical style bearing an oval cartouche in the centre with intertwined initials] / A Paris, / de l'imprimerie de Didot jeune. / 1791.

18°, i: 2 ff. (halftitle and titlepage) + [5]-37 + [39], [40], [41]-232 pp.

ii: 3 ff. (halftitle, titlepage and long halftitle for *Jeannot et Colin*) + [7-9], [10], [11]-234 pp.

iii: 2 pl + [j]-xj + 1 f. (long halftitle for *La Bonne mère*) + [3], [4], [5]-234 pp.

The pagination recorded above reflects two 'avant-propos' for vols i and iii, and preliminary pieces/halftitles for the first plays of each volume. The volumes begin with halftitles: 'Œuvres / de / M. de Florian.' The versos of the halftitles to vols i and iii only bear: '[rule] / A Paris, / Chez Guillaume, rue du Bacq, n°.940; / Fabre, rue du Hurepoix, n°. 11.' There are no catchtomes on the halftitles; those in the volumes are for 1, 2 and 3, respectively. As with most of the in-18° works of Florian, this edition was doubtless sold as part of a collection, and separately (with and without the halftitles).

A three-volume collection of Florian's *Théâtre italien* first appeared in 1784 (Didot) according to Cohen (col.403). But what seems to be the case is that vols i and ii of this collection appeared in 1784 and vol. iii in 1786 (with a reedition of vols i and ii). (See the BNC, lii, col.974, nos 545-46, 547.) The *Théâtre* described here seems to be listed in the NUC (Library of Congress, Indiana University, Harvard). This edition is not listed in the BNC or BLC.

Here is a list of the plays in this edition:

1. *Les Deux billets, comédie*, one act in prose, i.[39]-84;
2. *Le Bon ménage, ou la suite des Deux billets, comédie*, one act in prose, i.[85]-150;
3. *Le Bon père, ou la suite du Bon ménage, comédie*, one act in prose, i.[151]-232;
4. *Jeannot et Colin, comédie*, three acts in prose, ii.[5]-86;
5. *Les Jumeaux de Bergame, comédie*, one act in prose, ii.[87]-137;
6. *Héro et Léandre, monologue lyrique*, no scenes or acts indicated, ii.[139]-155;
7. *Le Baiser, féerie*, one act in verse, ii.[157]-189;
8. *Blanche et Vermeille, pastorale*, two acts in verse, ii.[191]-234;
9. *La Bonne mère, comédie*, one act in prose, iii.[1]-78;
10. *Le Bon fils, comédie*, three acts in prose, iii.[79]-192;
11. *Myrtil et Chloé, pastorale*, one act in prose, iii.[193]-234.

The last piece is an imitation from Gessner.

The 'avant-propos' at the head of vol. iii is the introduction to the entire volume, which appeared sometime after the publication of the first. The explanatory note at the bottom of the first page is revelatory: 'Cet avant-propos, qui n'est qu'une suite à celui de la premiere édition, lui est réuni dans la nouvelle qui paroît. Mais l'auteur a eu grand soin de le placer à la tête de ce troisieme volume, afin que les personnes qui ont déja les deux premiers de son théâtre puissent, en y ajoutant celui-ci, avoir une édition aussi complete que la nouvelle. C'est dans les mêmes vues qu'il a fait tirer à part un certain nombre des estampes destinées à la nouvelle édition, pour ceux qui voudroient les placer dans l'ancienne. Il n'y aura donc de différence entre cette ancienne et la nouvelle, qu'un autre ordre dans les pieces, et quelques retranchements à l'opéra du *Baiser*. L'auteur se fera toujours une loi de compléter ainsi par des suppléments tous les ouvrages auxquels il pourroit ajouter.'

For further information concerning the first dates of publication of these plays, see the 1792 *Œuvres*. Although *Héro et Léandre* was staged, Florian's dramatic monologue, recounting the tragic story of Hero and Leander, is more of a prose poem and could easily be considered part of the 'genre romanesque'.

These three volumes are illustrated with a dozen exquisite engravings designed by Quéverdo and executed by Dembrun (or Dambrun) and De Longueil.

Fables:

Fables / de / M. de Florian, / De l'académie françoise, de celles de Madrid, / Florence, etc. / [rule] / Je tâche d'y tourner le vice en ridicule, / Ne pouvant l'attaquer avec des bras d'Hercule. / La Font. Fables, liv. V, 1. / [rule] / [woodcut decoration in the neoclassical manner, oval centre with initials 'PD' intertwined] / A Paris, / de l'imprimerie de P. Didot l'aîné. / 1792.

18°: 2 ff. (halftitle and titlepage) + [5]-33 + [35]-220, [221]-224 pp. + 1 f. (1 p.)

The first piece is an introductory essay, 'De la fable'. Then follow the fables, a table of contents and a final folio containing a priced list of Florian's individual works, in-8° and in-18°, ordinary paper and 'papier vélin'; prices are also given for the collections.

There is a halftitle for the 'Œuvres / de / M. de Florian.' On the verso is the following indication: '[rule] / A Paris, / Chez Girod et Tessier, rue de la Harpe, / au coin de celle des Deux-Portes, / n° 162; / Et chez Debure, rue Serpente, hôtel / Ferrand.' There are no catchtomes in this volume.

I could find no copy of these *Fables* listed in the BLC, BNC, NUC (or NUC:S).

This volume contains illustrations by Gaucher, De Longueil, Delignon and perhaps Giraud (signature barely decipherable) after Villers and Flouest.

These engravings are not in the first state. All the pieces in this volume are in verse. At the end, is 'Tobie, / poëme / tiré de l'écriture sainte.' (halftitle), pp.[201]-220 (including the halftitle).

Cohen cites the first edition as above, with the same pagination, although he makes no mention of the advertisement leaf. Since he notes that the illustrations are 'd'une finesse remarquable', we probably have here an edition different from the first (cols.398-99).

There is a collection of Florian's *Œuvres choisies* listed in the Messkatalog which is not listed in the usual bibliographies; nor is it to be found in the BNC, BLC or NUC: 'Œuvres choisies de Mr. de *Florian*; recueillies à l'usage de la jeunesse. 8. Berlin, Unger', OM 1797, p.234.

Incipits: (*Les Deux billets*) 'Voici la premiere fois que je suis / bien aise de savoir lire.'

(*Héro et Léandre*) 'Enfin la nuit étend ses voiles sur / toute la nature. Mon cher Léandre'.

('Fable première: La Fable et la Vérité') 'La Vérité toute nue / Sortit un jour de son puits.'

116

Florian: *Œuvres*, 1792

Jean Pierre Claris de Florian (1755-1794): (half titlepages) Œuvres / de / M. de Florian.

12 vols in-18°, Paris: Didot, 1792. See the commentary for details.

Commentary: This is a very rare collection of Florian's works; most volumes in it containing items of prose fiction appear to be unique copies. The volumes are bound in early nineteenth-century, half calf, and bear the indications of vols 1-12 for the collection on the spines, which do not necessarily match their 'proper' place in the *Œuvres*, should one care to place one's faith in the catchtomes. As MMF point out (83.26), it is next to impossible to establish a list of Florian's *Œuvres*. Bookdealers published individual works and collected works, usually selling the items separately (as well as in collections). Publishers also added to their collections of the works as necessary, and most eighteenth-century owners seemed to make up their own sets by buying works as they appeared in the various formats. For a list of the contents of what would comprise a complete collection of Florian's works, in-18° (which would lead well into the nineteenth century), see Cohen, col.403.

The works included in this 1792 edition, as extant in my collections, are:

1. *Galatée* (vol. i);
2. *Numa Pompilius* (vols ii-iii);
3. *Nouvelles nouvelles* (vol. iv);
4. *Théâtre* (vols v-vii);
5. *Mélanges de poésie et de littérature* (vol. viii);
6. *Estelle* (vol. ix);
7. *Gonzalve de Cordoue* (vols x-xii).

For details concerning the individual items, see the appropriate entries in this bibliography. Since Florian's plays do not fall into the category of the 'genre romanesque', with the possible exception of *Héro et Léandre* (see below), and in the interest of completeness, here is a description of the *Théâtre*.

Théatre / de / M. de Florian, / De l'Académie françoise; de celles de / Madrid, Florence, etc. / Troisieme édition. / [rule] / Tome cinquieme [second, troisieme]. / [rule] / C'est là tout mon talent: je ne sais s'il suffit. / La Fontaine. [La Fontaine, V. for ii] / [rule] / A Paris. [Paris, for ii, iii]. / De [de for ii, iii because of the preceding comma] l'imprimerie de Didot l'ainé. / 1792.

i: 2 ff. (halftitle and titlepage) + [5]-36, [37-38], [39]-216 pp.

ii: 3 ff. (halftitle, titlepage and long halftitle for *La Bonne mère*) + [7], [8], [9]-228 pp.

iii: 3 ff. (halftitle, titlepage and long halftitle for *Jeannot et Colin*) + [7-9], [10], [11]-216 pp.

As can be seen by the information given on the titlepages, either this collection of plays consists of two editions or the printer made a mistake, calling the first volume vol.v of the collected works, then vols ii and iii, vols ii and iii of the *Théâtre*.

The halftitles of i and iii bear the catchtomes 5 and 7, respectively; none appears on the halftitle of vol. ii. Catchtomes within the books themselves are for 5, 6 and 7.

Vols i and ii bear, at the end, 'Fin du tome premier [second].' At the end of iii, is simply 'Fin.'

At the head of vol. i, bound in between the halftitle and titlepage, is a frontispiece engraving, unsigned, titled at the top 'Théatre.' This edition is not listed in Cohen or Reynaud. This is a poor copy of the pretty frontispiece designed by Quéverdo and engraved by Dambrun issued with various editions of the *Théâtre*. (The banner unfurled by the flying cupids at the top does not bear the motto 'castigat ridendo mores' inscribed on the original illustration.)

i.[5]-36 is an 'Avant-propos.' The rest of the pagination as recorded reflects halftitles and preliminary pieces to the first plays in the vols.

This edition of Florian's collected plays is not listed in the NUC, BLC or NUC (or NUC:S).

Here is a list of the plays, followed by the date of the first edition, according to Brenner (where recorded), and the date of the first performance according to the information supplied with the plays in the edition described here.

1. *Les Deux billets*, *comédie*, one act in prose, i.[37]-81; 1780. 9/2/1779, Comédie italienne.

2. *Le Bon ménage, ou la suite des Deux billets*, *comédie*, one act in prose, i.[83]-146; no date of publication given in Brenner (Paris: Brunet, 1783; BNC, NUC). 28/12/1782, before the king and queen, performed by the 'comédiens français et italiens'.

3. *Le Bon père, ou la suite du Bon ménage*, *comédie*, one act in prose, i.[147]-216; 1784. 2/2/83, 'sur un théâtre de société' (chez d'Argental; Brenner).

4. *La Bonne mère*, *comédie*, one act in prose, ii.[5]-82; 1785. 2/2/1785, 'sur un théâtre de société' (d'Argental; Brenner).

5. *Le Bon fils*, *comédie*, three acts in prose, ii.[83]-194; 1786. 1/11/1785, 'sur un théâtre de société' (d'Argental; Brenner).

6. *Myrtil et Chloé*, *pastorale*, one act in prose, ii.[195]-228; listed in Brenner, but no information whatsoever given, [1784 or 1786?].

7. *Jeannot et Colin*, *comédie*, three acts in prose, iii.[5]-84; 1780. 14/11/1780, Comédie italienne.

8. *Les Jumeaux de Bergame*, *comédie*, one act in prose, iii.[85]-132; 1782. 6/8/1782, Comédie italienne.

9. *Héro et Léandre*, *monologue lyrique*, no scenes or acts indicated, iii.[133]-148; 1784. 23/9/1784, Ambigu-comique (information derived from Brenner).

10. *Le Baiser*, *comédie*, one act in verse, iii.[149]-174; not in Brenner. The first edition listed in the BNC (*Le Baiser, ou la Bonne fée*, three acts in verse, 'comédie mêlée de musique') is for Paris: Brunet, 1782. 26/11/1782, Comédie italienne.

11. *Blanche et Vermeille, pastorale*, two acts in verse, iii.[175]-216; 1781. 5/3/1781, Comédie italienne.

Although it was actually staged, *Héro et Léandre* could well be considered a piece of prose fiction. It is as much a prose-poem as a dramatic monologue in which Hero relates her misfortunes. (At the end, she throws herself into the sea.) Note that there is no introduction to any but the first volume and that vols ii and iii contain the material (aside from the 'avant-propos') to be found in vols iii and ii of the 1791 edition described in the 1786-1801 *Œuvres* above.

For more collections of Florian's plays, see his other *Œuvres* below.

Incipits: (*Les Deux billets*) 'Voici la premiere fois que je suis / bien aise de savoir lire.'

(*Héro et Léandre*) 'Enfin la nuit étend ses voiles / sur toute la nature. Mon cher Léan- / dre, voici l'heure'.

117

Florian: *Œuvres complètes*, 1796.

Jean Pierre Claris de Florian (1755-1794): Oeuvres / complètes [completes for ii and vi] / de / M. de Florian. / De l'académie françoise, de celles de Madrid, / Florence, etc. / Tome premier [second, troisième, quatrieme, cinquieme, sixieme, septieme, huitieme]. / [rule] / Nouvelle édition. / [rule] / Leipsic, 1796. / Chez Gérard Fleischer.

8°, i: 2 pl (halftitle and titlepage) + 2 ff. (blank leaf and halftitle for 'Vie / de Cervantes.', dedication verso) + [1]-263 pp.

ii: 2 pl + 2 ff. (blank leaf and 1 p. dedication to Marie-Antoinette) + 1 f. (halftitle for *Numa Pompilius*, 'sommaire' verso) + [3]-311 pp.

iii: 3 ff. (vol. halftitle and titlepage, halftitle for 'Théatre.') + [9]-295 pp. (A blank leaf is bound in between pp.14-15, which presumably belongs to the preliminaries).

iv: 3 ff. (vol. halftitle, titlepage and a halftitle for 'Myrtil et Chloé, / pastorale.') + [11]-205 pp. (Two blank leaves are bound in between pp.14-15, which presumably belong to the preliminaries.)

v: 3 ff. (vol. halftitle, titlepage, halftitle for *Ruth*) + [9]-367 + 1 f. (2 pp.) pp. (A blank leaf is bound in between pp.14-15; this presumably belongs to the preliminaries. After the last folio recorded, a table, there is a blank leaf.)

vi: 3 ff. (vol. halftitle and titlepage, halftitle for 'Précis / historique / sur les Maures / d'Espagne.') + [9]-293 pp. (Although there is a blank leaf at the end, there is a folio of the first gathering missing, presumably a blank leaf, unless the frontispiece is part of that gathering, which I could not ascertain in the present copy.)

vii: 3 ff. (vol. halftitle and titlepage, halftitle for 'Gonzalve / de Cordoue. / [rule] / Livre quatrieme.') + [9]-227 pp. (There is a blank leaf bound in between pp.14-15, presumably part of the preliminaries.)

viii: 3 ff. (vol. halftitle and titlepage, and halftitle for 'Nouvelles.') + [9]-386, [387]-390 pp. (There is a folio missing from the first gathering, presumably a blank leaf unless the frontispiece is part of that gathering. However, there is a blank leaf at the end.)

Commentary: The collection halftitles read: 'Oeuvres / de / M. de Florian. / [rule] / Tome premier [... huitieme].' MMF largely list the prose fiction works in this collection. I have included it because they left out a couple of items of prose fiction contained in these *Œuvres* and because, with all the other works/editions of Florian described in the present bibliography, it seemed to me that this entry would be a welcomed addition. Also I have not been able to find any description of this hard-to-come-by collective edition (no copy listed in BNC, one in BL, four locations in NUC, one location in Krauss-Fontius [no.990]) that might be termed adequate.

My copy is printed on fine paper ('papier vélin'). There were at least two issues of these *Œuvres*, for the Messkatalog records: 'Œuvres complettes de Florian. 8 Vol. Pap. velin, av[ec] fig. de Chodowiecki. 8vo. à Leipsic, Gerh. Fleischer'. The next entry is for 'Les mêmes. 8 Vol. Pap. à écrire, sans fig. 8vo. Chez le sus-dit' (MM 1795, p.304).

This collection apparently appeared in two series: one beginning in 1796 (as described here) and the other beginning in 1799. The editors of the 1796 (and on) edition termed it 'complete' in 1796 because it contained all works by Florian published to that date. The posthumous publication of Florian's translation of Cervantes' *Don Quichotte* caused the continuation of these *Œuvres*. 'Amateurs' could at that point either add on to the 1796 edition or buy the 1799 reprint (possibly a reissue with cancel titlepages) with the later additions. *Don Quichotte* formed vols ix-xi (1800), as is clearly indicated in the Messkatalog: 'Don Quichotte de la Manche, traduit de l'Espagnol de Michel de Cervantes, par Florian. Ouvrage posthume. 3 Vol. av[ec] fig. 8vo. à Leipzig, Fleischer le cadet. Aussi sous le titre: Œuvres complettes de Florian. Tom. 9eme 10eme 11eme av[ec] fig. 8vo.' (MM 1799, p.34).

Two volumes of *Œuvres posthumes* were added later, to form vol. xii (1801) and xiii (1803). This information is deduced particularly from the BL copy and the entries in the NUC. Thus the collection described here comprises the complete series of Florian's *Works*, as available in 1796, but excluding the posthumous additions.

These *Œuvres* are unusual in that they were issued as a whole and obviously so sold. Catchtomes throughout indicate the appropriate volume. (Gesamtverzeichniss lists the *Œuvres complètes* in 13 vols, with thirteen illustrations, in-8vo, for Leipzig, '[1]799-801. Er. Fleischer', xxxix.139a). However, when reissued and/or reprinted 1799 and on, the individual volumes were also available separately. See MMF, Heinsius and Kayser under the individual titles. (Apparently, too, some volumes of the 1796 edition were also sold individually.)

Here are the items of prose fiction in the collection described here. With the exception of those contained in the *Mélanges de poésie et de littérature*, these are listed in MMF under the appropriate headings. (Pagination recorded here includes halftitles and liminary material, where extant.)

Vol. i: *Galatée* (1 f.: 2 pp. + [1]-122 pp.) and the *Six nouvelles* with a halftitle for 'Six nouvelles / de / M. de Florian.' (pp.[123]-263).

Vol. ii: *Numa Pompilius* (1 f.: 1 p. + [1]-311 pp.).

Vol. iii: *Théâtre*: 'Avant-propos'; *Les Deux billets*; *Le Bon ménage*; *Le Bon père*; *La Bonne mère*; *Le Bon fils*.

Vol. iv: *Théâtre*: *Myrtil et Chloé*; *Jeannot et Colin*; *Les Jumeaux de Bergame*; *Héro et Léandre* (pp.[131]-142); *Le Baiser*; *Blanche et Vermeille*.

Vol. v: *Mélanges de poésie et de littérature*, with *Éloge de Louis douze* (pp.[33]-70) and *Léocadie* (pp.[119]-133); *Estelle* with the *Essai sur la pastorale* (pp.[177]-367).

Vol. vi: *Gonzalve de Cordoue* (pp.[7]-293).

Vol. vii: *Gonzalve de Cordoue*, suite (pp.[7]-227).

Vol. viii: *Nouvelles nouvelles*, with a halftitle for 'Nouvelles.' (pp.[7]-188) and *Fables en vers* with a halftitle for 'Fables.'

There are several pretty engravings accompanying this collection, as follows:

1. frontispiece to vol. ii by Mansfeld after Chodowiecki;
2. frontispiece to vol. iii, same artists;
3. frontispiece to vol. iv, same artists;
4. frontispiece to vol. v, same artists (depicting Voltaire and the serf of mount Jura);
5. frontispiece to vol. vi, same artists;
6. frontispiece to vol. vii by C. Schule after Chodowiecki (dated 1796);
7. frontispiece to vol. viii by Chodowiecki after Penzel [Pentzel?], dated 1796.

The seven engravings bear the volume indication as well as the artists' names. 1 through 5 also bear 'Vienna' (variously spelled). This edition is not listed in Cohen or Reynaud. Since there is no illustration for volume i, perhaps a frontispiece portrait was planned, but never executed?

For first dates of publication and further information, see the main entries for each work in these *Œuvres* below.

For the incipits, see the appropriate entries below.

It might be noted that Gesamtverzeichniss has some 'Œuvres choisies, recueillies à l'usage de la jeunesse. 8vo. Berlin, Unger. [a[uch] Schade]. [1]797' (xxxix.139a). Not mentioned in MMF, these *Œuvres* probably contain some prose-fiction items. See too the end of the commentary on 115.

118

Florian: *Les Six nouvelles*, 1786

Jean Pierre Claris de Florian (1755-1794): Les / six nouvelles / de M. de Florian, / Capitaine de dragons, et Gentilhomme de / S.A.S. Mgr le Duc de Penthievre; / des acad. de Madrid et de Lyon. / [rule] / L'ennui naquit un jour de l'uniformité. Lamot, fabl. / [woodcut decoration in the neoclassical style, oval centre with intertwined initials] / A Paris, / de l'imprimerie de Didot l'ainé. / M. DCC. LXXXVI.

18°: 2 ff. (halftitle and titlepage) + [5-6], [7]-228 pp.

Commentary: The pagination recorded here reflects a two-page, verse dedication to Marie-Antoinette's friend, the hapless princesse de Lamballe. Then follow the six novelle. This collection first appeared in 1784 (MMF 84.24; however, the BL copy of the first edition, 634.a.19[1] is in-18°, and not in-12°).

Moreover, MMF list a Didot edition, a 'troisième édition' for 1786, 228 pp. in-12°, citing the BN and BL copies. While I was unable to see the BN copy, it was possible to justapose the book described here with the BL copy (12513.a.15). Both represent entirely different editions, in spite of the same pagination and format (both are in-18°), so neither is a reissue of the other. It is possible that there are copies of this edition (or that in the BL) listed in the NUC with locations for Harvard and the Rosenbach Foundation (Philadelphia).

The book described here has a halftitle for the 'Œuvres / de / M. de Florian.' The verso bears: '[rule] / A Paris, / Chez Guillaume, rue du Bacq, n°.940; / Fabre, rue du Hurepoix, n°. 11.' There are no catchtomes present. This volume is part of an interesting collection of Florian's works. See his *Œuvres*, 1786-1801 above.

The six tales are:

1. *Bliombéris, nouvelle françoise*, pp.[7]-84;
2. *Pierre, nouvelle allemande*, pp.[85]-104;
3. *Célestine, nouvelle espagnole*, pp.[105]-144;
4. *Sophronime, nouvelle grecque*, pp.[145]-168;
5. *Sanche, nouvelle portugaise*, pp.[169]-192;
6. *Bathmendi, nouvelle persane*, pp.[193]-228.

There are six pretty engravings accompanying the tales, each signed, captioned and bearing the name of the story illustrated: 1. facing p.[7], by de Longueil after Quéverdo; 2. facing p.[85], by Delignon after Quéverdo; 3. facing p.[105], by Dembrun after Quéverdo; 4. facing p.[145], by de Longueil after Quéverdo, dated 1786; 5. facing p.[169], by Dembrun after Quéverdo; 6. facing p.[193], by de Longueil after Quéverdo. (Note that the fourth one bears the date of 1786.)

Concerning the first edition, Cohen remarks that there is '1 frontispice par Pernotin, gravé par Guyard et 6 jolies figures de Quéverdo, gravées par de Longueil (3), Delignon (2) et Dambrun (2)' (col.402). However, he then mentions only *six* for 1786: 'Réimprimé chez le même éditeur [Didot] en 1786: 228 pp., plus les mêmes 6 figures'. Reynaud states: 'Le front., par Pernotin, gravé par Guyard, manque assez souvent. On a vu 2 exemplaires de l'époque qui ne le possédait pas. Delignon a gravé 1 figure' (col.184). It is probably a question of a portrait frontispiece, printed later (much later?) than the book, and sometimes bound with it, parallelling what probably also occurred, for example, with the illustrated, Paris edition of the *Mélanges de poésie et de littérature*, 1787, listed above. (Also, when several volumes were issued as an *Œuvres*, it would be logical to have only the first carry a portrait frontispiece.)

To editions of the *Six nouvelles* listed in MMF and in the current bibliography, I would add:

1. *Les Six nouvelles*, 1785. 'Nouvelles, les six, de M. de *Florian*. 4 Voll. 8. à Basle, chez J. J. Flick', Messkatalog, OM 1785, p.119. There is some sort of mistake here. Four octavo volumes, if true as stated, would have contained much more than the *Six nouvelles*. Perhaps the *Nouvelles nouvelles* and maybe other tales were included? Heinsius has the following entry: 'Les six Nouvelles. [in-]12. Basel, Flick. [1]785' (i, col.900 and Romane, col.152). This information is also largely contained in Heinsius, *Handbuch* (p.812) and in Heinsius, 1793 (iv.535).

2. *Les Six nouvelles de M. de Florian*. Londres, 1786. 264 pp. No size or format specified. Halftitle for 'Œuvres de M. de Florian'. Source: OCLC for California State College at San Bernardino and Cleveland Public Library.

Incipits: (*Bliombéris*) 'J'ai toujours aimé les romans de che- / valerie, sur-tout ceux dont les héros / sont françois.'

(*Pierre*) 'La langue allemande est trop diffi- / cile; presque aucun François ne l'ap- / prend'.

(*Célestine*) 'Les Espagnols ont été nos maîtres / en littérature'.

(*Sophronime*) 'Il faut être plus Grec que je ne le / suis pour oser parler des Grecs'.

(*Sanche*) 'Les Portugais avoient bien leur mé- / rite quand ils doubloient le cap des / Tourmentes'.

(*Bathmendi*) 'Les *Mille et une Nuits* m'ont / toujours paru des contes charmants'.

119

Florian: *Les Six nouvelles*, 1789

Jean Pierre Claris de Florian (1755-1794): Œuvres / complettes / de M. de Florian, / Capitaine de Dragons, et Gentilhomme de / S. A. S. Mgr. le Duc de Penthievre; / Membre de l'académie française, et de / celles de Madrid et de Lyon. / Tome second. / Contenant les Six Nouvelles. / [rule] / L'ennui naquit un jour de l'uniformité. / Lamot. fab. / [rule] / [complex composite woodcut ornament with flower in basket in centre] / A Paris; / Et se trouve à Bruxelles, / Chez Emm. Flon, Imprimeur-Libraire. / [double rule] / M. DCC. LXXXIX.

18°: 2 ff. (halftitle and titlepage) + 1 f. (2 pp.) + [7]-224 pp.

Commentary: I have been unable to find any other trace of this edition which is part of a 'recueil factice' of Florian's *Œuvres*. For other volumes from this collection and for further information, see the Flon, 1788 *Estelle* above and the other pertinent Flon editions.

There is a volume halftitle for the 'Œuvres / complettes / de / M. de Florian.' Bound in before the titlepage is a captioned frontispiece: 'C'est un enfant qui m'apprit ces nouvelles'.

This volume contains, after the two-page poem to the princesse de Lamballe:

1. *Bliombéris, nouvelle française*, pp.[7]-80;
2. *Pierre, nouvelle allemande*, pp.[81]-99;
3. *Célestine, nouvelle espagnole*, pp.[100]-136;
4. *Sophronime, nouvelle grecque*, pp.[137]-157;
5. *Sanche, nouvelle portugaise*, pp.[158]-178;
6. *Bathmendi, nouvelle persane*, pp.[179]-211;
7. 'Ruth, / églogue sainte / Qui a remporté le Prix de Poésie de / l'Académie française, en 1784. / Par M. de Florian.' (halftitle) + [215]-224 pp. (This piece is in verse.)

Incipits (*Bliombéris*): 'J'ai toujours aimé les romans de / chevalerie, sur-tout ceux dont les hé- / ros sont Français.'

(*Pierre*) 'La langue allemande est trop dif- / ficile; presque aucun français ne l'ap- / prend'.

(*Célestine*) 'Les Espagnols ont été nos maîtres / en littérature'.

(*Sophronime*) 'Il faut être plus Grec que je ne le / suis pour oser parler des Grecs'.

(*Sanche*) 'Les Portugais avoient bien leur mé- / rite quand ils doubloient le cap des / Tourmentes'.

(*Bathmendi*) 'Les *Mille et une Nuits* m'ont / toujours paru des contes charmans'.

120

Fontette de Sommery: *Lettres de la comtesse de L****, 1786

Mademoiselle Fontette de Sommery (?-1790): Lettres / De madame / la comtesse de L*** / a monsieur / le comte de R***. / Nouvelle édition / corrigée et augmentée. / [woodcut: rustic decoration in the form of a swag] / A Paris, / Chez Barrois l'aîné, Libraire, quai des / Augustins. / [double rule] / M. DCC. LXXXVI. / Avec approbation, et privilège du roi.

12°: 2 pl + [j]-iv + [1]-318, [319]-365, [366] pp.

Commentary: This novel first appeared in 1785 (MMF 85.28). MMF do list this edition, after Barbier, Quérard and Aspin catalogue no. 46. The volume described here was the Aspin copy, which I list since it exists nowhere else that I know of. P.[366] contains some legal material. The 'approbation', by Blin de Sainmore, is dated 4 April 1785. The 'privilège' is for Barrois the Elder, which is here only partially extant. A final folio (f. [Q4]) is missing, and 'Fin' has been inked in by a previous owner. F.Q4 would have contained the continuation and end of the official documents.

The preliminary pages are an 'Avertissement de l'éditeur'. Then follow the novel and its continuation. The latter bears the following head title: 'Lettres de madame la comtesse de L*** a madame la marquise de R***, sa belle-fille'. There is a half titlepage for the novel: 'Lettres / de madame / la comtesse de L*** / a monsieur / le comte de R***'. On the verso is a list of 'Livres qui se trouvent chez le même Libraire.'

The 'Avertissement de l'éditeur' insists that the letters are real, explains how the 'editor' obtained them and draws a parallel with those of Mme de Sévigné. Mme de Sévigné's are 'preferred', in so far as nicety is concerned: 'Ces Lettres plairont moins, ce me semble, aux personnes d'esprit qu'aux personnes sensibles: elles n'ont ni la légèreté, ni la variété, ni les tours de celles de madame de Sévigné; mais il est facile de s'appercevoir que madame de Sévigné écrivoit pour la postérité, et que madame de L***, au contraire, ne mettoit aucune prétention dans ses Lettres' (p.ij). (The novel and its continuation extend from 4 June 1674 to 15 August 1680.)

In passing I note that there were two editions for 1785 apparently, one for 2 preliminary leaves + iv + 324 pp. + 1f., in-12° (NUC: New York Public Library) and another as listed by MMF (iv + 360 pp., extant in the Newberry Library and the Free Public Library of Philadelphia [NUC]). The edition described here also seems to be listed in Giraud, 1785.7, p.81 (for 4 ff. + 365 pp. + 1 f.).

In addition to all the editions mentioned here, Giraud, if he be accurate, also has another edition for 1785, which he lists as the first: 'Paris, Barrois, 1785, in-12, 2ff-IV-355p.-2ff. (1785.7.a). This could conceivably be, however, the same as MMF's entry (after copies in the Newberry and Free Public Library of Philadelphia).

Incipit: 'Je le sais, je le sens, mon cher Adolphe, le regret de vous éloigner de moi, absorbe tous ceux que vous y pourriez joindre'.

121

Fougeret de Monbron: *Le Canapé couleur de feu*, 1745

Louis Charles Fougeret de Monbron, sometimes Montbron (1720?-1761): (*red and black titlepage*) Le / *canapé*, / couleur / *de feu*. / Par M. de *** / *nouvelle edition*. / [woodcut of flying cherub reading book] / A Londres, / *Chez Samuel Harding*, / MDCCXLV.

8°: 1 f. (titlepage) + [3]-112 pp.

Commentary: Jones lists the first edition of this amusing para-fairy tale for: La Haye, Papi, [n.d. 1714?] 115 p. (p.23). He also lists it for 1741. All of Fougeret de Monbron's other works appeared after 1740 and the author died in 1761. His birthdate is a subject of considerable speculation, but it seems illogical that he would write a piece in a rather mature style at a very young age and then wait nearly thirty years before doing anything else. And in light of what he did write, I doubt that his 'later' writings are those of an old or ageing man. For further information concerning the first edition of *Le Canapé*, see Katherine L. Gee's most interesting article, '*Le Canapé*: une erreur bibliographique rectifiée' (*Revue d'histoire littéraire de la France* 78 (1978), pp.[790]-92); she argues quite convincingly that 1741 is the date of the first edition and has meticulously traced the source of previous errors.

Pia states that the *Canapé couleur de feu* is not by Fougeret de Monbron, referring to Saillet (Pascal Pia, *Les Livres de l'Enfer: bibliographie critique des ouvrages érotiques dans leurs différentes éditions du XVIe siècle à nos jours*, Paris 1978, i, col.154). Saillet writes: 'En fixant la naissance de Fougeret de Monbron à partir de 1704 – date un peu flottante, mais plus exacte, malgré tout, que celle proposée jusqu'ici – nous lui retirons sans trop de regret la paternité du *Canapé couleur de feu*, paru à Amsterdam en 1714, et réimprimé plusieurs fois sous son nom' (in a 'postface' by Maurice Saillet appended to Fougeret de Monbron, *Margot la ravaudeuse*, Paris 1958, p.160). Since Saillet bases his conclusion on an erroneous first date of publication, it may quite safely be discarded.

The only copy of the above edition I could find, very recently acquired and catalogued to boot (assuming it be the same edition), is in the Library of Congress (source: OCLC). Weller seems to indicate a Parisian printing ('Amsterdam (Paris), n. ed. Londres, Sam. Harding (ib.), 1742 et 1745', p.108), but this book was not produced in Paris. Samuel Harding was a well known

London bookdealer of the time (1726(?)-1755; Plomer p.115) and published other French works. There are no press figures apparent in the copy described here, possibly because it has been trimmed by the binder (Parisian) to fit with Chevrier's *Minakalis*. (The latter work bears an imprint for 'A Londres' on the engraved titlepage, but was printed in Paris, 1752, with a 'permission tacite'; see Barbier, iii, col.303a.) However, this Harding *Canapé* was probably produced in England (catchwords on every page, signatures in arabic, woodcut decorations, etc.).

Incipit: 'Un Procureur qui avoit consumé toute sa jeunesse à ruïner de pauvres Plaideurs'.

122

Fougeret de Monbron: *Le Canapé couleur de feu*, 1776

Louis Charles Fougeret de Monbron, sometimes Montbron (1720?-1761): Le / canapé / couleur / de feu, / histoire galante. / Par M. D***. / [symmetrical woodcut decoration] / A Paris, / Rue Saint-Honoré, ou à l'Hôtel Soissons. / [rule] / M. DCC. LXXVI.

8°: 2 ff. (halftitle and titlepage) + [5]-50 pp.

Commentary: I have found no trace of this edition anywhere. There is a half titlepage reading: 'Le / canapé / couleur / de feu, / histoire galante.' Decorations, pagination and signatures all bespeak a genuine, Parisian printing or a provincial one closely following Paris norms. For further information about this work and the first edition, see the preceding entry.

Incipit: 'Un Procureur qui avoit consumé toute sa jeunesse à ruiner de pauvres Plaideurs'.

123

Genlis: *Les Veillées du château*, 1785

Stéphanie Félicité Ducrest de Saint-Aubin, marquise de Sillery, comtesse [Brulart] de Genlis (1746-1830): Les veillées / du château, / ou / cours de morale / a l'usage des enfans, / par l'auteur d'Adele et Théodore [Theodore for iii]. / [rule] / "Come raccende il gusto il mutare esca, / "Così mi par che la mia Istoria quanto / "Or quà, or là più variata sia, / "Meno a chi l'udirà nojosa sia. / Orlando Furioso, Canto terzo decimo. / Traduction Littérale. [Litterale. for ii] / Comme le changement de nourriture ranime le goût, / ainsi il me semble que plus mes récits seront variés, moins / ils paroîtront ennuyeux à ceux qui les entendront. / [rule] / Tome I [II, III]. / [rule] / A Paris, [Paris: for iii] / De l'Imprimerie de Lambert et Baudouin, [Baudoüin, for iii] / rue de la Harpe, près S. Côme. / [short swell rule] / M,DCC,LXXXV.

12°, i: 1 f. (titlepage) + 1 f. (1 p.) + [vii]-xvi, [17]-360 pp.
  ii: 1 f. (halftitle) + 1 f. (titlepage) + [5]-400 pp.

iii: 1 f. (titlepage) + [3]-266, [267]-[270], [271]-[272] pp.

Commentary: Vol. i contains an 'Epitre A Cesar D***, mon Neveu' (p.[v]); a 'Préface' (pp.[vii]-xvi); the first part of the work. Vol. ii continues the work. Vol. iii contains the 'Suite des veillées du château. Contes moraux a l'usage des jeunes personnes' (headtitle, pp.[3]-266); legal material (pp.[267]-[270]); a 'Catalogue Des différens Ouvrages de Madame la Comtesse de Genlis, qui se trouvent à Paris chez Lambert, Imprimeur-Libraire, rue de la Harpe, près Saint Côme' (headtitle, pp.[271]-[272]). Pages [268]-[270], [272] have their numbers enclosed in brackets.

The legal material comprises: 1. a flattering 'approbation' (Paris, 4 May 1784, 'Guidi'); 2. the 'Privilege du roi' to the comtesse de Genlis for her 'Œuvres' following the controversial system established by royal decree 30 August 1777 (Versailles, 14 January 1784, 'Le Begue'); 3. the registration (Paris, '20 Février 1748 [*sic*, for 1784]', 'Valleyre jeune, Adjoint').

The *Contes moraux* in vol. iii, with an untitled one-paragraph introduction (p.[3]), consist of 1. *Les Deux réputations* (p.[4]-130); 2. 'Daphnis et Pandrose, / ou / les Oréades, / conte moral.' (halftitle + p.[133]-134 ['Avertissement'], 135-137 [preliminary material], [138: blank], [139]-162, [163]-172 ['Notes']); 3. 'Le palais / de la vérité / conte moral. / I3 [signature]' (halftitle leaf + the tale, pp.[175]-266).

F.A1 appears to be missing from vol. i (presumably a halftitle). In the present copy, the leaves of the first gathering in vol. ii have been shuffled about. I have given the pagination as it should be. The first gathering of vol. iii is signed 'B' ([B1: titleleaf], B2-B5, [B6-12]).

Whoever put the present copy together (handsomely bound in contemporary English calf) made the serious, albeit interesting mistake of substituting cancels for vol. ii into vol. i (f.I4, I9, K7, K8). The signatures of these leaves are preceded by an asterisk, and each recto also bears the catchtome 'Tome II.' Thus the pertinent pages are missing from vol. i, and vol. ii retains its cancellanda. The cancellantia (new leaves) were printed to add some note numbers which had inadvertently been omitted from the cancellanda (p.200, '(51)'; p.210, '(52)'; p.230, '(53)'; p.231, '(54)').

Although these volumes contain no press figures, it is possible to state unequivocally that they were produced somewhere in Great Britain. Here are my reasons, aside from the fairly insignificant 'evidence' of the binding. The paper is British (English?). Signatures go through the fifth leaf; thus ff.6-12 of each gathering are unsigned. Catchmaterial appears between text and notes. Signatures are in the centre of the page. The first gathering of vol. iii is signed 'B'. Note too that vol. iii has a colon after the supposed place of publication and that 'Baudouin' has an accent. Both would be typical of a British printing. There are no ornaments whatsoever. The rules on the titlepages are thin lines, with the exception of that setting off the date (short swell rule, again typically English, but also typical of French imitations of English practices). The date is given as recorded: with commas instead of periods, and no spaces, a practice that was not imitated in France. As for the asterisked cancels, Chapman remarks that 'this type of signature [starred to indicate cancellantia] is, I believe, very rare in the eighteenth century' (pp.23-24). It was, however, the standard practise in France (and in other countries on the continent), and frequent enough in Great Britain that it would be impossible to claim the compositors of this *Veillées du château* were deliberately imitating a continental (or French) style rather than just following their own norms.

The first edition of this collection appeared in 1784, also for Paris, de l'imprimerie de Lambert et Baudouin, 3 vols in-octavo (MMF 84.26). The edition described here is a British (English?) contrefaçon of the original (or *an* original) Paris edition. MMF list an edition for 1784 and another for 1784-85, but not this one. I could find no other copy of the edition described here, nor any mention of it.

To editions of the *Veillées* listed in MMF, I would add: '[...] IV Vols. 8vo. Bern. [1]784. Haller' (Gesamtverzeichniss, xlv.142a).

Incipits: (*Les Veillées du château*) 'Le Marquis De Clémire, au moment de / partir pour l'armée, recevoit les tristes adieux de sa / femme' (vol. i, text).

(*Les Deux réputations*): 'Luzincour, satisfait d'une modique for- / tune & d'une existence obscure, mais heureuse / & paisible'.

(*Daphnis et Pandrose*): 'La nuit sombre & tranquille régnoit sur l'U- / nivers; le Dieu du jour, dans le sein de Thétis'.

(*Le Palais de la vérité*): 'La charmante Reine Altémire épousa le plus / beau des Génies, l'aimable & tendre Phanor.'

124

Genlis: *Les Veillées du château*, 1795

Stéphanie Félicité Ducrest de Saint-Aubin, marquise de Sillery, comtesse [Bru-lart] de Genlis (1746-1830): Les veillées / du château, / ou / cours de morale / a l'usage des enfans, / par l'auteur d'Adele et Theodore. / "Comme raccende il gusto il mutare esca, / "Cosí mi par che la mia Istoria quanto / "Or quà, or là piú variata sia, / "Meno a chi l'udirà nojosa sia. / Orlando Furioso, Canto terzo decimo. / Traduction Litterale. / Comme le changement de nourriture ranime le goût, / ainsi il me semble que plus mes récits seront variés, moins / ils paroîtront ennuyeux à ceux qui les entendront. / [rule] / Tome I [II, III]. / [rule] / A Dublin: / chez Wogan, 23 old-bridge, et / Jones, 86 dame-street. / [short rule] / M,DCC,XCV.

12°, i: 2 ff. (halftitle and titlepages) + 1f. (1p.) + [vii]-xvi, [17]-358 pp.

ii: 2 ff. (halftitle and titlepages) + [5]-392 pp.

iii: 2 ff. (halftitle and titlepages) + [5], [6]-271 pp.

Commentary: The volume halftitle pages read: 'Les veillées / du château.' (i-ii); 'Les veillées / du château, / ou / cours de morale,' (vol. iii).

These volumes contain the same items as those described in the previous entry, with the same pagination as far as the preliminaries in vol. i are concerned. MMF list an edition in two volumes, presumably the same (but incomplete), with a location for the University of Virginia, Charlottesville. The NUC lists the same. I include this entry to clarify the situation: there were definitely three volumes issued. I do not doubt that my three books were Dublin printed: primitive paper and inking, stark simplicity of presentation, no press figures (but largely following the compositorial practices as described for the previous entry). The binding is contemporary speckled calf, with titlepieces in red and green, a minimum of gilt decoration (probably Irish).

Incipits: (*Les Veillées du château*): 'Le Marquis De Clemire, au moment de / partir pour l'armée, recevoit les tristes adieux de sa / femme' (vol. i, text).

(*Les Deux réputations*, iii.[6]-131): 'Luzincour, satisfait d'une modique fortune / & d'une existence obscure, mais heureuse & pai- / sible'.

('Daphnis et Pandrose, / ou / les Oreades, / conte moral,': halftitle + pp.[135]-177): 'La nuit sombre & tranquille regnoit sur l'- / Univers; le Dieu du jour, dans le sein de Thétis'.

('Le palais / de la vérité, / conte moral.': halftitle + pp.[181]-271): 'La charmante Reine Altémire épousa le plus / beau des Génies, l'aimable & tendre Phanor.'

125

Gessner (Huber transl.): *Daphnis*, 1766

Salomon Gessner (1730-1788), translated by Michael Huber (1727-1804): Daphnis, / poëme / de / M. Gessner, / Traduit de l'Allemand / par M. Huber. / Nouvelle édition, / Revue & corrigée. / [symmetrical composite ornament] / A Amsterdam, / Chez J. H. Schneider, Libraire. / [double rule] / M. DCC. LXVI.

12°: 1 f. (titlepage) + [iij]-v, [vj], [vij]-viij + [1]-148 pp.

Commentary: There is an epigraph on the verso of the titlepage: 'Me juvet in gremio doctæ [...] Propert. Lib. II.' The first item is the 'Avertissement du traducteur'; the second, an unsigned letter (obviously to Gessner); the third, the reply to the latter (obviously by Gessner, although the authenticity of the letters as letters is by no means certain); then *Daphnis*. The first edition of this translation appeared in 1764 (MMF 64.25). The original first appeared in 1754 according to MMF, Max Schneider, *Deutsches Titelbuch* (1927), etc. (Huber, in the 'Avertissement du traducteur', gives 1755.) MMF list what appears to be a very similar edition of this work for 1766 (BN), in-16, vii + 148 pp. (which they seem to indicate includes *Le Premier navigateur*, Gessner-Huber; the above volume does not). I know of no other copy of the above described edition. (I was unable to examine the BN copy.)

In passing, to MMF's list, I would add a 'nouvelle édition, revue & corrigée', Paris: Vincent, 1764 (BN Y2.38805).

Incipit: 'Au milieu du Neætus*, fleuve qui prend sa source dans les monts Clibaniens'. (A note gives further information about the river.)

126

Gessner (Huber transl.): *Idylles et poèmes champêtres*, 1762

Salomon Gessner (1730-1788), translated by Michael Huber (1727-1804): Idylles / et / poëmes champêtres / de M. Gessner, / traduits de l'allemand / Par M. Huber, Traducteur de la / Mort d'Abel. / [symmetrical composite woodcut decoration] / A Lyon, / Chez Jean-Marie Bruyset, / Imprimeur-Libraire. / [double rule] / M. DCC. LXII. / Avec Approbation & Privilege du Roi.

8°: 1 f. (titlepage) + iij-xxxviij, xxxix-xlvj + 1 f. (2 pp.; table) + [1]-110, [111]-154 pp. + 2 ff. (4 pp.)

Commentary: The first item is an 'Avertissement du traducteur'; the second, a 'Préface de l'auteur'; the third, the 'Table'. The first item of the work proper is the *Idylles*, the second is the *Poèmes champêtres* (in prose). At the very end are four pages of legal material: an approbation for the *Idylles* signed 'Saurin' (18 October 1760), a privilege granted to Huber, signed 'Lebegue', for the *Idylles* (17 February 1761), a note in which Huber cedes his privilege to Bruyset of Lyon (3 March 1761), and the registration (9 March 1761 by G. Saugrain). There are a frontispiece by Watelet after Poussin and various vignettes and culs-de-lampe scattered throughout, mostly by Watelet after Poussin (and others). The unsigned engravings are probably by Watelet, too. (The choice of Poussin to illustrate a prose-poem adaptation of Gessner is an interesting one.)

MMF list this work after the BN copy (62.18), and their description matches the copy described here. However, my book consists of a different edition. There are very small differences in the type, some of the composite decorations have been reset, and so on. Here are a couple of the more describable differences. The BN edition, p.xxxix: the page number is the same size as the rest; in my book, the type of this page number is markedly smaller than the other preliminary page numbers. The BN edition, p.xlvi: the decoration has at the centre a sunburst with lines and cut lines around it; my copy has a circular decoration in the centre consisting of eight lines separating eight thicker, wedge-shaped devices. P.117, BN: an ornamental rule of sorts, interrupted in the centre by another decoration. The ornamental rule in my copy presents a single series of decorations (discreetly set off at the beginning and end), with no interruption in the middle. And so it goes... I do not doubt that there exist other copies of the edition represented by the book described here. I hope that my description will enable bibliographers and cataloguers to differentiate between the two. And perhaps there were more.

In passing I note that MMF list an *Œuvres* for 'Zuric, Orell et Gesner et Compagnie, 1768, in-8, ?, 348p. (Lausanne: t.ii seulement)' (60.16). Kayser lists 'œuvres, trad. pr. Mich. Huber. III vols. avec vign. 8. [...] Zürich [1]768-72. Orell' (ii.374b; also in Heinsius, ii., col.111; in Heinsius, *Handbuch*, p.814, and in Heinsius, 1793: iv.537). The Messkatalog has 'Œuvres de Mr. S. *Gesner* [*sic*] trad. de l'Allemand par Mr. Huber. 2 Tomes. av. des vignettes gravées par l'auteur. 8. à Zuric, chez Orell, Gessner & Comp.' (MM 1768, p.1039-40). It would appear that the third volume of this collection was published several years later, in 1772. See no.5 just below.

Here is a list of some editions and/or issues of works by Gessner in French which have escaped the attention of modern bibliographers:

1. *Idylles*, 1762. 'Idylles de Mr. Gesner [*sic*], av. fig. 8. à Zuric et à Leipsic, chez les her[ritiers] de Weidemann et Reich', Messkatalog, OM 1762, p.267. The next entry is for 'les mêmes sans figures, aux mêmes [endroits, chez les mêmes éditeurs]'.

2. *Idylles* and *Daphnis*, 1780. 'traduction libre des nouvelles Idylles et du Daphnis. [in-]12. Berl[in]. Rottmann. [1]780' (Heinsius, ii, col.111). Conceivably in verse.

3. *La Mort d'Abel*, 1761. 'la Mort d'Abel, Poeme en cinq chants, traduit de l'Allemand de Mr. *Gessner* par Mr. *Huber*. 8. Berlin, chez Fred. Nicolai', Messkatalog, MM 1761, p.193; also in Heinsius, 1793 (iv.534).

4. *La Mort d'Abel*, 1794. 'la mort d'Abel trad. p[ar] Huber av[ec] fig[ures]. [in-]12. Paris, Sommer, Lips.) [for 'Paris (Sommer in Leipzig)'?] [1]794' (Heinsius, *loc. cit.*).

5. *Œuvres*, 1768-1772. 'le même sans vign[ettes]. III Vol. [in-]16. ibid.' (in reference to the 1768-72 edition mentioned above; Heinsius, *loc. cit.*).

6. *Œuvres choisies*, 1774. 'œuvres choisies. [in-]12. Paris u[nd] Leipz. [1]774' (Kayser, ii.374b). However, this is conceivably a translation in verse, there existing a Paris (only) edition dating to the same year: *Œuvres choisies de M. Gessner, contenant la Mort d'Abel, la Nuit, & autres poèmes; avec des Idylles, des Pastorales, & autres pièces mises en vers françois par différents auteurs, et les meilleurs poètes en ce genre* (etc; containing much not by Gessner, observations on German literature, and so on, according to the titlepage), Paris: chez les libraires associés, 1774, lxxxiv + 342 pp., 17 cm [in-12?] (OCLC: State University of New York, Stony Brook).

7. *Œuvres*, 1791. 'œuvres III Vol. av[ec] fig[ures]. [in-]16. Bern, Haller. [1]791' (Heinsius *loc. cit.*; Kayser *loc. cit.*; Heinsius, *Handbuch*, p.814; Heinsius 1793, iv.537).

8. *Œuvres*, 1792. 'œuvres. III Vol. [in-]16. Zürich, Orell. [1]792' (Heinsius *loc. cit.*; Heinsius, *Handbuch*, p.814; Heinsius 1793, iv.537). MMF list an edition for 'Züric, Orell, Gessner, Füssli et Compagnie, 1793, 3t. [...] (Neuchâtel)' (60.16). There is also a 'Zuric 1792', 3 vol. edition in NUC (Library Company of Philadelphia).

9. *Œuvres*, 1793. 'le même trad. p[ar] Huber. III Vol. [in-]16. Zürich, Tourneisen, Cassel.) [for 'Zürich (Tourneisen in Cassel)'?] [1]793' (Heinsius, *loc. cit.*). MMF list what might be the same: 'Züric, Orell, Gessner, Füssli et Compagnie, 1793, 3t., 315, 303, 319p. (Neuchâtel)', 60.16.

10. *Œuvres*, 1797. 'œuvres compl. av[ec] fig[ures]. III Vol. [in-]18. Strasb[ourg]. König. [1]797' (Heinsius, *loc. cit.*, and Kayser: ii.374b).

There is a three-volume, in-12 edition (according to MMF; I was unable to see the BL copy) for Paris: Bossange, Masson et Besson, an V-1797 (MMF 60.16). MMF remark that, 'selon Brissart [*Manuel du Cazinophile*, 1879], cette édition a paru aussi in-18'. It is so listed in the Messkatalog: 'Œuvres complettes de S. Gesner [*sic*]. Magnifique edit. de l'imprimerie de Crapelet, ornée de grav. 3 Vol. 18. Strasbourg, König' (OM 1797, p.235), There was also, apparently, an in-24 issue according to Gason, who is generally very accurate (Librairie

Pierre-M. Gason, cat. 'Livres anciens et modernes', no. 115, no. 150, p.15-16). For a complete description, with pagination (and a list of sources in addition to those mentioned by MMF), see Gason. There are additional translations and editions listed in Gesamtverzeichniss (xlvi.607-09), but not knowing whether some of these are in verse or in prose, I simply refer the reader to them.

Incipits: (*Idylles*, 'A Daphné') 'Ce ne sont ni les Héros farouches & teints de sang, ni les champs de bataille couverts de morts'.

(*Poèmes champêtres*, 'La Ferme résolution') 'Où s'égarent mes pieds déchirés à travers ces épines & ces broussailles entrelacées?'

127

Gessner (Huber transl.): *La Mort d'Abel*, 1792

Salomon Gessner (1730-1788), translated by Michael Huber (1727-1804): La mort / d'Abel, / poëme, / traduit de Gessner. / [woodcut decoration: bouquet of three roses] / A Paris. / [double rule] / M. DCC. XCII.

18°: 2 pl + [1]-175 pp.

Commentary: I could find no trace of this edition anywhere. I have two identical copies. This work first appeared in 1760, in the French (MMF 60.16) and was, like all works by Gessner in French and other languages, very successful.

At the end of the volume there is a colophon for: '[rule] / A Paris. De l'Imprimerie de C. Glisau / & J. Pierret, rue du Murier, N°. 8.' There is a volume halftitle for 'La mort / d'Abel, poëme'.

For two more, hitherto unrecorded editions of *La Mort d'Abel*, see the commetary on the preceding entry.

Incipit: 'Je voudrois chanter en vers sublimes les aventures de nos premiers parens, après leur triste chûte'.

128

Gilbert: *Œuvres complètes*, 1798

Nicolas Joseph Laurent Gilbert (1751-1780), edited by Nicolas Le Moyne Desessarts (1744-1810): Œuvres / complètes / de / Gilbert, / nouvelle édition, / Où se trouvent insérés plusieurs Morceaux du même / Auteur, qui n'avoient pas encore été publiés; / suivies / de Remarques Critiques et Littéraires. / [rule] / Nascitur Poeta. / [rule] / [rule] / A Paris, / Chez les principaux Libraires. / [double rule] / An VI. (1798.)

4°: 1 pl (halftitle or titlepage) + 1 f. (halftitle or titlepage) + [iij]-viij, [ix]-xij + [1]-176, [177]-192 + [195]-212, [213]-214 pp.

Commentary: The pagination reflects:
  1. 'Notice sur la vie de Gilbert';
  2. 'Préface';
  3. assorted poems;

4. *Le Carnaval des auteurs, ou les masques reconnus et punis*, (pp.[177]-192);

5. halftitle: 'Remarques / critiques et littéraires / sur les œuvres / de Gilbert.', pp.[193-94], and the remarks;

6. a table.

There is a halftitle for the volume: 'Œuvres / completes / de / Gilbert.' The frontispiece portrait of Gilbert by J. Beniry or possibly Benizy (signed) is captioned with the poet's name and initials in the picture, and inludes the following lines: 'Rousseau fut son modèle, et Desprèaux son Maître; / Le talent lui dicta des vers purs et nerveux, / Et moissonné plus tard, il auroit su, peut-être, / De l'aveu d'Apollon, se placer auprès deux [*sic*].' The first two leaves of the 'Notice' are signed 'aij'. No chainlines or water marks. Assuming the preliminary gathering to have six leaves (vs. seven), the halftitle or titlepage (probably the former) is a preliminary leaf. This is reflected in the pagination recorded.

The *Carnaval des auteurs* first appeared in 1773 (MMF 73.21). The edition described here is not listed in MMF, however. Nor is it listed by Barbier, Quérard (etc.) and there is no copy recorded for the BN, BL or in the NUC. Indeed, the first edition of Gilbert's *Œuvres* recorded by MMF is for Paris: Gay, an IX-1801, in-8°, xii, 214 pp. Although there is an edition of the *Œuvres* in the BN for 1788 (Paris, Le Jay, [v]-[xvj] + [i]-iv, [5]-232 pp. in-8°; Ye.10002), it does not contain the *Carnaval des auteurs*, so the authors were quite right not to list it. However, the edition described here is mentioned by Cioranescu (ii.864, no. 31086). It is also cited by Escoffier who lists a copy bearing titlepages for 1798 and 1801: 'Œuvres complètes; nouvelle édition, où parmi plusieurs pièces de cet auteur, se trouve le Carnaval des Auteurs; suivies de remarques critiques et littéraires. *A Paris, chez les principaux libraires, an VI* (1798); in-4 [binding description]. –Exemplaire en grand papier de format in-4 contenant un second faux-titre et un second titre à l'adresse du libraire Gay, an IX-1801' (no.87, p.25). See below for further information.

So, who was the editor and author of the critical notes, introduction, and so forth? Although this book is not listed in most modern bibliographies, it can be found in a few contemporary sources. Ersch reports that we owe this edition to the efforts of Nicolas Le Moyne Desessarts. But Ersch lists an octavo edition (*Supplément à la France littéraire de 1771-1796, contenant les additions et corrections, les nouveaux articles jusqu'en 1800* Hambourg 1802, titlepage in German too, pp.149 and 216). In the *Journal général de la littérature de France* we find: 'Œuvres completes de Gilbert*, avec son portrait, contenant ses poésies diverses, & ses ouvrages en prose; II.^{de} édition, volume in-8, 50 fols, pap. vélin 5 liv.' (germinal an VI - avril [March/April] 1798, p.117). In Thermidor an VI [July/August 1798], yet *another* edition is listed: 'Œuvres complétes de Gilbert*, contenant ses satyres du XVIII siècle; Didon à Enée, héroïde, ses autres poësies & ouvrages en prose; quatrième édition, 1 vol. in-12. 1 fr. 75c. Morin' (p.244). Then follows a paragraph praising Gilbert's works.

What seems to be the case is that the 'second' edition was issued in duodecimo, in octavo and in quarto. Furthermore, the 1801 edition is a reissue of the 1798, octavo one, with a cancel titlepage substituted by Gay (BN: Ye.10003). I was able to juxtapose my copy with the BN 1801 edition. Barring differences of chainlines and so forth indicating the different formats, and barring a few accidents which are normal for hand-press books, they are alike. (It is of course possible that the two issues could have been pulled at quite different times.) Quérard mentions that there were three issues of the 1801 edition (in any format an item of considerable rarity today): in-8°, in-12° and in-4° ('papier vélin'). My copy consists of a mixture of different kinds of paper. All this doubtless means that there were at least three formats issued in 1798, possibly consisting of two different editions or, more likely, of two issues for one bookdealer (octavo and quarto) and one issue (possibly with a cancel titlepage) in duodecimo for another.

Why would it be claimed in my copy that this is an edition 'où se trouvent insérés plusieurs morceaux du même auteur qui n'avaient pas encore été publiés'? And why would the 1801 edition bear 'nouvelle édition, où parmi plusieurs pièces inédites de cet auteur, se trouve le Carnaval des auteurs'? First one must bear in mind that the 1788 edition of the *Œuvres* did not contain the latter piece. Second, the *Carnaval des auteurs* first appeared in the form of a flimsy pamphlet, in 1773. The copies in the BN are in contemporary wrappers and were probably not acquired by the king's librarian at the time they appeared. Thus the first edition could easily have been unknown to Desessarts.

Finally I might mention that p.13, 'que' has been struck in ink both in my copy and in the BN, 1801 edition. It is possible that these two copies are from a hand-corrected edition, a rather rare phenomenon made even more so since the two copies represent different issues. (This occurs in a line from 'Le Dix-huitième siècle': 'Sans doute [que] c'est ainsi que *Turenne* et *Villars*'.) Chapman notes that this sort of thing was most unusual, remarking that in the 'Duchess of Newcastle's Life of her Duke, 1667, a line on page 9 has been heavily deleted' (p.2).

Incipit: (*Le Carnaval des auteurs*) 'Depuis quinze jours mon corps se refusait au sommeil: vainement j'avais lu le poëme des Saisons'.

129

Godard d'Aucour: *Mémoires turcs*, 1787

Claude Godard (sometimes Godart) d'Aucour (1716-1795): Mémoires / turcs, / Par un Auteur Turc, de toutes les / Académies Mahométanes, Li- / cencié en Droit Turc, & Maître / ès Arts de l'Université de Cons- / tantinople. / Nouvelle Edition, revue & corrigée. / [rule] / Premiere [Seconde] partie. / [rule] / [composite, symmetrical woodcut ornament, same for both volumes] / A Amsterdam, / Par la Société. / [segmented double rule] / M. DCC. LXXXVII.

12°, i: 2 ff. (halftitle and titlepages) + [v]-xxij + [1]-146 pp.
    ii: 2 pl (halftitle and titlepages) + [1]-198 pp.

Commentary: The volume halftitles read: 'Mémoires / turcs. / [rule] / Premiere [Seconde] partie. / [rule]'. The preliminary pages in vol. i comprise an 'Épitre a mademoiselle D* T**'. Quérard, *Supercheries*, remarks concerning the 1776 edition that this 'épître dédicatoire ajoutée à cette édition est adressée à mademoiselle Duthé, courtisane célèbre, alors existante. L'auteur, sous le voile d'une ironie piquante et bien soutenue, y fait la critique du luxe impertinent des Laïs de la capitale. Ce persiflage contribua à la vogue de ce petit roman' (i, col.411d). This information is largely repeated in Barbier (iii, col.261f), Quérard (iii.388) and in Gay (iii, col.190). Gay gives some further information and curiously seems to indicate that quite a few editions of the *Mémoires turcs* appeared under the title of *Voyage galant dans les cours de l'Europe et particulièrement dans celle de France*. However, there is no such title listed in Gay (or MMF), and it is not listed in Barbier.

The Paris: à la librairie ancienne et nouvelle, 1822 edition has an interesting introduction. After explaining that the 1787 edition was chosen since it was 'publiée sous les yeux de l'auteur', the editor gives some tidbits of information concerning Mlle Duthé, which could well be the Gay's, Quérard's (and so on) source. For example, we learn that for her most important customers, 'elle se couchait dans des draps de satin noir, qui faisaient ressortir encore sa blancheur naturelle' (etc., p.iv).

MMF (58.R24), who list after Jones (1743, p.81), do not include the edition described here. I could not find a copy in a public library. I have two copies, one with manuscript notes. (These are largely humourous, comprising sarcastic editorial comments.)

I do not know what the legal status of this work was when it first appeared, but do know that a 'permission tacite' was granted to Prault in December of 1766 to sell copies of it, and other works like *Le Sultan Misapouf*, *Tant mieux pour elle*, *Les Trois voluptés*, etc. Charles Georges Coqueley de Chaussepierre was the censor ('Registre des livres d'impression étrangère présentés à monseigneur de Maupeou, vice-chancelier et garde des sceaux de France, pour la permission de débiter', BN ms F.F.21993, no.34, p.8).

Incipit: 'Puisque je me trouve dans un pays / si fertile en auteurs, on me permettra / bien de l'être aussi.'

130

Goethe (Deyverdun transl.): *Werther*, 1786

Johann Wolfgang von Goethe (1749-1832), translated by Georges Deyverdun (1734?-1789): Werther, / traduit de l'allemand. / [rule] / Premiere [Seconde] partie. / [rule] / [woodcut decorations: medallion in ornamental decoration for i; overgrown ruins with figure for ii] / A Maestricht, / Chez Jean-Edme Dufour & Phil. / Roux, Imprimeurs-Libraires, associés. / [double rule] / M. DCC. LXXXVI.

12°, i: 1 pl + j-v, (p.[vj] is blank), vij-viij + [1]-(201) pp.
  ii: 1 pl + [1]-(201), (p.[202] is blank), (203)-(230) pp.

Commentary: The preliminary pages in vol. i comprise a 'Préface du traducteur' and Goethe's 'Préface de l'auteur'. The last item in vol. ii is some interesting 'Observations du traducteur sur *Werther*, & sur les écrits publiés à l'occasion de cet ouvrage'. MMF list a similar edition or issue in octavo, with locations for the Goethemuseum, Frankfurt and the Bibliothèque municipale of Bordeaux (according to the 1837 printed catalogue). The former copy was examined by the authors (MMF 76.27). This would indicate at least two issues for 1786, if it be a question of the same edition. They also cite Baldensperger's *Bibliographie critique de Goethe en France* (1907) and the *Année littéraire* for 1786, ii.116. Baldensperger also mentions the latter source, which is erroneous. 1786, ii.116 is the middle of a short article devoted to Mme de Montolieu's *Caroline de Lichtfield* (see the two entries for Montolieu, *Caroline*... below) and has nothing to do with this edition of *Werther*. The only connection with Goethe is that *Caroline de Lichtfield* was published by 'le traducteur de *Werther*'. I have examined all volumes of the *Année littéraire* and the *Mercure de France* for 1786 and could find no trace of a 1786 edition of *Werther* in them. (The volumes described here are not listed in the NUC, the BLC or the BNC.) *Die Leiden des jungen Werthers* first appeared in 1774 and, in this particular French version, in 1776 (MMF 76.27).

Incipit: 'Que je suis content d'être parti! Qu'est-ce que le cœur de l'homme?'

131

Graffigny, anonymous, and Lamache-Courmont: *Lettres d'une Péruvienne*; a 'suite'; *Lettres d'Aza*, 1751

Françoise [Paule] d'Issembourg d'Happoncourt de Graffigny (sometimes Grafigny or Huguet de Graf[f]igny; 1695-1758), an anonymous author, and Ignace Hugary de Lamache-Courmont (often spelled 'Lamarche-Courmont'):

  i: Lettres / d'une / Péruvienne. / [symmetrical woodcut ornament] / A Amsterdam, / Aux de'pens du De'laisse'. / [treble rule] / M. DCC. LI.

  ii: Lettres / d'Aza / ou / d'un Péruvien. / [symmetrical woodcut ornament, different from that in i] / A Amsterdam, / Aux de'pens du De'laisse'. / [treble rule] / M. DCC. LI.

  in-12, i: 1 pl (halftitle) + 1 f. (titlepage) + [iij]-x + [1]-240 pp.

  ii: 2 pl (halftitle and titlepages) + 2 ff. (4 pp.) + [1]-124 pp.

Commentary: The first volume contains: halftitle page ('Lettres / d'une / Péruvienne, / Augmentées de celles du Chevalier / De'terville. / Premiere partie.'); the titlepage; an 'Avertissement'; the novel in thirty-eight numbered letters, plus Déterville's reply (pp.[1]-206, 207-210; the last letter forms the first of the next sequence); the sequel (seven letters between Déterville, Céline and Zilia the first of which is Déterville's unnumbered reply to Zilia, p.207-240).

The second volume contains a halftitle ('Lettres / d'Aza / ou / d'un Péruvien. / Seconde partie.'); the titlepage; 2 ff. (4 pp.) of an 'Avertissement'; the *Lettres d'Aza* in thirty-five numbered letters.

These books were probably printed in Holland (Amsterdam?): signatures in arabic (8s plus 4s), catchwords on every page (although catchwords at the end of each signature sequence would be somewhat more usual for 1751), ornaments, paper, etc.

I could find no trace of the edition described here in the usual bibliographies, much less another copy. For further information concerning this work, and editions of it, see the next entry.

Incipits: (*Lettres d'une Péruvienne*) 'Aza! mon cher Aza! les / cris de ta tendre Zilia, tels / qu'une vapeur du matin'.

(The first letter of the seven-letter 'suite', 'Réponse de De'terville à Zilia, & à la trente-huitiéme & derniére Lettre imprimée'): 'Ah, Zilia! à quel prix m'est-il / permis de vous revoir?'

(*Lettres d'Aza*): 'Que tes larmes se dissipent / comme la rosée à la vûë du / Soleil'.

132

Graffigny, anonymous, and Lamache-Courmont: *Lettres d'une Péruvienne*; a 'suite'; *Lettres d'Aza*, 1760

Françoise [Paule] d'Issembourg d'Happoncourt de Graffigny (sometimes Grafigny or Huguet de Graf[f]igny; 1695-1758), an anonymous author, and Ignace Hugary de Lamache-Courmont (often spelled 'Lamarche-Courmont'):

i: Lettres / d'une / Péruvienne. / Premiere partie. / [woodcut ornament: two medallion portraits facing each other in center, ornamental border surmounted by three roses] / A Amsterdam, / Aux dépens du Delaissé. / [double rule] / M. DCC. LX.

ii: Lettres / d'Aza, / ou / d'un Péruvien. / Seconde partie. / [woodcut ornament: flaming urn centred in an extensive ornamental border, a rose at top, bottom, left and right] / A Amsterdam, / Aux dépens du Delaissé. / [double rule] / M. DCC. LX.

i: 2 ff. (halftitle and titlepage) + [v]-xij + [1]-240 pp.
ii: 2 ff. (halftitle and titlepage) + [v]-viij + [1]-124 pp.

Commentary: The preliminary pages to vol. i are an 'Avertissement'; those to vol. ii, also an 'Avertissement'. The halftitles read: 'Lettres / d'une / Péruvienne. / Augmentées de celles du Chevalier / Déterville. / [rule] / Premiere partie.'; and: 'Lettres / d'Aza, / ou / d'un Péruvien. / [rule] / Seconde partie.' There is a large thick 'Z' stamped on the titlepage of the first volume; I don't know what, if anything, it signifies. But see below in this commentary. (Catchtomes for 'I. [II.] Partie.', respectively.)

The last letter of the original novel by Mme de Graffingy is numbered 38. (This is the first version.) Then follow seven separately numbered letters of correspondence between Déterville, Zilia and Céline (p.207-240). This is an anonymous 'suite' which first appeared in 1747 according to Nicoletti (no. 3), if we accept the particular edition he describes as dating to that year. (Nicoletti adds a question mark to the date; it conceivably appeared some time later.) It might be remarked that one of the 'A Peine' editions listed by Nicoletti for [1747?], viii + 248 pp., is followed by a second volume for the 'Suite des lettres d'une Peruvienne'. Vol. i ends with 'Fin de la Première Partie', 'e reca in basso la parola "suite"' (Nicoletti, no. 3). It is further added: 'cioè il romanzo sarebbe stato ristampato apposta per allegarvi la "suite"'. Vol. ii, with the same woodcut ornament on the titlepage (both titlepages are reproduced in Nicoletti, p.80), is in vi, 7-44 pp. (Giraud lists what is surely this edition for [1747?]; 1747.d). The NUC (NH0588814) lists yet another edition of the *Suite des Lettres d'une Péruvienne*, 'A Peine [Paris? 1747]. vi, [7]-60p. 15 cm. [...] Bound with (as issued?) Lettres d'une peruvienne' (location: University of Pennsylvania). Could this be a sequel to yet another edition of Mme de Graffigny's novel dating to around 1747 or later?

The *Lettres d'Aza*, containing thirty-five numbered letters, are by Hugary de Lamache-Courmont and first appeared in 1749 (Jones). They were often republished with the original novel.

Mme de Graffigny's work first appeared in 1747 (Jones, Nicoletti), and went through a considerable number of editions indeed: in the French, in translation (especially the English), in the French together with the Italian translation, and in the French with the English. (See the two 'Graffigny-Deodati' items below).

There are two versions of the novel: the first, in thirty-eight letters; the second, augmented and somewhat modified, in forty-one. (See Nicoletti).

MMF (52.R24) list one edition for 1760, after Nicoletti. However, there were two editions for 1760, both for Amsterdam, Aux dépens du delaissé. The NUC lists the other for 'viij, 183 p. 15 1/2 cm.' A note remarks: 'Accompanied by a sequel, Lettres d'Aza, by Hugary de Lamache-Courmont (Amsterdam, 1760). The two works are designated "première" and "seconde & dernière partie" respectively, but have no collective title'. (Locations: Library of Congress and Princeton.) Under Hugary de Lamache-Courmont, the NUC lists what is surely the second volume of this edition (containing the *Lettres d'un Péruvien*) for 1 pl, iij, 86 pp. (Library of Congress and Princeton Theological Seminary). This is obviously an edition entirely different from the one described here.

Barbier remarks: 'Souvent réimprimées avec le nom de l'auteur. L'abbé G.-L. Calabre Pérau assurait avoir eu une grande part dans la composition et dans la rédaction de ces "Lettres". Cet ouvrage a été mis à l'*index* le 28 juillet 1765' (ii, col.1246c).

I list my copy of this edition to note that there were two for 1760 and to remark that my copy represents an edition variant. The titlepage reproduced in Nicoletti (p.106) shows the titlepage vignette in vol. i upside-down. In my copy, the error has been corrected (three roses at the top, medalion portraits right-side up, etc.) The other pages reproduced in Nicoletti seem to match my copy of these two volumes. A point of speculation: perhaps the heavy 'Z' stamped on the titlepage has something to do with this correction?

No location is given in Nicoletti. The only trace of the two volumes described here that I have been able to find, assuming we are dealing with the same edition (which we probably are) is in Sabin, with a location for the Library Company of Philadelphia (Joseph Sabin, *A dictionary of books relating to America from its discovery to the present times*, rprt. Amsterdam 1961-62, vii.372, no. 28192).

I would like to add the following comments and editions to Nicoletti's bibliography and to MMF's list:

1. *1747*. Nicoletti, and MMF after Nicoletti, list three editions for this date. However, there were four: A Peine, no date, vi + 278 pp.; vi, 304 pp.; and two for viii + 337 pp. (See too 1749 below.)

Concerning the two editions with identical pagination: the NUC entry reads: 'Lettres d'une Peruvienne. A Peine [i.e. Paris? 1747?] p.l., viii, 337p. 15cm. (12°.) Brunet, II, 1690. Title vignette of ten type-ornaments. Signatures: [*]¹, a⁴, A-Y⁸⁻⁴, Z⁸, Aa⁴, Bb-Ee⁸⁻⁴, Ff¹. Imperfect: pp.31-34 wanting. The Bridgewater library copy. – Another edition. Title vignette of eleven "sun-burst" type ornaments. Signatures: [*], a⁴, B-P¹², [**]¹. The paper has vertical screen-marks. The Bridgewater library copy'. (Brunet does nothing more than state that the first edition 'a paru en 1747, sous cette indication: *A Peine*, sans date'.) Indeed, perhaps there were more than four editions for 'Peine, [1747]', for neither of the titlepages reproduced by Nicoletti has anything to do with the description furnished by the NUC entry. (However, the second titlepage reproduced by Nicoletti might date later than 1747; see below.)

2. *1748*. Nicoletti lists two editions. MMF indicate three: two as per Nicoletti, another in the Arsenal (which I have not been able to examine).

Krauss-Fontius list a two-volume edition for Peine, 1748, VIII, 337 pp., the second volume of which comprises the *Lettres d'Aza*, with no indication of a different date for that volume (no. 4274; location: Sächsische Landesbibliothek Dresden). This would open the possibility of four editions for 1748. It might be noted that the Grimm/Diderot/Meister *et al. Correspondance littéraire* reviews the *Lettres d'Aza* in a section just preceding an analysis of Crébillon's *Catilina*, 10 December 1748. In a note Tourneux adds: 'Par Hugary de Lamarche-Courmont. Amsterdam, 1748' (1877, i.251-52). The *Lettres d'Aza* probably appeared late in 1748, even if the first edition might have borne 1749 on the titlepage. The question of an edition explicitly dated 1748 remains open. Moreover, the NUC lists a '2. ed. Lausanne, Chez Marc.-Mic. Bousquet, 1748. 2 v. in 1' (location: Berkeley; not in Nicoletti). If neither that edition nor the one listed in Krauss-Fontius matches the one in the Arsenal, this would open the possibility of there having been five editions for 1748.

3. *1755*. Nicoletti lists a 'nouvelle édition, augmentée [etc.]', for Paris, Duchesne (no. 11). MMF also list only one edition, after Nicoletti. The NUC has yet another edition for that date: 'Lettres d'une Péruvienne [augmentées de celles du chevalier De'terville] Amsterdam, Aux de'pens du De'laisse', 1755. x, 240p. 17 cm. Accompanied by a sequel, Lettres d'Aza, by Hugary de Lamache-Courmont (Amsterdam, 1755). The two works are designated "première" and "seconde & dernière partie" respectively, but have no collective title' (location: Duke University). The second volume is listed, under Hugary de Lamache-Courmont, for 124 pp. Krauss-Fontius list an 'Amsterdam: Delaisse [*sic*] 1755' edition, no pagination recorded (no. 4275; location: Universitäts- u. Landesbibliothek Sachsen-Anhalt, Halle).

4. *1758*. MMF list an edition after the copy in the Arsenal (brought to their attention by English Showalter). Giraud lists a 1758 edition for Amsterdam, aux dépens du délaissé (1749.5.d). Perhaps it is the same? I was unable to see the Arsenal copy.

5. *1764*. MMF list an edition for 1764 (pointed out to the authors by English Showalter) with locations for the Arsenal and the University of Pennsylvania. (No details are given.) I was unable to see those copies, but Krauss-Fontius list an edition, implying that the second volume is [or contains] the *Lettres d'Aza*,

as: '–I.II. Amsterdam: Delaissé 1764' (no. 4276; location: Sächsische Landesbibliothek Dresden).

6. *1787*. MMF list one edition for that date. Nicoletti lists two: Lyon, Bruyset frères, and another, with Deodati's translation, for the same place and publishers.

7. *1790*. 'nouv. éd. A Bruxelles, Olivier Le May et Co., M. DCC. XC. 1pl., xvi, 246p. 17 1/2 cm'. With the *Lettres d'Aza*. Not in Nicoletti or MMF (NUC: University of Massachusetts at Amherst).

8. *1797*. Among editions dated 1797, Nicoletti lists one bearing the mention of various engravings on the titlepage. That is listed for the only copy known to him in the Bibliothèque municipale de Nancy, having apparently 487 pp. Nicoletti reproduces the titlepage of the Paris: Durand, 1802 edition, which contains four plates. I have a copy of the rare, octavo 1797 Migneret edition, which is in French and in Italian (Deodati's), a copy which includes an unpaginated page of errata (for the French and the Italian, p.[488]) at the end. Furthermore, the illustrations are those reproduced by Nicoletti for the 1802 edition, meaning that they were reissued with the later edition. My copy of the Migneret edition, beyond the six plates called for on the titlepage (after Le Barbier), also has a fine portrait-frontispiece of the author (also mentioned on the titlepage), engraved by Gaucher after the picture in the possession of Mme Helvétius. For more information concerning the engravings, see Cohen and Reynaud. (In passing, MMF list only one edition for 1797.)

9. *1798*. MMF list a 1798 edition, after the Library of Congress and Quérard. The BLC, five-year supplement (1966-1970) lists a French and Italian edition, 'Edizione novissima, corretta, e ricorretta dal Dott. Antonio Montucci. [...] Da' Torchi del Baylis; trovasi appresso Boosey, etc.: Londra, 1798', 371 pp. in-12° (two copies, the second imperfect: 1507/1667 and 1507/1108). There is no such edition listed in the NUC. There is one for 'Léttere d'una peruviana [...] Nuova ed. ... Parigi, Duchesne, anno VII [1798?] 242 p. 17 1/2 cm' with a location for the Library of Congress. ('Anno VII' would more likely coincide with 1799, in any case.) If this refers to MMF's entry, there were two editions for 1798 (if the French is included with the Duchesne, an VII edition and if it dates to 1798), or one for 1798 and another for 1799.

Furthermore, Heinsius lists the Leipzig (actually Paris and Leipzig appear on the titlepages; Nicoletti no. 19), 1765 edition and a couple of others, with no date, but which are not cited in Nicoletti (with those publishers):

'Lettres d'un Pérouvien [*sic*] et d'une Pérouvienne, publ. par Mad. de Grafigny. II Vol. 12mo. Leipz. Joachim' (Romane, col.126).

'– – le mêmes. II Vol. Leipz. Sommer' (*loc. cit.*).

Such entries must, of course, be treated with caution.

And here are a couple of editions of the *Lettres d'Aza* not recorded by Nicoletti (or MMF):

1. *1749*. Amsterdam, 1749. 250 pp. NUC, location: Indiana University.

2. *1749*. Londres: R. Wilson, [1749]. 156 pp. P.[135]-156 comprise a catalogue of new books for sale by Robert Wilson. NUC, location: Newberry.

For additional information, see the other Graffigny entries in this bibliography.

Incipits: (*Lettres d'une Péruvienne*) 'Aza! mon cher Aza! les / cris de ta tendre Zilia, tels / qu'une vapeur du matin'.

(The first letter of the seven-letter 'suite', 'Réponse de Déterville à Zilia, & à la trente-huitieme & derniere Lettre imprimée'): 'Ah, Zilia! à quel prix m'est-il / permis de vous revoir?'

(*Lettres d'Aza*): 'Que tes larmes se dissipent / comme la rosée à la vue du / Soleil'.

133

Graffigny and Lamache-Courmont, with the participation of Bret: *Lettres d'une Péruvienne*; *Lettres d'Aza*, 1761

Françoise [Paule] d'Issembourg d'Happoncourt de Graffigny (sometimes Grafigny or Huguet de Graf[f]igny; 1695-1758) and Ignace Hugary de Lamache-Courmont (often spelled 'Lamarche-Courmont'), with the participation of Antoine Bret (1717-1792): (engraved titlepages) Lettres / d'Une [dUne for ii?] / Peruvienne. [no period for ii] / Nouvelle Edition [Edition. for ii] / Augmentée de plusieurs Lettres, [no comma for ii] / et [Et for ii] d'une Introduction à l'Histoire. [no period for ii] / Premiere [Seconde] Partie / A Paris. [AParis for ii] / Chez Duchesne Libraire ruë [rue for ii] S^t. [no period for ii?] / Jacques au dessus des Mathurins, / au Temple du Gout. [no period for ii] / Avec Approbation et Privilege du Roy. / M.DCC.LXI.

12°, i: 2 ff. (frontispiece and engraved titlepage) + 1 f. (halftitle) + [ij verso halftitle, iij]-ix, [x-xij] + [3]-10, [11]-36, [37]-328. [329]-336 pp.

    ii: 2 ff (frontispiece and engraved titlepage) + 1 f. (halftitle) + [3]-152, [153]-156 + halftitle + [159]-364, [365]-372 pp.

Commentary: The pagination reflects, i: 'Vers a madame de Grafigny sur Cénie' (p.[ij], verso of the halftitle]; a 'Vie de madame de Grafigny, de l'académie de Florence, tirée de quelques ouvrages périodiques' (p.[iij]-ix); an approbation for the *Lettres d'une Péruvienne* and *Cénie*, a 'nouvelle Edition, corrigée & augmentée de plusieurs Lettres', 8 May 1751 signed 'Saurin' (bottom of p.ix); an 'Extrait du privilege du roi' to Mme de Graffigny for the same works, ten years, 20 December 1751, signed 'Sainson'; registration information (24 December 1751, 'Coignard'); an 'Extrait de la Cession de Madame de Grafigny' (of the privilege to Duchesne, which curiously antedates the privilege itself; this document is dated 23 June 1751). The last three documents occupy p.[x-xij]. Then follow Mme de Graffigny's 'Avertissement' (pp.[3]-10); the 'Introduction historique...' (pp.[11]-36) which is by Antoine Bret in all likelihood (see Nicoletti), and the first part of the novel through letter 27 (pp.[37]-328), with a table at the end (pp.[329]-336). Vol. ii contains: a halftitle; the second part of the novel through letter 41 (pp.[3]-152); a table (p.[153]-156); a halftitle for the 'Lettres / d'Aza, / ou / d'un Péruvien; / Pour servir de suite à celles d'une / Péruvienne.'; an 'Avertissement' (pp.[159]-162); the letters, 35 in all (pp.[163]-364), with an 'Avis' at the end; a table (pp.[365]-372), with an approbation at the end for the *Lettres d'Aza*, 14 September 1759 [*sic*], signed 'Crébillon, fils'.

Some peculiarities concerning these books: the preliminary leaves in vol. i (exclusive of the engravings, which are 'hors texte') comprise six leaves ([a], aij, aiij-[avj]). Then the 'Avertissement' begins with f.Aij. F.Ai is not here present and conceivably comprised an original titlepage, here cancelled. Thus we are conceivably dealing with some kind of a reissue. Indeed, the date on the engraved titlepages reads 1761 because there seems to have been a modification of the plates to read 'XI.' at the end of the roman number. Although signed in 12s (barring prelims), the original novel and its table in vol. ii end with G, Gij, Giij-[Gvj]; then follow gatherings H12, I12, etc. The catchtomes throughout are for 'Tome I. [II.]'. The last gathering of vol. ii is complete (Q[j]-[Qxij]), but there is a catchword 'PRIVILEGE' which leads nowhere. Note that the legal documents are bound in their correct place, after the 'Vie...' in vol. i. A catchword – 'Avertissement.' – leads from the bottom of p.[xij] to the piece in question. (And the documents begin on a verso).

The halftitle to volume i reads: 'Lettres / d'une / Peruvienne. / Nouvelle edition; / Augmentée de la Vie de Madame de / Grafigny, de plusieurs Lettres, & / d'une Introduction Historique aux / Lettres d'une Péruvienne. / Tome premier.' That to vol. ii bears: 'Lettres / d'une / Peruvienne. / Nouvelle edition; / Revûe, corrigée, & augmentée des / Lettres d'Aza. / Tome second.'

The first frontispiece is signed 'C. Eisen inv.'-'De lafosse Sculp'. The frontispiece to ii bears similar signatures. Neither titlepage is signed. The headpiece at the beginning of the first letter, vol. i, is a woodcut by (or after) Caron (signed). That to vol. ii is an engraving by Delafosse after Eisen (signatures barely legible). Cohen reports that the original illustrated edition appeared in 1752 (Paris, Duchesne) with two frontispieces, two engraved titlepages and vignettes, 'réimprimées avec les mêmes illustrations en 1756, 1760 et 1761' (col.447). The 1752 edition includes *Cénie* instead of the *Lettres d'Aza*, and two engraved vignettes (which are the same, according to my copy). Evidently, rather than repeat the same pictures for the edition described here, the printer or publisher decided to substitute a pretty woodcut after Caron. But why the engraved vignette would be put in vol. ii (instead of, more logically, in vol. i) is anyone's guess. (Perhaps this change concerning the illustrations occurred in an edition earlier than the one described here.) Some of the composite woodcut ornaments scattered throughout are unusual. (In spite of signatures in lower-case roman, there is an outside possibility we have here some sort of non-Parisian piracy).

MMF list three separate editions of the *Lettres d'une Péruvienne* for 1761 after Nicoletti. Nicoletti lists two for Amsterdam (etc.) and one for Paris: Duchesne, 1761 and remarks concerning the latter: 'Edizione in quarantuno lettere, la stessa (anche per formato e illustrazioni) del 1752, 1753 e 1755, di cui però alla Nazionale [BN] di Parigi esiste solo la *Seconde Partie*' (p.53, no.16). Although the pagination for that volume seems to agree with vol. ii as described here, Nicoletti makes no mention of the table for the *Lettres d'Aza*, or of the somewhat incongruent legal material (for the latter, obviously because that information is contained in vol. i). Nicoletti further remarks that 'non essendo riuscito a trovare altrove il primo tomo, presumo che nel 1761 si stato stampato solo questo secondo volumetto, da vendere insieme a giacenze invendute del primo', which is, of course, not true.

Conceivably this edition exists in the BL (C.30.d.36) and in the Newberry (NUC). I was not able to examine those volumes, or that in the BN for that matter; the NUC and BLC entries are most perfunctory. An edition which might refer to the same one as described here is also inadequately listed in Quérard. I have included my volumes in this bibliography as a step towards clarifying the situation.

Incipits: (*Lettres d'une Péruvienne*) 'Aza! mon cher Aza! / les cris de ta tendre / Zilia, tels qu'une va- / peur du matin'.

(*Lettres d'Aza*) 'Que tes larmes se dis- / sipent comme la rosée / à la vûe du Soleil'.

134

Graffigny, anonymous, and Lamache-Courmont: *Lettres d'une Péruvienne*; a 'suite'; *Lettres d'Aza*, 1767

Françoise [Paule] d'Issembourg d'Happoncourt de Graffigny (sometimes Grafigny or Huguet de Graf[f]igny; 1695-1758), an anonymous author, and Ignace Hugary de Lamache-Courmont (often spelled 'Lamarche-Courmont'):

i: Lettres / d'une / Péruvienne. / Premiere partie. / [symmetrical, composite woodcut ornament] / A Amsterdam, / Aux dépens du Delaissé. / [double rule: thick, thin] / M. DCC. LXVII.

ii: Lettres / d'Aza, / ou / d'un Péruvien. / Seconde partie. / [symmetrical, composite woodcut ornament: different from vol.i] / A Amsterdam, / Aux dépens du Delaissé. / [double rule: thick, thin] / M. DCC. LXVII.

in-12, i: 2 ff. (halftitle and titlepages) + [v]-xij + [1]-240 pp.
ii: 2 ff. (halftitle and titlepages) + [v]-vij (for viij) + [1]-124 pp.

Commentary: The first halftitle page reads: 'Lettres / d'une / Péruvienne. / Augmentées de celles du Chevalier / Deterville. / [rule] / Premiere partie.' The second reads: 'Lettres / d'Aza, / ou / d'un Péruvien. / [rule] / Seconde partie.'

The first volume contains the 'Avertissement', followed by the novel (thirty-eight numbered letters, pp.[1]-206, plus Déterville's reply to Zilia, pp.207-10), and then the sequel (seven numbered letters between Zilia, Déterville and Céline of which the first is the last mentioned for the novel, pp.207-10, 211-40). Vol. ii contains an 'Avertissement' and then thirty-five numbered letters of La Mache-Courmont's continuation.

It seems fairly certain that these volumes were printed in Holland (probably Amsterdam): signatures in arabic (8s plus 4s), composite ornaments, type, paper, etc. (The binding is contemporary English calf.)

I could find no trace of this edition elsewhere (Nicoletti, MMF, etc.).

Incipits: (*Lettres d'une Péruvienne*) 'Aza! mon cher Aza! les / cris de ta tendre Zilia, tels / qu'une vapeur du matin'.

(The first letter of the seven-letter 'suite', 'Réponse de Déterville à Zilia, & à la trente-huitieme & derniere Lettre imprimée') 'Ah, Zilia! à quel prix m'est-il / permis de vous revoir?'

(*Lettres d'Aza*) 'Que tes larmes se dissipent / comme la rosée à la vue / du Soleil'.

135

Graffigny (Deodati): *Lettres d'une Péruvienne*; *Lettere d'una peruviana*, 1774

Françoise [Paule] d'Issembourg d'Happoncourt de Graffigny (sometimes Grafigny or Huguet de Graf[f]igny; 1695-1758), with the translation by G. L. Deodati and Antoine Bret's 'Introduction historique'. Double titlepages (in French and Italian) facing each other:

Lettres / d'une / Péruvienne [Peruvienne for ii], / Traduites du François en Italien, / dont on a accentué tous les mots, / pour faciliter aux étrangers le / moyen d'apprendre la prosodie de / cette langue. / Par Mr. Deodati. / Tome premier [second]. / [woodcut ornament: spray of flowers, same for both volumes] / À [possibly A] Paris, / Chez / [open brace] Briasson, rue S. Jacques, à la Science. / Prault fils, quai de Conti, à la / descente du Pont Neuf [Pont-Neuf for ii], à la Charité. / Duchesne, rue S. Jacques, au temple / du goût. / Tillard, quai des Augustins, à S. Benoît. / [double rule] / M. DCC. LXXIV. / Avec Approbation & Privilége [Privilege for ii].

Lettere / d'una / peruviana, / Tradotte dal Francese in Italiano, / di cui si sono accentuate tutte le / voci, per facilitar agli Stranieri [stranieri for ii] il / modo d'imparar la prosodia di / questa Lingua. / Dal Signor Deodati. / [rule, none for ii] / Fluxere huc Latio Veneris Phœbique lepores; / Donorum partem versio tusca refert [no epigraph for ii] / [rule; none for ii] / Tomo primo [secondo]. / [woodcut ornament: spray of flowers; same motif, different ornament for ii] / In Parigi. [Parigi, for ii] / [double rule] / M. DCC. LXXIV. / Con Approvazione e Privilegio.

2 vols in-12°, i: 1 pl (French halftitle verso) + 1 pl (Italian halftitle recto, French titlepage verso) + 1 pl (Italian titlepage, beginning of text verso; no pagination or signatures) + [1]-335 pp.

ii: 1 f. (French halftitle recto, titlepage verso) + 1 f. (recto, Italian titlepage, verso, p.[4] of text) + [5]-243 pp.

Commentary: Nicoletti could only find volume i of a Paris edition for 1774 (BN; Z15597), presumably the same volume i as described here, although neither his transcription nor his explanations mention a titlepage in Italian. I have found a complete copy of the edition described here in the Benson Latin American Collection at the University of Texas at Austin, and, because of its rarity, have included it in this bibliography.

These volumes contain:
1. Deodati's dedicatory letter to Mme de Graffigny (1 p. and [1]-5 pp.);
2. 'Avis aux etrangers' / 'Avviso per gli stanieri [*sic*]', i.[6]-15;
3. 'Avis au lecteur' / 'Avvertimento al Lettore', i.[16-17];

4. 'Introduction historique aux lettres péruviennes' / 'Introduzione istorica alle lettere peruviane', i.[18]-45;

5. the novel, through letter 23, i.[46]-335;

6. the novel, through letter 41, ii.[4]-243;

The 'Avis' / 'Avviso' stresses the necessity of correct pronunciation of foreign langages (and, in passing, the originality of Deodati's version). It is worth noting that Mme de Graffigny's editorial 'Avertissement', containing the usual claims concerning the veracity of the novel, is omitted. Perhaps Deodati considered it inappropriate in light of his dedicatory letter to the author, naming her as such, even though the novel had already appeared with Mme de Graffigny's name on the titlepage (editions including the 'Avertissement').

In spite of signatures in lower-case roman (signed in 12s), there is a chance that these volumes comprise a pirated edition.

Deodati's biblingual publication first appeared in 1759 (Nicoletti no. 13, p.52) and was very successful. (For further information, see the next two entries.)

My thanks go to Jane Garner (rare books and manuscripts librarian) for her kindness in permitting the photocopying of key pages. (The Benson Latin American Collection is one of the richest extant, *sui generis*, and any French work of Latin American – or American – interest is often represented there in a handsome plurality of editions.)

Incipits: 'Aza! mon cher Aza! les cris de ta / tendre Zilia, tels qu'une vapeur du / matin'.

'Aza! mico [*sic*] cáro Aza! le grida, / i gémiti délla túa ténera Zília, / símili ái vapóri délla mattína'.

136

Graffigny (Deodati): *Lettres d'une Péruvienne*; *Lettere d'una peruviana*, 1792

Françoise [Paule] d'Issembourg d'Happoncourt de Graffigny (sometimes Grafigny or Huguet de Graf[f]igny; 1695-1758), with the translation by G. L. Deodati and Antoine Bret's 'Introduction historique'. Double titlepages (in French and Italian) facing each other:

A. Lettres / d'une / Péruvienne, / traduites en italien, / Avec des accens pour faciliter aux Etran- / gers la prononciation de l'Italien, & les / moyens de se familiariser avec la pro- / sodie de cette Langue. / Par Monsieur Deodati. / [rule] / Fluxêre hùc Latio [Latiò for ii] Veneris Phœbique lepores; / Donorum partem versio tusca refert. / [rule] / [woodcut ornament: branch with two flowers; same for both volumes] / A Lyon, / Chez Bruyset Freres. / [rule] / 1792.

B. Lettere [Léttere for ii] / d'una / peruviana, / tradotte / Dal Francese in Italiano, / di cui si sono / accentate [*sic*] tutte le voci, per facilitar agli / Stranieri il modo d'imparare la prosodia / di questa Lingua. / Dal Signor Deodati. / [rule] / Fluxêre hùc Latio Veneris Phœbique lepores; / Donorum partem versio tusca refert. / [rule] / [woodcut ornaments: lyre, branch with flowers, hills and rising sun; bouquet for ii] / Lione, / Appresso li [*sic*] fratelli Bruyset. / [rule] / 1792.

2 vols in-12°, i: 1 pl (first titlepage, halftitle recto) + 1 f. (titlepage; text begins verso, p.[2]), [3]-7, 8-15, [16]-55, [56]-407 pp.

ii: 2 ff. (titlepages: halftitle recto of the first; text begins verso of the second, p.[4]), [5]-375 pp.

Commentary: The rectos of the first titlepage in each volume bear halftitle information: 'Lettres / d'une / Péruvienne, / En Italien et en François. / [rule] / Tome I [II]. / [rule]'. The first halftitle to volume i is conjugate with a preceding blank leaf. The titlepage in volume ii is f.[A1], conjugate with f.[A12]. (My copy of this edition is in original wrappers, as issued, untrimmed.)

The pagination reflects the same contents as the preceding item: Deodati's dedicatory letter to Mme de Graffigny (i.[2]-7); 'Avis...' / 'Avviso...' (i.8-15); 'Introduction...' / 'Introduzióne...' (i.[16]-55; letters 1-21 (i.[56]-407); letters 22-41 (ii.[4]-375).

Sabin lists a 1792 edition as follows, with a location for the Library of Congress: Paris: Migneret, 1792, 8vo, 487p. This is doubtless a mistake, Sabin confusing the date for 1797. However, it could be a question of a 1797 (or later) piracy, with a printer's mistake on the titlepage (Sabin: *A dictionary of books relating to America...*, rprt. Amsterdam 1961, vii.372, no. 28193).

The 1792 edition described here is not listed in the usual bibliographies concerned with prose fiction, or in Nicoletti. It is also not to be found in the BLC, NUC or BNC. The only mention of it I have been able to find is in OCLC, assuming those books comprise the same edition (location: University of New Mexico at Albuquerque; no pagination recorded).

For further information, see the other Graffigny entries in this bibliography.

Incipits: 'Aza! mon cher Aza! les cris / de ta tendre Zilia, tels qu'une va- / peur du matin'.

'Aza! mío cáro Aza! le grída, i gé- / miti délla túa ténera Zília, símili ái va- / póri délla mattína'.

137

Graffigny (Deodati): *Lettres d'une Péruvienne*; *Lettere d'una peruviana*, 1795

Françoise [Paule] d'Issembourg d'Happoncourt de Graffigny (sometimes Grafigny or Huguet de Graf[f]igny; 1695-1758), with the translation by G. L. Deodati and Antoine Bret's 'Introduction historique'. Double titlepages (in French and Italian) facing each other:

A. Lettres / d'une / Péruvienne, / traduites / Du François en Italien, où l'on a accentué / tous les mots, pour donner aux Etrangers / la facilité d'en apprendre la prosodie. / Par M. Deodati. / Nouvelle edition. / [rule] / Fluxêre hùc Latio Veneris Phœbique lepores; / Donorum partem Versio Tusca refert. / [rule] / [woodcut ornament: vase with flowers 'swagging' out from centre, stylised leafage flowing out from vase pedestal on bottom] / [double rule] / A Londres, / Chez I. Herbert; F. Wingrave; T. / Boosey; Molini & Cie.; M. Stace; / & Vernor & Hood. / [short rule] / 1795.

B. Lettere / d'una / peruviana, / tradotte / Dal Francese in Italiano, di cui si sono / accentuate tutte le voci, per facilitar agli / Stranieri il modo d'imparar la prosodia / di questa lingua. / Dal Signor Deodati. / Nuova edizione. / [rule] / Fluxêre hùc Latio Veneris Phœbique lepores; / Donorum partem Versio Tusca refert. / [rule] / [woodcut ornament: similar to that on the French titlepage, but quite different as for the details] / [double rule] / In Londra, / Presso I. Herbert; F. Wingrave; / T. Boosey; Molini & Co.; M. Stace; / & Vernor & Hood. / [short rule] / 1795.

12°: 2 ff. (2 titlepages; for contents on recto and verso, see the commentary) + [5]-9, [10]-17, [18]-41, [42]-455, [456] pp.

Commentary: The French titlepage is on the verso. Recto is the following halftitle, with the printer's colophon: '[rule] / Lettres / d'une / Peruvienne, / avec / la traduction / italienne. / [rule] / A Londres, / Imprimé par R. Hindmarsh, Imprimeur à [*sic*] Son / Altesse Royale le Prince de Galles, / rue Old Bailey.'

The text, a dedicatory letter from Deodati to Graffigny, begins on p.[4], verso of the Italian titlepage. The pagination reflects the dedicatory letter (pp.[4]-9); an 'Avis aux etrangers' / 'Avviso per gli stranieri' (pp.[10]-17); an 'Introduction historique aux lettres peruviennes' / 'Introduzione istorica alle lettere peruviane', by Bret (pp.[18]-41); the novel proper (pp.[42]-455). At the end is a page of 'Books printed for the proprietors' (eleven items of foreign language interest, including *Il Castello di Otranto*, with cuts, on three different kinds of paper).

It is of considerable interest to note the large number of editions of the Deodati/Graffigny work published in England. It seems that the English preferred to learn Italian pronunciation via a French-Italian work, rather than an English-Italian one. (And it wasn't until nearly a half century after the publication of the Deodati/Graffigny work that there appeared a bilingual version in English and French: 1802; listed in Monglond, v, cols.1153-54; republished at least once, in 1807: Sabin, no. 28196, vii.373.)

The volume described here is not listed in the NUC, BLC or BNC, or in the usual sources. The only reference I have found to this edition (assuming it be the same) is in the BLC ten-year supplement (1956-1965), 455 pp. in-12° (1489.ff.52; under '*H*uguet de Graffigny', 'Huguet' being the name of Mme de Graffigny's husband). I have not been able to examine that book. In any case, my volume was in every likelihood printed as indicated by the halftitle and titlepages. (Corroboration: press figures; the paper is English.)

The edition described here contains forty-one numbered letters. For further information, see the preceding entries.

Incipits: 'Aza! mon cher Aza! les cris de ta / tendre Zilia, tels qu'une vapeur du matin'.

'Aza! mío cáro Aza! le grída, i gé- / miti délla túa ténera Zília, símili ái va- / póri délla mattína'.

138

Graffigny: *Lettres d'une Péruvienne*, 1800

Françoise [Paule] d'Issembourg d'Happoncourt de Graffigny (sometimes Grafi-gny or Huguet de Graf[f]igny; 1695-1758): Lettres / d'une / Péruvienne, / Par Madame de Graffigny. / [figurative woodcut ornament: rural manor-house] / A Avignon, / Chez la Ve. Seguin, Imprimeur-Libr. / et a Paris, / Chez C. Pougens, Imprimeur-Libraire, / rue Thomas-du-Louvre, N°. 246. / [short thin rule] / An VIII.

18°: 2 ff. (halftitle and titlepages) + [5]-16, [17]-235 pp.

Commentary: This book contains a halftitle for the novel ('Lettres / d'une / Péru-vienne.'); the titlepage; an 'Introduction historique aux Lettres péruviennes', and the novel in forty-one numbered letters.

I could find no trace of this book anywhere. It is a good example of one of those post-revolutionary provincial editions – also distributed in Paris – that seems to have survived in only one copy.

Incipit: 'Aza! mon cher Aza! les cris de ta / tendre Zilia, tels qu'une vapeur du ma- / tin'.

139

Gueullette: *Mémoires de mademoiselle de Bontems*, 1781

Thomas Simon Gueullette (1683-1766) *et al.*: Mémoires / de / mademoiselle / de Bontems, / ou / de la comtesse / de Marlou, / Rédigés par M. Gueullette, / Auteur des Contes Tartares, Chinois / & Mogols. / [rule] / Premiere [Seconde] partie. / [rule] / [circular woodcut ornament: eight wedge-shaped devices between eight lines] / Londres. / [double rule] / M.D.C.C. LXXXI.

18°, i: 3 pl (two halftitles and a titlepage) + [j]-vj, [1]-212 pp.

ii: 2 pl + 2 ff. (2 + 2 pp.) + [1]-119, 120, 113-166, [167]-262 pp. (See the commentary.)

Commentary: The pagination reflects: an 'Avis au lecteur' and the first part of the novel for vol. i. Vol ii contains two pages of an 'Avis aux amateurs'; two pages of 'Ouvrages qui paroissent', and the remainder of the novel. Then follow two additional pieces of prose fiction, as described below. Volumes i and ii have halftitles for 'Bibliotheque / amusante.' Then follows a halftitle for 'Mémoires / de / mademoiselle / de Bontems.' for vol. i. Catchtomes on the collection halftitles read 'Tome I [II]'. In vol ii, p.120 leads to p.113, and the book continues from there. Thus there is a duplication of pp.113-20.

This edition is listed in MMF, after the BN copy. The BN copy appears to be the same as that described here, but with a somewhat different ordering of the preliminary items. (None is listed in the NUC and it does not exist in the BL. However, this edition does appear to be listed in Krauss-Fontius, no. 3710, with a location for the Landesbibliothek Gotha.) The *Mémoires de Mlle de Bontems* first appeared in 1738 (Jones, p.66). I list my copy to remark that there are two additional stories included at the end of vol. ii, viz. the *Histoire de Polydore et d'Emilie* and the *Histoire d'Agnès de Castro*. No mention of these tales is made by A. D. Coderre (*L'Œuvre romanesque de T.-S. Gueullette*, Montpellier 1934) or J.-E. Gueullette (*Un magistrat du XVIIIᵉ siècle ami des lettres, du théâtre et du plaisir: T.-S. Gueullette*, Paris 1938). These two stories are by George, lord Lyttelton and Aphra Behn, presumably Mme Thiroux d'Arconville's translation. I was able to compare the incipits recorded here with the book in the Arsenal (*Romans traduits de l'anglois*, Amsterdam, 1761; 8vo B.L.29935), and they are the same. *Polydore* is from Lyttelton's '*Persian letters*', and *Agnès de Castro* is from Behn's *Recueil de romans et de pièces fugitives*. (These are listed in MMF whence I have derived my information.) Vol. ii, first p.120 contains the following 'Avis': 'On ne saura pas mauvais gré à l'Editeur de mettre à la suite de ce volume, pour le terminer, les deux Histoires dont le sujet s'accorde à présenter le vice sous les traits les plus odieux, & à faire respecter la vertu.'

The interesting 'Avis aux amateurs' introduces the collection which was to be known as the *Bibliothèque amusante*. This was to contain a group of curious novels, printed in a small format (presumably in-18°). The end of the 'Avis' reads: 'Cet ouvrage s'imprime à Londres', which is not true. (Everything about the two volumes described here bespeaks a Parisian or at least French printing.)

Incipits: (*Mémoires de mademoiselle de Bontems*) 'Vous ne vous contentez pas, Madame, du récit que je vous ai fait, à diverses reprises, des différentes aventures de ma vie'.

(*Histoire de Polydore et d'Emilie*) 'Sous le regne de Charles premier, roi d'Angleterre, deux gentilshommes dont je cacherai les véritables noms sous ceux d'*Acaste* & de *Septimius*'.

(*Histoire d'Agnès de Castro*) 'Qu'une passion naissante a de charmes, & qu'on se laisse facilement entraîner aux plaisirs que l'amour semble nous promettre!'

140

Gueullette: *Les Sultanes de Guzarate*; *Les Mille et une soirées*, 1733 and 1749

Thomas Simon Gueullette (1683-1766), two sets of titlepages as follows:

A. i, ii, iii: Les sultanes / de Guzarate, / ou / les songes / des / hommes éveillés. / Contes mogols. / Par M. G**** / tome premier [second, troisie'me]. / [symmetrical woodcut ornaments: with basket of flowers in centre for i and ii; surmounted by what looks like a burning heart (or two)] / A Paris, / Chez Denis Mouchet, Grand'Salle du / Palais, à la Justice. / [rule] / MDCCXXXIII. [M. DCC. XXIII. for iii] / Avec Approbation & Privilege du Roy.

B. i, ii, iii: Les mille / et une / soire'es. / Contes mogols. / Tome premier [second, troisie'me]. / [symmetrical woodcut ornament: fleur-de-lys vaguely resembling a shell for i; same as A. iii for ii; same as A. i and ii for iii] / A la Haye, / Chez Jean Neaulme. / [rule] / M. DCC. XLIX.

12°, i: 3 pl (halftitle and two titlepages) + 9 ff. (3 + 13 + 2 pp.) + 2 ff. (one blank, the second a halftitle) + [1]-348 pp.

ii: 3 pl (halftitle and two titlepages) + 2 ff. (4 pp.) + 1 f. (halftitle) + [1]-391 pp.

iii: 3 pl (halftitle and two titlepages) + 2 ff. (4 pp.) + 1 f. (halftitle) + [1]-356 pp. + 2 ff. (4 pp.)

Commentary: There are two halftitles and two titlepages for each volume. The halftitles read 'Contes / mogols. / Tome I [II, III].' The second halftitles are bound in right before the begininng of the text of the novel. Vol. i is preceded by a dedicatory letter to the duchesse d'Estrées, signed 'Gueullette' (3 pp.), an 'Avis au lecteur' (13 pp.), a two-page 'table', the blank and halftitle mentioned above. The preliminary gathering is [aviij], [biv], including the original halftitle and titlepages. Vols. ii and iii are preceded by the three leaves of a halftitle and two titlepages, 4 pp. of 'tables' and the second halftitle. At the end of vol. iii are four pages of legal material: a laudatory approbation signed 'de Beauchamps' (9 November 1731), a privilege (to Pierre Prault for six years, signed 'Sainson', 1 May 1732) and the registration (2 May 1732, 'Le Mercier, syndic'). From this, one might assume that Prault sold the rights to Muchet, or shared them with him.

This work is listed in Jones, who mentions two editions, one with only the date (1733), the other as per the above titlepages for 1749. (No pagination details are provided for the 1749 edition or issue.) The novel (or collection) first appeared in 1732 (Jones p.49). I list this work to remark that the 1749 'edition' is an issue of the 1733 edition, with 'Néaulme's' titlepages added as cancels. (I know of no other copy with both sets of titlepages and the two sets of halftitles.) It would seem most doubtful indeed that Néaulme acquired the left-over copies of the first edition, and then reissued them in Holland. Indeed, the evidence of the identical woodcut ornaments leads me to believe that the second set of halftitles and titlepages was printed by Prault. Without having access to documents concerning the booktrade, it does not seem farfetched to surmise that, since Prault's original six years were up (and during a very difficult time with respect to the novel and censorship), he obtained some sort of 'permission tacite' to reissue the collection. Of course, he might have reissued them with no permission at all.

This work parallels the *Arabian nights* and is divided into eighty-four 'soirées'. Like most of Gueullette's other attempts at imitating fairy tales, and the *Arabian nights*, it was quite popular, translated into several languages, and was especially appreciated by readers of English.

To editions of this work listed in modern bibliographies I would add:

Les Sultanes de Guzarate, ou les songes des hommes éveillés. Contes mogols. Par M. G****. Paris: André Morin, 1732 (possibly 1731 for vol. ii, but that is highly unlikely; part of the titlepage is missing). Avec approbation et privilège du roy.

in-12°, i: 2 pl (halftitle and titlepage) + 10 ff. (4 + 13 + 3 pp.) + [1]-372 pp. + 2 ff. (2 + 2 pp.)

ii: 2 pl + 2 ff. (4 pp.) + [1]-423 pp.

iii: 2 pl + 2 ff. (4 pp.) + [1]-386 pp + 1 f. (2 pp.)

The halftitles read 'Contes / mogols. / Tome I [II, III]'. This edition includes the legal material and Prault's colophon ('A Paris, de l'Imprimerie de P. Prault.

1732'). BL, 1093.aa.6 (Ashbee). Conceivably we are dealing with an issue of the first edition.

Incipit: 'Oguz Roi de Guzarate (*a*), ayant établi dans ses Etats la Religion du grand Prophete, & fait abattre tous les Temples des Idoles'. (A note gives explanations about Guzarate.)

141

Guilleragues *et al.*: *Recueil de lettres galantes et amoureuses,*
1706

Gabriel Joseph de La Vergne, vicomte de Guilleragues (1628-1685), Roger de Rabutin, comte de Bussy (1618-1693) after Caius Petronius Arbiter (?-66 A.D.), *et al.*: Recueil / de / lettres galantes / et amoureuses / d'Heloise a Abailard, / d'une / religieuse portugaise / au chevalier *** / Et celles de Cleante & de Belise / & leurs Réponses. / Avec l'Histoire de la Matrone / d'Ephese. / [woodcut sphere] / A Amsterdam, / Chez François Roger, à l'Enseigne / de l'Imprimerie. / [rule] / M. DCCVI.

12°: 1 pl (titlepage) + 1 f. (2 pp.) + [1]-428 pp.

Commentary: This volume contains, according to the head titles (where applicable):

 1. an 'Avertissement au Lecteur', 2 pp.;
 2. 'Lettre d'Heloise a Abailard', pp.[1]-28;
 3. an 'Avertissement' and 'Lettre a Heloise [...]', pp.[29-32], [33]-58;
 4. an 'Avertissement' and 'Lettre seconde a Abailard [...]', pp.[59-60], 61-80;
 5. 'Avertissement' and 'Seconde réponse d'Abailard [...]', pp.[81-82], 83-100;
 6. 'Avertissement' and 'Lettre troisième d'Heloise a Abailard', pp.[101], 102-20;
 7. (half titlepage) 'Lettres / d'amour / d'une / religieuse / portugaise, / ecrites / au / chevalier de C*** / Officier François en Portugal. / Avec les Réponses dudit Chevalier / ensuite de chacune des Lettres / de ladite Religieuse.' + pp.[123-24] ('Au lecteur'), 125-294 (twenty-three letters in all: twelve from the nun to the chevalier, with eleven replies; the last remains unanswered);
 8. (half titlepage) 'Recueil / de / lettres galantes / de / Cleante / et / Belise.' + pp.[297-98] ('Au lecteur'), 299-388 (seventy-two letters in all);
 9. (half titlepage) 'Lettres / galantes / et / amoureuses, / Tirées des meilleurs Auteurs. / Avec l'Histoire de la Matrone / d'Ephese.' + pp.[391-92] ('Avertissement au lecteur'), 393-417;
 10. 'Histoire de la matrone d'Ephese', pp.417-22;
 11. 'Des lettres, & de leur stile', pp.422-28.

According to Barbier, the first letter from Heloïse to Abelard (no. 2) and Abelard's reply (no. 3) are by Rémond des Cours (Barbier, iii, col.508f and ii, col.1136f). But these letters presumably match the 1695 edition, which might not be by Rémond des Cours. (See Rémond des Cours, *Histoire d'Héloïse et d'Abélard* below.) The rest of the Abelard and Heloïse correspondence is anonymous, still according to Barbier. (See too Barbier, i, col.144d-f.) There were other adaptations of the Abelard-Heloïse correspondence dating to the 1690s by Alluis, Du Bois and anonymous authors. See Charrier, p.605-06, nos 42-51. (See too Bussy-Rabutin, *Lettres* above.)

The *Lettres d'amour d'une religieuse portugaise* were, for the first five, often previously attributed to the nun, Mariana Alcoforado. But these are by Guilleragues, as Deloffre and Rougeot have convincingly shown (Frédéric Deloffre and Jacques Rougeot eds., *Lettres portugaises*, Geneva 1972). The history of the continuation of the letters and the replies is fairly complex. The author is today unknown. See Lever pp.250-51. See too the section 'L'Histoire des *Lettres portugaises*', pp.61-93 in Deloffre-Rougeot (*op. cit.*).

The *Recueil de lettres galantes de Cléante et Bélise* are supposedly the real-life letters of Anne Ferrand, née Bellinzani to the baron de Breteuil. They were published as a sort of addendum to the *Histoire des amours de Cléante et Bélise, avec le recueil de ses lettres* (first edition of the story, 1689; with the letters, 1691. See Lever p.213.) However, I doubt the letters are real. The parallels with the *Princesse de Clèves* and other fiction of the period seem too deliberate, and the thread of events too 'romanesque' in style, even if the facts be more or less 'true-seeming'. See too Barbier iii, col.509a and ii, col.738f.

The *Lettres galantes et amoureuses* are probably just what the editor claims they are, with probable modifications for many, if not most (or all) of the letters: 'Comme l'on a commencé dans cet Ouvrage par les Lettres les plus tendres & les plus delicates qui aient jamais paru, l'Auteur qui les a compilées, a jugé à propos de joindre dans ce Recueil, les Lettres les plus passionnées & plus amoureuses, que Voiture, Bussi-Rabutin, Montreüil, Scaron, le Chevalier d Her [obviously Fontenelle's *Lettres diverses de Mr. le chevalier d'Her****, Lever p.249] & Boursault ont mis [*sic*] au jour' ('Avertissement', p.[391]). Indeed, the thirteenth letter, p.409, is the first part (with variants) of Fontenelle's first letter ('Il y a longtems, Madame, que j'aurois pris la liberté de vous aimer, si vous aviez eu le loisir d'être animée [for aimée] de moi [...]').

The *Histoire de la matrone d'Ephèse* is an adaptation from Petronius (an excerpt from the *Satiricon*) by Bussy-Rabutin. For more information, see the latter's *Lettres* above.

As for the last piece in this collection: I do not know who authored it (quite conceivably the editor). It consists of twelve 'remarques' on letters and their style.

This 'recueil' first appeared in 1699 (Lever p.361; Charrier p.606, no. 51), and went through a considerable number of editions. Its popularity was not only the result of the entertainment value of the pieces contained in it: by the addition of the *Des lettres et de leur style*, the editor wilfully associated his book to the many 'secrétaires' of the time. (And, as we know now, epistolary fiction in part if not largely grew out of sixteenth-century 'secrétaires' and their analogues. See particularly Bernard A. Bray's most interesting *L'Art de la lettre amoureuse: des manuels aux romans, 1550-1700*, La Haye, Paris 1967.) This edition is not listed in Lever or Charrier and it is not recorded in the BLC, BNC or NUC.

Incipits: (Heloïse to Abelard) 'On m'aporta par hazard, il y a quelques jours, une Lettre de consolation'.

(*Lettres portugaises*) 'Il est donc possible que vous aïés été un moment en colere contre moi'.

(*Lettres galantes de Cléante et Bélise*) 'Je ne crois pas que la tendresse que j'ai pour vous'.

(*Lettres galantes et amoureuses*, 'A mademoiselle***') 'Mademoiselle, / Si je pouvois, vous auriez plus souvent de mes nouvelles'.

142

Haller (Tscharner transl.): *Poésies de M. Haller*, 1760

Baron Albrecht von Haller (1708-1777), Christoph Martin Wieland (1733-1813), *et al.*, translated by Vincenz Berhard von Tscharner (1728-1778) *et al.*: (vol. i) Poesies / de / Mr. Haller / Traduites de l'Allemand. / [double rule] / Édition / retouchée et augmentée. / [double rule] / Non omnis moriar / Horat. / [symmetrical woodcut decoration, different from vol. ii] / Berne, / aux dépens de la societé. / [decorative rule] / Chez Abr. Wagner Fils, / 1760.

(vol. ii) Seconde partie. / Ou / traductions, / qui peuvent servir de Suite / aux / poesies / de / Mr. Haller. / [composite symmetrical woodcut decoration, same elements but different from vol. i] / Berne, / aux dépens de la societé. / [decorative rule] / Chez Abr. Wagner Fils, / 1760.

12°, i: 1 f. (titlepage) + [jjj-jv], [v]-[vj], [vjj]-x, [11.]-350., [351.-352.] pp.
ii: 1 f. (titlepage) + [3.]-166. + 169.-353., [354.-355.] pp.

Commentary: I list these two volumes, which also exist in the BL (242.l.37), because they have escaped the attention of bibliographers of the 'genre romanesque'. My copy and the BL's differ radically from the two copies of Haller's *Poésies* to be found in the BN (Yh.924-25 and Yh.1260-61). The titlepages and pagination are different. The BN's books – both sets are identical – are in octavo. And, in spite of carrying 'Berne' on the titlepages, they were, in every likelihood, printed in Paris. Thus the BN books would represent a Parisian piracy of a Swiss edition. BN vol. i carries 'A Berne, / aux dépens de la société. / [double rule] / M. DCC. LX.' Note the absence of Wagner's name. Vol. ii does, however, bear 'Chez Abr. Wagner Fils. / 1760.' (The title for this volume begins with: 'Traductions qui peuvent servir de suite [...]').

Vol. i of the edition described here contains: 1. the translator's dedicatory letter, 'A madame***'; 2. 'Au Lecteur'; 3. 'Dédicace de Mr. Haller, a son excellenece [*sic*] Isaac Steiguer, avoyer de la république de Berne'; 4. Haller's poems, translated into prose. Some of these might be considered as falling within the scope of the 'genre romanesque', for example 'Doris' (p.172.-181.). The last unnumbered pages in each volume are the tables (called 'indices').

The verso of the titlepage, vol. ii, contains the following 'Avis': 'Les quatre traductions suivantes ne sont pas de la même main que celles de la premiére partie du présent recueil. Nous les avons tirées du premier Volume du *Choix littéraire de Genève*; page 174.' None of these is of particular interest to the 'genre romanesque'. Tscharner included in this volume a verse translation of the 'Doris' mentioned above, by Duclos, 'Capitaine d'Infanterie, attaché à la cour de M.

le Duc des Deux-Ponts', which he mentions had first appeared in the *Année littéraire* (true: 1759, vi.233-38; in the above collection, ii.36.-44.). The second volume also contains a verse translation/adaptation by a chevalier de Vatau titled 'L'Eternité, ode' (p.48.-56.) and 'Trois / epitres / de / Mr. de Haguedorn.' (half titlepage + pp.59.-166.), of no great interest to the 'genre romanesque'.

Of interest to students of French prose fiction is: 'IV. contes, / et le / fragment d'une himne / sur / dieu; / par / Mr. Wieland.' (half titlepage), especially the four tales. There is a notice on the verso of the half titlepage: 'Les traductions suivantes, à l'exception du fragment d'une Hymne &c. sont tirées du *Journal Etranger* de Paris.' These stories are: 1. 'Balsore', pp.169.-207.; 2. 'Zemin et Gulhindy', pp.208.-255.; 3. 'La Vertu malheureuse', pp.256.-285.; 4. 'Firnaz et Zohar', pp.286.-330. And they did indeed appear in the *Journal étranger*, with some brief liminary material: *Zemin et Gulhindy*, July 1756, pp.51-76; *Le Mécontent* (i.e., *Firnaz et Zohar*), August 1756, pp.175-99; *Balsore*, October 1756, pp.209-29; *La Vertu malheureuse*, November 1756, pp.50-68. According to a note at the end of *Balsore*, the editors were originally unaware that these tales are by Wieland: 'Nous apprenons d'Allemagne que l'auteur de ces Contes s'appelle M. *Wieland*, et qu'il demeure actuellement à *Zurich* en Suisse' (October 1756, p.229).

There were other editions of the *Poésies de M. Haller* in the eighteenth century, with varying contents, but this appears to be the first edition of this version. Beyond the usual catalogues and source books, see Kayser, iii.20a and Heinsius 1793, iv.541.

In passing, I might mention that Heinsius lists some 'Poésies chois. trad. en Prose. [in-]8. Zür[i]ch, Orell, F[üssli?]. et C[ompagnie?]. [1]750' (ii, col.244). Kayser lists the 1750 edition, and indicates that it was republished (or reissued) in 1758, also giving yet another, prose translation for 1750:

1. *Poésies choisies*, 1750 and 1758. 'poésies choisies trad. en prose. [in-]8. Zürich [1]750 u[nd] [17]58. Orell' (iii.20a).

2. *Poésies choisies*, 1750. 'poésies, chosies trad. en prose p[ar] V. E. Tscharner. [in-]8. Göting. [1]750. Vanderhöck u[nd] R[ein, Reich?]' (*loc. cit.*). None of these is listed in the NUC, BLC or BNC.

A cursory search reveals several other editions of the *Poésies de M. [de] Haller*:

1. *Poésies de M. Haller*, 1752. Zuric: Heidegger, 1752 (BNC).

2. *Poésies de M. Haller*, 1755. Berne: Société typographique, 1755 (NUC, three locations).

3. *Poésies de M. Haller*, 1759. Zuric: Heidegger, 1759 (NUC: Cornell University).

4. *Poésies de M. Haller*, 1775. Berne: Société typographique, 1775 (BNC).

The Messkatalog also has entries for Haller's *Poésies* which are not listed in the BLC, BNC or NUC:

1. *Poésies de M. Haller*, 1750. 'Les Poesies de Monsieur de Haller, traduit [*sic*] en Francois par Mr. de Tscharner, 8. Gottingue, chez Abram. Vandenhoeck', OM 1750, p.53. (This is probably Kayser, no.1[A] listed above).

2. *Poésies de M. Haller*, 1751. 'Poesies de Mr. de Haller, Traduit[e]s de l'allemand. 2de Edition. 8. Zuric chez Heidegguer & Comp.', OM 1751, p.167. (This is possibly BN, for 1752, mentioned above.)

3. *Poésies de M. Haller*, 1762. 'Poesies de Mr. *Haller*, edit. retouchée et augmentée. 12. 2 Voll. Berne, chez la societé typographique', OM 1762, p.269.

See too Gesamtverzeichniss, liv.144b.

Incipits: ('Doris') 'La lumiére du jour s'est obscurcie; le pourpre, qui brilloit au couchant'.

('Balsore') 'La Perse gémit jadis sous un Prince, qui surpassoit en cruauté les tyrans, dont les crimes étonnèrent autrefois les bords de la Sicile.'

143

Hamilton: *Mémoires du comte de Grammont*, 1746

Count Anthony (or Antoine) Hamilton (1645?-1719): Memoires / du comte / de / Grammont, / Par Monsieur le Comte / Antoine Hamilton. / Nouvelle edition, / Augmentée d'un Discours préliminaire / mêlé de Prose & de Vers, par le même / Auteur, & d'un Avertissement contenant / quelques Anecdotes de la Vie du Comte / Hamilton. / [woodcut decoration: a somewhat irregular triangle formed by five rows of snowflake-like decorations, viz. 7, 6, 5, 3, 1] / A Paris, / Chez la Veuve Pissot, Quay de Conti, à la / Croix d'Or. / [rule] / M. DCC. XLVI.

12°: 1 f. (titlepage) + iij-vj, vij-xxij, xxiij-xxiv + [1]-407 pp.

Commentary: This novel first appeared in 1711 or 1713; in all likelihood the latter date is correct (Jones p.20 and 22). See too Conlon, iv.356, no. 16811. The pagination recorded here reflects an 'Avertissement', an 'Epitre a monsieur le comte de Grammont' (in prose and verse, as was the fashion of the day for 'literary' letters), a 'Table' and the novel. This edition is listed in the usual bibliographies after the copy in the BL. I have not been able to locate another one in a public library. (I have two.)

I list this book simply to remark that it was printed in England (in London in all likelihood), which is evident not only from the woodcut decorations (particularly the woodcut headpiece and decorative capital), paper and type, but because of the press figures scattered throughout. This edition represents a genuine effort on the part of the printer(s) to imitate, superficially anyway, a Parisian printing: signatures in lowercase roman (terminal 'js' for 'is'), first gathering of the novel proper signed with uppercase 'A', catchwords leading from the last folio of each gathering to the first of the next only, etc. For another, albeit more complex example of this sort of thing, see Rousseau, *Emile*, 'Francfort', 1762 below.

To editions of these *Mémoires* listed in Ruth Clark, *Anthony Hamilton (author of 'Memoirs of count Grammont'): his life and works and his family* (London, New York 1921; Jones and MMF list after Clark), I would add:

1. *Mémoires du comte de Grammont*, 1716. Rotterdam: Bos, 1716. 304 pp. Krauss-Fontius, no. 587. Location: Sächsische Landesbibliothek Dresden.

2. *Mémoires du comte de Grammont*, 1749. s.l. [sans lieu], 1749. 2 vols. Krauss-Fontius, no. 590. Location: same as no. 1.

Under the rubric of the *Mémoires du comte de Grammont*, Krauss-Fontius list 'I-VII. s.l. 1760-1777', which surely refers to an edition (perhaps a composite one) of the *Œuvres* (no. 591; location: Thüringische Landesbibliothek, Weimar).

Incipit: 'Comme ceux qui ne lisent que pour se divertir, me paroissent plus raisonnables que ceux qui n'ouvrent un Livre que pour y chercher des défauts'.

144

Hamilton: *Œuvres diverses*, 1776

Count Anthony Hamilton (1645?-1719): Œuvres / diverses / du comte / Antoine Hamilton. / [nearly symmetrical woodcut decoration] / A Londres. / [double rule] / 1776.

12°: 1 pl + [1]-[2], [3]-236, 237-383 pp.

Commentary: The first item is an 'Avis du libraire'; the second, various pieces in prose and verse. The last is *Zénéide* (here spelled 'Zeneyde'), which first appeared in 1731. This is actually part of a seven volume collection of Hamilton's works, each with a titlepage for the individual volume, and with varying half titlepages for the *Œuvres* (for most volumes). Meant to be part of the entire collection, certain practices were followed virtually insuring that individual volumes would turn up, purportedly as complete pieces. Each volume, for example, carries 'Fin.' at the end (or 'Fin' of the pieces involved). And each volume is complete unto itself. Each gathering begins with the usual capital letter, with no indication of the 'tomaison', i.e. no catchtomes.

No bibliography that I know of gives the particulars of this potentially confusing bibliographical problem. (For one example alone, the BLC cites the above described volume as a separate entity, since it too lacks the important half titlepage.) Here then is a description of the seven volume collection, as per the BN copy (Z.23402-08). Ruth Clark, in her generally meticulous bibliography appended to *Anthony Hamilton (author of 'Memoirs of count Grammont'): his life and works and his family* (London, New York 1921) states that this is an edition with the collective title of *Œuvres du comte Antoine Hamilton, Nouvelle Edition, Corrigée et augmentée d'un volume...* (BN, BL), which is not quite true, as can be seen below.

i: 1. (half titlepage) Œuvres / du comte / Antoine Hamilton, / tome I. / Nouvelle édition, / corrigée & augmentée d'un Volume.

2. Then the titlepage as described above.

ii: 1. (half titlepage) Œuvres / du comte / Antoine Hamilton. / Tome II.

2. (titlepage) Fleur / d'épine, / conte. / [woodcut decoration] / A Londres. / [double rule] / 1776. 2 pl + [1]-205 + [207]-318 pp.

iii: 1. (half titlepage) Œuvres / du comte / Antoine Hamilton, / tome III.

2. (titlepage) Les quatre / facardins, / conte. / [woodcut decoration] / A Londres. / [double rule] / 1776. 2 pl + [1]-256, 257-318 pp.

iv: 1. (half titlepage) Œuvres / du comte / Antoine Hamilton, / tome IV. / Nouvelle édition, / Corrigée & augmentée d'un Volume.

2. (titlepage) Le bellier, / conte. / [woodcut decoration] / A Londres. / [double rule] / 1776. 2 pl + [1]-[2], [3]-262, [263]-335 pp.

v: 1. No half titlepage

2. (titlepage) Memoires / du comte / de Grammont. / Par le C. Antoine Hamil-

ton. / Tome Premier. / [woodcut decoration] / A Londres. / [double rule] / 1776. 1 f. (titlepage) + [iii]-ix, [x]-xxxiv + 1f. (2 pp.: Table) + [1]-315 pp. ('Fin du premier Tome.')

vi: 1. No half titlepage

2. Memoires / du comte / de Grammont, / Par le C. Antoine Hamilton. / Tome Second. / Nouvelle édition, / Corrigée & augmentée d'un Volume. / [woodcut decoration] / A Londres. / [double rule] / 1776. 1 pl + 1f. (2 pp.: Table) + [1]-340 pp. ('Fin.')

vii: 1. (half titlepage) Œuvres / du comte / Antoine Hamilton. / Tome VII.

2. Œuvres / diverses / du comte / Antoine Hamilton. / [woodcut decoration] / A Londres, / Et se trouve à Paris, / Chez Le Jay, Libraire, rue S. Jacques, / au grand Corneille. / [double rule] / M. DCC. LXXVI. 2 pl + [1]-272 pp. + 1f. (2 pp.: Table) pp.

Pagination has been given above with particularly the 'genre romanesque' in mind. The 'Avis du libraire' at the head of i mentions several volumes (other than vol. i) of the collection, and explains the division of the 'œuvres mêlées'. The bookdealer (possibly the firm of Le Jay; the books were certainly not printed in London and were in every likelihood printed in Paris) obviously also wanted vol. i to be able to stand alone, selecting the best 'pièces diverses', etc.

To editions of the *Œuvres* listed in Clark (and bibliographies dealing with prose fiction), I would add:

'Œuvres du comte d'Hamilton, auteur des "Mémoires du comte de Grammont". I-V. -Utrecht: Neaulme, 1731', Krauss-Fontius (no. 1013), with a location for the Thüringische Landesbibliothek Weimar.

Incipit: (*Zénéide*) 'Vous me demandez, Madame, une longue Lettre, & des particularités de notre Cour: vous allez être satisfaite'.

145

Haywood: *La Spectatrice*, 1750-1751

Eliza (Fowler) Haywood (1693?-1756); for the translator, see the commentary: (titlepages in red and black) La / *spectatrice*. / Ouvrage / *traduit de l'anglois*. / Premier [Second, Troisieme, Quatrieme] volume. / [good quality engraved fleuron, Scheurleer's device; in a much poorer state for vol. iv; bears the motto: 'erudit et ditat' indicating 'F.H.S. Lib[r].'] / A la Haye, Chez [chez for vol. iii; no 'chez' at all for iv] / *Frederic Henri Scheurleer.* / M DCC L. [M DCC LI. for vol. iv]

12°, i: 1 pl (titlepage) + 1 f. (2 pp.) + [1]-512 pp. + 6 ff. (12 pp.)

ii: 1 pl + [1]-502 pp. + 5 ff. (10 pp.)

iii: 1 pl + [1]-485, [486] pp. + 7 ff. (11 pp., continued from p.[486] + 3 pp.; see the commentary)

iv: 1 pl + [1]-488 pp. + 5 ff. (10 pp.)

Commentary: This is conceivably a translation by Jean Arnold Trocheneau (sometimes Trochereau) de La Berlière. The original first appeared from 1744-1746 as *The Female spectator*. The edition described here is a complete translation of the periodical, barring some dedicatory material of no particular importance.

(The edition with which I compared my copy of this translation is the self-styled fifth, London: printed for T. Gardner, 1755, 4 vols in-12°.)

I could find no other copy of this edition. Indeed, the only other editions in four volumes I could find are those listed in Krauss-Fontius: La Haye: Scheurleer, 1749-1751 (no. 183; location: Romanisches Seminar der Universität Jena), and same place/publisher, 1750 (no. 184; location: Universitäts- und Landesbibliothek Sachsen-Anhalt, Halle).

The last sets of pages in vols i, ii and iv, and the penultimate set in iii are alphabetical tables. The last sets of pages in each volume comprise folios which are part of the final gatherings. In vol. iii, the table begins on a verso, p.[486]. The last three pages of vol. iii contain a 'Catalogue de quelques livres, Imprimés chez Frederic-Henri Scheurleer'.

Kayser mentions what appears to be a one-volume edition or, in every likelihood, a one-volume, abridged version, in-8°, for Dresden: Walther, 1750 ('*Spectatrice*, la, trad. de l'Anglois. [in-]8. Dresd. [1]750. Walther', v.285a). This information is also in Heinsius (iii, col.780), who might well have been the source for the information in Kayser. And Heinsius might in turn have abstracted his entry from the two entries in the Messkatalog:

1. 'La Spectatrice, traduite de l'Anglois, 8. [La] Haye, & à Dresde chez George Conrad Walther', OM 1750, p.54.

2. '[...] ouvrage traduit de l'Anglois. Nouvelle Edition revuë & corrigée. 8. [La] Haye, & à Dresde, chez George Conr. Walther', MM 1750, p.105. The next entry is for 'Le meme Livre, 2 Vol. 12. chez Arkstée & Merkus'. Perhaps all three entries refer to two issues of the same edition?

Rochedieu has the following entries for French version[s?] (following his order, p.143):

1. 'La Spectatrice, traduction abrégée du *Spectateur féminin* d'Eliza Haywood. Paris: Rollin fils, 1750. 2 vol. in-12'.

2. 'La Nouvelle Spectatrice [ouvrage traduit de l'anglois d'Eliza Haywood, par J. A. Trocheneau de la Berlière]. Paris: Rollin fils, 1751. 2t. en 1 vol. in-12'.

3. 'Ibid. La Haye, 1749-51. in-12'.

Of all the editions cited by Rochedieu, Heinsius and Kayser, the only one that I have been able to find is Rochedieu no. 2 (BNC, NUC). Possibly there were two Paris editions, for the NUC lists Paris: Rolin, Bauche and Pissot, 1751 (2 vols, frontispiece; Harvard), whereas BNC lists only Paris: Rolin, 1751 (R.20112-13; in lxix.608). I was unable to examine these. In any case, there is obviously some confusion in Rochedieu at least. To say anything further would be tantamount to pure speculation.

The first volume of the edition described here is preceded by an 'Avertissement du traducteur'. The points covered are: 1. the considerable success of the original in England; 2. it was viewed in England as a 'livre à clef', which is not pertinent to its success elsewhere; 3. justification of the word 'spectatrice' – 'quoique le terme [...] ne soit pas nouveau' – instead of 'authrice'. (However there was no real reason to justify the use of the word 'spectatrice', there being at least two periodicals antedating this translation using the same noun in the title: *La Spectatrice* [March 1728-March 1729] and *La Spectatrice danoise, ou l'Aspasie moderne*

[September 1748 on]; see the *Catalogue collectif des périodiques*, Jean Sgard's *Dictionnaire des journalistes*, Sgard's forthcoming *Dictionnaire des journaux* and the NUC.)

As far as prose-fiction is concerned, *La Spectatrice* is sprinkled with tales, stories woven into the 'narrative' and set off. These pieces were supposed to be largely based on fact: 'Je dois [...] informer le Public que, pour m'assurer des intelligences qui ne manquent jamais, j'ai placé des Espions, non seulement dans les lieux les plus fréquentés de cette Capitale [Londres] & de ses environs, mais encore à *Bath Tunbridge* & *Spaw*, & que j'ai trouvé le moyen d'étendre mes correspondances, jusques en *France*, à *Rome*, en *Allemagne* & dans d'autres parties du Monde' (i.8). Some of these stories are quite substantial, for example *Le Triomphe de la patience & de la fermeté sur la barbarie & la fourberie. Histoire véritable*, supposedly a contribution from 'Elismonde' (iv.240-317).

Incipit: 'C'Est sur-tout le choix de nos Amusemens, qui distingue le goût épuré & délicat de celui qui est grossier & plus commun'.

146

Hervey *et al.* (Le Tourneur *et al.* transl.): *Méditations d'Hervey*, 1771

James Hervey (1714-1758), Edward Jerningham (1737-1812), Thomas Gray (1716-1771) *et al.*, translated by Pierre Prime Félicien Le Tourneur (1737-1788) and Jean François Peyron (1748-1784):

i: Méditations / d'Hervey, / traduites de l'anglois, / Par M. Le Tourneur. / Premiere partie. / [woodcut ornament, Le Jay's device, with the following line from Corneille: 'Je ne dois qu'à moi seul toute ma renommée'] / A Paris, / Chez Le Jay, Libraire, rue Saint Jacques, / au-dessus de celle des Mathurins, / au grand Corneille. / [rule] / M. DCC. LXXI. / Avec Approbation & Permission.

ii: (half titlepage) Méditations / d'Hervey. / Seconde partie. / Traduites par M. Peyron, & revues par / M. Le Tourneur.

12°, i: 2 pl + [1]-202 pp.

ii: 1 pl (halftitle) + [1]-191 p.

Commentary: This work is not listed in MMF, and since the piece in French after Jerningham, at least, must be styled 'prose fiction', I have included it. The two volumes contain the following works, all in prose:

1. Vie d'Hervey, recteur ou curé de deux villages dans la province de Northampton, pp.[1]-73.

2. Les Tombeaux d'Hervey, with the following epigraph: 'Plurima mortis imago. (Virg.)', pp.[75]-162.

3. Two letters from Hervey to his sister, pp.[163]-173.

4. Lettre d'Hervey à une dame, pp.[174]-186.

5. Méditation composée par une jeune dame angloise en 1750, à l'imitation de celles d'Hervey, pp.[187]-192.

6. Elégie écrite sur un cimetière de campagne, traduite de l'anglois de M. Cray [*sic*], pp.[193]-202.

In vol. ii:

7. Méditations au milieu d'un parterre, pp.[1]-92.

8. Méditations sur les cieux étoilés, pp.[93]-136.

9. L'Hiver, pp.137-55.

10. Hymne sur la création, pp.156-68.

11. Hymne, pp.169-71.

12. (half titlepage) Les / funérailles / d'Arabert, / religieux de la Trappe. / Poëme / Traduit de l'Anglois de M. Jerningham, / par M. Peyron. + pp.[174], [175]-191.

The first volume is preceded by a half titlepage: 'Méditations / d'Hervey. / Premiere partie.' Then follows a nice, portrait frontispiece of Hervey (no signatures; caption in the picture giving Hervey's name, title and dates).

The BLC lists a *Méditations d'Hervey* for 1770 (4409.bbb.25; Paris, Lacombe). In spite of what the BLC reports (and Rochedieu too for that matter, p.146), this is not Le Tourneur's translation, but one by Mme Thiroux d'Arconville. The Le Tourneur (with Peyron) translation first appeared in 1771 and completely overshadowed Mme d'Arconville's version. The first edition is for Paris, Le Jay, and was issued in-8° and in-12°, 4 livres and 2 livres 10 sols respectively. See the *Catalogue hebdomadaire*, 8 June 1771, item 6. (Part of this confusion might be due to Quérard who lists the first edition of the Le Tourneur-Peyron version for Paris: Lejay, 1770 and that by Mme Thiroux d'Arconville for 1771; iv.100.)

There were considerably more editions of the *Méditations d'Hervey* than indicated in Rochedieu, as the next entries amply demonstrate. A word of caution: all editions do not have the same contents (e.g. BL 1607/3112: halftitle indicating 1780; no titlepage; one volume only; perhaps incomplete?).

On the verso of the half titlepage of the *Funérailles d'Arabert* in the edition described here, there is an 'Avertissement' in which the adaptor draws a parallel between Jerningham's piece and d'Arnaud's famous play, *Les Amants malheureux, ou le comte de Comminges*, pointing out Jerningham's debt to d'Arnaud.

As for the *Méditations* proper: Le Tourneur followed fairly closely the modus operandi he had adopted for his celebrated version of Young's *Night thoughts*. As he explains: 'On trouvera que j'ai beaucoup abrégé les *Tombeaux*, si on en juge sur l'original, ou même sur une traduction [Mme Thiroux d'Arconville's] qui a précédé la mienne. Je suis loin de vouloir rabaisser son mérite; mais je ne l'ai point imitée dans les emprunts qu'elle a faits des *Nuits*, dans les morceaux qu'elle a ajoutés d'imagination, & dans les longueurs qu'elle a laissé subsister. A quoi bon réimprimer de nouveau un nombre de lieux communs bien mieux exprimés dans *Young*' (i.70-71).

There were many editions of this work. (See below for several more.) The above described copy seems to match BN R.19715-16. BN R.19717-18 is an octavo, 1771 Le Jay edition. (I am grateful to Professor François Moureau for his kind reply to my queries.)

Incipits: (*Les Tombeaux*) 'Je voyageois sans affaires dans la Province de Cornouaille'.

(*Les Funérailles d'Arabert*) 'La belle Léonore, conduite par la douleur, cherche les demeures souterraines & sombres consacrées à la mort.'

147

Hervey *et al.* (Le Tourneur *et al.* transl.): *Méditations d'Hervey*, 1771

James Hervey (1714-1758), Edward Jerningham (1737-1812), Thomas Gray (1716-1771) *et al.*, translated by Pierre Prime Félicien Le Tourneur (1737-1788) and Jean François Peyron (1748-1784): Méditations / d'Hervey, / traduites de l'anglois, / Par M. Le Tourneur. / Premiere [seconde] partie. / [composite wood-cut decoration with a funny little bust, 'à la romaine', in the centre, and rose hanging at the bottom; same for both volumes] / A Paris, / Chez Le Jay, Libraire, rue Saint Jacques, / au-dessus de celle des Mathurins, / au grand Corneille. / [rule] / M. DCC. LXXI. / Avec Approbation & Permission.

12°, i: 2 ff. (halftitle and titlepage) + [5]-156 pp.
  ii: 2 ff. (halftitle and titlepage) + [5]-202 pp.

Commentary: There are half titlepages for 'Méditations / d'Hervey. / Premiere [seconde] partie.' The *Funérailles d'Arabert* occupy ii.[192], [193]-202, with the same information on the half titlepage (p.[191]) as given in the preceding entry (different type). In spite of the information given on the titlepage, these volumes were not printed by the firm of Le Jay, or, in every likelihood, even in Paris for that matter.

The only complete copies of this edition I could find are in the collections of the University of Texas at Austin and in the BL (1607/4359), assuming both copies be identical. The second part of this book exists in the BN (R.58487), without the half titlepage. (My thanks go to Professor François Moureau who was kind enough to supply me with detailed bibliographical information and appropriate photocopies concerning the BN copy.) For further information, see the preceding entry.

Incipits: (*Les Tombeaux*) 'Je voyageois sans affaires dans la Province de Cornouaille'.

(*Les Funérailles d'Arabert*) 'La belle Léonore, conduite par la douleur, cherche les demeures souterraines & sombres consacrées à la mort.'

148

Hervey *et al.* (Le Tourneur *et al.* transl.): *Méditations d'Hervey*, 1771

James Hervey (1714-1758), Edward Jerningham (1737-1812), Thomas Gray (1716-1771) *et al.*, translated by Pierre Prime Félicien Le Tourneur (1737-1788) and Jean François Peyron (1748-1784): Méditations / d'Hervey, / traduites de l'anglois, / Par M. Le Tourneur. / Première [Seconde] partie. / [woodcut ornament of a cock crowing over two books, hourglass to the right, signed 'Neveu'] / A Amsterdam. / [rule] / M. DCC. LXXI.

12°, i: 2 ff. (halftitle and titlepage) + [5]-59, 60-256 [for 156] pp.
  ii: 2 ff. (halftitle and titlepage) + [5]-189 + [193]-212 pp.

Commentary: The pagination reflects:

1. a 'Vie d'Hervey, Recteur ou Curé des deux Villages dans la Province de Northampton';

2. the same contents as the first entry for vol. i of the *Méditations*, including Gray's *Elegy* (i.150-256 [for 156]; 'Gray' is spelled 'Cray');

3. again the same contents (vol. ii) as per the first entry above, including (halftitle) 'Les / funérailles / d'Arabert, / religieux de la Trappe, / poëme / Traduit de l'Anglais de M. Jerningham, / par M. Peyron.', the 'Avertissement' verso, and then the prose-poem (ii.[193]-212);

There are volume halftitles as follows: 'Méditations / d'Hervey, / première [seconde] partie.'

I could find no trace of this edition anywhere. (I have two copies.) Although most of the material contained in these two volumes might be considered quite marginal to the 'genre romanesque', the French prose translation of Jerningham's poem is definitely narrative fiction. For further information, see the first entry for Hervey.

Incipits: (*Les Tombeaux d'Hervey*) 'Je voyageois sans affaires, dans la Province de Cornouaille: ma route me conduisit dans un de ses Villages les plus peuplés, & je m'y arrêtai.'

(*Les Funérailles d'Arabert*) 'La belle Léonore, conduite par la douleur, cherche les demeures souterraines & sombres consacrées à la mort.'

149

Hervey *et al.* (Le Tourneur *et al.* transl.): *Méditations d'Hervey*, 1781

James Hervey (1714-1758), Edward Jerningham (1737-1812), Thomas Gray (1716-1771) *et al.*, translated by Pierre Prime Félicien Le Tourneur (1737-1788) and Jean François Peyron (1748-1784): Méditations / d'Hervey. / Traduites de l'anglois, / Par M. Le Tourneur. / Premiere partie. / [woodcut decoration, Le Jay's device with the slogan taken from Corneille: 'Je ne dois qu'à moi seul toute ma renommée'] / A Paris, / Chez Le Jay, Libraire, rue S. Jacques, / au-dessus de celle des Mathurins, / au grand Corneille. / [rule] / M. DCC. LXXXI. / Avec Approbation & Permission.

12°, i: 2 pl + [1]-72, [73]-202 pp.
  ii: [1]-246 + [249]-274 pp.

Commentary: Vol. i has a halftitle for 'Méditations / d'Hervey. / Premiere partie.' There is no titlepage (or halftitle) for vol. ii. The pieces contained in these volumes are the same as those to be found in the first edition of this collection listed above, including Gray's *Elegy* (i.[193]-202; 'Gray' is spelled 'Cray'). The main item of prose fiction here is Jerningham's *Les Funérailles d'Arabert*, with a halftitle as follows: 'Les / funérailles / d'Arabert, / religieux de la Trappe. / Poëme / Traduit de l'Anglois de M. Jerningham, / par M. Peyron.' (with the 'Avertissement' verso), ii.[249]-274.

The only trace I could find of this edition (assuming it be the same) is an entry in the NUC (University of Minnesota). For further information, see the first entry for the *Médidations d'Hervey* above.

Incipits: (*Les Tombeaux d'Hervey*) 'Je voyageois sans affaires dans la Province de Cornouaille: ma route me conduisit dans un de ses Villages les plus peuplés, & je m'y arrêtai.'

(*Les Funérailles d'Arabert*) 'La belle Léonore, conduite par la douleur cherche les demeures souterraines & sombres consacrées à la mort.'

150

Hervey *et al.* (Le Tourneur *et al.* transl.): *Tombeaux et méditations d'Hervey*, 1792

James Hervey (1714-1758), Edward Jerningham (1737-1812), Thomas Gray (1716-1771), *et al.*, translated by Pierre Prime Félicien Le Tourneur (1737-1788) and Jean François Peyron (1748-1784): Tombeaux / et méditations / d'Hervey, / suivis / des Funérailles d'Arabert, / et autres pièces du même genre; / Traduits de l'anglois par Letourneur. / [rule] / Tome premier [second]. / [rule] / A Paris, / Chez Favre, Libraire, Maison- / Egalité, Galeries-de-bois, N°. 220. / [double rule] / 1792.

18°, i: 2 pl + [1]-216 pp. + 1 f. (1 p.)

ii: 2 pl + [1]-208, [209]-210 pp. + 1? ff., 2? pp.

Commentary: These volumes contain largely the same pieces as the volumes described in the preceding entries, but in a different order. There are a couple of signature errors. I have found no trace of the edition described here anywhere. The only possibility – and a rather vague one at that – seems to be the following mention in Monglond: 'Méditations sur les Tombeaux, traduits de l'anglais par Le Tourneur et Peyron. Nouv. éd. 2 vol. in-12' (for 1792; ii, cols.693-94). There are two engravings in the volumes described here, a portrait frontispiece for i and a fine quality frontispiece for ii. The last page of vol. i is a table. The last set of pages in vol. ii is also a table, but the second leaf is missing; ergo the question marks. For further information concerning this collection, see the first entry for Hervey above.

Incipits: (i.[71]-154, *Les Tombeaux d'Hervey*) 'Je voyageois sans affaires dans la province de Cornouaille: ma route me conduisit dans un de ses villages les plus peuplés, et je m'y arrêtai.'

(i.[193]-216, *Les Funérailles d'Arabert*) 'La belle Léonore, conduite par la douleur, cherche les demeures souterraines et sombres consacrées à la mort.'

151

Hervey *et al.* (Le Tourneur *et al.* transl.): *Méditations d'Hervey*, 1792 or 1793

James Hervey (1714-1758), Edward Jerningham (1737-1812), Thomas Gray (1716-1771) *et al.*, translated by Pierre Prime Félicien Le Tourneur (1737-1788) and Jean François Peyron (1748-1784): Les tombeaux / et / les méditations / d'Hervey, / précédés de sa vie; / Traduit de l'Anglois / Par M. Le Tourneur [Letourneur for ii]. / Plurima mortis imago. Virg. / [rule] / Premiere [Seconde] partie. / [rule] / [small, symmetrical woodcut ornament, different for each volume] / A Paris, / De l'Imprimerie des Freres-Amis, rue des / Hommes-Libres, [rue / des Hommes-Libres, for ii] à l'Égalité [Egalité for ii]. / [double rule] / L'an 4ᵐᵉ. de la Liberté, & le premier de la / République Française.

18°, i: 1 f. (titlepage) + [3]-62, [63]-151, [152] pp.
     ii: 1 pl + [153]-325, 326-342 pp.

Commentary: The pagination reflects:
    1. a *Vie d'Hervey*;
    2. *Les Tombeaux d'Hervey*;
    3. one page of advertisements for books available at Cailleau's, with prices;
    4. the second part of the *Méditations d'Hervey* (beginning vol. ii), and other pieces;
    5. the *Funérailles d'Arabert, religieux de La Trappe*.
Gray's *Elegy* is also included with this collection (i.145-51; 'Gray' is again spelled 'Cray').

This edition comprises a rare example of a work bearing the mention of the first year of the republic on the titlepage, antedating the decree which created the revolutionary calendar (5 October 1793 or 14 vendémiaire an II).

I could find no trace of this edition anywhere. For further information concerning the contents of these volumes, see the first entry for Hervey above.

Incipits (*Les Tombeaux d'Hervey*) 'Je voyageois sans affaires dans la Province de Cornouaille: ma route me conduisit dans un de ses Villages les plus peuplés, & je m'y arrêtai.'

(*Les Funérailles d'Arabert*) 'La belle Léonore, conduite par la douleur, cherche les demeures souterraines & sombres consacrées à la mort.'

152

Inchbald (Deschamps transl.): *Simple histoire*, 1791

Elizabeth Simpson Inchbald (1753-1821), translated by Jacques (sometimes Jean) Marie Deschamps (1750?-1826): Simple histoire. / [rule] / Traduction de l'anglois, / de / mistress Inchbald. / Par M. Deschamps. / [rule] / Tome premier [second]. / [rule] / [small symmetrical woodcut decoration, same for both volumes] / A Paris, / Chez les Marchands de Nouveautés. / [rule] / 1791.

8°, i: 1 f. (titlepage) + [iii]-ix + [xj]-xvj + [1]-(247) pp. + 1 f. (1 p.)
     ii: 1 f. (titlepage) + [3]-(295) pp. + 1 f. (1 p.)

Commentary: The preliminary pages in vol. i contain a 'Preface de l'auteur anglois' and the 'Avertissement du traducteur'. (P.[x] is blank.) The final leaves, not part of the last gatherings, contain one page each of errata. At the end of the text, the two volumes described here contain the following colophon: 'De l'Imprimerie de du Pont, hôtel de / Bretonvilliers, isle Saint-Louis.' (Then follow the tipped-in leaves, one per volume, of the errata.)

MMF list as the first edition of the French translation a *similar* title (*Simple histoire, traduite de l'anglais par M. Deschamps*), for Paris: Dupont, 1791, 2 vols in octavo, after a copy that has disappeared from the Bibliothèque de Nantes (91.28). The two other copies listed for 1791 in MMF seem to be amalgams of different editions; both copies, or pertinent photocopies, were examined by the authors (Eleutherian Mills Historical Library and the Helsingin Yliopiston Kirjasto, Helsinki). Helsinki, vol. ii seems to match the vol. ii described here.

Assuming the information in MMF to be exact, I propose the following: first, that the above described volumes represent the first edition of the French version, with the possibility that a duodecimo edition might have been issued simultaneously (vol. i in the Eleutherian Mills Historical Library). Second, if the pagination reported in MMF is correct, that there was another octavo edition of vol. i anyway printed for the 'marchands de nouveautés' in Paris, 1791 (Helsinki). Third, that there was yet another edition for Paris, Buisson, 1791, 12° (Eleutherian Mills H. L., vol. ii). Fourth, depending here on the accuracy of the Nantes Library catalogue, that a certain number of the copies of the first edition were reserved for Du Pont, and carried Du Pont's titlepages, unless the Nantes Library catalogue reports the printer instead of the publisher, which seems most unlikely.

Monglond also lists Paris, Dupont, 2 vols in-8, after the *Mercure*, 28 January 1792, pp.91-99 (ii, col.364). And, from the information reported in the *Mercure français*, it would seem that some copies not only carried 'les marchands de nouveautés' as listed here, but Dupont's name *and* 'marchands de nouveautés': 'Simple Histoire, Traduction de l'Anglais de Mistress Inchbald, par M. Deschamps. A Paris, chez Dupont, Libr. rue de Richelieu, N°. 14; & chez les Marchands de Nouveautés. 2 Vol. in-8°. Prix, 4 liv.' (28 January 1792, p.91). The article is highly favorable; by a 'M. G... de l'Académie Française, l'Auteur & le Traducteur de ce Roman ayant désiré qu'il se chargeât d'en rendre compte dans le *Mercure*' (a 'nota', p.99). Thus it would appear a good possibility that Deschamps and Inchbald were acquainted.

The 'Avertissement du traducteur' mentions that two successive editions in England attest to the beauties of Inchbald's novel. After praise of the novelist's style, Deschamps goes on to say that the 'simple histoire' isn't that simple, and that he has limited himself to the first story, with certain modifications explained in the notes. The translation was continued; see MMF 92.18 and 00.26, and Monglond ii, cols.705-06; v, col. 346. The first 'suite' is titled *Lady Mathilde* and comprises a true sequel to *Simple histoire*. The second is anonymous, *Mistress Walter, ou nouvelle et dernière suite de 'Simple histoire'*, par Madame de S*** [Monglond].

In passing I note that Rochedieu gives yet a third title variant in his listing of the first edition: *Simple histoire, roman traduit de l'anglois* (Paris, 1791, 2 vols in-octavo; no publisher recorded).

Incipit: 'Dorriforth avoit reçu au collége de Saint-Omer, une éducation aussi sévère que l'est elle-même la règle de cette maison'.

153

Johnson (Belot transl.): *Rasselas, prince d'Abyssinie*, 1797

Samuel Johnson (1709-1784), translated by Octavie Guichard du Rey de Mey-nières, dame Belot: Rasselas, / prince d'Abyssinie. / Ouvrage / traduit de l'anglais, / du célebre / Samuel Johnson. / Tome premier [second]. / [swell rule] / A Paris, / Chez J. Baillio, Imprimeur-Libraire, / Vieille rue du Temple, N° 76. / [double rule] / An V de la république.

18°, i: 1 f. (titlepage) + [5]-178 pp.
ii: 1 f. (titlepage) + [5]-165 pp.

Commentary: This edition is not listed in MMF (60.19), and I could find no other copy of it. Note that the first pages are [5]-6 for each volume. A leaf seems to be missing in each case, I assume a halftitle, perhaps for some sort of collection? No further evidence is available from the volumes as extant (contemporary, pretty calf, usual gilt ornaments). There are no catchtomes, extra leaves, discernable cancels, and so on. (For an example of blank leaves used as endpapers, yet still part of the printed book, see d'Aulnoy, *Histoire d'Hypolite*.)

This work first appeared in the original as *The Prince of Abissinia* (1759).

Incipit: 'Que ceux qui se laissent séduire / par les prestiges de l'imagination; / qui poursuivent'.

154

Kimber: *Mariane*, 1780

Edward Kimber (1719-1769); for the translator, see the commentary: Mariane / ou / la nouvelle / Pamela. / Histoire veritable / traduite de l'anglois, / Enrichie de Figures en taille douce. / Nouvelle edition. / Tome premier [second]. / [composite, symmetrical woodcut decoration, same for both volumes] / A Leide, / Chez Les freres Murray, / M. DCC. LXXX.

8°, i: 2 pl + 2 ff. (2 + 2 pp.) + [1]-266 pp.
ii: 2 pl + 1 f. (2 pp.) + [1]-266 pp.

Commentary: It is possible to see in the present copy – original marbled wrappers, untrimmed – that the half titlepages and titlepages are conjugate. The half titlepages bear 'Mariane / ou / la nouvelle / Pamela.'

This is a translation of *Maria: the genuine memoirs of a young lady of rank and fortune* (1764). MMF list two different translations (65.27, 65.28; translators unknown) and note that subsequent editions seem to follow that of 65.28, in spite of the title changes. See too Rochedieu, p.177. No prefatory material is mentioned for 65.27. In 65.28, the authors mention an 'Avertissement', which does not appear with the above edition. But there is a two-page 'Préface' which opens with: 'Le lecteur ne doit s'attendre à rien d'extraordinaire, à rien de merveilleux. Des faits constatés, dont les témoins respectables, & les acteurs vivent encore, une narration simple & naturelle, c'est tout ce qu'offrent ces Mémoires'. And 'Puissent la bienveillance, la droiture, la patience, la résignation dont ces Mémoires offrent de si beaux modeles, passer dans l'ame des jeunes personnes qui les liront?' I do not know which translation the above is: perhaps a new one? (It does not, however, follow the additional, BL edition listed at the end of this commentary.) In any case, this edition is a toned down version of the often harshly expressed original. (The third and fourth preliminary pages in vol. i and the two in ii are tables.)

I have found no trace of the above edition anywhere. I note in passing that, if one can place any faith in the plurality of the editions, the French version was more popular than the English original, probably because the translator made a deliberate attempt to avoid wounding the delicate sensibility or notion of 'bienséance' (in the sense of 'propriety') of his readers. Each volume contains two rather pleasant, albeit conventional engravings by J. V. Schley, with captions.

To editions of *La Nouvelle Paméla* listed in MMF (assuming the pagination they record in 65.28 is correct), I would add: *Maria, ou les véritables mémoires d'une dame illustre par son mérite, son rang & sa fortune. Traduits de l'anglois.* Londres; Paris: chez Bauche, L. Cellot, 1765. 2 vols in-12°: 2 ff. (halftitle and titlepage) + 5-6, 7-8, 9-256 pp. and 2 ff. (halftitle and titlepage) + 5-246 pp. (BL: 1606/609). The first two items in vol. i are the 'Préface de l'auteur' and an 'Avertissement du traducteur'. A 'nota bene' p.8 begins with: 'Comme on achevoit l'impression de cet Ouvrage, on m'en apporta une traduction presque littérale, qui vient d'être faite à *Rotterdam*, sous le titre de Marianne, ou la Nouvelle Paméla. Les Lecteurs curieux de comparer les deux versions, seront à portée de le faire, & de décider de leur mérite', etc. Thus it seems highly likely that this edition follows the anonymous translation listed by MMF (65.28).

Incipit: 'Le bienfaisant Mr. *Worthy*, / homme puissamment riche / & d'un cœur au dessus de / la fortune, avoit passé quel- / ques heures agréables chez / son intime ami Mr. *Welldone*'.

155

La Beaumelle: *L'Asiatique tolérant*, 1779

Laurent Angliviel de La Beaumelle (1726-1773): L'Asiatique / tolérant. / Traité a l'usage / de / Zéokinizul, roi des Kofirans, / surnommé le chéri. / Ouvrage traduit de l'Arabe du Voyageur / Bekrinoll. / Par M^r. de ****. / [rule] / J'excuse les erreurs & non les cruautés. / [rule] / [small symmetrical composite ornament] / A Londres. / [double rule: thick, thin] / M. DCC. LXXIX.

12°: 1 pl + [j]-xxiij + [1]-124, (125)-(130) pp.

Commentary: This book contains a dedication 'A madame la comtesse de B**' (pp.[j]-ij); a 'Préface assez nécessaire' (p.iij-xiv); a satirical approbation (p.[xv]); a satirical privilege (p.xvj-xvij); a 'Lettre a Zeokinizul. Roi des Kofirans' (pp.(xviij)-xxj, signed 'Bekrinoll'); 'Plan de cet ouvrage' (pp.xxij-xxiij); the novel, with a 'Clef des noms Contenus dans cet Ouvrage' at the end (pp.(125)-(130)).

I could find no trace of this edition: it is not listed by MMF (55.R40) or Jones (1748, pp.97-98).

Drujon reproduces a key, and only lists editions for 1748, 1755 and 1799 (i, cols.91-93).

This volume was certainly not produced in London. It was probably produced in a Germanic country, and by the same firm that did *Les Amours de Zéokinizul*. See that entry above, under anonyms. In any case, both works deal with the life, loves and reign of Louis XV.

Quérard, *Supercheries*, states that there were two editions for 1748, and gives the pagination (i, col.498e). The same source states that the first edition is a duodecimo and implies that the other 1748 one is also. Tchemerzine, under Crébillon fils, gives yet different pagination for the first edition and claims it is an octavo. (Tchemerzine is often erroneous concerning formats.) He includes a photo-reproduction of the titlepage (iv.194, fig. 1).

Incipit: 'Ristkesusi n'a fondé son / Empire, que pour unir les / hommes'.

156

La Bruyère *et al.*: *Les Caractères de Théophraste*, 1724

Jean de La Bruyère (1645-1696), Theophrastus (370 B.C.?-287 B.C.?) translated by La Bruyère and Pierre Jacques Brillon (probably; see the commentary; dates: 1671-1736): (titlepages in *red* and black) Les / *caracteres* / de Theophraste / traduits du grec, / avec / *les caracteres* / ou / *les mœurs* / de ce siécle. / *Par Mr de la Bruyere de l'Academie* / *Françoise*. / Et la clef, / *En marge &* / *Par ordre Alphabétique*. / Tome premier [second]. / *Nouvelle Edition Augmentée*. / [small, symmetrical woodcut ornament, same for i and ii] / *A Paris,* / Chez *Estienne Michalet,* premier / Imprimeur du Roy, ruë saint Jacques. / [rule] / *M. DCC. XXIV.* / Avec Privilége de Sa Majesté.

(half titlepage in *red* and black for vol. iii) *Suite* / des / *caracteres* / de / *Theophraste,* / et des / *pensées* / de / *Mr Pascal*. / Tome troisie'me.

12°, i: 1 pl + 3 ff. (4 + 2 pp.) + 1-466 pp. + 5 ff. (9 pp.)
ii: 1 pl + 1 f. (2 pp.) + 1-163, [164] pp.
iii: 1 pl + 3 ff. (5 + 1 pp.) + 1-272 pp.

Commentary: The titlepage to vol. i is f.[ã1]; that to ii, f.[A1]. Vol. iii's halftitle is f.[ã1].

These volumes contain:

i: 1. *Eloge de M. de La Bruyère* (4 pp.);
2. 'table', vol. i;
3. *Discours sur Théophraste*, pp.1-24;
4. *Les Caractères de Théophraste traduits du grec*, pp.25-65;
5. a halftitle (curiously on the verso), 'Les / caracteres / ou / les mœurs / de ce siecle. / Admonere voluimus [...] / Erasm...' (p.[96]), *Les Caractères* proper, pp.97-466;
6. 'Clef des *Caractères de ce siècle* par ordre alphabétique', 9 pp.
ii: 1. 'Clef des *Caractères de ce siècle* par ordre alphabétique', 2 pp.;

2. the continuation of *Les Caractères*, pp.1-126;

3. halftitle for 'Discours / prononcé / dans / l'academie / françoise.', and the *Discours*, pp.129-46, 147-63. (The pagination includes a preface.);

4. a 'table', p.[164].

iii: 1. an 'Avertissement', 5 pp.;

2. a 'table', 1 p.;

3. *Ouvrage nouveau dans le goût des Caracteres de Theophraste, et des Pensées de Pascal* (according to the headtitle; the running title is for the 'Suite des Caracteres / de Theophraste.') pp.1-272.

The collection described here might be considered marginal to the 'genre romanesque'. But, because of the rarity of this edition and since it contains fictitious portraits, I have chosen to include it.

The first edition of the *Caractères* dates to 1688 (Paris, Michallet). There were various revised and augmented editions. See Julien Benda ed., La Bruyère, *Œuvres complètes* (Paris, 'Pléiade', 1951; 1962), pp.x-xvii and especially G. Servois ed., the *Œuvres* (Paris 1865-1878), 3 vols (and one volume of an 'album'), iii.130-56. (Also listed in Conlon, i.491, no. 3940.) The first edition to have carried some sort of key seems to have appeared right in 1688 (Servois, p.139, no. 1 bis).

The edition listed here is not recorded by Servois, or by Benda in his 'Bibliographie: éditions principales des *Œuvres* de La Bruyère' (pp.[731]-733). Nor is a copy of it listed in the BNC, BLC, NUC, etc. The only mention I could find of this 1724 edition – assuming, and only assuming, it refers to the same one – is hidden away in the 'avertissement' to Adrien Destailleur's edition of the *Caractères*. He writes: 'Les presses de Hollande continuèrent d'exploiter le livre. Les frères Wetsteins [*sic*], d'Amsterdam, produisirent, en 1720, une édition véritable, en trois volumes, dont le premier contient l'ouvrage de La Bruyère, les deux autres des *Suites*, la *Défense des Caractères*, par Coste, et la *clef*, avec des notes explicatives. Cette édition n'empêcha pas une contrefaçon de paroître encore en Hollande, l'année 1724, sous le nom d'Etienne Michallet. Elle est en trois volumes, et dans le dernier se trouve la *Suite des Caractères et des Pensées de Pascal*, que Michallet n'imprima jamais' (Paris 1854, i.xviij-xix).

Concerning the third volume: the contents are not by La Bruyère. The 'Avertissement' quite clearly indicates that the anonymous composer wished to imitate both Pascal and La Bruyère: 'Il est hazardeux d'entreprendre d'écrire comme les Pascals & les La Bruyeres. Il est impossible d'attraper l'air de leur stile, leur élevation & leur netteté: A qui dit-on cela? Plus j'ai lû leurs Ouvrages, plus je me suis défié de mes forces, il a falu l'autorité d'une personne connuë & éclairée pour me fixer au titre que j'ai choisi. Sans la crainte d'éfraïer les Lecteurs, je n'aurois pas manqué de l'illustrer encore du nom de Mr de Saint-Evremond, & du P. Rapin. La plûpart des aplications que je fais, mes remarques sur Tacite, mon Traité de la Comedie, quelques autres Chapitres, entrent assez dans leur maniere d'écrire. [...] Pourquoi s'est-on servi du titre de *Diversitez*, *d'Œuvres mêlées*, &c. Je ne puis plus choisir, c'est ma faute d'être venu un peu tard, & de composer peut-être de trop bonne heure', and so on. The work itself is by no means lacking in interest, containing sections on women (pp.119-36),

'Les auteurs' (pp.144-61), 'Le Procès' (pp.208-16), 'Le Pour et le contre de la comédie' (pp.226-55), etc.

Who was the author? Servois states that Brillon composed this work and gives solid reasons for his attribution (iii.182-83, no. 20). It first appeared in 1697, and was often republished with the *Caractères*. Barbier also attributes it to Brillon (iii, col.755c-d). For reasons perhaps best known only to himself, Quérard attributes this work to Guillaume Amable Valleyre (Paris 1698; x.29), in spite of what he indicates under La Bruyère's name. This work is entirely different from the *Suite des caractères de Théophraste et des mœurs de ce siècle*, which first appeared in 1700. See Barbier, iv, col.577d and especially Servois, iii.184-87, no. 25 for attibution(s) and a discussion of contents and significance.

Incipits: ('Des ouvrages de l'esprit' from La Bruyère's own *Caractères*) 'Tout est dit, & l'on vient trop tard depuis plus de sept mille ans'.

('*Ouvrage nouveau...*, 'L'Homme') 'L'Homme ne se peut définir au juste.'

157

La Bruyère *et al.*: *Les Caractères de Théophraste*, 1741

Jean de La Bruyère (1645-1696), Theophrastus (370 B.C.?-287 B.C.?) translated by La Bruyère, and edited with additions by Pierre Coste (1668-1747): (titlepages in *red* and black) Les / *caracteres* / de / *Theophraste*, / Avec les Caractéres ou les Mœurs / de ce Siécle, / *Par M. de la Bruyere*. / Nouvelle Edition augmentée de la Défense / de M. de la Bruyere, & de ses / Caractéres. / *Par M. Coste*. / Tome premier [second]. / [woodcut decoration, different for each volume] / *A Amsterdam*, / Chez *F. Changuion*, / 1741.

12°, i: 1 f. (titlepage) + 2 ff. (4 pp.) + 1 f. (2 pp.) + 1-48 + 1-32, 33-487 pp.

ii: 1 pl + 1 f. (2 pp.) + 1-318 + halftitle leaf + 321-364 + halftitle leaf + 367-571, 572-580 pp.

Commentary: Vol. i contains the titlepage; an 'Avertissement Sur cette Nouvelle Edition' (4 pp.); a two-page table; a 'Clef des caracteres de la Bruyere' (pp.1-48); the 'Discours sur Theophraste' (pp.1-32); the first part of the work. Vol. ii contains the titlepage; a two-page table; continuation of the work. The first halftitle in vol. ii (p.[319]) is the 'Discours / prononce' / dans l'academie / françoise. / O4 Pre'face [signature and catchword]'; then follows the work. The second halftitle (p.[365]) reads: 'Défense / de M. / de la Bruyere / et de ses / caracteres, / Contre les Accusations, & les Objections de / M. de Vigneul-Marville, / Par M. Coste. / Troisiéme Edition revûë & corrigée / par l'Auteur. / Q3 [signature]'; then follows that work. The last set of pages in vol. ii represents the 'table' (index) to the *Défense*.

Although the general titlepage description and the pagination are the same, these books differ markedly from BN R.18848-49. The incipit to vol. ii is the easiest way to differentiate between the two.

BN: 'Ne nous emportons point / contre les hommes en / voyant leur dureté, leur / ingratitude, leur injustice, / leur fierté, l'amour d'eux-mêmes, & / l'oubli'.

Dawson: 'Ne nous emportons point con- / tre les hommes en voyans [*sic*] / leur dureté, leur ingratitu- / de, leur injustice, leur fier- / té, l'amour d'eux-mêmes, & l'ou- / bli'.

As for vol. i: BN the first page of the 'clef' is paginated '1'; Dawson, 'Page 1'.

Servois, in the commentary on the Amsterdam: Changuion, 1739 edition mentions 'Autres éditions du même libraire: 1741, Amsterdam, 2 vol. in-12; 1741, 2 vol. in-12 (différant de la précédente de même date)' (iii.158, no. 37). Since there is no way of telling whether he is referring to the two editions discussed here ('BN' and 'Dawson'), I have chosen to include this item in the present bibliography.

For further information, see the other La Bruyère entry in this bibliography.

Incipits: ('De la dissimulation', from Theophrastus' *Characters*) 'La(a) dissimu- lation n'est pas ai- / sée à bien définir'. (A note explains the precise significance of 'dissimulation').

('Des ouvrages de l'esprit' from La Bruyère's own *Caractères*) 'Tout est dit, & l'on vient trop / tard depuis plus de sept mille ans'.

158

La Fontaine: *Les Amours de Psyché et de Cupidon*, 1793

Jean de La Fontaine (1621-1695): Les amours / de Psyché / et / de Cupidon, / Par J. de Lafontaine. / Édition conforme à celle de 1768, / et ornée de 4 figures, d'après le / tableau de M. Schall. / [short swell rule] / A Paris, / Chez Lepetit, Libraire, quai / des Augustins, n°. 32. / [double rule] / 1793.

18°: 1 f. (titlepage with advert verso) + [iij]-xij + [1]-240 pp.

Commentary: This edition is not listed in MMF (58.R31) and is also not listed in count René Rochambeau, *Bibliographie des œuvres de La Fontaine* (Paris 1911). The only trace I have been able to find of this edition is an entry in Reynaud, if indeed it is the same: 'Paris, Lepetit, 1793. 2 vol. in-18' (col.288). He mentions that 'cette rare petite édition imprimée sur papier médiocre est ornée de 4 charmantes figures fort bien gravées d'après Schall par un artiste qui ne les a pas signées'. My book does contain four pretty plates, numbered and captioned. Yet my book is quite complete in one volume. But perhaps there was another edition in two volumes for Paris: Lepetit, 1793? The advertisement at the end of d'Arnaud's *Loisirs utiles* (described above) indicates: 'Amours (les) de Psyché et Cupidon, 2 vol. in-18, fig.'.

Pages [iij]-xij are a preface. The advertisement on the verso of the titlepage, 'On trouve chez le même libraire', presents several items of considerable interest.

1. *Lucie et Mélanie* by d'Arnaud, in-18, 4 fig. MMF (67.17) list a Paris: Lepetit, 1792 edition, followed by *Clary* after the *Journal de Paris* and Quérard.

2. *Nauly* [*sic*] *et Anne Bell* by d'Arnaud, in-18, 4 fig. MMF (67.18) list a *Nancy* for 'Hambourg, 1792, in-8' after the *Feuille de correspondance du libraire*. Under *Anne Bell* they list a Hambourg, 1792, in-18 edition after the same source (69.12).

3. *L'Arcadie* by Bernardin de Saint-Pierre, in-18, 2 fig. This edition is not listed in MMF (88.101).

4. *La Nouvelle Sapho*, anonymous, in-18, 6 figs. There is no Lepetit or Fauche edition listed in MMF (89.2).

5. *Lettres galantes de deux nones*, in-18, 4 figs. This is surely the *Lettres galantes et philosophiques de deux nonnes, publiées par un apôtre du libertinage, avec des notes* (Paris, l'an IIe; Cohen col.642). MMF (77.2) list a 'Paris, an II, in-18' edition after Cohen, Gay and Tricotel (nineteenth-century ms catalogue in the BL). For further information concerning the d'Arnaud items, see the commentary on his *Epreuves du sentiment*, 1789.

La Fontaine's *Psyché et Cupidon* first appeared in 1669.

Incipit: 'Quatre amis, dont la connoissance / avoit commencée par le Parnasse, liè- / rent une espèce de société'.

159

Lambert: *Œuvres*, 1758

Anne Thérèse de Marguenat de Courcelles, marquise de Lambert (1647-1733): Œuvres / de madame / la marquise / de Lambert, / nouvelle edition / augmentée / [fairly extensive composite ornament surmounted by funny little head; sun burst in centre] / A Amsterdam, / Par la Compagnie. / [double rule] / M. DCC. LVIII.

12°: 1 f. (titlepage) + [iij]-xvj + [1]-427 pp.

Commentary: The preliminaries comprise an 'Avertissement' (pp.[iij]-vj); 'Abregé de la vie de mad. la marquise de Lambert' (pp.vij-xiv, 'Tirée du Mercure de France du mois d'Août 1733'); a 'Table...' (pp.xv-xvj). This work contains Mme de Lambert's tale, *La Femme hermite. Nouvelle nouvelle*, pp.279-360.

MMF (51.R28) and Jones (1747, p.95) list no such edition of Mme de Lambert's *Œuvres*. The only trace of it I could find, assuming it be the same, is that listed in OCLC (Cornell University).

Incipit: (*La Femme hermite*) 'Adelaïde & ses Amies, qui / étoient venues voir Bellamirte / à sa Campagne'.

160

La Roche-Guilhen: *Histoire des favorites*, ca.1700

Anne de La Roche-Guilhen (or La Roche-Guilhem; 1644-1707): (*red* and black titlepages) *Histoire* / des / *favorites*, / contenant ce qui s'est / passé de plus remarqua- ble / sous / *plusieurs regnes*, / Par Mademoiselle D***. / *Premiere* [*Second*] *partie*. / [woodcut ornaments, i: two pigeons drinking from goblet in a decorative medal- lion; ii: upside-down shield with three rows of decorations, six in all] / Imprimé / *a Constantinople* / cette Année presente.

12°, i: 1 pl + 1 f. (2 pp.) + 1-205, [206] pp.
  ii: 1 pl + 1 f. (2 pp.) + 1-229, [230] pp.

Commentary: There were various editions of this popular collection for the end of the seventeenth century / beginning of the eighteenth. My copy differs from all those I have seen, especially BN (G.28574) and Arsenal (8vo B.L.17688). It would appear that the above edition is copied from the BN edition, or vice-versa. This work first appeared in 1697 according to Lever (p.201) and to Conlon (ii.348, no.8230).

There are eight engravings in my copy of poor quality, plus a frontispiece. The illustrations are numbered I-VIII, and the frontispiece bears 'Histoire des favorites'. The engravings, although in order, do not all match the stories they are supposed to illustrate. What seems to be the case in the present copy is that the engravings to the nineth and tenth tales are missing. The binder forgot to put no. IV with tale no. 4, so the rest of the engravings are out of order by one story. (Possibly, though, there were only eight numbered engravings issued.) The contents of the different editions of this collection vary. The above copy contains the following (transcribed according to the head titles):

1. *Marie de Padille sous Pierre le Cruel, Roi de Castille*, i.1-54;
2. *Leonor Tellez de Menese, sous Ferdinand Roi de Portugal*, i.55-97;
3. *Agnez Soreau, sous Charles VII. Roi de France*, i.99-158;
4. *Julie Farnese, sous Alexandre VI. Pontife de Rome*, i.159-205;
5. *Roxelane sous Soliman II. Empereur des Turcs*, ii.1-56;
6. *Marie de Beauvilliers Abbesse de Montmartre, sous Henri IV. Roi de France*, ii.57-88;
7. *Livie sous l'empereur Auguste*, ii.89-146;
8. *Fredegonde sous Chilperic, Roy de France*, ii.147-72;
9. *Nantilde sous Dagobert Roy de France*, ii.173-200;
10. *Marozie sous plusieurs papes*, ii.201-29.

The 'Table' for i erroneously reports p.519 for the last tale; it should read 159. This edition dates to ca. 1700, although quite possibly to a few years earlier.

For a brief outline of the contents of each tale, see Alexandre Calame, *Anne de La Roche-Guilhen, romancière huguenote: 1644-1707* (Geneva 1972), pp.60-65. Calame points out that two additional tales were added to a 1703 edition (a 'nouv. éd. rev., cor. & augm. de deux nouvelles histoires: divisée en deux parties'; Yale, source: OCLC), namely the *Histoire d'Hercilie* and that of *Arsinoé*. Two others, probably not by La Roche-Guilhen, were added in 1714 (*Anne de Bolen* and *Eronime*).

Weller mentions that the [1699] edition was printed in France, which is quite possible here too. Barbier, on the contrary, indicates that the 'Constantinople', 1699 edition was printed in Amsterdam (ii, col.751e). In any case, it is obvious that neither edition was printed in Constantinople.

The two preliminary pages in each volume are prefaces, each apparently written at a different time. Indeed, the second notice indicates that vol. ii appeared some time after vol. i. But it is not possible to ascertain whether this is true for the above described edition.

Incipit: (*Marie de Padille*) 'Si jamais un homme dût être / détesté pour ses vices, ce fut / Dom Pedre surnommé le Cruel, / Roi de Castille.'

161

La Roche-Guilhen: *Histoire des favorites*, 1708

Anne de La Roche-Guilhen (or La Roche-Guilhem; 1644-1707): (titlepage in *red* and black) *Histoire* / des / *favorites,* / contenant ce qui s'est / passé de plus remarquable / sous / *plusieurs regnes,* / Par Mademoiselle D***. [appears to be D*** for ii] / *Premiere [Seconde] partie.* / [woodcut decorations, i: hand extending from a cloud holding a sphere; ii: just a sphere, but different from vol. i's] / *A Amsterdam,* / Chez *Paul Marret,* dans la Beurs- / straat, près le Dam, à la Renom- mée. / [rule] / *M. DCCVIII.*

12°, i: 1 pl (titlepage) + 1 f. (2 pp.) + 96 [for 1]-206 pp. + 1 f. (1 p.)
   ii: 1 pl (titlepage) + 1 f. (2 pp.) + 1-129 [for 229], [230] pp.

Commentary: The first two pages recorded for each volume are prefaces. The last page recorded for each volume is a table. There is a primitive frontispiece to vol. i bearing 'Histoire / des / favorites' in the centre. These two volumes contain all the tales listed in the previous entry, viz. (according to the head titles):

   1. *Marie de Padille, sous Pierre le Cruel, Roi de Castille,* i.96 [for 1]-54;
   2. *Leonor Tellez de Menese, sous Ferdinand Roi de Portugal,* i.55-97;
   3. *Agnez Soreau, sous Charles VII. Roi de France,* i.99-158;
   4. *Julie Farnese, sous Alexandre VI. Pontife de Rome,* i.159-206;
   5. *Roxelane sous Soliman II. Empereur des Turcs,* ii.1-36 [for 56];
   6. *Marie de Beauvilliers Abbesse de Montmartre, sous Henri IV. Roi de France,* ii.98 [for 57]-88;
   7. *Livie sous l'empereur Auguste,* ii.89-146;
   8. *Fredegonde sous Chilperic, Roy de France,* ii.141 [for 147]-172;
   9. *Nantille [sic] sous Dagobert Roy de France,* ii.173-200;
   10. *Marozie sous plusieurs papes,* ii.201-129 [for 229].

As is obvious, there are numerous pagination errors. Curiously the signatures in volume i are in arabic and those in volume ii are in lower-case roman (barring mistakes in both volumes). Catchwords are printed on every page.

This edition is not mentioned by Lever or Jones and is not listed in the NUC, BLC or BNC, so I have chosen to include it. MMF list a 1708 edition after Quérard (77.R55). Quérard records 'Nouv. édit. Amsterdam, 1700, 1703 et 1708, in-12' (iv.569a). Calame, in the bibliography appended to his study, lists an *Histoire des favorites* for 1708 as follows: 'réédition: Amsterdam, Compagnie, s.d; (1705) et 1708' (Alexandre Calame, *Anne de La Roche-Guilhen, romancière huguenote: 1644-1707,* Geneva 1972, p.93, in no.18). If this be accurate, there was yet another edition for 1708. (I could not find an 'Amsterdam, compagnie' edition for 1708 and suspect that Calame lists after Quérard's inaccurate or, at best, incomplete entry.)

The edition described here seems, however, to exist in the BN (8°Z.Le Senne 13692, with a card in the file entitled 'Auteurs: ouvrages entrés avant 1960 ne figurant pas au catalogue général imprimé'). I was unable to juxtapose my copy with that in the BN.

This collection first appeared in 1697 (Lever and Calame). For further information, see the preceding entry.

Incipit: (*Marie de Padille*) 'Si jamais un homme dût être / détesté pour ses vices, ce fut / Dom Pedre surnommé le Cruel, / Roi de Castille.'

162

La Sale: *Petit Jehan de Saintré*, 1724

Antoine de La Sale (b.1388?), Thomas Simon Gueullette (1683-1766) ed.: L'histoire / et / plaisante cronicque / du petit Jehan / de / Saintre, / De la jeune Dame des Belles Cousines, / sans autre nom nommer. / Avecques deux autres petites Histoires de Messire Floridan / & de la Belle Ellinde, & l'Extrait des / Cronicques de Flandres. / Ouvrage enrichi de Notes critiques, historiques & cro- / nologiques, d'une Préface sur l'origine de la Che- / valerie & des anciens Tournois, & d'un Avertisse- / ment pour l'intelligence de l'Histoire. / Tome I [II, III]. / [woodcut decoration, same for the three volumes] / A Paris, au palais. / Chez Pierre-Jacques Bienvenu, Grand- / Salls [Salle for ii, iii], à la Fortune. / [rule] / MDCCXXIV. / Avec Approbation & Privilege du Roy.

12°, i: 1 pl (titlepage) + 36 ff. (45 + 22 + 5 pp.) + [1]-196 + 1-7 pp.

  ii: 1 pl (titlepage) + [1]-9 + 2 ff. (first blank; second 1 + 1 pp.) + 197-510 pp.

  iii: 1 pl (titlepage) + 511-688, [689]-727 + 72[9]-757 + 11 pp.

Commentary: The first three items in i are an 'Avertissement', a 'Préface', and legal documents. The postliminary pages in i and iii are 'Tables'. ii.[1]-9 are a 'Table', and the next two pages are 'Errata' and an 'Avis au relieur'. Although there are three separate volumes, with three titlepages (bound in three tomes; contemporary calf), signatures and pagination are consecutive for the main body of the text. This piece of prose fiction was first published between 1502 and 1511. See Charles A. Knudson, 'Les anciennes éditions du *Petit Jehan de Saintré*' in *Mélanges de linguistique romane et de philologie médiévale offerts à M. Maurice Delbouille* (Gembloux 1964), ii.337-48.

The *Histoire de messire Floridan & de la belle Ellinde* included with the above edition (iii.[697]-727) is the story of *Floridan et Elvide* by Nicolas de Clemanges (or Clamanges; Nicolaus de Clemangiis) translated from the Latin *De raptoris raptæque virginis lamentabili exitu* into the French by Rasse de Brinchamel or Brunhamel (information largely derived from Knudson and OCLC). But see especially H. P. Clive's *'Floridan et Elvide': a critical edition of the 15th-century text, with an introduction* (Oxford 1959). He posits that La Sale had a hand in reworkings of *Floridan et Elvide* and in the *Extrait des Chroniques de Flandres* (pp.xv, xxv et passim). The tale was also included in the *Cent nouvelles nouvelles*, novella no. 98 (pp.xxiv-xxviii) and in other collections by Masuccio and Malespina.

There were other issues of the edition described here, with different imprints. This does not mean that there were several editions, however. The legal notice after the privilege indicates that the original publisher, Morel, had shared the proceeds with Mouchet, Saugrain Guillaume Huet and Bienvenu, each for a fifth of the whole (20 July 1722). Each then had his name on the particular copies destined for his own trade. This had been a work of extreme rarity, and the publishers hoped to reap a tidy profit from their venture. The original was a copy of the Paris, Philippe Le Noir, 1523 edition (Knudson no. 3), which had cost the publishers the very handsome sum of 180 'livres'. For further information, see Dawson, ii.479-80 and note 128. The above is the only copy of this particular issue that I have been able to find.

I do not know where the *Addicion extraicte des cronicques de Flandres* (iii.72[9]-757) comes from, but 'Anthoine de la Salle's' name appears at the end.

The editor and author of the copious notes and prefatory material is Thomas Simon Gueullette (or Gueulette), largely known today as the author of a long list of fiction, in the 'marvelous' tradition. He is also an important figure in the first stage of the eighteenth-century Gothic revival in France. The approbation is dated 12 May 1722 (Blanchard). The privilege, to Morel, is dated 5 June 1722 (Carpot); registered 21 July 1722 (Delaune).

Incipits: (*Petit Jehan*) 'Ou temps du Roy Jehan de France (a) fils aisné du Roy Philippes de Valois, estoit en sa Court, le Seigneur de Pouilly en Touraine'. (A note gives information about the king.)

(*Histoire de Floridan et Ellinde*) 'LEs haulx & courageux faicts, des nobles & vertueuses personnes, sont dignes d'être racomptez'.

163

La Sale (adapted by Tressan): *Histoire du petit Jehan de Saintré*, 1792

Antoine de La Sale (b.1388?), adapted by Louis-Elisabeth de Lavergne, comte de Tressan (1705-1783): Histoire / du petit / Jehan de Saintré / et de la dame / des Belles-Cousines; / Extraite de la vieille Chronique de ce nom, / Par M. de Tressan. / Edition ornée de figures en taille douce dessinées / par M. Moreau le jeune. / [rule] / A Paris, / Chez Lepetit & Guillemard l'aîné, / commissionnaires en librairie, rue de / Savoie, N° 10. / 1792.

18°: 2 pl + [1]-4, [5]-227 pp. + 1 f. (2 pp.)

Commentary: This version of the *Petit Jehan de Saintré* first appeared in 1780 (MMF 80.32; they do not mention this edition). There are four engravings by Carrée, dated 1791, with captions. Although this edition is not mentioned by Cohen, it is by Reynaud (col.529). The illustrations are copied from those after Moreau in the 1791 edition; 'Carrée' retained the pagination and dates. The engravings in the above edition carry the pagination, which does not fit. The first item is an 'Avant-propos' in which Tressan gives his reasons for believing that the work was composed during the reign of Charles VI.

I have two copies of this edition, both alike, except that in one, there is an added, final leaf comprising two pages of 'On trouve chez Lepetit & Guillemard, l'aîné'. (Then follows a list of books, with prices.) In the other, there is a half titlepage: 'Histoire / du petit / Jehan de Saintré / et de la dame / des Belles-Cousines.' (The pagination recorded above reflects these factors.) I know of no other location for this edition, and, indeed, the only mention of it I have been able to find is in Reynaud.

Incipit: 'La cour du roi Jean étoit une des plus brillantes de l'Europe, non-seulement par la puissance'.

164

Le Brun: *Apollonius de Tyr*, 1711

Antoine-Louis Le Brun (1680-1743), i: Apollonius / de Tyr. / Seconde edition, / augmentée de la Réponse à une / Critique sur ce Livre. / Par Monsieur Le B... / Le prix est de 40. sols. / [woodcut ornament: five flowers forming a symmetrical design] / A Paris, / Chez Pierre Ribou, Quay des / Augustins, à la Descente du Pont- / Neuf, à l'Image S. Loüis. / [rule] / M. DCC. XI. / Avec Approbation, & Privilege du Roy.

ii: (head title) Re'ponse / a une / lettre critique / sur / les avantures / d'Apollo-nius / de Tyr.

12°, i: 1 pl + 9 ff. (4 + 9 + 5 pp.) + [1]-351 pp.

ii: [3]-32 pp.

Commentary: This edition is not cited by Jones. MMF 97.R72 list two editions for 1710 (BN; the novel first appeared in 1710) and one for 1797 (BN) under the title of *Les Aventures d'Apollonius de Tyr*. Indeed all other editions I have seen are for *Les Aventures* (or *Avantures*) instead of the above. The only trace of the above edition that I have found is in Quérard:SD, ii, col.716b (who cites a second edition in-8, with no date, 'augmentée de la Réponse à une lettre critique sur les Avantures, etc. 32 pp.') and in Brunet (*Manuel du libraire et de l'amateur de livres contenant...*), i, col.352 (under Apollonius), who mentions a 1710, in-12 edition, 'ou avec une réponse à une critique de ce livre et un nouveau titre daté de 1711'. (Gay repeats some of Brunet's information, i, col.244.)

The book contains: a dedicatory 'épître' in prose and verse, 'A monsieur de...' (4 pp.); 9 pp. of a preface; 5 pp. of legal material; the novel with the following head title: 'Les avantures d'Apollonius de Tyr.' Then follows the second piece described here. Although I was unable to juxtapose my copy with a copy of the first edition, I am inclined to suspect that the book described here is a reissue of the first edition, with the addition of the second piece and a cancel titlepage, as Brunet suggests.

The preface contains the following explanation: 'je ne garantirai point la vérité de cette Histoire, qui paroîtra peut-être Romanesque à ceux qui ne sont point intiez dans les secrets vénérables, & mystérieux de l'antiquité. Cependant, quelque fabuleuse qu'on puisse la croire, par les faits singuliers, & peu vraisem-blables qu'elle contient, les Sçavans à qui l'on doit déférer en ces matieres, prétendent qu'elle n'est point apocryphe, & qu'Apollonius a composé lui-même l'histoire de sa vie, & de ses avantures, dont il reste encore quelques fragmens traduits en Latin. Je m'en suis servi comme de mémoires. J'ai lié ensemble, du mieux qu'il m'a été possible, ces incidens divers, dont le tissu paroît si bizarre, & si touchant' (pp.[1-2]).

Concerning the five pages of legal material: the approbation is dated 5 November 1709 (signed 'Burette'); the privilege to Pierre Ribou, 21 December

1709 (signed 'Lecomte'); registered 31 December 1709 (signed 'Delaunay'). The title mentioned is 'Les Avantures d'Apollonius de Tyr'.

The *Réponse à une lettre critique* begins with p.[3], f.Aij which means that A1 is missing, probably being a cancelled title- or half titlepage. At the end, p.32, is a very short approbation: 'Veu par ordre de Monseigneur le Chancelier. A Paris ce 6. Janvier 1711. Signé, Burette.' (The last piece is Aij-Aiiij, [A5-A8], B, Bij-[B4], C, Cij-[C4]; chain lines horizontal for A and B, vertical for C.) The *Réponse* is signed 'LE BR.' and is obviously by Le Brun.

Incipit: 'Antioche, Capitale de la Syrie, & célebre par le commerce de ses habitans'.

165

Le Prince de Beaumont: *Les Américaines*, 1769

[Jeanne] Marie Le Prince de Beaumont (1711-1780): Les / Americaines, [no comma for the remaining volumes] / ou / la preuve / de la / religion chrétienne / Par les lumieres naturelles. / Par Mde. Le Prince de Beaumont. / TOME [Tome for the rest] I [II, III, V, VI]. PREMIERE [Seconde, Troisieme, Cinquieme, Sixieme] PARTIE [Partie for the rest]. / [composite ornament: much larger for vol. i; some repeated for the rest] / A Anneci / Chez C. M. Durand Impr. / du Roi. / [segmented thin rule with finials] / Avec Approbation & Permission. / M. DCC. LXIX.

12°, i: 1 f. (titlepage with list of female characters verso) + 2 ff. (4 pp.) + (I)-(II) + 2 ff. (4 pp.) + 1-331 pp.
　　ii: 1 pl (titlepage) + 1-310 pp.
　　iii: 1 pl (titlepage) + 1-310 pp.
　　v: 1 pl (titlepage) + 1-389 pp. + 1 blank leaf
　　vi: 1 pl (titlepage) + 1-2[87]. [288] pp. + 4 ff. (7 pp.)

Commentary: Vol. iv is not here present. There are a number of blank leaves. Vol. i contains: the titleleaf with a list of characters verso; dedication 'A son altesse royale madame la duchesse de Savoie' signed 'de Beaumont' (4 pp.); an 'Avis de l'auteur' (pp.(I)-(II)); an 'Annonce d'un ouvrage intitulé le Mentor moderne, ou Instruction pour les Garçons, & pour ceux qui les élevent. Par Mde. Le Prince de Beaumont' (headtitle; 4 pp.); then the first part. *Les Américaines* ends vi.275. Then follow two 'déclarations de l'auteur' (religious in nature). P.[288] contains the 'Approbation' (high praise; Paris, 18 November 1766, signed 'Genet Docteur de la Maison & Société de Sorbonne'); V. Joudon's name after that, 'Chanoine de la Cathédrale de Geneve, Professeur de Théologie & Censeur Royal'; a permission to print the work (Annecy [*sic*], 17 March 1769, signed 'J. B. Garnier'). Then follows a list of subscribers (4 ff, 7 pp.), which includes a slew of religious dignitaries and such bastions of genteel society as the comtesse de Polignac, the duke of Württemberg, M. Le Cat, etc. (A note at the end explains that the people are listed in the order they subscribed).

The only entry in the 'old' Sabin for this work (it is not listed in the *New Sabin* yet) is for the 1811 edition (anonymous, title given as *Les Américains...*; i.129, no. 1033).

The first edition is given as 1770 by all bibliographers I have consulted. I could find no other trace of the edition described here.

In passing, I might mention that Krauss-Fontius list an edition that has escaped the attention of bibliographers of the 'genre romanesque': '2ᵉ éd.', Lyon; Liège: Bassompierre, 1791, 6 vols (no.1988; Location: Universitäts- und Landesbibliothek Sachsen-Anhalt, Halle).

This long-winded, didactic work contains various tales. Incipits are given for the work and for the stories listed in MMF 70.58.

Incipits, (*Les Américaines*): 'La Providence, Mesdames, / qui dispose tout avec sagesse / & avec bonté'.

(*Histoire de Melicourt*, i.103-65): '*Melicourt* naquit dans les Cévennes / d'une Famille honnête'.

(*Histoire de Leontine*, i.220-37, 240-50): 'Pendant mon séjour en France, je / fus témoins [*sic*] d'une avanture fort ex- / traordinaire.'

(*Histoire de Bervile*, v.3-35): 'Mon pere, qui se nomme Ber- / vile, est bon Gentil-homme.'

166

Le Prince de Beaumont: *Arrêt solennel de la nature*, 1748

[Jeanne] Marie Le Prince de Beaumont (1711-1780): (headtitle) [triple rule broken in the middle] / Arrest / solemnel [*sic*] / de la nature, / par lequel le grand Evénement de l'Année 1748. est / sursis jusqu'au premier Aoust 1749. / Donné aux Champs Elysées près Paris le 31. Juillet 1748. à onze heures du soir. / Par Madame le P. de B.*** [Paris 1748]

4°: [1]-(8) pp. (The numbers of p.(4), (5) and (8) are enclosed in parentheses).

Commentary: I have been unable to find any trace whatsoever of this interesting piece (BL, NUC, BN, Quérard, Quérard:SD, Cior., Barbier, Gay, etc.). Perhaps the work described here is a unique copy of a single edition. It is one of those items which appeared in the wake of the abbé Gabriel François Coyer's anti-feminist *Année merveilleuse*. Mme Le Prince de Beaumont replied with a *Lettre en réponse à l'*'*Année merveilleuse*' (see the entry immediately below).

The *Arrêt solennel* is addressed to the same lady as the *Lettre en réponse*. Seated under a tree in the verdant section outside Paris then known as the 'Champs Elisiens', the author falls into a state of rêverie, thinking about her appeal. Suddenly she notices that it is night, that the crowds have left, so she jumps up to return to the city: 'tout à coup les ténébres firent place à une lumiére éclatante; l'air me paroissoit tout en feu, la terre trembla sous mes pas, les arbres s'agitérent, une horreur secrette s'empara de mes sens' (p.2). To shorten, Nature in all the splendid beauty of pristine simplicity appears, together with a crowd. The 'Silphide' changes into a lady of fashion right in front of the bewildered Parisienne: 'je ne vis plus qu'une poupée, où les momens précédens j'avois crû voir une Divinité' (p.(4)). Finally the generous fairy grants a delay in the changing of women into men. This is followed by a code of behaviour, which shows that Mme Le Prince de Beaumont was considerably less liberated than she thought she was, by current standards at least!

Coyer's *Année merveilleuse* was extremely successful in its day. Gay reports that 'cette pièce eut beaucoup de vogue, et il en circula en France un si grand nombre d'exemplaires dans l'année où elle parut qu'on prétendait que la poste seule y avait gagné deux mille écus' (i, cols.227-28). And the pieces surrounding the *Année merveilleuse* were very popular, too. (For a list of some of these, see Barbier, i, col.202b-c; in connexion with the *Arrêt du conseil de Momus*, see Quérard, ii.327.) For further information, see above, Coyer, *Lettre à une jeune dame nouvellement mariée*, and Le Prince de Beaumont's *Lettre en réponse* just below. (For interesting information and analyses of Coyer's debts to Swift, Arbuthnot and others, see Louise Elsoffer-Kamins, 'Un imitateur original de Jonathan Swift: l'abbé Coyer et ses *Bagatelles morales*', *Revue de littérature comparée* 1949, xxiii.[469]-81.)

Incipit: 'Madame, / Je croirois manquer à l'amitié que je vous ai jurée, si je / tardois à vous faire part de l'étonnante Vision dont je sors à / peine'.

167

Le Prince de Beaumont: *Lettre en réponse à l'"Année merveilleuse'*, 1748

[Jeanne] Marie Le Prince de Beaumont (1711-1780): Lettre / en réponse / a / l'année / merveilleuse. / [double rule broken in the centre] / Par Mad. Le Prince D. B. / [extensive woodcut ornament bearing the following motto: 'non norunhæc monumenta mori'] / Se vend a Nancy, / Chez [open brace] H. Thomas, Imprimeur-Libraire, rüe de la Boucherie, Ville-Neuve. / Georges Henry, Marchand Libraire, proche la Porte Royale, Ville-Neuve. / Bertheau, où réside l'Auteur, rüe saint Michel, Ville-Vieille. [end of material set of by the brace] / [rule] / Avec permission. [1748]

4°: (titlepage, see the commentary), (2)-(7), (8) pp.

Commentary: The actual text begins on the verso of the titlepage. (There are no signatures.) The first section is the main body of the text, in the form of a letter addressed to 'Madame'. The BNC lists two copies of this rare work (for Nancy, H. Thomas, s.d., 8 pp. in quarto; 4° Li3.12 and Rés. Z Fontanieu.167(8)). I have not been able to juxtapose my copy with those in the BN. (Not listed in the BLC or NUC.) This is a work which might be considered marginal to the 'genre romanesque'.

It appeared shortly after the publication of the abbé Coyer's satire, *L'Année merveilleuse* (1748). In the *Lettre en réponse*, Mme Le Prince de Beaumont indignantly attacks Coyer's principles that men: 1. talk little; 2. think a lot; 3. like to dominate. She cites the examples of Deborah, Semiramide, Judith, Esther, queens Elizabeth and Anne: 'Si les Loix de ce Royaume nous excluent du Gouvernement, c'est qu'elles furent données dans un tems où les François étoient encore Barbares' (p. (5)). She then compares the two sexes. What woman in her right mind would consent to becoming a man? 'Pourrions-nous regarder comme un gain, le privilége de devenir volages par nature, indiscretes par honneur, fourbes par nécessité?' (p.(7)). The *Lettre en réponse* ends with an ersatz legal appeal, set off from the main body of the text: (headtitle) 'A dame nature' (p.(8)), begging that no such metamorphosis be permitted. See Mme Le Prince de Beaumont's *Arrêt solennel de la nature* just above.

Incipit: 'Madame, / vous me demandez mon sentiment sur l'étonnante méta-/morphose que nous annonce l'Auteur de l'*Année Merveilleuse*.'

168

Lemarié: *Nouveau dictionnaire d'anecdotes*, 1789

François Lemarié: Nouveau / dictionnaire / d'anecdotes, / ou / l'art / d'éviter l'ennui, / contenant / Une Collection nouvelle & intéressante de traits cu- / rieux, historiques, littéraires, politiques, moraux, / critiques, satyriques, tragiques & comiques; sans / aucune indécence, pour l'ornement de l'esprit & de / la mémoire des lecteurs de toutes les conditions. / Pour servir de suite à l'ancien Dictionnaire / d'Anecdotes de M. Lacombe. / Troisieme Édition. / [rule] / Tome premier [second]. / [rule] / [small woodcut decoration, different for each volume] / A Liege, / Chez D. de Boubers, Imprimeur-Libraire, / à l'Homme-Sauvage, rue du Pont. / [rule] / M. DCC. LXXXIX.

12°, i: 2 ff. (halftitle and titlepage) + v-vj + [1]-360 + 4 pp. [paginated 38, 382, 383, 84]
ii: 2 pl + [1]-374, 375-380 pp.

Commentary: This alphabetical work first appeared in 1783 and went through several editions. The only trace of the edition described here I could find (assuming it refer to the same edition) is in Krauss-Fontius, with a location for the Universitäts- und Landesbibliothek Sachsen-Anhalt, Halle (no. 501). MMF do not list this work, but the two volumes do contain snippets of fiction. The first item reported in the pagination is an 'Avant-propos', thanking the public for its support and hoping that the new, modified edition will also meet with its approval. The last item in each volume is a 'Table'. There are numerous pagination errors. There is a half titlepage for each volume: 'Nouveau / dictionnaire / d'anecdotes. / [rule] / A-H [I-Z for ii] / [rule].

Incipit: ('Abbés') 'A La représentation d'*Abdilly*, tragédie, un instant avant qu'elle commençât, le parterre voyant un abbé'.

169

Leroy: *Aventures divertissantes du duc de Roquelaure*, 1800

Antoine Leroy: Aventures / divertissantes / du duc / de Roquelaure, / Suivant les Mémoires que l'Auteur / a trouvés dans le Cabinet du / Maréchal D'H.... / [rule] / A Paris, / Chez Le Prieur, Lib. rue Saint-Jacques, / N.° 278, à côté de l'hôtel de Lyon. / [double rule] / An VIII.–1800.

18°: 2 ff. (halftitle and titlepage) + [5]-(8), [9]-(140), [141]-142 pp.

Commentary: I have found no trace of this edition anywhere (NUC, BLC, BNC, Gay, etc.) The half titlepage carries: 'Aventures / de / Roquelaure.' The first edition dates to 1718, and appeared under the title of *Le Momus français, ou les aventures divertissantes*... There were other titles as well; see Jones, MMF 59.R20 and Gay, especially i, cols.327-28. Jones states that the earliest edition he could find dates to 1727, although Gay lists 1718 (Jones, p.30 and 38). MMF list 1718 (and 1720) with question marks (59.R20). Proof of the 1718 date lies in Krauss-Fontius, no. 3624, who list: Cologne: Marteau, 1718, 143 pp. (Title: *Le Momus français, ou les aventures divertissantes du duc de Roquelaure* [...] *par le Sr. L. R.*; location: Universitäts- und Landesbibliothek Sachsen-Anhalt, Halle.)

The edition described here carries an amusing frontispiece of respectable quality (not cited in Cohen or Reynaud), with the following caption: 'Soyez les biens venus, foi d'honnête-homme, / je ne vous attendois pas si tot'. There is a preface of sorts, the 'Portrait du duc de Roquelaure', pp.[5]-(8), and, at the end, a 'Table'.

This work has also been attributed to F. A. Chevrier (Jones, p.39, after BN), which is of course not possible. (He was born in 1721.)

To editions of this work listed in Jones and MMF, I would add: *Le Momus français*, 1758. Cologne: Marteau, 1758. 180 pp. Krauss-Fontius, no. 3627. Location: Universitäts- und Landesbibliothek Sachsen-Anhalt, Halle.

Incipits: ('Portrait') 'Ce duc avait de petits yeux noirs, et, comme l'on dit, des yeux de cochon'.

('Aventure I.ere': 'La Corbeille de Pêches') 'Ce duc, qui n'était uniquement appliqué qu'à faire des siennes, se trouvant un jour dans l'antichambre de la reine'.

170

Lesage: *Gil Blas*, 1735

Alain René Lesage (1668-1747): Histoire / de / Gil Blas / de Santillane. / Par M. Le Sage. / Tome IV. / [symmetrical woodcut ornament signed with an 'N'] / A Paris, / Chez Pierre-Jacques Ribou, vis-à-vis [vis-à vis for copy A] / la Comedie Françoise, à l'Image S. Loüis. / [rule] / M. DCC. XXXV. / Avec Approbation & Privilege du Roy.

12°, iv: 1 pl + 3 ff. (6 pp.) + [1]-347, [348-50] pp.

Commentary: The first six pages are a table; the last three (unpaginated, beginning on a verso, p.[348]), legal material. I have two copies of the above first edition of the fourth volume of Lesage's *Gil Blas* and list them to comment on the engravings. Barring accidents which normally result with the printing of handpress books (e.g. copy A reads 8 for p.68; copy B reads 68; A reads 339 while B reads 33), the two volumes are alike except for the engravings. There are only seven engravings in A and none is signed. B has eight engravings, and all are signed 'Dubercelle In. et Fecit'. The frontispiece to A is actually the second engraving in B; the frontispiece in B is entirely lacking in A. The two states of the plates are also obvious from the engravings themselves: the unsigned ones did not undergo the final touching up that the signed ones did, as is evident from particularly the lack of certain hatching and crosshatching in the unsigned engravings.

Concerning the illustrations: Cohen states that there are eight for the volume described here. According to the same source, of the twenty-seven meant to accompany all four volumes of *Gil Blas* (in the first editions), eight are signed 'Dubercelle' (col.630). Cohen doesn't specify which eight.

This is presumably the first edition of vol. iv, the titlepage of which is reproduced in Jules Le Petit, p.485. There are a couple of minor differences which probably have to do with the reproduction process used for the Le Petit: the rule is a bit shorter, the 'E' of 'Santillane' differs slightly, the 'vis-à-vis' reads 'vis à vis'. (In my copies, the dashes are very faint.)

There is at least one other edition of *Gil Blas* listed in Krauss-Fontius which has escaped the attention of bibliographers of the 'genre romanesque' (and of Lesage): 4 vols, Amsterdam: Uytwerf, 1733-1735. No. 4196; location: Universitäts- und Landesbibliothek Sachsen-Anhalt, Halle. (See the other entries in Krauss-Fontius for possibly another edition or two.)

Another edition which is not listed in the usual bibliographies is: '[Histoire] de Gil-Blas de Santillane, par le Sage, nouv. edit. IV Vol. 8vo. Dresde, Walther, [1]786' (Heinsius, *Handbuch*, p.796). MMF list an edition for 1786-87 after Cordier (55.R48). The latter's entry is for Paris: par la compagnie des libraires, 1786-87, 4 vols in-12 (copy in the BN).

Incipit: 'Dans le tems que je me disposois à partir de Madrid avec Scipion'.

171

Lesage: *Gil Blas*, 1771

Alain René Lesage (1668-1747): (*red* and black titlepages) *Histoire* / de / *Gil Blas* / de Santillane. / Par M. *Le Sage*. / Derniere Edition, revue & corrigée. / *Tome premier* [*second, troisieme, quatrieme*]. / [woodcut decoration, different for each volume] / *A Paris*, / Par les Libraires Associés. / [double rule] / *M. DCC. LXXI.* / Avec Approbation & Privilége du Roy.

12°, i: 2 pl + 2 ff. (2 + 2 pp.) + [1]-402 pp. + 3 ff. (6 pp.)
   ii: 2 pl + [1]-342 pp. + 2 ff. (3 pp.)
   iii: 2 pl + [1]-381 + 7 (beginning with p.[382]) pp.
   iv: 2 pl + [1]-369 + 7 (beginning with p.[370]) + 4 pp.

Commentary: MMF list four editions for 1771 (55.R48). But I have checked the titlepages of my copy against the pertinent copies in the BL (12518.t.9) and BN (Y2.9994-5-6(ii-iv), Y2.9997bis, Y2.9998-9-10,000) and my copy is different. My copy is also not listed in Cordier. It is therefore a hitherto unknown edition. There is a stamp on the first page of the novel, vol. i, reading Rouen, 1777 with the book inspector, Havas's signature, meaning that we have here a legalised copy of a contraband edition. See the commentary on d'Arnaud's 1777 *Œuvres* for further explanation. All four volumes are embellished with that kind of popular, not very good quality engraving that so often accompanied duodecimo novels (thirty-two in all: 8, 9, 8, 7, for each volume respectively).

The legal material comprises the last four pages of vol. iv. The approbation, for the fourth volume only of *Gil Blas*, is signed 'Danchet' for 29 October 1738. The privilege, by Sainson to Jean Baptiste Juin, is dated 30 January 1739. Registered by Langlois 8 March 1739 (vol. iv, last two leaves, 4 pp.). Certain rights were ceded to other bookdealers 19 January and 6 December 1740. Beyond the evidence of the legal stamp, paper and type, this indicates a non Parisian piracy, for many bookdealers, when pirating a book, faithfully copied everything contained in the book, including titlepages, official documents, and the like. There is a copy of *Gil Blas* listed in the NUC (Yale) for 1771: i, A Paris, Chez Brocas, libraire, rue S. Jacques [De l'imprimerie de Le Breton, premier imprimeur ordinaire du Roi]; for ii-iv, A Paris, Par la Compagnie des Libraires. This is obviously an amalgam of two editions, and neither appears to be the one listed above.

The first two pieces in i are a 'Déclaration de l'auteur' and 'Gil Blas au lecteur'. The postliminary pages are tables. These are all part of the last gatherings. The tables at the end of vols iii and iv begin on versos. There are volume half titlepages reading: 'Histoire / de / Gil Blas / de Santillane. / Tome premier [second, troisieme, quatrieme].'

Incipits: ('Gil Blas au lecteur') 'Avant que d'entendre l'Histoire de ma vie, écoute, ami Lecteur, un conte'.

(*Gil Blas*) 'Blas de Santillane, mon pere, après avoir long-tems porté les armes pour le service de la Monarchie Espagnole'.

172

Lesage: *Gil Blas*, 1798

Alain René Lesage (1668-1747): Histoire / de / Gil Blas / de Santillane. / Par Le Sage. / Tome V [VI]. / [rule] / A Paris, / Chez T.-P. Bertin, Libraire, / rue de la Sonnerie, N°. 1. / [rule] / An VI. (1798.)

18°, v: 2 pl + [1]-220, [221]-225 pp.

vi: 2 pl + [1]-147, [148]-153, [154]-(157) [for 159; p.[158] reads '(156)'] pp.

Commentary: MMF list *Gil Blas* for 'an V, an VI, 1798, 1800 (Quérard)' (55.R48), so it would appear that the authors were unaware of a 'An VI. (1798.)' edition. Cordier does list two editions for an VI, 1798, among which no. 29, six volumes in-18, with seven engravings by Bovinet and Copia, after Challiou and Angelica Kauffmann (p.257 no location given). His source was possibly an edition of Cohen anterior to S. de Ricci's refurbishment, or Monglond's source. Monglond lists a 6 volume, in-12 edition (an VI (1798)), after a Lardanchet catalogue, with a frontispiece by Angelica Kauffmann and six illustrations after Challiou by Bovinet and Copia (iv, cols.599-600). Since this edition does not exist in the BN or BL, and is not listed in the NUC, I have included it. Although my copy is incomplete, I thought a detailed description of the last two volumes of this edition might prove of use to scholars working on Lesage.

There are two frontispiece engravings after Challiou, engraved by Copia (vol. v) and Bovinet (vi). Each volume has a 'Table' at the end. At the very end of vi is a long, interesting list of books, mostly novels, available at Bertin's, preceded by the following announcement: 'L'éditeur de ce roman se propose de réimprimer tous les meilleurs ouvrages de littérature française et étrangère, sous le titre d'éditions de Bertin, dans le même format avec les mêmes caractères, et la même exécution dans le type et la gravure que le Gil Blas, à 12 sols le volume. / On peut dès ce moment se procurer à son adresse, rue de la Sonnerie, N°. 1, presque tous les livres du Catalogue ci-dessous, à 10 sols le volume.' (Follows the list.)

The volume half titlepages read: 'Histoire / de / Gil Blas / de Santillane.' On the versos is '[rule] / De l'Imprimerie de Delance, rue / de la Harpe, n°. 133, à Paris. / [rule]'.

Incipit: ('Livre neuvième') 'Un soir, après avoir renvoyé la compagnie qui étoit venue souper chez moi'.

173

Lichtwehr (Pfeffel transl.): *Fables nouvelles*, 1763

Magnus Gottfried Lichtwehr (sometimes Lichtwer; 1719-1783), translated by Gottlieb Conrad (or C[K]onrad Gottlieb [Théophile]) Pfeffel (1736-1809): Fables / nouvelles / Divisées en quatre Livres. / Traduction libre de l'Allemand de / Monsieur Lichtwehr. / [composite woodcut decoration, nine sections forming a square of sorts laid on its side] / A Strasbourg, / Chez Jean Godefroy Bauer. / Et se trouve à Paris, / Chez Langlois, Libraire, rüe de la Harpe, / près de la rüe percée, à la Couronne d'or. / [double rule] / M DCC LXIII.

8°: 1 f. (titlepage) + 3-8, 9-14 + 1 f. (halftitle) + 1-267, [268] pp.

Commentary: The contents comprise a letter 'A monsieur Lichtwehr, conseiller de sa majesté prussienne à la régence de Halberstadt', a 'table' of the four books of fables, a halftitle 'Livre premier.', the fables proper, and a one-page list of errata. At the end is the following colophon: 'A Colmar, / De l'Imprimerie Royale.'

MMF list this as a work marginal to the 'genre romanesque', after the copies in the BN and BL. They further state that the *Fabeln* first appeared in 1748, with an augmented edition in 1761 (63.34). I list my edition since it contains two extra leaves bound in at the end, pp.47-48 and 55-56. Pages 48-49 and 55-56 are correctly bound in the text, but slashed from the bottom up. The two slashed sheets were supposed to have been cancelled and substituted by the leaves at the end. Chapman remarks that 'the survival of a mutilated *cancellandum* must be (again, relatively) a very rare accident' (p.29).

The variants represented by the new leaves are not very important. Here are a couple: p.48, up three lines from the bottom, cancellans (original leaf) reads 'Hélas! lui dirent en le voyant, les écloppés, / pourquoi nous as-tu donc abandonnés de la'. The same lines in the cancellandum (replacement leaf) read 'Hélas! lui dirent, en le voyant, les éclop- / pés, pourquoi nous as-tu donc abandonnés de la'. P.55, lines 6-8 read '*Comme cela*, répondit un convive, qui appa- / remment n'avoit point perdu son tems aux pre- / miers services; ce n'est pas là, je vous assure,'. P.55, cancellandum, lines 6-8: '*Comme cela*, répondit un des convives (vous / remarquerez que le pauvre homme avoit le mal- / heur d'être aveugle,) & ce n'est pas là, je vous'. These consist of ff.[C8] and D4.

This work contains 120 short fables translated into prose.

MMF mention that this work and edition is listed in Quérard [v.299]. It is also listed in the Messkatalog for 'Fables nouvelles divisées en quatre Livres, traduction libre de l'Allemand de Mr. Lichtwehr. 8vo. à Strasbourg, chez J. God. Bauer' (OM 1763, p.367; also in Heinsius 1793, iv.505). This book was printed in Strasbourg, and not in Paris.

Incipit: ('A la Muse') 'O Muse, o Toi, pour qui la langue même des Dieux n'a rien de difficile!'

174
Macpherson (Le Tourneur transl.): *Ossian, fils de Fingal,*
1797

James Macpherson (1736-1796), translated by Pierre Prime Félicien Le Tourneur (1737-1788): Ossian, / fils de Fingal, / barde du troisième siècle: / poésies galliques, / Traduites de l'Anglois de M. Macpherson, / Par M. Letourneur. / [rule] / Tome premier [second]. / [rule] / [swell rule] / A Paris, / Chez [brace] / Favre, libraire, rue de Savoie, / N°. 19; et au Palais-Egalité, gale- / ries de bois, N°. 220. / B.-Duchesne, imprimeur, rue des / Fossès-Montmartre, N°. [n° for ii] 42. / [end of material set off by the brace] / [short rule] / L'an V.

18°, i: 2 pl (halftitle and titlepages) + [1]-216 pp.
    ii: 1 pl (titlepage) + [1]-227 pp.

Commentary: This work is a translation of the *Works of Ossian* (1765) and first appeared in this French version in 1777 (MMF 77.49). MMF list reeditions for Paris: Dufart an VI-1798 and Paris: Dantu, an VIII (various sources). They also list a continuation by John Smith, translated by Griffet de La Baume and David de Saint-Georges (vf. 95.40). It is doubtful that the edition listed here would have contained that 'suite'.

The books listed here contain about half of Le Tourneur's *Ossian*; I assume that two more volumes were printed to complete the collection. Vol. ii goes through the 'Description d'une nuit du mois d'octobre dans le nord de l'Écosse'. At the end of each volume, there is printed 'Fin du Tome premier [second]'. The contemporary calf binding – both volumes are bound in one – has a volume piece on the spine, indicating '1-2', from which nothing conclusive can be deduced. I could find no trace of these books anywhere.

Each volume has a pretty frontispiece, unsigned, captioned, bearing at the top left 'Tom. 1 [2].' (not in Cohen or Reynaud).

The halftitle to vol. i reads: 'Ossian, / poésies galliques, / traduites de l'anglois. / [rule] / Tome premier. / [rule]'. There is none present for vol. ii.

Glued onto the inside of the first board is an interesting, contemporary label: 'Se vend à Nancy, chez Vincenot, Rue de l'Esplanade, n.° 210. // Ce Libraire tient un Cabinet littéraire, donne à lire, tant en ville qu'à la campagne, toutes les nouveautés, fait des échanges, achète des Bibliothèques, fournit celles qui ne sont pas complètes, se charge de toutes les commissions concernant la Librairie, et de fournir les bureaux tant en Cire, et Pains à cacheter, qu'en Papier, Plumes, Encre, Crayons etc.'

Incipit: 'Près des murs de Tura, Cuchullin (I) / étoit assis au pied d'un arbre au trem- / blant feuillage.' (A note at the end of the canto explains 'Cuchullin'.)

175

Mareuille[?]: *Histoire des princesses de Bohème*, 1750

Variously attributed to madame de Mareuille and to André François Boureau-Deslandes (1690-1757): Histoire / des princesses / de Boheme. / Par Madame *** / [double rule: thick, thin] / Premiere [seconde] partie. / [double rule: thick, thin] / [symmetrical woodcut ornament, same for both volumes: lamp-shade hanging in centre, vase of flowers to either side, in an ornamental border forming part of the same structures] / A la Haye. / Chez Jean Neaulme. / [double rule] / M. DCC. XLX. [M. DCC. L. for ii]

in-12, i: 1 f. (titlepage) + 1 f. (1 p., 'Avis de l'éditeur') + [5]-(143) pp.

ii: 1 f. (titlepage) + [3]-(147) pp.

Commentary: Jones lists the first edition for 'La Haye, [n.d.], 2v. in 1, 221p., 230p.' (1749, p.102). He also cites another 1749 edition (BN) for La Haye, J. Neaulme, 221p. and 230p. as well. His commentary runs as follows: 'B[arbier] and BN. attribute this work to Mme. de Mareuille. B[arbier] adds the note: "Note de l'exempt de police d'Hemery du 19 mars 1750. Van-Thol dit qu'une autre note signale Andr. Franç. Boureau-Deslandes, comme l'auteur". Q[ué-rard] attributes this work to Deslandes [ii.516]'. (Mareuille is not listed in Quérard.) Barbier further clarifies by explaining that Mme de Mareuille was 'séparée de son mari, âgé de soixante ans', according to d'Hémery (ii, col.762a).

I would not presume to make a definite statement about the authorship of this novel. However, it would not be inappropriate to point out that it is certainly not in the vein (or style) of other works by Boureau-Deslandes. And the reader is reminded that a 'Mme de ***' is cited on the titlepage. I list it under de Mareuille's name because Jones has done so and because logic seems to lean much more heavily in her favor than in Boureau-Deslandes'. (This work is not listed in MMF.)

I could find no trace of this edition in the usual sources, nor another copy.

Incipit: 'De toutes les passions qui / tirannisent les hommes, / l'ambition'.

176

Marmontel: *Bélisaire*, 1767

Jean François Marmontel (1723-1799): Belisaire. / Par M. Marmontel, / De l'Académie Françoise. / [rule] / Non miror, si quandò impetum capit / (Deus) spectandi magnos viros colluctantes / cum aliquâ calamitate. / Sénec. De Provid. /

[rule] / [assymetrical woodcut decoration: ornamental border, with four squares inside formed of four snowflake-like decorations; the right-hand side of the composite, ornamental border is missing] / A Paris, / Chez Merlin, Libraire, rue de la Harpe / à l'Image S. Joseph. / [rule] / M. DCC. LXVII. / Avec Approbation, & Privilége du Roi.

12°: 1 pl + [j]-x + [1]-272 + [274], [275]-340 pp. + 2 ff. (3 pp.)

Commentary: The first section is a 'Préface', Then follows the novel. After that come the 'Fragmens / de / philosophie morale.' (half titlepage, p.[273]), an 'Avis' (p.[274]), the 'fragments' proper and three pages of legal material. The approbation, signed 'Bret', is dated 20 November 1766; the privilege, signed 'Le Begue', is dated 10 December 1766 and was issued to Merlin for *Bélisaire*; registered 16 December 1766 ('Ganeau, Syndic'). The verso of the half titlepage of the *Fragments* (p.[274]) has an 'Avis' explaining that they had been published before, but in a hard-to-come-by book and that they quite naturally find their place with *Bélisaire*. P.340 contains a colophon: 'De l'mprimerie [*sic*] de P. Alex, [*sic*] le Prieur, / Imprimeur du Roi, rue S. Jacques.'

Assuming the first edition in-duodecimo be an issue of the first edition generally speaking, i.e., that the duodecimo would match the octavo in all respects except format and size (thus signatures would differ, but ornaments would be the same), none of the editions of *Bélisaire* described in this bibliography is the first. However, see the commentary on the next entry. MMF note that 'selon le *Catalogue hebdomadaire*, l'ouvrage se vendait en 1 volume in-12 avec figures (notre princeps), en un volume in-12 sans figures (BN), ou en un volume in-8 avec figures (BM, BN). Mornet donne deux éditions pour 1767, sans autres précisions' (67.39). The BN edition without illustrations that they mention is surely Y2.51305, in-12, which is in all likelihood a counterfeit edition.

Although the *Catalogue hebdomadaire* mentions a *Bélisaire* without illustrations, I am sure that the periodical is listing an edition variant, and not a separate edition. It was often the custom to issue a work with and without illustrations at different prices, in a larger, more expensive format (here octavo) and in a cheaper format (here duodecimo), and on different kinds of paper, a practice still followed today. The non-illustrated edition in the BN has nothing to do with the first edition, as I see it. The *Catalogue hebdomadaire* actually mentions a duodecimo with illustrations (price: three livres), without illustrations (two livres) and an octavo with illustrations (five livres; *Cat. hebdo.* 7 February 1767, no.6, item 2).

The first octavo edition is doubtlessly that represented in the BN by Rés. Y2.3666 and BL, G[renville].17757. It is printed on good paper, the illustrations are in the first state and, just as important, there is no addition to any note (as described for the next entry). The octavo edition's titlepage is reproduced in Tchemerzine, iv.441. I am unable to affirm which is the first duodecimo edition. But it too would carry the illustrations in a good state and contain no addition to any note. It seems logical that there was then a new edition, in-12, with the 'Addition à la note de la page 237'. The copies and piracies of *Bélisaire* multiplied rapidly: some were copied from one of the first editions (without the addition), or copied from copies of those! The book described here is probably an example of one of these editions, for I am convinced that it does not represent the first edition, or even sure that it was printed in Paris. Most editions were copied from editions with the note. That note was first issued as a fly-sheet, and then printed with subsequent editions of the book. (I do not doubt but that copies of the first edition, whether a dudecimo or an octavo will turn up, with the 'Addition à la note' tipped in.)

The third probable stage in this confusing progression consists of editions with the note incorporated directly into the text. See below for a couple of examples of such editions.

Just how many editions in French of *Bélisaire* were there for Paris, Merlin, 1767 (x + 340 paginated pages in-duodecimo) alone? At least four, all listed in this bibliography. There is also an edition bearing 1765. (See below.) Reynaud seems to list four, different Paris, Merlin editions, with engravings, one with 'Françoise' spelled 'Française', 350 pp. + 2 ff. of legal material. (All this is over and beyond the first octavo edition, or issue.) The edition described here seems to be one of the last ones listed by Reynaud, with the appropriate Gravelot engravings. (As usual, Reynaud is not very clear in his explanations or transcriptions.) The above volume contains an unsigned frontispiece, column bearing 'Belisaire / par / M. Marmontel / de l'Acad^e Franc.' to the right, plus three other pictures (mirror images of the signed versions described in the next entry).

In spite of the colophon (yet partially because of it: note the spelling errors) and signatures numbered in roman, it is possible that the above book was not produced in Paris (Holland perhaps?). Since the doctors at the Sorbonne were quick to condemn *Bélisaire*, one rather wonders how many editions were really put out by Merlin and co., and how many represent pirated, or counterfeit editions. There was in all likelihood a Merlin edition with the 'Addition' incorporated directly into the text; in fact, there might have been several. MMF list two additional Merlin editions, with different pagination: xii + 352 pp. (Newberry Library) and a 'nouvelle édition, revue et corrigée', xii + 249 + 22 + xi + 33 + 54 pp. (Yale, Harvard, etc.). The last three sequences of arabic numerals doubtless represent some of the works which appeared in the wake of *Bélisaire*, such as the abbé Coger's *Examen du 'Bélisaire'*, for which see the next entry.

Then, or at about the same time that the Parisian presses were churning out copies and editions of *Bélisaire*, the novel fanned out across Europe, in French and in translation, often with copies of Gravelot's designs executed with varying degrees of success. (For a brief introduction to the many translations of *Bélisaire*, the interested reader might begin with Graesse, iv.406.) S. Lenel, in his *Un homme de lettres au 18e siècle: Marmontel d'après des documents nouveaux et inédits* (1902; Slatkine 1970) asserts, without citing his sources or presenting documentation, that 'en moins d'une année, il s'en répandit en Europe plus de quarante mille exemplaires' (p.[316])! His source is doubtless Marmontel's *Mémoires*, book 8; in the critical edition edited by John Renwick, i.241. If by the figure 'forty thousand', translations were meant to be included, I have little doubt but that the estimate is conservative.

I was unable to juxtapose my editions of *Bélisaire* with those to be found in the BN and Arsenal, though I have no doubt that those libraries possess copies

Ecce spectaculum dignum, ad quod respiciat
intentus operi suo Deus: ecce par Deo dignum,
Vir fortis cum mala fortuna compositus. *Senec.*

BELISAIRE,

PAR M. MARMONTEL,

De l'Académie Françoise.

'Non miror , si quandò impetum capit
(Deus) spectandi magnos viros colluctantes
cum aliquâ calamitate.
Sénec. De Provid.

A PARIS,

Chez MERLIN, Libraire, rue de la Harpe
à l'Image S. Joseph.

M. DCC. LXVII.

Avec Approbation, & Privilège du Roi.

No 176: Marmontel, *Bélisaire*, 1767

of some of them. I list mine as a step towards identifying *Bélisaire* editions for especially the year of the first edition. There were obviously more editions and issues of Marmontel's controversial novel than anyone has yet suspected, for 1767 alone.

To the listings in MMF of 1767 editions of *Bélisaire* must be added this entry, several of the next few entries, possibly BN Y2.51304 (I was unable to examine it), BN Y2.51305 (see the commentary on the 'Paris', 238 pp. edition below) and Reynaud's '350 pp. + 2 ff.' 1767 edition. MMF list a Paris, Merlin, 1767 edition, xii + 352 pp., Newberry Library, a copy they examined. The entry in the NUC gives further information: 18cm – thus probably in-12° – 'Fragmens de philosophie morale', p.[191]-238; 'Pièces relatives à Bélisaire', pp.[239]-352; 'Seizième chapitre de Bélisaire. Constantinople, 1768', 56 pp. bound in at the end. (This could conceivably be the edition recorded by Reynaud, but that doesn't seem likely.) If someone tackles this problem armed with appropriate photocopies, I am sure that more editions will come to light. (See too the next entries devoted to *Bélisaire*.)

To the list of the various eighteenth-century editions of *Bélisaire* to be found in MMF (67.39) and in this bibliography, I would add the following:

1. *Bélisaire*, 1767. Paris: Merlin; Francfort: Esslinger, 1767. 282 pp. Krauss-Fontius no. 4339, with locations for the Universitäts- und Landesbibliothek Sachsen-Anhalt, Halle and a subsidiary of the Deutsche Akademie der Wissenschaften zu Berlin (B.692).

2. *Bélisaire*, 1770. Paris: Merlin, 1770. 341 pp. Krauss-Fontius no. 4341, with a location for the Romanisches Seminar der Universität Leipzig.

3. *Bélisaire*, 1795. 'gr. [in-]12. Vienne, Tendler, [1]795' (Heinsius, Romane col.27).

4. *Bélisaire*, 1798. 'Belisaire, par Mr. Marmontel, avec des lettres relatives au Belisaire. Mit den Sinn erläuternden Noten zum Schulgebrauch u[nd] Selbslunterricht herausg. 8. Koburg, Sinner', Messkatalog, MM 1798, p.383.

There is also a 1770 *Bélisaire*, 3. éd. Leipzig, Crusius, xvi, 478 pp. listed in Krauss-Fontius (no. 4345), with two locations. However, this seems to refer to a German translation, rather than the French original. (Krauss-Fontius are not quite clear).

See too the commentary on the 1775 edition of the *Contes moraux* listed below for yet another edition.

The BNC ten-year supplement lists a *Bélisaire* for Paris: Merlin, 1765, in-8°, XII, 343p., ill. (16° Y2.26197; in xiv.402a). The date is correctly recorded ('M. DCC. LXV.', doubtless for '...LXVII.'), but the book is a duodecimo. It is a piracy of one of the 'Merlin', 1767 editions (the punctuation error in the colophon is the same as that for the fourth *Bélisaire* listed in this bibliography: '... P. Alex, [sic] le Prieur ...'). There are good copies of the original Gravelot designs, unsigned. (The column in ruins of the frontispiece is on the right.) This edition is not listed in the usual bibliographies.

For an interesting and thorough discussion of the events surrounding *Bélisaire*, see John Renwick, *Marmontel, Voltaire and the 'Bélisaire' affair*, Studies on Voltaire and the eighteenth century, cxxi (1974). There is a useful 'Chronological table' (pp.319-23).

Incipit: 'Dans la vieillesse de Justinien, l'Em- / pire, épuisé par de longs efforts, ap- / prochoit de sa décadence.'

177

Marmontel: *Bélisaire*, 1767

Jean François Marmontel (1723-1799): Belisaire. / Par M. Marmontel, / De l'Académie Françoise. / [rule] / Non miror, si quandò impetum capit / (Deus) spectandi magnos viros, colluctan- / tes cum aliquâ calamitate. / Sénec. De Provid. / [rule] / [woodcut ornament; see the commentary] / A Paris, / Chez Merlin, Libraire, rue de la Harpe, / à l'Image S. Joseph. / [rule] / M. DCC. LXVII. / Avec Approbation, & Privilége du Roi.

12°: 2 pl + [j]-x + [1]-272 + [274], [275]-340 pp. + 3 ff. (2 + 3 pp.)

Commentary: There is a half titlepage for 'Bélisaire.' Then follow the titlepage, the preface, the novel, a half titlepage for 'Fragmens / de / philosophie morale.' (with the 'Avis' verso, p.[274]), the 'fragments' proper, a two-page (1 f., unnumbered) 'Addition à la note de la page 237' (meant for the controversial chapter xv), and, at the end, 2 ff., 3 pp. (again unnumbered) of legal material, for which see the preceding entry. At the end of the text, before the addition and legal material (p.340), is Le Prieur's colophon: 'De l'Imprimerie de P. Alex. le Prieur, / Imprimeur du Roi, rue S. Jacques.' (One wonders if anyone at the time was amused by the fact that the king's printer produced a book so roundly condemned by the Sorbonne!)

The composite woodcut ornament on the titlepage consists of a series of geometrical patterns within an ornamental border, viz. (outside to inside) ornamental border, five boxes with dark squares inside on the top and bottom, four to either side; three crosses (vertical-horizontal) on the top and bottom, two to either side (with an 'x' in each corner); dot-lines in the interior roughly forming four 'x's on the top and bottom. (This woodcut is repeated, for example, on p.68.)

There are four engravings by various artists after Gravelot. The first (frontispiece) is by Le Vasseur. The second does not bear an engravor's signature. The third is by Le Veau, and the fourth by Masquelier. (All have captions.) The ruined column on which are engraved the author's name and the title is on the left-hand side of the frontispiece. Bound with this book is the *Examen du Bélisaire de M. Marmontel* by the abbé François-Marie Coger (Paris: H. C. De Hansy le jeune, 1767) also printed by Le Prieur (source: colophon), with an approbation signed 'Riballier' dated 14 April 1767. The reason I mention this work is that the woodcut decorations seem to be composed of the same elements as those of the ornaments in the novel, but reset into different patterns. (There were apparently two issues of this work: duodecimo and octavo, perhaps in order to be able to be bound with the two formats of *Bélisaire*. Vide the *Catalogue hebdomadaire*, 25 April 1767, no.17, item 3.)

The titlepage of this edition or issue is remarkably similar to that of the first, octavo edition. Even the woodcut ornament is the same. The one difference is

BÉLISAIRE.

PAR M. MARMONTEL,

De l'Académie Françoise.

Non miror, si quandò impetum capit
(Deus) spectandi magnos viros, colluctan-
tes cum aliquâ calamitate.

Sénec. De Provid.

A PARIS,

Chez MERLIN, Libraire, rue de la Harpe,
à l'Image S. Joseph.

M. DCC. LXVII.

Avec Approbation, & Privilége du Roi.

No 177: Marmontel, *Bélisaire*, 1767

the first line of the epigraph. The octavo edition reads 'Non miror, siquandò impetum capit' (BL, G.17757). Everything leads me to believe that the titlepage of the edition described here was pulled from the same forme, after a slight correction was effected, involving shifting 'Non miror, si' to the left in order to create a space between 'si' and 'quandò'. The leaf containing the 'Addition' in the copy described here has been tipped in. Could this then be the first, duodecimo edition?

For further information, see the Paris: Merlin, 1767 *Bélisaire* described right above.

Incipit: 'Dans la vieillesse de Justinien, l'Em- / pire, épuisé par de longs efforts, ap- / prochoit de sa décadence.'

178

Marmontel: *Bélisaire*, 1767

Jean François Marmontel (1723-1799): Belisaire. / Par M. Marmontel, / De l'Académie Françoise. / [rule] / Non miror, si quandò impetum capit / (Deus) spectandi magnos viros, colluctan- / tes cum aliquâ calamitate. / Sénec. De Provid. / [rule] / [composite woodcut ornament; see the commentary] / A Paris, / Chez Merlin, Libraire, rue de la Harpe, / à l'Image S. Joseph. / [rule] / M. DCC. LXVII. / Avec Approbation, & Privilége du Roi.

12°: 1 pl + [j]-x + [1]-272 + [274], [275]-340 pp. + 3 ff. (2 + 3 pp.)

Commentary: The pagination reflects a preface, *Bélisaire*, halftitle for 'Fragmens / de / philosophie morale.' (with the 'Avis' verso), the *Fragments* proper, 1 f. (2 pp.) of the 'Addition à la note de la page 237' and 2 ff. (3 pp.) of legal material. At the end is Le Prieur's colophon: 'De l'Imprimerie de P. Alex. le Prieur, / Imprimeur du Roi, rue S. Jacques.' For the 'addition' and the legal material, see the first entry above dealing with *Bélisaire*.

This is yet another edition of Marmontel's controversial novel for 1767, 'x + 340 pp.' The woodcut decoration on the titlepage, going outside inwards, consists of an ornamental border; a rectangle formed by five boxes with dark boxes inside top and bottom, four to either side; five xs on top and bottom, four to either side; two rows of four dot-line xs in the centre.

I have three copies of this edition. All have four illustrations. Two sets are in poor states (copies B and C), and one is sharp and clear (copy A). The pictures comprise: a frontispiece by Le Vasseur after Gravelot (column to the left); facing p.57, after Gravelot (no signature for the engraver); facing p.69 by Le Veau after Gravelot; facing p.255 (copies A and B) by Masquelier after Gravelot (facing p.149 in copy C). The last picture is bound in facing p.149 in copy C doubtless because the chapter indicator is fuzzy and the binder (or 'brocheur') read 'Ch. XII' for 'Ch. XVI'. All pictures bear captions. It might interest the reader that copy A was obviously printed before the others, and that it is bound in contemporary English calf. Copies B and C are bound in contemporary continental calf (French – possibly Parisian – for C; no geographical provenance is possible for B).

There is no half titlepage for the volumes. For further information, see the first entry for *Bélisaire* above.

Incipit: 'Dans la vieillesse de Justinien, l'Em- / pire, épuisé par de longs efforts, ap- / prochoit de sa décadence.'

179

Marmontel: *Bélisaire*, 1767

Jean François Marmontel (1723-1799): Belisaire. / Par M. Marmontel, / De l'Académie Françoise. / [rule] / Non miror, si quandò impetum capit / (Deus) spectandi magnos viros, colluc- / tantes cum aliquâ calamitate. / Sénec. De Provid. / [rule] / [composite woodcut ornament; see the commentary] / A Paris, / Chez Merlin, Libraire, rue de la Harpe, / à l'Image S. Joseph. / [rule] / M. DCC. LXVII. / Avec Approbation, & Privilége du Roi.

12°: 2 pl + [j]-x + [1]-272 + [274], [275]-340 pp. + 3 ff. (3 + 2 pp.)

Commentary: There is a halftitle for the volume reading 'Belisaire.' The pagination reflects a preface, *Bélisaire*, halftitle for 'Fragmens / de / philosophie morale.' (the 'avis' verso), the *Fragments* proper, 2 ff. (3 pp.) of legal material, 1 f. (2 pp.) of the 'Addition à la note de la page 237'. At the end of the *Fragments* is Le Prieur's colophon; 'De l'Imprimerie de P. Alex, [*sic*] le Prieur, / Imprimeur du Roi, rue S. Jacques.' For the legal material and the 'Addition', see the first entry for *Bélisaire* above.

The woodcut ornament on the titlepage consists of (going from outside inwards): an ornamental border; a square formed by boxes within boxes, five on each side; four sides of three double-line xs with stars in the corners; three rows of dot-line xs, four on the top, four on the bottom, the middle row having two (one irregular) laid on their sides. This decoration is repeated on p.68.

There are the following illustrations, in a mediocre state: frontispiece by Le Vasseur after Gravelot (column to the left); facing p.57, after Gravelot (no name of an engraver); facing p.69 by Le Veau after Gravelot; facing p.149 by Masquelier after Gravelot. All engravings are captioned.

The last gathering consists of P, Pij, [P3-4]. The leaf containing the 'Addition' is tipped in at the end.

It might amuse the reader to learn that this volume bears the gilt arms of a cardinal (on the front and back covers of the binding) and that, although the title pieces on the spine are missing, the embossed residue reads something like: 'Vertu de [illegible]'. (The volume indication was evidently ii, or possibly iii.)

For further information concerning *Bélisaire*, see the first entry in this bibliography dealing with the novel.

Incipit: 'Dans la vieillesse de Justinien, l'Em- / pire, épuisé par de longs efforts, ap- / prochoit de sa décadence.'

BÉLISAIRE.

PAR M. MARMONTEL;

De l'Académie Françoise.

Non miror , si quandò impetum capit
(Deus) spectandi magnos viros , colluctan-
tes cum aliquá calamitate.

Sénec. De Provid.

A PARIS,

Chez MERLIN , Libraire , rue de la Harpe,
à l'Image S. Joseph.

M. DCC. LXVII.

Avec Approbation , & Privilége du Roi,

No 178: Marmontel, *Bélisaire*, 1767

180

Marmontel: *Bélisaire*, 1767

Jean François Marmontel (1723-1799): Bélisaire. / Par M. Marmontel, / De l'Académie Française. / [rule formed of line of decorations] / Non miror, si quandò impetum capit / (Deus) spectandi magnos viros, colluctantes / cum aliquâ calamitate. / Sénec. De Provid. / [rule formed of line of decorations] / [composite, symmetrical woodcut ornament: square formed of 8x8 little crosses, each side containing triangular shaped decorations on outside topped by finials] / A Paris, / Chez Merlin, Libraire, rue de la Harpe, à / l'Image S. Joseph. / [double rule] / M. DCC. LXVII. / Avec Approbation & Privilege du Roi.

12°: 1 f. (titlepage) + iij-ix + 1-191, [192], 193-238 pp. + 2 ff. (3 pp.)

Commentary: The pagination reflects a preface, the novel, an 'Avis' (p.[192]), the *Fragments de philosophie morale* and 2 ff. (3 pp.) of legal material. There is no colophon. The 'Addition à la note' is incorporated into the note proper (pp.165-66).

This edition is not listed in MMF (67.39). It is different, too, from a similar edition to be found in the BN (also not listed in MMF; Y2.51305). The pagination is similar, but far from identical: 1 f. (titlepage) + [iij]-xij + [1]-189 + [193]-238 pp. + 2 ff. (2 + 2 pp.), in-12°. Pages [191-92] are the halftitle for the *Fragmens*, with the 'Avis' verso. Le Prieur's colophon appears on p.238. The penultimate folio (2 pp.) is the 'Addition', for p.164. The last folio (2 pp.) comprises the legal material. There are no illustrations present in either copy, and none seems ever to have been bound with my book anyway. Regardless of the legal material and the indication of an 'approbation' and 'privilege' on the titlepage, my book is a piracy, and the legal documents would have had no effect.

In spite of the pagination, the signatures in my book are consecutive from the beginning. Curiously this edition is signed in 6s (A6, B6-X6); BN, Y2.51305, is signed in 8s plus 4s.

For further information concerning the novel (and the many editions for 1767), see the first entry for *Bélisaire* above.

Incipit: 'Dans la vieillesse de Justinien, l'Em- / pire, épuisé par de longs efforts, / approchoit de sa décadence.'

181

Marmontel (and Lezay-Marnézia): *Bélisaire* (and *L'Heureuse famille*), 1767

Jean François Marmontel (1723-1799) and François Adrien, marquis de Lezay-Marnézia; edited by Siegfried Lebrecht Crusius: Belisaire / Par / Mr. Marmontel, / de l'Académie Françoise. / [rule] / Non miror, si quandò impetum capit (Deus) spectan- / di magnos viros, colluctantes cum aliquâ calamitate. / Senec. De Provid. / [rule] / Nouvelle Edition, / Enrichie de nouvelles remarques et de /

très-belles figures, et augmentée / de / l'heureuse famille, / Conte moral, par le même. / [woodcut ornament: military trophy of shield and crossed weapons surmounted by a plumed helmet] / Avec Privilége de S.A.S. l'Electeur de Saxe. / [rule] / A Leipsic, / chez Siegfried Lebrecht Crusius. / MDCCLXVII.

8°: 1 pl + 3 ff. (6 pp.) + [1]-217 [for 317], [318-19] pp.

Commentary: The contents of this volume are as follows: titleleaf; preface (the six preliminary pages); *Bélisaire*, pp.[1]-218; halftitle page for 'L'heureuse / famille. / Conte moral. / [rule] / Il laboure le champ que labouroit son pere. / Racan.', p.[219]; 'A madame la ....', p.[220]; *L'Heureuse famille*, pp.[221]-262; halftitle page for 'Fragmens / de / philosophie morale. / R4 [signature]', p.[263]; 'Avis', p.[264]; *Fragmens de philosophie morale*, pp.[265]-217 (for 317); 'Addition A la Note de la Page 187.', pp.[318-19]. P.217 (for 317) has the following colophon: 'a Leipsic, / de l'Imprimerie de Breitkopf. 1767.'

There are the following fine illustrations, copies of the Gravelot originals:
1. facing the last page of the preface, the frontispiece, 'nach Gravelot von J. F. Bause gest.'; ruined column to the left, with no inscription;
2. facing p.44: 'Gravelot inv. / C. Crusius [sp.?]'; 'Chap. 6.' on top right;
3. facing p.54: 'Gravelot inven / C. G. Giyset sc.'; 'Chap. 7.' top right;
4. facing p.204: 'H. Gravelot Inv. / IMStock Sculp.'; 'Ch.XVI.' top right.

There are numerous notes by the 'editor', presumably Crusius himself.

L'Heureuse famille is a tale by Lezay-Marnésia which, doubtless because of its superficial resemblance to some of Marmontel's 'contes moraux', was falsely attributed by the editor.

This edition seems to be listed in the NUC (location: University of Wisconsin at Madison), in Krauss-Fontius (no. 4338, with three locations), and is also cited by the Messkatalog (OM 1767, p.848). It is not mentioned by MMF, who do however give a Vienne: J. Thomas, 1767 edition (BN, 16° Y2.18977). That copy also contains illustrations after Gravelot, and the interesting 'Notes de l'éditeur de Leipsic, pour le XVme chapitre' (8 pp. at the end). Those notes are very conservative in nature, so it is little wonder that they were reprinted with an edition of *Bélisaire* in Vienna. (The court at Vienna was known for its conservatism.) For example, where Marmontel has written that 'les vérités mystérieuses, & qui ont besoin d'être révélées, ne tiennent point à la morale. Examinez-les bien: Dieu les a détachées de la chaîne de nos devoirs, afin que, sans révélation, il y eût par-tout d'honnêtes gens' (pp.193-94), Crusius begins his diatribe with: 'La religion de Bélisaire n'est qu'un mélange de fanatisme & de libertinage. Ses vérités de sentiment, ses préceptes de morale ne sont que la simple Loi naturelle [etc.]' (p.194). That is indicative enough of the rest.

In passing, the Messkatalog has an edition of *L'Heureuse famille* which seems to have escaped the attention of modern bibliographers: 'L'heureuse Famille, Conte Moral de Mr. de *Marmontel*. 8vo. Amsterd. & à Leipsic, chez Arkstée & Merkus', Messk., OM 1767, p.850.

Incipits: (*Bélisaire*) 'Dans la vieillesse de Justinien, l'Em- / pire, épuisé par de longs efforts, / approchoit de sa décadence.'

(*L'Heureuse famille*) 'Le jeune Basile étoit le fruit d'une union / mal assortie.'

Ecce fpectaculum dignum ad quod refpiciat
intentus operi fuo Deus ecce par Deo dignum.
Vir fortis cum mala fortuna compofitus.

BÉLISAIRE.

PAR M. MARMONTEL,

De l'Académie Françoise.

*Non miror, fi quandò impetum capit
(Deus) fpectandi magnos viros, colluctantes cum aliquâ calamitate.*
            Sénec. De Provid.

A PARIS,
Chez MERLIN, Libraire, rue de la Harpe,
à l'Image S. Joſeph.

M DCC. LXVII.
Avec Approbation, & Privilége du Roi.

No 179: Marmontel, *Bélisaire*, 1767

BÉLISAIRE.

PAR M. MARMONTEL,

DE L'ACADÉMIE FRANÇAISE.

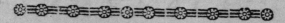

*Non miror, si quandò impetum capit
(Deus) spectandi magnos viros, colluctantes
cum aliquâ calamitate.*

Sénec. De Provid.

A PARIS,

Chez MERLIN, Libraire, rue de la Harpe, à
l'Image S. Joseph.

M. DCC. LXVII.

Avec Approbation & Privilege du Roi.

No 180: Marmontel, *Bélisaire*, 1767

182

Marmontel: *Bélisaire*, 1767

Jean François Marmontel (1723-1799): Bélisaire. / Par M. Marmontel, / De l'Académie Françoise. / [treble rule] / Non miror, si quandò impetum capit (Deus) / spectandi magnos viros, colluctantes cum aliquâ / calamitate. / Sénec. de Provid. / [treble rule] / [woodcut ornament: bouquet of flowers tied with ribbon] / A Neuf chatel [*sic*], / [double rule] / M. DCC. LXVII.

8°: 1 pl + [j]-viij + [1]-225 + [228], [229]-283 pp. (P.[226] is blank).

Commentary: The pagination reflects a preface, the novel, a halftitle for 'Fragmens / de / philosophie morale.' (p.[227], with the 'Avis' verso, p.[228]; p.[226] is blank), the *Fragments* proper. There are no illustrations. This edition was in all likelihood printed in Neuchâtel, as indicated on the titlepage.

MMF list what is probably this edition (67.39), with the only location for the Bibliothèque publique of Neuchâtel. I could find no other copy. Because of its rarity and because of the many editions of *Bélisaire* listed in this bibliography, I have chosen to include it. For further information, see the first *Bélisaire* listed above.

The 'Addition à la note' is not here present, either in the text or as an addendum.

Incipit: 'Dans la vieillesse de Justinien, l'Em- / pire, épuisé par de longs efforts, / approchoit de sa décadence.'

183

Marmontel: *Bélisaire*, 1767

Jean François Marmontel (1723-1799): Belisaire. / Par M. Marmontel, / De l'Académie Françoise. / [double rule] / Non miror, siquandò impetum capit [vertical bar; typographical separator?] (Deus) / spectandi magnos viros, colluc- tantes cum aliquâ / calamitate. / Sénec. De Provid. / [double rule] / [woodcut ornament, largely symmetrical: baldaquin in ornamental border with globe in centre on a table/pedestal and with what look like urns to either side] / A Amsterdam, / Aux Dépens de la Compagnie. / [double rule] / M. DCC. LXVII.

12°: 1 pl + [i]-vj + [1]-204 + [206], [207]-296 pp.

Commentary: The first item is a 'Préface'; then follow *Bélisaire*, a half titlepage for the 'Fragmens / de / philosophie morale.', with the 'Avis' verso (p.[206]), and finally the *Fragments* themselves. There are no illustrations. The addition to the note is incorporated into the main body of the work (chapter XV, note, pp.177- 78). MMF list what might be this edition, 'Amsterdam, Compagnie, 1767' (67.39) after the Lille and Nantes library catalogues. Since it is not to be found in the NUC, the BNC or the BLC, I have chosen to list it. For further information, see the first entry for *Bélisaire* above.

Incipit: 'Dans la vieillesse de Justinien, l'Empire, / épuisé par de longs efforts, approchoit de sa dé- / cadence'.

184

Marmontel: *Bélisaire*, 1769

Jean François Marmontel (1723-1799): Belisaire. / Par Mr. Marmontel, / De l'Académie Françoise. / Nouvelle Edition Augmentée. / [rule] / Non miror, si quando impetum capit (Deus) / spectandi magnos viros, colluctantes cum aliquâ / calamitate. / Senec. De Provid. / [rule] / [woodcut decoration: circular garland] / A Lausanne, / Chez François Grasset & Comp. / [rule] / M. D. CC. LXIX.

8°: 2 pl + [I]-VIII, [1]-173, [174], [175]-217, [218-19] pp.

Commentary: The pagination reflects a preface, the novel, the one paragraph introduction to the 'Fragmens de philosophie morale' (the 'Avis', p.[174]) with, at the end, the 'Addition A la Note de la page 150' which corresponds to the correct page in this edition. There is a halftitle to the volume reading simply: 'Belisaire.' This edition seems to be listed in MMF (67.39), after the only known copy in Lausanne (Bibliothèque cantonale et universitaire) and after Quérard. The latter indicates: 'Lausanne, 1769, in-12, fig.; ou 1771, et 1784 in-8 fig' (v.548b). If Quérard be accurate, he lists another edition or issue for 1769. Because of the extreme rarity of the edition described here and because of the many items of Marmontel interest in this bibliography, I have chosen to include this item.

Although it is not listed in Cohen or in Reynaud, there are several engravings of somewhat primitive quality (copies of the original Gravelot designs), as follows:
1. frontispiece by L. A. Chovin after Gravelot; signed; column to the left;
2. facing p.36, by Chovin (signed), after Gravelot (unsigned);
3. facing p.43, by [Chovin?; unsigned], after Gravelot (unsigned);
4. facing p.161, by [Chovin?; unsigned], after Gravelot (unsigned).

Incipit: 'Dans la vieillesse de Justinien, l'Empire, / épuisé par de longs efforts, approchoit de sa / décadence.'

185

Marmontel: *Contes moraux*, 1775

Jean François Marmontel (1723-1799): Contes / moraux / et / pieces choisies / de / M. Marmontel / de l'academie françoise. [françoise, for iii] / [rule] / Tome premier [second, troisieme]. / [small woodcut ornaments, i: rococo; ii: very simple, a kind of rule; iii: backwards version of that to be found in ii] / Avec Privilege de S.A.S. l'Elect. de Saxe. / [rule formed of little decorations] / A Leipsic, / chez S. L. Crusius, Libraire, / 1775.

12°, i: 1 pl + [1]-12 + 1 f. (1 p.) + [1]-243 pp.
   ii: 1 pl + 1 f. (1 p.) + [1]-275 pp.
   iii: 1 pl + 1 f. (1 p.) + [1]-223 pp.

Commentary: The only trace of this edition I have been able to find is in the Messkatalog, which once again underscores the importance of the series: 'Contes

H. Gravelot Inv.   I.A Choven Sculp.
Ecce fpectaculum dignum, ad quod refpiciat
intentus operi fuo Deus: ecce par Deo dignum,
Vir fortis cum mala fortuna compofitus.   Senec.

Biergio e M. 3. 5.

BELISAIRE.

PAR Mr. MARMONTEL,

De l'Académie Françoife.

NOUVELLE EDITION AUGMENTÉE.

Non miror , fi quando impetum capit (Deus)
fpectandi magnos viros , colluctantes cum aliquâ
calamitate.
        Senec. De Provid.

A LAUSANNE,

Chez FRANÇOIS GRASSET & Comp.

M. D. CC. LXIX.

No 184: Marmontel, *Bélisaire*, 1769

moraux & Pieces choisies de Mr. *Marmontel*. Nouv. Ed. augm. & corrigée, av[ec] tres-belles fig. 3 Tomes. 12. Leipsic, chez Siegfr[ied] Lebr[echt] Crusius', OM 1775, p.882. The next entry is for 'Les mêmes sans fig. 12. chez le même'. Thus it would appear that there was an issue with engravings as well as the one described here.

This edition contains the following tales (according to the headtitles):

1. *Alcibiade, ou le moi*, i.[1]-35;
2. *Soliman II*, i.36-59;
3. *Le Scrupule, ou l'amour mécontent de lui-même*, i.60-91;
4. *Les Quatre flacons, ou les aventvres d'Alcidonis de Megare*, i.92-121;
5. *Lausus et Lydie*, i.122-36;
6. *Le Mari sylphe*, i.137-74;
7. *Heureusement*, i.175-99;
8. *Les Deux infortunées*, i.200-19;
9. *Tout ou rien*, i.220-43;
10. *Le Philosophe soi-disant*, ii.[1]-32;
11. *La Bergere des Alpes*, ii.33-68;
12. *La Mauvaise mere*, ii.69-89;
13. *La Bonne mere*, ii.89-117;
14. *L'Ecole des peres*, ii.118-47;
15. *Annete et Lubin, histoire véritable*, ii.148-62;
16. *Les Mariages samnites, anecdote ancienne*, ii.163-87;
17. *Laurette*, ii.188-238;
18. *Le Connoisseur*, ii.239-75;
19. *L'Heureux divorce*, iii.[1]-46;
20. *Le Bon mari*, iii.46-82;
21. *La Femme comme il y en a peu*, iii.82-119;
22. *L'Amitié a l'épreuve*, iii.120-75;
23. *Le Misanthrope corrigé*, iii.176-223.

These tales comprise the entire first series of the 'contes moraux'. The first editions date to 1755-1759, 1761 and 1765. See MMF, 61.12.

The first item in i is the preface; the unpaginated folios contain one page each of 'Tables'. The catchword 'CON-' at the end of the preface leads to the head title of vol. i ('Contes moraux'). The first table is on the 'verso' of its folio. None of the folios containing the 'Tables' is part of the gatherings of the respective volume. (Neither are the titlepage leaves.) These are tipped in. The end of iii carries 'Fin du Tome troisième'. There are no 'pièces choisies' present. Perhaps the collection was continued? (The woodcut ornaments scattered through the three volumes are, many of them, rather interesting.)

There are several editions of Marmontel's *Contes moraux* which do not seem to be listed in MMF (61.12, 65.35, 92.28), one with *Bélisaire*:

1. *Contes moraux*, 1778. 'Contes moraux & Belisaire par *Marmontel*. IV Volumes. 12. Bale, chez C. A. Serini', Messkatalog, MM 1778, p.578.

2. *Contes moraux*, 1788. 'Contes moraux, par *Marmontel*. Edn. exactement corrigée. 4 Vol. 8. à Paris & à Leipzig & à Nuremberg, en comm[ission]. chez C. Weigel & Schneider', Messkatalog, MM 1788, p.288.

3. *Nouveaux contes moraux*, 1799. 'Contes, nouveaux contes moraux, p. Marmon-

tel. Nouv. edit. 8. à Marbourg, n. libr. acad. [nouvelle librairie académique?]',
Messkatalog, OM 1799, p.205.

While on the subject of *Contes moraux*: to the editions of Mlle d'Uncy's
compilation, the *Contes moraux dans le goût de M. Marmontel* I would add a four
volume edition, 'gr. [in-]12. Francf[ort]. Esslinger. [1]763' (Heinsius, i, col.597;
Heinsius 1793, iv.486; Kayser i.480b. The latter adds the mention of '(Schäfer)',
the bookdealer.) This is listed (apparently) in Krauss-Fontius: 'Contes moraux
dans le goût de ceux de M. Marmontel, recueillis de divers auteurs, publiés par
Mlle Uncy. 4 vols. Francfort: Knoch, Eslinger, 1763' (no. 4485, vol. i in a
subsidiary of the Deutsche Akademie der Wissenschaften zu Berlin).

There are other 'contes' of interest to students of the 'genre romanesque'
which have escaped the attention of modern bibliographers:

1. *Nouveaux contes à rire*, 1722. '[contes] –nouveaux, à Rire avec figures et
avantures plaisantes II Tom. [in-]8. Cologne. [1]722' (Heinsius *loc. cit.*; not
listed in modern bibliographies dealing with prose fiction). The first edition of
this work I could find (without having access to the BN anonyms or the Arsenal)
is for Amsterdam: G. Gallet, 1699, with the title of *Nouveaux contes à rire et aventures
plaisantes de ce temps, ou récréations françaises* (NUC: several locations; further
information is given in OCLC; also in Krauss-Fontius no. 4393). There were
quite a number of editions of this collection. A cursory search yields Amsterdam,
George Gallet, 1700 (BL; listed in the BLC in the fairly extensive listings of
'Contes', xliii, cols.313-16); Cologne: Roger Bontemps, 1702, a 3ᵉ édition
(OCLC: Cleveland Public Library, BL); 1709 (same place and publisher: NUC,
Library of Congress); idem., 1713 (NUC: Princeton); etc. (1722 [NUC and BL;
probably the same as that cited in Heinsius and Heinsius 1793, iv.486], 1733
[BLC], 1762 [NUC], 1775 [NUC], 1781 [NUC]...). Lever lists a *Nouveaux contes
à rire de Bocace, de Douville et autres personnes enjoüées*, Paris: J. B. Loyson, 1692
(p.316). All this does not include editions of *Contes à rire, ou récréations françaises*
(for example, 3 vols, Paris: Aux dépens de la Compagnie, 1769, in-12; BL). The
latter work (not listed in MMF), while mostly containing short recitals of
dubious veracity, also includes some long tales, e.g. 'Nouvelle plaisante et
récréative', iii.[1]-66. The editions of the *Nouveaux contes à rire* vary somewhat
with respect to the contents.

2. *Histoires, ou contes du temps passé*, 1748. 'Histoires ou Contes du Tems passé,
avec des moralitez par Mons. Perrault, grand 8. à Celle, chez *G. Conrad Gsellius*',
Messkatalog, OM 1748, f.H1v. Not in BNC, BLC, NUC.

3. *Histoires, ou contes du temps passé*, 1750. 'Histoire[s] ou Contes du Tems passé,
8. Celle, chez George Conr. Gsellius', Messkatalog, OM 1750, p. 52; also
Heinsius 1793, iv.516. By Perrault; not in BNC, BLC, NUC.

4. *Contes des fées*, 1761. 'Contes des Fées, avec des moralités, par Mr. *Perault*.
Franz. u[nd] Deutsch. m[it] K[upfern]. 12. Berlin, bey Arnold Wewer', Messkatalog, OM 1761, p.147. Not in NUC, BNC, BLC.

5. *Contes du temps passé*, 1767. *Contes du temps passé de ma Mère l'Oye* [...] Londres:
S. van den Berg, 1764. BL: Ch.760/7.

6. *Histoires, ou contes du temps passé*, 1767. 'Histoires ou Contes du tems passé
avec des moralités par Mr. *Perault*. Edit. nouv. französisch und deutsch. m[it]

K[upfern]. 8. Berlin, chez Arn. Wewer', Messkatalog, MM 1767, p.897. Not in the BNC, NUC, BLC.

7. *Contes de ma mère l'Oye*, 1770. 'Contes de ma Mere l'Oye. Nouv. Ed. franc. & allem. av[ec] fig. 8. à Berlin, chez A. Wever', Messkatalog, OM 1770, p.76. Heinsius, *Handbuch* has a '*Histoires, ou contes du tems-passé*, avec des moralités, francois & allemand par Mr. Perrault, avec fig. 8vo. Berl[in]. Wever, [1]770' which might be the same (p.798). See too Heinsius 1793, iv.516.

8. *Contes à sentiments*, 1781. '[contes] à Sentimens, ou recueil des jolies pièces les plus récentes. [in-]8. Nuremb. Grattenauer. [1]781' (Heinsius *loc. cit.*; Heinsius 1793, iv.486; not in Barbier, Jones, MMF, NUC, BLC). The pieces contained in this collection could well be in verse.

9. *Le Conteur*, 1785. 'Conteur, le, No. 1-6. [in-]8. Dessau, Librairie des Savans. [1]785' (Heinsius, *loc. cit.*; Heinsius 1793, iv.486). This seems obviously to be a periodical, perhaps containing pieces of prose fiction. The only copy of this, if it be the same, I could find, and only one issue of that, is listed in the *Catalogue collectif des périodiques*: 'Le Conteur. s.l. 8° BN. Z.46118 (1784: no. 4)' (ii.252b). The NUC has an entry for *Le Conteur*, Londres; Paris: Hôtel de Boutihillier [...], 1789, 2 vols, 17 cm (University of Michigan), which I have not been able to see. The BL also has a *Le Conteur*, Londres, 1789 in one volume (v-x + [1]-366 pp. in-12° with a halftitle for 'Le Conteur.', verso: 'A Paris, / Hôtel de Bouthillier, rue des Poitevins.'), the contents of which are a mixture of reflexions, second-hand, factual(?) stories and the like.

10. *Contes des fées*, 1792. 'Contes des fées, p[ar] Charles Perrault, et Mad. la Comt. de Murat, avec fig. 8vo. à Vienne, chez F. I. Kaiserer' Messkatalog, OM 1792, p.153; also in Heinsius, *Handbuch*, p.780 and in Heinsius 1793, iv.486. (See too Heinsius 1798, p.483-84).

Incipit: ('Alcibiade, ou le moi') 'La nature & la fortune sembloient avoir conspiré au bonheur d'Alcibiade.'

186

Marmontel: *Contes moraux*, 1778

Jean François Marmontel (1723-1799): Contes / moraux, / par M. Marmontel, / suivis / D'une Apologie du Théatre. / Nouvelle édition, / Corrigée et augmentée. / Tome premier [second, troisieme, quatrieme]. / [woodcut decoration, different for each volume] / A la Haye. / [rule] / M. DCC. LXXVIII.

12°, i: 1 f. (titlepage) + [iij]-xij + [1]-135, [136] pp.
  ii: 1 f. (titlepage) + [3]-175, [176] pp.
  iii: 1 f. (titlepage) + [3]-163, [164] pp.
  iv: 1 f. (titlepage) + [3]-44 [for 78], 79-417 [for 174], [175] pp.

Commentary: The first item in vol. i is the preface; the last page of each volume is a 'table'. Included are the first series of the 'contes moraux' which appeared between 1755-1765. See MMF 61.12. (See too the preceding entry. The same tales are included in this collection, albeit in a different order.) The second item in vol. iv (p.79-[174]) is the 'Apologie du théatre, ou analyse de la Lettre de M.

Rousseau, Citoyen de Geneve, à M. d'Alembert, au sujet des Spectacles' (according to the head title). This piece has its own running title for 'Apologie [versos] / du théatre [rectos]'. I know of no other copy of this edition, which is not mentioned in any bibliography I have consulted. Curiously vol. iv pp.[3]-4 are f.A[1?], and pp.5-6 are f.B[1].

MMF mention no edition for 1778, but there is yet another one listed in the NUC, a 'nouv. éd., rev., corr., & considérablement augm.' […] for Paris: Merlin, 1778, 3 vols (Library of Congress). I might mention that the preface in the edition recorded here differs somewhat from that in the preceding entry.

In passing, I note that MMF list a '*Suite des contes*…, Paris, 1762, in-8' after Freund (Max Freund, *Die Moralischen Erzählungen Marmontels*, Halle 1904, MMF 61.12). The OCLC contains the following, somewhat enigmatic entry: '*Contes moraux par M. Marmontel. Suivis d'une apologie du théâtre*. [s.l. Hare, 1762,' 2 vols, 17 cm (location: SUNY at Binghamton).

Incipit: ('Alcibiade, ou le moi') 'La nature & la fortune sembloient avoir conspiré au bonheur d'Alcibiade.'

187

Marsy: *Semaines amusantes*, 1750

Abbé François Marie de Marsy (1714-1763): Semaines / amusantes / ou / nou- / veaux / essais periodiques, / contenant / Un mélange curieux de Contes, d'A- / necdotes, de Pensées ingénieuses, / d'Observations, d'Analyses inté- / ressantes, &c. / [rule] / ....Deus nobis hæc otia fecit. / Ille meas errare boves, ut cernis, & ipsum / Ludere quæ vellem calamo permisit agresti. / Premiere Partie. / [small woodcut ornament: symmetrical, stylised flower] / A Bruxelles, / Chez la Veuve Tonnins. / [rule] / M. DCC. L.

12°: 1 f. (titlepage) + iij-vj + [3]-[52] pp. (The page numbers are enclosed in brackets.)

Commentary: The first part is a preface titled 'A M..... Conseiller au Parlement de Rennes'. The head title, p.[3], reads: 'Semaines amusantes. N°. I.' (The signatures are highly irregular.) This work does not fall squarely into the category of the 'genre romanesque', but it does contain snatches of fiction in prose, amongst which adaptations/extracts of Martial's *Arrêts d'amour* (pp.[23]-[46], continuing with commentary to p.[48]). It is actually the beginning of a periodical venture started by Marsy; to my knowledge, no more of it appeared.

Hatin cites it up to the word 'périodiques', further giving 'Bruxelles, 1750, in-12, Louvre'. Unfortunately the imperial library of the Louvre went up in smoke, together with most of the Tuileries Palace which housed it, in the nineteenth century. (This is an entry only to be found in Hatin's index, since the *Semaines amusantes* came to his attention while his bibliography was in the press.) I have been unable to locate another copy (*Catalogue collectif des périodiques du début du XVIIe siècle à 1939* [BN, iv, Paris 1967]; the *Union list of serials*, 3rd edition [v 1965]; *British union-catalogue of periodicals*; NUC; BLC; BNC, etc.) It is however listed in the *Dictionnaire des journalistes (1600-1789)*, Jean Sgard director, with the collaboration of Michel Gilot and Françoise Weil, and a team (Grenoble 1976) p.262. The editors attribute this work to Marsy, after Arsenal, ms [Archives de la Bastille] 10,302. (Needless to say, it is not listed in Quérard, Barbier or any other bibliography I have examined.)

In that particular box of papers having to do with censorship affairs is an announcement of sorts: 'Semaines Amusantes, ou nouveaux Essais Périodiques. C'est le titre qu'il donne a son ouvrage qui a parû pour la p^e fois le 19 fevrier 1750'. This is scribbled on a letter by Marsy to the police (probably to Duval, Berryer's secretary). It is an interesting document, both for the light it sheds on the *Semaines amusantes* and for showing what tight controls were exercised by the authorities: 'Je n'ai reçu votre lettre, monsieur, qu'hier au soir en rentrant. Quoique mon titre soit le même pour le fond, cependant comme j'en ai un peu changé la forme, je dois vous en avertir.

Semaines amusantes / ou / Bibliotheque des gens du Monde, Contenant un mélange curieux de contes, d'anecdotes, de pensées diverses, d'observations, d'analyses intéressantes &c / Ouvrage d'un goût nouveau. à Brusselles, chez La veuve Tonnins.

Outre Les articles que j'ai eu l'honneur de vous communiquer, il y en aura un autre, sous le titre de Nouveautez courantes. il comprendra pour cette semaine 1° L'annonce et la description (mais un peu mitigée) de l'hermaphrodite, d'après la dissertation de M. Mer[tru?]d, approuvé de la police. 2° Les livres nouveaux surtout les Romans. 3°. Les nouveautés du Theatre, Comme Galatée pour les derniers jours du Carnaval, Tancrede pour le commencement du Carême, La Force du Sang comedie de M. Destouches pour &c. Mes nouvelles ne sortiront point de cette sphere. j'ai l'honneur d'etre avec le plus respectueux attachement, Monsieur, votre tres humble & très obeissant serviteur. / L'abbé de Marsy'.

A note further along in the box indicates that Ballard fils was the actual printer, meaning of course that the *Semaines amusantes* appeared in Paris. (The work is again mentioned in a couple of miscellaneous pieces, including one titled '*1750* Ouvrages permis ou non permis': 'abbé de Marsy. semaines amusantes ou Bibliotheque des gens du monde'.)

There is nothing concerning new plays or novels in the present copy, but there is a section on the hermaphrodite, one Michel-Anne Drouart. (And also such tidbits as the description of a new kind of wig made of curled, iron wire; the automata at the foire St Germain, etc.) The preface claims that the periodical was started at the instigation of one of the author's provincial friends and that it was going to contain tales to please his friend's daughters, aged 10 and 15, analyses of *good* books, and not '*des modernes*', etc.

Incipit: ('Brusquet, fou de Henri II') 'Brusquet ne conçut pas comme Memnon (a), le projet insensé d'être sage.' (A note quotes the opening of Voltaire's tale.)

188

Matthieu: *Ælius Séjanus, histoire romaine*, 1618

Pierre Matthieu (1563-1621): Ælivs / Seianvs. / Histoire romai- / ne, recveillie / de diuers Autheurs. / Seconde edition. / [woodcut decoration] / A Roven, / Chez Iacqves Besongne, / ruë aux Iuifs, pres le Palais. / [rule] / M. DC. XVIII.

12°: 1 pl (titlepage) + 1 f. (2 pp.) + 1-304 pp.

Commentary: The first two pages recorded (1 f., ãij, actually part of the first gathering) are a dedication 'Av roy', signed 'P. Matthiev'. This novel first appeared in 1617, and went through several editions (Lever, pp.189-90). Lever lists the 'second' edition as above, citing the two copies in the BN (J.14998 and J.16490), further explaining that the latter copy has had its date changed to 'MDCXXVIII' in ink. Arbour mentions two copies in the BN and one in the BL (Roméo Arbour, *L'Ere baroque en France: répertoire chronologique des éditions de textes littéraires*, 2ᵉ partie: 1616-1628, Geneva 1979, no.8993.) I list my copy simply to remark that there were two editions of the 'seconde édition'; the two copies in the BN are of different editions and mine matches BN J.16490, which also seems the same as the BL copy (587.a.21[1-2]; I was unable to juxtapose my copy with the BL copy). Among the various differences, J.14998's titlepage reads '[...] / Histoire romaine, / [...]' vs. '[...] / Histoire romai- / ne [...]'.

As with the BN and the BL copy, mine is followed by an adaptation after Boccaccio authored by Matthieu, viz. 'Histoire / des prosperitez / malhevrevses, / D'vne femme Cathenoise, grande / Seneschalle de Naples. / En suite de AElius Seianus. / Par P. Matthiev. / [woodcut decoration, same as for *Ælius Séjanus*] / A Roven, / Chez Iacqves Besongne, / ruë aux Iuifs, pres le Palais. / [rule] / M. DC. XVIII.' + 1 f. (1 + 1 pp.) + 1-120 pp. in-12. The first two pages, 1 f. (not part of the first gathering), are a dedication to the king and an 'Advertissement' explaining that the tale is purportedly true, taken from Boccaccio's *De casibus virorum illustrium*. Purportedly, too, it actually recounts the fortunes and misfortunes of Concino Concini, maréchal d'Ancre – assassinated in 1617 – and his spouse; NUC. It seems certain that both works were issued together.

It might also be pointed out that the 'qvatrisme edition' (Roven: Iean Berthelin, 1626) was published not only with the *Histoire des prosperitez malheureuses* (titlepage with same place, publisher and date), but also with *Remarques d'estat et d'histoire, sur la vie et les seruices de monsievr de Villeroy* (titlepage with same publisher, place and date; signatures and pagination consecutive for all pieces, 1pl + 1 f. (2pp.) + 1-307 + titlepage + [311-12], 313-428 + titlepage + [431-32], 433-434, 435-548 pp. in-12°. BL: 587.a.22). Lever does not mention this edition. Possibly the *Remarques d'estat* appeared earlier with *Ælius Séjanus*?

Incipits: (*Ælius Séjanus*) 'Encores que les Princes disposent souuerainement de leurs cœurs, qu'ils y formēt l'amour & la haine'.

(*Histoire des prospérités malheureuses*) 'Les Estats se destruisent aussi tost par des foibles instrumens, que par des efforts violens'.

189

Meissner, Goethe, Gray and Bion (Cabanis transl.):
Mélanges de littérature allemande, 1797

August Gottlieb Meissner (1753-1807); Johann Wolfgang von Goethe (1749-1832); Thomas Gray (1716-1771); Bion of Phlossa, near Smyrna; translated by Pierre Jean Georges Cabanis (1757-1808): Mêlanges / de / littérature / allemande, / ou / choix de traductions / de l'allemand, etc. / [rule] / Les Lettres et les Arts nous consolaient encore. / [rule] / [small swell rule] / A Paris, / Chez J. J. Smits et Cᵉ., Imp.-Lib., rue de Tournon, / Nᵒ. 1133, Faubourg Germain. / [thin swell rule] / L'an V. de la république (1797.)

8°: 2 pl + [j]-xv + 1 f. (halftitle) + [3]-419, [420] pp.

Commentary: The volume halftitle reads 'Mêlanges / de / littérature / allemande.' Then follow the titlepage, and a dedication to Mme Helvétius in the form of a preface (pp.[j]-xv). Each item has its own halftitle which I transcribe, giving the incipits and pagination:

1. 'Gustave Lindau. / Fragment / Extrait du Voyage de Branko. / Traduit de l'allemand de Meissner. / A [signature]' + p.[3]-125; 'Branko avoit employé beaucoup de / tems à parcourir beaucoup de pays.'

2. 'Roxane. / Épisode de l'histoire / de Massoud.' + pp.[129]-153; 'Massoud prononça, durant le cours de / son règne long et paisible'.

3. 'Les filles / de / Guillaume d'Albanak. / Traduit de l'allemand de Meissner.' + pp.[157]-179; 'Alfred, roi d'Angleterre, était chéri / ou plutôt adoré de ses sujets.'

4. 'Le / chien de Melaï. / Traduit / de l'allemand de Meissner. / M3 [signature]' + pp.[183]-220; 'Depuis les violences trop célèbres des / iconoclastes, la sculpture ne s'était point / relevée chez les Grecs du moyen âge.'

5. 'La / vertu héroïque / chez / les peuples / de l'Orénoque. / Traduit de l'allemand de Meissner.' + pp.[223]-232; 'Xotilaqua: Nous voici donc encore / une fois!'

6. 'Diego / de Colmenarès. / Anecdote / traduite de l'allemand / de Meissner.' + pp.[235]-287; 'Rien de plus commun que de voir de / jeunes Espagnols, entreprenans ou légers, / aller'.

7. 'Stella, / pièce de théâtre / traduite / de l'allemand de Goéthe. / T [signature]' + pp.[291]-396; 'La Maîtresse de poste. / Charles, Charles!'.

8. 'Le cimetière / de campagne, / élégie de Gray. / Traduite de l'anglais.' + pp.[399]-408; 'Le son mélancolique de la cloche du / soir, annonce le départ du jour.'

9. 'Idylle de Bion, / sur / la mort d'Adonis, / traduite du grec.' + pp.[411]-419. 'Je déplore la mort d'Adonis; le bel Ado- / nis n'est plus'.

The last page is a table.

This volume is a very large octavo, exquisitely printed on special 'papier vélin'. I have listed it under Meissner's name, since he is the main author. Items 1-6 are prose-fiction. Goethe's *Stella* is a play. Gray's *Elegy* and Bion's *Idyll* are both rendered into prose. I leave it up to the reader to decide whether he wishes to classify them as pieces of prose fiction, or prose-poems.

Barbier attributes this series of translations/adaptations to Cabanis (iii, col.113).

This volume is not listed in major library catalogues (BNC, BLC, NUC, together with all supplements), and is not in MMF. In 1786 there appeared a collection titled *Choix de petits romans imités de l'allemand* [...], containing material after Meissner, H. P. Sturz and others, adapted by Nicolas de Bonneville. (See MMF 86.49.) Included is *Le Sultan Massoud*, but that compendium seems to have nothing to do with the book described here.

Finally, none of these items is contained in Cabanis's *Œuvres complètes* (5 vols, Paris 1823-1825).

190

Mercier de Compiègne: *Les Concerts républicains*, 1795

Claude François Xavier Mercier, called Mercier de Compiègne (1763-1800): Les concerts / républicains, / ou / choix lyrique / et sentimental. / Ouvrage orné de 4 gravures, dessinées et / gravées par Quéverdo. / [rule] / A Paris, / Chez Louis, libraire, rue Severin, n°.29. / Et se trouve chez Charon, libraire et / marchand d'estampes, passage du théâtre de / la rue Faydeau, N°. 8. / [rule] / L'an IIIe. de la République. / Ere vulgaire 1795.

18°: 2 pl + [1]-2, [3]-210 pp. + 1 f. (2 pp.)

Commentary: The pagination given above reflects an 'Avis des éditeurs', the collection with the 'table' (pp.[205]-210) and then an 'Avis'. There is a volume halftitle for 'Les concerts / républicains.' At the end of the table (p.210), there is the following colophon: 'De l'Imprimerie de J. B. Imbert, rue de / la Calandre, vis-à-vis le Palais, n°. 47.' The 'Avis' at the end explains that the publisher (author?) did not include the music to the songs in order to keep the price of the book at a reasonable level. But this was available, and appropriate information is given. This work, which contains pieces of prose fiction, is not in MMF, so I have chosen to include it. There are copies in the BN (Ye.12484) and in the BL (11481.aaa.4). The only copy listed for the United States by the NUC is defective (University of Chicago).

Barbier mentions that this is a 'recueil formé par Claude-François-Xavier Mercier, de Compiègne, qui a signé les premières pièces' (i, col.664b). I assume that the unsigned pieces are by him as well.

Here is a list of the principal items in the collection; those comprising prose-fiction are starred:

1. *Le Prix de la bienfaisance, pastorale*, 1 acte en vaudevilles, pp.[14]-36;

2. (halftitle) 'Le tombeau / du jeune Silvain.', a 'pastorale', 1 act in verse and prose, pp.[37]-63 (including the halftitle);

3. (halftitle) 'La première / requisition, / ou / le serment / des Français', scène patriotique, 1 act in verse and prose, pp.[65]-81 (including the halftitle);

4. *Lettre[s] d'Adèle à Isidore, volontaire de la première requisition dans l'armée d'Italie*, pp.[82]-84 and 101-29. Pages 85-100 comprise a 'Recueil d'odes, hymnes, chansons, ect. [*sic*] envoyés par Adèle' (in verse);

5. *Paul et Zénie, ou les couronnes civiques, pastorale*, pp.130-53. This piece is a prose effusion, intermingled with verse and is not a piece which would fall into the category of 'dramatic literature'.

6. *Les Nuits de Zélarie et Claudoé, ou les concerts mélancoliques de l'isle des peupliers*, pp.154-83. In prose and verse, divided into four 'nights'.

At the end is a collection of poems by various authors.

Here is a list of the exquisite engravings, designed and engraved by Quéverdo (signed), to be found with this book (Cohen col.703):

1. frontispiece, 'La liberté guide nos pas.';
2. an engraved titlepage, 'Les concerts / républicains. / Amour / sacré / de la patrie. / L'an Troisieme';
3. facing p.[39], 'Le tombeau / du jeune Sylvain.';
4. facing p.[67], 'Le serment des Français.'

In the present copy (in original wrappers as issued, untrimmed), it is possible to see that the first two illustrations are printed on the same sheet, i.e. are conjugate.

Incipits: (*Lettre[s] d'Adèle à Isidore*) 'Lorsque dans le temple de la liberté, je t'entendis prononcer, avec tes camarades, le serment auguste d'affranchir l'Univers'.

(*Paul et Zénie*) 'Le temps étoit beau, l'air frais, et le soleil vers son déclin'.

(*Les Nuits de Zélarie et Claudoé*) 'Fatigué du tumulte de la capitale, rebuté de la légèreté de mes amis, de leur insouciance'.

191

Montesquieu: *Considérations sur les causes de la grandeur des Romains* with *Dialogue de Sylla et d'Eucrate*, 1750

Charles-Louis de Secondat, baron de La Brède et de Montesquieu (1689-1755): (titlepage in *red* and black) *Considerations* / sur les causes / de la / *grandeur* / des / *Romains,* / et de leur / *decadence.* / Nouvelle edition, / Revue, corrigée & augmentée par l'Auteur. / A laquelle on a joint un Dialogue / *de Sylla et d'Eucrate.* / [woodcut decoration by Papillon: flying cupid bearing large, swaddled bouquet tied with ribbon; radiant something-or-other in the back; a mirror image of this ornament is on the titlepages of Cailleau, *Lettres ... d'Héloïse*, ca.1780; see that entry] / *A Lausanne,* / Chez Marc-Michel Bousquet / & Compagnie. / [red rule] / M D C C L.

8°: 1 f. (titlepage) + [III]-XII + 1 f. (2 pp.) + [1]-298, 299-339, [340]-352 pp. (P.340 is numbered within brackets.)

Commentary: The preliminary material (pp.[III]-XII) is a dedicatory letter 'A messieurs messieurs les avoyer [*sic*], petit et grand conseil, de l'etat exterieur, de la ville de Berne' (head title) by Marc-Michel Bousquet. Then there are two pages of an analytical 'Table des chapitres', the *Considérations* proper, an analytical 'Table des matieres' (pp.299-339) and, at the end, the dialogue. There is only one other copy of this edition that I could find – assuming that it be the same – listed in the NUC for the University of Chicago. (It is not recorded in

Vian.) I have thus chosen to include it. The dialogue is marginal to the 'genre romanesque' and was first published in the *Mercure*, February 1745 (February, [i].61-72), then with the *Considérations* in 1748 (source: R. Callois in the Pléiade edition of the *Œuvres complètes*, 1956). A note in the *Mercure* has an explanation: 'Ce qu'on fait dire dans ce Dialogue à Sylla n'est que pour développer son caractere, qui étoit celui d'un homme cruel, & d'un mauvais Citoyen, & en même tems pour inspirer de l'horreur & du mépris' (p.61).

There is a nice frontispiece engraving, differing radically from the one designed by Eisen (frequently copied and usually the one to be found with the *Considérations*), and a pretty, engraved vignette by Joubert after Delamonce (signed) at the head of the dedicatory letter. (The frontispiece is unsigned; not in Cohen or Reynaud.) At the end, p.352, is an 'Approbation' for the *Considérations*, 'avec des *Augmentations*, dans lesqelles je n'ai rien trouvé qui ne soit digne de la réputation de ce Livre & de celle de l'Auteur', given at Versailles, 12 August 1747, signed 'Demoncrif'.

In passing I note that Heinsius lists what appears to be a piece of prose fiction, under Montesquieu's name because of the association with that philosophe's famous novel, which is an edition not listed in bibliographies of prose fiction, or for that matter in Barbier, BLC, BNC, NUC, etc.: 'Le Persan en Angleterre pour Guide des Lettres Persanes. [in-]8. Francf. Brönner. [1]771' (ii, col.1057). This is also probably in Heinsius, Romane as: 'Persan, le, en Angleterre, pour suite et paroli [*sic*] aux lettres persannes de Montesquieu. 8vo. Frcft. Gebhardt et K[ayserer?]. [1]771' (col.159). Heinsius, *Handbuch* carries much the same information ('...pour suite des lettres Persannes...', p.816). What could conceivably be the same edition is listed in the Messkatalog as: 'Le Persan en Angleterre pour suite des Lettres Persannes de Mr. *Montesquieu*. 8[vo]. Francfort, chez Jean Gottl. Garbe' (MM 1771, p.291; also in Heinsius 1793, iv.540). This is in all likelihood a French translation of George, lord Lyttelton's *Letters from a Persian in England...* (1735). The first French version (a partial one) listed in MMF dates to 1761 (*Lettres d'un Persan en Angleterre...*, 61.5). The first full translation appeared in 1770 (MMF 70.61), by Jean François Peyron. No edition for 1771 is mentioned in MMF, nor do they list any printed in Frankfurt.

To editions listed in MMF, I would also add 'Nouvelles Lettres Persanes par Myl. Littleton. Nouv. traduction. gr. 12. à Paris & Leipsic, chez J. Joach. Kessler', Messkatalog, OM 1771, p.231.

Incipit: (*Dialogue*) 'Quelques jours après que Sylla se fut démis de la Dictature, j'appris'.

192

Montesquieu: *Considérations sur les causes de la grandeur des Romains*, etc., 1792

Charles Louis de Secondat, baron de La Brède et de Montesquieu (1689-1755): Considérations / sur les causes / de la / grandeur / des Romains, / et de leur /

décadence. / Nouvelle édition, / A laquelle on a joint / Un Dialogue de Sylla et d'Eucrate, le / Temple de Gnide, et l'Essai sur le Gout, / Fragment. / [woodcut decoration: child, globe, books, shrub] / [rule] / M. DCC. XCII.

12°: 2 pl + [1]-284 + [287]-300 + [303]-306, [307]-(361) + [365]-407, [408]-440 pp.

Commentary: I could find no trace of this edition anywhere. There is a halftitle for 'Considérations / sur / la grandeur / des Romains.'

The contents are as follows:

1. *Grandeur et décadence des Romains*, p.[1]-284;
2. (halftitle) 'Dialogue / de Sylla / et / d'Eucrate.' + pp.[287]-300;
3. (halftitle) 'Le temple / de Gnide. / [rule] / ....Non murmura vestra columbae, / Brachia non hederae, non vincant oscula / conchae. / [rule] / Fragment d'un Epithalame de l'Empereur / Gallien.' + pp.[303]-306, [307]-(361);
4. (halftitle) 'Essai / sur le goût. / Fragment.' + pp.[365]-407;
5. various tables, pp.[408]-440.

The *Temple de Gnide* first appeared in 1725. The *Dialogue de Sylla et d'Eucrate*, which might be considered marginal to the 'genre romanesque', first appeared in the *Mercure* in 1745, and then with the *Considérations* in 1748. For further information, see the preceding entry.

Incipits: (*Dialogue de Sylla et d'Eucrate*) 'Quelques jours après que Sylla se fut démis de la dictature'.

(*Le Temple de Gnide*) 'Vénus préfere le séjour de Gnide à celui de Paphos & d'Amathonte.'

193

Montolieu: *Caroline de Lichtfield*, 1786

Elisabeth Jeanne Isabelle Pauline de Bottens, dame de Croussaz, baronne de Montolieu (sometimes Montaulieu; 1751-1832): Caroline / de Lichtfield. / Par / madame de ***. / Publié par le / traducteur de Werther. / [rule] / Idole d'un cœur juste, & passion du sage, / Amitié, que ton nom soutienne mon ouvrage; / Regne dans mes écrits, ainsi que dans mon cœur, / Tu m'appris à connoître, à sentir le bonheur. / Voltaire, Mêlanges de Poésies. / [rule] / Tome premier [second]. / [symmetrical woodcut ornaments, quite similar but different for each volume] / A Paris, / Chez les libraires associés. / M. D. CC. LXXXVI.

8°, i: 2 pl + [1]-(272) pp.
   ii: 2 pl + [1]-(232) pp.

Commentary: Here is yet another edition of this popular novel, appearing the same year as the first edition. In spite of the indication on the titlepage, I have no doubt that the above two volumes were not printed in Paris. On the verso of the titlepages, one finds the following indication ('conger'): 'Cet Ouvrage se debite / A Amsterdam, Chez [open brace] D. J. Changuion. / B. Vlam. / J. A. Crayenschot. / J. van Gulik. / C. N. Guerin. / T. van Harrevelt. / A Leide. / les Freres Murray. / A Utrecht. / B. Wild. / A Rotterdam. / L. Bennet [close brace] /

Libraires.' There is a half titlepage for each volume reading 'Caroline.' I could find no trace of this edition in the usual bibliograhies. There is an entry in OCLC which might refer to the same edition. I write 'might' because little information is given – no pagination or format for example – and I was unable to see the copy referred to (location: University of Delaware at Newark).

For further information, see the four volume *Caroline* just below.

Incipit: 'Caroline, dit un jour le Baron de Licht- / field, (grand chambellan de la cour de Prusse, / & l'un des ministres du Roi,) à sa fille'.

194

Montolieu: *Caroline de Lichtfield*, 1786

Elisabeth Jeanne Isabelle Pauline de Bottens, dame de Croussaz, baronne de Montolieu (sometimes Montaulieu; 1751-1832): Caroline / de / Lichtfield. / Par / madame de***. / Publié par le Traducteur de Werter [*sic*]. / Troisieme édition. / [double rule] / Premiere [Seconde, Troisieme, Quatrieme] partie. / [double rule] / [woodcut ornament, two pigeons kissing, etc., same for all volumes] / A Paris, / Chez Buisson, Libraire, Hôtel de Mes- / grigny, rue des Poitevins. / [double rule] / M. DCC. LXXXVI.

12°, i: 1 f. (titlepage) + [3]-(156) pp.
  ii: 1 f. (titlepage) + [3]-(132) pp.
  iii: 1 f. (titlepage) + [3]-(112) pp.
  iv: 1 f. (titlepage) + [3]-(138) pp.

Commentary: The verso of the titlepages carries the epigraph by Voltaire which is the same as that to be found on the titlepage of the preceding entry. This was a very popular novel in its day, and beyond. 1786 is the date of the first edition (MMF 86.52), and there were many editions for that year alone. For a discussion of the editions and the changes undergone by these, see Dawson, ii.675-76.

To the various editions of this popular novel listed in MMF, I would add:

1. *Caroline de Lichtfield*, 17??. 'la même [Caroline de Lichtfield, histoire], par le traducteur de Werther. 2 Vol. [in-]8. Vienne. (Kupferberg à Mayence.) [1]785'. (Heinsius, Romane col.126. The date is obviously a mistake, but there are no editions listed in MMF for 'Vienne'.)

2. *Caroline de Lichtfield*, 1786. 'Lichtfield, Caroline de; Histoire. [in-]12. Basel, Flick. (Ettinger à Gotha.) [17]786'. (Heinsius, *loc. cit.*, and Heinsius 1793, iv.525). Kayser lists: '[v[on] Lichtfield] Histoire. [in-]12. Gotha [1]786. Ettinger' (Romane, p.86a).

3. *Caroline de Lichtfield*, 1786. 'Caroline de Lichtfield par Mad. de ***, publié par le traducteur de Werther. 2 Vol. gr. 12. à Basle, chez J. J. Flick', Messkatalog, OM 1786, p.381. (This is conceivably the same as no. 2 just above.) The next two entries in the Messkatalog show how widespread the circulation of *Caroline* was, from the onset: '*Le même livre*, à Gotha, chez G. G. Ettinger'; '*Le même livre*, à Lausanne et se trouve à Strasbourg, chez Treuttel'. It is of course possible that the entries in Heinsius and Kayser (no.2 just above) derive from those in

the Messkatalog. Heinsius, *Handbuch* also has: 'Lichtfield, Caroline de; Histoire, 12mo. Basle, Flick, [1]786' (p.805).

4. *Caroline de Lichtfield*, 1792. *Caroline de Lichtfield: ou mémoires d'une famille prussienne rédigés par M. le baron de Lindorf, & publiés par mme. la baronne de Montaulieu*. 3ᵉ éd., revue, corrigée, & changée par l'auteur, avec la musique des romances. Rouen: J. Racine, 1792. 3 vols, 14 cm (OCLC: BOCES Monroe 2/Orleans, Spencerport, New York).

The 'traducteur de *Werther*' often mentioned on the titlepages, of particularly the early editions, is Georges Deyverdun. (The baron de Lindorf is one of the characters; 'Montolieu' was frequently spelled 'Montaulieu'.)

Incipit: 'Caroline, dit un jour le baron de / Lichtfield, (grand chambellan de la cour / de Prusse, & l'un des ministres du roi) / à sa fille'.

195

Montolieu: *Caroline de Lichtfield*, 1787

Elisabeth Jeanne Isabelle Pauline de Bottens, dame de Croussaz, baronne de Montolieu (sometimes Montaulieu; 1751-1832): Caroline / de / Lichtfield. / Par / madame de *** / Publié par le Traducteur de Werther. / Nouvelle Édition, / Avec des Corrections considérables. / [double rule: thick, thin] / Tome second. / [double rule: thin, thick] / [woodcut ornament: two branches tied together] / A Toulouse, / Chez Manavit, Libraire de Monsieur, / Frère du Roi, rue Saint-Rome. / [double rule: thick, thin] / M. DCC. LXXXVII.

12°, i: (no titlepage), [1]-264 pp.
  ii: 1 f. (titlepage with quote verso) + [3]-215, [216] pp.

Commentary: The verso of the titlepage carries the epigraph by Voltaire which is the same as that to be found on the titlepages of the first *Caroline* listed in this bibliography.

Note that there is no titlepage for the first volume, which begins with pp.[1]-2, f.A[1]. The last page of vol. ii comprises the 'permission simple' accorded to Manavit for the production of 2,000 copies of the novel, to follow strictly the Paris, 1786 edition; signed Dumirail, for Vidaud (director-general of the booktrade); given in Paris, 24 August 1786; registered in Toulouse, 18 December 1786, 'Pijon, Syndic'. For further information concerning this 'permission simple', its purport and significance, see Robert L. Dawson, 'The permission simple of 1777 and the bibliographical evidence of its register', forthcoming.

I could find no trace of this edition anywhere. For further information concerning *Caroline*, see the other pertinent entries in this bibliography.

Incipit: 'Caroline, dit un jour le baron de / Lichtfield, (grand chambellan de a [*sic*] cour de / Prusse, & l'un des ministres du roi) à sa / fille'.

196

Mouhy: *La Paysanne parvenue*, 1767 and 1771

Charles de Fieux, chevalier de Mouhy (1701-1784): La / paysanne / parvenue, / ou les / mémoires [memoires for iii, iv] / de madame / la marquise de L. V. / Par M. le Chevalier de Mouhy. / Tome premier [troisieme, quatrieme]. / [woodcut decoration which varies for each titlepage] / A Amsterdam, / Aux dépens de la Compagnie. / [double rule] / [i:] M. D CC. LXVII. [M. DCC. LXXI. for iii, iv]

12°, i: 1 f. (titlepage) + 3-4, [v]-viij + 1-240 pp.
  ii: 1-206 pp.
  iii: 1 pl + 1-222 pp.
  iv: 1 pl + 1-260 pp.

Commentary: The titlepage to ii is missing. MMF list an edition for 1767 (56.R46), after Jones (p.56) and one for 1771, Châteauroux and the Library Company of Philadelphia. The latter's copy is listed in the NUC as being in two volumes. My copy obviously consists of an amalgam of two editions, each in four volumes. Feeling that there is every chance that one or both sets are unique, I have chosen to include them here. The first edition dates to 1735-1737 (Jones p.56). The two preliminary pieces are a letter ('A monsieur, Monsieur d'Abbé d'Opede, Aumônier de chez le Roi', signed 'Le Chevalier de M.') and a 'Préface'.

To editions of this work listed in Jones and MMF, I would add:

1. *La Paysanne parvenue*, 1735-1736. '[...] par monsieur le chevalier de M.' 12 vols. Paris; Liège: Kints, 1735-36. Krauss-Fontius no. 3673. Location: Universtäts- und Landesbibliothek Sachsen-Anhalt, Halle. Jones (p.56) lists an incomplete edition for Paris: Prault, 1735-36, another for 1735-37 (Paris, i.e. La Haye, etc.) and various composite editions (but none for Liège). MMF echo Jones.

2. *La Paysanne parvenue*, 1736. 12 vols. La Haye: Neaulme, 1736. Krauss-Fontius no. 3674. Location: Romanisches Seminar der Universität Jena.

3. *La Paysanne parvenue*, 1740. 12 vols. Amsterdam; Leipzig: Arkstée, Merkus, 1740. Krauss-Fontius no. 3676. Location: Universtätsbibliothek Leipzig. (Partly listed in MMF.)

Incipit: 'Il m'en coûte infiniment d'avouer / ma naissance; le rang que je tiens / aujourd'hui dans le monde, en est peut-être la cause.'

197

Musset and Bourgoing: *Correspondance d'un jeune militaire*, 1798

Louis Alexandre Marie de Musset, marquis de Cogners (1753-1839) and Jean François de Bourgoing (1748-1811): Correspondance / d'un / jeune militaire. / Nouvelle édition. / [rule] / Ut patriæ sit idonæus, utilis agris, / utilis et bellorum, et pacis / rebus agendis. / Juv. / [rule] / Tome premier. / [double rule] / Première

LA
PAYSANNE
PARVENUE,
OU LES
MÉMOIRES
DE MADAME
LA MARQUISE DE L. V.

Par M. le Chevalier DE MOUHY.

TOME PREMIER.

Carlo Agostino Barraia

A AMSTERDAM,

Aux dépens de la Compagnie.

M. D. CC. LXVII. *1767*

No 196: Mouhy, *La Paysanne parvenue*, 1767 and 1771, t.1

LA
PAYSANNE
PARVENUE,
OU LES
MEMOIRES
DE MADAME
LA MARQUISE DE L. V.

Par M. le Chevalier DE MOUHY.

TOME TROISIEME.

A AMSTERDAM,
AUX DÉPENS DE LA COMPAGNIE.

M. DCC. LXXI.

No 196: Mouhy, *La Paysanne parvenue*, 1767 and 1771, t.3

partie. / [double rule] / A Paris. / Chez Dupont, Imprimeur- / Libraire, rue de la Loi, N° 1231. / [double rule] / An VI. de la république française.

12°, i: 2 ff. (halftitle and titlepage) + [v]-vi, vij-viij + [1]-(127) pp.

 ii: [1]-[172] pp. (The first page is unnumbered; the last is enclosed in brackets. The rest are enclosed in parentheses.)

Commentary: There is a halftitle to vol. i reading 'Correspondance / d'un / jeune militaire.' There is no halftitle or titlepage for vol. ii, in the present copy anyway. There is a frontispiece to vol. i, of respectable quality, 'Lanier [possibly Lonier] invenit'. The pagination reflects an 'Avis de l'éditeur' (pp.[v]-vi), followed by two pages of errata for both volumes. The novel first appeared in 1778 (MMF, 78.28).

 This edition/version of the *Correspondance d'un jeune militaire* is not listed in any modern bibliography I have consulted. For March 1798, the *Journal général de la littérature de France* lists '*Correspondance d'un jeune militaire*; roman. 2 volumes in-4. *Dupont* [bookdealer and publisher]', with no price however. If this information be exact, that means that there was another issue at least for this date, an in-quarto. The commentary runs as follows: 'Ce n'est pas comme la plupart de nos romans modernes, un tissu d'aventures étranges, plus propres à effrayer l'imagination qu'à émouvoir le cœur. L'intrigue en est peu compliquée & cependant attachante; le style est pûr & les sentimens n'ont rien d'exalté; il y a de la vérité dans tous les caractères & de la vraisemblance dans tous les événemens' (p.88).

 Quérard cites this novel and gives the following reference: 'pour un historique de ce roman, voy. une lettre de M. de Musset, insérée dans le Journal de la librairie, 1822, p.158-9' (vi, col.369). This interesting letter is to be found in the *Bibliographie de la France, ou journal général de la librairie* (no. 10, 9 March 1822, pp.158-59). It merits transcription:

 Au rédacteur. / Cogners, ce 28 janvier 1822. / Monsieur,

 Permettez-moi, je vous prie, de vous adresser les détails qui me sont demandés sur un livre intitulé: *Correspondance d'un jeune militare, ou Mémoires du marquis de Luzigny et d'Hortense de Saint-Just.*

 J'étais sous-lieutenant au régiment d'Auvergne avec Jean-François de Bour-going, que vous avez vu depuis ambassadeur en Espagne. Il avait pris son congé de semestre au mois d'octobre 1771, et m'écrivait de Paris le 8 février 1772, une lettre dont j'extrais ce qui suit:

 'En quittant le bal de madame la Dauphine, je suis parti seul pour Paris; et, pour charmer les ennuis et le froid de ce trajet, j'ai beaucoup déclamé, et me suis occupé du canevas de ce roman conçu dans mon pélerinage de Calais à Arras. Le voici, puisque tu le désires.

 'Julie est retirée du couvent par une amie de sa mère que des affaires retiennent en province. Le marquis de ***, jeune officier, et fils de la maison, prend peu à peu du goût pour Julie. Les progrès de cette passion sont la matière ordinaire des lettres des deux dames. Le marquis a une sœur, amie de la personne qu'il adore, et qu'il voudrait adorer à l'insu de tout le monde. Sa mère rit de ses efforts, et l'amène, après plusieurs circonstances épisodiques que j'ai déjà conçues, à lui faire l'aveu de sa passion. Il faut dans ce moment que le marquis aille prendre possession d'une compagnie de cavalerie qu'on vient de lui acheter. Il part avec la plus grande peine. Tout plein de son amour, il devient dans son corps plus bouillant que jamais; il relève avec aigreur des propos libertins, injurieux à la vertu des femmes, à laquelle il croit; et, mourant d'un coup d'épée que sa vivacité lui attire, il dicte à son ami une lettre pathétique pour sa mère et pour Julie qui, de douleur, renonce au monde.'

J'étais à Vendôme lorsque Bourgoing m'écrivait; je lui répondis le 23 février 1772:

'Faire mourir un personnage coupable malgré lui, comme le fut la chère Clarice, voilà un moyen puissant de nous arracher des larmes; le faire mourir lorsqu'il est près d'être heureux, frappé de la main d'un rival, son sort pourra nous attendrir; mais priver cette pauvre Julie de son amant, vouloir qu'il périsse victime d'un moment d'emportement et du juste respect que lui inspire la vertu des femmes, sans lier ce fatal événement au fond de l'histoire, ton roman sera triste et sans intérêt.

'Qu'un amant dédaigné de Julie parle mal de cette aimable fille; que le marquis soit tué par son rival, ou, mieux encore, qu'il ne soit que blessé, et qu'après sa guérison, il soit heureux, cela pourra produire quelqu'effet.'

Telle fut, Monsieur, la première idée de la *Correspondance d'un jeune militaire*. Le plan de ce petit ouvrage resta sans exécution jusqu'en 1776. Nous étions alors en garnison à Valenciennes. Nous convînmes, vers les premiers jours de septembre, des noms que nous donnerions à nos acteurs, dont le nombre fut fixé à six. Nous convînmes également des sujets que nous traiterions, et de l'ordre dans lequel chaque pièce serait inscrite au recueil. Je me chargeai d'écrire toutes les lettres attribuées à la marquise de Luzigny, à M. de Saint-Just et à Hortense. Mon ami eut pour son lot celles qui devaient être au nom du marquis de Luzigny, de Mme de Saint-Just et de M. de Lansal.

L'ouvrage entier fut terminé au 1er octobre; Bourgoing me quittait pour aller à Nevers. Notre manuscrit resta entre mes mains pendant l'hiver, et j'y fis des corrections, des notes, dont mon ami profita lorsqu'il le mit au net, avant son premier départ pour l'Espagne en 1777.

M. Blondeau, professeur à Brest, que je consultai, me donna par écrit, sur chaque lettre, des observations qui me furent très-utiles; et, d'après le consentement de mon collaborateur, je refis en entier le dénouement, depuis la trente et unième lettre de la seconde partie jusqu'à la fin.

Je demandai, au mois de décembre 1777, ce qu'on appelait alors une *permission tacite d'imprimer*; elle me fut accordée sur le rapport du censeur *M. Pidansat de Mairobert*.

Au mois de mars 1778, M. Dorat, dont nous étions connus, Bourgoing et moi, imprima dans son *Journal des Dames* 17 lettres de notre *Correspondance*, et annonça que les *Mémoires du marquis de Luzigny* étaient l'ouvrage *de deux jeunes militaires* unis par le goût des lettres. Plusieurs journaux du tems l'ont répété.

J'ai depuis, sur un privilége obtenu le 27 septembre 1787, au nom de M. Dériaux, fait imprimer la *Correspondance* que j'ai refondue en entier, d'après les conseils de Bourgoing et ceux de nos amis communs, MM. *Blin de Saint-Maur*, *Dorat* et autres. M. Artaud a été mon censeur.

Mme veuve Ballard a imprimé la première édition que M. Dériaux, rue de

Tournon, à Paris, a été chargé de vendre. Il y a eu contrefaction, 1° à Paris, 2° à Mastricht, et 3° en Suisse. M. Regnault a débité ce qui restait de l'édition originale, en y joignant un titre nouveau en 1784.

La seconde édition, imprimée au Mans par M. Charles Monnoyer, fut mise en vente à Paris, chez M. Savoye, au mois de juillet 1789; et M. de Bourgoing fit choix, en 1800, d'un autre libraire. L'ouvrage se trouve à présent chez M. L. Colas.

J'ai survécu à mon ami; les *Mémoires de Luzigny*, que nous avons composés en commun, sont pour moi une sorte de monument. Si, à l'avenir, des biographes y impriment le nom de Bourgoing, je leur demande d'y inscrire aussi le mien.

J'ai l'honneur d'être, etc. / Louis A. M. de Musset.

Would that we had so many interesting details concerning more novels of the time!

So it would appear that there were several more editions than those listed in MMF. The one described here differs considerably from the first edition. From Musset's letter, it would appear to represent a version that he had worked on himself, even though he makes no mention of this edition.

The Messkatalog lists what is probably the first edition ('2 Parties. 12[°]. Paris & se trouve à Leipsic, chez la veuve H. Merkus') and also what is possibly another edition (note the different format): 'Le même livre. 8[°]. Berne, chez Eman. Haller' (both listed in the OM 1778, p.700). The latter could well be MMF's entry for 'En Suisse, libraires associés, 1778, 2 part., 170, 158 p.', with a location for Neuchâtel (no format recorded; 78.28).

Furthermore, MMF list an edition for 'Paris, 1779, 2 part. in-12' after the Besançon library catalogue. They also note: 'CatH [*Catalogue hebdomadaire*] xxxvi 1779 annonce une édition portant la mention Yverdon & Paris'. Giraud lists 'P[aris], 1779, 2 t. en 1 v. in-12, viii-173p. + 2 ff.-158p.' (1778.3.b). In his preceding entry, Giraud does mention 'l'auteur' ('Yverdon-P., l'auteur, 1778 [...]', 1778.3.a). Krauss-Fontius give Paris: auteur, 1779 (no. 3972), with a location for the Romanisches Seminar der Universität Leipzig. Could that then constitute another edition?

Incipit: 'Mes craintes étoient fondées, ma chere cousine; la derniere lettre de ma fille'.

198

Nogaret: *Podalire et Dirphé*, 1800 or 1801

François Félix Nogaret (1740-1831): Podalire et Dirphé, / ou / la couronne / tient a la jarretière; / Par l'auteur de l'Aristenète français, / et de Contes en vers, mis à l'index de la Cour / de Vienne. / [rule] / "Une merveille absurde a pour moi peu d'appas;" / La Nature, en tout tems, étonne.... et ne ment pas. / (Aris.) / [rule] / Tome premier [second]. / [woodcut ornament: cloud, sunrise, cupid, with centre oval with intitials 'FL' entwined] / A Paris, / Chez Louis, Libraire, rue St.-Séverin, N.° 110. / [rule] / Nivôse, IX.

12°, i: 2 pl + [j]-xxiv, [25]-318 pp.

ii: 2 pl + [1]-289, [290-92] pp.

Commentary: The preliminary material comprises an 'Épitre dédicatoire. A Nestor Adanson, philosophe naturaliste, membre de l'institut national' (pp.[j]-v, signed 'Félix Nogaret'); the 'réponse' (pp.[vj]-viij); 'Narré préparatoire', which is a sort of preface (p.[ix]-xxiv. The last three pages of vol. ii are a list of errata for both volumes.

The volumes halftitles read: 'Podalire et Dirphé, / ou / la couronne / tient a la jarretière.' The verso of the first one has a notice: '[rule] / On a tiré quelques Exemplaires de cet / Ouvrage, in-8.°, sur vélin. / [rule]'. What is surely meant is 'papier vélin'.

There are two frontispiece engravings, 'avant la lettre' for the captions, by Bovinet after Bornet (signed). Curiously Cohen gives 'Paris, Louis, 1801' and states that the two engravings are not signed.

This work is not listed in MMF, doubtless because of the date. However, nivôse embraces December and January (22 December to 20 January, to be more precise), so it seems to me this work should form part of a bibliography devoted to eighteenth-century French prose fiction. I have thus chosen to include this entry. There is a copy in the BN (Y2.75978-79). None is listed in the NUC, BLC (and all supplements).

Incipit: 'Dans ces tems de simplicité où les / Princesses'.

199

Nougaret: *Lettre d'un mendiant au public*, 1765

Jean Pierre (or Pierre Jean) Baptiste Nougaret (1742-1823): Lettre / d'un mendiant / au public, / Contenant quelques-unes de ses Aventures / & ses Réflexions morales. / [double rule] / Nouvelle Edition. / [double rule] / [symmetrical woodcut decoration with an upside-down fleur-de-lys at the bottom] / A Paris, / aux depens du public, / Et se vend / Chez la Veuve Valleyre, Libraire, Quai / de Gêvres, à l'entrée par le Pont au / Change, à la Nouveauté. / [double rule] / 1765.

12°: 1 pl + 1 f. (2 pp.) + [1]-[39] pp. (The first page bears no number. The rest are numbered within brackets.)

Commentary: The first edition and version of this satirical piece appeared in 1764 (MMF 64.36, Quérard, etc.). MMF cite what is doubtless the edition described here, after Barbier. (Barbier lists only this edition, with no commentary; ii, col.1159b.) I could find no other copy of it. Indeed the first edition is, itself, very rare (not in NUC or BLC).

The 1765 edition is reworked and augmented. For one example alone, the penultimate paragraph (before the 'post-scriptum') is new, and is of interest to any scholar who might wish to study the author: 'Je ne conçois pas comment les Auteurs ont la bonté d'écrire, pour ne rien tirer de leurs productions; ils veulent sans doute avoir la gloire d'enrichir les Libraires, qui se moquent souvent d'eux. On croit peut-être que cette Lettre m'a valu de légers profits, puisque la premiére édition s'est bien vendue. Je puis assurer que je n'ai rien eu du tout. Au reste, grace à ma chere *Javotte*, qui est à-présent ma femme, je n'attends pas pour dîner le succès d'un Livre. Je travaille aussi. Elle fait des bourses, des bonnets à la *Grecque*, &c. &c; & moi je suis Colporteur. Cela vaut mieux que le rude & stérile métier d'Homme de Lettres.'

Incipit: 'J'espere que le Public daignera m'écouter, & pardonner la liberté que je prends de lui écrire.'

200

Parny: *Œuvres complètes*, 1788

Evariste Désiré Desforges [sometimes de Forges], vicomte de Parny (1753-1814): (engraved titlepages) Œuvres / complètes / du Chevalier / de / Parny. / A Paris. / Chez Hardouin et Gattey. Libraires de S.A.S. / Mad.^me la Duchesse d'Orléans. au Palais Royal. N°. 14. /M. DCC. LXXXVIII.

18°, i: 1 pl (half titlepage with note verso) + engraved titleleaf + [1]-(180) pp.
ii: 1 pl (half titlepage with note verso) + engraved titleleaf + [1]-(190) pp.

Commentary: The halftitles read 'Œuvres / complètes / du chevalier / de Parny. / [rule] / Tome premier [second]. / [rule]'. On the versos is the following annoucement: '[rule] / Cette Edition, ornée de six figures et / de deux frontispices en taille-douce, est / la seule avouée par l'Auteur. / [rule]'.

My books have five exquisite illustrations (unsigned), beyond the two engraved titlepages. Cohen calls for six (plus the titlepages) and mentions that they are the same as Monnet's (by Anselin, after Monnet in *Opuscules*, 1784; col.785). Reynaud seems to list another edition or issue, in-16, and states that he has seen a copy 'en 2 vol. in-18 comprenant 1 titre gravé (répété) et 5 figures par Coulet' (col.399). None of the illustrations in my books is signed. But, as mentioned, there are five plates, and none seems missing.

The second volume of perhaps an issue of this edition seems to exist in the BN ('...Paris, Hardouin et Gattet, 1788. In-12, titre gravé et pl.', vol. ii only; 8vo Ye.535; BNC). The NUC has a very perfunctory entry for a 2 vol. edition, 1788 (Ohio State University, Columbus). And the BLC lists 'Œuvres complètes. 2 tom. [Paris, 1788] 12°. Imperfect; wanting the titlepages and the plates' (1477.cc.15).

Although Parny is not listed in MMF, these two volumes contain several items of prose fiction:

1. *Les Ailes de l'Amour* (i.(39)-(42));
2. 'Chansons / madecasses, / traduites en françois. / Tome II. E [catchmaterial]' (halftitle + (51)-(52) ['Avertissement'], (53)-(72) pp. in vol. ii);
3. *Le Promontoire de Leucade* (ii.(105)-(115)).

At this writing, I do not have access to collections that would permit me to ascertain when these pieces first saw the light.

Les Ailes de l'Amour is a short piece of fiction (not to be confused with Montesquieu's tale by the same title). The highly romantic and rather lovely *Chansons madécasses* are a series of twelve prose-poems, each comprising a short tale or fable, some in dialogue form, one to two pages each. These are supposedly real translations, but it is obvious that the author has read Gessner and

Macpherson: 'J'ai recueilli et traduit quelques chansons, qui peuvent donner une idée de[s] ... usages et de[s] ... mœurs [des Madécasses]. Ils n'ont point de vers; leur poésie n'est qu'une prose soignée. Leur musique est simple, douce, et toujours mélancolique' ('Avertissement', ii.(52)). The *Promontoire de Leucade* is a short story.

Because of the rarity of this edition and because Parny is not listed in MMF, I have chosen to include a description of my books in this bibliography.

Incipits: (*Les Ailes de l'Amour*) 'Un jour, Éléonore et moi, nous rencontrâmes / l'Amour, dormant sur un lit de fleurs.'

(*Chansons madécasses*) 'Quel est le roi de cette terre?'

(*Le Promontoire de Leucade*) 'Je suis né dans un village d'Étolie, sur les bords / du fleuve Achéloüs.'

201

Parny: *Opuscules*, 1781

Evariste Désiré Desforges [sometimes de Forges], vicomte de Parny (1753-1814): (engraved titlepage) Opuscules / de M. le Ch^{er}... / de Parny / Troisieme Edition / Corrigée et / augmentée. / A Londres / M. DCCLXXXI.

12°: 1 f. (halftitle) + engraved titlepage + [1]-284 pp.

Commentary: This volume contains a series of poems, letters and miscellaneous pieces, with a table at the end (pp.281-84). There are letters concerning a voyage, erotic (love) poems and, what is of interest to us here, a short prose-fiction tale titled *Les Ailes de l'Amour* (pp.250-54).

Parny is not listed in MMF. At this writing, I do not have access to collections that might permit me to state when *Les Ailes de l'Amour* first appeared. (This *Ailes de l'Amour* is not to be confused with a short, prose-fiction piece by Montesquieu with the same title.) For further information concerning prose fiction and Parny, see the preceding entry.

The edition described here contains a series of exquisite illustrations. Cohen lists what is possibly this edition, but as in-18 (col.783). Reynaud remarks that this work – he does not write 'édition' – 'existe pet. in-12' (col.399), which is here the case. As the discerning reader might surmise, this volume was not printed in London.

This edition is not listed in the BLC, NUC, BNC (and all supplements). I have included my book in this bibliography because of its rarity and in order to help complete MMF.

Incipit: (*Les Ailes de l'Amour*) 'Un jour, Éléonore & moi, nous ren- / contrâmes l'Amour dormant sur un lit de / fleurs.'

202

Passerat: *Le Bel Anglais*, 1695

François Passerat: Le bel / Anglois, / nouvelle / galante. / Par Mr. Passerat. / [elaborate woodcut ornament with three figures in centre; Backer's device?] / A Brusselles, / Chez George de Backer, Im- / primeur & Marchand Libraire, aux / trois Mores, à la Berg-straet. 1695. / [rule] / Avec Privilege du Roy.

12°: engraved titlepage + 1 f. (titlepage) + 5-82 pp.

Commentary: Although the pagination and preliminary folio seem to indicate that a leaf is missing, it is not. It was often the custom in Germanic countries of the seventeenth century – and in adjacent territories – to include the frontispiece in the first gathering, a practice reflected by the pagination.

This piece of prose fiction is part of Passerat's *Œuvres*. Lever lists *Le Bel Anglais* according to a copy in the Arsenal (8° B.L.18689), and makes no mention of the *Œuvres*. Cioranescu lists *Le Bel Anglais* for Brussels, 1695 in-12°. He then lists two editions of the *Œuvres*, and gives a very imperfect breakdown of the contents of the first edition (17e siècle, iii.1585, nos 53507-08-09). Conlon lists *Le Bel Anglais* as above (ii.237, no. 7293). The next entry is for the first edition of the *Œuvres* (no. 7294). No breakdown is given or mention made of the novel's place in the collection. He also does not list the plays; see below. Conlon is evidently listing after a copy of the novel in the Arsenal, bound as a unit, Lever's 8vo B.L.18689.

There were two editions of the *Œuvres*, one as described here and a 'Seconde Edition, revûë & corrigée' (La Haye: Henry van Bulderen, 1695, 302 pp. in-12°). Although the signatures and pagination are consecutive for the collection, each piece has a titlepage for La Haye: Henry van Bulderen, 1695. The engravings are copies of the original ones. *Le Bel Anglais* occupies pp.201-50. The second edition is the more common of the two (NUC: Library of Congress, Yale, Princeton, Indiana, University of Delaware at Newark; BN: Yf.10582). The BL has a copy of the first edition which matches mine (243.b.4), and it also appears to be listed in Krauss-Fontius (no. 1083). I list this work to clarify the situation. The items found in the first edition were in all likelihood available for purchase individually at the time of publication.

Here is a description of the first edition of the collection.

Volume titlepage in *red* and black: *Œuvres* / de / monsieur / *Passerat* / dediées a son / *altesse electorale* / de / *Baviere*. / [same woodcut ornament as on the titlepage of *Le Bel Anglois*] / *A Brusselles*, / Chez *George de Backer*, Im- / primeur & Marchand Libraire, aux / trois Mores, à la Berg-straet. 1695. / [rule] / *Avec Privilege du Roy*.

This is followed by 5 ff., 8 + 1 + 1 pp. comprising a letter to the elector of Bavaria, signed 'Francois Passerat', an 'Extrait du privilège du roi' (to de Backer for nine years, 31 January 1695, signed 'Loyens'), and a table of contents for the pieces contained in this volume. Each piece has its own titlepage preceded by an engraved titlepage (excluded from the pagination recorded, but actually f.A1). All items are separately signed and paginated. As mentioned, these were doubtless sold separately and as a collection.

The contents of these *Œuvres* are as follows:

1. Sabinus. / Tragedie. / Par Mr. Passerat. / [elaborate woodcut ornament with three figures in centre; Backer's device?] / A Brusselles, / Chez George de Backer, Im- / primeur & Marchand Libraire, aux / trois Mores, à la Berg-straet. / [rule] / M. DC. XCV. 1 f. (titlepage) + [5-12], 13-60 pp.

2. L'heureux / accident, / ou / la maison / de / campagne. / Comedie / Par Mr. Passerat. / [elaborate woodcut ornament with three figures in centre; Backer's device?] / A Brusselles, / Chez George de Backer, Im- / primeur & Marchand Libraire, aux / trois Mores, à la Berg-straet. 1695. / [rule] / Avec Privilege du Roy. 1 f. (titlepage) + 5-48 pp.

3. Le / feinct / campagnard, / comedie / Par Mr. Passerat. / [elaborate woodcut ornament with three figures in centre; Backer's device?] / A Brusselles, / Chez George de Backer, Im- / primeur & Marchand Libraire, aux / trois Mores, à la Berg-straet. 1695. / [rule] / Avec Privilege du Roy. 1 f. (titlepage) + 5-36 pp.

4. Amarillis / petite / pastoralle, / Mêlée de Recit, de Musique & de / Danse. / Compose'e / Pour étre [*sic*] representée par des Personnes / de Qualité. / Par Mr. Passerat. / [elaborate woodcut ornament with three figures in centre; Backer's device?] / A Brusselles, / Chez George de Backer, Im- / primeur & Marchand Libraire, aux / trois Mores, à la Berg-straet. 1695. / [rule] / Avec Privilege du Roy. 1 f. (titlepage) + 5-20 pp.

5. Le / grand ballet / d'Alcide / et / d'Hebe' / de'esse de la jeunesse. / Par Mr. Passerat. / [elaborate woodcut ornament with three figures in centre; Backer's device?] / A Brusselles, / Chez George de Backer, Im- / primeur & Marchand Libraire, aux / trois Mores, à la Berg-straet. 1695. / [rule] / Avec Privilege du Roy. 1 f. (titlepage) + [5], [6], 7-12 pp.

6. *Le Bel Anglois*, as described above.

7. Receuil [*sic*] / de / poesies diverses / sur / differens sujets. / Par Mr. Passerat. / [elaborate woodcut ornament with three figures in centre; Backer's device?] / A Brusselles, / Chez George de Backer, Im- / primeur & Marchand Libraire, aux / trois Mores, à la Berg-straet. 1695. / [rule] / Avec Privilege du Roy. 1 f. (titlepage) + 3-46, [47-48] pp.

There is a halftitle for the whole volume, in *red* and black: 'O*Euvres* / de / monsieur / *Passerat*.' Then follows a pretty engraved titlepage for the 'OEuvres / de / monsieur / Passerat.', signed 'Harrewyn invenit / et fecit.' On the verso of the engraved titlepage of my copy is glued Vatar's label: 'Se vend / a Nantes, / Chez J. Vatar, Libraire, au bas de la Grand- / Ruë, entre le Puits-Lory & les Changes. / On trouve aussi chez le meme Libraire toutes sortes de / Livres anciens & nouveaux, sur differentes ma- / tieres, tant de Paris que des Païs étrangers.'

Each piece is preceded by a pretty engraving by Harrewyn (signed in the picture like the volume frontispiece); each is captioned with the title. Following compositorial practices of seventeenth-century Germanic countries in particular, the engravings are fitted in each piece as ff.[A1], with the exception of the last item. Thus the titlepages are ff.[A2], followed by ff.A3. The pagination reflects this.

P.[11] of *Sabinus* is a notice, 'Le libraire au lectuer [*sic*]', which runs as follows: 'On donnera bien-tôt au Public un Recueil des Oeuvres du même Auteur, dans lequel il entrera quelques Comedies, & plusieurs autres Pieces de Poësie sur differens sujets.' To my knowledge, such a collection never appeared.

Incipit: (*Le Bel Anglais*) 'Ce n'est pas seulement en Espagne & en Italie, que les Dames font les premiers pas, la mode en est venüe jusqu'en France'.

203

Pigault-Lebrun: *Adèle et d'Abligny*, 1803

Charles Antoine Guillaume Pigault de L'Epinoy, called Pigault-Lebrun (1753-1835): Adèle / et / d'Abligny. / Par / Pigault-Lebrun. / [rule] / A Paris, / Chez Barba, Libraire, Palais du Tri- / bunat, Galerie derrière le Théâtre de la / République, N°. 51. / An XI.-1803.

12°: 2 pl + [1]-171 pp.

Commentary: There is a signed frontispiece of good quality by Bovinet after Challiou (chain lines vertical). It indicates 'Page 131', but the caption in the picture is actually to be found on p.130: 'Et vous chanteriez cela?' The half titlepage reads: 'Les / cent-vingt jours, / ou / les quatre nouvelles. / Tome IV.' On the verso is a conger listing twenty-six cities (largely in France) together with twenty-six bookdealers, as follows (bookdealers in parentheses): Londres (De Boff), Vienne (Degen), Francfort (Essinger), Bruxelles (Le Charlier), Caen (Chalopin), Genève (Paschoud), Poitiers (Fatou), Brest (Belloy-Kardowick), Lille (Castiaux), Bordeaux (Lafitte), Basle (Deker), Arras (Delacroix), Avignon (Joly), Amiens (D'Aarras), Montpellier (Fontanel), Dijon (Marin), Limoges (Bargeas), Toulouse (Devers), Lyon (Bohairs), Metz (Devilly), Nismes (Maux-Buche), Manheim (Fontaine), Rouen (Hue), Rennes (Front), Clermont (Roussel), Strasbourg (Jung).

The beginning of each signature sequence bears a catchtome, signed with the volume indication of a series: 'N°. 4.' This novel first appeared in 1800 (MMF 00.119 and Monglond v.338-39). The edition described in this entry might well be one listed in the OCLC, with a location for the University of Delaware, Newark. For further information, see Pigault-Lebrun's *Théodore* below.

Incipit: 'Monsieur d'Alleville avait servi trente ans avec distinction.'

204

Pigault-Lebrun: *Métusko*, 1802

Charles Antoine Guillaume Pigault de L'Epinoy, called Pigault-Lebrun (1753-1835): Métusko, / ou / les Polonais; / troisième nouvelle, / Par Pigault-Lebrun. / [rule] / A Paris, / Chez Barba, Libraire, Maison-Égalité, / galerie derrière le théâtre de la République, / n°. 51. / [rule] / An onze.-1802.

12°: 2 pl + [1]-168, [169]-172 pp.

Commentary: The half titlepage reads: 'Métusko, / ou / les Polonais.' There is a signed frontispiece by Bovinet after Challiou, bearing the following caption in the picture's frame: 'Ils sont à peine à cent toises de leurs escadrons, qu'ils se chargent avec fureur.' (This illustration runs sideways; chain lines vertical.) The beginning of each signature sequence bears a catchtome, being signed with the volume indicaton of a series: 'N° 3.' The second piece reported in the pagination is a poem, *Les Ages*. This novel first appeared in 1800 (MMF 00.120 and Monglond v, col.339). For further information, see Pigault-Lebrun's *Théodore*.

Incipit: 'Les Sarmates avaient perdu une partie de ces coutumes barbares, qui avaient rendu la moitié de l'univers connu méprisable aux anciens Romains'.

205

Pigault-Lebrun: *Monsieur de Kinglin*, 1802

Charles Antoine Guillaume Pigault de L'Epinoy, called Pigault-Lebrun (1753-1835): Monsieur / de Kinglin, / ou / la prescience; / Par Pigault-Lebrun. / [rule] / In varietate voluptas. / [rule] / A Paris, / Chez Barba, Libraire, Maison-Égalité, / galerie derrière le théâtre de la République, / n°. 51. / [rule] / An dix.-1802.

12°: 2 pl + [1]-180 pp.

Commentary: The interesting frontispiece (chain lines vertical), by Bovinet after Challiou (signed), bears on the top right: 'Pag. 40'. The actual quotation in the picture ('Que veux-tu de moi?') is to be found on p.37. The half titlepage reads: 'Les cent vingt jours, / ou / les quatre nouvelles; / Par Pigault-Lebrun. / [rule] / Tome second. / [rule]'. The beginning of each signature sequence bears a catchtome, the series number 'N°. 2.'

This novel first appeared in 1800 (MMF 00.122 and Monglond v, cols.339-40). For additional information, see the next item.

Incipit: 'L'avenir est au présent un peu moins que le passé, qui laisse au moins des souvenirs.'

206

Pigault-Lebrun: *Théodore*, 1800

Charles Antoine Guillaume Pigault de L'Epinoy, called Pigault-Lebrun (1753-1835): Théodore, / ou / les Péruviens; / Par Pigault-Lebrun. / [rule] / In varietate voluptas. / [rule] / A Paris, / Chez Barba, Libraire, Maison-Egalité, / Galerie derrière le Théâtre de la République, / N°. 51. / 8. 1800.

12°: 2 pl + [1]-202 pp.

Commentary: The frontispiece (chain lines vertical) by Bovinet after Challiou indicates that the quotation is to be found on p.54; that is correct: 'Bel étranger, que veux-tu?' This is the first in a series of four novels which were to have formed part, apparently, of a longer series. See the three preceding entries.

MMF give locations for editions of *Métusko* and *Adèle et d'Abligny* which appear to be the same as my copies described above. But *Monsieur de Kinglin* and *Théodore* seem to be here in unique editions. Indeed, the BN copy of *Théodore*, aside from other differences, bears '9. 1800' on the titlepage (Y2.59974), and is so listed in Monglond, v, col.340. If the information on the titlepage is true, then my copy is for the 8th year of the Republic, and that of the BN, for the 9th year, meaning mine represents an earlier edition. Anyway, the 'an IX' edition could well have appeared in 1801. According to MMF and Monglond, all four volumes first appeared in 1800. For further commentary, see MMF 00.123 and Monglond v, cols.338-40.

The half titlepage to the above copy reads: 'Les / trente jours, / ouvrage périodique.' There is a conger on the verso of the half titlepage containing a list of twenty-six cities around Europe (mostly in France), with a list of twenty-six bookdealers. (These match the cities and dealers to be found with the *Adèle et d'Abligny* listed above.) The beginning of each signature sequence bears the series part, 'N° I.'

My copy of Pigault-Lebun's *Mon oncle Thomas* (Paris: Barba, [an-]8, 4 vols in-12°) has 4 pp. (2 leaves) tipped in after the titlepage of vol.iii, comprising an advertisement and announcement concerning *Les Trente jours, ouvrage périodique.* (This is not to be found with the BN copy of the novel, Y2.59193-96, or with the BL copy, 1458.b.18-21.) In it, the author (probably Pigault-Lebrun himself), after much praise of his works, writes: 'Les *Trente Jours* formeront un corps d'ouvrage de douze volumes in-12, en cicéro, qui paraîtront de mois en mois. Chaque volume, de 170 pages environ, contiendra une nouvelle, un conte, ou un petit roman détaché des numéros suivans, et pourra par conséquent s'acheter isolément' (pp.(2)-(3)). He then goes on to explain that each tome will contain abstracts of the literary news which appeared during the course of the preceding month. Barba was the publisher and owner of the enterprise. (Specific details are given concerning subscription rates, etc.) Much of this information is repeated in the *Journal général de la littérature de France*, germinal an VIII (1800), iii.124. This venture never went further than the publication of the four novels described in the present bibliography (as far as I know).

These four novelle were grouped under the title of *Les Cent vingt jours* when published in the *Œuvres* (vol. v, Paris 1823). A note on the halftitle explains: 'Ces quatre Contes ont paru périodiquement; mais seulement pendant quatre mois. Voilà pourquoi ils sont intitulés: *Les Cent vingt jours*'.

Incipit: 'Sous le règne de Louis XIV, dont on a dit trop de bien & trop de mal, le commerce maritime'.

207

Porée: *Histoire de dom Ranucio d'Alétès*, 1752

Abbé Charles Gabriel Porée (1685-1770): (titlepages in red and black) *Histoire* / de / dom Ranucio / d'Alétés. / Histoire véritable. / *Premiere [Seconde] partie.* / [very similar woodcut decorations of baldaquin, flowers, foliage in symmetrical decoration, on each titlepage] / *A Venise,* / Chez Antonio Pasquinetti. / *M. DCC. LII.*

12°, i: 1 pl + 5 ff. (2 + 2 + 4 + 2 pp.) + [1]-208 pp.

ii: 1 pl + 1 f. (2 pp.) + [1]-186 pp.

Commentary: This satirical novel first appeared in 1736 (Jones p.60). MMF list an edition for 1752, with no explanation. (The other 1752 edition was published as the *Histoire de D. Ranucio d'Alétès écrite par lui-même*.) Gay lists rather perfunctorily an edition for Venice, 1752 (ii, col.499), with a commentary which is elaborated in an extensive article by M. Alleaume in Fernand Drujon's *Les Livres à clef* (i, cols.436-39) who records what is perhaps this edition somewhat inaccurately. Alleaume mentions that the 'Venise' of the titlepage is a false imprint, and that the novel was printed in Rouen, probably basing himself on the fact that Weller reports the Venice of the first edition as being a trumped-up place name for Rouen (p.99; also in Quérard who only mentions editions for 1736 and 1738, vii.280). I do not know where the above volumes were printed, certainly not in Venice or Paris, however.

In spite of what Barbier reports (and Quérard in the *France littéraire*: 'Quelques exemplaires de ce roman contiennent une clef imprimée'), according to Alleaume there never did appear a printed key to the characters' identities. But it was possible to establish one for this 'véritable *Satyricon* antimonastique' with the help of several manuscript keys. I have included this edition since it is not elsewhere available, as far as I am able to ascertain (no location for BNC, BLC or NUC). The above described volumes are illustrated with four amusing engravings, of mediocre quality, including an allegorical frontispiece. Cohen lists editions for 1736, 1738, 1752 and 1758 (2 vols in-12°), stating that all contain two, pretty engravings (unsigned, the last edition also containing an engraved titlepage vignette; col.487).

The four preliminary pieces consist of: 1. 'Monitioné dell editoré' (in atrocious Italian); 2. 'Avertissement de l'éditeur'; 3. 'Préface de l'auteur'; 4. 'Table des chapitres'. (The first two pages of vol. ii are another table.) The 'Monitioné' (and 'Avertissement'; one is a translation of the other) claims that the manuscript of the *Histoire de Dom Ranucio* was bought at a sale in Padua: 'non bavévo l'intentioné d'i far[ne] uz anza nissúna', but two French friends of the 'publisher' judged otherwise. (Note the somewhat less-than-perfect Italian!)

Incipit: 'Dom Pedre d'Ale'te's, après avoir fait une fortune considérable au Brésil, revint à Lisbonne'.

208

Prévost d'Exiles: *Le Doyen de Killerine*, 1739-1740

Abbé Antoine François Prévost, called Prévost d'Exiles (1697-1763): Le doyen / de Killerine, / histoire morale [morale. for v, vi] / Composée sur les Mémoires d'une / Illustre Famille d'Irlande, & or- / née de tout ce qui peut rendre / une lecture utile & agréable. / Par l'Auteur des Mémoires d'un / Homme de Qualité. / Premiere [Seconde, Troisie'me, Quatrieme, Cinquie'me, Sixie'me et derniere] partie. [Partie. for vi] / [woodcut decoration, vase of flowers in fairly extensive decoration, same for all volumes] / A la Haye, / Chez Pierre Poppy. / [rule] / M. DCC. XXXIX. [M. DCC. XL. for iv, v, vi]

12°, i: 1 pl + [j]-jv + 1-4, 5-222 pp.

ii: 1 f. (titlepage) + 3-212 pp.
iii: 1 f. (titlepage) + 3-213 pp.
iv: 1 f. (titlepage) + 3-192 pp.
v: 1 f. (titlepage) + [3]-204 pp.
vi: 1 f. (titlepage) + 3-237, [238]-[239] pp.

Commentary: This novel first appeared from 1735 to 1740 (Jones p.57). The BNC lists three editions of the *Doyen de Killerine*, vol. ii of which is for La Haye, Poppy, 1739. These are different, however, from vol. ii above, having 239 pp. See Harrisse, *L'Abbé Prévost*, p.298. I have found no trace of the above described edition. That is surprising – assuming 'Poppy' was the real publisher – since so many editions of Prévost's works appeared with the name 'Poppy' on the titlepage. The two preliminary pieces are a 'Préface' and an 'Avant-propos'. The last piece reported (vi.[238-39]) is an untitled postface of sorts. (vi.[239] might be paginated 239; the upper corner where the page number ordinarily would be is not present due to a defect in the paper.) For further information concerning the significance of this edition, see Aurelio Principato's introduction to the text of the *Doyen de Killerine* in the *Œuvres complètes*, Jean Sgard general editor, iii (Grenoble 1978), and his bibliographical notes.

To editions of this novel listed in bibliographies dealing with prose fiction, I would add:

1. *Le Doyen de Killerine*, 1735-1740. '[...] par l'auteur des "Mémoires d'un homme de qualité"'. 6 vols. s.l. [sans lieu], 1735-1740. Krauss-Fontius, no. 3677. Locations: Universitäts- und Landesbibliothek Sachsen-Anhalt, Halle and Romanisches Seminar der Universität Leipzig (vol. i only at the latter location).

2. *Le Doyen de Killerine*, 1741. 6 vols. La Haye, 1741. Krauss-Fontius, no. 3678. Location: Universtätsbibliothek Greifswald (vols i-iv only). BN apparently has vol. i (Jones, p.57; no such volume is listed in the BNC).

3. *Le Doyen de Killerine*, 1777. 3 vols. La Haye: de Hondt, 1777. Krauss-Fontius, no. 3679. Location: Thüringische Landesbibliothek Weimar.

Incipit: 'C'est moins mon Histoire que je donne au Public, que celle de mes deux Freres & de ma sœur.'

209

Prévost d'Exiles: *Le Doyen de Killerine*, 1783-1784

Abbé Antoine François Prévost, called Prévost d'Exiles (1697-1763): Le doyen / de Killerine, / histoire morale, / Composée sur les Mémoires d'une Illustre / Famille d'Irlande, & ornée de tout ce / qui peut [ce qui / peut for vols ii-vi] rendre une lecture utile & / agréable. / Par [utile & agréable. / Par for vols ii-vi] l'Abbé Prevost. / Nouvelle édition, / Avec Figures. / [rule] / Premiere [Seconde, Troisieme, Quatrième, Cinquième, Sixième] partie. / [rule] / Prix, 15 liv. relié. / [woodcut decorations, i: stylised plant; ii: spray of flowers; iii: same as ii; iv: plants, ribbon and lyre of sorts; v: flowers; vi: same as iv] / A Lyon, / Chez Amable Le Roy [Leroy for iv, v, vi], Libraire. / [double rule] / M. DCC.

LXXXIII. [M. DCC. LXXXIV. / Avec Approbation & Permission. for iv, v, vi]

12°, i: 1 f. (titlepage) + iij-xv + [1]-4, 5-239 pp.

  ii: 1 pl + [1]-230 pp.
  iii: 1 pl + [1]-230 pp.
  iv: 1 pl + [1]-210 pp.
  v: 1 pl + [1]-211 pp.
  vi: 1 pl + [1]-243, 244-245, [246] pp.

Commentary: The first item in vol. i is a preface (the running title p.xiij reads 'prefece'). Then follow the 'Avant-propos' and the novel itself. The very last piece reported (vi.[246]) is an 'approbation' for '*le Doyen de Killerine, Roman de feu M. l'Abbé Prévôt*', Paris, 11 January 1771, signed 'Arnoult'. Each volume has a frontispiece which carries the 'partie' indication at the top right. Although in the tradition of the duodecimo, cheap illustrations, these are of interesting quality (not in Cohen or Reynaud).

MMF mention an edition for '/?1783/' and 1784, surely after Jones, p.57 (MMF 60.R50). The doubtful 1783 edition is listed by Jones according to the Library of Congress, the 1784 according to BN and Arsenal. The recent NUC does list what is presumably the six-volume edition described here (Oberlin College), but no edition is listed for 1783. I have included a description of my copy in order to clarify the confusion. I have found no trace of it elsewhere. This edition has nothing to do with the BN, 1784 edition. For the first edition and the preliminary pieces, see the preceding entry. (The type of the first three volumes' titlepages differs markedly from that of the last three.)

Incipit: 'C'Est moins mon Histoire que je donne au Public, que celle de mes deux Frères & de ma Sœur.'

210

Prévost d'Exiles: *Mémoires et aventures d'un homme de qualité*,
1738

Abbé Antoine François Prévost, called Prévost d'Exiles (1697-1763):
  i and ii: Memoires / et / avantures / d'un homme / de qualité, / Qui s'est retiré du Monde. / Tome premier [second]. / [woodcut ornament: symmetrical with baldaquin for i; symmetrical, vase of flowers at centre, with baldaquin, for ii] / A Paris, / Chez Theodore Legras, Grand'Salle / du Palais, à l'L couronnée. / [rule] / M. DCC. XXXVIII. / Avec Approbation & Privilege du Roy.
  iii and iv: Suite / des / memoires / et / avantures / d'un homme / de qualite', / Qui s'est retiré du monde. / Tome trosie'me [quatrie'me]. / [primitive woodcut decoration: smiling sun in centre of elaborate décor, with baldaquin, same for both volumes] / A Paris au palais, / Chez Theodore Legras, Libraire, / Grand'Salle, à l'L couronnée. / [rule] / M. DCCXXXVIII. / Avec Approbation & Privi lege [Privilege for iv] du Roi.
  v and vi: Suite / des / memoires / et / avantures / d'un homme / de qualité, / Qui s'est retiré du monde. / Tome cinquie'me. [sixie'me, or sixie'me.] / [woodcut

ornament, symmetrical, primitive with vase? in centre for v; intertwined branches forming initials of sorts, in heavy border for vi] / A Amsterdam. / Aux
dépens de la Compagnie. / M.DCCXXXVIII [M. DCCXXXVIII for vi]

    vii and viii: Suite / des / memoires / et / avantures / d'un homme / de qualité, /
Qui s'est retiré du monde. / Tome septie'me [huitie'me]. / [woodcut decoration
of 28 'stars', of an entirely different variety for each volume, forming inverted
pyramids] / A Amsterdam, / Aux dépens de la Compagnie. / MDCCXXXVIII.

12°, i: 2 pl (halftitle and titlepage) + 1 f. (2 pp.) + [1]-274 pp. (Preliminaries
include: halftitle, titlepage which is f.[aj], 1 f. (2 pp.) which is f.aij; then begin
ff. A[j], Aij, etc.)

    ii: 2 pl + [1]-214, 215-262, [263-264] pp.

    iii: 1 pl + 1-372 pp.

    iv: 1 pl + 1-196, 197-234, [235-236] pp.

    v: 1 f. (titlepage) + [3-6], 7-356 pp.

    vi: 1 f. (titlepage) + 3-330, 331-456 (for 356) pp. (pp.351-356 are paginated
451-456).

    vii: 1 pl (titlepage) + 7 ff. (6 + 8 pp.) + [1]-268 pp.

    viii: 1 pl (titlepage; see commentary) + [269]-470 pp. + 6 ff. (12 pp.).

Commentary: Vols i and ii have half titlepages for 'Memoires / et / avantures / d'un
homme / de qualité. / Tome premier [second].' (There are no half titlepages for
the remaining volumes, in the present copy anyway.) The first two pages of vol.i
are the 'Avis de l'éditeur'. P.274 contains the approbation. The second item in
ii is the 'Table' (for vols i and ii), followed by legal documents, which begin on
the last numbered page. The same pattern is repeated for vol. iv ('Table' pp.197-
234 for vols iii and iv, legal material 234-[236]). The first item in vol. v is a
'Lettre de l'éditeur'. The last item in vol. vi is the table (for v and vi).

    Vols vii and viii (here bound together) are separated by a titlepage, but are
consecutively paginated and signed. The last two folios of vii are M and M2
respectively (signed). M2 bears the catchword 'Suite', which matches the
titlepage of viii and not the head title. Vol. viii's titlepage is not signed, and the
last volume begins with f.N[1]. As can be seen, the titlepage of vol. viii is not
included in the pagination. I have seen what appears to be this edition in a
bookstore containing a blank leaf after the last page of vol. vii. I assume then
that a complete copy of vii would end with M, M2, [M3: blank], [M4: titlepage
to vol. viii]. (Or M3 might be the titlepage, M4 blank.) This could indicate a
separate printing for viii, or some fairly last-minute changes in book production
for the last two volumes. Vol. vii opens with a 'Lettre de l'éditeur. A Messieurs
de la Compagnie des Libraires d'Amsterdam' (head title; signed 'd'Exiles').
This is followed by an 'Avis de l'auteur'. The last item is vol. viii is a 'Table
des matières contenues dans ce volume' (which covers vii and viii).

    The head and running titles for i and ii are 'Memoires du marquis de ***'.
The head and running titles for iii-iv are 'Suite des Memoires du Marquis de
***'. For v-vi the head title is 'Suite et conclusion des memoires du marquis de
***'. The running title is 'Suite des Memoires du Marquis de ***'. The running
title for vii-viii is 'Memoires du Marquis de ***'. The head title is 'Memoires
d'un homme de qualité qui s'est retiré du monde. [rule] Histoire Du Chevalier

des Grieux, & de Manon Lescaut.', first and second books for each volume respectively.

The NUC lists a Paris, 1738 edition in six volumes (Indiana University, Yale University), with no pubisher recorded. There is no copy listed of the above edition in the BLC. The BN has only vols vii and viii, with the titlepage to viii missing and no blank leaf between the volumes (8° Y2.25346). The above edition appears to be listed in Max Brun's bibliography appended to his and Claire-Eliane Engel's edition of *Manon Lescaut* (Paris: Club des Libraires de France, 1960) and, then again, in the Deloffre and Picard edition of *Manon* (Paris: Garnier, 1965). I list these volumes, recording exactly what appears in them and on the titlepages. (The entries referred to in the bibliographies mentioned above present certain differences, which might be inaccuracies.) Henry Harrisse, although he does not mention the entire edition described here, does imply that the last volumes, comprising *Manon Lescaut*, were available separately when issued (*Bibliographie de 'Manon Lescaut' et notes pour servir à l'histoire du livre, seconde édition*, Paris 1877, no.15, pp.57-58). Harrisse mistakenly states that this edition comprises two segments: vols i-iv, Paris, veuve Delaulne, 1738 and vols v-viii, Amsterdam, 1738, unless he be referring to another edition. (See too his *L'Abbé Prévost*, pp.290-99.) The various parts of the novel first appeared between 1728 and 1731 (Jones).

There appear to be at least two editions of the *Mémoires et aventures d'un homme de qualité* which have escaped the attention of modern bibliographers:

1. *Mémoires et aventures*, 1765. '[Mémoires et aventures] d'un homme de qualité. II Tom. av[ec] fig[ures]. [in-]8. Augsb. Stage. [1]765' (Heinsius, Romane col.141). Kayser lists 'II Tom. av[ec] fig. [in-]8. Augsb. [1]765. v. Jenisch u[nd] St.' (Romane p.94a).

2. *Mémoires et aventures*, 1766. '[Mémoires et aventures d'un homme de qualité.] [in-]12. Basle, Thurneisen. [1]766' (Heinsius, loc. cit; also in Kayser, *loc. cit.*). The NUC lists a Paris: Emanuel Tourneisen, 1766 edition, 7 vols, 15 cm (location: Joint university libraries in Nashville, Tennessee). If 'Paris' does indeed appear on the titlepages, it would appear to be a false place of publication, unless it be a question of two editions (not likely) or of two issues (a possibility). MMF list '1766 (BM)' (51.R44). The BLC records '3 tom. 1766. 12°' (838.a.38). I have not been able to see the BL edition which, if it is complete in those volumes, would constitute yet another edition for 1766.

Those interested in further elucidations and possibly additional editions of this novel might consult Krauss-Fontius, nos 3639-43.

Incipits: (vol. i, *Mémoires et...*) 'Je n'ai aucun interêt à prévenir le Lecteur sur le récit que je vais faire des principaux évenemens de ma vie.'

(*Manon*) 'Je suis obligé de faire remonter mon Lecteur au tems de ma vie où je rencontrai pour la premiere fois le Chevalier des Grieux.'

2 1 1

Prévost d'Exiles: *Le Philosophe anglais*, 1785

Abbé Antoine François Prévost, called Prévost d'Exiles (1697-1763): Le / philo-sophe / anglois, / ou / histoire / de monsieur / Cléveland, / fils naturel / de Crom-wel; / Ecrite par lui-même, & traduite de l'Anglois par / l'Auteur des Mémoires d'un Homme de Qualité. / Tome premier [second, troisieme, quatrieme, cin-quieme, sixieme, septieme, huitieme]. / [woodcut ornament, some repeated] / A Rouen, / Chez Jean Racine, Libraire, rue / Ganterie. [Libraire, / rue Ganterie. for vols v-viii] / [rule] / M. DCC. LXXXV. / Avec permission.

12°, i: 1 pl + [j]-x + [1]-174 pp.
  ii: 1 pl + [1]-170 pp.
  iii: 1 pl + [1]-192 pp.
  iv: 1 pl + [1]-180 pp.
  v: 1 pl + [1]-216 pp.
  vi: 1 pl + [1]-187 pp.
  vii: 1 pl + [1]-224 pp.
  viii: 1 pl + [1]-235, [236-237] pp.

Commentary: The first ten, numbered pages of vol. i are a preface. The last two pages of vol. viii comprise: a 'permission simple' to Jean Racine for an edition of 750 copies of the work, 4 vols in-12. This information was duly recorded in the register of 'permissions simples'. Racine's edition was supposed to copy strictly the contents of the 1776, Amsterdam edition. The document is dated 22 February 1785; granted by Pierre Charles Laurent de Villedeuil, director-general of the booktrade, signed for him by de Sancy, 'Secrétaire général'; registered at the 'chambre syndicale' of Rouen, 24 February 1785, by Louis Oursel, 'Syndic'. (For further information concerning this 'permission simple', its purport and significance, see Robert L. Dawson, 'The permission simple of 1777 and the bibliographical evidence of its register', forthcoming.)

MMF (57.R40) list a 1785 edition after Berenice Cooper, 'Variations in the texts of eighteenth-century editions of *Le Philosophe anglais*', *Transactions of the Wisconsin academy of sciences, arts, and letters* (1940) xxxii.287-98. Cooper lists a Rouen: Racine, 1785 edition, with no further bibliographical details. But she does cite from those books, and the spelling varies from mine. For example, v.118 'P.' is given for 'Pere'; 'sçavoir' for 'savoir', etc. Cooper further states that 'the Rouen texts were based upon the Amsterdam text. This relation may indicate a business connection between the two publishing houses. [That is not true.] The 1785 Rouen edition of Racine contains, in the official permission for publication, the stipulation that the Amsterdam text of 1778 [*sic*] is to be followed, and the comparison made in this study shows that they do agree page for page, line for line' (p.292). Perhaps then there were two editions for 1785, since the 'permission simple' printed with my books clearly indicates that the edition was to follow the Amsterdam, *1776* edition. For further information, see the article referred to above (forthcoming). Since I could not find another copy of the edition described here, I have chosen to include this entry.

In any case, I am positive that the eight volumes described here were printed in Rouen.

Finally, in order to clarify some confusion concerning a 1788 version: MMF give '1788 (version abrégée) (CtY, Cooper, Gove, Weller)'. At the end of their entry, they write: 'V. aussi BUR 1788, août-oct.' (57.R40). The abridged version listed by Cooper is that which appeared in the *Bibliothèque universelle des romans*. Yale (CtY) has what appears to be an extract from that compendium (NUC).

Incipit: 'La réputation de mon Pere me dispense du / soin de m'étendre sur mon origine, personne n'i- / gnore quel fut le caractere de cet homme cele- / bre'.

212

Rémond des Cours(?): *Histoire d'Héloïse et d'Abélard*, 1693

Nicolas Rémond des Cours(?) (?-1716): (red and black titlepages) *Histoire / d'Eloïse* / et / *d'Abelard*. / Avec la Lettre passionnée / qu'elle lui écrivit. / *Traduite du Latin*. / Et accompagné [*sic*] de deux autres Avan- / tures Galantes fort singulié- / res. / [woodcut decoration: swag of sorts with hanging fruit] / *A la Haye*, / Chez *Jean Alberts*, Marchand / Libraire prés la Cour. / [rule] / *M. DC. XCIII*.

12°: 1 pl + 1 f. (2 pp.) + 1-24, 25-86 + 89-106 + 109-140 pp.

Commentary: Barbier attributes this work to Rémond des Cours, cites another edition for 1697 in-12 (ii.656d), but does not mention the 'Avantures galantes'. (The last word in his transcription of the title is 'latin'.) Charlotte Charrier lists what is presumably this work, but not this edition, under the rubric 'Traductions fantaisistes' (no. 43, p.605). Conlon, too, under Rémond des Cours's name, lists what appears to be 'Charrier's' edition, with a title variant: 'Histoire abregée d'Eloïse et d'Abélard. Avec la lettre passionnée qu'elle lui écrivit, traduite du latin, et accompagnée de deux autres avantures galantes fort singulières. La Haye, Louis & Henry van Dole 1693' (ii.121, no.6310). In his indexes, under Rémond des Cours, Lever lists a *Lettre d'Héloïse à Abailard*, 1693 (pp.480 and 551), but I could not find a main entry for any 1693 edition, under 'Histoire' or 'Lettre'. Giraud also lists the Van Dole edition (p.24, 1693.2; see too 1711.2).

In a note in the text of her book, Charrier discounts Bussy-Rabutin's possible plagiarisms from Rémond des Cours (p.418 n.3). What seems certain is that Rémond des Cours is the author of the *Lettre d'Héloïse à Abailard*, published supposedly at Amsterdam, chez Pierre Chayer in 1693. (This is part of a series of publications that appeared in the second half of the seventeenth century, beginning with Alluis' *Les Amours d'Abélard & d'Héloyse*, 1676; see Lever p.45.) The *Avantures galantes* were excluded from the 1695 edition of Rémond des Cours's *Lettre d'Héloïse*, and, what is just as important, the preliminary material and the adaptation of Heloïse's first letter to Abelard – the only one that concerns us here – is considerably different. There are two possibilities: 1. that Rémond des Cours did extensive plagiarising from the 1693 book; 2. that he is the author of the 1693 version and simply wrote a revised adaptation. I am not entirely convinced that he is the author of both books; ergo the question marks above.

Whoever composed the 1693 *Histoire d'Eloïse* possibly also wrote the two tales at the end of the book.

There is no copy of the 1693 book described here listed in the NUC, BLC or BNC. But I have come across another copy of it in the BN, with a card tucked away in the 'fichier des anonymes' (Ln27.27007). Since it is of extreme rarity, and the only known public copy so difficult to find, I have chosen to include it. (Also there is no accurate description of the book.) The first two pages are a preface, 'Au lecteur'. The author 'modestly' begins: 'Voici une piéce qui ne sauroit manquer de plaire; puis qu'elle joint aux charmes de la vérité toutes les autres beautez dont elle a été susceptible'. He then explains that the two tales have been added because they are too short to be published separately and because the reader will enjoy the variety formed by the collection. Follows an 'Histoire abrégée d'Eloise et d'Abelard' (head title). Then come the 'Lettre d'Eloise à Abelard' (head title), 'Le / marquis / de / Basin / ou / le barbare / epoux.' (half titlepage), and 'Le / chevalier / de la / Tour-Landry / ou / l'amant dupé.' (half titlepage).

In *Le Marquis de Basin*, the marquise's rabid husband prepares his wife's funeral bed – he's in love with someone else – plunges a sword into the heaving bosom of a handmaiden who tries to save her mistress, and then cold-bloodedly murders his horrified spouse.

According to the author, *Le Chevalier de La Tour-Landry* is 'une Histoire tout à fait risible, & que l'on peut mettre au rang des plus plaisantes avantures' ('Au lecteur', p.[2]). Rémond des Cours, if indeed he be the author, had a strange notion of the word 'plaisant'! The hero encounters two masked ladies in the Tuileries. An assignation is arranged with the more noble appearing woman, who has allowed him to glimpse the most delicious of attributes. During the rendez-vous, his beloved's wax hand falls apart in his own. She trips, and her wig tumbles off, which 'laissa voir sa tête toute pélée comme celle d'un vieux singe' (p.136). Worse yet, a false eye pops out of its socket. Seeing she can no longer hide the truth, our 'heroine', screeching imprecations, yanks out her false teeth and hurls them at La Tour-Landry: 'Il eut tellement peur qu'elle ne continuat à se démonter ainsi piéce à piéce, qu'il sortit avec la derniere diligence par la premiere porte qu'il trouva' (p.137). He flees Paris, never to return.

Incipits: ('Lettre d'Eloïse à Abélard') 'C'est à son Maître & à à [*sic*] son Pére, c'est à son Frére & à son Epoux, qu'une servante, qu'une fille'.

(*Le Marquis de Basin*) 'Une fille de Turin de trés bonne maison, jeune, riche, belle & vertueuse'.

(*Le Chevalier de La Tour-Landry*) 'Le Chevalier de la Tour-Landry de la maison de Maillé Brézé qui a de l'esprit & du mérite avoit passé'.

213

Révéroni Saint-Cyr: *Nos folies*, 1800

Jacques Antoine, baron Révéroni (de) Saint-Cyr (1767-1829): Nos folies / ou / mémoires / D'un Musulman connu à Paris en / l'an VI. / Orné de gravures. / [rule] / Tome premier [second]. / [rule] / A Paris, / Chez Lemierre, Libraire, rue du Four- / Germain, N°. 293. / [double rule] / Impr. d'Emm. Brosselard, rue André-des-Arts, n°. 73. / An VIII.

12°, i: 2 pl + [1]-194 pp.
  ii: 2 pl + [1]-182 pp.

Commentary: MMF list this novel as 'Nos folies ou mémoires d'un Musulman connu à Paris en 1798, recueillis et publiés par l'auteur de *Sabina d'Herfeld* Paris, Lemierre, an VII, 2t. in-12' (99.148), after the *Journal général de la littérature de France*, the *Journal typographique et bibliographique*, Barbier [iii, col.423f], Quérard [vii.554-55], Monglond [iv, col.1131, after Barbier and Quérard], Pigoreau and Dufrenoy (*L'Orient romanesque en France, 1704-1789*, Montreal 1946-47). MMF also cite another edition for 'Londres, Bell, 1799, 2 part. in-12, 194, 182p.' with the only location given being the château d'Oron. To the references given by MMF, I would add Cohen, who cites the 1799 edition, mentioning that it has two engravings by de Launay after 'Chaillou'. See below for the engravings accompanying the edition listed here. (For what it's worth, the novel is also listed in the advertisement leaf at the end of my copy of Pigault-Lebrun's *Mon oncle Thomas*, Paris: Barba, [an-]8., 4 vols in-12°: 'Folies (nos), *ou* Mémoire [*sic*] d'un Musulman, 2 vol. *in*-12, fig.; par Lemière'. Since the leaf is titled 'Livres qui se trouvent chez le même Libraire', Barba obviously meant 'published by Lemierre').

I have been unable to locate a copy of this work, much less the edition described here (BLC, NUC, BNC, etc.). The entry in the *Journal typographique et bibliographique* is for 'Nos folies, ou Mémoires d'un Musulman connu à Paris en 1798 (v. st. [vieux style]), recueillis et publiés par l'auteur de *Sabina*, d'*Herfeld*, de *Pauliska*, etc. etc. Deux vol. *in*-12, ornés de jol. fig. [...] Paris, *Lemierre*, libraire, rue du Four-Germain, n°. 293, près de l'Egout' ('Livres nouveaux', 10 brumaire an 8 [1 November 1799], p.37). This information is largely repeated in the *Journal général de la littérature de France, ou répertoire méthodique des livres nouveaux* [...], brumaire an VIII [October/November 1799], p.344.

There are two pretty engravings, bound in at the head of each volume, as follows: i, 'Tom. Ier.'-'Pag. 51', 'Challiou del.'-'De Launay direx.'. The caption within the border reads: 'Si la corde casse! .... Non, parbleu! / des cordes de Naples!' Vol. ii: 'Tom. IIe'-'Pag 139.', 'Challiou del.'-'De Launay direx^{t}.'. The caption within the border reads: 'C'est Fatmé! Fatmé elle-meme!' The citations match the pagination indicated on the pictures.

Each volume is preceded by a halftitle: 'Nos folies, / ou / mémoires / D'un Musulman connu à Paris en / l'an VI.' On the versos is to be found the following annoucement: '[double rule] / On trouve chez le même Libraire, *Lettres / sur l'imagination*, par *M. Meister*, deuxième / édition, 1 vol. *in* 8°. 2 fr. 50 c.; et 3 fr. 50 c. / franc de port. / *Mon Histoire au Trente un*, et celle de / tous ceux qui le jouent, 1 vol. *in*-12 1 f. 20 c. / et 1 fr. 50 c. franc de port.'

Incipit: 'J'ai joué mon rôle *d'automate*; ainsi qu'il a plû aux *merveilleuses* de me nommer'.

214

Riccoboni: *Lettres de milady Juliette Catesby*, 1759

Marie-Jeanne Laboras de Mezières, madame Riccoboni (1713-1792): Lettres / de milady / Juliette Catesby, / a milady / Henriette Campley, / son amie. / Seconde e'dition. / [woodcut decoration of two cupids embracing over a burning torch, quiver, bow, stylised decoration] / A Amsterdam. / [double rule] / M. D. CC. LIX.

12°: 1 pl + (1)-(250) pp.

Commentary: This novel first appeared in 1759 (MMF 59.22). I have been unable to find this particular edition anywhere. The only possibility is BN Y2.62636, which is a volume the staff informed me has been missing now for quite some time. I have chosen to list an edition which, at the moment, is a unique copy. If this holds true for the future, it means that there were at least six editions for this amusing, highly readable novel for 1759 alone (including the one mentioned in the commentary just below).

There are several editions of works by Mme Riccoboni which have escaped the attention of bibliographers dealing with prose fiction:

1. *Lettres d'Adélaïde de Dammartin*, 1767. 'Lettres d'Adélaide de Dammortin [for Dammartin] etc. II Part. [in-]8. Frcf. [Francfort] Brönner et Hermann. [1]767' (Heinsius, iii, col.379). Heinsius lists what might be another edition or issue of the same: '[Dammartin] d'Adelaide de, Lettres, à Mr. le Comte de Nance, p[ar] Mad. Riccoboni. II Part. [in-]8. Francf. Garbe. (Gebhardt et K[eyserer?] a[uch] Hermann.) [1]767' (Romane, col.47). Heinsius' source might have been the Messkatalog, which has: 'Lettres d'Adelaide de Damartin, Comtesse de Sancerre, à Mr. le Comte de Nancé, par Mad. *Riccoboni*. 2 Parties. 8. à Francfort, chez J. Gottl. Garbe', OM 1767, p.852. A few items down is the following entry: 'Lettres de Sancerre. 12. Londres & à Leipsic, chez Arkstée & Merkus'.

2. *Lettres d'Adélaïde de Dammartin*, 1767. Lettres d'Adélaïde de Dammartin, comtesse de Sancerre, à monsieur le comte de Nancé, son ami, par madame Riccoboni. Amsterdam: M.-M. Rey, 1767 (OCLC: California State University, Long Beach).

3. *Lettres d'Elisabeth Sophie de Valière*, 1773. Lettres d'Elisabeth Sophie de Valière à Louise Hortense de Canteleu [misspelled as 'Cantelieu'], 2 vols, in-8, Leipzig: Schwickert, 1773 (Kayser, Romane p.112b). Heinsius gives: '[Valiere] d'Elisabeth, Sophie de, Lettres, à Louise Hortense de Canteleu, p[ar] Mad. Riccoboni. II Tom. [in-]8. Lpz. Schwickert. [1]773' (Romane col.217; same information in Heinsius, *Handbuch*, p.778, and in Heinsius 1793, iv.525).

4. *Lettres de milady Juliette Catesby*, 1759. Lettres de milady Juliette Catesby, à milady Henriette Campley, son amie. 13 éd. [*sic*, probably for '3ᵉ éd.']. Amsterdam, 1759. 216 pp., 16 cm (OCLC: California State University, Chico).

5. *Œuvres*, 1780. 'Œuvres, collect. compl. [in-]8. Basle, Flick, [1]780' (Heinsius iii, col.379; also in Heinsius *Handbuch*, p.778, and Heinsius 1793, iv.484). Kayser, under Mme 'Riccobini' gives 'Neukirch' instead of 'Flick' (iv.502a). Perhaps their source was the Messkatalog, which contains: 'Collection complete des Œuvres de Mad. *Riccoboni*. Nouvelle Edit. 8 Voll. 12. à Berne, chez Eman.

Haller; il se trouve aussi à Basle chez Jean Jaque [!] Flick', OM 1780, p.913.
Note the different formats. Perhaps there were two issues?

Moreover, MMF list an edition of Mme Benoist's *La Vertu persécutée, ou lettres
du colonel Talbert* ('par madame ** auteur d'"Elisabeth"') for 'Dresde, 1767, 4
part. in-12 (BM)' (67.20). Kayser erroneously lists Mme Benoist's novel under
Mme Riccoboni's name and gives 4 vols in-8°, Dresden: Walther, 1767 (Romane,
p.112b; also in Heinsius, Romane, col.220, and in Heinsius 1793, iv.559). This
corresponds to the BL copy (1102.c.9) which is in two tomes, four parts
(volumes), in-8°. (These four parts were issued in two tomes: titlepages to i and
iii in red and black, to ii and iv in black only; catchtomes for Tom. I. I. [and
II.] Partie, Tom. II. I. [and II.] Partie). Giraud lists the first edition of this
novel, with the title of *Lettres du colonel Talbert*, for Amsterdam; Paris: Durand,
1766 (1766.2.a), possibly after an amalgam of Barbier, Quérard and Mornet.
(MMF mention these sources, state they were unable to locate a copy, and thus
have listed the first edition under 1767; 67.20).

The Messkatalog has the following entry relating to Mme Riccoboni's *Catesby*,
which I cold not find in the usual bibliographies and about which I know
nothing: 'Reponse de Sir Manley à Mylady Comtesse de Sunderland. Dans les
Lettres de Mylady Catesby. 8. Francfort, chez Knoch et Esslinger', MM 1760,
p.90. Could it possibly be a heroïd?

Incipit: 'C'Est au grand trot de six forts chevaux, avec des relais bien disposés'.

215

Riccoboni: *Lettres de milady Juliette Catesby*, 1782

Marie-Jeanne Laboras de Mezières, madame Riccoboni (1713-1792): Lettres / de
milady / Juliette Catesby, / a milady / Henriette Campley, / son amie. / [elaborate
woodcut decoration with symmetrical garlands] / A Paris, / Chez Briasson, rue
S. Jacques, à la / Science. / [double rule] / M. DCC. LXXXII.

12°: 1 f. (titlepage) + [3]-(153) pp.

Commentary: The only mention I have been able to find of this edition is in
Giraud, assuming that represents the same edition (p.45, 1759.4.f). For further
information, see the preceding item.

Incipit: 'C'est au grand trot de six fort bons chevaux, avec des relais bien
disposés'.

216

Richardson (Prévost): *Lettres anglaises (Clarisse Harlowe)*, 1784

Samuel Richardson (1689-1761), Antoine François Prévost, called Prévost d'Exiles (1697-1763), trans.: Lettres / angloises, / ou / histoire / de miss / Clarisse
Harlove, / Augmentée de l'Eloge de Richardson, / des Lettres Posthumes & du

Testament / de Clarisse. / Avec figures. / [rule] / Tome troisieme. / [rule] / [small woodcut ornament] / A Londres. / [double rule] / M. DCC. LXXXIV.

24°, iii: 2 ff. (halftitle and titlepage) + [5]-380 pp.

Commentary: Unfortunately I only have vol. iii. There is a half titlepage bearing: 'Lettres / angloises. / [rule] / Tome troisieme. / [rule]'. The bottom of the spine – the binding is of contemporary mottled calf – bears 'edition Cazin' in gilt letters. The 'Eloge' mentioned on the titlepage is of course Diderot's well known effusion. Jean Baptiste Antoine Suard also had a hand in this French rendition; see MMF 62.31. Cohen mentions a 1784 edition, 11 volumes in-18, A Londres [Paris, Cazin] (col.892), vol. iii having 380 pp. and two illustrations. Reynaud further elaborates, citing his source, Corroënne. Reynaud states that Corroënne 'mentionne un portrait et 23 figures; il faudrait selon lui au tome iii 3 figures et au tome v, 6 figures' (col.457). But Reynaud goes on to give the 'placement des *21* figures', and for vol. iii, only two at pp.230, 331 (col.458).

Thus the volume described here takes on a certain importance, since it does contains three engravings, and the second one, which is here unique or completely 'unfindable', is by Chapuy after Marillier. The other two (nos. 1, bearing 'Tom. 3.'-'Pag. 230' and 3, bearing 'Tom. 3'-'Pag. 331.') are in an entirely different style from no. 2. No. 2 appears to be a reduction of probably an octavo or duodecimo illustration (woman seated with paper in hand conferring with two other women, elegant interior, carpet, painting on wall of a standing cupid in loin cloth). This illustration faces p.253 and bears on the top left: 'Tom. III. Pag. 253'. The caption, in the picture, reads: 'Ayez la bonté Mademoiselle, de fortifier le cœur de cette chere / fille, pendant une lecture qui ne peut manquer de l'attendrir'. (This citation is not on p.253.) Then follow the artists' signatures.

The NUC lists an 11 volume edition ('Harlove' spelled 'Harlowe') '...Londres [Paris, Succrs de Valade, et Cazin]...' for the Library of Congress, Detroit Public Library and University of Oregon at Eugene. The listing in MMF is for Londres, 1784, 10 volumes in-12 according to BN and Quérard. The BNC lists 11 volumes in-12, and vol. iii has been lost. In the BNC ten-year supplement we find: 'Lettres anglaises [...], nouvelle édition [...]. Londres 1784, 10 vols in-12' (16°Y2.25530) with the remark: 'Ne contient pas les lettres posthumes ni le testament de Clarisse' (xvii.833a; I was unable to examine those books). Giraud lists 11 vols in-18 (p.41, 1751.6.j). It is probable that the above volume is part of both NUC and BN, but it is doubtful that NUC contains the Marillier illustration. (As mentioned, vol. iii of the BN copy is missing.) The translation first appeared in 1751 (MMF 51.40) and the original in 1747-1748.

I would like to take this occasion to mention a couple of editions of the *Lettres anglaises* which have escaped the attention of modern bibliographers of the 'genre romanesque':

1. *Lettres anglaises, ou histoire de Miss Clarisse Harlowe*. 3 vols. Dresde: Walther, 1764. Krauss-Fontius, no. 7035. Location: Universitäts- und Landesbibliothek Sachsen-Anhalt, Halle.

2. *Lettres anglaises*, 1766-1780. '[Lettres] angloises, ou Histoire de Miss Clarisse Harlove, traduites de l'Anglois de Mr. Richardson. 7 Vol. en 13 Parties, avec

fig. [in-]8. Dresd[e]. Walther. [1]766-80' (Heinsius, Romane col.125). Much the same information is given in Heinsius, *Handbuch*, but with no mention of the number of 'parties' (p.802). Heinsius 1793 gives 'XIII Part. en VII Vol.' (iv.521). Perhaps what is meant by the listing is that two editions were put out by Walther: one in 1766 and another in 1780. This information is repeated in Kayser, who specifically mentions twenty engravings (Romane, p.112b).

There are also several editions and/or issues of Le Tourneur's translation, which first appeared in 1785-86 (MMF 85.41), that have escaped the attention of modern bibliographers:

1. *Clarisse Harlowe*, 1787. '[Clarisse] Harlowe, histoire de, nouvelle traduction de Mr. le Tourneur, av. fig. de Chodowiecky. X Vol. [in-]8. Winterthur, Steiner. [1]787' (Heinsius, Romane col.43; incomplete listing in Kayser, Romane, p.112b).

2. *Clarisse Harlowe*, 1787. The next entry in Heinsius is for 'le même en XIV Vol. avec fig. de Schellenberg. [in-]12. ibid.' (also Kayser, Romane p.112b).

3, 4. *Clarisse Harlowe*, 1792 (and 1793?). 'VIII Vols. gr. [in-]8. Basel [1]792, 93' (Kayser, Romane, *loc. cit.*; what seems to be meant is two editions, one for 1792 and another for 1793, or perhaps one for 1792-93).

Kayser also mentions a *Paméla* not listed in the usual, modern bibliographies: 'Histoire de Pamela. II Vols. [in-]8. Frankf. [1]771 (Herrmann)' (Romane p.112b).

Incipit: (Miss Howe to Miss Harlove) 'Une visite imprévue a détourné le cours de mes idées'.

217

Rousseau: *Emile*, 1762

Jean Jacques Rousseau (1712-1778): (titlepages in *red* and black)

i and iii: *Émile*, / ou / de l'éducation. / *Par J. J. Rousseau*, / Citoyen de Genève. / [rule] / Sanabilibus ægrotamus malis; ipsaque nos in rectum / genitos Natura, si emendari velimus, juvat. / Sen: de irâ. L. II. c. 13. / [rule] / *Tome premier*. [*troisieme*.] / [woodcut decoration consisting of five symmetrical decorations in a row on top – the middle one is different – surmounting three rows of three (comprising nine similar decorations except that the one in the middle is different), positioned to form a square laid on its side, with the top point just under the middle one of the row above; same for all four volumes] / A Francfort. / [treble rule] / *M. DCC. LXII*.

ii and iv: *Émile*, / ou / de l'éducation. / *Par J. J. Rousseau*, / Citoyen de Genève. / [rule] / *Tome second*. [*quatrieme* no period] / [woodcut decoration described above] / A Francfort. / [treble rule] / *M. DCC. LXII*.

12°, i: 1 pl + (i)-(vi) + [1]-228 pp.
ii: 1 pl + [1]-186 pp. + 14 ff. (27 pp.)
iii: 1 pl + [1]-179 pp.
iv: 1 pl + [1]-231, [232], [233]-248 pp.

Commentary The first set of pages in vol. i is an untitled preface. The last sets of

pages in vols ii and iv are tables, each for the corresponding two volumes. These
are part of the normal signature sequences. (Note that the pages of the tables
in vol. ii are not numbered and that those in iv are.) i.228 is the end of the text
and also contains a list of errata for that volume. iv.[232] contains the errata
for vol. iv.

MMF list this edition according to the Harvard copy (62.33). The NUC lists
that copy and two others, assuming they all be the same (for Princeton and the
University of Illinois, Urbana). Dufour describes this edition (i.174-75, no. 192),
with a couple of fairly minor errors, according to the BL copy (1030.d.15-16;
Dufour's errors are 'Sanalibus' for 'Sanabilibus' and part of the errata to vol.
iv reads 'dans les qualitéz' instead of 'dans les qualitez'). Sénelier lists this
edition too (under the rubric of editions printed in Germany), with no commentary except a reference to Dufour (p.119, no. 857). Sénelier's entry is either very
inaccurate or he had in hand another edition; I strongly suspect the former!

The BLC claims the BL copy is in octavo, erroneously. The NUC notes that
this is 'a pirated edition; the imprint may be false' and reference is made to
Gagnebin. Bernard Gagnebin, in the bibliography appended to his critical
edition of *Emile* (Paris 1969), lists the above edition according to the copy in the
Library of Geneva, noting that that copy 'ne comporte pas de gravures. Il s'agit
certainement d'une contrefaçon anglaise' (p.1869). And he is quite right. Not
only is this evident from the paper, frequency of catchwords and decorations –
the copy described here is also bound in two tomes, in contemporary English
calf, and bears the signature of an eighteenth-century owner, one 'Miss
Clements' – but by the press figures sprinkled throughout. (However, there are
none in vol. iv.) Also the four volumes (obviously issued in two tomes) contain
a very large number of errors indeed, which the errata do not even begin to
correct. Giles Barber was the first to remark upon the significance of the press
figures in the identification of this edition as an English 'piracy' ('Catchwords
and press figures at home and abroad', *The Book collector* [autumn 1960] p.307
and n.18).

Professor William Todd was kind enough to supply me with the names of the
real printer and publisher. This edition of *Emile* was printed by William Strahan,
well known in the trade of the time (he did Gibbon's *Decline and fall*, participated
in the Johnson *Dictionary* venture, and so on; vide Plomer pp.239-40). *Emile* was
printed for Thomas Becket who not only dealt in French literature, both British
printed and imported from abroad (Plomer p.21-22), but also published the
English translation of Rousseau's explosive treatise (see below), printed by
Strahan as well. This information is derived from the Strahan printing ledger
(BL ms Additions 48800, opening 117, or f.116*v*, originally numbered 131
[struck], then 129). The publisher, Becket, was charged for eight sheets of the
French work – which would not have comprised the entire *Emile* of course – and
750 copies of those. This entry is dated August 1762. The item following *Emile*
is the English *Emilius*, vol. i (14 sheets). Several items down, a few months later
(December) is *Emilius*, vol. iv (14 and a half sheets). Strahan also did other
works by Rousseau, works by Voltaire, pieces dealing with the Hume-Rousseau
controversy, etc. (The Strahan ledgers are to be published by Professor Patricia
Hernlund. See William B. Todd, 'David Hume: a preliminary bibliography' in

Hume and the enlightenment, William B. Todd editor, Edinburgh 1974, pp.189-205.)

Vol. i begins with ff.[a1: titlepage], a2-a4. Then the text begins with gathering B. Vols ii and iii each begin (for the text) with a gathering signed 'A'. Vol. iv reverts to B. Bearing in mind the English custom of beginning signature sequences for the main text proper with B regardless of preliminaries (vide for example the anonymous *Secret memoirs* and Crébillon fils, *Le Sopha* above), the compositors seem to have had a hard time remembering that they were supposed to be producing a 'German' book!

But why would the English printer have tried to manufacture a book which, upon first glance, would look like a German piracy of a highly controversial French work or a clandestine edition printed in Paris? (The absence of publishers' names on titlepages indicating a foreign city – usually 'Londres', 'Amsterdam' or 'La Haye', though German cities so used are not infrequent – and date only was commonly used for books printed in Paris with a 'permission tacite', and for books printed there and elsewhere with no permission at all.) Several possible reasons come to mind. Commerce between France and England, never mind London and Paris, had been severely disrupted by the Seven years' war. Yet there had been no particular lessening of interest for things French in England. (A study of the influence of patriotic sentiment in both countries on Franco- and Anglophilia respectively, wrought by the war, would be an interesting one.) Then too anything pertaining to someone as famous as Jean-Jacques would have aroused considerable interest all over Europe, England included. (One need scarcely remind the present reader of *Emile*'s fate and Rousseau's hasty flight.)

There would probably have been relatively few copies of *Emile* in French available in England, whether printed in France or in Holland, during the last, full year of the war. Yet the reading public across the channel would have been anxious to read a work, in the original language, which was creating such a furor. Of course Britons had available an English version right from 1762, but most educated Englishmen had a good working knowledge of French and would have desired access to the original, especially in light of the inadequacies of the English translation.

The public's appetite was whetted by enticing anouncements and tidbits appearing in British periodicals of the time. The English translation (by William Kenrick) was announced hither and thither (e.g. *The London magazine*, November 1762, p.632, Becket and co.; *The Scots magazine*, October 1762, p.542 [same edition]). And *The Scots magazine* reported, in news from Rome (November 1762), that 'the holy office had just prohibited, under the pain of excommunication, the importation of two books printed in Holland, and written by the celebrated M. de Rousseau; one his well known treatise on education; the other a disquisition upon nature' (p.611; no mention is made of an English printed edition). The *London magazine* provided an excerpt, 'Advice of a Father to his Daughter. From the French of Rousseau' (August 1762, pp.404-406) and, in the next month, the second article comprises yet another pithy extract: 'A Parallel between Jesus-Christ and Socrates. From Æmilius: or, the Treatise on Education. By Rousseau'. (I have chosen these items at random. For some information concerning particularly the *Monthly review* and the *Critical review*, see Henri Roddier, *J.-J. Rousseau en Angleterre au XVIIIe siècle*, Paris 1950, pp.[133]-34, 136. Roddier also points out that the 1762 English translation was not highly regarded at the time, and gives the reasons.) Interest of course continued throughout 1763 and beyond. (See for example part of Rousseau's letter to Néaulme, [5 June 1762], Englished in the *Gentleman's magazine*, published in the 1763 supplement, pp.644-45 [part of Leigh 1830]. Etc.)

The need for an English edition of the French original must have struck more than one publisher, regardless of the availability in England of continental editions (which were doubtless inadequate in number to supply the demand, and would also have been more expensive). But why was this one printed under the rubric of 'Francfort', with no names of publishers or printers? Aside from possibly desiring to avoid the expense and bother involved with legal depositories, Becket might have wanted to add to the titillation of his edition by making it seem a continental contrefaçon. Perhaps he expected sales on the continent, and he might have erroneously thought it a bit easier, in war-time France, to circulate a prohibited work purportedly of German (or even French) manufacture, rather than English. In all this, an important question lies unanswered: how aware were the educated public, agents of the police and customs officials in France and elsewhere about diverging compositorial practices? (Writers in contact with publishers in various countries would have known, but others...).

There are several editions of *Emile* which do not seem to be listed in the usual, modern bibliographies:

1. *Emile*, 1781. 'Emile, ou de l'Education. IV Tom. av[ec] fig. gr. [in-]8. Lond. [Société?] Typ. [1]781' (Heinsius, iii, col.442). This information is also in Heinsius, *Handbuch* for '... Londres, Typograph. [1]781' (p.786). MMF list a 'Londres, 1780-81, 4t. in-8' edition after the copy at Harvard and Charles Antoine Brissart-Binet, *Manuel du cazinophile*, Paris 1879. (There are three locations of the latter *Emile* listed in the NUC.)

2. *Emile*, 1781. 'Emile, ou de l'education, par J. J. *Rousseau*. IV Tomes. Nouv. Edit. 12. Geneve & Berne, chez la nouv. soc. typographique', Messkatalog, OM 1781, p.120. Perhaps issued from an *Œuvres*?

3. *Emile et Sophie*, 1781. 'Emile & Sophie, ou les Solitaires, par J. J. *Rousseau*. 12. à Leipsic, chez la Ve H. Merkus', Messkatalog, OM 1781, p.120. This is conceivably a Société typographique edition.

4. *Emile*, 1799. 'l[e] m[ême]. IV Tom. [in-]12. L[ei]pz[ig]. G. Fleischer (a[uch] Turneiseo [for Turneisen or Tourneisen] à Cassel) [1]799' (Heinsius, *loc. cit.*). The NUC has an entry for Leipsic: G. Fleischer, 1799-1800, in 4 vols (location: Cornell University). This is also listed in the Messkatalog: 'Emile, ou de l'education, par I. I. *Rousseau*. 4 Tomes. 12. à Leipsig, Fleischer le cadet', OM 1799, p.207.

5. *Emile*, 1799. 'l. M. IV Vol. [in-]12. L[ei]pz[ig] Rein. [1]799' (Heinsius, *loc. cit.*). This information is also in the Messkatalog, with a different format recorded: 'Le même livre [*Emile*...]. Nouv. edit. 4 Vol. avec fig. 16. à Leipsig, Rein', OM 1799, p.207.

Much of this information is repeated in Kayser (iv.558b).

Incipit: 'Tout est bien, sortant des mains de l'Auteur des choses'.

218

Rousseau: *Emile*, 1762

Jean Jacques Rousseau (1712-1778): (titlepage in *red* and black) *Émile*, / ou / *de l'éducation*. / Par J. J. Rousseau, / Citoyen de Genève. / [rule] / Sanabilibus aegrotamus malis; ipsaque nos in rectum / genitos natura, si emendari velimus, juvat. / Sen: de irâ. L. II. c. 13. / [rule] / *Tome troisiéme*. / [symmetrical woodcut decoration with sun in centre] / *A Amsterdam*, / Chez Jean Néaulme, Libraire. / [treble rule] / *M. DCC. LXII*. / Avec Privilége de Nosseigneurs les Etats / de Hollande & de Westfrise.

12°, iii: 2 pl + 1-201 pp.

Commentary: Unfortunately I only have vol. iii of this edition. There is a half titlepage as follows: 'Émile, / ou / de l'éducation. / Tome III.' This edition does not seem to be listed in either Dufour or Sénelier, assuming that Dufour no. 197 is the same as Gagnebin no. 16 ('Notices bibliographiques' in *Œuvres complètes*, Paris 1969, p.1870). The latter (no. 16) is purportedly a Rey piracy (in-12), of which vol. iii has 201 pp. Gagnebin, known for his accuracy, lists: 'A Amsterdam, / Chez Jean Néaulme. / M.D.CC.LXII.' whereas, as can be seen from the above transcription, my copy bears '[...] Jean Néaulme, Libraire. / [treble rule: Gagnebin does not usually report rules] / M. DCC. LXII.' (Gagnebin transcribes the titlepage of vol. i.) The book described here is a 'contrefaçon', but I cannot say for certain whether it was printed by Rey. (There is no illustration, and never seems to have been one; contemporary calf binding.)

Incipit: ('Suite du Livre quatriéme') 'Il y a trente ans que dans une ville d'Italie, un jeune homme'.

219

Rousseau: *Emile*, 1793

Jean Jacques Rousseau (1712-1778): Émile, / ou / de l'éducation. / Par J. J. Rousseau, / Citoyen de Genève. / [rule] / Tome premier [second, quatrième, cinquième, sixième]. / [rule] / [short rule] / A Paris. / [double rule: thick, thin] / 1793.

18°, i: 1 f. (titlepage) + iij-x, [11]-222 pp.
  ii: 1 pl + [1]-244 pp.
  iv: 1 pl + [1]-278 pp.
  v: 1 pl + [1]-240 pp.
  vi: 1 pl + [1]-238 pp.

Commentary: Vol. i contains a 'Préface d'Émile' (pp.iij-x). Vol. iv contains the 'Suite du livre quatrième. Profession de foi du vicaire savoyard' (pp.[1]-157). *Emile* ends vi.140. Then follow 'Émile / et / Sophie, / ou / les solitaires.' (halftitle, p.141); 'Avis des éditeurs Sur le fragment qui suit' (pp.[142]-146); *Emile et Sophie* (p.[147]-238). Vol. iii is missing.

There are no ornaments, except for rules. These volumes are printed on generally flimsy paper, but of different weights.

This edition is not listed in Dufour or Sénelier, and I could find no other copy of it.

Incipits: (*Emile*) 'Tout est bien, sortant des mains de l'Auteur des choses'.

(*Emile et Sophie*) 'J'étois libre, j'étois heureux, ô / mon maître!'

220

Rousseau: *Julie, ou la nouvelle Héloïse*, 1785

Jean-Jacques Rousseau (1712-1778): Julie, / ou / la nouvelle / Héloïse. / Lettres de deux amants / Habitants d'une petite Ville aux / pieds des Alpes. / Recueillies et publiées / Par J. J. Rousseau. / [large swell rule] / Premiere [Seconde, Troisieme, Quatrieme, Cinquieme, Sixieme] partie. / [large swell rule] / Édition augmentée des Amours de Milord / Edouard Bomston. [Édition augmentée d'une seconde Préface / de l'Auteur. for vol. v] / [thin rule] / Non la conobbe il mundo, mentre l'ebbe: / Conobill' io ch' a pianger qui rimasi. / Petrarc. / [thin rule] / [small symmetrical ornament, same for all volumes] / A Amsterdam, / Chez les Libraires Associés. / [swell rule] / 1785.

12°, i: 1 f. (titlepage) + [iij]-xxviij, 29-156 pp.
ii: 1 f. (titlepage) + 3-142 pp.
iii: 1 f. (titlepage) + 3-119 pp.
iv: 1 f. (titlepage) + 3-167 pp.
v: 1 f. (titlepage) + 3-178 pp.
vi: 1 f. (titlepage) + 3-168 + [169], [170], 171-191 pp.

Commentary: The contents are as follows: 'Préface' (i.[iij]-iv); 'Seconde préface de Julie, ou entretien sur les romans' (i.v-xxviij); then the novel, from i.29 through vi.168. Follow 'Les amours / de milord / Édouard Bomston. / [large swell rule] / Par J. J. Rousseau. / [large swell rule] / Part. VI. P [catchmaterial]' (halftitle, vi.[169]); an 'Avant-propos' verso which is a summary (vi.[170]); *Les Amours* ... (vi.171-191). The last item (*Les Amours...*) is double spaced. The end of the novel (vi.168) bears 'Fin de la Nouvelle Héloïse.', and the halftitle for the *Amours*, with the 'Avant-propos' is f.P[1]. The end of that piece bears 'Fin.' (vi.191). It is possible that copies of just the last bit might show up by themselves. (Unless it was separately issued with special pagination and signatures, with the catchtomes deleted – which seems unlikely – it would be easy to recognise.) It is also possible that copies of this edition which would appear complete might turn up without the *Amours*.

Each part has a good-sized, somewhat primitive woodcut vignette on the first page of text. II.3, iv.3 and vi.3 are the same. III.3 and v.3 are the same. The vignette in volume i (p.29) is not repeated, and is signed 'Chenet'. (There are only a couple of other ornaments in the book.) The paper is of a cheap, nondescript variety. All this, plus the quality of the type, would bespeak more a French provincial printing (Lyon?, Avignon?, Toulouse?) than of volumes produced in Amsterdam.

This edition is not listed in Dufour or in Sénelier, and I could find no other copy of it.

Incipits: (*La Nouvelle Héloïse*) 'Il faut vous fuir, mademoiselle, je le sens / bien'.

(*Les Amours de milord Bomston*) 'Les bizarres aventures de milord Edouard / à Rome, étaient trop romanesques'.

221

Rousseau: *La Nouvelle Héloïse*, 1795

Jean-Jacques Rousseau (1712-1778): La nouvelle / Héloïse, / ou / lettres / de deux amants, / habitants d'une petite ville / au pied des Alpes, / Recueillies et publiées par J. J. Rousseau, / Citoyen de Geneve. / [rule] / Tome premier [second, troisieme, quatrieme]. / [rule] / [wooodcut decoration, i: foliage with shell? in back; ii: symmetrical, with two swirls on either side; iii: bunch of grapes on stalk with two leaves; iv: flowers and foliage tied together] / A Rouen, / Chez la Veuve de Pierre Dumesnil, / & Comp. Impr.-Libr. rue de l'Union, N°. 20. / [double rule] / L'an troisieme de la République Françoise.

8°, i: 2 pl + [I]-V, VI, [VII]-LXII + [1]-342, 343-356 pp.

ii: 2 pl + [1]-453, 454-464 pp.

iii: 2 pl + [1]-413, 414-419 pp.

iv: 2 pl + [1]-349, 350-376, 377-383 pp.

Commentary: Item no. 1 in i is the preface; i, no. 2 is an 'Avertissement Sur la Préface suivante'; no. 3, 'Seconde préface de la nouvelle Éloïse' [*sic*]; no. 4, the first part of the novel. The last set of pages in each volume is a 'Table'. The second item in iv is *Les Amours de milord Edouard Bomston*. The copy described here has four half titlepages, 'La / nouvelle / Héloïse. / [rule] / Tome premier [second, troisieme, quatrieme]. / [rule]'.

MMF (61.18) list a Rouen edition after Sénelier. But Sénelier's no. 411 (p.81) seems entirely different. (Sénelier gives no location for that particular item.) The edition described here is not listed in Dufour. There is no copy recorded in the NUC, BNC or BLC. The only listing I have been able to find, and somewhat faulty at that, is in Reynaud. He reports: 'Il existe une autre édition: A Rouen, chez la Veuve de Pierre Dumesnil et Comp. Impr. Libr., rue de l'Union, n° 20. L'an troisième de la République française (soit 1794), 4 vol. in-8. Edition rare illustrée d'un portrait de Rousseau par Degault et de 5 très jolies figures par de Prudhon, le tout gr. par Copia' (col.464).

The exquisite illustrations in my copy are as follows (captions in the pictures): i, frontispiece by Copia after J. M. Degault (signed): 'Vitam impendere vero', a sculpted bust, à la romaine, much stylised, of Rousseau. This is similar to, but not quite the same as Lemoyne's bust of Rousseau pictured in the *Album Rousseau* compiled by Bernard Gagnebin (Gallimard 1976) p.165, no. 261. Then, facing the first page of the novel, 'Le premier baiser de l'amour' by Copia after Prud'hon (signed). In vol. ii, frontispiece, 'Ma Fille, respecte les Cheveux Blancs de ton Malheureux Pere.', by Copia (signed; no signature for the artist). Facing the first page of part 3 (ii.[257]), 'Il appliqua sur sa main malade des baisers

LE PREMIER BAISER DE L'AMOUR

No 221: Rousseau, *La Nouvelle Héloïse*, 1795, frontispiece by Copia

de Feu', by Copia (signed; no signature for the artist). Vol. iii also has a frontispiece (part 4 of the novel): 'Je ne me bats point contre un insensé', by Copia after Prud'hon (signed). Then an illustration facing the beginning of part 5 (iii.[275]): 'l'Héroïsme de la valeur', by Copia (signed; no signature for the artist). There are no engravings in the fourth volume. Each 'partie' has a running title for it and the novel. The *Amours de milord Bomston*, however, has a running title for the sixth part of the main novel ('La Nouvelle [versos] / Héloise. VI. Part. [rectos]'). At the end of iv we find: 'Fin de la Table du quatrieme et dernier Volume'.

Reynaud mentions that all the engravings are by Prud'hon [or after him rather], and that these are also to be found in the 1804 and 1808 Paris editions of the novel. (I have not been able to examine them).

Girardin reports that 'cette suite [de gravures] est dessinée par Prudhon et gravée par Copia. Elle parut en 1804, mais l'édition ne parut qu'en 1808' (p.146). Concerning the first plate (which Girardin terms the fifth): 'cette vignette est de beaucoup supérieure aux quatre autres; elle passe pour être un des chefs-d'œuvre de Prudhon. Elle est fort rare, même avec la lettre' (p.148). Girardin also states that these illustrations are in octavo. But the first five in my copy are somewhat smaller than the actual leaves of the books (my copy is untrimmed), and the chain lines are horizontal. The last engraving is on a bigger sheet, with vertical chain lines.

Edmond de Goncourt states that the five illustrations (excluding the frontispiece) were engraved by Copia, 'pour l'édition de la *Nouvelle Héloïse* publiée par Bossange, Masson et Besson' (in *Catalogue raisonné de l'œuvre peint, dessiné et gravé de P. P. Prud'hon*, Paris 1876, p.234; it is only fair to state that much of the information in Girardin concerning these illustrations seems to be derived from E. de Goncourt although neither the latter's name nor work is mentioned.)

The novel first appeared in 1761 (MMF 61.18). *Les Amours de milord Bomston* was first published in 1780 (MMF 80.30). The head title to the latter piece is asterisked, and a note states: 'Cette piece qui paroît pour la premiere fois, a été copiée sur le manuscrit original et unique de la main de l'Auteur, qui appartient et existe entre les mains de *Mad. la Maréchale de Luxembourg*, qui a bien voulu le confier' (iv.350).

I would like to mention that Monglond lists a *Nouvelle Héloïse* for Leipsic, G. Fleischer le cadet, 1796, 4 vols in-12° (iii, col.659; location: Bibliothèque de Neuchâtel), which was republished as a new edition in 1801. (This is not listed in Dufour, Sénelier or MMF). Kayser gives 'Julie, ou la nouvelle Héloïse. IV Vols. [in-]8. Leipz. [1]796. N. Aufl. [1]801. Er. Fleischer' (Romane, 117a; the 1801 edition is reported in Monglond after Kayser). And Kayser's source could well have been Heinsius: '[Julie] ou la nouvelle Heloise, p[ar] J. J. Rousseau, nouv. Ed. 4 Vol. [in-]8. Lpz. Gerh. Fleischer. (a[uch] Levrault in Strasb.) [1]801' (Romane, col. 109). Elsewhere he reports: '[Héloïse,] la nouvelle, p.Rousseau. 4 T[omes] gr. [in-]12. Lpz. Gerh. Fleischer. [1]796' (Romane, col.97). The same information, together with a Bâle, Thurneysen, 1796 edition (4 vols, gr. in-12) is reported in Heinsius 1798, p.490. See too no. 4 directly below.

Further, MMF give an edition for 'Bâle, s.d. [1796], 4t.' (61.18), after Sénelier who in turn reports 'octavo' after Monglond (iii, col.659). Kayser's entry is for 'gr. 12. Basel [1]796. Thurneisen' (*loc. cit.*). Kayser also lists a *Julie* in 4 vols, in-12°, Leipzig: Rein, 1799, and another – no date mentioned – 4 vols in-12° for Leipzig, Hinrichs (ibid.). Kayser's source could well have been the Messkatalog, which lists the two editions, with varying formats: 'nouvelle Heloise. Nouv. édit. 4 Vol. avec fig. 8. à la même ville [Leipzig], le même [G. Fleischer]', OM 1796, p.187. As the Messkatalog also lists a new edition in-12°, there were probably two issues: 'Heloise, la nouvelle, ou Lettres de deux amans, par J.-J. Rousseau. 4 Tomes. Nouv. edit. gr.-in 12. à Leipsig, G. Fleischer' (MM 1796, p.325). Since it is a question of 'grand in-12°', perhaps a mistake was made concerning the octavo format? As for the 1799, Rein edition, it too is listed in the Messkatalog which could thus also have been Kayser's source: 'Heloise, la nouvelle, ou lettres de deux amans, habitans une petite ville aux pieds des Alpes, recueillies & publ. par I.-I. Rousseau. Nouv. edit. avec fig. 6 Vol. [in-]16. à Leipsig, *Rein*', OM 1799, p.209.

Here are a few more editions of *La Nouvelle Héloïse* which have escaped the attention of modern bibliographers:

1. *La Nouvelle Héloïse*, 1762. 'La nouvelle Heloise par Mr. J. J. *Rousseau*. VI Tomes 12. à Berne, chez la societé typographique', Messkatalog, OM 1762, p.266.

2. *La Nouvelle Héloïse*, 1781. 'Heloise, la nouvelle, ou lettres de deux amans par J. J. *Rousseau*. IV Tomes. 12. Geneve & Berne, chez la nouv. soc. typogr.', Messkatalog, OM 1781, p.122. There are several editions for Geneva in and about 1781 listed in the NUC.

3. *La Nouvelle Héloïse*, 1784. 'Heloise, la nouvelle, ou lettres de deux amans. IV Voll. pet[it] in[-]18. à Kehl, chez la soc. litt. typogr. & à Leipsic, en commiss[ion], dans la libr. des Savans', Messkatalog, OM 1784, p.902. This is conceivably part of an *Œuvres*.

4. *La Nouvelle Héloïse*, 1800. 'Rousseau, I. I. la nouvelle Heloise. 4 Voll. avec fig. Nouv. edition. 8. à Leipsic, Fleischer le jeune', Messkatalog, OM 1800, p.247. The NUC has a Leipzig, 1801 edition (sub *Julie, ou...*), vols i-iii only, which might refer to the same edition (Harvard).

The Messkatalog also lists an edition of *Les Amours de milord Bomston* which has escaped the attention of modern bibliographers: 'Les Amours de Mylord Bomston par J. J. *Rousseau*. 12. à Leipzig, chez la Ve H. Merkus', OM 1781, p.117.

In passing: MMF list the 1769 edition of Brument's *Henriette de Wolmar*, according to Gay, for Münster, 1769, in-8° (MMF 68.17; Gay ii, col.461). Gay lists after a Scheible catalogue of 1867. Kayser, listing the work under Rousseau's name, indicates the publisher: Coppenrath (Romane, 117a).

Incipits: (*La Nouvelle Héloïse*) 'Il faut vous fuir, Mademoiselle, je le sens bien'.

(*Les Amours de milord Bomston*) 'Les bizarres aventures de Milord Edouard à Rome, étoient trop romanesques'.

222

Saint-Lambert: *Les Saisons*, etc., 1778

Jean François, marquis de Saint-Lambert (1716-1803):

i: Les saisons, / poëme. / [rule] / Puissent mes chants être agréables à l'homme / vertueux & champêtre, & lui rappeller quel- / quefois ses devoirs & ses plaisirs. Wieland. / [rule] / Nouvelle Édition. / [elaborate, composite ornament, symmetrical, made of many little 'flowers'] / A Amsterdam. / [two thin rules] / 1778.

ii (halftitle): L'Abenaki, / Sara Th.... / Ziméo. / Contes. / [at bottom, catchtome: 'II. Partie' and signature 'A']

12°, i: 2 pl + [j]-xxxvj + [1]-215 pp.
ii: 1 f. (halftitle) + [3]-240 pp.

Commentary: The volume halftitle reads 'Les saisons, / [ornamental rule] / Poëme.'

This edition contains: a 'Discours préliminaire' (pp.[j]-xxxvj); *Les Saisons* (i.[1]-215); *L'Abenaki* (ii.[3]-7); *Sara Th....* (ii.[8]-54); *Ziméo. Par George Filmer, né primitif* (ii.[55]-98); 'Piéces / fugitives. / Eij [signature]' (halftitle with a note verso + pp.[101]-134); 'Fables / orientales.' (halftitle + pp.[137]-240).

The following leaves are asterisked cancellantia, i: A[1], Biij, Bvj, C[1], D[1], E[1], G[1], H[1], Hiij; ii: [K6?; no asterisk], [K7-K9]. These two volumes were probably produced in Paris, and perhaps Saint-Lambert himself was involved in the final corrections.

Not listed in MMF, the only mentions I could find of presumably this edition are two entries in OCLC (College of Charleston and State University of New York at Binghamton). Very little information is given for the Charleston copy. The Binghamton entry is for one vol., 17 cm, xxxvi and 240 pp. which could well be a mistake.

MMF (69.58) point out that *L'Abenaki* and *Sarah Th....* first appeared in 1765. (See 65.47 and 65.48.) The *Fables* first appeared in 1769, as did *Ziméo*. The former were augmented by four fables in 1771 (MMF 69.78). All the fables are in prose, and most comprise short prose-fiction narratives.

A slight clarification: MMF (69.58) list an edition for Hambourg, 1797 (BL; copy personally examined). I was unable to see that book, but Krauss-Fontius list Hambourg: Fauche, 1797 (same pagination; no.3451; location: Universitätsbibliothek Leipzig).

Furthermore, Krauss-Fontius have another edition to add to those contained in MMF and described here: 'Œuvres. 4. éd.', Amsterdam, 1771, xxxvi, 211 pp. (no.1114; location: Romanisches Seminar des Universität Leipzig).

Incipits: (*L'Abenaki*) 'Pendant les dernières guerres de l'A- / mérique, une troupe'.

(*Sara Th....*) 'Il y avoit plus de cinq ans que j'avois / achevé mes voyages'.

(*Ziméo*) 'Les affaires de mon commerce m'a- / voient conduit à la Jamaïque'.

('Préface de Saadi') 'Louange au Dieu tout-puissant, père / de tous les étres'.

('L'homme vrai', the first actual fable) 'Un Roi avoit condamné à mort un de / ses Esclaves'.

223

Saint-Réal: *Conjuration des Espagnols contre Venise*, 1788

César Vichard (sometimes Vischard), abbé de Saint-Réal (1639-1692): Conjura-tion / des Espagnols / contre Venise, / en 1618. / Par M. l'Abbé de Saint-Réal. / [woodcut ornament: shield with three fleurs-de-lys, star, crown; d'Artois' de-vice] / A Paris, / de l'imprimerie de monsieur. / [double rule] / M. DCC. LXXXVIII.

18°: 2 ff. (halftitle and titlepages) + [v]-xxiv + [1]-168 pp.

Commentary: The preliminary material is an interesting 'Préface de l'éditeur' (pp.[v]-xiv) and Saint-Réal's 'Introduction' (pp.[xv]-xxiv). The volume halftitle reads 'Conjuration / des Espagnols / contre Venise.'

There are a portrait frontispiece (of Alphonse de la Cueva) and two folding plates. (Not in Cohen or Reynaud).

The historical novel first appeared in 1674.

This edition is not listed in MMF (57.R44), in G. Dulong, *L'Abbé de Saint-Réal...* (Paris 1921), or in Andrée Mansau's bibliography in her edition of *Don Carlos* and the *Conjuration* (Geneva: Droz, 'Textes littéraires français', 1977). The only other copy I could locate (assuming it represent the same edition) is at Johns Hopkins University (source: NUC).

Incipits: ('Introduction') 'De toutes les entreprises des / hommes, il n'en est point de si / grandes que les conjurations.'

(The main body of the novel) 'Le différend de Paul V et / de la république de Venise ayant été / terminé par la France'.

224

Saint-Réal: *Œuvres mêlées*, 1690

César Vichard (sometimes Vischard), abbé de Saint-Réal (1639-1692): Œuvres / mêlées, / Comprenant / l'usage de l'histoire. / Dom Carlos nouvel- / le historique. / Conjuration des Espagnols / contre la republique / de Venise. / & / entretiens histori- / ques et moraux. / Par Monsr. / l'abbe de St. Real. / [woodcut ornement] / A Utrecht, / [rule] / Chés Antoine Schouten, / Marchand Libraire. M DC XC.

12°: 1 f. (titlepage) + 3-156 + 1 f. (half titlepage) + [3-4], 5-178 + 1 f. (half titlepage) + [3-4], 5-176, [177] + 1 f. (half titlepage) + 3-238 pp. + 1 f. (2 pp.)

Commentary: I have found no trace of this edition anywhere. The earliest edition of Saint-Réal's *Œuvres mêlées* I could find is listed in the NUC with locations for Yale and the William Andrews Clark Memorial Library at the University of California, Los Angeles, viz.: *Œuvres mêlées de Mons'. l'abbé de S'. Real. suivant la copie*. A Paris, Chez Claude Barbin, 1689. Since the titlepage bears 'suivant la copie', there is every chance of there having been an edition anterior to that of 1689, as extant at Yale and UCLA. The edition described here is definitely not a reissue of the one described in the NUC. (Pagination and signature details are given in the NUC, following the UCLA copy.) The first edition of the *Œuvres mêlées* listed by Lever is for 1693 (Bibliothèque municipale de Lille). Lever of course did not have access to vol. cccccxv (1977) of the NUC. The contents of the 1690 edition described here are as follows:

1. titlepage;
2. De l'usage de l'histoire. A M**** (head title), pp.3-156;
3. Dom Carlos / nouvelle / historique / et / galante. (half titlepage);
4. Avis, p.[3];
5. Untitled discussion of sources, p.[4];
6. Dom Carlos nouvelle historique, pp.5-178;
7. Conjuration / des / Espagnols / contre la / republique / de Venise, / En l'Année M. DC. XVIII. (half titlepage);
8. Avis, 1 f. (2 pp.);
9. Conjuration [...], pp.5-176;
10. A citation from 'Monsieur de la Noüe dans ses Memoires', 1 f. (1 p.; p.[177]).
11. Entretiens / historiques / et / moraux. (half titlepage) + pp.3-238;
12. Catalogue de Livres Nouveaux, qui sont imprimées [*sic*], & qui se trouvent chez ledit Schouten. (head title) 1 f. (2 pp.).

The signatures for the first two major pieces (*De l'usage* and *Dom Carlos*) are consecutive. Thereafter each piece, with the material meant to accompany it, is separately signed. The publisher probably issued the several pieces individually and as a collection. For the first editions of the prose-fiction pieces contained in the edition described here, see Lever.

Incipits: (*Dom Carlos*) 'LOrsque Charles-Quint résolût de quitter ses Etats, pour se rétirer dans une solitude'.

(*Conjuration des Espagnols*) 'De toutes les entreprises des hommes, il n'en est point de si grandes que les Conjurations'.

225

Souza: *Adèle de Senange*, 1798

Adélaïde Marie Emilie Filleul, comtesse de Flahaut, then marquise de Souza (or Sousa), or marqueza do Souza-Botelho (or Sousa-Botelho) Mourão e Vasconcellos (1761?-1836): Adèle / de Senange, / ou / lettres / de / lord Sydenham. / Tome premier [second]. / [rule] / If thou remenberest [*sic*] not the slightest Folly / That ever love did make thee run into, / Thou hast not Loved. / Shakfpeare [corrected to Shakespeare in ii]. / [rule] / A Genève, / Chez J. J. Paschoud, Libraire. / A Paris, / Chez Maradan, Libraire, rue du Cimetière / André des Arts, N°. 9. / [rule] / An VI.

12°, i: 2 ff. (halftitle and titlepage) + [5]-23 + [25]-240 pp.
ii: 2 ff. (halftitle and titlepage) + [5]-193 + [196], [197]-231 + [5] pp.

Commentary: MMF list a similar edition of this novel for the collection of books formerly owned by Monglond and now in the Centre de recherches révolutionnaires et romantiques, Université de Clermont, Clermont-Ferrand; the Bibliothèque cantonale et universitaire, Canton de Vaud, Lausanne; the

Brotherton Library, University of Leeds; the Bibliothèque publique de Neuchâtel (MMF 94.13; see too Monglond, iv, cols.606-07). This novel first appeared in 1794. (MMF were unable to track down a copy of the first edition, but there are four listed in the NUC, for Londres, chez Debrett, 1794: Berkeley, Duke, University of North Carolina at Chapel Hill, and Yale.) Curiously Giraud gives the 1794 edition as follows: 'L[ondres]. s.n.i. [sans nom d'imprimeur], 1794, in-8°' (1794.2.a). Perhaps there were two editions for that year?

The volumes of the 1798 edition listed by MMF contain 240 and 232 pp. respectively, and are so listed by Monglond. The NUC also lists an edition for only 'Paris, Chez Maradan, an sixième' (2 vols in-12, ill., Princeton). Such a work, with no mention of Geneva or Paschoud, is also mentioned in the *Journal typographique*, 1 March 1798/11 ventôse an 6, no. XX, p.156, information repeated in Maradan's list, 16 March 1798/26 ventôse an 6, no. XXII, p.173. Further to complicate matters, Giraud lists a Paris, Maradan, 1798 edition, two vols in-12, with 1 f. + 248 pp. and 1 f. + 232 pp. (1794.2.b), which raises the possibility of there having been three editions or issues for 1798. But I doubt that is true. Gay lists a 1798 edition, 2 vols, in-12, ill., with no further information. He also gives a brief synopsis of the novel and mentions that it is 'analysé dans la *Nouvelle bibliothèque des romans*, tome IV, de la 2ᵉ année' (i, cols.20-21). Krauss-Fontius list a 2 vol., 1798 edition, with the same places and publishers as the copy described here. No pagination is given (no. 4058 with a location for the Universitäts- und Landesbibliothek Sachsen-Anhalt, Halle). Since the edition represented by my copy of the novel does not appear to be listed in the NUC, is not listed in the BNC and does not exist in the BL, I have chosen to include it.

Vol. i.[5]-23 is an 'Avant-propos', signed 'A. de F.....'. The second item in vol. ii is another tale, set off with a half titlepage: 'Aglaé. / Conte. / [rule] / Une morale nue apporte de l'ennui: / Le conte fait passer le précepte avec lui. / La Fontaine. / [rule]'. A note at the end of the novel explains that 'Le petit ouvrage qui suit, est celui que Mad. de Verneuil donna à lord Sydenham; nous l'avons placé ici afin de ne pas retarder la marche de ses lettres'. A short announcement on the verso of the half titlepage further explains: 'Ce conte a été fait pour une jeune personne que sa toilette occupait beaucoup; elle avait déjà tous les défauts d'Aglaé, que nous n'avons fait princesse que par égard pour la Fée, qui ne pouvait pas trop se mêler d'une éducation ordinaire'. There are half titlepages at the head of each volume for 'Adèle / de Senange.'

The last five pages of ii are a catalogue of 'Romans nouveaux et autres, qui se trouvent chez le même Libraire', followed by a shorter list of 'Livres divers'. The compiler of the booklist obviously took considerable pains accurately to report the titles of the items for sale, and these are quite interesting, including such rarities as *Louisa Beverley*, of which MMF could not find a copy (98.17). See too Monglond, iv, col.653. (The *Journal général de la littérature de France* lists *Louisa Beverley*, largely as per MMF, 98.17, mentioning it was available from or published by Lenormand; March 1798, p.88.) Of interest to the 'genre romanesque' are:

1. *Le Château mystérieux...* (anon., a translation from the English by Pierre-François Henry). MMF (98.8) list an edition, 2 vols in-12. The catalogue lists

that one, and a two-volume edition (or issue) in-18, with illustrations. (There also exists a play by the name of *Le Château mystérieux, ou l'héritier orphelin*, anon., staged the 8th frimaire an VII [28 November 1798], never published; Monglond, iv, col.695.)

2. *La Femme de bon sens, ou la prisonnière de Bohème...*, anon., translated by B. Ducos, 'receveur général des finances du département du Bas-Rhin et régent de la Banque de France' in 1818 (titles according to the BNC, xliii, col.309). MMF (98.12) list an edition of 4 vols in-18; the catalogue adds an edition (or issue) of 3 vols in-12, ill. This information is repeated in Maradan's catalogue, 'Romans nouveaux et autres, qui se trouvent...' in the *Journal typographique et bibliographique*, 26 ventôse an VI-16 March 1798, no. XXII, p.173.

3. *Folies de la prudence humaine*, 1 vol. in-12. Not in MMF. Repeated in Maradan's catalogue (see no. 2 above).

4. *Henry*, trad. de l'anglais par B. Ducos. Such is the listing in the present catalogue. MMF (97.19) state that this work by Richard Cumberland was translated by B. Ducos or Angélique Caze de La Bove, Mme Ducos. It seems certain that the French is due to the former. This information is repeated in Maradan's list (cited in no. 2 above). The title listed by Monglond for the 1798 edition is *Henry. Traduction de l'anglais par B. Ducos* (iv, col.654). See too Monglond, iv, col.218; a reference is given to the *Journal de Paris*, 29 November 1797, p.238-40. See too the short notice, largely bibliographical, devoted to B. Ducos and his wife in Antoine Vincent Arnault (*et al.*), *Biographie nouvelle des contemporains, ou dictionnaire [biographique]...*, vol. vi (Paris 1822), p.119-20.

5. *Jenny et Sophie, ou les méprises de l'amour*, tr. de l'anglais, 2 vols in-12, ill. Not in MMF. Gay adds 'traduit de l'anglais par L. M. –Paris, 1798, 2 vol. in-12, figures (Pigoreau)'. The *Journal typographique et bibliographique*, under 'romans nouveaux', has the following: 'Jemmy et *Sophie, ou les Meprises de l'Amour*; trad. de l'anglais, par L. M***. Très-jolie fig. (An 6.) [...] Paris, *Maradan*, libraire [...]. Cette jolie production sort des presses du citoyen *Crapelet*. Nous dirons de cet artiste, que son nom nous suffira pour faire l'éloge de l'exécution typographique, comme l'a si bien dit le Journal de Paris', etc., with more praise of Crapelet and his art (24 prairial an 6 [12 June 1798]).

6. *On ne s'y attendoit pas, ou histoire de Redi Ferea*, 2 vols in-12. MMF list this anonymous work in 72.6, 2 parts in-12, with an additional edition for 1773 (also 2 vols in-12). No subtitle is mentioned. The edition with the subtitle is obviously a new one and is probably contemporary, more or less, to the catalogue.

7. *Recherches du bonheur*, 1 vol. in-12. Not in MMF. (This item is listed with the novels, although it doesn't sound like one.)

The *Adèle de Senange* described here contains two pretty, albeit conventional engravings by Bovinet after Challiou (signed; Cohen, col.956). These are meant for i.149 and ii.188, and bear the following captions: i, 'Vous devriez ériger ici un tombeau / bientôt il vous ferait ressouvenir de moi'; ii, 'Vous aux pieds de Lord Sydenham!'

Finally I might mention that MMF list an edition of *Adèle* for 'Hambourg, Hoffman, 1796, in-8', after Quérard. The Messkatalog also seems to list this edition, with some additional information: 'Adèle de Senange. Edit. finie par des additions de l'auteur. 8. à Hambourg, *Hoffmann*', OM 1796, p.176. (A briefer entry in included in Heinsius 1798, p.[481].)

   Incipits: (*Adèle*) 'Je ne suis arrivé ici qu'avant hier, mon cher Henri'.

   (*Aglaé*) 'Il y avait une fois une reine qui croyait que rien ne pouvait s'opposer à ses desirs'.

226

Sterne and Combe (transl. unknown): *Lettres d'Yorick à Eliza et d'Eliza à Yorick*, 1784

Laurence Sterne (1713-1768) and William Combe (1742-1823), translator unknown: Lettres / d'Yorick / a Eliza, / et / d'Eliza / a Yorick. / Traduites de l'Anglois, de M. Sterne. / Nouvelle édition, / Augmentée de l'Eloge d'Eliza, par M. l'abbé / Raynal. / [small symmetrical woodcut ornament] / A Lausanne, / Chez Mourer, Cadet, Libr. / [double rule] / M. DCC. LXXXIV.

16°: 1 f. (titlepage) + [III]-VIII, [IX]-XVI + [1]-88 pp. (Initial pages of text are numbered within brackets).

Commentary: The preliminary pages comprise a 'Préface' and an 'Eloge d'Eliza Draper extrait de l'*Histoire philosophique et politique des établissemens et du commerce des Européens dans les deux Indes*, par M. l'abbé Raynal.' The work proper is a translation of the *Letters from Yorick to Eliza* (which first appeared in 1773) and the *Letters from Eliza to Yorick* (which first appeared in 1775).

   I list this work, which went through quite a few editions in French, because, although 'Yorick's' letters are real (or so it is believed), those by Elizabeth Sclater Draper (1744-1778) to Sterne are in every likelihood by William Combe, a friend of Sterne (who also forged other letters of his famous friend). Indeed, in listing an English edition, supposedly printed in London, the *Catalogue des livres nouveaux* (*Catalogue hebdomadaire*) reported: 'Lettres supposées écrites par Yorick & par Elisa' ('*en anglois*: 2 vol. in-12. A Londres, Chez Bew'; 10 June 1780, no.24, art.13). And Heinsius, for one, lists editions of this material in the volume devoted to novels (Romane, col.125; also under 'Sterne', iii, cols.831-32).

   Thus, we have here an interesting example of what might be termed a 'half novel', comprising a genuine correspondence and apocryphal replies, much as replies were written, for example, to the letters of a Portuguese nun. (Even if the 'Portuguese nun' turned out to be a Frenchman, contemporaries generally thought them real.) In a like fashion, the reading public took this correspondence at face value. See Wilbur L. Cross, *The Life and times of Laurence Sterne* (3rd edition, New Haven 1929), pp.605-606, 610 *et passim*, and the *Letters of Laurence Sterne*, ed. Lewis Perry Curtis (Oxford 1935), pp.189, 218-20 *et passim*. As for the 'Eloge d'Eliza Draper' included with this French edition: it was indeed inserted into the *Histoire philosophique des deux Indes*. The latter work is largely by Raynal, with the collaboration of Diderot and others, and the *Eloge d'Eliza* is possibly, if not quite probably, by Denis Diderot. The work described here contains twenty-two numbered letters.

As for the first edition of the French translation of the 'Yorick-Sterne' correspondence: Rochedieu lists 'Lettres d'Yorick à Eliza [traduites par J.-P. Frenais]. Paris, 1776. in-12' and 'Lettres d'Yorick à Eliza et d'Eliza à Yorick, augmentées d'un Choix de lettres de lord Chesterfield à son fils, traduites par Peyron. Londres; et Paris: Nyon l'aîné, 1776. 1 vol. in-12' (p.316). With no explanation, Giraud lists an edition for 1776, translated by Joseph Pierre Frénais?, or Jean François Peyron?, for Londres, Paris, Nyon, 1776, in-12. A cross-reference leads to some 1784 editions. No mention is made of the Poinçot edition. (See p.69, 1776.8 and p.80, 1784.12.; much of this information is doubtless derived from Rochedieu.) I have not seen, and indeed could not find an edition of these *Lettres* earlier than 1784. And I do not know who did the translation of the 1784 edition described here, or if there was more than one French version of these letters.

In passing, I note that Heinsius (iii, col.833) lists two editions of Sterne's *Sentimental journey*, in the French, not cited by modern bibliographers, namely:

1. *Voyage sentimental*, 1786. 'Voyage sentimental, trad. de l'anglois. [in-]8. Berne, Haller, [1]786.' (Also Kayser, v.330a). The same information is in Heinsius, *Handbuch*, for 'Suisse, Haller' (p.827).

2. *Voyage sentimental*, 1790. 'le même, trad. par Irenais [for Frénais]. gr. [in-]8. Strasb[ourg]. Koenig. [1]790'. (Also Kayser, v.330a). MMF list an edition for 'Strasbourg, imprimerie de la Société typographique, 1790, in-8' after BN and Quérard (69.64), which is also listed in NUC (Yale, Library of Congress, Drexel Institute of Technology [Philadelphia]).

French readers seemed to have very much appreciated the *Lettres d'Yorick à Eliza, et d'Eliza à Yorick*, for, beyond individual editions of the work, they were often published with the *Voyage sentimental* and with *La Vie et les opinions de Tristram Shandy*. (See particularly Rochedieu, p.316-17; MMF list a half dozen editions of the *Voyage sentimental* with the 'Yorick-Eliza' correspondence, 69.64; there were more).

The only other copy of the edition described here I could find is in the rare-books room of the BN (Rés. Y2.3524[2]).

Incipits: (Yorick to Eliza, no. 1) 'Eliza recevra mes livres avec ce billet.' (Eliza to Yorick, no. 2) 'J'ai reçu votre Voyage Sentimental. .... J'admire le pouvoir de votre imagination'.

227

Sterne (Frénais and Bonnay transl.): *La Vie et les opinions de Tristram Shandy*, 1784 [or ca.1794]

Lawrence Sterne (1713-1768), translated by Joseph Pierre Frénais (or Fresnais) and the marquis Charles François de Bonnay: La vie / et / les opinions / de / Tristram Shandy; [Shandy, for vol. iii] / Traduites de l'Anglois de Stern, / Par [Pa for iii]M. Frénais. / [rule] / [two-line citation in Greek; for vols ii-vi, the space between these rules is occupied by the volumniation: Tome second (troisième, quatrieme, cinquième, sixième).] / [rule] / Tome premier. [nothing for vols ii-vi] / [swell rule] / A Londres. / [double rule: thick, thin] / M. DCC. LXXXIV.

18°, i: 2 ff. (halftitle and titlepages) + v-viij + [j]-ix + [1]-178, 179-18[1] pp.
  ii: 2 pl + [1]-192, 193-196 pp.
  iii: 2 pl + [1]-182, 183-186 pp.
  iv: 1 pl (titlepage) + [j]-ij + [3]-186, [187]-189 pp.
  v: 1 pl (titlepage) + [1]-172, [173]-176 pp.
  vi: 1 pl + [1]-182, [183]-186 pp.

Commentary: The pagination reflects: an 'Avertissement' (i.v-viij); a 'Vie de Stern' (*sic*, i.[j]-ix); then the first part. The pages at the end of each volumes are the tables. The two preliminary pages in vol. iv are an 'Avis du traducteur' for the *Suite de la vie et des opinions de Tristram Shandy*, for which see below.

The first three volumes are preceded by halftitles: 'La vie / et / les opinions / de / Tristram Shandy. / [rule] / Tome premier [II, III]. / [rule]'.

Each volume is preceded by a pretty, captioned frontispiece which indicates the volume and page illustrated (with the exception of the first: a portrait of Sterne). This edition is not listed in Cohen or Reynaud.

MMF list two Londres, 1784 editions, one of which they remark is surely a Cazin. The other is for six volumes in-18, with the only location given being the BN (vol. iii only); mentioned by Barton and Rochedieu (76.47). MMF note that it includes 'la suite de Bonnay, ce qui fait croire que la date doit être fausse pour les derniers volumes au moins'. Indeed, the volumes described here do contain the 'suite', which occupies the last three volumes. MMF remark that this continuation of Sterne's work was, from 1785 on, more often than not published with Frénais' translation (85.44).

Francis Brown Barton, in his *Etude sur l'influence de Laurence Sterne en France au 18e siècle, thèse...* (Paris 1911; cited by MMF), writes concerning this edition: 'Edition [*sic*] incomplète; il n'est pas probable que tous les volumes de cette édition aient paru en 1784', etc., because the 'suite' appeared in 1785 according to all available information. As conclusive proof of that, I might mention that Bonnay's 'suite' was granted a 'permission tacite', 29 June 1785; approved by Demeunier (BN ms F.F.21866, f.182v). See too the *Journal de la librairie, ou catalogue des livres nouveaux*, 1786, no. 11, supplement, (18 March), art. 49 (the two volumes priced at 4 'livres', in wrappers).

As for the date: I quite agree with MMF's supposition that the volumes were printed at a date later than that indicated by the titlepages. Due to the evidence of the type, paper and the costumes of the characters portrayed in the illustrations, I would place this edition at somewhere around 1794 (or a bit later). This sort of thing seems to have happened not infrequently during the 1790s. For another example, see Florian, *Galatée*, 1784 [or 1799?] above.

Concerning the 1784, Cazin edition: MMF give the pagination after the BL copy, 2 vols in-18. They explain that the BL and BN copies also include Bonnay's continuation, and pagination is given for two more volumes. No mention is made of a date. I was unable to see those volumes, but OCLC has an entry for what is probably the 'Cazin' (Ohio University, Athens), giving 1784-1785 as the date. Since Bonnay's 'suite' didn't appear until 1785, there is a mistake someplace. Not having seen those volumes, I cannot of course presume to judge whether they are truly a 'Cazin'.

Barton states that three volumes of the edition described here exist in the BN. Doubtless he means Y2.69859-61. Y2.69860 is missing, and the staff at the BN were unable to locate it. The other two volumes have undergone some carefully executed, yet heavy-handed mutilations. The indication of 'Tome troisieme' on Y2.69859 has been carefully obliterated by a strip of paper being glued down over it; the last page has been glued down to the wrapper to hide the 'partie' indication at the end. As for volume vi, the titlepage was removed from the book, cut in two and the volume indication was cut away. The pieces were then glued together, and reinserted in the book. (These are only some of the mutilations: there are pages missing, etc.) Since the BN books can hardly be used for a bibliographical description, and since I could find no other copy of this edition, I have chosen to include this entry.

Incipits: (*La vie et les opinions de Tristram Shandy*) 'Je l'ai toujours dit; il auroit été à souhaiter / que mon pere ou ma mère, pourquoi pas tous / deux'.

(*Suite de la vie...*) 'Ces dissertations subtiles et savantes avoient / charmé mon père; et cependant, à propre- / ment parler'.

228

Swift (Desfontaines transl.): *Voyages du capitaine Gulliver*, 1778

Jonathan Swift (1667-1745), translated by Pierre-François Guyot Desfontaines (1685-1745): Voyages / du capitaine / Gulliver, / en / divers pays / éloignés. / [rule] / Tome second. / [rule] / Nouvelle édition. / [woodcut ornament: bouquet tied with ribbon] / A la Haye, / Chez Jean Swart, Libraire, dans / le Toornstraat. / [double rule] / M. DCC. LXXVIII.

8°, ii: 1 f. (titlepage) + [3]-80, [81]-189 + 3 pp.

Commentary: This edition is not listed in Teerink's *A bibliography of the writings of Jonathan Swift* (second edition, Arthur H. Scouten ed., 1963), but could conceivably be part of the edition listed in the NUC, with no details (Universities of Michigan and Virginia). The translation first appeared in 1727. Unfortunately I only have volume ii, out of a probable three-volume set. The third would contain the translation of the spurious continuation. (See Teerink.) The pagination above comprises the third part, 'Voyage à Laputa, aux Balnibarbes, à Luggnagg, à Gloubbdoubdrid & au Japon'; the fourth part, 'Voyage au pays des Houyhnhnms', and the 'Table' for these parts. At the end is 'Fin de la Table du Tome second'. Each part has a mediocre illustration, in-12 (chain lines horizontal), and considerably smaller than the leaves of the text.

Incipit: (third part: 'Laputa') 'Il n'y avoit que dix jours environ que j'étois chez moi, lorsque le Capitaine *Guill. Robinson*'.

229

Tasso (Fournier de Tony transl.): *L'Aminte du Tasse*, 1785

Torquato Tasso (1544-1595), Fournier de Tony trans., and Gilles Ménage (1613-1692): (engraved titlepage) L'Aminte / du Tasse, / Traduction Nouvelle. / A Paris, / M.DCC.LXXXVI. / Edition de Cazin, Rue des Maçons, N°. 31.

(regular titlepage) L'Aminte / du Tasse. / [rule] / Traduction nouvelle. / [small woodcut decoration: wooden structure, swag, monogramme of publisher's initials in the centre] / A Paris, / De l'Imprimerie de Ph.-D. Pierres, / Premier Imprimeur Ord. du Roi, &c. / [rule] / M. DCC. LXXXV. / Avec Approbation, & Privilége du Roi.

18°: 2 ff. (halftitle and titlepage) + [v]-xx, [xxj]-xxxvj + [1], [2], [3]-143 + 145-150, 151-162, 163-168 pp.

Commentary: There is a half titlepage for the volume reading 'L'Aminte / du Tasse.' The first item is a 'Vie du Tasse'. Then follow the 'Traduction de la préface Composée par Gile Ménage en 1655' (head title), the *Aminte* with a half titlepage for 'Aminte du Tasse, / pastorale. / Traduction Nouvelle.' (p.[1], with a list of characters on the verso, p.[2]), a short piece in prose titled *L'Amour fugitif*, some notes to the entire book, and, at the end, six pages of legal material. The legal material consists of an approbation (12 July 1785, signed 'Bret'), the privilege to Pierres (3 August 1785, signed 'Le Begue'); registered 9 August 1785 ('Le Clerc').

This translation is attributed to Fournier de Tony by Gay, who lists what appears to be this edition, but in-12 (i, col.98). Blanc, too, lists a 1785 edition, in-18, but makes no mention of the 1786 book: his next listing is for Londres, 1789 (Joseph Blanc, *Bibliographie italico-française universelle, ou catalogue méthodique de tous les imprimés en langue française sur l'Italie ancienne et moderne depuis l'origine de l'imprimerie: 1475-1885*, Milan 1886, ii, col.1339). The Cazin, 1786 edition (or issue) carries the translator's name on the titlepage (NUC: Harvard [Houghton]). I have not been able to find another copy of this first edition (BLC, NUC, BNC, etc.). The copy described here is printed on fine paper, and the engraved titlepage, signed 'AA. et P. D. R.', is probably the one meant to accompany the 1786, Cazin edition. (I was unable to see a copy of the 1786, Cazin edition.)

The *Aminta* is actually a dramatic pastoral which, in Fournier de Tony's French, reads like a sort of prose eclogue; I list this work particularly because of the second item, which might be considered marginal to the 'genre romanesque'. (Original Italian title: *L'Amore fuggitivo*.)

The play was first performed in 1573 and was first printed in 1581, according to Ferrazzi (Giuseppe Jacopo Ferrazzi, *Torquato Tasso: studi biografici-critici-bibliografici*, 1880; rpt. New York 1971, p.369-70). However, Parenti lists 1580, for Cremona (Marino Parenti, *Prime edizioni italiane: manuale di bibliografia pratica ad uso dei bibliofili e dei librai*, 2nd ed., Milan 1948, p.481). The *Amore fuggitivo* first appeared in 1581 (Bortolo Tommaso Sozzi ed., *Opere di Torquato Tasso*, Torino 1974, ii.895.) Sozzi also includes a brief discussion of whether the *Amore fuggitivo* was really a sort of epilogue to the pastoral. However, Sozzi does not

No 229: *L'Aminte du Tasse*, 1785, engraved titlepage

mention the date of the first edition of *Aminta*. His 'nota biografica' – a chronology of Tasso's life and works – a bit ambiguously carries: '1580-1581 Prima edizione dell'*Aminta* (Venezia, Aldo) e della *Parte prima* delle *Rime* (Venezia, Aldo)', i.32. The NUC lists an *Aminta* for 'In Vinegia, M. D. LXXXI [i.e. 1580]', Harvard [Houghton], with no reason given for contradicting the information presumably to be found on the titlepage. (This doubtless has to do with differences pertaining to the Julian and Gregorian calendars.)

Incipits: (*L'Aminte*, 'prologue') 'Qui pourroit soupçonner, sous une figure humaine & sous un habit de berger, la présence d'un dieu.'

(*L'Amour fugitif*) 'Souveraine Déesse de l'empire du ciel, je descends en ces lieux pour chercher un fils fugitif.'

230

Tasso (Mirabaud transl.): *Jérusalem délivrée*, 1784

Torquato Tasso (1544-1595), translated by Jean Baptiste de Mirabaud (1675-1760): Jérusalem / délivrée. / Poëme héroïque / du Tasse. / Tome premier [second]. / [woodcut ornament: swag of flowers, same for both volumes] / A Lille, / Chez C. F. J. Le Houcq, Libraire, rue / Neuve, la porte cochère à droite en entrant / par la Place. / [double rule: thick, thin] / M. DCC. LXXXIV. / Avec permission.

12°, i: 1 f. (titlepage) + [iij]-xlviij + [1]-186 pp.

ii: 1 f. (titlepage) + [189]-406 pp. + 1 f. (2 pp.)

Commentary: This book, obviously meant to form one tome with two titlepages (here bound in two volumes, though), contains a dedication 'A son altesse sérénissime monseigneur le duc d'Orléans, premier prince du sang', signed 'Mirabaud' (pp.[iij]-[vij]); a preface (pp.viij-xxxj); a 'Vie du Tasse' (pp.xxxij-xlviij); the work itself; two pages of legal material at the end of vol. ii. Note that the second titlepage is part of the normal printing sequence of the whole, constituting pp.[187-88]. The titlepages are 'encadrées' (squiggly line of ornaments, with finials at the four corners).

The legal documents at the end comprise a 'permission simple' to Lemmens of Lille to print 1000 copies of the work, one volume in-12, to reproduce faithfully the Rouen, 1780 edition; signed de Sancy, general secretary, for Néville (Le Camus de Néville, director of the booktrade); given in Paris, 11 December 1783. Registered in Lille 10 January 1784, L. Danel 'Syndic'. Then follows a note whereby H. H. J. Lemmens cedes his rights to C. F. J. Le Houcq of Lille, 1 April 1784. At the very end of the book is a colophon for 'A Lille, de l'Imprimerie de H. H. J. Lemmens'. For further information concerning this 'permission simple', its purport and significance, see Robert L. Dawson, 'The permission simple of 1777 and the bibliographical evidence of its register', forthcoming.

Incipit: 'Je chante cette guerre que la piété / fit entreprendre, & ce Capitaine / qui délivra le Saint Tombeau'.

231

Tencin (*et al.*): *Mémoires du comte de Comminges* (etc.), 1772

Claudine Alexandrine Guérin, marquise de Tencin (1682-1749), François Thomas Marie [de] Baculard d'Arnaud (1718-1805) *et al.*: Les / amants malheureux, / ou / le comte / de Cominges, / drame. / Par M. d'Arnaud, / Conseiller d'Ambassade de la Cour de Saxe, de / l'Academie royale des Sciences & Belles-Lettres de / Prusse, &c. / [rule] / .... Et qui pungit cor / Profert sensum. Ecclesiastic. cap. xxij, v. 24. / [rule] / Quatrieme édition. / [woodcut decoration of flowers] / A la Haye, / Chez Pierre Gosse junior, & Daniel Pinet. / [rule] / M. DCC. LXXII. 8°: 1 f. (titlepage) + [iij]-x, xj-ljv, lv-lxij + half titlepage + [1]-74 + [77]-(137) + [141]-147 + [151]-164 + [167]-176 pp.

Commentary: This volume contains: preliminary material dealing with Baculard d'Arnaud's play (two 'Discours préliminaires' and d'Arnaud's *Idée de la Trappe*); a half titlepage, 'Les / Amants / malheureux, / ou / le comte / de Cominges. / [rule] / Drame.'; the play; a half titlepage: 'Memoires / du comte / du [*sic*] Cominges.'; Tencin's novel, and two heroids by Claude-Joseph Dorat, preceded by an *Extrait des Mémoires du comte de Comminges*, also by Dorat. The heroids have their own titlepage: 'Lettre / du comte / de Cominges / a sa mere, / suivie / d'une lettre de Philomele / a Progné / [woodcut decoration: bouquet] / A la Haye, / Chez Pierre Gosse junior, & Daniel Pinet. / [rule] / M. DCC. LXXII.' (The pagination and signatures are nonetheless consecutive throughout; the titlepage for Dorat's material comprises f.[16], pp.[139-40].)

The novel first appeared in 1735, the play in 1764, Dorat's *Lettre de Philomèle à Progné* in 1759 (Cior. no. 25116) and his *Lettre du comte de Comminges* in 1764. All these items frequently were published together. The novel was published with the first edition of the play (Paris: L'Esclapart, 1764), and frequently thereafter. The edition described here is not in MMF (64.R77). Although the *Lettre de Philomèle à Progné* has nothing to do with the Comminges material, it was published with the *Lettre du comte de Comminges* in 1764, and subsequent publishers, largely pirates, simply copied both. For further information see the d'Arnaud *Œuvres complètes* above and Dawson, ii.651-58. The copy described here carries a frontispiece, which is a rather poor imitation, in a poor state, of the engraving which appeared with the first edition of d'Arnaud's play (designed by Restout). I have been unable to find this edition anywhere, though it is possibly the same as a book in the Arsenal. I was unable to juxtapose the copies.

Incipit: (*Mémoires du comte de Comminges*) 'Je n'ai d'autre dessein, en écrivant les mémoires de ma vie, que de rappeller les plus petites circonstances de mes malheurs'.

232

Thomson (Bontems transl.): *Les Saisons*, 1780

James Thomson (1700-1748), translated by Marie Jeanne de Châtillon de Bontem[p]s (1718-1768): Les saisons, / poeme / traduit de l'anglois / de Thompson. / [woodcut ornament with entwined initials in centre: 'DCE'] / A Londres. /

[double rule: thick, thin] / M. DCC. LXXX. / Avec Permission.

12°: 2 pl + [j]-xvj + [1]-262, [263]-268 pp.

Commentary: The halftitle reads: 'Les saisons. / Poëme.'

Printed largely on light-blue paper, this book was probably meant to imitate a Cazin. According to the register of 'permissions simples', on 24 July 1780 Cazin requested a 'permission' for 2000 copies of *Les Saisons*, in-18. (For further information, see Robert L. Dawson, 'The permission simple of 1777 and the bibliographical evidence of its register', forthcoming.) The volume described here contains an 'Avertissement' (pp.[j]-ix); a dedication 'A l'ami des hommes', signed 'Votre très-humble, &c. ***' (pp.[xj]-xvj); *Les Saisons* (pp.[1]-262); a final *Hymne* (pp.[263]-268). P.[x] is blank.

I could find no trace of this edition. For further information, see the following entry.

Incipit: 'Viens, doux Printemps, fraîcheur / éthérée, viens, descends dans nos plaines / du sein de la nue'.

233

Thomson (Bontems transl.): *Les Saisons*, 1788

James Thomson (1700-1748), translated by Marie Jeanne de Châtillon, dame de Bontem[p]s (1718-1768): Les saisons, / poëme / traduit de l'anglois / de Tompson. / [woodcut decoration: building with a tower on a rock; two bits of vegetation] / A Londres, / [rule] / 1788.

18°: 1 f. (titlepage) + [iij]-viij, ix-xij + [1]-239 pp.

Commentary: I could find no other copy or mention of this edition anywhere.

The pagination reflects:
1. an 'Avertissement';
2. an 'épître dédicatoire', 'A l'ami des hommes';
3. the text of the work.

The first collective edition of the *Seasons* in English dates to 1730. This French version first appeared in 1759, and went through many editions. Although this work is not listed in MMF, it is in prose and does contain a plot-line of sorts. If one lists prose-poem French versions of, for example, various works by Gessner, it seems to me that a bibliography dealing with the 'genre romanesque' ought to include *Les Saisons*.

For anyone who might be interested in compiling a complete bibliography of Thomson in French, the Messkatalog has the following entry: 'Les Saisons, Poëme trad. de l'Anglois de *Thompson*. 12. [in-12°] fig. Berl[in]. et à Leipz. chez Arkstée et Merkus', OM 1762, p.270. (The NUC has a Berlin, Amsterdam, 1760-1763, 2 vol. edition, 17 cm, various locations.) See too Krauss-Fontius, nos 7056-58, Heinsius 1793 (iv.549), etc.

Incipit: 'Viens, doux Printemps, fraîcheur éthérée, viens, descends dans nos plaines du sein de la nue'.

234

Torche: *Alfrède, reine d'Angleterre*, 1678

Abbé Antoine [de] Torche (1631-1675): Alfrede, / reyne / d'Angleterre. / Novvelle historiqve. / [woodcut ornament: basket of flowers] / A Paris, / Chez Estienne Loyson, au Palais, / à l'entrée de la Galerie des Prisonniers, / au Nom de Jesus. / [rule] / M. DC. LXXVIII. / Avec privilege dv roy.

12°: 1f. (titlepage) + 1-193, [194] pp.

Commentary: The last page contains the 'Extrait du Privilege du Roy': to Estienne Loyson, 'Marchand Libraire à Paris', for six years, 'à commencer du jour que ledit Livre sera achevé d'imprimer pour la premiere fois', given in Chaville 18 May 1678, signed Desvieux. The registration (same page) is dated 1 June 1678 (signed by the 'syndic' Couterot). At the very end: 'Achevé d'imprimer pour la premiere fois le 11. Iuillet 1678'.

Lever lists this work for Lyon: A. Demen, 1678, in-12, iv + 104p. and cites the legal material which corresponds to that printed in my book (p.33, after the B.N. copy: Y2.12516). He mentions 'Attr. par Mercier de Saint-Léger (*Magasin encyclopédique*, 3ᵉ année, t. VI, p.186)'.

I was unable to see the B.N. copy. Since the Lyon book also bears the 'achevé d'imprimer' and legal material (I assume), it seems not farfetched to deduce that *Alfrède* was 'contrefait' in Lyon. In any case, there is little doubt that my book is the first edition. The discrepancy in pagination can be explained by the fact that the Paris edition is small in-12, big print, with some sixteen lines of text per page.

Incipit: 'Comme les inju- / res que nous re- / cevons des Personnes / qui nous sont cheres, / sont ordinairement cel- / les qui nous touchent / le plus'.

235

Toussaint: *Mémoires secrets pour servir à l'histoire de Perse*, 1745

abbé François Vincent Toussaint (1715-1772): (titlepage in *red* and black) Memoires / *secrets* / pour servir / a / *l'histoire* / de / *Perse*. / .... Vitiis nemo sine nascitur, optimus ille est / Qui minimis urgetur. / Horat. / [very large, symmetrical woodcut ornament with empty shell in centre, signed 'I'] / *A Amsterdam*, / aux depens de la compagnie. / *MDCCXLV*.

8°: 1 pl (titlepage) + 2 ff. (4 pp.) + 4 ff. (8 pp.) + [1]-265, [266] pp. + 18 ff. (32 pp.)

Commentary: This volume contains a four-page, unnumbered 'Avertissement'; a 'Liste ou clef, des noms propres de ces mémoires' (4 ff., 8 pp.); the 'memoirs'; a 'Table des principales matieres Contenues dans ce Volume' (p.[266] to the end). The catchword at the end of the 'Avertissement' is 'ME'MOI-', leading to p.[1]. The 'key' is a separate gathering ((A)1, (A)2, A3, [A4]), and has been placed more or less arbitrarily in the book described here between the

'Avertissement' and the text. (Contemporary full calf binding.)

This work has been variously attributed to Antoine Pecquet, to Mme de Vieux-maisons (or Vieuxmaisons), to the chevalier de Rességuier and even to Voltaire! Most modern bibliographers attribute it to Pecquet, basing themselves on previous bibliographers and scholars who have stated that Pecquet was thrown into the Bastille for having composed this work. Jones lists it as anonymous, with some explanations. But he only lists one edition for 1745 (p.89). MMF list after Jones (59.R2). Krauss-Fontius list an edition under Nicolas Fromaget, which seems to be a mistake for Pecquet (no. 4254). In their index, they also list this work under Toussaint, with no explanation. Paul Fould, after having shown that the *Mémoires secrets* are the same as the *Anecdotes curieuses de la cour de France sous le règne de Louis XV*, has convincingly shown that the author is the abbé Toussaint. See his edition of the latter from a manuscript, the third edition (Paris: Plon, 1908).

In the bibliography appended to his excellent work, Fould lists a *Mémoires secrets* largely as given here, but with the major difference being that the titlepage bears an engraved vignette, with the motto 'vis unita major', the device of the company of bookdealers of Amsterdam. (Various versions of that vignette do appear on books bearing 'aux dépens de la société'; see for example Paul Delalain, *Inventaire des marques d'imprimeurs et de libraires de la collection du Cercle de la librairie...*, 2e éd, rev. et corr., Paris: Cercle de la librairie, 1892, p.282-83. See too the commentary on Auvigny, with Desfontaines, *Mémoires de madame de Barneveldt* above. I might here remark that that device was also copied and printed on the titlepages of counterfeit editions.) The copy Fould describes is BN Lb38.45c which I was unable to juxtapose with my book. As is obvious, the titlepage decoration differs considerably. Since the *Mémoires secrets* created quite an uproar when they first appeared, and went through many editions (sometimes page-by-page copies), it seems safe to assume that my book differs from that in the BN. In any case, I could find no edition with the titlepage decoration as described here (of the books I was able physically to examine, that is).

As for the attribution to Pecquet: various 'Pecquets' were thrown into the Bastille in and about the mid-'40s (for cheating at cards, overt homosexuality in the Tuileries, purportedly over-charging one captain Belmont of the king's own for his horse-drawn taxi, etc.). With the aid of various source materials relating to the Bastille and its prisoners, I did finally track down a 'literary' Pecquet (sometimes Pequet), a 'marchand-libraire', who was incarcerated in the Bastille for having printed works by Mouffle d'Angerville and Rochon de Chabannes. (Date of entry: 27 August 1750.) The trials and tribulations of Pecquet were many, until he was divested of his livelihood entirely. See Arsenal, ms 12564; 11722, f.22; BN n.a.f.1891, ff.451-52 (ms dealing with 'Auteurs et imprimeurs de mauvais livres'); etc. In fact, it is not without interest to note that Claude Crespy, widow of Charles Pierre Bienvenu, was held in Fort l'Evêque and was subsequently fined a thousand 'livres' plus being deprived of her qualities forever in 1747 – her shop had already been closed for four months 7 August 1746 (500 'livre' fine) – for dealing in various works 'contre les bonnes mœurs'. These had been seized by the commissaire La Vergée (15, 17 and 18 November 1747). The list includes our *Mémoires secrets*:

'Œuvres de Grecourt.

Memoires secrets pour servir a l'histoire de Perse.

Biblioteque des Damnés [not in Barbier or Gay].

Zensoli et Belma, ou le Triomphe de la Nature [anon., *Zensoli et Bellina* ...,
1746; Jones p.93].

Le Parfait Maçon &c. [not in Barbier or Gay].

Essay historique et politique sur les gouvernemens des Stathouders.

La Vie de Marianne [by Marivaux, 1731-1745; Jones p.46].' (BN, ms
n.a.f.1891, f.395-96). It goes without saying that the *Mémoires secrets*, dealing
with the life, reign and loves of Louis XV, were banned as soon as the authorities
got wind of them, and the title was duly inserted into the register of 'livres
prohibés' (BN ms F.F.21928, f.35vo).

The key can be perused in Drujon (i, cols.606-13). It is reproduced from a
1746 edition. (There are variants.)

To editions of this work listed in Fould and in MMF, I would add: '[Mémoires]
secrets, à l'Hist. de Perse. 8vo. Basle. [1]745' (Heinsius, ii, col.993).

Incipit: 'Le Règne de *Cha-Abas I.*, qui mé- / rita le surnom de *Grand*, a été / un
des plus glorieux dont l'His- / toire de Perse fasse mention.'

236

Toussaint: *Mémoires secrets pour servir à l'histoire de Perse*,

1745

abbé François Vincent Toussaint (1715-1772): (titlepage in *red* and black)
Memoires / *secrets* / pour servir / a / *l'histoire* / de / *Perse*. / .... Vitiis nemo sine
nascitur, optimus ille est / Qui minimis urgetur. / Horat. / [pretty engraved
ornament, the central action being a bust crowned by a cupid; motto worked
into the top on a banner: 'vita sine litteris mors est'; signed P. Tanje: f:'] / *A
Amsterdam,* / aux depens de la compagnie. / *MDCCXLV.*

12°: 1 pl (titlepage) + 3 ff. (5 pp.) + [1]-(11) + [1]-265, [266]-302 pp.

Commentary: This volume contains an unpaginated 'Avertissement'; an eleven-
page 'Liste ou clef, des noms propres de ces mémoires'; the memoirs; a 'Table
des principales matieres Continues [*sic*] dans ce Volume.'

The motto on the titlepage vignette was used by different bookdealers, with
various pictures involved. See Paul Delalain, *Inventaire des marques d'imprimeurs et
de libraires de la collection du Cercle de la librairie...* (2e éd., rev. et corr., Paris: au
Cercle de la librairie, 1892, pp.282-83, 286-87).

This edition seems to be listed in Fould, after his personal copy. The NUC,
under the title, lists various locations for what might be this edition: '4 p.l., 302,
11p.' Since there are a couple of errors in Fould's transcription, and since there
is no way of telling whether the NUC entry refers to the same edition (which
does not exist in the BL, BN or Arsenal, that I could ascertain), I have chosen
to include a description of my copy.

For further information, see the preceding entry.

Incipit: 'Le Règne de *Cha-Abas I.*, qui mé- / rita le surnom de *Grand*, a été / un des plus glorieux dont l'His- / toire de *Perse* fasse mention.'

237

Vadé: *Œuvres badines*, 1799

Jean Joseph Vadé (1720-1757): Œuvres / badines / de J. J. Vadé, / et / de l'Écluse. / [short swell rule] / A Paris, / Chez tous les marchands de nouveautés. / [short double rule] / An septième.

18°: 2 ff. (halftitle and titlepages) + [1]-176 pp.

Commentary: This volume contains the volume halftitle: 'Œuvres / poissardes / de J. J. Vadé, / et / de l'Écluse.'; the titlepage; a synopsis of Vadé's life (pp.[1]-3); 'La / pipe cassée, / poeme / epi - tragi - poissardi - héroi - comique / en quatre chants. / A5 [signature]' (halftitle with 'Avertissement' verso + pp.[7]-42); 'Les / bouquets poissards, / par / Vadé. / C6 [signature]' (halftitle with 'Avertissement' verso + pp.[45]-61); 'Le / déjeune [*sic*] / de la Rapée, / ou / discours / des halles et des ports; / par / l'Écluse.' (halftitle leaf + p.[65]-115); 'Lettres / de / la grenouillère, / entre / M^r. Jérosme Dubois, / Pêcheux du Gros-Caillou, / et / Mlle. Nanette Dubut, / Blanchisseuse de linge fin. / Par Vadé.' (halftitle + pp.[119]-159); various poems (pp.[160]-174); 'table' (pp.[175]-176). The *Déjeuner de la Rapée* contains a series of interconnected pieces in prose and in verse. (Not indicated in MMF.)

There is a pretty frontispiece engraving with a caption: 'la Pipe cassée.' (This edition is not listed in Cohen or Reynaud.)

MMF (55.R71) list an edition of the *Lettres de la Grenouillère* for 1799, with locations for Amsterdam (Universiteitsbibliotheek) and the Library Company of Philadelphia. I assume they cite from the NUC for the American location. The latter is for the 'Œuvres poissardes de J. J. Vadé, et de l'Ecluse. A Paris, 1799'. No pagination is given. That would seem to have little to do with the edition listed here, unless the Library Company of Philadelphia compiled its entry from a combination of the halftitle and titlepages, which seems highly unlikely.

Those interested in bibliographical problems concerned with Vadé might consult Georges Lecocq's interesting, if rather incomplete 'Essai bibliographique' appended to his edition of Vadé's *Poésies et lettres facétieuses* (Paris 1879).

Incipits: (*Le déjeuner de la rapée*) 'Le dernier jour de carnaval'.

(*Lettres de la Grenouillère*) 'Quand d'abord qu'on n'a plus son cœur à / soi, c'est signe qu'une autre personne l'a' (the first lines of the letter, after the salutation, 'Maneselle').

238

Villeneuve: *La Jardinière de Vincennes*, 1767

Gabrielle Suzanne Barbot, Mme Jean-Baptiste de Gallon de Villeneuve (1695?-1755): La / jardiniere / de / Vincennes, / Par Madame de V***. / Nouvelle Edition, revue & corrigée. / Premiere [Seconde, Troisieme, Quatrieme, Cinquieme] partie. / [composite woodcut decorations, different for each vol.: circular design with four roses, different designs in centres] / A Londres, / Et se vend à Francfort en Foire, / Chez J. F. Bassompierre, Pere & Fils [Fils, for ii, iii, iv, v] / Libraires à Liege. / [double rule] / M. DCC. LXVII.

12°, i: 1 f. (titlepage) + [iij]-vj + [1]-125 pp.
  ii: 1 f. (titlepage) + [3]-132 pp.
  iii: 1 f. (titlepage) + [3]-119 pp.
  iv: 1 f. (titlepage) + [3]-122 pp.
  v: 1 f. (titlepage) + [3]-114 pp. + 1 f. (1 p.)

Commentary: The first item in vol. i is a dedicatory letter 'A madame la marquise de Senneterre'. Gay lists what is possibly this edition for simply 'Londres, 1767' (ii, col.698), information which is repeated in MMF 53.34 (after Gay, who remarks upon the rarity of these books). I have been unable to find another complete copy of the edition described here. (See the commentary on no.3, 1759 below in this entry.) The last folio contains a short, one-paragraph approbation signed 'Crébillon', dated 22 September 1752; this is for *Les Caprices de l'amour et de la fortune, ou la jardinière de Vincennes*. Gay notes: 'On voit dans l'approbation royale [...] que le manuscrit primitif de l'ouvrage avait pour titre: *Les Caprices* [...]' (ii, col.698). The novel first appeared in 1753 (MMF 53.34). Perhaps there was a change in title after the approbation was granted, but before the printing of the work? In any case, these volumes were not printed in either London or Frankfurt. And were they actually printed for, or available at the Frankfurt book fair? There is no mention of this novel in the sections of the *Messkatalog* devoted to works not in German or Latin for 1766, 1767 or 1768.

To editions of the *Jardinière de Vincennes* listed in MMF, I would add the following comments and editions:

1. 1757. 'La jardiniére de Vincennes, par madame de V***. Nouvelle édition, revue & corrigée... Londres [Liege] 1757.' 2 vols. (NUC: Newberry Library.) MMF list two editions for 1757, but both in five volumes.

2. 1758. 'Jardiniere de Vincennes par Mad. de V*** 5 parties, 12. chez les mêmes [Arkstée et Merkus; thus doubtless Leipzig]', Messkatalog, OM 1758, p.877.

3. 1759. 4 vols. Londres; Francfort: Bassompierre, 1759. Krauss-Fontius, no. 3811. Location: Universitäts- und Landesbibliothek Sachsen-Anhalt, Halle. Krauss-Fontius list vols 'I-IV' and make no statement concerning the completeness (or incompleteness) of the copy recorded. MMF list an edition for 'Londres, 1759', after Gay. Gay lists 'Londres, 1759, 5 parties in-12' (ii, col.698). Furthermore, the BNC seems to list yet another edition for 1759: Liège: J. F. Bassompierre, 2 vols in-12 (Fb.9073-74). This is actually 5 vols, in-12, with an imprint for A Londres, et se vend a Francfort, en Foire, Chez J. F. Bassompierre, pere

& fils, libraires à Liége, M. DCC. LIX. (for i, iii-iv) and M. DCC. LVII. (for ii and v). I strongly suspect that all entries refer to the same edition. Furthermore, although I was unable to juxtapose my volumes with those owned by the BN (housed at Fontainebleau), the pagination of vols ii and v are the same, so I suspect they are from the same edition.

4. 1771. 'La jardinière de Vincennes / par Madame de V***. --Nouvelle éd., revue & corrigée. --A Londres: Chez J. F. Bassompierre (Liège), 1771.' 5 vols; 17 cm. (NUC: University of Wisconsin, Madison.) MMF list a 1771 edition for Avignon (number of volumes not specified) and a 'Londres, 1771, 2t. in-12' edition after Quérard. Quérard lists only 'Londres, 1771, 2 vol. in-12' (x.189b). If that be true, the Wisconsin copy comprises an additional edition.

Incipit: 'Quoique la Marquise d'Astrel fût veuve depuis vingt ans, elle n'en avoit cependant que trente-six'.

239

Villeneuve: *La Jardinière de Vincennes*, 1778

Gabrielle Suzanne Barbot, Mme Jean-Baptiste de Gallon de Villeneuve (1695?-1755): La / jardiniere / de / Vincennes, / Par Madame de V***. / Nouvelle Édition, revue & corrigée. / Premiere [Seconde, Troisieme, Quatrieme, Cinquieme] partie. / [woodcut ornament; see the commentary] / A Londres, / Et se vend à Francfort, en Foire. ['Francfort, en Foire,' for ii-iii; 'Francfort en Foire,' for iv-v] / Chez J. F. Bassompierre, Pere & Fils, / Libraires à Liege. / [rule; see the commentary] / M. DCC. LXXVIII.

12°, i: 1 f. (titlepage) + [iij]-iv, [5]-117 pp.
 ii: 1 f. (titlepage) + [3]-120 pp.
 iii: 1 f. (titlepage) + [3]-108 pp.
 iv: 1 f. (titlepage) + [3]-111 pp.
 v: 1 f. (titlepage) + [3]-104 pp.

Commentary: The first item in vol. i is a dedicatory letter 'A madame la marquise de Senneterre'.

MMF list an edition for 'Londres, 1778, 5t. in-12' after the *Catalogue de livres* (1837) of the Bibliothèque municipale of Bordeaux. I was unable to examine those books, and since I know of no other copy of a 1778 edition, I have chosen to include mine in this bibliography. (It is quite possible that the Bordeaux books differ from mine.)

A peculiarity about the edition described here: the first three volumes are similarly printed. The woodcut decoration is a distinctive spray of foliage with a flower in the centre. There is a double rule: thick, thin. The type is the same. The headpiece of the first page of text is the same for all three volumes.

The titlepages of iv and v are 'encadrées'. The decoration is composite, and the rule ornamental. The headpieces are composite (basically the same), and the type differs from that on vols i-iii. (It is larger, for example.)

The first three volumes are characteristic of Rouen; the last two of Liège (for example). In any case, it is obvious that the two sets were printed by different firms. The imprint in each case follows the tradition of the first, 'Francfort en foire' edition.

For further information, see the first Villeneuve entry above.

Incipit: 'Quoique la Marquise d'As- / trel fût veuve depuis vingt / ans, elle n'en avoit cependant / que trente-six'.

240

Voiture: *Lettres* (*Œuvres*), 1668

Vincent [de] Voiture (1597-1648): (engraved titlepage) Les / lettres / de M^r de / Voitvre / A Wesel, / chez Andre Hogenhuyse / A° j668

12°: 1 pl (titlepage) + 10 ff. (3 + 17 pp.) + 1-642 pp. + 6 ff. (12 pp.)

Commentary: The only copies of this edition I could find – assuming they be the same – are those listed in the NUC (University of Southern California, Cornell, Library Company of Philadelphia, Duke, University of Minnesota). Since there are no copies in the BN or BL and because the NUC description is incomplete, I thought it best to bring the above edition to the attention of the public. (I have not been able to find it in the usual bibliographies, except Weller who mentions that the book was actually printed in Holland, p.21.) As mentioned, the titlepage is an engraving, and the whole is preceded by a portrait frontispiece bearing the following lines: 'Tel fut le Celebre Voiture, / L'Amour de tous les beaux Espris: / Mais bien mieux qu'en cette peinture, / Tu le verras dans ses escris. D.P.'

The first item is a dedicatory letter to 'Berhardt comte de Sain et Witgenstein [...]', signed 'Andre de Hoogenhuysen'. The second is a preface of sorts, 'Au lecteur', unsigned, but by Etienne Martin, sieur de Pinchesne. F.[Z5], pp.[537-38] is a half titlepage for: 'Seconde partie / ou suitte des / nouvelles / oeuvres / et / lettres / de / monsieur / de Voiture.' This section is preceded by a notice, 'Le libraire aux lecteurs' (pp.539-42). Several of Voiture's works are of interest to the 'genre romanesque', for example, the 'Lettres amoureuses' (pp.361-412), his 'Métamorphoses' (pp.575-77), containing such lovely whimsies as the 'Métamorphose de Julie en diamant, pour madame la marquise de Montausier'. But of especial interest is the *Histoire d'Alcidalis et de Zélide*, dedicated to Mme de Rambouillet (pp.580-633, preceded by a one-page introduction, p.[579]). This incomplete novella first appeared in the *Nouvelles œuvres de monsieur de Voiture* (1658; Lever p.190). The last twelve pages cited above are the tables to the pieces contained in both parts.

The signatures are consecutive throughout, exception made of those delimiting the ten preliminary leaves. The first folio of the book proper is signed '*2', which might make a bibliographer familiar with problems relating to eighteenth-century France think that there is a folio missing. He might further speculate that it might have been a printed titlepage. However, it was frequently the practice in the seventeenth century (which continued well into the eighteenth century), particularly in the Low Countries and the German states, to sign the first folio of a book containing an engraved titlepage with a '2' (and appropriate symbol or letter). An engraving would then have occupied the first folio. The above copy is quite complete. F.*2, [*3], *4, *5, [*6-*11] (the unpaginated, twenty preliminary pages) and the two engravings comprise a complete gathering.

Incipit: (*Histoire d'Alcidalis et de Zélide*) 'Dv temps que l'Espagne estoit divisée, non seulement entre plusieurs Roys, mais aussi entre plusieurs Nations'.

241

Voltaire: *Candide*, 1759

François Marie Arouet, called Voltaire (1694-1778): Candide, / ou / l'optimisme, / traduit de l'allemand / de / M^r. le Docteur Ralph. / [woodcut ornament] / [double rule] / M. DCC. LIX.

12°: 1f. (titlepage) + [3]-237 + 3 pp.

Commentary: The last three pages are a 'Table des chapitres'. I list this rare, Parisian edition of *Candide* simply to remark that the above copy seems to match in all particulars the BN copy, Rés. Z. Beuchot 131. To the description in the BN catalogue's remarkable volumes dealing with Voltaire, I would like to add that the running title on p.43 carries: 'de l'Optimisme' and not 'ou l'Optimisme'.

In passing, one might note that MMF list a *Candide* for 'Berlin, 1778' after Bengescu and Morize (59.25). Heinsius is a bit more complete, and seems to list two editions for 1778, although in all likelihood it is a question of the same edition, with a mistake on Heinsius' part:

1. '[Candide] ou l'Optimisme, par Voltaire. II Vol. av[ec] fig[ures]. [in-]12. Berl[in]. (Levrault à Strasb[ourg].) [1]778.'

2. 'le même, av[ec] 5 fig. [in-]8. Berlin, Himb[o]urg. [1]778.' (Heinsius, Romane, col.39 for both; Bengescu no.1452 and André Morize, *Candide, ou l'optimisme, édition critique* Paris 1931, p.lxxiii, no.41). Cohen simply lists 'A Berlin, 1778. 2 part. en 1 vol. 8°. Chodowiecki [the name of the illustrator] (titre gr. et 5 fig.)'. Kayser lists: 'Candide, ou l'optimisme. II Vols., av[ec] 5 fig. [in-]12. Berl. [1]778. Himburg [...] (Levrault in Strassb.)' (vi.107a). Heinsius 1793 lists an edition, 'avec figures, II Vol. 8[vo]. Berlin, Himbourg, [1]788' (iv.481).

Further, MMF (70.38) mention an edition of Jean Louis Castilhon's *Le Mendiant boiteux* with the title of '*Candide anglois ou aventures tragi-comiques d'Ambroise Gwinett*, Francfort et Leipzig, 1771' after the Columbia University libraries (NUC), Brown University (NUC) and Gove (Philip Babcock Gove, *The Imaginary voyage in prose fiction*, New York 1941: 'A Francfort Et Leipzig, Aux Depens De La Compagnie. M.DCC.LXXXI.'; Gove p.363). NUC lists M. DCC. LXXI. (same locations as listed in MMF), so Gove has probably made an error which MMF have corrected.

To the editions listed in MMF, one might add:

Le Mendiant boiteux, 1770. 'le mendiant boiteux. [in-]8. Frankf. [1]770. Varrentrapp' (Kayser, Romane p.25a; Kayser also gives a new edition of Castilhon's 'Zingha, Reine d'Angola. [in-]12. (Frankf.) [1]769. Varrentrapp' ibid.).

Heinsius lists a *Candide anglois*, 1771 as follows: 'Candide Anglois, ou aventures tragi-comiques d'Ambr. Guinet [*sic*] avant et dans ses voyages aux deux Indes'. 2 vols in-8°, Francfort: Kessler, 1771 (Romane col.39). This is possibly the Leipzig, 1771 edition mentioned above in the commentary.

And Heinsius gives a few more details for one edition of the anonymous *Candide en Dannemarc, ou l'optimisme des honnêtes gens*, for which MMF (67.3) list two 1767 Geneva editions (various locations for each) with no publisher: '[...] des honnêtes gens, p[ar] le Bar[on] de Maubert. [in-]8. Génève. Esslinger. [1]767' (Romane col.39; also in Heinsius 1793, iv.482). I was unable to find any trace of this 'baron de Maubert' (Q, Q:SD, Barbier, Cioranescu, etc.). None of the 'usual' eighteenth-century Mauberts was a baron. It is conceivable that this work might have been, at one time, attributed to Maubert de Gouvest (who died in 1767).

Incipit: 'Il y avait en Westphalie, dans le Château de Mr. le Baron de Thunder-ten-trunckh'.

242

Voltaire: *Nouveaux mélanges philosophiques, historiques, critiques*, 1772-1776

François Marie Arouet, called Voltaire (1694-1778), with some pieces, letters and so forth by others; vols i-x: Nouveaux / mélanges / philosophiques, / historiques, / critiques, / &c. &c. / Premiere [Seconde, Troisieme, Quatrieme, Cinquieme, Sixieme, Septieme, Huitieme, Neuvieme, Dixieme] partie. / [woodcut ornament] / [double rule] / M. DCC. LXXII.

xi: [...] / critiques, / &c. &c. &c. / Onzieme partie. / [woodcut ornament] / [double rule] / M. DCC. LXXIV.

xii: [...] / critiques, / &c. &c. / Douzieme partie. / [woodcut ornament: sprig of flowers] / [double rule] / M. DCC. LXXIII.

xiii, xiv: [...] / critiques, / &c. &c. &c. / Treizieme [Quatorzieme] partie. / [woodcut ornament] / [double rule] / M. DCC. LXXIV.

xv: Nouveaux / mélanges / philosophiques; / historiques, / critiques, / &c. &c. / Quinzième partie. / [woodcut ornament] / [double rule] / M DCC. LXXII.

xvi, xvii: Nouveaux / mélanges / philosophiques, / historiques, / critiques, / &c. &c. / Seizième [Dix-septième] partie. / [woodcut ornament] / [double rule] / M. DCC. LXXV.

xviii: Nouveaux / mélanges / philosophiques, / historiques, / critiques, / &c. &c. / Tome dix-huitieme. / [woodcut ornament] / [double rule] / M. DCC. LXXVI.

8°, i: 2 ff. (halftitle and titlepage) + [j]-ij (tipped-in leaf; see the commentary) + [5]-372, (373)-376 (table) pp.

ii: 2 ff. (halftitle and titlepage) + [5]-6, [7]-384, (385)-388 (table) pp.

iii: 2 ff. (halftitle and titlepage) + [5]-426, (427)-430 (table) pp.

iv: 2 pl + (I)-XVI + [1-2; halftitle for *Les Scythes* with characters verso], [3]-411, (412)-416 (table) pp.

v: 2 ff. (halftitle and titlepage) + [5], (6) [halftitle for *La Princesse de Navarre* with beginning of the 'Avertissement' verso], 7-362, (363)-365 (table) pp.

vi: 2 ff. (halftitle and titlepage) + [5]-374, (375)-376 (table) pp.

vii: 2 ff. (halftitle and titlepage) + [5]-357, (358)-364 (table) pp.

viii: 1 f. (titlepage) + (III)-XXII + (3), 4-306, (307)-312 (table) pp. (The titlepage is actually f. [A1]; pp. (III)-XXII comprise ten preliminary leaves, and are so signed, in appropriate lowercase letters; a, [a2], b-b4, [b5-b8]. P.(3)-4 comprise f.A2).

ix: 1 pl (titlepage) + [1]-330, (331)-334 (table) pp.

x: 2 ff. (volume titlepage and halftitle for *Sophonisbe*) + (5)-398, (399)-404 (table) pp.

xi: 1 pl (titlepage) + 1 f. (2 pp.; table) + [1]-355 pp.

xii: 2 pl + 1 f. (halftitle for *Le Dépositaire*) + [3]-(346), 347-348 (table) pp.

xiii: 1 f. (titlepage) + (III)-VIII (table) + [1]-344 pp.

xiv: 2 pl + [I]-IV (table) + (1)-100 (for 400) pp.

xv: 2 pl + j-xxxij, [33]-348 pp. (No table.)

xvi: 2 pl + [1]-356 pp. (No table.)

xvii: 2 pl + [1]-362, [363]-364 (table) pp.

xviii: 2 pl + [1]-380 pp. (No table. See the commentary.)

Commentary: The information recorded on volume halftitles varies. All volumes bear catchtomes for the appropriate part or volume. This series has a very complicated history indeed. The Voltaire Foundation is currently engaged in massive efforts to compile a complete and scientific bibliography of the works of Voltaire. So, rather than enter into a discussion of the *Nouveaux mélanges* (which first began publication in 1765, were reissued and republished as the series was continued, eventually forming nineteen volumes in all, 1765-1776), I would simply like to mention that these volumes contain several pieces, and editions of pieces of prose fiction which are not to be found in MMF. (See below.)

Some of the volumes listed here do not seem to exist in another library (as far as I could ascertain, without being able to juxtapose copies). While awaiting the new bibliography of Voltaire's works, the interested reader might consult Georges Bengescu, *Voltaire: bibliographie de ses œuvres* (1882-90, with an index by Jean Malcolm, 1953), especially iv.230-39, and William H. Trapnell, 'Survey and analysis of Voltaire's collective editions' *Studies on Voltaire* 77 (1970), especially pp.124-25. A glance at the BNC would also be of help. It might be pointed out that Bengescu lists the contents of the entire collection, but that his list is not complete. For example, he left out *Du gouvernement et de la divinité d'Auguste* here in iv.(185)-187; *Des conspirations contre les peuples ou des proscriptions* here in iv.(188)-209; *Diatribe à l'auteur des 'Ephémérides'* here in xviii.[201]-226 (first pagination series), etc. Also there are sometimes considerable title differences (e.g. *Dieu et les hommes* according to Bengescu and BNC; *Ouvrage raisonnable traduit de l'anglais* in my copy, ix.[1]-201). To supplement the information given concerning the contents, see the BNC (ccxiv, cols.81-95), although the BNC is also incomplete, having omitted, for example, *Du gouvernement et de la divinité d'Auguste, Des conspirations contre les peuples, ou des proscriptions* in vol. iv; *Dialogue de Pégase et du vieillard* (with the 'Notes de M. de Morza', here xiv.381-386, 387-397); *Lettre de monsieur de Voltaire à un académicien de ses amis* here xiv.398-400, etc.

However, many of these pieces could be considered liminary.

It might be noted that Bengescu states that the 'Avertissement de l'éditeur', by Voltaire, at the head of vol. i (pp.[j]-ij) constitutes 'pages 3, 4 (paginées i, ij)'. In this edition anyway, that leaf is tipped in and bears an asterisk on the bottom right recto. This leaf bears the catchtome 'Tome I.' whereas the rest of the catchtomes are for '*Nouv. Mél.* I. Part.' ('Partie' for ff. D[1], E[1], L[1], S[1], Aa[1]). The halftitle and titlepages are ff. [A1] and [A2], respectively.

As is obvious by the dating of the volumes listed here, most are not the first edition for the collection. The above collection seems to be a composite one, formed of two or more editions (as is nearly always the case for copies of the *Nouveaux mélanges* that have come down to us).

Listed here are the more obvious pieces of prose fiction contained in the eighteen volumes described above, with succinct information concerning their place in the collection, first date of publication and other pertinent facts. I have left out a good deal of marginal material: the *Sermon du Rabin Akib*, *La Défense de mon oncle*, and so on. I have included prose-fiction works in this collection listed by MMF and those listed in René Pomeau's interesting edition of Voltaire's *Romans et contes* (Paris 1966).

MMF list a 'Nouveaux mélanges [...]. dix-septième partie. 1775, in-8, 364 pp.' (For prose-fiction items in that volume, see below.) However, MMF seem not to have been aware of the various editions/issues of this collection and were also not aware of all the tales and so forth that it contains, in spite of the thorough index to Bengescu's bibliography and in spite of Trapnell's explanations.

Titles are given here as they appear in the *Nouveaux mélanges*.

1. *Pot pourri*, iii.(33)-54. First appeared in the *Nouveaux mélanges* in 1765 (Pomeau, p.[291]). Not listed in MMF.

2. *Petite digression*, iv.(331)-332. First appeared in 1766 with the *Philosophe ignorant* (Pomeau, p.[309]). Not in MMF.

3. *Avanture indienne, traduite par l'ignorant*, iv.(333)-336. First appeared in 1766 with the same piece as the preceding item (Pomeau, p.[313]). Not in MMF.

4. *L'Ingénu, histoire véritable tirée des manuscrits du P. Quesnel*, vi.[5]-99. First appeared in 1767 (MMF 67.52). No edition for the *Ingénu* in the *Nouveaux mélanges* is listed in MMF.

5. *L'Homme aux quarante écus*, vi.(100)-192. First appeared in 1768 (MMF 68.55). MMF list an edition for the *Nouveaux mélanges*, 1768, but not this one.

6. *La Princesse de Babilone*, vi.(193)-292. First appeared in 1768. MMF list a *Nouveaux mélanges* edition for 1768 (68.55), but not this one.

7. *Les Lettres d'Amabed, &c., traduites par l'abbé Tamponet*, viii.(188)-260. First appeared in 1769. MMF list a *Nouveaux mélanges* edition for that date (69.69), but not this one.

8. *Conte nouveau traduit du syriaque: par dom Calmet*, xiv.342-380. First published in 1774 under the title of *Le Taureau blanc* [...]. MMF list an edition for the *Nouveaux mélanges*, same volume, 1774 (74.33).

9. *Aventure de la mémoire*, xvii.139-144. First appeared in 1775. MMF (75.45) list an edition in the *Nouveaux mélanges*, 1775, vol.xvii.

10. *Eloge historique de la raison, prononcé dans une académie de province par M......*,

xvii.189-203. First appeared in 1775. MMF cite the *Nouveaux mélanges*, 1775, vol. xvii (75.46).

11. *Les Oreilles du comte de Chesterfield, et le chapelain Goudman*, xvii.333-362. First appeared in 1775, in the *Nouveaux mélanges*. So cited by MMF (75.46).

12. *Histoire de Jenni, ou le sage et l'athée. Par M. Sherloc. Traduit par M. de La Caille*, xviii.[1]-200 [i.e. 100]. First appeared in 1775. MMF cite a *Nouveaux mélanges*, 1776, vol. xviii edition (75.44).

It is worth noting that the pagination of vol. xviii is highly irregular. Pages 65-129 are numbered 165-229. Page 130 reads as it should, and the pagination resumes from there, correctly. Pages 373-376 appear to be missing in the copy described here. (The last gathering, as extant, contains Aa, Aa2, [Aa3?-Aa4? or Aa5?-Aa6?]). Also, the first *Anecdote sur 'Bélisaire'* is printed twice: vii.(33)-39 and ix.223-230. The latter is dated 'A Paris, 20 Mars 1767' and has a couple of notes not published with the piece as extant in vol. vii.

This collection also contains *Le Cathecumene, traduit du chinois* (xi.175-202, 1774) by Charles Borde, which first appeared in 1768. MMF only mention a 1772 edition for the *Nouveaux mélanges* (68.16; the volume described here is dated 1774).

Incipits: (*Pot pourri*) '*Brioché* fut le pere de *Polichinelle*'.

(*Petite digression*) 'Dans les commencemens de la fondation des Quinze-Vingt'.

(*Aventure indienne*) '*Pythagore*, dans son séjour aux Indes'.

(*L'Ingénu*) 'Un jour *St. Dunstan* Irlandais de nation & Saint de profession'.

(*L'Homme aux quarante écus*) 'Un vieillard qui *Toûjours plaint le présent & vante le passé*, me disait'.

(*La Princesse de Babylone*) 'Le vieux Bélus Roi de Babilone se croyait le premier homme de la terre'.

(*Les Lettres d'Amabed*) 'Lumiere de mon ame, pere de mes pensées, toi qui conduis les hommes'.

(*Conte nouveau; Le Taureau blanc*) 'La jeune princesse Amaside, fille d'Amasis roi de Tanis en Egypte, se promenait'.

(*Aventure de la mémoire*) 'Le genre-humain pensant, c'est-à-dire, la cent millieme partie du genre-humain'.

(*Eloge historique de la raison*) 'Erasme fit au seizième siècle l'éloge de la Folie.'

(*Les Oreilles du comte de Chesterfield*) 'Ah! la fatalité gouverne irrémissiblement toutes les choses de ce monde.'

(*Histoire de Jenni*) 'Vous me demandez, Monsieur, quelques détails sur notre ami le respectable *Freind*'.

(*Le Cathécumène*) 'Des affaires de commerce m'avaient engagé à faire un voyage sur mer'.

243

Voltaire: *Romans et contes*, 1780

François Marie Arouet, called Voltaire (1694-1778): Romans / et / contes. / Par M. de Voltaire. / [short rule] / Tome premier [second, quatrieme, cinquieme]. / [woodcut decoration, same for all volumes: bouquet of three flowers tied together with a ribbon; Caron's name appears on the ribbon, and is barely legible for most volumes] / A Paris. / [short rule] / M. DCC. LXXX.

18°, i: 2 pl + [1]-189 pp. + 1 f. (1 p.)
  ii: 2 ff. (halftitle + titlepage) + [5]-180.
  iv: 2 pl + [1]-178 pp. + 1 f. (1 p.)
  v: 2 ff. (halftitle + titlepage) + [5]-178 pp. + 1 f. (1 p.)

Commentary: The halftitles read 'Romans / et / contes. / [short rule] / Tome premier [second, quatrieme, cinquieme].' The last page of vols i, iv-v is a 'Table...' for the particular volume. There is no table for vol. ii.

The contents are as follows: *Zadig, ou la destinée: histoire orientale* (i.[1]-136); *Babouc, ou le monde comme il va* (i.[137]-172); *Les Voyages de Scarmentado, écrits par lui-même* (i.[173]-189); *La Princesse de Babylone* (ii.[5]-152); *Le Blanc et le noir* (ii.[153]-180); *Le Huron, ou l'ingénu* (iv.[1]-140); *Memnon, ou la sagesse humaine* (iv.[141]-153); *Autre temps, autre façon de voir* (iv.[154]-156); *Songe de Platon* (iv.[157]-162); *Les Deux consolés* (iv.[163]-166); *Bababek, ou les fakirs* (iv.[167]-172); *Le Roi de Boutan, ou jusqu'à quel point on doit tromper le peuple* (iv.[173]-178); *L'Homme aux quarante écus* (v.[5]-132); *Micromégas, histoire philosophique* (v.[133]-173); *Les Aveugles, juges des couleurs* (v.[174]-176); *Le Hibou et les oiseaux* (v.[177]-178). (The *Aveugles juges des couleurs* first appeared in the *Philosophe ignorant* as *Petite digression*; for the first editions of these pieces, see Bengescu.)

There appear to be at least two volumes missing: iii and vi. This collection is in the vein of the Didot, 1780, six-volume *Romans et contes*, and the volumes described here might well represent an issue versus another edition, although some cursory comparisons (with photocopies) indicate that the decorations are not all the same. In any case, the type is Didot's and these volumes were doubtless produced by his firm. The six-volume *Romans et contes*, in-18, for 1780 which is recorded in Bengescu (and elsewhere) bears the indication of 'de l'imprimerie de Didot l'aîné', and was printed by order of the comte d'Artois. (Copy in the BN, for example, réserve, printed on vellum.) What is probably the case is that Didot printed a limited edition of a whole series of works upon orders from the comte d'Artois, and then reprinted (possibly reissued) the collection for more general consumption. Another, parallel volume is listed in this bibliography, with some commentary about the similarity of decorations. See Eustathius Macrembolites, *Ismème et Ismémias* (Beauchamps transl.) above. Like that book, the *Romans et contes* have no catchwords at all. (Catchtomes are for 'Tome I [II, IV, V].') For a succinct list of the Didot works printed by order of the comte d'Artois, see, for example, Brunet, ii, cols.137-38 (sub 'Collection d'Artois').

I could not find a mention of these volumes elsewhere, much less another copy.

Incipits: (*Zadig*) 'Du temps du Roi Moabdar, il y avoit / à Babylone un jeune homme'.

(*Babouc*) 'Parmi les Génies qui président aux em- / pires du monde, Ituriel'.

(*Les Voyages de Scarmentado*) 'Je naquis dans la ville de Candie en 1600.'

(*La Princesse de Babylone*) 'Le vieux Bélus, Roi de Babylone, se / croyoit le premier homme de la terre'.

(*Le Blanc et le noir*) 'Tout le monde, dans la province de / Candahar'.

(*Le Huron*) 'Un jour Saint Dunstan, Irlandois de na- / tion, & Saint de profession'.

(*Memnon*) 'Memnon conçut un jour le projet in- / sensé d'être parfaitement sage'.

(*Autre temps, autre façon de voir*) 'Que je suis malheureux d'être né! disoit / Ardassan Ogli, jeune Ichoglan'.

(*Songe de Platon*) 'Platon rêvoit beaucoup, & on n'a / pas moins rêvé depuis.'

(*Les Deux consolés*) 'Le grand Philosophe Cynophile disoit / un jour à une femme désolée'.

(*Bababek*) 'Lorsque j'étois dans la ville de Béna- / rès sur le rivage du Gange'.

(*Le Roi de Boutan*) 'C'est une très grande question, mais / peu agitée, de savoir'.

(*L'Homme aux quarante écus*) 'Un Vieillard, qui toujours plaint le pré- / sent & vante le passé'.

(*Micromégas*) 'Dans une de ces planetes qui tournent / autour de l'étoile nommée *Sirius*'.

(*Les Aveugles, juges des couleurs*) 'Dans les commencements de la fon- / dation des Quinze-vingts'.

(*Le Hibou et les oiseaux*) 'Un Aigle gouvernoit les Oiseaux de tout / le pays d'Ornithie.'

244

Voltaire: *Zadig*, 1799

François Marie Arouet, called Voltaire (1694-1778): Zadig, / ou / la destinée, / histoire orientale / par / mr. de Voltaire. / [double rule: thin, thick] / Londres, 1799. / Imprimé chez G. Sidney, in Leadenhall / Street, pour G. Polidori. / [double rule: thick, thin] / Il se vend chez le Propriétaire, No. 42, / Broad Street, Carnaby Market.

18°: 1 f. (titlepage) + [3]-7, 8, [9]-203, (204) pp. + 1 f. (1 p.)

Commentary: The ESTC was kind enough to check the records, and no such *Zadig* is listed in the short-title data-base (as of August 1982). The recent *Provisional handlist of separate eighteenth-century Voltaire editions in the original language* (Oxford: The Voltaire Foundation, 1981) does list a similar edition for Londres: Sidney, 1799, 1 vol. in-12, 204 pp. (various locations). The Humanities Research Centre at The University of Texas at Austin has a copy of presumably that edition (Ellery Queen, PQ2082.Z3.1799). A comparison between my copy and that in the HRC reveals that my book is a considerably different issue. The titlepage is entirely different: '[...] histoire orientale / par M. de Voltaire. / [short swell rule] / Il n'y a point de hasard; tout est epreuve, ou / punition, ou recompense, ou prevoyance. / [short swell rule] / M.DCC.XCIX. / Londres: imprimé par G. Sidney / pour les proprietaires. / [double rule] / Se trouve chez G. Polidori, No. 42, / Broad-street, Carnaby Market.' (Note that my copy mentions 'Propriétaire', and the other 'proprietaires'.)

Furthermore my book has some very pretty illustrations (in aquatint) as follows: a portrait-frontipiece of Voltaire bearing a caption: 'Drawn & Engraved by Le Cœur, & Published by G. Polidori, London, Mar: 29 1799'; a tailpiece, p.7; another tailpiece, p.8. Cohen lists an edition, in-32, '1 portrait de Voltaire, 13 figures dessinées et gravées à l'aqua-tinte par Le Cœur, et deux vignettes. Jolie petite édition peu commune de ce roman. Les figures existent imprimées en couleurs' (col.1038). The HRC copy has the fourteen illustrations called for by Cohen, but not the tail-pieces. (Plates seem to have been removed from my book).

A peculiarity of both the HRC copy and my book is that the first 'gathering' is signed 'B', with only f.B2 (pp.[3]-4) bearing a signature. The second second set of signature sequences begins with 'B' again (B-B3, [B4-6]). In both books, there has been some tampering with the first six leaves, some of which are cancels. In the HRC copy it is possible to see that folios [B3-4] (pp.5-8) are conjugate.

Zadig first appeared as *Memnon* in 1747 (Bengescu, Jones, MMF, etc.).

The pagination reflects an 'Épitre dédicatoire de Sadi à la sultane Sheraa' signed 'Sadi'; a humourous 'approbation' (p.8); the novel; a 'table' (p.(204)); and a final leaf bearing, on the recto, the following information: 'London, 1799. Printed in Leadenhall Street, by *G. Sydney*, for *G. Polidori*, Italian Master and Publisher, No. 42, Broad Street, Carnaby Market.' (That is unique to my copy.) P.203 (both copies) also contains a list of errata at the bottom.

Incipit: 'DU tems du roi Moabdar, il y / avoit à Babylone, un jeune homme / nommé Zadig'.

245

Young (Le Tourneur transl.): *Les Nuits d'Young*, 1793

Edward Young (1683-1765), translated by Pierre Prime Félicien Le Tourneur (1737-1788): Les nuits / d'Young, / traduites de l'anglois, / Par M. Le Tourneur. / [rule] / Sunt lacrymae rerum et mentem mortalia / tangunt. Virgile. / [rule] / Cinquième édition, corrigée et augmentée / du Triomphe de la Religion. / Tome premier [second, troisième, quatrième]. / [short rule] / A Londres; / Et se trouvent à Paris, / Chez Favre, Libraire au Palais / de l'Égalité, ci-devant Palais-royal, / galeries de bois, N°. 220. / [double rule: thick, thin] / M. DCC. XCIII.

18°, i: 1 f. (titlepage) + [3]-156 pp.
    ii: 1 f. (titlepage) + [3]-215 pp.
    iii: 1 f. (titlepage) + [3]-248 pp.
    iv: 1 f. (titlepage) + [3]-219 pp.

Commentary: The first volume has a long 'Discours préliminaire', together with some other preliminary material (pp.[3]-62). The work then continues through to iv.54 (twenty-fourth 'nuit'). Then follow 'Le jugement dernier, poème' (pp.[55]-106); 'Jeanne Gray, ou le triomphe de la religion sur l'amour. Poème [...]', preceded by an 'extrait' from Voltaire's *Essai sur l'histoire générale* (pp.[107]-152); 'Paraphrase d'une partie du livre de Job' (pp.[153]-176); 'Épitre a Voltaire' (pp.[177]-180); 'Revue de la vie' (pp.[181]-192); 'Pensées sur différens sujets' (pp.[193]-209); 'Eusebe, ou le riche vertueux' (pp.[210]-214); 'Extrait d'un poème intitulé la résignation' (pp.[215]-219).

All items in this collection are in prose, and several of them might be considered prose-fiction. The *Nuits* proper are religious meditations intermingled with a plot-line. The *Jugement dernier* is religious, but with dialogue and a plot of sorts (quite marginal to the 'genre romanesque'). *Jeanne Gray* is decidedly prose-fiction. The *Paraphrase de Job* is fictionalised, and *Eusèbe* is somewhat marginal. (Young is not listed in MMF.)

Vols i and ii each have a frontispiece plate engraved by Bovinet: the first is a portrait of Young; the second is actually meant for vol. i, p.147.

This edition seems to be listed in the NUC for Georgetown University Library. It is not listed in any other library catalogue I have consulted, or in Cohen and Reynaud.

Incipits: (*Les Nuits*) 'Doux sommeil, toi dont le baume / répare la nature épuisée....'.

(*Le Jugement dernier*) 'Tandis que d'autres chantent la / fortune des grands'.

(*Jeanne Gray*) 'Muse, quitte le séjour des cieux, et / ce ton solemnel'.

(*Paraphrase d'une partie du livre de Job*) 'Long-temps Job vécut sur le trône, / environné du faste'.

(*Eusèbe*) 'Eusebe a de l'esprit; il connoît l'art / de varier les plaisirs'.

246

Young (Le Tourneur transl.): *Œuvres diverses*, 1773

Edward Young (1683-1765), translated by Pierre Prime Félicien Le Tourneur (1737-1788): (titlepages in *red* and black) *Œuvres* / diverses / du / *docteur Young*, / traduites de l'anglois / *Par M. le Tourneur*. / [rule] / Sunt lacrymae rerum, & mentem mortalia tangunt. / Virgile. / [rule] / Derniere Edition, corrigée & augmentée du / Triomphe de la Religion. / *Tome premier* [*second*]. / [symmetrical, composite woodcut ornament, same for both volumes] / *A Amsterdam,* / Chez E. van Harrevelt. / *MDCCLXXII.*

12°, i: 1 pl + [I]-LVI + [1]-295, [296] pp.
    ii: 1 pl + [1]-310, [311-12] pp.

Commentary: These volumes contain the same items as those in the 1793 *Nuits* described above. However, *Jeanne Gray* is titled *Le Triomphe de la religion* only.

The first edition of the *Œuvres diverses*, adapted by Le Tourneur, appeared in 1770 and was destined to complement the *Nuits* (1769). See the comment in the BNC, ccxxviii, col.1069. This particular edition contains both the original 'œuvres diverses' and the *Nuits*.

I could find no other copy of this edition (OCLC, NUC, BNC, BLC, including all supplements).

There are two handsome frontispiece plates. The first, captioned 'Young offrant son livre a l'eternel', is signed 'Vinkeles, sculp. 1769.' The second bears the same signature and date, and is captioned 'Young enterrant sa fille.' (This edition is not listed in Cohen or in Reynaud.)

Incipits: (*Les Nuits*) 'Doux sommeil, toi dont le baume répa- / re la nature épuisée........'

(*Le Jugement dernier*) 'Tandis que d'autres chantent la fortune / des grands'.

(*Le Triomphe de la religion*) 'Muse, quitte le séjour des cieux, & ce / ton solemnel'.

(*Paraphrase d'une partie du livre de Job*) 'Longtems Job vécut sur le trône, envi- / ronné du faste'.

(*Eusèbe*) 'Eusebe a de l'esprit: il connoît l'art de / varier les plaisirs'.

247

Young (Bertin transl.): *Satyres d'Young*, 1797

Edward Young (1683-1765), translated by Théodore Pierre Bertin (1751-1819): Satyres d'Young, / ou l'amour / de la renommée, / passion universelle. / Traduction libre de l'Anglois, / Par T. P. Bertin. / [rule] / ...Fulgente trahit constrictos gloria curru / Non minus ignotos generosis. Hor. / [rule] / [short swell rule] / A Paris. / Chez T. P. Bertin, Libraire, / rue de la Sonnerie, N°. 1. / [short rule] / An V. (1797.)

18°: 1 f. (titlepage) + [5]-20, [21]-141, [142] pp.

Commentary: Pages [5]-20 are a preface; the last page is a list of errata. The first leaf seems to be missing, probably a halftitle.

This translation first appeared in 1787. The original was first published from 1725 to 1727 with the title of *The Universal passion*. It was then collectively published as *Love of fame* (1728).

This work is not listed in MMF. It contains fictitious characters, some dialogue, and plot-lines of sorts. Thus I have included this item. I could find no other copy of this edition.

Incipit: 'Je compose une Satyre; / Dorset, prêtes l'oreille et daignes / protéger une muse'.

Chronological index

The following is a chronological index of the main entries. Items spanning two or more years are placed at the first year recorded.

List of incipits

The following index of incipits has been modernised to facilitate reader consultation. However, names have not been tampered with. Only enough of the incipit is included to make it unique. For expanded incipits, with original spelling (and lineation, where deemed important), see the end of the entry involved.

Index

This index is as comprehensive as possible. It includes proper names mentioned in titles; all minions of the censorship and police; publishers slogans as recorded on titlepages; all eighteenth-century titles (authors only for the rest); publishers and bookdealers; all place-names, etc. Names of libraries have been indexed too, under the library name if it has (or had) a special name (e.g. Lilly Library), or under the place if the library is named after it (e.g. Sachsen-Anhalt). The same holds true for institutions. Thus the University of Texas at Austin is indexed under 'Texas'. Certain items are listed under an abbreviation, e.g. BN for Bibliothèque nationale; NUC for National Union Catalogue; ESTC for Eighteenth-century short-title catalogue, and so on. This should pose few problems for the user. In any case, cross-references have been given where deemed necessary.

Roman numbers refer to pages in the introductory sections; arabic numbers refer to the entries themselves.

Alternate titles are treated like main titles. If a title is given followed by a date, that usually indicates an additional edition not recorded in prose-fiction bibliographies. Rather than an entirely new edition, this also sometimes means that a comment on a previously recorded edition has been deemed significant. A number in parentheses after the date indicates the number of editions for that year.

Some modernisation was considered essential. Thus 'avanture' is listed under 'aventure'. Anomalies are cross-referenced. In the case of *Œuvres* and the like, the main author is given within parentheses.

In short, no effort has been spared to render the general index as comprehensive, yet as efficient as possible.